Selected Native Groups and Trading Sites, ca. 1825–1850

BEAUFORT
SEA

CHUKCHI
SEA

BERING SEA

Point
Barrow

Niġliq

Barter
Island

Herschel
Island

MACKENZIE ESKIMO

Mackenzie River

Peel's River Post,
later Fort McPherson
(est. 1840)

La Pierre's House
(est. 1846)

GWICH'IN
in summer

Icy Cape

Cape
Lisburne

Point
Hope

GWICH'IN

Fort Yukon
(est. 1847)

Porcupine River

Yukon River

Yukon Flats

Colville River

Noatak River

Kobuk River

Sheshalik

IÑUPIAQ ESKIMO

Kotzebue
Sound

Buckland
River

Koyukuk River

KOYUKON

Yukon River

TANANA

Tanana River

Nuklukayet

Cape Serdtse
Kamen

St.
Lawrence
Bay

Cape Dezhnev

Diomede
Islands

Bering Strait

Mechigmensky
Bay

Indian
Point

St. Lawrence
Island

SIBERIAN YUPIK
ESKIMO

Seward
Peninsula

Port Clarence

King
Island

Sledge
Island

Cape
Rodney

Norton
Bay

Nulato (est. 1839)

Unalakleet (est. 1836)

NORTON SOUND

Stuart
Island

Mikhailovsky Redoubt (est. 1833)

Pastuliq

CENTRAL ALASKAN YUP'IK ESKIMO

Kuskokwim River

Nunivak
Island

FURS AND FRONTIERS IN THE FAR NORTH

RECENT TITLES

War of a Thousand Deserts: Indian Raids and the U.S.–Mexican War, by Brian DeLay
"Liberty to the Downtrodden": Thomas L. Kane, Romantic Reformer, by Matthew J. Grow
The Comanche Empire, by Pekka Hämäläinen
Frontiers: A Short History of the American West, by Robert V. Hine and John Mack
    Faragher
Bordertown: The Odyssey of an American Place, by Benjamin Heber Johnson and
    Jeffrey Gusky
Emerald City: An Environmental History of Seattle, by Matthew Klingle
Making Indian Law: The Hualapai Land Case and the Birth of Ethnohistory,
    by Christian W. McMillen
The American Far West in the Twentieth Century, by Earl Pomeroy
Borderlines in Borderlands: James Madison and the Spanish-American Frontier,
    1776–1821, by J. C. A. Stagg
Fugitive Landscapes: The Forgotten History of the U.S.–Mexico Borderlands,
    by Samuel Truett
Bárbaros: Spaniards and Their Savages in the Age of Enlightenment, by David J. Weber
The Spanish Frontier in North America, Brief Edition, by David J. Weber

FORTHCOMING TITLES

The Bourgeois Frontier, by Jay Gitlin
Defying the Odds: One California Tribe's Struggle for Sovereignty in Three Centuries,
    by Carole Goldberg and Gelya Frank
Under the Tonto Rim: Honor, Conscience, and Culture in the West, 1880–1930,
    by Daniel Herman
William Clark's World: Describing America in an Age of Unknowns, by Peter Kastor
Geronimo, by Robert Utley

FURS AND FRONTIERS IN THE FAR NORTH

*The Contest among Native and Foreign
Nations for the Bering Strait Fur Trade*

John R. Bockstoce
Foreword by Felipe Fernandez-Armesto

Yale University Press
New Haven & London

Published with assistance from the foundation established in memory of
Philip Hamilton McMillan of the Class of 1894, Yale College.

Set in Electra type by Tseng Information Systems, Inc.
Printed in the United States of America.

Library of Congress Cataloging-in-Publication Data
Bockstoce, John R.
Furs and frontiers in the far north : the contest among native
and foreign nations for the Bering Strait fur trade /
John R. Bockstoce ; foreword by Felipe Fernandez-Armesto.
p. cm. — (Lamar series in Western history)
Includes bibliographical references and index.
ISBN 978-0-300-14921-0 (hardcover : alk. paper) 1. Bering Strait Region (Alaska)—
History—19th century. 2. Fur trade—Alaska—Bering Strait Region—History—19th
century. 3. Merchants—Alaska—Bering Strait Region—History—19th century.
4. Alaska—Commerce—Russia—History—19th century. 5. Russia—Commerce—
Alaska—History—19th century. 6. Great Britain—Commerce—Alaska—History—19th
century. 7. Alaska—Commerce—Great Britain—History—19th century. 8. Eskimos—
Hunting—Alaska—Bering Strait Region—History—19th century. 9. Russians—Alaska—
Bering Strait Region—History—19th century. 10. British—Alaska—Bering Strait
Region—History—19th century. I. Title.
F951.B63 2009
911'.1645109034—dc22
2009001944

A catalogue record for this book is available from the British Library.

This paper meets the requirements of ANSI/NISO Z39.48-1992 (Permanence of Paper).

10 9 8 7 6 5 4 3 2 1

For Howard Lamar,

*who introduced me to the history of the North American West
and who encouraged me to pursue my studies of the Bering Strait
region, with highest regards and fondest memories of a
generous teacher and a true gentleman*

Other Publications by
John R. Bockstoce

Eskimos of Northwest Alaska in the Early Nineteenth Century (1977)

Steam Whaling in the Western Arctic (1977)

The Archaeology of Cape Nome, Alaska (1979)

*The Voyage of the Schooner Polar Bear: Whaling and Trading in the
North Pacific and Arctic, 1913–1914*, by Bernhard Kilian (editor) (1983)

American Whalers in the Western Arctic (with William Gilkerson) (1983)

*Whales, Ice, and Men: The History of Whaling in
the Western Arctic* (1986, 1995)

*The Journal of Rochfort Maguire, 1852–1854: Two Years at Point Barrow, Alaska,
Aboard H.M.S.* Plover *in the Search for Sir John Franklin* (editor) (1988)

*Arctic Passages: A Unique Small Boat Voyage through the
Great Northern Waterway* (1991, 1992)

Arctic Discoveries: Images from Voyages of Four Decades in the North (2000)

*High Latitude, North Atlantic: 30,000 Miles through
Cold Seas and History* (2003)

CONTENTS

FOREWORD

Furs were the black gold of the far north in the pre-industrial era of global trade. Russians called them "treasure of the land of darkness." Europe demanded huge amounts, but China craved even more. Because the balance of trade between China and the West heavily favored the Chinese—and continued to do so, while the gap gradually narrowed, until the second half of the nineteenth century—any product saleable in Chinese markets attracted European merchants. Furs were of critical importance because Westerners had so little to offer the Chinese. From the sixteenth century to the late eighteenth, they struggled as shippers around the coasts of maritime Asia to scrape together silver bullion for China. Meanwhile, the trade gap widened, as Europe's demand grew for formerly inaccessible Chinese treats, such as tea, porcelain, and rhubarb (prized for supposed medicinal magic). Europeans had not yet learned how to pry open Chinese markets for opium or to limit their dependence on China by growing tea elsewhere. Furs, however, could help to fill the gap. Fur-yielding frontiers in Siberia and North America were early nurseries of a changed world, in which the distribution of wealth and power would shift toward the West.

Siberia was Russia's Eldorado. The conquests of Kazan and Siberia in the sixteenth and seventeenth centuries gave Russia privileged access to the bulk of the fur-producing regions China had traditionally relied on. The opening up of the New World, however, transformed the situation. The abundance of under-exploited fur-bearing creatures in the forests of northern and eastern North America was unprecedented in European experience. French trappers went native in search of them. British explorers penetrated deep into the recesses of the far north to track them. Britain and France fought over them. The British and Russian empires risked war to acquire them. The fledgling United States—

which, until well into the nineteenth century, had few resources suitable for the China trade — pursued and acquired an enormous stake in them. The last great fur-producing region to be incorporated in the modern global system of trade was the area of the Bering Strait. In the half-century or so before the acquisition of Alaska by the United States, native peoples and Westerners colluded and collided to revolutionize the trade. John Bockstoce has at last given us a book worthy of a vital, fascinating, and neglected theme in the making of modern America and of the modern world: the story of the efforts of Britain, Russia, and the United States to garner what, before the exploitation of undergound oil, was the greatest resource in the tundra and taiga. For the author, this is just the beginning — the first volume — of what promises to be a comprehensive history of the riveting of the region to the world.

He never lets the romance and spectacle seduce him. With patient, painstaking scholarship he reconstructs a story that is irrepressibly lively with adventure and excitement. John Bockstoce knows the world he writes about too well to be dazzled by the glare of the ice or daunted by the scale of the task. He has piloted an umiaq amid the ice floes of the Arctic, bedded down on 'bergs, and survived on a diet of old blubber and other Inuit treats and challenges. No other living historian can rival him in intimate knowledge of this milieu or mastery of the sources for the story. Among the book's most impressive features are the confidence the reader acquires in the author's familiarity with his world and the closeness of his narrative to the accounts participants left. Almost every page is alive with detailed allusions to or quotations from the journals and letters of participants. Familiar stories of Arctic exploration, such as those of Alexander Mackenzie, Peter Pond, and John Franklin, become more intelligible and more resonant than formerly in the context set by John Bockstoce.

No aspect of the story escapes him: the ecology of the furs, the politics and economics of the trade, the techniques of exploration and hunting and trading, the sometimes frightening logistics of the expeditions. But the core of the book is a tale of encounters between traders and the native communities who supplied them with their stock. I know of no work so helpful for anyone trying to understand why the interchanges between traders and Eskimos (as some peoples are properly called in some parts of what is now northwestern Canada and Alaska) were so violent and so riven with misunderstandings — far more so than encounters between natives and intruders in many other parts of the Americas. The book is full of revealing anecdotes: Alexei Lazarev's failure to impress Eskimos with his guns in 1820; or the tales of Chukotkan ingenuity in protecting their monopoly as key middlemen in fur dealing; or the evidence of the canniness of the Chukchi in general in eluding tribute and fixing favorable terms of exchange; or the intriguing mystery of how O-mi-ga-loon, a chief of the Point Barrow people in 1849, got his musket; or recollections of the days when a marten skin could buy a glassful of vodka at the Ostrovnoe Fair.

Rather like Confucius recounting in his devastatingly deadpan fashion the iniquities of ancient Chinese courts, John Bockstoce does not need to draw out the morals of the story for us. The facts are enough: the effects of the fur trade and whale fishery brought human tragedy and ecological catastrophe, where good intentions failed, heroism got perverted for evil ends, and malign ambitions triumphed. Now, as a new phase of overexploitation threatens the Beringian wilderness, John Bockstoce's account of the nineteenth-century phase is instructive and even admonitory, as well as engaging and enlivening.

Felipe Fernandez-Armesto

PREFACE

In the summer of 1969 I first became aware of the complexity of the historical Bering Strait fur trade. I was an assistant on an archaeological survey near the village of Gambell on St. Lawrence Island, where many of the Eskimos routinely dug in the ancient middens nearby for saleable artifacts and curios. I was offered several collections of glass beads, which, they said, had been traded to their ancestors by other Eskimos who lived forty miles across the northern Bering Sea, at Indian Point (Mys Chaplina) on the Chukchi Peninsula of what was then the Soviet Union. When I asked why these excavators had recovered so many beads, I was told, "Most of the people died here a hundred years ago." One of the Eskimos showed me a figurine he had carved from a piece of walrus tusk. The small sculpture was a stylized form of an Eskimo warrior wearing Chukchi-type armor. I asked if those people who had died a century before had been killed in warfare. "No, they starved to death," was the reply.

I left the island puzzled and curious about the region's history, and although I thought about these questions from time to time, no ready answers presented themselves. But in the following years, as I studied many museum collections from the Bering Strait region and western arctic America, I saw beads and other artifacts that could have originated only in Asia, and my interest grew about why and how these things had arrived in North America.

At the same time I began to grasp how vast were the distances that the Bering Strait fur trade encompassed. In the 1970s I traveled by small boat throughout the region, descending the Tanana and Yukon rivers by canoe from Fairbanks to Cape Nome and traveling along the coast by walrus-hide umiaq from there to Somerset Island in arctic Canada. Later I twice traversed the Northwest Passage by boat. On these journeys I met a number of natives who many years before had participated in the fur trade, and I began to appreciate what their lives had been like as frontier trappers in an earlier era, when their existence had been simpler and harder, yet to them was remembered fondly.

The fur trade of Bering Strait was one aspect of the European expansion into the most remote regions of Asia and America. At times it involved the contest for dominion between Russia and Great Britain, but at its basis was always the search for profit—in whatever way it was defined by the participants. Far beyond the Europeans and Americans who sought to buy furs, ivory, and whalebone for the markets in the south, members of fifty native nations provided these commodities to one another—and to foreigners—in return for goods that they required or desired. Manufactured goods, coastal products, inland products, tobacco, tea, alcohol, and hundreds of other things changed hands many times in the immense region between the Kolyma River in the west and the Mackenzie River in the east.

No matter which goods were exchanged, these transfers were almost universally regarded as advantageous by both parties. The belief that the native peoples were grossly exploited by foreign fur traders has long been current; yet the natives of the Bering Strait region willingly participated in these exchanges, and on both sides of the exchanges the participants thought they were receiving a favorable reward—by whatever scale of values they chose to measure that reward. The fur trade was an agent of massive change in the region, and this book is my attempt to answer those questions that I first pondered on St. Lawrence Island forty years ago.

A NOTE ON NAMES

My use of the ethnonym *Eskimo* is carefully chosen. In Canada *Inuit* has largely replaced *Eskimo*. If applied to all Eskimo peoples across the Arctic, as it often is, the term *Inuit* is inexact. For example, in Greenland the natives refer to themselves as *Greenlanders* or *Kalaallit*; in western arctic Canada they refer to themselves as *Inuvialuit*. In Alaska, however, *Eskimo* is commonly used as a broad reference to include the Iñupiat (adjective: Iñupiaq) of northern and western Alaska, as well as the Siberian Yupik of St. Lawrence Island and a few settlements on the coast of the Chukchi Peninsula, the Yup'ik [*sic*] of southwestern Alaska, and the Alutiiq (Sugpiaq) of the Pacific coast. For discussions of Eskimo synonymy see Goddard (1984, 5–7), Kaplan (1999), and Carpenter (1997, 310).

Russian names and words in the text have been transliterated using a slightly modified version of the standard Library of Congress system, simplifying some vowels and making certain combinations more accessible and easier to pronounce for the nonspecialist. Exceptions have been made for familiar names and phrases: for example, Cape Dezhnev, Koryak, and Tsar Peter.

ACKNOWLEDGMENTS

I have been working on various aspects of this book since the late 1960s, and through the years many persons have aided me in its development. I am grateful to all of them, and I hope this book in some small way is recompense for their kind assistance.

I thank most gratefully those who have helped with the research and those who have patiently read drafts of this book: Katherine Arndt, William Barr, Jack Borrebach, Ernest S. Burch, Jr., Eliza Childs, Paul Comstock, Maida Counts, Laura Davulis, Felipe Fernandez-Armesto, Patricia Fox, James R. Gibson, C. Ian Jackson, Christopher Rogers, and David H. Stam.

Others have been equally generous with their thoughts and help: Virginia Adams, the late Herbert Apposingok, the late Terence Armstrong, Serghei Aroutiounov, Jerry Austin, the late Elsie Backland, Hans-Georg Bandi, Judith Hudson Beattie, the late Lydia Black, the late Waldo Bodfish, Serghei Bogojavlensky, Naomi Boneham, Nadine Bonsor, Daniel Botkin, Nicole Bouche, Bill Boucher, Stephen Braund, Lawson Brigham, the late Thomas Brower, Sr., Bern Will Brown, Jennifer Brown, John J. Burns, Michael Carey, Edmund and Adelaide Carpenter, the late Fred Carpenter, Terrence Cole, the late Alan Cooke, Jeremy Coote, Bruce Courson, Aron Crowell, the late Thomas B. Crowley, Sr., Andrew Crow, Elizabeth Crownhart-Vaughan, C. A. Dana III, Susan Danforth, Andrew David, the late Mike Dederer, Gary and Pat Dederer, the late Richard von Doenhoff, Jacqueline Astor Drexel, Michael Dyer, the late Frank and Ursula Ellanna, Glenn Farris, Ann Fienup-Riordan, Norman Fiering, the late Richard Finnie, William Fitzhugh, Clare Fleming, David Forbes, Stuart Frank, the late Scotty Gall, Freddy Garfunkel, Craig George, Lile Gibbons, Ives Goddard, Archie Gottschalk, David Gregg, Bonnie Hahn, Cyrus Hamlin, Charles Hanson,

Jr., Todd Hanson, John Hattendorf, Robert Headland, Austen Hemion, George Hobson, Jacquline Hollister, the late Al Hopson, Pat Hostetter, the late James Houston, David Hull, Richard Hurley, the late Harold Huycke, Sven Johanssen, Lawrence Kaplan, Susan Kaplan, the late Herbert Kinneeveak, the late Jimmy Killigivuk, Jonathan C. H. King, the late H. G. R. King, the late Laurie Kingik, Bill Kooiman, Luke and Angeline Koonook, Michael Krauss, Shepard Krech III, Igor Krupnik, Richard Kugler, Karen Ordahl Kupperman, Michael LaCombe, Michael Lapides, Dennis Landis, Patricia Lai, Sue Largent, Molly Lee, the late Father Robert LeMeur, Genevieve LeMoine, Margaret Lennie, Dee Longenbaugh, Tom Lowenstein, Judith Navas Lund, Eona MacLean, Ross MacPhee, David Malaher, Mary Malloy, Carolyn Marr, Zena McGreevy, the late Dwight Milligrock, Craig Mishler, the late Lionel Montpetit, Ann Morton, the late Kivetoruk and Bessie Moses, Evelyn Stefansson Nef, Bill Nelson, the late Cornelius Osgood, David Owsley, the late Charles Pedersen, the late Ted Pedersen, Laura Peers, Laura Pereira, Ethan Pollock, the late Dorothy Cottle Poole, the late George W. Porter, George and Effie Porter, Suzi Prior, the late Thomas Pullen, the late Philip Purrington, Adeline Peter Raboff, the late Elmer Rasmuson, the late Dorothy Jean Ray, Carolyn Reader, Richard Ring, the late Tom Robinson, Jean-Loup Rousselot, Diana Rowley, the late Graham Rowley, Laura Samuelson, Peter Schweitzer, the late Slim Semmler, Peter and Alma Semotiuk, the late Chester Sevek, the late Leon Shelabarger, Ann Savours Shirley, the late William E. Simon, the late Shirlee A. Smith, Verbeck Smith, the staff of the Southworth Library, Rose Speranza, Deirdre Stam, Marcia Stentz, John Tichotsky, the late James VanStone, Thomas Vaughan, Louise Vietor, the late Roy Vincent, Brian Walsh, the late Lincoln and Tahoe Washburn, Bruce Watson, Candy Waugaman, Nicholas Whitman, Anne Witty, Edward Widmer, the late Robin Winks, the late Jim Wolki, Martin Wolman, Gordon Wood, and William Workman.

I am also deeply indebted to the explorers, traders, and scholars who have recorded and enlightened the history of the Bering Strait region—among them: Douglas D. Anderson, Waldemar Bogoras, Ernest S. Burch, Jr., Charles D. Brower, Don C. Foote, Edward William Nelson, John Murdoch, Froelich Rainey, Dorothy Jean Ray, James VanStone, Ferdinand von Wrangell, and Lavrenty Zagoskin.

Eskimos of Kotzebue Sound, 1816 (Choris 1822).

Part 1

$$\text{———●————}$$

THE ORIGINS OF THE FUR TRADE IN
THE BERING STRAIT REGION

The first foreign commercial voyage to Bering Strait took place in 1819, when the American trading brig *General San Martín* explored the region and discovered an active intercontinental native trade network carrying manufactured goods from Asia and furs from Alaska. This trade, nevertheless, was a comparatively recent development in the region and was the outcome of events that began centuries before in western Siberia and resulted in China becoming the primary market for the Alaskan furs.

THE OPENING OF THE MARITIME
FUR TRADE AT BERING STRAIT

As a summer fog lifted in Bering Strait on July 21, 1819, the American trading brig *General San Martín* lay near the towering, flat-topped island that would be known as Big Diomede. Twenty-five miles to either side rose the great headlands that are the gates of the Arctic Ocean—Cape Dezhnev, the easternmost point of Asia, and Cape Prince of Wales, the westernmost point of continental North America. The *General San Martín* had sailed north from Hawaii on an audacious voyage to scout the potential of the Bering Strait region for the fur trade. The brig was more than 3,000 miles from Hawaii, probably more than 800 miles from the nearest ship, and heading to Kotzebue Sound, an area that had been unknown to Europeans only three years before.

But the exotic grandeur of the scenery was probably lost on the *General San Martín*'s crew because a crowd of more than two hundred hostile Chukchi and Eskimos confronted their small brig with a fleet of eighteen walrus-hide umiaqs. A trading vessel was a convenient source of foreign goods—and one might assume that the natives would have welcomed it—but the Chukchi were not at all glad to see the *General San Martín* at Big Diomede. For thirty years they had controlled the cross–Bering Strait fur trade, carrying knives, tobacco, and beads to the natives of Alaska and returning with cargoes of furs that they then sold to other Chukchi, who would haul them overland to a rendezvous with Russian traders 800 miles west of Bering Strait. The Chukchi, one of the fiercest and most belligerently independent peoples of Asia, fully understood the implications of a foreign trading vessel's presence at Bering Strait, and they intended to protect their monopoly.

The *General San Martín*'s crew probably numbered about two dozen, but they had been warned that the natives of Bering Strait were aggressive and dangerous, and they were prepared for hostilities. In fact, two weeks earlier, as the brig worked its way northeast along the coast of Kamchatka, the captain, Eliab Grimes, had put the crew to work making cartridges for their muskets and over-hauling their four small cannons.

For four or five days the Chukchi blocked the Americans and prevented them from trading at Big Diomede. Grimes finally gave up and headed twenty miles northwest to Cape Dezhnev hoping to have better luck, but the Chukchi flotilla followed the ship and blocked it there too. "Finding myself foiled in this I bore up through Bering Straits," he reported, and headed northeast, toward Kotzebue Sound, in search of easier opportunities to trade for furs. But despite this setback, Grimes had already acquired important information. He had learned that Big Diomede Island served as a rendezvous where the Chukchi traders bartered their goods with Alaskan Eskimos, and the fact that the Chukchi had so aggressively protected their trade meant that a substantial amount of furs probably changed hands at the island.[1]

This information itself encouraged the American traders to conduct further reconnaissance, and, unknown to all parties, the *General San Martín's* voyage was the beginning of a commercial invasion that would overwhelm the region and its inhabitants throughout the nineteenth century.

Although the *General San Martín* was almost certainly the first trading vessel to reach Bering Strait, the voyage was the result of the forces that began forty years before, with Captain James Cook's third voyage of discovery. In Canton (today, Guangzhou) in 1779 Captain Cook's men were astonished to find that the sea otter pelts they had acquired for trifles from the natives on the North-west Coast of North America fetched phenomenal sums from the merchants of China, and when accounts of the Canton sea otter sales appeared in print in the 1780s, they set off a rush to the Northwest Coast.

For the Americans in particular, John Ledyard's unauthorized report of Cook's voyage, published in 1783 in Hartford, Connecticut, was a powerful lure to enter the maritime fur trade in the Pacific. Before that date American merchants in East Asia had been blocked by the East India Company's monopoly, but after the colonies achieved independence, American ships could trade throughout the Pacific without restraint. Ledyard's exaggerated report of skins "which did not cost the purchaser sixpence sterling [on the Northwest Coast] sold in China for 100 dollars" drew New England merchants to a new enterprise while Great Brit-ain — in the aftermath of the War of Independence — embargoed the products of the American whale and cod fisheries. To the Americans' advantage, however, the British traders in the Pacific soon found more lucrative opportunities in the opium trade (among other endeavors), and from about 1790 onward American ships dominated the maritime fur trade via highly lucrative triangular voyages, carrying manufactured goods and rum from the northeastern states to the Northwest Coast, carrying furs from there to Canton, and returning with Chinese products.[2]

By 1810, however, the boom years were in the past. Sea otter skins were in shorter supply, hence more expensive, and President Thomas Jefferson's Embargo Act of 1807—an effort to keep the United States out of the war between Britain and France—had prevented American vessels from sailing for foreign ports. "How Congress failed to throw out this absurdity is a mystery," wrote Paul Johnson. "While American ships remained in harbor, their crews idle and unpaid, smuggling flourished and British ships had a monopoly of legitimate trade." To make matters worse, the War of 1812 brought both a British blockade of the United States' ports and the capture of American merchantmen.[3]

But when the war ended in 1815, the Americans returned to the trade in force, and their voyages to the Pacific took on new dimensions and destinations in the search for profits. Sea otters—and later, beavers—were only two of the furs they bought on the Northwest Coast and traded to China. American ships also began carrying cargoes from Russian America to China and trading throughout the Pacific for a wide variety of commodities, such as betel nut, sugar, bird nests, *bêche de mer* (trepang), sandalwood, "and anything else that would catch an eye and open a purse in Canton."[4]

"The vessels were on the alert to add any other venture that gave a reasonable prospect of a saving voyage," wrote the historian F. W. Howay. "It followed that the ship owner could do no more than indicate in a general way the conduct to be pursued by the master. So much depended upon the conditions prevailing when the vessel reached the coast or other place at which she was to call. The result was that the maritime fur-trade had become, as one ship-owner expressed it, 'a voyage of adventure.'"[5]

At the same time, the emerging political revolutions against the rule of Spain in South America created new opportunities for the American traders. In 1817, as a stepping stone to an attack on the Viceroyalty of Peru, an Argentine general, José de San Martín, crossed the Andes "in one of those supreme feats of war" and defeated a Spanish army—an act that led to Chile's independence and the opening of its ports to foreign shipping. American merchant vessels, some of which had hitherto been involved in smuggling in Chile, soon began to visit its ports to take on cargoes of copper for the China trade.[6]

John Jacob Astor of New York, the central figure in the American fur trade, was always quick to seize new opportunities. Astor had entered the Pacific trade at the very beginning of the nineteenth century and operated a number of vessels. Shortly after Chile's liberation, an American fleet, including Astor's *Enterprise*, arrived at Coquimbo, Chile, from Hawaii early in 1818. Captain John Ebbets, Astor's trusted agent and associate, commanded the *Enterprise*. At Coquimbo, Ebbets took on a load of copper and bought a ship for William Heath Davis and Thomas Meek. The ship was a brig, the *General San Martín* (150 tons, 4 cannon), a prize that a revolutionary privateer had recently captured.[7]

Davis had arrived in Chile in command of the ship *Eagle*, which was owned by the Boston firm of Boardman and Pope. Boardman and Pope often cooperated in Pacific trading ventures with Astor. While the fleet was in Chile, Thomas Meek took command of the *Eagle* from Davis. Eliab Grimes, a widely experienced mariner and trans-Pacific trader, took command of the *General San Martín*. The *Enterprise* and the *General San Martín* then departed for Hawaii.[8]

The *General San Martín* stopped in Hawaii only briefly and then sailed for the coast of Asia. In September 1818, the brig touched at Okhotsk, the Siberian trading settlement on the northwest coast of the Sea of Okhotsk. Okhotsk lay at the terminus of the land route across Asia from St. Petersburg and was the transshipment port for the Russian-American colony. Failing to find a buyer for his cargo at Okhotsk, Grimes headed for Petropavlovsk on the east coast of the Kamchatka Peninsula. There, on behalf of Astor and Boardman and Pope, he sold Peter Dobell 25,000 rubles' worth of trade goods, which Dobell then loaded aboard Astor's brig *Sylph* for shipment to Manila. Grimes then took aboard another of Astor's captains, William J. Pigot, with a consignment of 60,649 of Astor's fur seal skins, which for three years Pigot had been unable to sell. During that time Pigot, however, had kept Astor and his associates apprised of the potential of the Siberian trade. The *General San Martín* sailed for Hawaii in October.[9]

Ebbets, Davis, Meek, Grimes, Pigot, and a few others made up a loose commercial fraternity of Pacific Ocean merchant mariners. This group of experienced Northwest Coast traders and entrepreneurs operated throughout the Pacific in the early years of the nineteenth century. They not only acted as agents and captains for several American trading companies but also, as opportunities arose, owned trading vessels outright or in partnership with those companies and with one another. Eliab Grimes, for example, was an agent not only for Astor but also several other firms, including Boardman and Pope, and Marshall and Wildes, both of Boston.[10]

But peerless among them in entrepreneurial energy was Peter Dobell, who led several of them into an attempt to create a whaling operation in Kamchatka to help feed the population there. Dobell was an Irish-American who went to sea after serving as an Indian fighter in western Pennsylvania. He landed in China in 1798 and spent thirteen or more years in the Canton area. From there, in 1805, he assisted Captain Ivan Fyodorovich Kruzenshtern during the round-the-world voyage of the Russian ship *Nadezhda* (*Hope*) and consequently established a relationship with the Russians in eastern Asia and was rewarded by the tsar. Much later he learned of a severe shortage of supplies in Kamchatka and in 1812 sailed to Petropavlovsk with two ships loaded with provisions. He traveled aboard one of them, John Jacob Astor's brig *Sylph*, and stayed on in Kamchatka. Dobell then traveled throughout the region, seeing firsthand its poverty and its potential.[11]

Provisions were always a problem for the Russians in those regions. In fact, almost as soon as they achieved their remarkably swift conquest of northern Asia and parts of Alaska, they faced the critical difficulty of supplying food to their own people. In particular, "on the Okhotsk Seaboard and the Kamchatka Peninsula," James R. Gibson wrote, "the Russians were beset with a chronic question of how, in such a harsh and distant region, to provision not only fur traders but also state servitors, missionaries, convicts, serfs, and scientific expeditions." For example, despite government efforts to encourage farming in Kamchatka, the experiment was a failure, and not only was state aid insufficient to sustain the population, but the catches of fish and animals were continuously poor. Confronted with these dismal prospects, in 1817 Captain of the First Rank Pyotr Ivanovich Rikord, a capable and honest naval officer who had recently been appointed as the commandant of Kamchatka, was forced to consider any opportunities available to him to acquire food and provisions.[12]

The year before, Dobell, "the tireless promoter," had proposed a plan to the governor-general of Siberia, Ivan Pestel, to supply foodstuffs to Kamchatka from the Philippine Islands, and Pestel had directed Rikord to discuss the matter with Dobell. Previously Dobell had traveled to St. Petersburg, where he became a subject of the tsar and arranged to be appointed as both a court councilor and the Russian consul general in Manila. The Spaniards, however, did not accept his credentials, and in 1818 he returned to Petropavlovsk, Kamchatka, where, with his trading business there in disarray, he "pestered" his friend Rikord with a plan to create a whaling operation as a way of providing meat for the indigenous population.[13]

Dobell must have sent word of his proposal to his associates in Hawaii, because on June 16, 1819, the *General San Martín*, with Eliab Grimes in command, arrived for the second time in Petropavlovsk. Dobell purchased the cargo, part of which he kept at Petropavlovsk, another part of which he sent to Okhotsk, and the rest of which he intended to sell in Manila. Aboard the *General San Martín* was William J. Pigot, as well as a crew for the *Sylph*, which was to sail at once under Pigot's command for Manila with Dobell aboard.[14]

Pigot carried with him powers of attorney from William Heath Davis, John Ebbets, and Thomas Meek to conclude a contract, with Rikord and Dobell signing for the Russian government—subject to the tsar's confirmation—to have exclusive rights to conduct a whale fishery for ten years, beginning in 1821, "on the eastern shores of Siberia." In return Pigot and his associates were to sell their whale products to the Russians and to teach a number of Russian sailors how to catch and process whales.[15]

But Rikord unfortunately had an enemy in Aleksandr Nikolaev, the Russian-American Company's resident agent in Petropavlovsk. "Both at that time and later, the trade of foreigners in Kamchatka and their protector, Rikord, were under strict supervision of the company's agents," wrote the historian V. Vagin. "Its Kamchatkan commissioner, Nikolaev, reported to the board of directors in all detail not only the actions but sometimes even the words of Rikord and the foreigners. In Kamchatka he was completely justifiably called a spy."[16]

Although Rikord had acted in the interest of the welfare of the people of Kamchatka, in St. Petersburg the Russian-American Company's directors immediately attacked the arrangement, seeing it as a dangerous infringement on the company's monopoly in its territories, which included all of Kamchatka, most of the Kurile Islands, and the shores of the Okhotsk Sea, as well as much of present-day Alaska. The company protested that this group of foreigners would use the whaling operation as a cover for hunting sea otters and fur seals, among other prohibited activities.[17]

The Russian-American Company was not, however, a private enterprise as it is understood today; rather, it was "an important auxiliary of the Imperial Russian government," "a de facto agency of the . . . government." In St. Petersburg the government nullified the contract, but because of the immense distance (more than 8,000 miles of overland travel) and slow communications between St. Petersburg and the East Asian settlements (six months or more, one way), Rikord, as we shall see, did not receive this order until September 1820.[18]

Most important for the history of the Bering Strait region, however, the *General San Martín*'s visit to Petropavlovsk was the departure point for a commercial reconnaissance in the North. The idea of searching for furs at Bering Strait had almost certainly occurred to John Ebbets and his associates in Hawaii in 1817. In October of that year, the Russian naval officer Otto von Kotzebue reached Honolulu aboard the 180-ton brig *Riurik* during his round-the-world voyage of discovery (1815–18). Kotzebue's expedition had probed the waters north of Bering

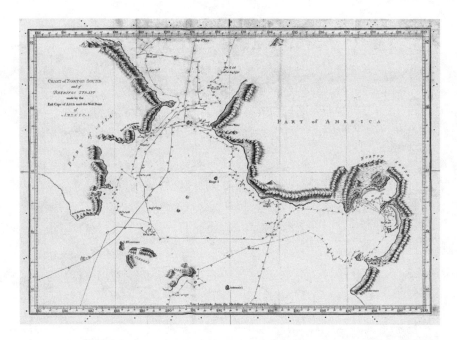

Map 1.1. Captain James Cook's chart of Bering Strait, 1878 and 1879. Captain James Cook's third voyage of discovery was the first non-Russian foreign visit to Bering Strait. The expedition's surveys produced a highly accurate chart of the region, but Cook's ships did not close with the coast immediately northeast of the strait, an area in which Otto von Kotzebue's expedition would chart Kotzebue Sound.

Strait and, in an area where Captain Cook had not closed with the American shore—but where earlier Russian maps had indicated that there might be a large embayment—he discovered the sound that bears his name. There the Russians encountered highly aggressive Eskimos. The explorers found that the Eskimos were expert, cunning, traders who held many furs—among them, red and black fox, muskrat, marten, river otter, and caribou—which, the Russians correctly assumed, were destined to be traded to the Chukchi.[19]

At that time Russians were unpopular in Hawaii because of a clumsy intrusion into Hawaiian politics by a German employee of the Russian-American Company. Despite this unpleasantness, Kotzebue proved to be a skillful diplomat in Honolulu, and he and his officers got on particularly well with the American traders William Heath Davis, John Ebbets, and Thomas Meek, among others. In fact, the Americans sent their ships' boats to help tow the *Riurik* out of the harbor on its departure. Because of these good relations, it is highly likely that the Russians told the Americans about their discoveries in the North—and it is

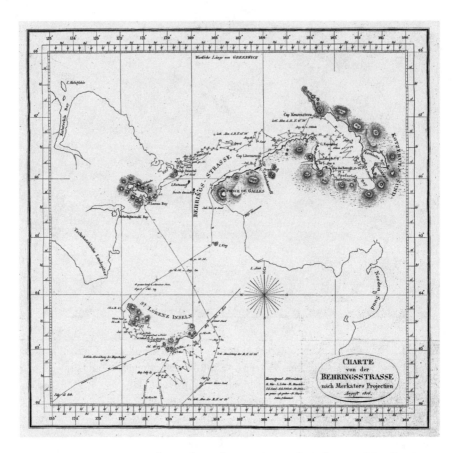

Map 1.2. Otto von Kotzebue's chart of Bering Strait, 1826. Otto von Kotzebue's expedition probed the waters immediately northeast of Bering Strait in search of a northwest passage. There, in an area that Captain James Cook's ships had not investigated, the Russians charted Kotzebue Sound.

significant that in December 1817, Ebbets, Davis, Meek, and others left Hawaii for Chile, where, as we have seen, Ebbets bought the brig *General San Martín.* In fact, Ebbets may have bought the *General San Martín* specifically to carry out a reconnaissance based on Kotzebue's discoveries because before the brig's arctic voyage of 1819 the owners entered into an agreement with the king of Hawaii, Kamehameha I, to sell the brig for 2,500 piculs of sandalwood on its return from the North.[20]

Count Nikolai Petrovich Rumiantsev, the chancellor of Russia, had sponsored Kotzebue's expedition at his own expense and sent it in search of a northwest passage, a northern water route between the Pacific and Atlantic oceans. On Au-

Figure 1.1. Eskimos of Shishmaref Inlet, 1816. The artist Louis Choris accompanied Otto von Kotzebue's round-the-world voyage of discovery (1815–18). In 1816, north of Bering Strait, the Russians encountered aggressive Eskimos who were deeply involved in the intercontinental fur trade. The men wore labrets piercing their cheeks. Labrets with blue glass beads attached were signs of wealth. The beads were probably made in China and had been carried across Bering Strait by native traders. Ludovik Choris Collection, Beinecke Rare Book and Manuscript Library, Yale University.

gust 15, 1818, the *Riurik* ended its voyage and anchored off Rumiantsev's palace in the river Neva. There can be little doubt that Kotzebue reported his discoveries to his patron then. Not long after that, judging from Grimes's correspondence, Rumiantsev must have written to Rikord in Kamchatka, suggesting further research on Kotzebue's discoveries at Bering Strait. In fact, Rumiantsev's original plan for a traverse of a northwest passage had included sending two expeditions, one ship from the west and another from the east. Kotzebue wrote that it was to be "under the direction of some enterprising American captain, for which purpose the Count had already opened a correspondence with America. This latter attempt was not made."[21]

During the *General San Martín*'s visit to Petropavlovsk in 1818, Grimes must have discussed with Rikord the possibility of a voyage to Bering Strait, and the following year Rikord, having received Rumiantsev's request for further investigations, must have viewed the *General San Martín's* planned northern voyage as a convenient opportunity to confirm Kotzebue's surveys for Rumiantsev, at no cost to the Russians. In fact, to assist the *General San Martín's* expedition Rikord not only gave Grimes a copy of Kotzebue's chart of the Bering Strait region but also provided him with an interpreter to help in communicating with the natives there.[22]

THE VOYAGE OF THE *GENERAL SAN MARTÍN*

In Petropavlovsk on June 29, 1819, Grimes wrote, "After gitting the necessaries ready, . . . at 2 PM Capt Ricord very politely set me onboard, after passing a little time took his leave wishing me a prosperous voyage." The *General San Martín* then weighed anchor and stood out of the bay. Grimes paused briefly to receive a letter from Thomas Meek, from a Russian brig inbound from Novo-Arkhangelsk, the Russian-American Company's headquarters on the Northwest Coast of America.[23]

Continuing onward, on July 4 Grimes wrote, "This being a remarkable day, the people was [regaled?] with fresh pork and an extra glass of grogg." But with Kotzebue's report of the aggressive natives at Bering Strait no doubt in mind, the next day he began preparing for the encounter. "We lost no time in getting ready to meet any hostile intentions from natives," he added. "Should we meet with any [we] put our large guns in order and muskets, making cartridges."[24]

Grimes pushed ahead to the northeast, parallel to the Asian coast. On the eleventh, in thick fog, the *General San Martín* reached the northwest corner of St. Lawrence Island and hove to where Kotzebue had paused. Grimes sent his boat to shore and an hour later it returned accompanied by several native umiaqs. "When along side," he wrote, "I found they had a considerable quantity of horse teeth [walrus tusks] and a few fox skins which we bought for a little tobacco." The following day twelve umiaqs arrived with twelve to fourteen persons in each boat. "We bought what they had for sale," Grimes continued, "which in all amounted to about forty skins and about thirty hundred weight of teeth. I bicame quite elated with the good success I had met with which led me to believe I should make a good voyage."[25]

"You might naturally ask the reason I did not continue about the Island longer," he wrote to John Ebbets in September. "I was anxious to git the fur and teeth at the Bay of St. Lawrence and its neighbouring places before they were carried to the Russian settlements, and having been presented one of Kotzebues chart of

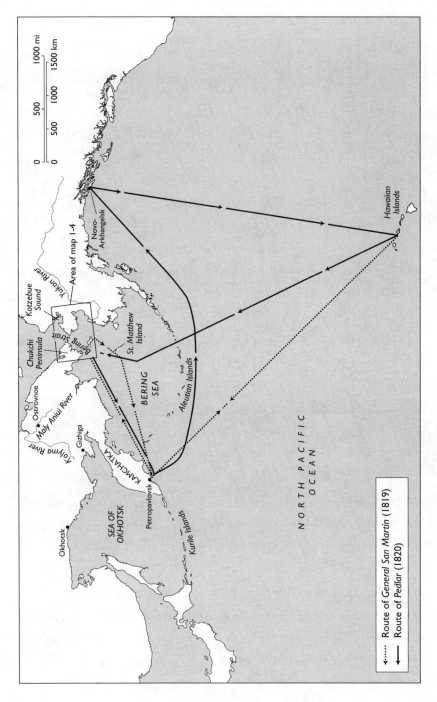

Map 1.3. Routes of the *General San Martín* (1819) and *Pedlar* (1820) in the North Pacific.

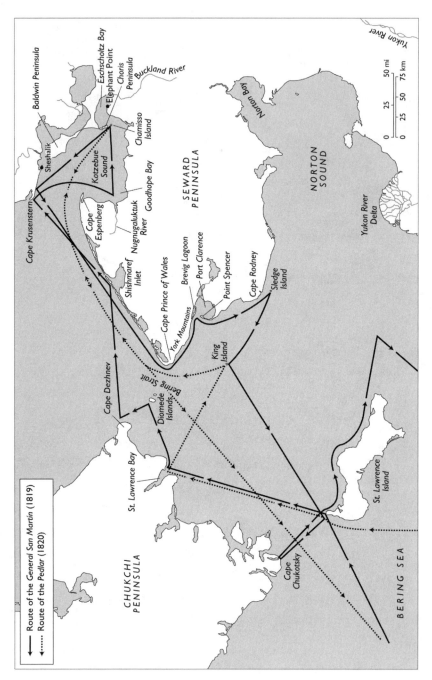

Map 1.4. Routes of the *General San Martín* (1819) and *Pedlar* (1820) in Bering Strait.

Figure 1.2. Interior of a Chukchi dwelling at St. Lawrence Bay, 1816. Louis Choris sketched the inhabitants of a Chukchi house when Kotzebue's expedition visited the west shore of Bering Strait. A large iron pot, which probably entered Chukchi hands at one of the trade fairs in Chukotka, hangs above the fire. Ludovik Choris Collection, Beinecke Rare Book and Manuscript Library, Yale University.

his sound and Chesmurofs straits [Shishmaref Inlet] by Capt Ricord and strongly recommended to visit the place as it would be the most likely to reward me for my labour while the season was favorable."[26]

So Grimes, prompted by Rikord and aided by a copy of Kotzebue's chart, headed first to St. Lawrence Bay on the eastern coast of the Chukchi Peninsula. After three days at anchor, the word of the brig's presence had spread, and "there were great numbers alongside, however I found there was no one had fur or teeth of any consequence except the chief and his brother and in order to trade I was requested to go ashore."

"I must confess the invitation was not so pleasing as it would have been for New York or Boston," he continued, "however during my stay I was treated very well and after examining their property it was sent on board after agreeing and paying them which was forty skins of the same bulk of tobacco moderately stowed into the same bag which contained the skins."

Grimes then steered directly to the Diomede Islands, the two small, vertical-sided rocks that stand midway in Bering Strait about twenty-five miles from either shore. There, as we have seen, he quickly learned the central reality of commerce in that region. He discovered the existence of a robust and well-organized intercontinental native trade between America and Asia and learned that its participants did not welcome foreign competition. "I fell in with two of the Tschutski [Chukchi] chiefs with an hundred men each which comes from the East Cape [Cape Dezhnev] of the Asiatic coast yearly and makes this Island called Imjacklima [*Imaqłiq*, Big Diomede Island] there central place of trade and receiving all the fur near Cape Prince of Wales and as far to the southward as Norton Sound."[27]

Thus Grimes found that Big Diomede Island served as an entrepôt between the Eskimos of Norton Sound and the Chukchi of northeasternmost Asia. Grimes's observation was confirmed in 1833 by Mikhail Tebenkov, who was a captain of Russian-American Company trading vessels in the Bering Strait region and, later, chief manager of the colony. "The main place of barter for the Chukchi with the Americans," he wrote, "is Imaklit Island, where they either go themselves or send agents from among the sedentary Chukchi."[28]

Grimes continued, "After spending four or five days with them and not being able to do any thing for want of proper trade I left for an Island about twenty miles to the NNW." Kotzebue's chart of Bering Strait shows another island (which does not exist), northwest of the two Diomedes and their neighbor, Fairway Rock. I believe that Grimes, aided by a copy of Kotzebue's chart, thought he was heading for this island when in fact he was heading for "East Cape" (Cape Dezhnev). The bold headland of Cape Dezhnev is joined to the Chukchi Peninsula by a twenty-mile-wide lowland. From a distance it appears to be an island. To judge from his course when leaving the Diomedes, it can be assumed that Grimes headed to Cape Dezhnev, where the Chukchi traders, more than two hundred strong, again blocked his attempt to intercept the furs.

"I had no sooner arrived than I saw the whole fleet to the number of eighteen boats carrying twelve and thirteen men each following in order to prevent my trading, as they had done at the one I had just left. Finding myself foiled in this I bore up and passed through Bering Straits." The Chukchi traders once again showed Grimes that they understood full well that his presence at Bering Strait threatened their trade monopoly.

As Grimes approached Shishmaref Inlet, he must have remembered Kotzebue's report of the difficult encounter there with the Eskimos, but his visit was uneventful. "On the 27 July fell in with Chesmerofs straits [Shishmaref Inlet] . . . having a large village on the western shore and not seeing any natives I concluded they were curing their winter stock of fish. On the 29th I left for Kotzebues Sound and on the 30th we made Cape Cruzenstern [Krusenstern], the northern point latitude 67°10 where we saw a few natives but owing to the heavy surf were not able to land. I stood for the southern shore and in the evening came to an anchor [in] 4½ fathoms water . . . our distance from shore fourteen to fifteen miles bearing from west to SE." The *General San Martín* was anchored in Goodhope Bay, the southwestern embayment of Kotzebue Sound.[29]

"The following morning I sent Mr. Dyrkee to examine the shores so far as was practicable. He returned after being twenty four hours without seeing any natives. I than made sail for the head of the sound keeping the northern shore in view but did not see any natives untill we arrived at the head, where we fell in with about one hundred and fifty of them."[30]

The *General San Martín* was probably now near the Choris Peninsula and Chamisso Island, where Kotzebue had anchored in 1816, in the inner waters of Kotzebue Sound. This area was within the territory of the Buckland River Eskimos, the Kaŋiġmiut nation, one of approximately thirty nations of indigenous peoples in northwestern Alaska. Grimes no doubt encountered the Eskimos in Eschscholtz Bay, where the Kaŋiġmiut gathered to hunt the great numbers of beluga whales that enter the estuary each summer.[31]

"I bought eighty skins," Grimes continued, "but no [walrus] teeth except three small ones which they esteemed much more valuable than their skins, for pointing their spears and using them as a pick ax. . . . I found they had the Russian long knife and large blue bead also a small piece of iron about [word omitted] inches long stub answering for an adz."[32]

There Grimes confirmed two things that Kotzebue had learned: that the Eskimos' foreign trade goods came from Asia and that glass beads and iron were in demand. Grimes then headed on, in search of more trading opportunities. "I left this keeping the southern shore in sight and when we ware about half way to the entrance, came to in four fathoms. Sent Mr. Durkee in the direction SW where hee saw a few natives that were a fishing. They not having any fur nor seeing any other, he shortly returned."[33]

Grimes added a note to Ebbets about the depth of water and the low, tundra-covered shores surrounding inner Kotzebue Sound and about the advantage of having a small boat (which, in fact, he did carry aboard the *General San Martín*) to approach the coast: "The situation of the sound is such and from that to Cape Prince of Wales in regard to shoal water making off to such a distance . . . [requiring] a tender to examine where we were hardly able to see the shores which are low, the land in the country rising to a moderate hight entirely destitute of shrub or tree."

"On the 9th of August anchored of Cape Cruzenstern abrest of a Village when we were visited by a number of natives. Finding they had no fur or teeth I left for Chesmerofs straits and arrived on the eleventh, where we saw a number of natives and bought what skins they had, which was about twenty but no teeth and have every reason to believe they seldom, or ever, see any of the sea horses [walruses] in the sound or about the shores north of the Cape." Walruses are rarely found in Kotzebue Sound.

The reason that Grimes could buy no furs at Cape Krusenstern and only a few at Shishmaref Inlet was because the Eskimos had just returned from their great annual trade fair at Sheshalik (*Sisualiq*), the sandspit in the northeastern corner of Kotzebue Sound. More than seventeen hundred persons from most of the Eskimo nations of northwestern Alaska (as well as a few natives from farther away) met there annually—in a season of truce—to trade, dance, feast, and engage in athletic competitions, among other activities. Most of the furs had been exchanged by then, and the traders were on their way to their homelands. In fact, many of the furs were no doubt already on their way to the Chukchi Peninsula when Grimes stopped at Big Diomede.[34]

"I left here with a fresh gale from NW, thick weather, and passed Prince of Wales during the night . . . brought in a little to the southward of Cape Prince of Wales. In the afternoon it became more moderate with pleasant weather. Stood to south there, keeping near the shore but saw no natives nor the appearance of any as it is barren and mountainous, rising abruptly from the water's edge until you get to the latt 65°22 where it trends to the E by S."[35]

Grimes continued his reconnaissance along the southwestern coast of what is today the Seward Peninsula. He wrote, "After running about thirty miles, came to. In the morning I found we had anchored near a fine beach covered with driftwood. On landing we saw some natives which informed me by signs they had been with their boats and sold their fur, pointing to the north of west [toward Bering Strait]. A few miles to the south by east I found a good harbour. Although formed by low land, it [is] of a sufficient hight to keep the sea off."[36]

Grimes had found the large, sheltered embayment of Port Clarence, which is enclosed by Point Spencer's long gravel spit. Another native trade fair took place in Port Clarence. Here members of more southerly Eskimo nations, from as far south as the Yukon River delta, met annually with King Islanders, Diomeders, Seward Peninsula Eskimos, Asiatic Eskimos, and Chukchi.[37]

"I left this and examined the shores [as] far as Cape Rodney and Sledge Island and all the natives we saw informed me the same as before mentioned. I found it to correspond exactly to what the Tchutski chiefs had informed me; that they get most of their fur from the Americans.[38]

"Finding I was not able to do anything in this quarter I run for Kings Island and arrived on the 18th of August. Here I bought . . . a hundred skins, thirty of them silver grey [foxes] and half of thoes we had to buy with the boat anchored near the shore, owing to a fresh breeze which [raising?] a short sea." The King Island Eskimos were traders themselves. The only fur products locally available at King Island—a tall, vertical-sided speck of rock, nearly forty miles off the coast of the Seward Peninsula—were seals, polar bears, and arctic foxes.

Grimes then warned Ebbets of another reality of trading with the Eskimos of the Bering Strait region. Referring to the steep swell—and, by extension, to its accompanying breakers—he encountered at King Island, he explained, "when [a heavy swell and breakers] is the case the natives will not visit you, and to trade with them on shore you run a great risque of your boat and people being captured, as they have made two attempts and it will always be found difficult to trade in thoes seas for want of a harbour where they can visit you with ease and you then feel yourself safe on board, trading the usual way with natives." Grimes was no doubt drawing on his experiences in trading with the natives on the Northwest Coast, where traders always had to be on their guard in case of hostile action and consequently trading usually took place aboard ship in carefully controlled situations.

To judge from Grimes's reference to two attempts by the Eskimos to capture his longboat and crew, the *General San Martín*'s men may have had difficult encounters with the Eskimos in Kotzebue Sound and at King Island. This is not surprising. In 1816, when the *Riurik* was on the west side of Bering Strait at St. Lawrence Bay, a Chukchi man told Otto von Kotzebue that the natives on the American side of the strait were treacherous. "The Tschukutskoi live in eternal enmity with the [Eskimos]; and my venerable guest, without hesitation, declared them all to be bad men. As a proof of his assertion, he said, that they behaved friendly as long as they considered themselves weaker; but robbed and murdered strangers without hesitation, if they were strong enough, and were able to do it without danger; and, for this reason he thought they wore knives in their sleeves, and use their wives to entice them."[39]

Grimes continued his report to Ebbets. "I left here for Clark's Island [St. Lawrence Island] and on my arrival at the Village where I sailed first the chief informed me that the Tchutska traders from Cape Anadyr had been to the island during my absence and bought all there was, both teeth and fur of any size, as they all know where to meet the traders, which is at the NW part of the Island. I amediately left in hopes to fall in with them and on the 22nd arrived at the cape, where I fell in with a number of natives. They inform me the traders had arrived and that they had sold them their fur and teeth and had mounted their raindeer and were on there way to the Russian settlements. (I forgot to observe that I had a linguist which was through the [word omitted] of Capt Ricord) however I got about thirty teeth that had lately been taken and about four hundred weight of whalebone."[40]

Grimes wanted to buy a supply of reindeer meat and spent two days trying to find a harbor nearby on the Chukchi Peninsula, but he finally gave up and returned to St. Lawrence Island to conduct further explorations. At the northeastern corner of the island he learned from the natives that they also had already sold all their "furs and teeth" to the traders. Realizing that the *General San Martín* had arrived after most of the native trade had concluded, he wrote, "I was now convinced, . . . there was nothing more to be done to advantage on the north." On August 28 he headed south. After searching for "Preobragenia" Island, a nonexistent island that his Arrowsmith chart indicated to be southwest of St. Matthew Island, on September 9 the *General San Martín* returned to Petropavlovsk. There Grimes immediately wrote his long report to John Ebbets in New York.[41]

Ebbets—who, as we have seen, had bought the *General San Martín* in Chile in 1818—arrived in New York in September 1819, still in command of John Jacob Astor's *Enterprise*. There he concluded a four-year voyage during which he had traveled throughout the Pacific, carrying cargoes of sea otter and seal skins, sandalwood, and copper to Canton. But Ebbets learned on his arrival that John Jacob Astor had departed from New York in June for extended travels in Europe, leaving the conduct of his business affairs in the capable hands of his son, William Backhouse Astor. Ebbets must have informed the younger Astor of Eliab Grimes's activities in the Pacific in 1818 and of his plans for a northern cruise in 1819.[42]

Grimes continued his letter to Ebbets with succinct advice about the Bering Strait trade. "In attempting to carry on a trade in those seas the vessel should arrive by the first of July or before, if the ice will admit. Collect all that can be got at Clarks Island [St. Lawrence Island], touch at Cape Anadyr and St. Lawrence Bay, proceed to the island in the straits [Big Diomede Island], where you may stand a chance of getting a part of the fur that comes from the American coast, but not all untill they are tought to believe that a vessel will visit them yearly, as they all know at what time to meet the traders, and the whole business is all over by the first or tenth of August. They amideately leave this for the East Cape [Cape Dezhnev] and from that to the Russians settlements on the river Kovima [Kolyma] and Ingiga [Gizhiga] at the head of ochotska sea, where they dispose of their fur."

Thus Grimes had confirmed Kotzebue's observation and identified for Ebbets the substantial flow of furs that annually were carried west, out of Alaska and across Bering Strait to the Asian mainland, where they were traded to Chukchi, who carried them to the Russian trading centers. He also called for intercepting the furs by encouraging the Eskimos to anticipate annual visits by trading vessels. As we shall see, this sensible advice was identical to the conclusions that the Russian-American Company's traders would draw during the next forty years.[43]

Grimes then listed the trade goods that the natives sought: "[They] receive in return large knives from 18 to 24 inches long and one fourth of an inch thick, ornamented with brass near the Handle, also a lance in the form of a spontoon [halberd] having a bar on each side similar to that of an . . . Index on a Quadrant inlaid with brass, large scissors, small adzes, hatchets, iron pots, copper tea kettles, looking glasses, sewing needles, large blue and dark glass beads, size of a nutmeg, sheet lead and the best Cazan Tobacco." Grimes's instructions no doubt directed him to estimate the amount of walrus ivory and fur seal skins that might be available in the Bering Strait region. But first he corrected a misconception about walruses shedding their tusks: "The idea of finding Sea Horse teeth about these shores is equally absurd as that of finding guineas in the streets of New York—or that they shed their teeth any oftener than a Bullock does his horns, as has been mentioned by some, is equally erroneous, as I have bought them standing in the upper part of the head, weighing from 1 to 8 pounds, the size of the head in proportion to that of the teeth as the small ones belong to the younger animals."

The idea that walrus ivory could be collected on the shores of Bering Strait probably began with the reports of Semyon Dezhnev's expedition. Dezhnev and his men discovered a walrus rookery near the mouth of the Anadyr and collected walrus ivory in quantity on the beaches there in the years after his voyage of 1648. The report received attention in the English-speaking world when William Coxe published a description of Dezhnev's voyage in 1780.[44]

Then Grimes turned to the question of fur seals, which at that time were a valuable commodity. "I can with safety inform you there is no fur Seal in any place or Island that I have visited, which is all to the Northward of Clark's, including the one in Kotzebues Sound." Fur seal (*Callorhinus ursinus*) skins sold well in China because of their soft and warm fur. Their primary range is, however, in the central and southern Bering Sea and throughout the northern North Pacific. They are only rarely found near Bering Strait.[45]

Grimes then tallied the results of his barter: "I have subjoined a list of fur and teeth, and what I gave: 226 Red Foxes, 34 Silver Grey, 32 White, 17 Blue, 3 Black, 85 Martin [marten] skins, 10 pack same 19 each, 9 Small beavers, 1 land Otter, 1 Cat Skin [lynx], 66 Muskrats, and 1 kind I am not acquainted with but is said to be of Value [possibly a wolverine] and should say from 2½ to 3 tons of Horse [walrus] teeth."[46]

For these Grimes paid "145 large knives, 30 of those belonging to yourself, a pr Old Pistols, 5 Looking Glasses, 1 carp[enter']s Adze, 1 Hammer, 1 Pick Axe, 3 Iron pots, 11 of those Iron Kettles from the Sultan, 4 lb of those small blue Beads, and about 3 poods of Cazan Tobacco that I got of Mr. Dobell, shirt and 1 pr trousers."[47]

Grimes noted elsewhere in his business letter book—apparently to aid his memory—an inventory of desirable items to carry in "trade for the tschutkus." He listed "large thick knives from 10 to 20 inches in length, from 1½ eight to 2 [eighths?] of an inch thick on the back, 1½ inch wide, kazan tobacco, flints and [fire]steels, lead, scissors—iron pots, sewing needles, round blue and red beads about the size of large buck shot. Black [beads of the same size], looking glasses, dark and light sky blue beads size of a nutmeg, and of prunes and cast in the form of this [he sketched a cylindrical bead] made of glass (some white), best of cazan tobacco, a few pick axes, knives 3 feet long, lances about a foot long with a bar in the center projecting . . . each side [a halberd], iron pots holding from 4 to 5 gallons, small axes and adzes."

Most important, Grimes estimated that a trading cruise to the Bering Strait region could be carried out as a segment of a more comprehensive voyage to the North Pacific: "A voyage to the North connected with business at this place or with a North West Voyage as it would not take more than 2½ [months] I should think might answer. . . . I think there might be about $10,000 worth of fur and teeth collected for $1,000 of trade."[48]

Beyond the fact that the *General San Martín*'s gross fur returns were worth ten times the cost of the trade goods, the northern cruise had produced a valuable cargo of commercial intelligence. Grimes had learned that Eskimos carried furs and walrus tusks to Big Diomede Island and bartered them there to Chukchi traders in return for knives, pots and other metal goods, beads, and tobacco. The Chukchi then carried the furs farther, to trade with Russians on the Kolyma River and at the head of the Sea of Okhotsk. But Grimes had also learned that two valuable commodities he almost certainly sought for the Chinese market were more difficult to acquire: fur seal skins were not available in the Bering Strait region and walrus ivory did not litter the shores, waiting to be collected.[49]

In Petropavlovsk, Grimes reported the details of his cruise to Pyotr Rikord and agreed to continue the Bering Strait survey the following summer, 1820. Grimes promised that, should he himself not be able to carry out the survey, an associate would come north to do it. Grimes placed his furs in Peter Dobell's care and arranged to have them shipped to Joseph H. Gardner, his agent in Okhotsk, instructing Gardner to sell them "to the best advantage" and to forward the proceeds to Meyer and Bruxner, agents in St. Petersburg, Russia, who would divide the credit equally between "Messrs Boardman and Pope of Boston and John Jacob Astor of New York."

The *General San Martín* then headed to Hawaii, and there, on December 15, for $10,000 William J. Pigot bought the brig from its owners, William Heath Davis and Thomas Meek. As we have seen, however, before the *General San Martín*'s northern cruise, her owners had agreed to sell the brig to the king of Hawaii for 2,500 piculs of sandalwood, payable on its return, but King Kamehameha died on May 8, 1819, and the agreement was not concluded. Pigot immediately sent the ship to Manila.[50]

THE VOYAGES OF THE *PEDLAR* AND THE *BLAGONAMERENNY*

On December 15, 1819, the same day that the *General San Martín* arrived in Honolulu, Eliab Grimes wrote to Pyotr Rikord, answering a letter that Rikord had sent to Pigot (which Grimes himself probably carried to Hawaii). No doubt as a consequence of the agreement that Rikord and Grimes had reached in September, Rikord had written to Pigot asking about undertaking further "surveys and discoveries for and on Acct of Count Romanzoff [Rumiantsev]." Grimes replied to Rikord that it was necessary for him (Grimes) to "proceed to America for the Purpose of procuring a suitable Vessel of Cargo for this Ocean," adding, with his eye firmly focused on the bottom line, that "it is very uncertain that I shall go to the North, as the amount of property that can be collected is so small it will not be worth going for while there is other business of more profit, but should I go that way, I will give you all the information that I am capable of, should I have time and not interfere with my business." Despite Grimes's gross returns of ten times the cost of the trade goods, he apparently could find better profit margins elsewhere. As we shall see, however, Pigot did in fact agree to Rikord's request and did go north in 1820.[51]

Shortly after replying to Rikord, Grimes took passage to Boston aboard Boardman and Pope's ship *Eagle*, with Thomas Meek in command. Later, in Canton, Grimes wrote to Dobell in Manila, reaffirming his reluctance to return to Bering Strait. Grimes asked Dobell to send word to Rikord via one of his vessels, informing Rikord again that it would not be possible for him (Grimes) to carry out Count Rumiantsev's request for further explorations in that region because "it is not certain that I shall go to the North on Acct of the small Amt of property that can be collected."[52]

While in Canton, Astor's agent Nicholas Gouverneur Ogden gave Grimes a letter from John Ebbets in New York. Ebbets reported that Astor was in Europe and that it was unlikely that he (Ebbets) would "be able to send a Vessel out this season." Astor, farsighted as always, was reassessing his commitment to the Pacific trade. "I have understood," Grimes continued, "that Mr. Astor is not pleased with the result of the Voyage—We understand that Mr. Astor is getting rather indifferent about business however he has probably gone to Europe to make future arrangements."[53]

But Grimes probably knew that another of Astor's vessels would fulfill his promise of a further survey in the North: the brig *Pedlar* (225 tons, with eight three-pound guns) by then was about to arrive in Hawaii. Late in 1819 the *Pedlar* had set out from New York under the command of John Meek, Thomas Meek's brother, carrying a cargo of "gin, brown sugar, cloth and other goods." The brig reached Honolulu on May 23, 1820, where, John Walters, the boatswain, glad to be there, noted in his journal, "wee got our yellow legged lasses on board." The *Pedlar* also took aboard William J. Pigot, who would serve as the ship's agent and supercargo and who would consequently direct the vessel's movements during the trading cruise in the North.[54]

During June the *Pedlar* cruised among the Hawaiian Islands and sold part of the cargo to "the vassal king of Kauai" for 191 piculs of sandalwood. The *Pedlar* then returned to Honolulu, took on fresh provisions and water, and headed north with, Walters wrote, "a fine breeze to leave our copper coulard lasses." On July 20 the *Pedlar* reached St. Lawrence Island ("Clarks Island") "at the entrance to the straits" and, after having sailed nearly 3,000 miles from Hawaii, "came to anchor in 10 fathoms. Wee got the natives off to trade. They brout furs and sea horse teeth and wee gave them small quantity of tobaco and beads and so forth in return. While lying to anchor saw A ship. We got under way and spoke her. She was A Russian on discovery."[55]

Acting on Grimes's information, Pigot had directed Captain Meek to anchor the *Pedlar* at the northwestern tip of St. Lawrence Island, where Kotzebue and Grimes had paused. This is where the brig lay when the Russian naval vessel *Otkrytie* (*Discovery*) came upon it. The *Otkrytie* was under the command of Captain-Lieutenant Mikhail Nikolaevich Vasiliev, the leader of the northern section of a four-ship voyage of discovery. The *Otkrytie*, inbound from Petropavlovsk, was headed to Kotzebue Sound to rendezvous with the *Blagonamerenny* (*Benevolent*), and from there they were to search for a northwest passage across northern North America to the Atlantic. The *Otkrytie* overhauled the *Pedlar* to ask whether the Americans had seen its partner.[56]

The Americans had not seen the ship, and the *Pedlar* moved onward, almost certainly to St. Lawrence Bay on Grimes's advice. Walters continued, "We stood for the continent Asia and hove two off a village and a few of the natives came off but not willing to trade. We sent one man on shore to see if they would trade, we keeping some of the natives on board till the man returned which was the next morning and they would not trade with us." Perhaps the Chukchi traders were protecting their monopoly by refusing to trade with the *Pedlar*'s man or, more likely, had already traded their furs to middlemen who were on their way west.[57]

On July 25 the *Pedlar* arrived at King Island. The fact that Pigot headed there before going to Kotzebue Sound suggests that he was acting on Grimes's advice and trying to intercept the furs before they reached the Chukchi traders. "The natives came on board," wrote Walters, "and we traded for fur and ivory and giving tobacco and beads in return. The natives seem to be friendly."

The Americans thought that the King Island Eskimos were not hostile — contrary to Grimes's apparent assessment of their intentions the year before. Some of the King Islanders, were, of course, on board the *Pedlar*, where they were presumably outnumbered by the brig's crew of about thirty, and probably therefore behaved passively. On shore, however, with the numbers reversed, they might have acted very differently, as Grimes had warned. In any case, Pigot must have felt comfortable enough to allow one of them to have a firearm. The King Islanders apparently had not seen such a weapon. "We let the chief have a musket. They not knowing the use of it, but we showed them by firing it off." Two years later, in 1822, the chief's son, Kunaginyn, asked Vasily Stepanovich Khramchenko (who was in command of the Russian-American Company's brig *Golovnin*) for gunpowder, presumably for this firearm. The Russian-American Company's policy forbade trading firearms or alcohol to the northern natives.[58]

Walters then witnessed the first recorded encounter between an inhabitant of the Bering Strait region and a pig. "I see one of them come forward and we had some hages [hogs] under the boat which grunted. That frightened the fellow that he run aft in such a hurry that he fell his lenth on the deck as if the divil was after him."

The King Islanders had "broad faces and eyes resembling the chinius [Chinese], Walters wrote. "It is hard to till the woman from the man by their dress, but I see some of them very handsome featured. Their clothing is of rain deer skin and cama links that is made of sea lion guts and throtes neatly sewed together which is fine for standing water. Their ornaments is ivory curiously carved which they do with stones."

He added, "They are employed in hunting and fishing for sea horse and whale, seal and so forth. All this done with spears and bows and arrows made of sea horse teeth. Their boats is slightly formed and covered with sea horse hide when dried. Their diet is of the sea horse, blubber, oil and fish. They [have] no bread or any thing of the like amongst them. They seem to live happy in their way."[59]

The *Pedlar* then continued north, through Bering Strait and toward Kotzebue Sound. The Americans were unaware that the *Otkrytie's* partner-in-discovery, the *Blagonamerenny*, was already in Kotzebue Sound. On July 22, 1820, the *Blagona-merenny*, about five days ahead of the *Otkrytie*, reached near Cape Espenberg, the southernmost of the two points of land that enclose Kotzebue Sound.[60]

Midshipman Nikolai Dmitrievich Shishmaryov recorded their first encounter with the Eskimos of Kotzebue Sound.

At 10:30 [PM] we saw a baidara [umiaq] coming toward us from Cape Espen-berg. On its approach we saw 7 people in it, all paddling hard. . . . We began to shout to them "Tavvakom," that is, tobacco, thinking that they were as fond of it as on [St.] Lawrence Island. Though they answered us, we did not under-stand; but soon they set course directly for us, meanwhile having held a red fox [skin] on a pole. We immediately could understand that they wanted to trade furs with us. As soon as they came alongside the captain immediately gave them a little tobacco, and for this they gave one fox. However, we could barter nothing from them, because they are so seasoned in trade that they are not inferior to our bazaar merchants. . . . For example, they did not want to take knives, scissors, needles, mirrors, and other such things; and if someone looked at something, he examined it with great attention and the slightest rust or damage did not appeal to them and they gave it back. Their demands were for axes.

The Eskimos then left the Russians.

At 12:30 we again saw 4 baidaras a little bigger than the first coming toward us, which soon fearlessly came alongside. In them were 42 people in all, the same sort of traders as the first. At the top of their voices they beckon toward them-selves and try to barter something, but they price their things so high that it was impossible to barter anything. Their demands were the same as those of the first, and in half an hour they all left the vessel. One must note that there was a woman in one baidara, a real fury; with disheveled black hair . . . she shouted ceaselessly with all her might.[61]

Lieutenant Aleksei Petrovich Lazarev, aboard the *Blagonamerenny*, also de-scribed meeting the Eskimos from Cape Espenberg and added some details about them, although he conflated the two encounters that Nikolai Shishmaryov reported.

We had an encounter with the American savages from the western settlement of Cape Espenberg. They came to us 48 strong in five baidaras [umiaqs] and wanted to barter their furs, but we did not take them and instead gave them gifts of tobacco and other trifles. The savages came directly alongside our sloop straightaway, but not one of them dared to come aboard no matter how much we tried to persuade them. They were dressed in ground squirrel or muskrat parkas, very neatly sewn, and almost all had perforations under the lower lip at the corners of the mouth in which was stuck a large sky blue bead set with bone or stones of various colors. It sccms that one can recognize their eldeis by this decoration because some of them had a bead of larger size and better set than the others. Near their ears and nose[,] down the whole length of the face were pricked various figures, and they are always ready to make a new hole any place in their face in order to pass through it a thread of worthless beads given to them; they especially chose sky blue ones. We wanted to barter weapons from them, but they tried to sell foxes instead, for each of which they requested either an ax or a large knife, but as we did not need this trade item of theirs to make up our collection of curios, we gave them gifts of tobacco alone, to which they scarcely paid attention. For each trifle they asked a very high price and tried to substitute another, poorer item for an item already sold, for example a dog's tail for a marten, etc.[62]

Shishmaryov's and Lazarev's reports reveal several things about the Cape Espenberg people: the Eskimos apparently had adequate supplies of tobacco, suggesting that they had already sold some of their furs to native traders that summer and had received tobacco in return. Iron tools and weapons were valued commodities, but the Eskimos' supply of iron—and their knowledge of its properties—was sufficient to allow them to be very particular about the quality of their purchases. The natives were also masterful traders, well acquainted with deceit. The fact that they approached the Russian ship without apparent hesitation suggests that they had by then become somewhat accustomed to the sight of foreign vessels, and the fact that they approached with a large number of persons suggests that they were more comfortable in force when encountering foreigners.

The *Blagonamerenny* then moved on into Kotzebue Sound and anchored at Chamisso Island. While awaiting the *Otkrytie*'s arrival, Captain Shishmaryov decided to send a shore party comprising a longboat and a three-hatch Aleutian baidarka to explore Eschscholtz Bay. Captain Shishmaryov no doubt remembered the antagonistic reception the Eskimos had given the *Riurik*'s men on the north coast of the Seward Peninsula in 1816, so he outfitted the longboat with, among other things, fifteen armed sailors and four falconets.[63]

And in the same frame of mind, when Lieutenant Aleksei Lazarev went ashore near Elephant Point, seeing a large number of Eskimos encamped there, he later wrote: "I was in high Aleut boots and was the first to get out to wade, having small pocket pistols loaded with bullets up my sleeves. The inhabitants immediately met me, but with great distrustfulness, especially the elder, who maintained an average of about a hundred paces between me and their throng. The savages tried by all means not to come close to me, though I showed them that I had nothing in my hands, to which the elder replied with the same sign."[64]

To judge from other encounters, this elder, like Lazarev, also had weapons concealed in his sleeves. Nevertheless, when Lazarev "showed them some tobacco and other things, all distrustfulness on their side apparently disappeared, the elder beckoned the others, and they all ran directly up to me." The Eskimos then "sat on the ground in a semicircle, and," Lazarev continued, "sat me before them in the middle and began to greet me, blowing their nose in their hand and then smearing it on the face, to which I responded in the same manner."[65]

The Russians must have been surprised to find so many natives at the place where Kotzebue had not reported anyone. In fact Kotzebue had arrived there in the latter part of August 1816, after the Buckland River Eskimos had dispersed following the conclusion of their annual gathering to hunt beluga whales. But the *Blagonamerenny*'s men had arrived there more than three weeks earlier in the season, probably just as the hunt was ending.[66]

Despite the friendly start to their encounter, the Eskimos soon turned aggressive, and when Lazarev and a few other Russians climbed the bluff behind the encampment, the Eskimos gathered around them and a few began to cut the gilt buttons from his uniform. In response Lazarev vigorously shoved one of the men away, stating in his journal, "one should by no means allow them impudence or boldness." On their way back to the longboat the Russians passed through the Eskimo encampment again and found an armed native standing in front of each tent and umiaq (which was ready for immediate launching). "Here the inhabitants again followed us and did not go away," he added, "very much desiring and even insistently demanding that we trade with them."

After the Russians had eaten a meal at the longboat, Captain Shishmaryov allowed the crew to trade with the Eskimos, and the Russians again witnessed the natives' hard-headed approach to bartering. "But no one of us could succeed in this trade," Lazarev wrote, "because the [Eskimos] charged much too high a price for each thing requested, an axe or large knife, which we did not have with us."[67]

The sailors began to return to the *Blagonamerenny*, but just as they had launched the longboat, an onshore wind sprang up and drove in such a steep sea that they could not tack offshore. The spray drenched the Russians and soaked their firearms. They had no choice but to return to shore to dry out and await a change in the weather. "One must admit that at this time our situation was very unpleasant," wrote Lazarev. "Our guns, musketoons, pistols, and even falconets had become completely drenched, so that it was necessary to unload, swab, and clean them. There remained only a few lances and cutlasses for our defense. [The Eskimos], as we later saw, each had several knives: one up the left sleeve, another down the right boot, and a third, about half an arshin long, along the back between the shoulder blades."[68]

The Russians now found themselves in a very dangerous situation. Forced ashore and unable to reach the safety of their ship, their firearms wet and useless, they were outnumbered roughly ten-to-one by a group of heavily armed, aggressive Eskimos. Unfortunately for the men from the *Blagonamerenny*, in the early nineteenth century it was a fact of life that the Eskimo nations of northwestern Alaska were constantly under the threat of attack from other native nations; consequently all strangers were considered to be enemies unless they could prove otherwise.

"In the popular literature of the twentieth century, Eskimos in general . . . have often been represented as never hostile, let alone warlike," writes the anthropologist Ann Fienup-Riordan. "This literature . . . pays little attention to the violence and warfare that are a very real part of Eskimo history and tradition." The ethnohistorian Ernest S. Burch, Jr., describes the Iñupiaq Eskimo attitude toward strangers: "The traditional Eskimos did not know how to interact with strangers outside the context of the summer fair [which was a time of general truce], and they usually either avoided them or killed them on sight." "The evidence from both oral and written sources confirms that the Iñupiat were not the happy, peaceful hunter-gatherers of anthropological perspective. Instead they were fiercely independent peoples who conducted external affairs in a very aggressive manner. Armed conflict, and the threat of armed conflict, were basic facts of life." When explorers outnumbered the natives, the Eskimos were usually docile, but when the Eskimos found themselves in superior numbers to the visitors, they rapidly pressed their advantage, becoming extremely belligerent and domineering.[69]

Lazarev tried to frighten the Eskimos by firing the Russians' only working gun, but his bluff failed. "Seeing our disproportion to them both in numbers and in strength," Lazarev went on, "it came into my head to inspire fear in them in advance. For this I pulled out of a box my own gun, the only one that had remained dry, and, having fired at a sea gull flying by, killed it. The inhabitants at first were frightened by this, and all shrieked from fright, but when they saw that the whole thing had ended with the death of one bird, they began to laugh loudly and one of them, having grabbed a stone, also killed a sea gull flying by, and rather high, after which he explained to us that the effect of both implements was the same.

His other comrades then demonstrated their skill in throwing stones by hand, hitting the mark at about fifty paces."[70]

Forced to spend the night ashore, the Russians set up a tent and posted sentries. Lazarev continued:

> It was already around 10 o'clock in the evening and we, desiring to set ourselves at ease, tried with all our might to convince the inhabitants to leave us. For a long time they did not understand us, or perhaps they did not want to obey. Seeing that they continued to surround the tent, one of the Aleuts with us who knew a few words of the Agalakhmut language, through it and pantomime made them understand our wishes. After that he ran very quickly and began to make a line in the earth around the tent right by the watchmen, explaining that during the night no one should cross it. Some of the inhabitants still stood near us and watched this work, but when the line was close to completing the circle they all threw themselves headlong outside it as if fearing some sorcery.[71]
>
> Having stood awhile near the line, they made a line of their own about five paces from ours and indicated to the watchmen through pantomime that they should not cross it. After this they made faces and laughed for another half hour and finally dispersed to the settlement and did not come all night. Seeing the savages dispersing, we lay down to sleep and spent the night rather peacefully, but in great caution, inspecting the watchmen very frequently and conducting the shift changes ourselves, giving them necessary instructions. At midnight all the wet guns were in order and in readiness in case of attack, for which, however, we had not given the slightest grounds, treating the inhabitants very kindly and having given them various things.

But the Russians got only a few hours' rest.

> At 3 AM, when it was just getting light, the inhabitants began little by little to gather . . . but the watchmen did not allow them to come farther. This apparently insulted the [Eskimos], and they told our sailors that they should not come up on them, either, laughed at them, and some even began to break through, waving and threatening with their large knives. The watchmen alerted us of this with their shout. All those sleeping in the tent were awakened by this noise and we feared bad consequences. I went out first and began to greet the inhabitants and soon after me appeared the captain, who . . . ordered our watchmen to come to the tent, having indicated to the savages that they too could come there. This restored calm and barter began, just as unprofitable for us as on the day before because for every little thing they requested from us either an axe or a knife. The captain wanted to barter a [kayak] and the deal

had already been made when suddenly the axe offered for it did not appeal to the seller because it bore several spots of rust.

Despite Lazarev's attempt to keep things peaceful, it was a very brittle situation, with the possibility of hostile action at any time.

During this trade I walked about between our people and the [Eskimos] watching that nothing unpleasant should happen between them, which in fact happened and could have led to very bad consequences if I had not averted them with presents. The barter, as I have already noted, took place at the persistent insistence of the inhabitants and we were forced, whether we wanted to or not, to buy what they offered us, even what was entirely unnecessary for us. It happened that one sailor, having bought one of two ermines that were tied together, began to cut away one with a knife and accidentally cut the hand of the seller, who was still holding both furs. Grumbling and noise immediately began and if I had not given a gift to their wounded man, all his comrades could have been outraged and then it would have been difficult for us, 15 men, to settle with 200 who had three knives apiece and were masterful users of slings etc.

Soon after this I stopped in at our tent and saw in it a savage [Eskimo], a robust man, who was examining a pistol I had left on the table. It was loaded, at half-cock, and the [Eskimo] was touching it without any caution and was looking directly into the muzzle. Fearing the consequences that could arise from this, I approached him, took the pistol and, pointing the muzzle away from him, tried to explain by signs that the pistol could fire and kill him. The savage probably understood me differently, i.e., that I would kill him for touching the pistol; in an instant he flew into a rage and with flashing eyes struck me in the left side near the stomach with his spear. Fortunately it only penetrated the warm overcoat, waistcoat, and trousers I was wearing and stopped after scratching the skin. I had not yet had time to think when he seized his long knife from behind his back and threatened me, while the spear remained with its shaft on the floor and the stone [spearhead] in me.

Seeing the brutality of the savage and his eyes, so to speak, flashing with malice, and fearing to be the reason for further quarrels between us and the [Eskimos] and through that, of course, guilty of the death of many, I was silent, waving my hand and indicating that I was not afraid of threats. Fortunately, at the same time one of the sailors, Salnikov, came into the tent, and soon another as well. The [Eskimo], having seen them, with a look of extreme cold-bloodedness, put the knife back in its sheath, extracted his spear, and very quietly left the tent.[72]

The tensions later cooled somewhat, and "at the invitation of the elder the captain and I crawled into his [tent] where sat two . . . women. Its interior was filled with fish, fat, guts, and every sort of filth. The master showed us his wealth, consisting of knives, cutlasses, and other iron things of very clean finish which, he explained, he had received from the Hudson's Bay Company."[73] Lazarev continued, "The weapons of this people are bows and arrows which they keep in sewn skin quivers and which have sharp worked flints on the ends. Their lances are also of plain wood and were often, it seems, of driftwood with worked flint on the end. As food they use, we saw, walrus, seal, and whale meat and fat, small fish which they roast simply, throwing them on the coals, and birds, roasted in the same manner. Near each hut there were no fewer than four dogs. Of furs they have red fox, beaver, arctic fox, and bear skins."

"On this stretch of shore grows [*Ledum*, 'Hudson Bay Tea' or 'Labrador Tea']," Lazarev added, "which the inhabitants mix with tobacco in order to get intoxicated more quickly. The local [Eskimos] are terribly fond of smoking-tobacco. Having filled a wooden pipe with it and having mixed it with [*Ledum*] (and when there is none, they are satisfied with the latter herb alone), the [Eskimos] when smoking draw in all the smoke and hold it for at least five minutes, until they become intoxicated and completely lose consciousness. In this condition they begin retching and it goes on for more than a quarter of an hour until they regain consciousness. When they stand up after this, judging from their faces one can suppose that they have come from great intoxication. We saw this more than once among the [Eskimos] in the settlement in Eschscholtz Bay."[74]

The Russians returned to their ship, and to their joy, a few days later the *Otkrytie* hove into sight. The *Otkrytie*, having visited Petropavlovsk, was carrying "news and letters from our friends and relatives," wrote Lazarev. Captain-Lieutenant Mikhail Nikolaevich Vasiliev and the officers of the *Otkrytie* then came aboard the *Blagonamerenny* to dine, when, to the surprise of the Russians, a third ship appeared. The strange ship was, of course, the *Pedlar*, and John Walters, a man of few words, noted its arrival: "anchored in scots pru [Kotzebue] sound . . . found two Russian ships on discovery."[75]

Lazarev also described the *Pedlar*'s arrival. "In the second hour there arrived from sea a brig under the flag of the United American States and, having anchored between our sloops, it saluted with seven shots, to which the *Otkrytie* replied with five per the regulations of Emperor Pyotr I.[76]

"In the seventh hour of the evening Clark, former supercargo with our consul Dobrel [*sic*] in Manila, came to our sloop from the American brig. He declared to us that the name of his brig was *Pedlar*, cargo owner Pigot, captain John Meek, that there were 30 men aboard, and that they had come here to barter furs from the inhabitants in exchange for leather, sabers, guns, powder, etc." "One must admit," Lazarev continued with a certain amount of admiration, "that the enlightened Americans are expeditious in trade; they scarcely hear of some new discovery before they appear there with trade goods. Captain Vasiliev, passing by St. Lawrence Island on the way to Kotzebue Sound, saw the aforementioned brig and questioned it. Clark brought us a few pineapples as a gift, a great rarity among the polar ice and snow."[77]

Lazarev then reviewed his understanding of why the *Pedlar* had appeared in Kotzebue Sound.

When the Otkrytie was in Kamchatka this summer, the commander of Kamchatka, Rikord, told Captain Vasiliev that the year before [1819] the American [Grimes], who was aboard a vessel also belonging to Pigot, allegedly went, on the commission of Count Nikolai Petrovich Rumiantsev, to verify the discoveries made in the north by Kotzebue. On his return to Petropavlovsk port in the fall, [Grimes] told the commander of Kamchatka that on his trip beyond Bering Strait he stopped at Shishmaryov Bay, whence he explored the whole area right up to Kotzebue Sound and the sound itself and went in a longboat near the whole coast, measuring the depth with a pole. According to him, these places are very incorrectly placed on the chart and are even not at all as they should be. Finally, with regard to the strait in Goodhope Bay, so named by Kotzebue, he expected from the name that this strait would lead to the north, as Kotzebue maintained. "From these stories," said Captain Rikord, "it is apparent that [Grimes] is a man who had taken on something that is not in his line of work."

Lazarev, apparently overlooking the fact that a longboat could work very close to shore in shallow water, then interjected, "In fact, can one measure depth in a sound with a pole when in some places it goes to 15 sazhens?"[78]

His account continues: "[Grimes] said also that next year, i.e., in 1820, if not he then another vessel would come for further explorations and the brig we met justified those words. Curiosity compelled Captain Shishmaryov to go aboard the American brig, having invited me with him, to look at the chart made by [Grimes], the more so as he himself [Captain Shishmaryov] had been a participant in placing the coast and sound on Kotzebue's chart. On arriving aboard the brig we saw that the aforesaid chart was nothing other than one crudely copied from Kotzebue's chart, on very thin transparent paper, and it was apparent that the Americans had not yet managed to transfer it to good paper. On it some insignificant changes were made with regard to capes and mountains, and in place of a strait in Goodhope Bay there was a lake."[79]

Although Lazarev believed correctly that Grimes had undertaken his voyage for a commercial reconnaissance rather than for a geographical survey on behalf of Count Rumiantsev (the Americans had, after all, borne the cost of the voyage themselves), the "strait" that appears in Goodhope Bay on Kotzebue's chart is, in fact, a saltwater lagoon, where the Nugnugaluktuk River enters Kotzebue Sound. "Showing us this chart," Lazarev continued, "the Americans tried with all their might to convince us of its correctness, confirming [Grimes's] story that he allegedly measured all the places near shore with a pole and although he went along the coast he did not see a strait. When Shishmaryov told them that he himself was in it and spent the night there, they immediately changed the subject and began to talk about the savages, asking us where we had seen them."

> Captain Rikord had given [Grimes] a sailor as an interpreter and that man was now aboard the Otkrytie. He said that the Americans did stop near Shishmarev Bay, but went no farther and though they went in a longboat, it was not for long enough to cover the whole distance from that bay to Kotzebue Sound. I do not think the merchant would have thought of covering this distance, nearly 200 versts, in a longboat when one could sail aboard a vessel, and without any profit besides. Therefore, one can justly agree with Rikord's opinion that the Americans' goal was not discovery, but trade with the inhabitants for which they solicited a mission from Count Rumiantsev in order not to be hindered by that captain [Rikord] or our expedition. In addition, the merchant-American really will not venture great expenditures without seeing personal profit.[80]

As we have seen, it was actually *Rikord* who had solicited Grimes's assistance, not the reverse. Lazarev may also have misunderstood the interpreter's account of where the *General San Martín* had gone while north of Bering Strait: the *General San Martín* did in fact reach the inner waters of Kotzebue Sound, and the crew did carry out some reconnaissance with the ship's boat. Lazarev was also partly confused about the genesis of Grimes's voyage aboard the *General San Martín*. It is true that American traders were always alert for new trading opportunities throughout the Pacific; nevertheless Grimes was simultaneously aided in his commercial reconnaissance by Rikord (who had been encouraged by Rumiantsev) as a way of gaining geographical information for the Russians at no cost.

The next day the *Otkrytie* and *Blagonamerenny* set off for explorations on the northwest coast of arctic Alaska, leaving the *Pedlar* alone in Kotzebue Sound. The Russians, however, had cautioned the crew of the *Pedlar* to be on their guard when dealing with the Eskimos in Eschscholtz Bay. "We advised [Pigot] to go to the smaller part of the sound as close as possible to the northeastern shores," Gillesem wrote, "but not to go on land, and to permit the Indians on the brig only after taking all precautions because these people were crafty and unreliable. As proof we related our adventures with them."[81]

On the day that the Russians departed, John Walters reported, "we sent our pinice, the chief officer, and 7 men to look for the natives to trade but being gon longer than was expected made us oneasy for fear of som accident . . . the boat returned with but little success. The same day we sailed down the straits." The *Pedlar* then headed for Kamchatka.[82]

The *Pedlar*'s lack of success in trading with the Eskimos near Chamisso suggests that having heard the cannon fire from the ships' salutes, and seeing now *three* ships at anchor, the Eskimos perhaps dispersed or hid, believing that the foreigners might be returning in force with superior numbers and firepower. On the other hand, Ernest S. Burch, Jr., offers a different explanation. Burch writes: "It is equally likely that the Eskimos had headed inland to hunt caribou, which they would have done about this time [of year]. They weren't yet so addicted to trade that they would forego proper winter clothing to get it."[83]

It is noteworthy that the *Pedlar*'s voyage to Bering Strait was concluded much more quickly than the *General San Martín*'s had been. If Grimes's and Walters's reports of their trading cruises included all the trading stops that each ship undertook, then it is clear that the *Pedlar* touched only at those places where the *General San Martín* had traded successfully: St. Lawrence Island, St. Lawrence Bay, King Island, and Kotzebue Sound. The *Pedlar*'s trading cruise within the Bering Strait region occupied only eleven days, whereas the *General San Martín*'s had taken forty-eight days. Thus Pigot almost certainly went north to confirm the conclusions that Grimes had drawn the year before. And the fact that the *Pedlar* seems to have acquired furs only at St. Lawrence Island and King Island, if true, would have confirmed to the American traders and to John Jacob Astor that the effort and expense of a voyage to Bering Strait were not worth the reward.

On August 29 the *Pedlar* anchored in Petropavlovsk's harbor, where they "made some trade with the govener [Rikord]. He is a fine man," wrote Walters, "and speeks good English. . . . We fired a salute on the Empirers birth day of 21 guns. The next day was visited by the govener and his lady which is a nice woman."[84]

William Pigot told Pyotr Rikord about the *Pedlar*'s cruise in Bering Strait and about his encounters with the *Otkrytie* and *Blagonamerenny*, and, no doubt, about their relative lack of success in trading for furs. In return Rikord gave Pigot a letter of introduction to Matvei Ivanovich Muravyov, the new chief manager of the Russian-American colonies in Novo-Arkhangelsk, the *Pedlar*'s next port of call.[85]

The *Pedlar* sailed from Petropavlovsk and endured a punishing eighteen-day (and nearly 3,000-mile) crossing of the North Pacific. When the brig reached Novo-Arkhangelsk it had sustained damage to its hull, its sails were in tatters, and the seas had demolished both boats, among other breakage. It took the crew a month to repair the damage and build a new boat. Before sailing for Hawaii, Pigot traded with Muravyov for some of the *Pedlar*'s cargo and took 2,620 fur seal skins in return for the trade goods.[86]

AFTERMATH

Shortly after the *Pedlar*'s departure for Russian America, startling news reached Commandant Pyotr Rikord in Petropavlovsk. A letter arrived from Count Mikhail Speransky, the new governor general of Siberia. Siberia was "notorious for bad administration," but Speransky was an honest and diligent civil servant and an energetic reformer who was greatly in favor of promoting Russian trade in the North Pacific. "These considerations," Marc Raeff wrote, "perhaps explain Speransky's favorable view of the Russo-American Company, whose monopolistic practices and plans were otherwise uncongenial to him." Nevertheless Speransky was simultaneously "distrustful of American enterprise, in particular that of whalers and traders in the North Pacific, whose better commercial and organizational talents might provide 'unfair' competition for the Russians."[87]

Speransky informed Rikord that by imperial order, confirmed on March 31, 1820, the entire region was hereby closed to foreigners, and trade with foreigners was forbidden. Rikord was ordered to annul the whaling agreement, which, as we have seen, he had entered into with Pigot, Davis, Meek, and Ebbets in 1819. Foreigners were now forbidden to settle in Kamchatka and Okhotsk, and their ships were prohibited from visiting the ports of Eastern Siberia. Foreigners living in Kamchatka and Okhotsk were to be assisted in selling their houses and leaving. Moreover, Peter Dobell should cease sending his ships from Manila and henceforth should use only Russian ships to send cargoes of vital supplies.

Virtually since its founding the Russian-American Company had protested to the Crown about the activities of American traders, who, it claimed, were infringing on its monopoly, but in 1817 the directors of the company had submitted to the government a "draft of proposed regulations to be imposed upon foreign vessels touching Russian-American shores," wrote Howard I. Kushner. "The directors raised the old cry against the American traders: United States citizens were procuring animal furs from the natives by selling firearms and gunpowder to them, and, to make matters worse, Americans were 'teaching them how to use them, to the detriment of our hunters.' The directors also complained, perhaps more to the point, that the Yankees set 'such low prices' on their goods that the same articles sent from Russia 'are much more expensive' to the Russian settlement because of the high cost of transportation through Siberia to Okhotsk." Thus the objections of the Russian-American Company (claiming infringement on its monopoly) had been fully upheld, despite the obvious hardship these restrictions would cause to the populace.[88]

This imperial order later reached Russian America. In a letter of January 21, 1821, Muravyov reported to the Russian-American Company's headquarters in St. Petersburg about the *Pedlar*'s visit to Novo-Arkhangelsk. While Muravyov no doubt welcomed the chance to acquire some supplies from the *Pedlar*, he clearly was sensitive to the company's position about maintaining its monopoly and about the stated undesirability of foreign trading vessels operating within the waters it claimed. Muravyov consequently emphasized that the *Pedlar*'s arrival was the result of force majeure and described the extent of the damage the brig had suffered.[89]

Muravyov explained that although Meek was the captain, "Pigott was the supercargo or owner; for the cargo was under his control, and he directed the movements of the ship."

> He brought with him a letter of recommendation from M. Ricord to me. . . . I could not refuse him permission to anchor in the roadstead here and to repair his ship. . . . If I had refused to allow him to do this, I should have been violating the usage of friendly nations. I took care, however, to place rafts near his ship, and I informed him that if he violated the rights of the Colony in any way, or had any communications whatever with the Indians . . . , he would be at once arrested, and his ship and her cargo confiscated. Of course this annoyed him, and he told me so. I replied that I was justified in being suspicious of the open enemies of the Company. There were at that time two men-of-war on the roadstead, and this fact afforded me frequent opportunities of meeting Pigott, for he was acquainted with the officers of both of them. They had met beyond Behring Strait in Kotzebue Sound, and had been anchored there together. He said in a hesitating way that he had been trading there, and complained that he had been unsuccessful; but are his statements to be believed?
> He had a quantity of guns and ammunition with him, and sold some guns to the officers of the men-of-war. I asked him whether he had sold any guns in the north, and he answered that he had not; but are we to believe him?[90]

To make matters worse for the inhabitants in eastern Asia and Russian America, Russia's isolationist policy of 1820 was strengthened by an imperial *ukaz* of September 4, 1821, "prohibiting foreign merchant ships from trading in the Russian colonies in the North Pacific." Thus, all whaling, fishing, and trading activities were forbidden to foreigners in waters that ran from Bering Strait south to 51° N on the American coast and to 45°50′ N on the Asian coast. Moreover, no foreign vessel could approach the coast closer than one hundred Italian miles. Thus the Northwest Coast of America, from Queen Charlotte Sound northward, as well as the northeastern coast of Asia, most of the Kurile Islands, and the entire Sea of Okhotsk was proclaimed closed to foreign men and ships. By decree the tsar had embargoed much of the northern North Pacific and adjacent waters as far north as Bering Strait. But the Russians lacked the ability to enforce this proclamation.[91]

On September 13, 1821, a second imperial ukaz granted the Russian-American Company a renewal of its charter for twenty years and a monopoly over all activities within its territories. This edict was underscored—specifically by the minister of foreign affairs—warning American merchants (some of whom had been involved with gunrunning and rum-running on the Northwest Coast) not to trade with the natives there. Ships of the Imperial Navy would now patrol those coasts, and any vessel sailing from port after March 1, 1822, would be liable under these regulations for the confiscation of the vessel and its cargo.[92]

The tsar's orders of 1820 and 1821—however shortsighted and unenforceable they may have been—had both defensive and offensive purposes. They were aimed at American traders who ignored the Russian-American Company's claimed monopoly on the Asian and American coasts, but they were also intended to block the advances of the Hudson's Bay Company, whose traders were then approaching the Northwest Coast from the interior of North America. Equally important, the ukaz of September 4, 1821, laid claim to large areas of the northeastern Asian coast, where the tsar's government was eyeing expansion toward the Amur River.[93]

The historian Glynn Barratt put it this way: "Since the fall of 1820, the authorities of Petropavlovsk and at Novo-Arkhangelsk had been obliged, despite their wishes, to enforce an isolationist and even xenophobic policy whereby all foreign ships and traders were excluded from the [Russian-American] Company's own settlements and waters. Semi-isolation from the outside world and periodic hunger in the settlements became inevitable."[94]

It took more than a year for Muravyov's letter of January 21, 1821, to reach the headquarters of the Russian-American Company in St. Petersburg and for the board of directors to draft its reply. Regarding Muravyov's report on the *Pedlar's* visit to Novo-Arkhangelsk in 1820, the board wrote to Muravyov on February 28, 1822: "It is a pity that you had not yet been informed of the right which has been officially declared and announced in the Regulations which have been sent to you by the 'Apollo' of the Imperial navy; if you had received these Regulations earlier, you would, no doubt, have searched Pigott's ship. Don't let these impudent fellows off so easily in the future."[95]

But the Imperial Navy ship *Apollon*, which was sent to patrol the coast and enforce the ukaz, reached Novo-Arkhangelsk in October 1822, two years after the *Pedlar*'s visit. The *Apollon* carried the orders that closed the Russian territories in eastern Siberia and North America to foreign trade. Of course, the enforcement of these orders resulted in a severe shortage of food in the Russian settlements, and these edicts also put Muravyov in a very difficult position: his only recourse—other than urgently to petition the company's directors for relief—was to send ships to Hawaii and California for supplies.[96]

The governments of the United States and Great Britain quickly protested Russia's unilateral closure of the coasts she claimed and the extension of her boundaries in the North Pacific. "The ukase of September 4, 1821, contained two features that were objectionable alike from the British and American point of view," wrote the historian Stuart R. Tompkins: "first, the exclusion of all foreign shipping from waters extending one hundred Italian miles from shore; secondly, the extension of Russia's territorial claims as far south as the 51st parallel of latitude." In fact, in 1823 the president of the United States had proclaimed the Monroe Doctrine, stating that foreign powers were prohibited from further colonization within the Western Hemisphere. And Russia backed down, first in 1824, in a convention with the United States, and soon thereafter, in 1825, with Great Britain. These conventions now fixed Russian America's southern boundary at 54°40′ N (the southern tip of Prince of Wales Island) and its eastern boundary at 141° west of Greenwich (from Mount St. Elias to the Arctic Ocean), but they allowed Americans and Britons free access to the coast for navigation, fishing, and trade for a period of ten years. Russia thus achieved a victory in gaining formal recognition of its boundaries in North America, but in all practicality the advantage was lost.[97]

No American trading voyages are known to have gone to the Bering Strait region in the three decades following the *Pedlar*'s voyage. Despite the fact that the imperial ukaz did not claim the coast of America north of Bering Strait, and despite the fact that the Americans learned that $1,000 of trade goods yielded $10,000 in furs and ivory, there simply was not enough trade at Bering Strait to justify the time and expense, and perhaps the danger, of the voyage. Better opportunities could be found elsewhere.

The closure of the coasts did not greatly affect the American traders. Some found profits in carrying supplies to Novo-Arkhangelsk on Muravyov's orders; others simply ignored the closure and continued their smuggling on the North-

west Coast. But it is indisputable that the hunting pressure had severely suppressed the sea otter population, making profits more difficult to come by. Although new opportunities for trade arose on the coast of the Californias, at the
same time Hawaii's sandalwood supply began to run low. By about 1825 John
Jacob Astor, suffering ill health, essentially withdrew from the Pacific trade: his
trade with the United States' ports was by then far more important.[98]

For the Russians, and for the naval explorers Vasiliev and Shishmaryov, the
voyage of the *Otkrytie* and *Blagonamerenny* was not considered to have been a
success because it had proceeded only twenty-two miles beyond Captain Cook's
farthest advance. This may explain why no detailed account of their expedition
was published in their lifetimes. Count Rumiantsev, however, continued in his
desire to expand on the discoveries he had sponsored via Kotzebue's voyage. He
proposed to Muravyov that the Russian-American Company should join with
him in underwriting the expense of another expedition.[99]

Rumiantsev knew that the British Admiralty, in response to the Russian explorations, was sending Captain John Franklin to descend the Mackenzie River and
to proceed west along the Arctic coast. Rumiantsev, as we shall see, understood
the advantage of having Russian explorers meet Franklin's expedition in northern Alaska, and he planned that this new Russian expedition should follow the
American coast as far as the Mackenzie River. Rumiantsev's proposed expedition might have been important and productive, but unfortunately for the Russians, Rumiantsev died in 1826, and his heir would not authorize the expenditure
for the project. In any case, the expedition would have set off too late to meet
Franklin.[100]

But that day in the summer of 1820—when the *Pedlar* lay at anchor in company with the Russian ships in Kotzebue Sound—was a highly significant moment in the history of the Bering Strait region. Trade and exploration had drawn
members of several nations into contact. Russians, Americans, Chukchi, and
Eskimos encountered one another, and a vigorous foreign maritime trade would
develop alongside the existing intercontinental native trade, a foreign trade that
the Americans had initiated, a trade that the Russians would expand in competition with the British, and a trade that the Americans would dominate in the
second half of the nineteenth century and thereafter.

2

Trapping and Hunting for Marketable Furs

The markets of Asia received a wide variety of furs and commodities from the Bering Strait region. Each type of furbearer had unique habitat preference and behavior, factors that were central to the devices and techniques that the hunters and trappers employed to capture the animals. The skills employed by the hunters and trappers were not only the result of careful attention to their elders' practices and a close study of animal behavior but also of painstaking trial and error in the field.

THE FURBEARERS AND OTHER SOURCES
OF SALEABLE MATERIALS

FOX AND WOLF

Fox skins probably made up the largest number of furs to cross Bering Strait westbound. "Foxes inhabiting very cold districts have coats of long, dense, downy fur and over-hair of exquisite fineness and beauty," wrote A. L. Belden. Chukchi and Eskimos captured two types of foxes, the arctic or white fox, which was also occasionally called "stone fox" or "ice fox" (*Alopex lagopus*), and the red fox (*Vulpes vulpes*). The arctic fox is a circumpolar animal, living not only on the tundra and the arctic shore but also on sea ice. It is "among the best adapted of all terrestrial mammals to the harsh Arctic climate." Arctic foxes often scavenge dead marine mammals and the remains of wolf and polar bear kills. They are omnivorous, feeding on lemmings, young seal pups, hares, birds, fish, eggs, berries, and flotsam seaweed. The lemming population is cyclical, moving through highs and lows, and the size of the arctic fox population is closely correlated with the lemmings. These foxes are small, weighing from five to fifteen pounds, and have short rounded ears and a rather short snout. Their winter coats are either white or "blue," which is actually a gray blue shade, "more on the order of the blue seen in the fur of maltese cats," wrote A. R. Harding. Depending on the market's changing tastes, at times "blue fox" skins have been extremely valuable. Arctic foxes are occasionally preyed upon by red foxes in areas where their ranges overlap.[1]

The other fox, the red fox, is "the most widespread and abundant carnivore in the world." The best red foxes are found in Kamchatka and interior Alaska, where it is very cold in the winter. "All of the northern foxes are well furred, except along the Pacific Coast," wrote A. R. Harding. "The . . . poorest red fox[es] in the world are caught on Kodiak Island, Alaska. . . . A silver fox caught on Kodiak Island is worth about as much as a good coyote and does not look any better. . . . The island lies in the warm Japan current."

An intelligent animal with keen senses, the red fox is about the size of a small dog. It is found throughout forested areas and far out onto the tundra as well. Cautious and shy, it is omnivorous, eating mice, squirrels, muskrats, insects, birds, hares, berries, carrion, arctic foxes, and other things. Trappers who sought white foxes were occasionally enraged by the depredations of red foxes ("colored foxes") which followed their traplines and ate the white foxes.[2]

The red fox has a number of color variations: the "red fox" is reddish yellow, with a white belly, dark feet, and a bushy tail that is white tipped; the "cross fox" has a dark stripe across the shoulders and down the back; the "silver fox" is black with white-tipped guard hairs and a white-tipped tail; and the "black fox" lacks white-tipped guard hairs. All of these color variations may be present in a single litter of pups. Other than man, the red fox's predators are wolves, coyotes, lynx, and wolverines.[3]

The other member of the dog (Canidae) family that was trapped and traded in the Bering Strait region was the wolf (*Canis lupus*), and it is likely that wolf skins were traded both ways across Bering Strait. Circumpolar in distribution, these highly intelligent, social carnivores usually live in packs ranging in size from two to more than twenty, although four to seven are common. They prey on a wide variety of game, from small mammals to beavers and moose, but in the North, caribou and reindeer are their principal quarry. Wolves also rob traplines. John Tetso, a Slavey trapper who lived near the Mackenzie River, wrote, "The wolf is number one on my bad list. It will eat its fill and cache what it cannot eat. Sometimes it does not go far to cache the stolen property, so I watch for that. I follow tracks leaving the trail after stealing and sometimes recover the stolen fur." He added, "One bad wolf on a trapline is just as bad as many."[4]

The northern wolves are generally whitish or light gray, although some can be black. Their coats are thick and rich, with long, coarse guard hairs and a dense underfur. A large male wolf can weigh 145 pounds. The Russian-American Company sold its wolf skins through Michailovsky Redoubt, near the Yukon delta (see front endpaper map).[5]

THE WEASEL FAMILY

In the weasel family (Mustelidae), wolverine, river otter, mink, marten, and ermine were the principal furs that the natives traded to market across Bering Strait. Of the group, the most impressive is the wolverine (*Gulo gulo*). The largest of the terrestrial mustelids, with a circumpolar distribution, wolverines weigh up to sixty pounds and have a dense, wooly underfur and coarse guard hairs. Wolverine skins are particularly prized by natives for trim on parka ruffs because the hairs resist matting by ice accumulation from the wearer's breath. Wolverine skins were probably both exported from and imported to Alaska. Like most of the weasel family—which includes skunks—wolverines have anal musk glands. The wolverine secretes a yellowish foul-smelling fluid, which it uses for scent marking but can also squirt up to nine feet.

Wolverines are renowned for their strength and stamina. These solitary creatures roam constantly, covering as many as forty miles a day over often difficult terrain. The wolverine's short, powerful legs do not give it great speed, but its large paws allow it to work in deep soft snow and to take young caribou and moose that are mired in it. Wolverines are omnivorous scavengers, eating beavers, rodents, larvae, eggs, hares, berries, and animal carcasses. They are famous for robbing traps and food caches. Wolverines are also expert tunnel diggers in snow, where they build long, intricate dens.[6]

Roderick MacFarlane, an early Hudson's Bay Company trader on the Mackenzie River, thoroughly disliked wolverines. "This comparatively powerful and very destructive animal is to be met with all over the northern continent and along the shores of the Arctic Ocean," he wrote. "They are first-class experts in persistently demolishing very extensive lines of deadfall, marten, and other traps, as well as hiding, eating, or otherwise injuring the animals found in them. They treat rabbits and lynx caught in snares in a similar manner. They will further break up well-built caches of meat, fish, and sundries. The wolverine is undoubtedly entitled to first place among the destructive animals of North America, and is also the most detested of them all."[7]

"The wolverine is universally execrated throughout the North as an inveterate and tiresome cache-robber," wrote the explorer Vilhjalmur Stefansson. "Hardly any kind of cache can be made strong enough to keep out a wolverine if he has plenty of time to work undisturbed; for the animal is strong enough to roll away heavy stones and logs, gnaw through timbers, climb to elevated caches, and excavate buried goods. . . . At Langton Bay [Northwest Territories] a wolverine ate a round hole through two plank doors to get into meat which we had stored in the old ice house. On attaining entrance to a food cache the animal will often remain until all the food is consumed." Stefansson also learned from a native that "if [a] wolverine knows of meat buried under frozen ground, it will lie down on top of the earth covering, thaw it a little, dig away the thawed part and lie down in the hole, thus finally thawing its way to the meat. As for stone covering, they will lift straight upward, if necessary, stones to uncover meat."[8]

Wolverines almost drove Robert Kennicott, a pioneering scientist of Russian America, off his trapline in 1862. "The rascally beasties, not content with breaking open the back of the traps to get out the bait, would often demolish the entire trap, as if in spite, and certainly without any object except its destruction," he wrote. Kennicott then placed baited "set guns," aimed at his marten traps, which the wolverines were destroying. "Sometimes they would not touch the bait; and, in two or three instances, they *went behind the gun and cut the lines that tied it, or gnawed off the line which attached the bait to the trigger*, after which they ate the bait with impunity."[9]

The ethnographer and naturalist Edward William Nelson had a similar opinion of the wolverine, referring to it as "one of the most detested animals found in all of the fur country." "They invariably steal bait from traps . . . and very rarely do they get caught. Should they find an animal in a trap they make short work of it, and in Northern Alaska, as else where in the fur country, they sometimes take up a line of traps so persistently that the hunter is forced to abandon it and look for a new route."

"The Yukon Indians have a superstitious dread of this animal," Nelson continued, "and one occasion . . . a hunter found a wolverine caught . . . in one of his lynx-traps. . . . Straight away the Indian returned home, and a grave consultation was held among the elders of the village. It was finally decided that the hunter might take the animal from the snare, but to avert possible bad consequences he was instructed to abuse the white men all of the time, so as to make the spirit of the wolverine believe it was owing to their agency that he had been trapped. The hunter then returned with a companion to the trap and removed the animal, repeating as he did so nearly his entire stock of English in saying 'G——d——the Americans, G——d——the Americans,' over and over again until well away from the accursed spot." The Russian-American Company sold its wolverine skins to the natives via Mikhailovsky Redoubt.[10]

The most valuable furs in the weasel family are the Asian sable (*Martes zi-*

bellina) and its American cousin, the marten (*Martes americana*). Martens and sables are about the size of a small house cat, with a typical weasel shape, a slender body, and a furry tail. Sables and martens have a silky, lustrous dense fur that ranges in color from a yellowish brown to dark brown and in some cases almost to jet black. "The value of a sable as well as the [marten] depends on the color and density of the top coat," wrote Marcus Petersen. "The skins of animals taken in the depths of the forests where the sun's rays never penetrate the gloom are almost black, and well nigh priceless in value." One Fort Yukon trader called it "the diamond of the northern fur, the orange-throated marten, with a pelt shading from a pale lemon to a chocolate brown, fur so fine it was like trying to touch moonbeams."[11]

Sables and martens live throughout the subarctic regions and spend much of their time in conifers and mixed wood forests, where they feed on mice, voles, squirrels, rabbits, insects, birds, carrion, and nuts, both above and below the snow cover. They do not store a layer of fat during the winter so must hunt year-round. Males are about 24 to 30 inches long and weigh 1.5 to 2.5 pounds; females are slightly smaller. They are preyed upon by foxes and probably by other predators as well.[12]

River otters (*Lutra canadensis*) are also members of the weasel family. The American river otter is found throughout the temperate and subarctic regions of North America. Its cousin is the Eurasian river otter (*Lutra lutra*). River otters can reach 35 pounds and 60 inches in length. With their short legs and powerful tail they can swim as fast as six miles per hour, and when running and sliding alternately, they are as fast as a man on hard-packed snow or ice. Otters live near rivers and lakes and eat fish, clams, snails, mussels, frogs, and occasionally birds. Their coat is rich brown on the back and slightly lighter on the belly, with a dense underfur and longer guard hairs. Otters are highly intelligent animals with a well-known ability to avoid traps.[13]

Ermine, or short-tailed weasels (*Mustela erminea*), and long-tailed weasels (*Mustela frenata*) were probably all considered to be "ermine" in the trans–Bering Strait fur trade. Ermine are six to nine inches long and during the winter are white with a black-tipped tail. Long-tailed weasels are slightly larger and in winter are also white with a white-tipped tail. They subsist on small rodents and nesting birds, and they often burrow in the snow, following the tunnels in which lemmings run. Ermines are hunted by wolves, foxes, wolverines, and snowy owls.[14]

"The great swiftness and prowess of this animal," Edward William Nelson wrote, "and the success with which it sometimes attacks and destroys such disproportionately large animals as the white ptarmigan or the northern rabbit, has a remarkable effect upon the native mind. The Eskimo look upon it with an almost superstitious fear. Its skin is often worn by them as a kind of fetich and it figures in their mythology."[15]

Mink (*Mustella vison*) pelts probably also entered the trans–Bering Strait native fur trade. Mink live throughout North America in a variety of wetland habitats, near the edges of streams, marshes, and ponds, and seem to "combine the traits of the wood-frequenting marten with those of the water-loving otter." Excellent swimmers, they are carnivorous, preying on muskrats, waterfowl, hares, and mice, and, on occasion, young mink. They are in turn preyed upon by wolves, foxes, hawks, lynx, and river otters. Otters will usually not tolerate minks in their territory. Large minks can be as long as 29 inches and weigh as many as 5 pounds. They have a dense, wavy, grayish brown underfur and, when prime, long dark brown guard hairs that are stiff and glossy. The Russian-American Company sold its mink pelts in Novo-Arkhangelsk.[16]

LYNX

Lynx (*Lynx canadensis* and *Lynx lynx*), members of the cat family (Felidae), are found in wooded areas throughout much of northern North America and Eurasia. One observer thought that "a lynx resembles a huge Manx cat, about the size of a retriever dog, and posseses no tail except a short stump about 3 inches long." Weighing up to 40 pounds, with long legs and large furry feet, a short black-tipped tail, and tufted ears, the lynx has large feet that allow it to move over soft snow, hunting hares and other small mammals, as well as grouse and ptarmigan and, occasionally, caribou, Dall sheep, and foxes. Lynx have a thick, extremely soft fur with creamy white tones that is mottled with black spots. Snowshoe hares are its primary prey, and both populations rise and fall in a cycle of approximately a decade.[17]

BEAVER AND MUSKRAT

Beavers (*Castor canadensis* and *Castor fiber*) were found in the forested regions of North America and Eurasia but were apparently quickly extirpated from northeastern Siberia. The beaver is the largest of the rodent family, growing throughout its life, and reaching 3 or 4 feet in length and as many as 100 pounds. Its dark brown coat, with its dense underfur, which allows it to work and swim in frigid water, made it highly valuable for clothing and for felt making. These intelligent animals live in dens near water, and if there is an insufficient depth of water in a stream for them to build lodges for a colony's home and food cache, gnawing with their formidable incisors, beavers will create dams, using logs and trees banked with mud to raise the water level. Their food is bark, aquatic plants, and grasses, and when they have exhausted the food supply in one area, the colony moves to another. Wolves, bears, and lynx prey on beavers.[18]

In northeastern Asia, beaver skins were highly valued for trim on clothing. Large numbers of beaver pelts were traded across Bering Strait in return for skins of domestic reindeer, which were used for clothing by Alaskan natives. Beaver castors, glands located near the anus, were also sought for their medicinal properties: castoreum contains salicin, the basic ingredient of aspirin.[19]

Muskrats (*Ondatra zibethica*), also called musquash, were another valuable rodent in the fur trade. About 10 inches long, with a scaly, ratlike tail, "rats" weigh up to 2 pounds and have a beautiful rich brown coat, which is nearly as fine as the beaver's. Their dense and downy underfur allows them, like beavers, to endure the cold waters in the sloughs and flats of rivers and lakes, where they burrow into the banks, making dens. They chiefly live on aquatic plants and occasionally on mussels, shrimp, and small fish. Muskrats store their food for the winter by making piles of vegetation ("pushups") which cover holes through the ice. The Russian-American Company sold its muskrat skins in Novo-Arkhangelsk and, later, Shanghai.[20]

MARMOT AND GROUND SQUIRREL

Two rodents that also provided skins for the trans–Bering Strait fur trade were the Alaska marmot (*Marmota broweri*) and the arctic ground squirrel (*Citellus parryi*). Alaska marmots weigh about 10 pounds and may be more than 2 feet long. They live in families, generally in talus slopes, amassing body fat during the summers and hibernating during the winters. The arctic ground squirrels are smaller, weighing only about 2.5 pounds. Ground squirrels also live in colonies, usually denning in soft earth. Like the marmots, they hibernate during the winter. Both eat a variety of vegetation and occasionally meat and bird eggs. They are preyed upon by eagles, foxes, wolves, wolverines, and bears. The skins of both were sought for clothing, particularly for parkas. Arctic ground squirrels are also found in northeastern Asia.[21]

HARE

Hare skins were also exported from Alaska to Chukotka. There are two species of hares in Alaska, the snowshoe hare (*Lepus americanus*) and the Alaskan hare (*Lepus othus*), both of which are white in the winter. The snowshoe hare is smaller than the Alaskan hare, which can weigh up to 12 pounds and reach 28 inches. Snowshoe hares prefer spruce forests and brushy areas, eating grasses, buds, and twigs. The Alaskan hare is more often found on open tundra, feeding on tundra plants and willow shoots. The population of snowshoe hares is cyclical, a cycle that is reflected in the numbers of their primary predators, lynx. Hares are also preyed upon by foxes, wolves, and occasionally hawks and ermines.[22]

REINDEER AND CARIBOU

Like some wolverine and wolf skins, reindeer (*Rangifer tarandus*)—called caribou in North America—were one of the few furs exported from Chukotka to Alaska in quantity, both as hides and as manufactured clothing. The Chukchi and other native groups in northeastern Asia not only kept herds of domestic reindeer but also hunted wild reindeer. Although the natives on the Alaskan side of Bering Strait did not practice reindeer husbandry, they hunted barren ground caribou for their meat and warm hides; but they preferred the hides of domestic reindeer from the Asian side of Bering Strait, which they considered to be finer and more durable for use in clothing. Domestic reindeer hides were also prized because of their vivid, mottled patterns of brown and white.

An adult bull caribou weighs about 350 to 400 pounds and a cow about 175 to 225 pounds. Caribou travel in herds and usually keep moving in search of new forage, eating willows, sedges, tundra plants, mushrooms, small shrubs, and lichens (reindeer moss).[23] Wolves, grizzly bears, and golden eagles prey on young caribou calves, and wolves often follow caribou herds, culling infirm or injured animals.

MOOSE

A few moose (*Alces alces*) skins were probably exported to Asia across Bering Strait. A circumpolar animal, the moose (called *elk* in Eurasia) is the largest living deer, reaching more than 9 feet tall and weighing up to 1,800 pounds. Males have enormous antlers that can weigh more than 60 pounds. The moose's long legs allow it to travel easily over most terrain and to evade most predators at speeds of up to thirty-five miles per hour. Moose also defend themselves with their sharp hooves, striking out with devastating force. They browse on twigs and shoots and on aquatic vegetation. Their coarse and heavy pelts provide warm sleeping skins.[24]

MUSK OX

A few musk ox (*Ovibos moschatus*) skins may have crossed Bering Strait as well. Mature male musk oxen usually weigh from 600 to 800 pounds. Until the mid-nineteenth century, musk oxen lived in northern Alaska but were hunted to extinction there. Their fine and soft underfur is extremely warm. Their horns were crafted into a variety of tools and were used for ladles and drinking vessels.[25]

DALL SHEEP

Like musk ox skins, a few Dall sheep (*Ovis dalli*) skins may have been exported to Asia via the native trade route. Like their Asian cousins, snow sheep (*Ovis nivicola*), Dall sheep are herbivorous, living in mountainous and upland areas of Alaska and the Yukon Territory. They have dense white pelts and may weigh more than 200 pounds. Their horns were also used for a variety of implements. Large numbers of sheep hides were traded in the 1880s at Point Barrow and at the Sheshalik trade rendezvous in Kotzebue Sound.[26]

BEAR

Some bear skins were also traded across Bering Strait. There are three species of northern bears. The polar bear (*Ursus maritimus*) is primarily a marine mammal, with a water-repellant coat of guard hairs and dense underfur. In the nineteenth century these bears roamed throughout the Arctic Ocean and its shores and, in the Bering Sea, as far south as St. Matthew Island and the Kuskokwim River delta. Their primary food is ringed seals, but they may also take bearded seals, walruses, beluga whales, and, along shore, other foods, as opportunities arise. Very large males may attain a weight of 1,500 pounds and a length of 10 feet.[27]

Brown bears, also called grizzly bears (*Ursus arctos*), ranged throughout Eurasia and northwestern North America. Extremely large male grizzlies can weigh more than 1,400 pounds and when standing on their hind legs are 9 feet tall. Their hides were probably traded across Bering Strait. Brown bears can run surprisingly fast when frightened or chasing game, and they are opportunistic and omnivorous feeders, eating berries, grasses, fish, roots, ground squirrels, lemmings, carrion, and even newborn moose and caribou.[28]

Black bear skins were also traded to Asia. Black bears (*Ursus americanus*), the smallest of the North American bears, are woodland dwellers that formerly lived throughout much of northern North America south of the tree line. Average-sized Alaskan males weigh about 180 to 200 pounds. They are about 5 feet from nose to tail and range in color from jet black to white, although the normal color is black, with a brown muzzle. Their fur is "smoother, glossier, and less shaggy" than a brown bear. Black bears eat almost anything they encounter: green vegetation, carrion, berries (especially blueberries), ants, and grubs, and males will occasionally eat bear cubs. The Russian-American Company exported its bear skins to St. Petersburg.[29]

WALRUS

Although sea mammal products—oil, hides, and lines—were exported from Alaska to Asia across Bering Strait, as were some minerals and soapstone lamps, the only non-fur item that reached the markets of Asia from Alaska in quantity was walrus ivory. Pacific walruses (*Odobenus rosmarus divergens*) live throughout the Bering and Chukchi seas, ranging from the Alaska Peninsula to the coast of Kamchatka. Walruses generally migrate north with the retreating ice floes in the spring and return south in the autumn, feeding as they go on clams and other invertebrates in shallow waters. Mature adults weigh from 2,000 to as many as 4,000 pounds. The coastal natives on both sides of Bering Strait have traditionally hunted these animals for their meat, hides, and tusks, the largest of which can weigh close to 10 pounds apiece. The natives captured walruses by harpooning them when they found them swimming, or by lancing and clubbing them when they were hauled out on an ice floe or on shore. Walrus hides were made into very strong rawhide lines. Walrus hides are so thick, however, that they must be split laterally for use as boat coverings. The Russian-American Company sent its walrus tusks to St. Petersburg.[30]

MAMMOTH

Substantial quantities of mammoth (*Mammuthus primigenius*) ivory also reached the markets of eastern Asia. Although it is likely that comparatively little of that mammoth ivory originated in Alaska, large amounts were excavated from the Arctic islands and eroding river banks of northeastern Siberia. Between 1825 and 1831, 50,000 to 70,000 pounds of ivory were sold in Yakutsk. Mammoth tusks, which can weigh 300 pounds or more, were sent to Europe and to China, where they were carved into a wide variety of objects. By the beginning of the twentieth century, the mammoth ivory that the Chukchi, Yukagir, and Even (Lamut) excavated was sold mostly to America, while that from the lands near the Okhotsk Sea went mostly to Japan. By that time about 70,000 pounds of mammoth ivory were exported annually from northeastern Asia.[31]

WHALEBONE

Some whalebone, also called "baleen," the long flexible keratinous plates that hang from the upper jaw of bowhead whales (*Balaena mysticetus*), was also exported from the Bering Strait region. Natives of the Bering Strait region captured bowhead whales by chasing them with umiaqs, fastening to them with harpoons and drag-floats, then lancing them. In Europe and the Americas whalebone was used as a flexible stiffener for, among many uses, brushes, skirt hoops, buggy whips, corset stays, and umbrella ribs.[32]

TRAPPING AND HUNTING TECHNIQUES

It took knowledge, energy, patience, skill, strength, endurance, and occasionally great bravery to capture the animals whose skins, tusks, and whalebone were marketable. Before the arrival of firearms and mechanical steel traps in the mid-nineteenth century, the trappers and hunters on both sides of Bering Strait used a variety of devices and techniques to acquire their pelts.

DEADFALLS

The deadfall trap, one of the most widely used devices, is essentially a heavy weight propped up by a pole, which is held erect by the weight of the deadfall but is easily destabilized when an animal wrenches bait from a trigger mechanism. This action knocks away the prop pole and allows the weight to fall, pinning the quarry to the ground or to another object. A deadfall was often surrounded by two walls to ensure that the animal would be under the fall weight when it tore at the bait. Depending on the location of the trap and the materials available to build it, the deadfall could be built of logs, rocks, ice, or a combination of these. Deadfalls ranged in weight from very heavy for capturing bears, for example, to heavy for beavers, to medium size for foxes and marmots, to light for marten, to very light for furbearers such as ermine—and they were built in hundreds of forms with an equally diverse number of trigger mechanisms. Some were raised on special platforms to keep them above the snow cover.[33]

"This kind of trap takes quite some time to make and set," wrote John Tetso, a Slavey trapper.

First the bottom log, which is cut three feet long and should be four inches thick. Next, the top one, four inches too, but this one is a whole tree. The bottom log lies between two standing trees and the top one sits and rests on it. The big end of the top log is the business end, and care is taken to see that top and bottom fit nicely together. Next comes the pen. This is cut from logs three inches thick and over a foot long. About a dozen is plenty and those are pushed and planted into a U-shaped pen. The pen is about two feet from the business end of the top log. Now comes more logs over the top one, these are long ones and their only job is to add weight, which should be in the neighborhood of forty pounds.

Our bait stick is a little piece of knife-planed wood, about nine inches in length and a quarter inch thick. The baited end is pointed to go through the bait. The next item is also a little piece of wood, a quarter of an inch thick, four inches long and round. Green willows are considered ideal for this. I might call this a trigger. It is the one piece that trips the set and makes the weight drop on the animal.

Now the weighted top is lifted, the stick holding the bait goes under it[,] over the bottom one, the piece that I call the trigger is put in a standing position on top of the bait stick at the empty end, which is over the bottom log. The trigger will stand upright under the forty-pound weight, and the opening of the pen is closed at the top with spruce bows, which are laid on top. The trap is now set and can be covered with more spruce bows. . . .

The size and weight vary according to the size of the animal it is intended for. I have caught wolverines in this kind of set, not marten sets but wolverine sets. The weight is very important and should kill the animal outright, no struggling in the trap.[34]

It was extremely annoying for a trapper to find his deadfall sprung by "whiskey jacks," gray jays, also called "camp robbers." "I found many . . . traps sprung," Charles Camsell recalled, "obviously by Whiskey jacks who in trying to take the bait had their tail feathers caught in the dead fall and had to leave them behind."[35]

And it required an especially sturdy deadfall to capture a wolverine. One type, in use among the Eskimos of Anaktuvuk Pass in Alaska's Brooks Range, was built of rocks. The ethnographer Nicholas J. Gubser wrote: "The trapper roams over the region on foot or by sled in search of an area where wolverine tracks abound, and then he builds a rock deadfall. He may have to go to a talus slope a quarter of a mile away for rocks not frozen into the ground. . . . The trapper then looks for a flat rock, 4 to 6 inches thick, large enough to cover the entire rectangle. Such a rock is so heavy that it must be transported by sled to the site. The hunter props it up with a trigger made from two long, slender pieces of rock. . . . Most of the trigger extends inside the enclosed area. As the wolverine reaches for the bait it touches the trigger and jars the very carefully balanced support, causing the cover rock to fall and crush the animal."[36]

In 1852, the British naval officer Rochfort Maguire saw several fox traps on the barrier islands east of Point Barrow, Alaska. "They are simple and in some way injenious," he wrote. "A Moderate sized log of driftwood, loaded about the Middle with a heavy block of ice, one end resting on the ground—the other supported on a thin stick about a foot long. . . . From the upright-stick another projects at right-Angles, to which the blubber used as bate is made fast, and the whole covered round with ice and snow—so that Mr Reynard to get at the bate

Figure 2.1. Alaskan deadfall. Edward Adams, 1850–51. Excerpts from the work of Edward Adams (MS 1115;BJ) appear by permission of the Scott Polar Research Institute, University of Cambridge.

must come under the loaded log, which falls and crushes him as soon as he pulls at the bate."[37]

PITFALLS

Hunters also built pitfalls to capture animals. Pitfalls could be dug amid broken sea ice and covered with a precisely balanced block of ice so that when an animal stepped on the block, it fell into the pit, with the block of ice falling on top of it and pinning it. Trappers also dug pitfalls in hard snow. Some also might put a sharp spike upright in the bottom of the pit and cover the top of the pit with a piece of thin crusted snow. For foxes, the walls of the pit were iced so that the animal could not clamber out. Similarly, hunters might excavate a pit so narrow that when a caribou fell into it, the animal's weight would jam it between the sides so that it would be unable to free itself. Human urine was used to attract caribou to these pitfalls.[38]

At Point Barrow, Alaska, in the early 1880s hunters also built another type of pitfall. John Murdoch described one: "A round hole is dug in the drifted snow. . . . This is about 5 feet in diameter and 5 or 6 feet deep and is brought up to within 2 or 3 inches of the surface, where there is only a small hole, through which the snow was removed. This is carefully closed with a thin slab of snow and baited by strewing reindeer moss and bunches of grass over the thin surface, through which the deer breaks as soon as he steps on it. The natives say they sometimes get two [caribou] at once."[39]

The anthropologist Knud Rasmussen learned of a similar trap used in northern Alaska. "[The pitfall] is built at the top of a gully slope, where the snow is deep and smooth; [the pit] must be no wider than a man can just stand in it with his legs closed, and it must be deep enough to reach to his chest. The bottom must reach the ground, so that the caribou cannot stamp his way out. The pit is covered with a thin crust of snow."[40]

And a special pitfall was built to capture foxes. "The pit, about 4 feet deep and 4 feet in diameter, is covered with baleen strips. These surround the opening, the broad . . . end on the outside and the narrow end reaching to the middle of the pit. . . . Water is poured over the [broad] end of the baleen freezing it into place. A piece of bait is attached to the baleen near the center of the pit. The fox approaches and attempts to get the bait, but falls through instead. The baleen springs back into position, blocking the exit for the captured fox, and in readiness for another."[41]

Another type of pitfall was used on the lower Kolyma to catch arctic foxes. "This trap is a square pit with perpendicular walls, about eight feet deep. . . . It is covered with pieces of ice so that only a small opening remains in the centre. As a bait a piece of flesh or fish is fastened to a square board, fixed on two wooden pivots projecting from the side walls some little distance below the level of the ground. It is so balanced by the pivots that it lies level, and comes back into its original position after it has been touched or swung. The fox cannot reach the tempting morsel from above; so he springs down on the board, which tips over, and he falls into the pit. After a few seconds the treacherous board is again in position and tempts another fox to make a grab."[42]

A variant of the pitfall was the tower trap, which was used on the northwestern coast of arctic Alaska. "On land, the tower trap is built of rocks, piled up to form a high (often over 6 feet) conical structure which is hollow inside and open at the top. A putrid seal or other smelly bait is laid in the bottom and some rocks are removed to open a hole in the base. This is often left open for a while to allow the foxes to come to feed 'free,' but then is closed up after they get used to jumping in through the top and escaping out the bottom."[43]

SNARES AND NOOSES

Snares also captured animals ranging in size from the largest bears and moose, to mountain sheep, to smaller mammals. "It takes little more than the thought of facing a bear at close range with a bow and arrow or spear to make one understand why snares were an important method of killing these animals in aboriginal times," wrote the anthropologist Richard K. Nelson about the Gwich'in of northern Alaska. "The best time for snaring bears is during the fall, when they are fat and seem to wander along well-defined trails. . . . The aboriginal [Gwich'in] made their snares from braided strands of babiche [rawhide]. . . . The bear snare is usually set in a trail, either a man-made trail intended for winter travel or a natural game trail. It is generally placed where a constriction is created by bushes or trees, so that the snare fills the whole trail. Another good place is where a log or tree has fallen over the trail, so that the bear is forced to go underneath."[44]

In the Brooks Range of northern Alaska the Eskimos also used snares to capture grizzly bears. "In timbered country bears were sometimes snared," according to the biologist Robert Rausch. "A noose was placed above the trail, with the line running upward over a branch of a tree or through a hole in the tree itself. The line was attached to a very heavy log carefully balanced on end against the side of the tree. When the bear pulled against the noose, the log was dislodged and its weight tightened the loop."[45]

The size and strength of the snare depended on the quarry. Snares were often set amid brush or trees at about the height of the quarry's head. Caribou were "snared with strong nooses of rawhide, which were tied to stout bushes and held open by light strings of grass or sinew connecting them with other bushes, or with small stakes planted in the ground," wrote the ethnographer Edward William Nelson. "In feeding, the [caribou] would entangle their antlers or thrust in their heads, so that they were held or strangled by the nooses closing around their necks."[46]

Edward Adams described Eskimo caribou snares near Norton Sound in 1851. "A thick thong of seal's skin is made into a noose, about 4 ft. in diameter, & set in some bushes with the end fastened to a large stone. They generally set a row of them in this way across the bottom of a ravine, where the deer are in the habit of passing—or if the deer are near, they drive them in that direction. Sometimes the snares are left & visited every day. I recollect a boy at a village where I was staying for the night, setting 4 snares—I went with him to see him set them—He set them across a ravine in the way I have mentioned, & in the morning we went to look at them. There were 3 fine deer lying dead, & a fourth snare was broken!"[47]

For the Eskimos of the Brooks Range in northern Alaska snares were particularly effective. Nicholas J. Gubser described the use of snares among the Eskimos of Anaktuvuk Pass.

Before the Nunamiut obtained guns, most hunters relied on snares to supply their families with meat. A caribou snare, typical of snares used for moose, mountain sheep, lynx, and other animals, was made from a strong piece of rawhide line 12 to 15 feet long and two willow poles 5 to 6 feet long. When possible, Nunamiut hunters traded bearded seal [*Erignathus barbatus*] rawhide line from the coast, already cut into proper lengths for snares, and packed twenty to a bundle. A good bearded seal line could easily hold a bull caribou and was just under a quarter of an inch in diameter. If bearded seal line was not available, a man braided three or four strands of bull caribou rawhide line together. The man setting the snare tied the line to the base of a large trunk in a stand of willows in a creek which caribou were likely to cross. Two poles were forced into the snow or ground, about 2 or 2½ feet apart, one of which was near the large willow trunk. If possible there were thick willows on both sides of the poles which would channel a caribou toward the opening. From the base of the large trunk the man wrapped the line once around a pole, bringing it up to shoulder height. Then he draped the line across the other pole and wound it down to knee height (for a cow). The line was then draped back to the first pole where a slipknot was tied, joining the line to itself to complete the loop.

When a caribou passed through the opening enclosed by the loop, its legs and chest pulled the line tight around its neck; it was usually killed by the hunter with a spear, or it was starved or froze to death. In the old days the Nunamiut relied very heavily on snares during winter months when caribou are difficult to approach. If a household moved into the timber, the men set much larger snares for moose. If they were in a region plentiful in mountain sheep, smaller snares were set high in the small creeks coming down between two mountains across which sheep tracks had been seen.[48]

A variety of trigger mechanisms could be used with snares. Some devices held a spring pole under tension until an animal put its head through the noose, releasing the pole to spring up and strangle the quarry. Stratford Tollemache described lynx snaring: "A spot on the trail is chosen where thick bushes prevail on each side, so that the snare can be made to harmonize more effectually with its surroundings. Brush or sticks are placed upright across the trail, leaving an opening where the snare has been set, while one end of the cord is attached to a pole which is placed across the trail above the snare." Snares could be made from very heavy sea mammal hide line to capture brown bears, for example, or made from progressively lighter materials to capture moose, Dall sheep, caribou, wolves, foxes, hares, marmots, ground squirrels, ptarmigans and other animals.[49]

Edward William Nelson noted, "I saw snares for catching lynxes made by building a dome-shape pile of brush, with one or more openings leading to the bait, which was placed on the ground under the center," while traveling on the lower Yukon. "At the mouth of each of these openings a rawhide loop was so arranged that the lynx could not reach the bait without getting its head or legs entangled, and as the animal drew back the snare would close and hold it fast."

Another common style of snare was made by setting a noose over a path used by animals and digging a deep hole in the ground below it. To the lower end of the snare a heavy stone was attached, hanging in the mouth of the pit; the upper part of the snare was held open by attaching it by strings to surrounding objects, and a trigger was so arranged that at a touch from a passing animal the stone would be freed and drop into the hole, causing the snare to close and draw the animal's neck down to the ground and hold it fast.

Sometimes a noose was set at the entrance to a tunnel made in the frozen snow, with a bait of meat at the rear end, and in endeavoring to reach this the animals were snared. I was informed that animals as large as reindeer, and even bears, were formerly caught by means of snares, and that they were in general use for taking red and white foxes.[50]

Edward Preble reported a similar arrangement for catching lynx in the Mackenzie River area. "The Indians capture the lynx mainly by snaring," he wrote. "In setting the snare, a circular inclosure about 5 feet in diameter is made by sticking pieces of brush into the crusted snow. One or more openings are left, in which the noose is placed at the proper height, so that the animal attempting to enter the pen will put his head into the loop. In the center of the inclosure is placed a split stick smeared with the contents of the musk glands of the beaver. . . . The snare is attached to the middle of a stout stick 3 or 4 feet long, which acts as a drag when the animal is caught. It thus generally becomes entangled in the brush and after a few struggles remains passive, and if the weather is cold quickly freezes to death."[51]

Some fox snares were made by attaching the snare line to a heavy stone that was balanced on a tripod of sticks above a small enclosure. The fox had to insert its head through a noose to reach the bait at the back of the enclosure. When the fox withdrew its head, the noose would close, and, the fox would jerk back, trying to free itself, thereby knocking the stone off its balance. The snare line would then haul the fox up by its neck to the apex of the tripod. Hares, marmots, and ground squirrels were also captured with snares.[52]

Eskimos also caught marmots by placing the noose of a lasso around the opening of a marmot's den. The lasso line might be as long as 300 feet, and the hunter would conceal himself at its end, waiting for a marmot to stick its head out of the entrance to its den. The hunter would then quickly jerk the noose closed, pulling the marmot to him, so that he could club it. The Point Barrow Eskimos also used a noose to capture ground squirrels. "The hunter carried a rawhide line about 30 feet long which was formed into a noose at one end. A stake was made from a willow stem about two feet in length, and a hole cut through one end, through which the snare line was passed. The stake was then placed firmly into the ground alongside the den. . . . The noose, approximately the same size as the

Figure 2.2. Eskimo ground squirrel snare, 1877–81 (E. W. Nelson 1899, 125).

entrance to the den, was placed directly in front of this opening. The hunter then stationed himself about 25 feet behind the hole and waited for the squirrels to appear."[53]

CARIBOU AND REINDEER DRIVE FENCES

Both in Chukotka and Alaska the natives built lines of manlike decoys from sod blocks, snow, rocks, or other materials, to serve as gradually converging fences to force migrating caribou and wild reindeer into rivers and lakes, where they could be speared by hunters in kayaks, or into corrals, where they would become entangled by snares as they sought to escape and, thus encumbered, could be speared or shot by hunters with arrows.[54] In the winter of 1885–86 George Stoney saw one of these caribou fences at the headwaters of the Kobuk River in northern Alaska.

> Running for miles in two converging lines they make piles of stones four feet high and having the general resemblance of a man. Beginning at the outer ends of these lines, which are miles apart, the piles are built every thirty yards; the distance gradually lessening as the lines converge, until at their inner ends, where the width is about forty yards, the piles occur every ten feet. Connected with the inner ends of these piles is a circular place marked out by bushes concealing a rope securely fastened at the ends and in other places along it. To this rope are made fast numerous laniards having slip nooses at their ends

Figure 2.3. Alaskan Eskimo caribou drive enclosure (*kangiraq*) (Ostermann and Holtved 1952, 33). Reproduced by permission of the Ethnographic Division, National Museum of Denmark, Copenhagen.

open and held up properly in the bushes by small stakes. The deer are driven inside the lines without observing the stones; the natives then close in shouting and frightening the deer, who mistaking the stones for men rush on and seeing the opening ahead dash at the brush and are caught in the nooses by the horns or legs when they are killed by spears. As many as twenty-five are caught at a time.[55]

The Eskimos also built converging fences to drive caribou into lakes where, swimming, they were speared by kayakers. George Stoney explained: "In the narrow mountain passes frequented by deer similar arrangements are made. One native caught ninety deer during the season. In the big lake near the limit of the mountains large herds of deer gather in the fall. It is shut in by the mountains, with the ends open and accessible, but the sides so very steep that only in places can the deer climb; at such points some natives conceal themselves while others drive the deer into the ends. The hidden natives rise and make a great noise and the deer becoming frightened take to the water, where they are speared from light canoes made of deer skins shaped like kyaks of the coast. Hundreds are killed in this way."[56]

Helge Ingstad learned from Simon Paneak that Eskimos in the Brooks Range of Alaska sometimes took several days to herd caribou into an enclosure, which they called a *kangiraq*. "When the caribou had at last been driven up the slope towards the enclosure," he wrote, "people ran up from both sides, clapping their hands, hooting, and yelling. The beasts rushed in panic through the opening and into the inner enclosure. A number went straight into the snares; others broke through the willows into the outer enclosures and were snared there. Some of the hunters sent a rain of arrows at the beasts trying to escape, while others were busy with their flint spears." After the caribou calving season the Eskimos in northern Alaska also used dogs to drive the herds into swift streams, where some fawns would be drowned.[57]

BOW AND ARROW AND SPEAR

The bow and arrow and the spear, of course, offered a variety of opportunities for capturing everything from bears, to mountain sheep, caribou, foxes, hares, birds, and fish. Near Norton Sound in the winter of 1851–52 Edward Adams reported, "The black bear they kill in fair fight with their bows & arrows, but the other bear, which I imagine from the skins to be a grizzly, they describe as so ferocious that they do not venture to disturb him unless several of them are together."[58]

But the bow and arrow was also used widely in northeast Asia as a stationary device for taking foxes, hares, and ermine, and even moose and reindeer. One type, a "kind of cross-bow set on the animal's usual route" was used by the Evenk (Tungus). "It is fixed in a cleft in a tree-stump, with a pile driven in about two and a half feet in front, pressing against it and protecting it from being disarranged. It is then hidden as far as possible with twigs so that animals do not notice it. The hunters bar the way to the right and left with tree trunks, and the animal has, therefore, to pass the desired spot," wrote E. W. Pfizenmayer. "On the cross-bow they set a featherless arrow which has usually a forked point like a swallow's tail, to make the wound and the loss of blood more severe. About two handbreadths down from the point it has two or three notches on alternate sides, so that it breaks off in the body and the animal, fleeing through the undergrowth, cannot get rid of it. . . . These bows are dangerous also to human beings who go heedlessly through the woods."[59]

The hunter could also mount a bow vertically in a rectangular frame with a cocked arrow that was designed to release when the animal tugged on a baited trigger string. A similar device for catching sables, ermines, and arctic foxes had a cross-bar mounted at the point of the arrow, which, when released, closed on the neck of the quarry. The natives probably acquired this device from the Russians.[60]

ENCLOSURES AND NETS

To trap the wolves that preyed on their reindeer herds the Evenk (Tungus) and Sakha (Yakut) also built concentric circular enclosures, which one observer called a "wolf's garden."

The wolf's garden is made of piles, the height of a man, driven into the ground in two circles, the inner one complete, and the outer having a door. The diameter of the whole thing is from eleven to thirteen feet. The natives build the "garden" in summer, with an opening, but no door. In the passage between the two circles they lay bait to tempt the wolves in and accustom them to the trap. When in the late autumn the wolf has his winter coat, they fit the door so that it opens inward only, and put a live puppy or young reindeer inside the inner circle, whose cries whet the wolf's appetite and tempt it inside.

He squeezes through the door, which is light on its hinges, and goes round the narrow space between the first and second circles of piles. He cannot turn round, as the space is too narrow; and when he comes past the door, he shuts it. The next wolf can easily open the door into the prison in which his comrade is slinking round and then keeps the first wolf company till the hunter comes.[61]

In the Brooks Range of northern Alaska an Eskimo "placed several old meat carcasses in a spot as bait and set up a fence of sinew and rawhide line around it. He left an opening several feet wide so animals could enter without having their suspicions aroused. He then constructed a small snow-block house on the leeward side of the enclosure. When an animal entered, the man pulled a section of fence across the opening and shot the animal with a bow and arrow."[62]

They also employed an analogous net device in the Brooks Range. "This net, tied from caribou sinew, was about six feet wide, and was placed upright in a semi-circle. Near the opening a small snow-house was built, just large enough to contain a man. A caribou carcass was placed inside the net, and the hunter would spend the entire night in the snow-house, watching through a small observation hole. When foxes or wolves came into the bait the hunter would burst from the blind, and in their frantic efforts to run in the opposite direction, the animals became entangled and could be killed. The mesh of this net was large enough to catch the head of a wolf, but not so large as to allow foxes to escape." Foxes were also netted this way on St. Lawrence Island and on the Yukon.[63]

In Kamchatka dogs were used to tree sables, "the hunter then surrounds the base of the tree with nets, and either shakes down his quarry or knocks it off the boughs with sticks. If it does not fall into the net it is run down by dogs." Eskimos of interior northern Alaska in summer set nets near their meat caches to capture foxes and wolverines and set nets, and chased foxes into them, where they would be entangled and clubbed. Hunters might also put nets across an otter's run or the underwater entrances to a beaver lodge, where the animals would "become entangled and drown."[64]

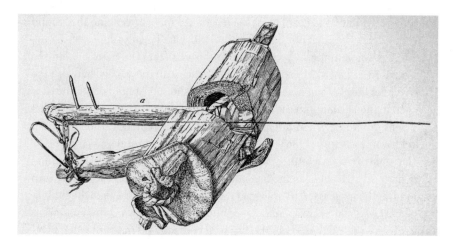

Figure 2.4. Chukchi torsion-spring trap (Bogoras 1904–9, 138).

TORSION-SPRING TRAPS

Another device, used on both sides of Bering Strait, was the torsion-spring trap, which was probably adopted via other Siberian groups or from the Russians. The "Uralo-Siberian torsion trap, or *klepi*" was a composite device made from a hollow log, inside of which a strong sinew cord was fastened and twisted so that, when it was tripped by an animal pulling at bait on a trigger cord, it released a spiked lever that struck the animal in the head. "This kind of trap is not very safe for the owner," Waldemar Bogoras wrote, "[because it] may occasionally strike him on the feet, since under the snow it is not easy to ascertain the actual place of the releasing-string trigger." The torsion-spring trap was used to take foxes and wolves. "I was told that formerly they were used to kill bears," wrote Edward William Nelson, who lived near the Yukon delta from 1877 to 1881.[65]

OTHER DEVICES AND TECHNIQUES

The natives of Chukotka and Alaska also used a mechanism called a "wolf killer." "This consists of a stout rod of whalebone [baleen] about 1 foot long and one-half inch broad, with a sharp point at each end," wrote the ethnographer John Murdoch about its use at Point Barrow. "One of these was folded lengthwise in the form of a Z, wrapped in blubber . . . and frozen solid. It was then thrown out on the snow where the wolf could find and swallow it. The heat of the animal's body would thaw out the blubber, releasing the whalebone, which would straighten and pierce the walls of its stomach, thus causing the animal's death." Hunters employed this device to capture foxes in the Norton Sound area. The

Figure 2.5. Eskimo wolf killer. Edward Adams, 1850–51. Excerpts from the work of Edward Adams (MS 1115;BJ) appear by permission of the Scott Polar Research Institute, University of Cambridge.

Chukchi were known to hang several wolf killers on a string and place them on a bush near a wolf's trail, high enough that foxes could not reach them, or the hunters would leave them on the ground, frozen into an icy matrix that kept them away from smaller animals.[66]

The Chukchi also made spiked blocks to capture bears. They drove several sharpened, barbed spikes into a wooden block and concealed it on a bear's trail. When a bear stepped on one of these it would be unable to withdraw the spikes and, thus crippled, would be relatively easy to kill. But no one considered hunting brown bears or polar bears to be easy. On both sides of Bering Strait, bears might be shot with arrows when emerging from their dens, or when fishing at rivers, or when brought up by dogs. Once the bear was wounded, it was often speared when it reared up on its hind legs.[67]

In Kamchatka, when the natives found a brown bear's den, they might pile logs and tree trunks in its entrance. The bear would then pull the timbers back inside the den to keep the entrance open. When the bear had nearly completely filled the den, and thus restricted his movement, the hunters would open the roof of the den and spear the bear.[68]

In the Brooks Range of Alaska "Grizzlies were killed in the winter whenever one could be found in a den," wrote the biologist Robert Rausch. "Before an effort was made to kill the bear, the hunters used to defecate upon the earth dug from the den. They believed that doing so would ensure their finding a bear inside. For killing the bear, a triangular frame was prepared by binding together three heavy willow sticks, with a fourth placed from the base to the apex to give additional strength. The apex of this frame was inserted into the den mouth, and a certain phrase ('*Nami kamna,*' meaning approximately 'Is anything in?') was called out. The aroused bear would seize the wood and try to pull it into the den, and while thus occupied it was speared."

The Brooks Range Eskimos also took grizzly bears in the open with spears. "The bear spear had a head made from flint or from the forearm bone of a bear, and a shaft about eight feet long. The butt of the spear was placed firmly against the ground, before the bear attacked, and when the animal lunged at the hunter, it became impaled."[69]

The Gwich'in of the Yukon drainage used a similar method for hunting bears. When they found a bear's den in the spring, they blocked its entrance with logs. "The bear is then stirred up until he awakes and rushes to the entrance of the den in a rage and receives a blow from an ax." "Whereas a black bear comes out slowly, not looking for a fight," wrote Richard K. Nelson, "the grizzly angrily charges out, trying to get anyone it can. The [Gwich'in of northern Alaska] say that grizzlies do not really hibernate; 'Maybe he don't even go to sleep in there.' Thus if a grizzly den is found, the hunter must expect trouble unless he decides to be prudent and leave it alone."[70] Across the circumpolar North it was a mark of considerable pride for a hunter to have killed a brown bear or a polar bear.

For the Chukchi and Koryak, red foxes and arctic foxes were the most important furbearers. For them the least complicated way to capture foxes was to run them down with reindeer teams or dog teams after a fresh snowfall had revealed their tracks. It often took two or three hours to overtake a fox, and when a hunter did, if he was using a reindeer-drawn sled, the reindeer might trample the animal with their hooves. In the Northwest Territories dogs were occasionally used to tree a lynx.[71]

When Chukchi hunters found a fox's burrow they might try to stun it by putting smoking debris in its hole and then dig it out with axes or ice picks. If the Yukagir found a fox's den, they blocked all but two of the openings, put a burning stick in one and, when the fox ran out the other, a dog would seize it. Hunters in Alaska also captured lynx, otters, and hares by chasing them on foot and clubbing them.[72]

In Alaska, when a hunter found a beaver lodge, he might cut a hole in its roof. If the beavers were absent, he would insert a light stick into the lodge, and then cover up the hole. The hunter then waited with a spear until he noticed the stick moving, indicating that beavers had returned to the lodge. The hunter would then throw aside the cover and spear the beavers inside. In this manner he might take half a dozen beavers at once. Lavrenty Zagoskin, in the 1840s, thought that this method had been introduced to the natives by Russian fur hunters. He felt that this practice was "so destructive that it promises to be the most effective way of exterminating the animal." In the open, beavers were also shot with bow and arrow.[73]

On the lower Yukon Nelson saw an unusual method of hunting beavers. "As winter advances and all of the lakes are covered with a heavy layer of ice," he wrote, "some of the small ponds drain away so that a sheet of ice covers the empty bed of the pond like a flat roof. The hunters cut a hole through the ice, and if beaver tracks are seen in the mud on the bottom, they take stout clubs and descend under the ice in search of the animals. The house is usually at one end of the lake, and the poor animals are soon routed therefrom. They are then pursued over the floor of their icy prison and brained by the hunter."[74]

The Gwich'in of northern Alaska captured muskrats by using a rawhide dip net which they placed across a muskrat's underwater swimming channel when the ice was clear shortly after the lakes froze. "Whenever one of these underwater trails was found, they made a hole [in the ice] and pushed sticks into the bottom on each side, making a small fence with a narrow opening for the runway right in the middle. Then a dip net was placed in the opening. One man went up on the shore 5 or 10 feet from the water's edge and jumped up and down, frightening the muskrat so it swam full speed through its tunnel into the runway and into the net." The Koyukon also used a wicker funnel-shaped trap under the ice from which the muskrat would be unable to back out.[75]

In the same region hunters captured minks by building a small fence across a stream, which forced swimming minks into a funnel-shaped fish trap, where they would be unable to find their way back and would drown. Edward William Nelson noted a number of instances where a trapper might retrieve ten to fifteen minks in one haul of his fish trap.[76] It is also likely that natives, aided by dogs, drove herds of caribou and mountain sheep over cliffs.[77]

One of the simplest methods of acquiring furs was to raise the animals in pens. When the natives captured young wolves or foxes alive, they might keep them in pens and feed them until their pelts became prime. At Point Barrow, Alaska, "wolf pups were often raised by hand," wrote the ethnographer Vilhjalmur Stefansson. "When their fur became good they were killed with flint-pointed arrows made for the purpose." In northeastern Asia Waldemar Bogoras reported that captive young foxes were kept in a state of semi-starvation because "if well fed, they would have thin and uneven fur."[78]

PELT HANDLING AND PREPARATION

The value of a fur depended not only on its size, pelt thickness, color, and tex-
ture, but also on the quality of its preparation. Consequently, the preparation of
furs for sale in effect began while the trapper was building his sets. The set had to
be built carefully. Damaged pelts were obviously less desirable; hence the trap
had to be put together to minimize hide punctures or fur loss. The use of snares,
especially, could result in badly abraded pelts if they were improperly set. The
trapper also had to visit his sets frequently to minimize the problem of other
animals scavenging the carcasses and to prevent the fur freezing to the trap or to
other objects.

The timing of the set was important. A pelt taken in the summer was shorter
and less dense than one taken in the winter. Prime pelts, with new guard hairs
and dense underfur, were far more valuable than pelts taken early in the winter
("early caught"), when the hair had not reached full growth, or late in the winter,
when the pelts had become "singed," with frizzy hairs, or "rubbed," having lost
their guard hairs. "Prime skins are fully furred," wrote A. L. Belden in his description of the American fur trade. "The leather is clean, clear and of maximum
strength; in color the fur is at its best, darkest or lightest, according to the nature
of the animal. . . . Unprime skins are only moderately well furred, tend to shed
the fur and hair . . . and the leather is weak, blue, and in instances nearly black."
He added, "blue pelts . . . which are blue on the pelt or leather side . . . are caught
early in the fall . . . ; such skins are 'unprime,' and the condition of the leather is
due to the fact that the blood which supplies 'life' to the fur and hair at the roots
during the period of growth, had not completed its purpose and been in due
course absorbed into the veins of the body. When the animal is killed in this stage
of development, the light strain of blood feeding the fur coagulates, corrupts,
turns the pelt blue, and weakens it as corruption progresses."[79]

With the exception of bear, otter, beaver, and muskrat, which become prime
in late winter, furs taken at the beginning of the depth of winter are best. "New
fur replaces the short summer hair in the fall, growing to its full length and completely covering the animal by late November or early December," wrote Terence
Ruttle in discussing damage to furs.

> Later on there is a tendency for some of the fur to wear off, especially the top
> hair in long-haired animals. An animal may rub this top hair off on bushes or
> trees or against the sides or top of a burrow or, in the case of a beaver or musk-
> rat, the entrance to its house. Sometimes when a fox sits or lies on the snow
> or a rock, some of the top hairs become stuck and pull out when the animal
> gets up.

The later in the season it gets, the looser both the top hair and the underfur become in their attachment to the skin and the more likely they are to come out. They also become more brittle and prone to break off. The rumps, shoulders and sides are the parts of an animal most likely to show this "rubbing."

Buyers are affected very much, either consciously or subconsciously, by the first flash appearance of a pelt. When they see a rubbed beaver, it automatically registers as a lower grade pelt. Such rubbing occurs much more frequently in a later "springy" pelt, and points to the likelihood of other defects. Buyers surmise that the rest of the fur is probably weak or loose and the pelt is to be avoided except at a low price.

One very common form of fur damage is tainting. It is caused by carcasses being left too long before skinning or by their being left piled together so that the body heat cannot escape. . . . What happens is that the dampness and the warmth . . . favor the growth of bacteria, which rot the roots of the hairs. . . . Once the roots rot, there is no longer anything to hold the hairs in tight and whole clumps of fur will come loose at the slightest pull.

Tainting occurs more often in beaver and muskrat than in mink. . . . A mink's skin gets brownish and reddish towards spring, as does that of the otter, and there are often dark marks between the shoulders. These are sure signs that the fur is past its prime and that it will be weak and flat, especially on the shoulders.[80]

There are four processes in pelt preparation: skinning, fleshing, stretching, and drying. Pelts were removed from the carcass in two ways, "open" and "cased." Caribou, bear, moose, beaver, and some wolf pelts were removed by the open pelt method of cutting lengthwise down the animal's underside. With the exception of beaver, a cut was then made along the legs, thus creating a flat skin. Beavers' feet were often cut off prior to skinning. Most of the other furbearers' pelts were cased, wherein the skin was cut across from one hind leg to the other and then pulled off the animal from the tail to the head in one tubular piece. All pelts were then scraped or "fleshed" to remove any fat and muscle adhering to the underside of the skin. This allowed them to dry properly, preventing them from spoiling. Fleshing was often done by placing the skin on a hard, flat or rounded surface and scraping off the fat and tissue. If this was not done, the pelt would dry slowly and become "grease burned," making the pelt worthless.

"Skinning Animals, a required part of the trapper's profession," wrote the Alaskan trapper Ray Tremblay, "has to be performed properly in order to obtain top money for furs. A slip of the knife, unfleshed hides, or those improperly stretched, will take many dollars off the price." "Most animals are found dead and frozen in the traps," he continued.

They are hauled back to the main cabin and carefully thawed before being skinned. At least 24 hours at room temperature is required for the smaller animals; larger ones take considerably longer. This is usually no problem for marten and mink. However, things can become very difficult with a frozen wolf in a small cabin. Wolves smell bad at times since they like to roll in the often rotten remains of a kill after eating, and they have to be hung out in the air before thawing. In cases like this it's best to go on a trip and tackle the skinning job upon returning without firing up the stove. A good cabin will retain heat in the log walls for several days, allowing a trapper on his return to skin a wolf in relative comfort. I must admit, however, that it was always a relief once the job was finished.

When dealing with the tough greasy hides of the beaver, otter, or wolverine there are two skinning methods employed. One is to rough skin the animal, removing the hide using the knife close to the carcass and leaving the tough gristle and fat on the skin. It can be finished in a short time and therefore is a method used out on the trail when it is inconvenient to pack the animals back to camp. Several large beaver can constitute a load too heavy to carry when using snowshoes to run a beaver line. Large adults weigh 40 or more pounds, so when more than one is taken, skinning is the only feasible way to get the hides back to camp. With a dog team weight is not a consideration, so hide can be peeled off in the comfort of a warm cabin. Rough skinned pelts are difficult to flesh properly and for this reason most trappers like to remove the hide clean. This takes longer, requiring about 45 minutes to handle a large beaver, but the end result is a skin ready for drying with little more work. Otherwise, a skin is layed across a smooth surface so flesh can be scraped off with a knife, broken glass, cabinet scraper, ax head or a moose shin bone. It's a tough job, and after trying it a few times, most trappers opt for the clean-skinning method."[81]

Any damage to the pelt was then mended before it was placed on a frame to stretch and dry. Pelts that were dried without stretching were wrinkled, stiff, and less valuable. The frames varied according to the species and its size. "A very important aspect to drying the skin is to stretch the skin enough, but not too much," wrote Terence Ruttle. "The fur on an understretched pelt may seem to be of better quality than most, because it has more top hairs and underfur fibres per square inch. However, any benefit gained in this way will quickly be offset if the pelt ends up in the Medium and Small category. . . . On the other hand, overstretching is just as bad or worse, since it inevitably weakens the fur." "Prior to selling," Ray Tremblay added, "the furs were always combed and fluffed to present the best appearance possible. There is nothing that upsets a fur buyer more than to have a bundle of skins brought in for grading that are greasy and matted with pitch and grime."[82]

The size, quality, and condition of the furs usually allowed them to be classified into several basic categories. "The various collections of 'wild' furs, except those caught by professional trappers, show more or less irregularity in skinning and handling, coming as they do from so many different persons," wrote A. R. Harding. "Among collections will be found not only blued skins, but torn, shot, dog chewed, rubbed, springy and otherwise damaged."

"During this examination," wrote Terence Ruttle, "you should stroke the whole of the back [of the pelt] lightly downwards toward the tail, then shake it up and stroke again. If you keep your fingers together, slightly bent but not stiff, you can judge the denseness of the fur with the sides of the fingers and the edge of your palm. . . . As you stroke the fur, you should get an impression of a cushiony effect that keeps you from being aware of the skin underneath the fur. . . . Furthermore, as your hand moves along, the displaced fur should spring back up again immediately, showing that it is supported by a dense underfur. On a well-furred fox the fur should flow over the tops of your fingers when it is stroked in the other direction—towards the head."[83]

"Firsts" were fully prime pelts with long, dense guard hairs and thick underfur and no thin spots. "Seconds" were inferior, lacking guard hairs and often having "wooly" underfur. "Thirds" were usually skins that were taken in the fall or spring: "early caught" or "late caught." "Fourths" were early or late caught skins of poor quality. "Damaged" were skins of all of these categories with nicks, cuts, or rodent damage.[84] These categories would, of course, have been reflected in the furs' prices at each place where they changed hands in the long chain from native trapper to retail customer.

3

THE RUSSIAN EXPANSION TOWARD ALASKA

The robust intercontinental fur trade that Eliab Grimes found at Big Diomede Island in 1819 was, in fact, a comparatively recent development in the
Bering Strait region. The Chukchi and Eskimos had been vigorously involved
with this trade for only about thirty years, a commerce which developed as a result of a Russian trade fair that began on a tributary of the Kolyma River in 1789.
This fair was one of the last elements of the Russian expansion across northern
Asia, an expansion that began a thousand years earlier and 4,000 miles to the
west.

BEGINNINGS

The early stirrings of a Russian state can be dated to the latter part of the ninth
century in Kiev, where a Slavic trading center developed on the Viking trade
route between the Baltic and the Black Sea. Less than two centuries later Kiev
had become an important commercial center, but the Tatar (Mongol) invasions
destroyed Kiev in the thirteenth century. By then, however, the states east of
the Baltic had grown, with Novgorod becoming a vigorous city-state in northern
Russia, and later Moscow emerged as well, with the defeat of the Tatars in 1380.
"This victory marked the beginning of the end of Tatar domination of Russia,"
David Warnes wrote. "The power of the Golden Horde never fully recovered
after Tamerlane's attack on the khanate in the 1390s, and in the fifteenth century
the Tatar state fell apart [although] the successor khanates remained a threat to
Russian lands."[1]

In the north, Novgorod's need for export products—among them, furs—drew
hunters northeastward, to the rivers that flow into the Arctic Ocean, and by the

mid-fourteenth century they regularly crossed the northern Ural Mountains. But in the next century Tsars Ivan III and Ivan IV (in the West, "Ivan the Terrible") conquered Novgorod. "The history of Moscow," according to Robert J. Kerner, "is the story of how an insignificant ostrog became the capital of a Eurasian empire. This insignificant ostrog, built in the first half of the twelfth century, on an insignificant river by an insignificant princeling, became, in the course of time, the pivot of an empire extending into two, and even three continents."[2]

"Pelts were a basic medium of exchange in medieval Russia," wrote E. A. P. Crownhart-Vaughan. "As Moscow prospered[,] her princes used furs to pay for personal services to the state. Peers were rewarded and diplomats bribed. Tsars sent sable gifts to foreign emissaries and rulers, sometimes in lieu of travel expenses. By the seventeenth century the Sable Treasury in Moscow, secure within the Kremlin walls, was the chief depository of government-owned pelts and functioned as a royal reserve." In 1586, for example, the "treasury received 200,000 sables, 10,000 black foxes, 500,000 squirrels, besides beavers and ermines from Siberia."[3]

The need for furs was a powerful inducement for expansion, and the sparsely inhabited lands east of Russia were full of valuable furbearers, but the way east was blocked by the Tatar khanate of Kazan, one of the successor states to the Golden Horde. Ivan IV conquered Kazan in 1552, and with its capture Russia became an imperial power. The Russians next approached the khanate of Sibir, which occupied the central reaches of the Ob River and from which the entire region of northern Asia between the Urals and the Pacific Ocean has become known in the West as *Siberia*. Ivan IV then enlisted the aid of the Stroganov family—wealthy entrepreneurs of Perm in the Urals—whom he encouraged to continue the expansion for him. The Stroganovs, in turn, received permission to employ Cossacks for their advance. These frontiersmen were led by Vasily Timofeevich Olenin, called Yermak, "a notorious river pirate with a price on his head," who commanded about eight hundred men. In 1582 Yermak captured the capital of the khanate. Soon the Russians began colonizing the new lands, founding towns on the middle Ob in 1585, on the Irtysh in 1587, and on the lower Ob in 1595. From the lower Ob the fur hunters moved on again, to the sable-rich lands surrounding the Taz River, founding Mangazeia in 1601.[4]

Russian *promyshlenniki*—frontiersmen who hunted, trapped, and traded for furs—were important participants in the expansion, and the furs they acquired helped to pay the expenses of the tsar's court. By the 1600s, however, the furbearers of European Russia had become so reduced that the hunters were forced to move farther east in the search for virgin fur territories. "There was an abundance of 'soft gold' in Siberia, prompting the adage 'Siberia is a gold mine,'" wrote the historical geographer James R. Gibson. "Other motives certainly induced the movement across Siberia, such as the desire for personal freedom and adventure and the search for gold and silver and mammoth and walrus ivory, but furs represented the overriding incentive, especially in eastern Siberia, the Russian Far East, and Russian America, where the finest furs were found and where alternate sources of wealth, particularly agricultural land, were very limited. It has been said, with little exaggeration, that the conquest of Siberia was one continuous hunt for sables."[5]

In general, the men obtained furs two ways. The first was by collecting *yasak*, annual tribute paid by natives in furs—sable, ermine, squirrel, and fox—to the Crown's agents, signifying their subjugation to the tsar. But the Crown also gathered pelts from fur hunters and traders, who were taxed 10 percent of their catch. "These persons did not always hunt the animals," wrote Terence Armstrong. "Instead, they often hunted the natives, because the latter were skilled in hunting the animals."[6]

Of course this hunting pressure quickly reduced the furbearers in one area after another and was in itself a cause for the rapid Russian advance across Siberia. The Russians moved on via the great rivers of Siberia, most of which flow north into the Arctic Ocean. The men used them as highways and, where necessary, portaged from one watershed to another. The fur hunters had probably rounded the northern tip of Asia, Cape Chelyuskin, by 1619. Soon they were on the Lena, one of the longest rivers in the world. Its outflow forms a huge delta on the shore of the Laptev Sea, and its watershed was critical to the Cossack advance in eastern Siberia. The Russians continued onward to the Kolyma and then to the shore of the Sea of Okhotsk in the early 1640s. In 1648 the Cossack Semyon Dezhnev, a government agent attached to Fedot Alekseev's merchant expedition to "procure sable and for trade," sailed east from the mouth of the Kolyma with seven vessels. Although Alekseev and his party vanished and were probably shipwrecked and killed by the Chukchi, Dezhnev rounded the eastern tip of Asia (today, Cape Dezhnev) and ultimately reached the Anadyr River, which flows east, into the Bering Sea, where he founded the Anadyr fort in 1649. Despite the importance of his voyage, Dezhnev's report was filed away in an archive in Yakutsk, only to be discovered in 1737.[7]

With the exception of Kamchatka, Dezhnev's voyage essentially concluded the amazingly swift Russian advance across Eurasia, an advance of more than 3,000 statute miles (5,000 km)—encompassing 17 degrees of latitude and 110 degrees of longitude—in only seventy years. At the same time the natives, who might have opposed such an advance, were very few, disorganized, and lacked the technological superiority of the Russians.[8]

BERING, GVOZDYOV, FYODOROV, AND DAURKIN

Although Dezhnev's report was filed away in a provincial archive for nearly a century, some information about the possibility of a land lying east of Bering Strait did exist. Tsar Peter the Great, who was unaware of Dezhnev's achievement, was curious about the exact nature of the easternmost part of his empire. He had received a sketch map from Ivan Lvov, the commandant at Anadyr, showing two islands and a large land east of what would later be called Chukotka, and in 1711 he sent the Cossack Pyotr Popov to explore the Chukchi Peninsula and to collect tribute from the Chukchi. Popov "every where met with a Denial with respect to their rendering themselves subject, and paying Tribute." Nevertheless he did learn from the Chukchi that to the east "an Island is said to be seen at a great Distance, which the Tschuktschi call a large Country, and say, that People dwell there who have large Teeth put into their Mouths that project thro' their cheeks. These People are different in their Language, and Manner of Living, from the Tschuktschi, who have waged War against them Time out of Mind. . . . Popov found ten Men of these People disfigured with their projecting Teeth; these were Prisoners of war among the Tschuktschi."[9]

Consequently, in December 1724, Tsar Peter, in the last weeks of his life, ordered a naval expedition—to be commanded by Vitus Bering, a Danish mariner in Russian service—to probe the regions beyond northeasternmost Asia. Peter's highly important initiative was carried out during the reigns of his widow, Catherine I (1725–27), and his grandson, Peter II (1727–30). His orders were to "build in Kamchatka or in some other place in that region one or two decked boats," to "sail on these boats along the shore which bears northerly and which (since its limits are unknown) seems to be part of America," and to "determine where it joins with America."[10]

The expedition set out from Russia early in 1725. Bering went overland to the Lena River, where his men built barges and boats during the winter. He and his men descended the Lena to Yakutsk, where, despite many difficulties, they set off again, overland to Okhotsk. Bering reached Okhotsk in October 1726, and the rest straggled in throughout the winter. An advance party had already built a sewn-plank vessel, the *Fortuna*. Bering and his men used her to carry their equipment and supplies to Kamchatka for the winter. On the east side of the peninsula they built another vessel, the *Sviatoy Arkhangel Gavriil* (*Saint Gabriel the Archangel*), in which they put to sea and headed northeast in July 1728. On August 10, St. Lawrence Day, they discovered and named St. Lawrence Island. Moving on in fog, they passed through Bering Strait. Fifty years later Captain James Cook would name the strait in Bering's honor.

Believing he had already sailed beyond the eastern tip of Asia, Bering nevertheless kept on until August 16 and then turned back, having reached 67°18′ N, "because the coast did not extend farther north . . . therefore it seemed . . . that the instructions of his Imperial Majesty . . . had been carried out." On the way south he sighted and named what would colloquially become called "Big Diomede," the westernmost of the Diomede Islands, which stand midway in Bering Strait. But fog, which is often present there in the summer, prevented him from seeing the Alaskan shore. On August 20, near the coast of the Chukchi Peninsula, forty Chukchi in four umiaqs paddled to the ship. They offered the Russians meat, fish, and fresh water, as well as fifteen furs, some of them arctic fox, and four walrus tusks. Bering paid with pins and steels for striking fires. Bering then returned to Kamchatka and wintered there.[11]

The following year, 1729, he sailed about a hundred miles east, searching for, but not finding, islands that were believed to lie in those waters. Bering returned to Okhotsk and then traveled overland to St. Petersburg, where he arrived on March 1, 1730. He was convinced that he had confirmed the separation of Asia and America, but he could not prove the fact, and the Admiralty deemed his investigation to have been inconclusive.[12]

Bering, as we shall see, was ordered to return to the Pacific, but meanwhile, in 1732, Dmitry Pavlutsky, the military commander at Anadyr who had failed to subjugate the Chukchi the year before, ordered a ship to sail from Kamchatka in search of the "large country" that was reported to lie east of Chukotka. Mikhail Gvozdyov, a geodesist (a land surveyor and mapper), and Ivan Fyodorov led the expedition aboard the *Sviatoy Arkhangel Gavriil*, to find "how many ostrogs there were, what kind of people live in them and to find and tax the ones that had not previously been taxed." They sailed along the Asian coast to the Chukchi Peninsula and on August 20 anchored in Bering Strait off Big Diomede Island. They were only the second group of Europeans to reach the Diomedes, and they received "a hail of arrows from the Eskimos on shore." Although the Russians responded with gunfire, Gvozdyov and Fyodorov must have eventually established some sort of communication with the Diomeders, because the explorers learned that some of the Eskimos there had joined the Chukchi and fought against Pavlutsky the year before, which explains the "hail of arrows."[13]

The next day Gvozdyov and Fyodorov crossed to Cape Prince of Wales, the westernmost promontory of North America. They saw huts on shore, but the wind prevented them from landing, so they moved southeast to King Island. There they met a man in a kayak who told them that the land they saw to the east was inhabited and that it had forests with deer, marten, fox, and beaver. That they were able to understand the kayaker suggests that many persons on both sides of

Bering Strait were bilingual. Again the Russians were unable to land, and they soon returned to Kamchatka. Gvozdyov's expedition was almost certainly the first Russian sighting of mainland Alaska, although Gvozdyov thought he had only seen several new islands.[14]

Meanwhile, in St. Petersburg, Vitus Bering had been unable to convince the Admiralty that he had proved the separation of Asia and America. Consequently he petitioned Empress Anna to appoint him to lead another expedition to probe the relation between Asia and the lands to the east. Anna agreed and ordered Bering to return to Kamchatka to continue his explorations. Bering's new expedition was part of one of the most ambitious explorations ever attempted. This bold initiative, the Great Northern Expedition, was a comprehensive, coordinated investigation comprising seven separate expeditions to chart the entire northern and eastern coasts of Eurasia, from Arkhangelsk on the White Sea to the Kurile Islands and Japan. Bering's segment was to go to the American coast. He left St. Petersburg in 1733 but encountered so many crippling difficulties that he did not reach Kamchatka until autumn 1740.[15]

At last, in 1741, Bering, commanding the *Sviatoy Pyotr*, with Aleksei Chirikov commanding the *Sviatoy Pavel*, left Petropavlovsk, Kamchatka. In July Chirikov reached the American mainland in southeastern Alaska, but the two boats he sent ashore disappeared, their crews either drowned or captured by the Tlingit. Lacking other boats, he returned home along the arc of the Aleutians and arrived in Petropavlovsk in October.[16]

While Chirikov was at sea Bering touched briefly at Kayak Island in the Gulf of Alaska, then headed back quickly. The reason for Bering's short stay and fast turnaround has been debated ever since. Working west along the islands in stormy weather, scurvy broke out and, much worse, in November they were shipwrecked east of Kamchatka in the Commander Islands. Bering died there in December, and his crew spent a miserable winter, scraping out an existence by eating, among other things, Steller's sea cows. In the spring the survivors built a boat from the remains of the *Sviatoy Pyotr* and at last reached Petropavlovsk in August. Only forty-five of the *Sviatoy Pyotr*'s crew of seventy-six returned alive. But in St. Petersburg the government was occupied with other challenges and had lost interest in further explorations eastward. "For the next twenty years," Lydia Black wrote, "exploration and gaining footholds on the American continent would be left solely to Russian private entrepreneurs and frontiersmen" (see chapter 5).[17]

Nikolai Daurkin undertook the next exploration that bears directly on the history of the Bering Strait fur trade. Daurkin was a Chukchi, born near Cape Serdtse Kamen on the north coast of the peninsula. As a boy he was captured by

Pavlutsky's troops and sent to Yakutsk, where he was baptized. Daurkin learned to speak and read Russian, and for a time he served Pavlutsky's family in Tobolsk, but the governor of Siberia, noting his exceptional intelligence and seeing in him an opportunity to improve relations with the Chukchi, freed him and sent him to Anadyr. At Anadyr the new military commander ordered Daurkin to scout Chukotka and nearby lands for the prospects of fur trade and tribute.

In 1764 Daurkin crossed Bering Strait to Big Diomede. "The inhabitants of the island gave us a friendly reception. Their first request was for tobacco," he wrote. "Having brought three poods [108 pounds] of this commodity with me, I presented them with several leaves, in return for which they gave me a whole suit of sable and marten fur." A comparison with the amount of furs received in trade for tobacco in later years makes clear that tobacco at that date was without doubt a scarce and highly desired commodity at Bering Strait.

More important, Daurkin learned about the large country lying east of the Diomedes. He reported, "The Chukchi Peninsula, lacking woods, has nothing except red foxes and wolves; but this other country contains all kinds of animals, such as sables, martens, ice foxes of all sorts (that is, both white and blue), gluttons [wolverines], bears, and also sea otters [probably river otters]. . . . The country is well forested with dwarf pine [spruce], red and white fir, and larch. . . . Streams of considerable size are said to flow from this country into the sea." His report also contained a map with an outline of the American shore. As a Chukchi, he was clearly able to gain more information than his predecessors.[18]

COOK, KOBELEV, BILLINGS, AND DAURKIN AGAIN

The first penetration of the region by an entity that had no connection with Russia was Captain James Cook's third voyage of discovery for Great Britain. Cook was sent in search of a northwest passage, a northern water route between the Pacific and Atlantic oceans. On August 9, 1778, Cook named Cape Prince of Wales, the westernmost point of continental North America. The next day, St. Lawrence Day, he arrived on the east coast of the Chukchi Peninsula and named St. Lawrence Bay. Captain Cook stepped ashore first, and three Chukchi men advanced toward him. Assistant Surgeon William Ellis described the encounter:

> Three of them came down; but upon captain Cook's approach (who landed by himself), they retired: he however followed them, and, by every sign of friendship, endeavoured to persuade them to lay aside their fears, and at the same time shewed them beads and various other articles. These seemed to engage

Figure 3.1. "The Tschuktschi and Their Habitations," St. Lawrence Bay, 1778. When Captain James Cook's ships visited St. Lawrence Bay, the Chukchi men carried iron spearheads which were made by Yakut, Evenk (Tungus), and Koryak blacksmiths (Cook and King 1784, pl. 51).

their attention. . . . Several of the officers who were in the boats now followed the captain; but the natives made signs that too many should not come at once . . . they fixed a line, made of skin of the sea-horse [walrus], across, and gave the gentlemen to understand that they were not to go beyond it. Having settled matters thus far, they brought out various articles of trade, such as sea-horse hides and teeth, seal skins, ropes made of hides, gloves, and half-boots.

It was a fact of life in the Bering Strait region that unknown foreigners were deeply mistrusted in trading encounters: the Chukchi stretched a rawhide line on the ground to establish a boundary between the two parties. "They were all armed with bows, quivers of arrows at their backs, and spears headed with iron exceeding sharp and bright, and inlaid with white and yellow metal," Ellis added. He also noted that "they saw neither women nor children."[19] In the usual manner of meeting unknown foreigners in the Bering Strait region the Chukchi, having sent their women and children away, were prepared for hostilities.

Daurkin was asked for tobacco on Big Diomede in 1764, but the Alaskan natives whom Cook met in 1778 on the Seward Peninsula and on the coast of Norton Sound apparently did not consider it of major importance. Neverthe-less, when Cook visited Nunyagmo (Nuniamo), a Chukchi settlement on the north shore of St. Lawrence Bay, less than one hundred miles from the Seward Peninsula, he noted, "Of the few articles they got from us knives and tobacco were what they most valued." And Captain Charles Clerke reported, "Their chief demand with our people in the course of traffick was for tobacco and Snuff." It appears that the spread of tobacco had only recently reached Bering Strait.

Cook remarked that "the spears or spontoons [halberds]" the Chukchi men carried "were of iron or steel and of European or Asiatic workmanship." He added later, "They must have a trade with the Russians either directly or by means of some neighboring nation or else how came they by the spontoons we saw in their possession?"[20]

In fact, knives (*palmas*), halberd heads, and other ironwork reached the Chukchi via trade from Yakut, Evenk (Tungus), and Koryak blacksmiths. These blades were often inlaid with copper or brass, skills that the ethnographer Walde-mar Jochelson thought had been acquired from people on the Amur River, which they in turn had learned from the Chinese. The palma, or "Tungus spear," a single-edge general-purpose tool and weapon, was particularly widespread in northeastern Asia and western Alaska. About two feet long, palmas could be used alone or mounted on a long shaft.[21]

Cook surveyed the northwest coast of arctic Alaska as far as Icy Cape (70° N), where pack ice prevented his ships from going farther. He then sailed west and charted the north coast of the Chukchi Peninsula before returning to the Pacific. Cook was, of course, killed in Hawaii that winter, but Charles Clerke took command of the expedition and returned north in 1779.

The British, however, were not the only foreigners in the Bering Strait region in summer 1779: Ivan Kobelev, a Cossack *sotnik* (company commander) had also been sent to Chukotka. At St. Lawrence Bay, Kobelev heard a report of two ships having visited there the previous summer: Cook's expedition. Kobelev also learned of two ships that had visited there many years before: this must have been a report of Vitus Bering's expedition of 1728. And Kobelev met a Chukchi man "who formerly, for trade and war, had gone as often as five times to the American mainland and had become very friendly with an inhabitant of the island of Ukipan [*Uivaq*, King Island]."[22]

Like Daurkin before him, Kobelev crossed to the Diomede Islands. There the natives told him that "the coast of America is very populous, having an abundance of fish and land animals, and also being blest with reindeer." Kobelev's investigations yielded a detailed map of the location of all the settlements on the American shore from the Yukon delta to Kotzebue Sound. "Kobelev's map is unique," wrote Dorothy Jean Ray, "not only for the fact of its being made without benefit of a base map or a personal survey of the Alaskan mainland, but because it includes bays, rivers, and islands 'discovered' much later by Europeans, and sixty-one settlements that have stood the test of twentieth-century inquiries." Kobelev's map is indeed remarkable for many reasons. Most important, however, it reveals the detailed geographical knowledge that the natives of the Bering Strait region possessed about the settlements on the American coast.[23]

The Russian government had been aware of Cook's expedition from the start and had received copies of his charts of Alaska and Kamchatka when the ships visited Petropavlovsk in 1779. Cook's expedition did not alarm the government in St. Petersburg, but when it learned that the French, in response to Cook's discoveries, were sending their own expedition to the North Pacific under the command of Jean-François de Galaup, comte de La Pérouse, the government ordered an expedition of its own. The Russian expedition was to be secret, and it was sent to gain a better understanding of Russia's possessions in northeastern Asia and Alaska and thus to strengthen its claims there. The Russians chose Joseph Billings, an Englishman who had sailed as an astronomer's assistant with Cook's expedition, to "try to find as much as possible about the Chukchi land, the strength and habits of this people, and if the case presents itself, to try to convince this people to become subjects of Russia."[24]

Billings and his assistants left St. Petersburg in autumn 1785, beginning their long overland journey toward the Pacific. In 1787, after exploring the Kolyma River, Billings and some of his men reached Yakutsk in mid-November. There they learned to their dismay that many of their supplies for building ships in Okhotsk were still behind them in Irkutsk. In fact, they were forced to overcome so many difficulties that it was not until 1790 that the expedition departed Kamchatka. Aboard the *Slava Rossii* (*Glory of Russia*), Billings first headed east, along the Aleutians, to Kodiak Island, where Grigory Shelikhov, a far-sighted and energetic merchant and the founder of the first permanent Russian settlement in Alaska, had built an outpost for collecting sea otter skins. In the absence of any governmental encouragement, for nearly fifty years enterprising merchants of Russia and Siberia had pushed east, along the Aleutians and farther, capitalizing on the information that Bering had acquired on his second voyage. The sea otter trade proved to be both highly lucrative and extremely cutthroat. Nevertheless, Shelikhov not only consolidated these competitive efforts but also received a grant of a ten-year hunting monopoly.

That summer, 1790, Billings sailed as far east as Prince William Sound in the Gulf of Alaska, returning to Petropavlovsk in the autumn. The following spring, 1791, the *Slava Rossii* headed via Unalaska and the Pribilof Islands to St. Lawrence Island, which Billings determined to be one island, not three or four as Cook had believed. On August 7, 1791, the *Slava Rossii* reached the southwest

Theil des kamtschatkischen Meeres, Ivan Kobelev, 1779

Before the nineteenth century, Russians in northeastern Asia mainly learned about the American coast of Bering Strait secondhand, via native informants. Ivan Lvov in 1711 and Nikolai Daurkin, a Chukchi, in 1764 were the first to record place names on the Alaskan coast, but it was Ivan Kobelev who compiled the first detailed map of the region. Kobelev visited the Diomede Islands in 1779 and with the help of the local Eskimos assembled a remarkably accurate map of settlements on the Alaskan shore of Bering Strait. It conclusively demonstrates the high degree of geographical knowledge possessed by residents of the region.

Kobelev's map delineates the Asian coast from Cape St. Thaddeus in the southwest and runs as far as the north coast of the Chukchi Penin-sula. It includes the estuary of the Anadyr River, Zaliv Kresta (Holy Cross Bay), and a shrunken St. Lawrence Island, which nevertheless indicates most of its settlements. Directly above the outline of St. Lawrence Island is the peninsula and village of Uŋaziq (Indian Point), labeled "Ugün." To its right is the embayment that is enclosed by Arakamche-chen Island, and further northeastward is St. Lawrence Bay, showing the place where Captain Cook's ships anchored in 1778 ("Ankerplatz der Englaender im Jahr 1778"). The Chukchi settlement of Uelen and its sandspit ("Uwtlen') are shown near Cape Dezhnev. In Bering Strait are Fairway Rock ("Usken") and the two Diomede Islands, where Kobe-lev gathered the information about settlements on the American shore: Big Diomede, Imaqłiq ("Imaglin"), and Little Diomede, Ingaliq ("Iaga-lin").

It is understandable that the outline of the Alaskan shore is much less accurately depicted than is the Chukotkan coast—Kobelev did not visit it and only learned about it from native informants. Beginning at the north (upper right), the embayment of Kotzebue Sound is shown. From there the settlements on the north coast of the Seward Peninsula are listed in order as far as Cape Prince of Wales, Kingigan ("Kigygmin"). The coast then leads southwest, and King Island is shown offshore as "Ukipen" (Uivaq). The great embayment of Port Clarence is confused

continued

with Captain Cook's Norton Sound. The "Cheuweren" (Kuzitrin) River flows into Port Clarence ("Norton Sound"). On its banks a fortress is indicated, which was not a Russian redoubt but rather the Eskimo settlement of Kauwerak (*Qaviaraq*). Southwest of Port Clarence is Sledge Island, "Ejech" (Aziaq). Coastal settlements are then identified as far as Norton Bay at the base of the Seward Peninsula, and the shoal water of the Yukon delta, incorrectly placed, is probably depicted as well. See also D. J. Ray 1971.

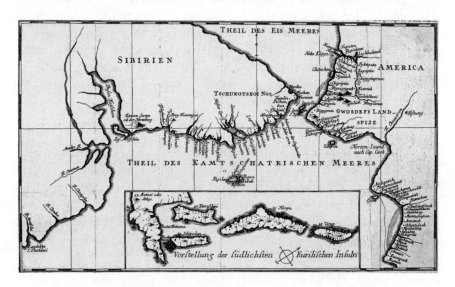

Map 3.1. Ivan Kobelev's map of Bering Strait, 1779. In Peter Simon Pallas, *Neue nordische Beyträge*, vol. 4, 1783. Alaska and Polar Regions Department, Elmer E. Rasmuson Library, University of Alaska, Fairbanks.

corner of the Seward Peninsula.[25] Billings went ashore with a few others. "We landed on a sandy beach near the discharge of a small river," one of the shore party reported to Martin Sauer, the expedition's secretary:

> hauled both boats on shore; and made a fire with driftwood, which was in great plenty. The Captain, Mr. Bakoff, the Doctor, and Draftsman, walked along a narrow path on shore, quite unarmed; and at a small distance from the boats, we saw two natives coming toward us. When advanced within a few fathoms, they made a stand; upon which beads were shewn them, and a few thrown on the ground. They were armed with lances, and advanced with the points toward us; but upon seeing the beads, and observing our signs of friendship, they turned the points of their lances behind them, and approached without hesitation.
>
> Upon the first sight of the natives, our interpreters were sent for, viz. the Oonalaskan, the American taken from Kadiak, and an Anadyrsky Cossac, whose mother was a Tshutski woman. This latter they understood perfectly well, and, embracing him upon speaking the language of the Tshutski, we concluded that they were of that nation, and not Americans.[26] We returned all together to the boats, and captain Billings gave each of them a copper medal and a few beads. Shortly after we were joined by two other Americans, and obtained of them, for beads and a few uniform buttons, their bows, arrows, and lances."[27]

The expedition's naturalist, Carl Heinrich Merck, noted that some of the men's spears were tipped with iron points "which originate in Tshika [Gizhiga]." "What they have for barter-trade are skins of wolf, wolverines and foxes, also marten-parkas or skins of rats, evrashka-parkas [marmot or ground squirrel], river otters, hermelin [ermine], seal and reindeer skins." "They in general love beads and other ornaments, but most of all they wish to have iron, and are ready to give everything that they have for it."[28]

While Billings and his party were on shore, an umiaq with nine natives came alongside the *Slava Rossii.* In the umiaq the natives had hung a bladder on a pole and two red fox skins on another pole, and they raised their arms above their heads, signs that they wanted to trade and that they were not concealing knives in their sleeves. Lieutenant Gavriil Sarychev, Billings's second-in-command, ordered the sailors to do the same and to hoist a flag in response. The natives, who apparently understood that these foreigners were friendly, then came aboard, leaving their bows, arrows, and spears in the umiaq. "They had some red foxes, some vests of young reindeer and alpine hares, wooden bowls, and different trifles, made of walrus' teeth, which they exchanged with our sailors for coral, pearl-enamel, and buttons, *but no tobacco.*"[29]

Sarychev continued: "In their ears they wore an ornament of pearl enamel, and in the perforations of the under lip, on both sides of the mouth, they stuck two alabaster stones in the form of a shirt-button." The fact that the visitors wore labrets piercing their lower lips confirms that they were Alaskan Eskimos, not Chukchi (who did not wear labrets). In the Bering Strait region and in the North American Western Arctic only Eskimo males wore labrets.[30]

Two days later the *Slava Rossii* moved on "and bore up to Sledge Island, called by the Americans Ajak [Aziaq]. Here the same Americans visited us as had come the day before, and with them many others whom we did not know. They brought us similar articles, and carried on a brisk trade with our sailors. Glass beads were in the greatest request with them, for which they paid most liberally. Captain Billings bought a single-seated baidar [kayak] for one row of them only. . . . This baidar was large and constructed in the same manner as that of the Kadjukers [natives from Kodiak], only with this difference, that it was not covered with the hides of the sea-lion, but with those of the walrus, which, on account of their thickness, had been parted three times."

On August 14 the *Slava Rossii* reached St. Lawrence Bay on the Chukchi Peninsula. Before their arrival, Ivan Kobelev and Nikolai Daurkin had been sent to inform the natives about the expedition's pending appearance and to rendezvous with Billings. First Kobelev and Daurkin were to travel to the northeastern corner of the Okhotsk Sea "and from thence to accompany the Tschukschians, who frequent that place every year for the purposes of trade, to Tsukotskoi-nos, in order to appraise the inhabitants of our arrival, and wait for us in Behring's straights," wrote Sarychev.

In June, Daurkin and Kobelev reached the settlement of Nunyagmo on St. Lawrence Bay, well before Billings's arrival, then had crossed Bering Strait to the Seward Peninsula in a fleet of seventeen umiaqs with a group of Chukchi in search of a mythical Russian settlement, "Kheuveren," which was supposedly inhabited by descendants of a shipwrecked group from Dezhnev's and Alekseev's expedition of 1648. The misinformation about "Kheuveren" had grown from Daurkin's expedition to the Chukchi Peninsula and the Diomedes in the 1760s. Daurkin, hearing secondhand information, confused the Eskimo settlement of Kauwerak (*Qaviaraq*) in the Imuruk Basin of the Seward Peninsula with a Russian outpost, and the myth grew from there.[31]

Kobelev's and Daurkin's flotilla touched first at Cape Prince of Wales, where Kobelev counted fifty houses but found the settlement deserted. As Dorothy Jean Ray observed, "The inhabitants probably hid when they saw a fleet of 17 skin boats coming from the west, bearing their old enemies, the Chukchi." When Kobelev reached King Island, the King Islanders, well acquainted with the realities of Bering Strait raid-and-trade, awaited their arrival wearing armor. In the Bering Strait region, the threat of a raid by other nations was sufficiently high that men often wore armor when suspicious strangers arrived. This armor was made of overlapping bone or ivory plates, or hide strips backed in places with wood.[32]

"The threat of amphibious attack was sufficiently high in the Bering Strait region for the peoples in the area regularly to post lookouts on high points of land during the season of open water," Ernest S. Burch, Jr., has written. "One special goal of the defenders was the complete or partial destruction of the invaders' boats. This isolated them in enemy territory, where they eventually would be out-numbered and killed. If those on the Iñupiaq side won, they presumably killed all of the enemy. If the Chukotkans won, on the other hand, they killed all of the men in the defeated force, took whatever booty they could, and captured some women to keep as slaves."[33]

Kobelev described their arrival at King Island: "In the morning at sunrise, we paddled to the island. . . . We stopped our baidaras [umiaqs] and dressed in *kuyak* [armor], spears in hand, arrows on the bowstrings as a warrior should. I asked why we were getting ready for war since we were not going to war with them. I was told that the [King Islanders] always have such greetings and that they will greet us in this way. Then the islanders stopped at the shore and dressed in *kuyak*, spears in hand, arrows on the bowstrings. . . . Afterwards the islanders took every-one to their yurts. . . . That same day there was trading between the two groups. [The King Islanders] exchanged marten parkas, foxes, wolves, wolverines, otters, lynxes and a few reindeer [skins], all of which they obtained from America. From our side they trade spears, knives, axes, [palmas], iron cauldrons, metal and some kinds of beads."

Most interestingly, on King Island Kobelev also met a few Eskimos from the Seward Peninsula. They were Qaviaraġmiut from the Imuruk Basin, a na-tion that historically had a close trading relationship with the King Islanders (Ukiuvaŋmiut). Kobelev added: "Whenever I would be with the Americans all of the visitors I came with [the Chukotkans] avoided us to keep from translating for me. The Americans also did not speak because my sinister companions would not translate. The Americans stroked and hugged my face and chest signifying a strong, unbreakable friendship with me. They pointed to their land and pulled my garments apparently inviting me to come to America. . . . My companions would not translate for the Americans and myself because if the Russians and Americans developed friendship, the Chukchi commerce would end. That is why an American came to see me after hearing that I had come to [Little Diomede Island] and that I would be spending a year in Chukotka. They would not let him see me and killed him at [Cape Dezhnev]."[34] It is clear from Kobelev's encounter that the Chukotkans were very serious about protecting their monopoly as middlemen in the trade with Alaska and wanted no one to interfere with it, as Eliab Grimes was to learn in 1819.

When Daurkin returned to St. Lawrence Bay he carved a brief account of this expedition on a piece of walrus tusk and left it for Billings. This tusk became part of Count Rumiantsev's collection and now is in the State Historical Museum in Moscow. Daurkin's tusk reads, "On 1 June 1791, in the settlement of Noniakhmun [Nunyagmo], awaiting vessels of the secret expeditions. On 11 June was on the American shores of the islands Imiakhdin [Big Diomede], Inel'lin [Little Diomede], Okibian [*Uivaq*, King Island] with seventeen bidaras of faithful Chukchi subjects and with companion sotnik Ivan Kobelev, the Siberian nobleman and Chukchi interpreter Nikolai Daurkin signed this the same 30 June. We were waiting and thus waited until 15 July."[35]

Kobelev also left a report for Billings. "We had no sooner dropped our anchor [in St. Lawrence Bay on the fourteenth of August]," Martin Sauer reported, "than a baidar [umiaq] full of Tshutski came along-side, and shewed us a paper from Kobeleff, who (they said) was now at the eastern promontory; and Dauerkin was with his relations toward Anadyrsk; but they added, that we must come on shore and give them some tobacco before they would let us have the paper."[36]

Captain Billings, Carl Heinrich Merck, and Sarychev went ashore. The Chukchi greeted them warmly, although they asked the Russians to leave their swords in the boat. The explorers went to one of the Chukchi dwellings, where they were given Kobelev's letter. They read that Kobelev had waited with a group of nomadic "Reindeer Chukchi" at St. Lawrence Bay and at Cape Dezhnev until August 4, but that his Chukchi companions could wait no longer because they had to return west to their reindeer herds.

The natives also told Billings that heavy ice on the north coast of Chuktoka would almost certainly prevent his ship from reaching the Kolyma River. Accepting their advice, Billings transferred command of the *Slava Rossii* to Lieutenant Sarychev and departed overland to continue his explorations. Billings not only charted the north coast of the peninsula as far as Chaun Bay, but also mapped the major rivers as well. He reached the Kolyma early in 1792.[37]

Daurkin was nearby when Billings reached St. Lawrence Bay. Alerted by the natives, he appeared two days later accompanied by twelve umiaqs full of Chukchi. Their "numbers increased hourly," wrote Martin Sauer. Sarychev ultimately put the number at seventy-two umiaqs. "They had plenty of skins of foxes, martins, hares, and the musk-rat of America," Sauer added, "whence, indeed, they obtain the greatest number of their furs . . . in exchange for such articles as they get from Izshiginsk [Gizhiga], and from the wandering peddling traders about the estuary of the [Kolyma], etc." He continued:

> The beach was now covered with the baidars [umiaqs] of the natives, hauled on shore and turned keel upwards, one gunnel resting on the ground, the other supported on their paddles: thus they served the purpose of tents; and old dressed deer-skins sewed together and used instead of curtains for the open side. Here the natives, men and women, slept indiscriminately. The former traded with their dresses, furs, tusks of the walrus, whales' fins ["whalebone"], and pieces of the gut of rein-deer stuffed with chopped meat, marrow, and fat. The latter were extremely happy to grant any favors for beads, buttons, tobacco, etc. and that even in the presence of the men, who actually introduced our people to the women when they had no other articles of trade. These, however, were not their wives, but prisoners taken from their American neighbours, with whom they are frequently at war. The cause of the last affair between them was this: both parties meeting, on the chace of sea animals, quarreled; an engagement commenced, in which the Americans took one baidar and made the crew prisoners; the other, returning, procured a reinforcement, made a descent on the American coast, carried off a few women, and then peace was restored."[38]

"But nothing could equal their astonishment at witnessing the effect of our guns, which we fired with balls into the sea for their entertainment," Sarychev wrote. "In the mean time they carried on a brisk trade with us; bartering their fox-skins, walrus' teeth, arms and utensils, for tobacco, enamel, and beads." "The Tschukschens are divided into Reindeer or nomadical Tschukschens and settlers," he added. "The former are the most numerous, and wander from place to place; but the latter, who are only a few in number, are altogether poor people; who having by some misfortune lost their reindeer, their only wealth, are compelled to fix their abode near the sea, and from whence to draw their subsistence. . . . They prepare, not only for themselves, but for the Reindeer Tschukschens, the fat of fish and marine animals; sew summer shirts and covering for the feet out of reindeer's entrails, for which they receive, from the latter, upper garments and winter covering for the feet; reindeer's skins, and others, fetched from Ischiga [Gizhiga]; also tobacco, and other Russian commodities."[39]

The Russian explorers and the American traders who visited Kotzebue Sound from 1816 to 1820 found that the natives on the American side of Bering Strait had developed a great fondness for tobacco, an item that Cook in 1778 and Billings in 1791 barely mentioned when they visited the American shore.[40] Tobacco probably did not reach the Bering Strait region until the second half of the eighteenth century. Its diffusion began when sailors carried tobacco to Europe from the Americas early in the sixteenth century. It spread rapidly across the continent in the seventeenth century, but in Russia Tsar Michael banned its use in 1634. This ban was repealed in 1697 by Peter the Great, but the Russian Tobacco Company, which held a monopoly on the importation of tobacco to Russia during Peter the Great's reign, was prohibited from selling it in Siberia. Nevertheless, tobacco may have already reached the Bering Strait region from the east. In the sixteenth century tobacco was carried west across the Pacific from Mexico to the Philippines, then via the Portuguese to Macau and from there onward, through many hands, to eastern Siberia.[41]

Cook and Billings also found that relatively small pieces of metal were extremely valuable to the Eskimos: in Norton Sound, for example, Cook bought four hundredweight (approximately 550 pounds) of fish for a few pieces of iron barrel hoops. But in Kotzebue Sound in 1816, 1819, and 1820, the sailors reported that the male Eskimos often carried as many as three iron knives and were very particular and demanding about the quality of the metal when they bartered with the Americans and Russians. It is clear that in the three decades following Billings's visit to the American shore things had changed dramatically, and this change, as we shall see later in this chapter, was the result of the Russians having established a trade fair on a tributary of the lower Kolyma River and at other places after the end of the wars in northeasternmost Asia.

THE CHUKCHI AND KORYAK WARS

In the latter seventeenth century Yukagir and Chukchi inhabited northeastern Asia from the Alazeia and Kolyma region east, and a few small groups of Siberian Yupik Eskimos lived on the shores of the Chukchi Peninsula and St. Lawrence Island. South and west of the Chukchi, the Koryak, Chuvan, Evenk, and others lived on the lands between the Kolyma River and the Bering Sea. East of Chukotka, on the Diomede Islands and in northern Alaska, were Iñupiaq Eskimos, and from Norton Sound southward were Alaskan Yup'ik Eskimos (see front endpaper map).[42]

In their expansion across Asia, the Russians advanced down the Kolyma River from Yakutsk and in 1644 founded the settlement of Nizhne Kolymsk ("Lower Kolymsk"), less than one hundred miles from the Arctic coast. It was from Nizhne Kolymsk that Dezhnev and Alexeev departed in 1648. Dezhnev built the fort on the Anadyr River the following year.

In their eastward advance the Russians had subjugated one native group after another and forced them to pay yasak, but when they penetrated northeasternmost Asia, they encountered native groups that were increasingly difficult to subdue. Before the Chukchi Wars, it was the Koryak who fought the Russians. Finding Chukotka very poor in furs, the Russians moved south from Anadyr fort, attempting to impose tribute on the Koryak. The Cossacks had learned from the Koryak that the natives of Kamchatka had sea otter and sea lion skins and sable pelts of great beauty. When the Russians eventually gained control of Kamchatka and its rich resources of furs, the Anadyr fort took on new importance by becoming a pivotal point in transporting the Kamchatkan furs overland to Yakutsk, via the "long and dangerous route" through Koryak territory.[43]

The Koryak quickly learned to use the firearms they had captured from the Russians. They made a practice of attacking the Anadyr fort and ambushing Russian caravans to steal their furs. In response the Russians mounted campaigns against the Koryak near the northern shore of the Sea of Okhotsk. The Koryak resisted ferociously, and then in 1714 those Yukagir who had been forced to fight alongside the Russians rebelled and joined the Koryak. They assaulted the Russian forts nearby, thereby putting the entire Russian overland supply line between Petropavlovsk and Okhotsk in jeopardy.

Afanasy Shestakov, a Cossack commander, was ordered to "subjugate the warlike tribes" and thus to bring the population under Russian control.[44] Aided by several native groups,

> he began his march along the coast [of the Sea of Okhotsk] to the home of the Koriaks. Those whom he met on the way, being generally few in number, he either conquered or killed. . . . [On the west shore of the Gulf of Penzhina] he learned that the Chukchi were in the neighborhood making war on the Koriaks. Shestakof followed them . . . [and] lined up his men in a military formation. On his right he stationed the Tungus [Evenk] . . . on the left were the Koriaks . . . , and the center was in the hands of the Russians and Jakuts. The battle opened by the discharge of firearms by the Russians. It was immediately answered by a cloud of arrows from the Chukchi. Before the Russians could reload the Chukchi swept down on them in a mass, and after driving off the left wing and then crushing the right, concentrated their efforts on the center, which gave way. Shestakof was in the midst of the fight and was wounded by an arrow entering his throat. He tried to save himself by escaping on a reindeer sled which stood nearby; but unfortunately for him the sled belonged to the Chukchi and the deer dragged him into the camp of the enemy where he was killed. . . . After helping themselves to the firearms and other stores of the enemy the Chukchi withdrew. . . . When the Russian forces reunited after the fight they were disorganized and disobedient to the second in command and quite useless for effective service.[45]

Of Shestakov, Waldemar Jochelson wrote, "His arrogance and self-reliance equaled his ignorance of local conditions and his cruelty." Soon all the Koryak knew of Shestakov's death and "the Koryak rose in a body."[46]

The Russians then turned to Shestakov's assistant, Major Dimitry Pavlutsky. "Pavlutski, who had reached the Anaduir fort on September 3, 1730, busied himself in strengthening the defenses," Frank Golder wrote, "and making ready for his fight against the Chukchi, who had become unusually bold since their victory over Shestakof. By March 12 [1731] all was in readiness. Taking with him one hundred sixty Koriaks, sixty Yukagirs, and two hundred fifteen Russians, he marched northwardly . . . and then eastwardly with the intention of going around the whole Chukchi country. At first he met with little resistance, but from about the middle of June the enemy appeared before him in large numbers. On June 17, he was opposed by seven hundred warriors, of whom four hundred fifty were killed and one hundred fifty were taken prisoners. Near Bering Strait, on June 30, one thousand Chukchi faced him, and of this number three hundred were killed and ten captured. Four thousand deer were also taken. Two weeks later another company of five hundred blocked his way, and these were also defeated."

"Shestakov was avenged fairly well," wrote Gerhard Friedrich Müller, "especially since not more than three Russians, one Iukagir, and five Koriaks were killed in all these encounters. We are assured that among the enemy's dead from the last battle one was found with two holes in his upper lip at each side of his mouth through which teeth carved from walrus tusks had been inserted." As we have seen from the hostile reception that explorers Gvozdyov and Fyodorov received on Big Diomede in 1732, Eskimos must also have been killed or captured in these engagements.[47]

Despite Pavlutsky's legendary cruelty he was nevertheless unable to conquer the Chukchi. "The expedition of Pavlutski against the Chukchi was a little better than useless," Frank Golder added. "Instead of subduing them it merely aroused their warring spirit. When he left in the fall of 1732 for Jakutsk his force became disorganized and lost its effectiveness. This gave the Chukchi their opportunity, and they waged bitter war on the Russians and their allies." In 1738 the Chukchi raised a force of two thousand to attack those Koryak who were allied with the Russians.

While Bering's second voyage was underway in 1741 the Russians went on the attack again, and the government ordered that the Chukchi and the nonallied Koryak should be "totally extirpated," to force them to "forget their restless way of life and be loyal subjects" and to pay yasak. Pavlutsky was again given command of the campaign, but the Chukchi had their revenge in 1742 and killed him in battle. Chukchi folklore states "for many years after that the Chukchi kept his head as a trophy."[48]

It became obvious to the Russians that to keep the Kamchatkan furs moving overland to market and to control Chukotka they had to conquer the Chukchi. The Russians nevertheless found it very difficult to locate the camps of the nomadic Chukchi and learned that "a detached band of Chukchi would prefer to die and kill their wives and children rather than consent to pay tribute or deliver hostages." In fact, the Russians never subjugated the Chukchi, who were described by an eighteenth-century writer as "the most savage, the most barbarous, the most intractable, the least civilized, and the most rugged and cruel people in all of Siberia." "They are more savage, coarse, proud, refractory, thievish, false, and revengeful, than the neighbouring nomads the Koryak. They are as bad and dangerous as the Tunguses [Evenk] are friendly. Twenty Chukches will beat fifty Koryaks."[49]

But the Russians' brutality eventually caused the native groups, who had formerly been enemies, to forge an alliance with one another: Chukchi, the Koryak, the Yukagirs, and some Itelmens came together against the Russians. In 1746 the natives attacked a Russian fort in northern Kamchatka, and in response the Russians mounted a reprisal campaign against the Koryak. Many were captured and forced to build the fortress at Gizhiga before the Russians executed them— and the Russians finally broke the Koryak resistance: by 1757–58 the remaining Koryak became tributary to the Russians and began paying yasak.[50]

Having subjugated the Koryak, the Russians renewed their onslaught against the Chukchi, and the fight went on, back and forth, with attacks and reprisals by both sides at Anadyr and in northern Kamchatka. Finally, however, it was the Russians who were worn down by the Chukchi, and the government concluded that the cost of maintaining the Anadyr fort was nearly fifty times more expensive than the revenues from the post. They abandoned the fort in 1764, concluding that in Chukotka "there is no game except wolves and red foxes, and even these are scarce because of the lack of wood [forests]." By then the Russians were carrying Alaskan and Kamchatkan furs to Okhotsk by sea.[51]

At last, without the threat of Russian attacks, the Chukchi moved into the lands from which the Koryak had been driven, expanding both west and south. But at about the same time they too concluded that there were, in fact, advantages in trading with the Russians. After 1764, the year that the Russians abandoned Anadyr fort, a few Chukchi groups offered to pay yasak if the Russians would agree not to take hostages from them. But it was not until 1779 that Empress Catherine II decreed that the Chukchi should be absolved of all yasak payment for a decade—if they would agree to conduct themselves peacefully.

Figure 3.2. A Chukchi warrior wearing armor. Lamellar armor, made of overlapping plates, was used throughout central and eastern Asia. One of the warrior's arms was also protected by a thick sheet of hide (Bogoras 1904–9, 92).

Although the Russians formally took claim to Chukotka, the Chukchi and Eskimos were officially listed as "natives not wholly subjugated." The Russians agreed that the Chukchi were to be "governed and judged according to their own customs and usages, and . . . subject to Russian law only in case of murder or pillage committed on Russian territory." Their semi-autonomous association with the Russians was affirmed by several agreements in the subsequent years, in which the Russians agreed not to erect settlements on their lands. In 1822 the Chukchi were relieved of all yasak and tax payments forever. To this day Chukotka is an autonomous region of the Russian Federation.[52]

THE OSTROVNOE TRADE FAIR

With the end of the Chukchi Wars—and with the Russian acceptance of the Chukchi's autonomous status—regular trade relations between the Russians and the peoples of northeastern Asia could at last begin. Like the Chukchi, the government in Yakutsk concluded that it would be best to encourage trade. "The policies of conquering the Chukchi with punitive military expeditions," wrote M. B. Chernenko, "were replaced with hopes of attempting to bring the Chukchi into the Russian realm by peaceful means."[53] This was a highly significant development, a development with far-reaching consequences for the intercontinental trade across Bering Strait, a trade that would, at its greatest extent, involve native groups that lived as far apart as the Kolyma River watershed and Coronation Gulf in the Canadian Arctic.

Despite these developments, trade had gone on across Bering Strait for several millennia. For example, about 1,500 years ago the Ipiutak people at Point Hope, Alaska, used burins with non-meteoric iron tips that were probably imported from Asia. On the Asian side of Bering Strait, the iron on the tip of an engraving tool, dating from early in the first millennium AD, probably originated on the Amur River or the coastal areas of the Sea of Japan. Similarly, pieces of Alaskan jasper and nephrite have been found in several prehistoric sites near Cape Dezhnev.[54]

Before the arrival of the Russians in northeast Asia, the Chukchi, Koryak, and some Asian Eskimos, as well as natives from Kamchatka, met at a trade fair northeast of the Sea of Okhotsk, near a southern tributary of the Anadyr River. The Chukchi brought reindeer meat and skins, and perhaps sea mammal products. In return they received spear heads and iron goods, which may have been made by the Evenk (Tungus), and armor, some of which had originated in Japan. The natives of Kamchatka also traded fly agaric—*Amanita muscaria*, a hallucinogenic mushroom—to the northern natives. Another early native trade fair took place east of the Kolyma River, where the Chukchi brought not only their own goods but also products from Alaska. In return they received, among other commodities, salt and iron products, including spear heads and palmas, from the Evenk and from the Yakut who lived west of the Indigirka River.[55]

The volume of foreign trade goods available to the natives of the Bering Strait region must have increased somewhat after the founding of Anadyr fort in 1649, but before the late eighteenth century the Bering Strait natives participated in these trade encounters very cautiously and "with considerable distrust," wrote the ethnographer Waldemar Bogoras. "I was told that in very ancient times there was a kind of fair [near Cape Dezhnev] which was held outside of the village, on the flat seashore, for fear of hostilities. . . . The people came to trade fully armed, and offered their wares to each other on their spear-points; or else they would hold a bundle of skins with one hand and with the other a bared knife, in readiness to raise a fight upon the slightest provocation." And the Chukchi in turn apparently engaged in a small amount of armed trade with the Russians. The explorer George Kennan was told of this when he traveled in Chukotka in the 1860s. "For many years [the Chukchi] would have no dealings with [the Russians] except at the end of a spear," he wrote. "They would hang a bundle of furs or a choice walrus tooth upon a sharp polished blade of a long Chookchee lance, and if a Russian trader chose to take it off and suspend in its place a fair equivalent in the shape of tobacco, well and good; if not, there was no trade. This plan guaranteed absolute security against fraud, for there was not a Russian in all Siberia who dared to cheat one of these fierce savages, with the blade of a long lance ten inches from his breast bone."[56]

It was under the same climate of suspicion that the natives of Chukotka engaged in a silent trade in Alaska. An Eskimo described the silent trade with the Chukchi to Otto von Kotzebue in 1816: "On my questioning whence he had the blue glass beads, an old knife, and the like European goods, he pointed [west, to the entrance of Kotzebue Sound], where people came to them in boats, who gave them beads, tobacco, and also wood for making bows and arrows, in exchange for furs and ready-made articles of dress. He knew very well how to instruct me in their manner of dealing: the stranger first comes, and lays some goods on the shore, then retires; the American [Eskimo] comes, looks at the things, puts as many skins near them as he thinks proper to give, and then also goes away. Upon this the stranger approaches, and examines what is offered him; if he is satisfied with it, he takes the skins, and leaves his goods instead; but, if not, then he lets all the things lie, retires a second time, and expects an addition from the buyer."[57]

The Chukotkans also brought spear heads, palmas, knives, reindeer skins and reindeer products, and perhaps wolverine and wolf pelts, for which they received primarily sea mammal oil, hides, rawhide lines, and, most important, furs.

Although these trade encounters were still fraught with tension, by the first half of the eighteenth century the volume of the trade had increased, no doubt as a result of a greater amount of manufactured goods reaching northeasternmost

Asia. Georg Wilhelm Steller, the naturalist on Bering's second voyage, learned "from quite reliable information" that the cross–Bering Strait trade was centered on the Diomedes, and that the Chukchi purchased "knives, axes, lances, and iron arrow points . . . at a very high price" from the Russians at Anadyr fort and exchanged them on the "second Chukchi island" [one of the Diomedes] with the Eskimos. "Although for some years this commerce was interrupted because a misunderstanding arose, this trade is still carried on by the inhabitants of the islands, who paid for the ironware at a many times higher price with [river otters], martens, and foxes, some of which are brought to Russia by way of Anadyrsk."[58]

At last, in 1788 the government made the decision to open trade relations with the Chukchi, and the result was that in 1789 the Russians established a trading rendezvous east of Nizhne Kolymsk, a trade fair that was ultimately located at Ostrovnoe, on the Maly Aniui River, a tributary of the Kolyma. The Ostrovnoe fair took place 800 miles west of Bering Strait, and to reach the rendezvous traders had to cover twice that distance overland, following the coast, the rivers, and mountain passes. The Ostrovnoe site was chosen because the Maly Aniui flows mostly through tundra, not forest; hence the wind-packed snow made sled travel much easier for the participants. Being extremely wary of the Chukchi, the Russians built one of their usual forts, surrounded by wooden palisades for protection against attacks (which never occurred).[59]

To entice the Chukchi to pay tribute, the Russians gave the natives "Chukchi presents," which often exceeded the value of the fur tribute they received in return. In 1791 these amounted to five hundred rubles' worth of tobacco, kettles, and knives, which were distributed to the Chukchi "as if in payment for their tribute." As we have seen, however, the natural resources of Chukotka were not sufficient to support the volume of this trade. "Chukotka was uniquely inaccessible and undesirable," wrote Yuri Slezkine. Lacking forests, it also lacked most of the desirable types of fur. Most important for the trans–Bering Strait trade was the fact that to obtain Russian trade goods, the Chukchi were forced to acquire their furs elsewhere.[60]

The Ostrovnoe fair immediately produced a dramatic change in Russian-Chukchi relations. Gavriil Sarychev, Joseph Billings's second-in-command, wrote: "On the demolition of the fortress of Anadyr, and the introduction of a government at Ischiga, these differences with the Tschukschens having been compromised, we tried to allure them by kind treatment, and found our efforts crowned with success. They now come yearly to Ischiga and Molne Kolymsk in order to deal with the Russians, upon which occasion many of them also bring their japak [yasak] or tribute. This commonly takes place at the close of February or the commencement of March; and when their trade is finished, they go off immediately to the Frozen Ocean, and spend their whole summer in catching fish and sea-animals."[61]

Ferdinand Petrovich Wrangell, a Russian explorer and naval lieutenant who later became the chief manager of the Russian-American colony, was in Nizhne Kolymsk in February 1821 — six months after the *Pedlar*'s voyage to Bering Strait. Wrangell witnessed the Russian traders' preparations for attending the trade fair at Ostrovnoe. A caravan arrived annually from Yakutsk, "consisting of about twenty merchants, each with from ten to forty horses loaded with goods," which included brandy, Circassian leaf tobacco, white sugar, Chinese sugar candy, an inferior quality of tea, thread, Chinese cotton, silk and linen, among other things.[62]

Wrangell's associate, Fyodor Matiushkin, visited the fair the same year:

The Russian merchants arrived . . . with 125 loaded pack horses. The Tschukt-schi were here before us, and had encamped on the islands and banks of the river. They came from the extreme eastern point of Asia, bringing furs and walrus teeth, which they had crossed Behring's Straits to procure from the inhabitants of the north-west coast of America. They brought with them their women and children, their arms, their household goods, and their moveable houses of reindeer skin, all conveyed on sledges drawn by reindeer. The journey occupies five or six months, for though the distance in a straight line is little more than a thousand wersts [versts], they make long circuitous routes in search of pasture. . . .

The trade with the Americans [Eskimos] is an exceedingly profitable one, both to the Russians and to the Tschuktschi; the latter are in truth only carriers, as they buy the furs and other articles with the Russian tobacco, hardware, and beads; they give half a pood [18 pounds] of tobacco to the Americans for furs, which they sell to the Russians for two pood of the same tobacco; thus their gain is 300 per cent. The same two pood of tobacco may cost the Russian trader 160 roubles at the outside, and he sells the furs bought therewith for at least 260 roubles, a profit of 62 per cent.

The furs consist chiefly of black and silver grey fox, stone [arctic] fox, lynx, wolverine, river-otter, beaver, and a species of marten unknown in Siberia, of remarkable beauty and nearly resembling the sable in the nature and colour of the fur. Besides these the Tschuktschi bring from America, bear-skins, thongs of walrus-skin, and a quantity of walrus teeth. They add nothing of their own, except whalebone [baleen] sledge-runners, a large quantity of clothing made by themselves from the skin of the reindeer, and a kind of bag of seal-skin in which they pack the American furs.

The Russian wares are suited to meet the demands of the Tschuktschi. . . .

They consist of tobacco and all kinds of iron and hardware, such as kettles, hatchets, knives, etc., and beads of various colours. The traders *would* bring a quantity of brandy if they were not restrained by a highly wise and beneficent regulation of the government, in consequence of which only a very small quantity is secretly smuggled, and is bought by the Tschuktschi at almost incredible prices; they call it *wild-making-water*; and some will give the most beautiful fox-skins, valued at 250 roubles, for a couple of bottles of bad brandy, which cost only a few roubles at Jakutsk.

The fair is visited besides by the various natives of the district of above 1000 wersts [659 miles or 1060 kilometers] in extent, Jukahiri [Yukagir], Lamuti [Evens], Tungusi [Evenks], Tschuwanzi [Chuvans] and Koraki [Koryak]. Their various clothing and equipages add greatly to the animation and variety of the scene.

Matiushkin described how the prices were established at the fair. "Before the fair begins the principal persons on both sides assemble to fix a tariff for the different wares. After much discussion it was settled that two pood [approximately seventy-two pounds] of circassian tobacco should be the price of sixteen fox, and twenty marten skins, and of other articles in proportion; any one who is known to sell for lower prices is made to pay a fine, and loses the right of trafficking during the remainder of the fair; without some such regulation the avidity of the Russian traders would lead them to spoil their own market by too eager competition."

Then the trading began. "The fair was opened by hoisting a flag over the gate of the Ostrog [fort]. At this signal the Tschuktschi advanced in order, fully armed with spears, bows and arrows, and ranged themselves, with their sledges and goods, in a semi-circle in front of the fort, where the Russians, and the other tribes awaited the ringing of a bell, which was to give notice that the traffic might commence. The moment it sounded, it seemed as if an electric shock had run through the whole party in the fort. Old and young, men and women, all rushed forward in mad confusion towards the Tschuktschi; every one endeavoured to be first at the sledges, to obtain the best, and to dispose of his own wares to the most advantage."

Although the prices had been fixed, the Russians competed with one another for the furs.

The Russians were much the most eager of the whole; they might be seen dragging, with one hand, a heavy bag of tobacco, and having in the other a couple of kettles, whilst hatchets, knives, wooden and metal pipes, long strings of beads, etc. etc. were stuck round their girdles, or thrown over the shoulders, as they ran from sledge to sledge proclaiming their wares, in a language which is a medley of Russian, Tschuktschi, and Jakuti.

The noise, the press, the confusion, would defy description. Some were thrown down by the throng in the deep snow, and run over by their competitors; some lost cap and gloves in the fall, and, not stopping to recover them, might be seen with bare heads and hands, in a temperature of –35°, intent only on making up for lost time, by a double activity.

The Chukchi, however, maintained great composure in the melee. "The excessive eagerness of the Russians was exhibited in remarkable contrast with the composure and self-possession of the Tschuktschi, who stood quietly by their sledges, and made no reply to the torrent of words of their customers, until a proposal met their approbation, when the exchange was effected at once. It appeared to us that their calmness gave them a great advantage over the Russians. They had no scales, but judged the weight very correctly by the hand. The average value of the goods brought to this fair is said to be nearly 200,000 roubles; the fair lasts about three days, and, at its close, the various parties disperse."[63]

Captain John Dundas Cochrane, a British naval officer and traveler, was also at the fair in 1821, the same year as Fyodor Matiushkin. "I never saw better judges of tobacco, nor of weight, than the Tchuktchi," he wrote. "I can confidently assert that they do not err one pound in the hundred weight; and the detection of the slightest fraud on the part of the Russians is sufficient to the Tchuktchi to cut the party short, and deal no more with him. Their mode of trying the strength of tobacco is this: a leaf of it is taken and squeezed in the hand as hard as possible, and if any appearance of moisture be left in the palm, it is well known that the tobacco has been watered; if the leaf preserves the compressed shape which the force of the hand has given it, it is weak, but if it recovers and expands quickly to its original size and shape the tobacco is deemed strong."

Cochrane also learned that recent visits to Bering Strait by foreign vessels (American traders and Russian explorers) had already been factored into the Chukchi's bartering tactics: "The last day's sale, although of course the best, was held back a little by the Tchuktchi wishing to make the Russians believe that they had no want of tobacco, as they could get it much cheaper in the bay of St. Lawrence, from the ships which casually call there. Whatever trade they may carry on with those vessels, the Tchuktchi appear to know the value of a more direct and first-hand trade; nor can this be doubtful, when the toils and dangers of their journey [to the Ostrovnoe fair] and the small profits are considered—at least, small when compared with the profits they sometimes receive from the few vessels which now and then visit their coast."[64]

Cochrane reported that the Chukchi were very careful about their transactions and had sold only about a third of their most valuable furs, carrying the remainder back with them. He added that the Chukchi visitors—more than 180 strong, with 250 sleds and 500 reindeer, each of which could draw 150 pounds—carried about four hundred bags of tobacco away from the fair. At the start of their return journey each man carried 40 or 50 pounds of goods on his back, until their provisions had been reduced enough to allow them to put the cargo on their sleds. The return journey to easternmost Chukotka would take from seventy-five to ninety days.[65]

By the 1830s the sale of alcohol had become a factor in the trade with the natives near the lower Kolyma. Mikhail Tebenkov, who had operated trading vessels for the Russian-American Company in the Bering Strait region and who would later serve as chief manager of the colony, reported on his investigations there. "Chukchi acquainted with the Russians love vodka and know all the tricks of our petty tradesmen and even a few words used by the Russians in swearing," he wrote.

> Some of them are enlightened by Christianity, but unfortunately those are also in general the biggest drinkers and drunkards. . . . I saw not a one who knows how to read. [Of] those who are in frequent relations with the Russians, some have testimonials, probably from those persons with whom they have had business. Among these are some very amusing ones. For example, I saw two such testimonials, the first "I warn everyone that the bearer of this, Chukcha (name), is the greatest scoundrel, a drunk, cheat, beggar, and in general a most intolerable person in trade," the second "one can buy the bearer of this, (name), himself for vodka and tobacco, however he is a good fellow and one can conduct business with him"—and they most diligently protect these testimonials.[66]

"To induce the Chukchee to pay tribute," the ethnographer Waldemar Jochelson wrote at the beginning of the twentieth century, "methods were used and probably are still used, which are as humorous as they are humiliating to the Russian Empire."

> The court treasury spent a certain sum yearly on presents for those Chukchee who paid their tribute voluntarily. The chief of the Kolyma district, on his way to the Chuckchee fair on the Anui River, would carry on special sledges presents consisting of iron kettles, tea-pots, tobacco, etc. In 1892 I witnessed on the Anui River the ceremony of the tribute presentation by the Chukchee. Ten or so Chukchee from various localities came to the official cabin, and in the presence of the district chief were entertained by the Cossacks with tea, sugar,

Figure 3.3. The Ostrovnoe trade fair, 1901. Waldemar Bogoras photographed the fair in its last years. American Museum of Natural History, New York, neg. 11125.

and biscuits. After a speech suitable to the occasion had been made by the chief through an interpreter, to the effect that the Czar loved the Chukchee and was sending them presents, each of the natives made his small contribution to the tribute with a red or arctic fox. Then the imperial presents were inspected and additions begged for, which were generally granted by the chief, who was anxious to get rid of his tiresome guests. The results of the barter were very favorable to the Chukchee. They had received presents which in value greatly exceeded their tribute; the hides meanwhile were ceremoniously stamped with the official seal and dispatched to the Court Treasury in St. Petersburg as a token of Chukchee submissiveness.

Jochelson added that in 1901 the chief of the Kolyma district did not bring any presents when he met the Chukchi. "On being informed of this, [the Chukchi] requested the return to them of the tribute skins which they had given to the chief. Their request was granted."[67]

To protect the Russian traders from competing against one another, the prices for the most expensive items (beaver, fox, marten, and walrus ivory) were fixed and rated in equivalents of prime red fox pelts. For example, one pud (approximately thirty-six pounds) of tobacco, or one pud of iron kettles, or one pud of copper kettles was equal to ten red foxes; furthermore, one black fox was equal to twenty red foxes. Similarly one gray fox, or one beaver, or one otter, was equal to two red foxes; one lynx was equal to three red foxes; three martens were equal to one red fox; four white foxes equaled one red fox; four average walrus tusks were equal to one red fox; and so on. The Chukchi traders' reindeer meat and sealskin line, being less valuable, were not price controlled and were freely bartered for "iron-work, sugar, etc."[68]

"Before opening the fair all the tobacco was divided, under the inspection of deputies, into piles of one or two puds, put into leather bags, and then sealed," wrote the ethnographer Waldemar Bogoras. "It had to be quite dry and of good quality. Sprinkling with water, which adds to the weight, was forbidden. Trade with objects of fixed value was permitted but one day. After that the less important trade began."[69]

At about the same time that the Russians established the Ostrovnoe fair, smaller fairs sprang up as well. For example, in 1788 Pyotr Andreevich Baranov, whose brother, Aleksandr Andreevich Baranov, became the first chief manager of the Russian-American colony, set up a trading post on a tributary of the Anadyr River, but the Chukchi destroyed it the following year. In 1803 Aleksandr Baranov ordered a post established near Gizhiga, but in 1806 the Chukchi destroyed that too. Undeterred, in 1810 Aleksandr Baranov tried again and gave his brother Petr authority, with Russian-American Company funds, to resume trade on the Anadyr. Baranov presumably wanted to intercept the furs that the natives were carrying across Bering Strait from Alaska.

"Operating from Gizhiga . . . Petr Baranov reestablished the post on the Anadyr," and soon thereafter bought it from the company for 30,000 rubles. "He hired employees at Gizhiga, erected dwellings, churches and a trading factory, surrounded by a stockade. The place began to be called a 'fort' and was a branch of the annual fair [at Ostrovnoe]. Now accustomed to Russian trade goods, the Chukchi welcomed the new establishment. From 1815, P. Baranov organized annual fairs at the new post. These lasted up to three weeks, and were visited by as many as 300 Chukchi and Koriaks at a time. Later he established another fair, held in August at the mouth of the Anadyr when the sedentary Chukchi gathered to hunt wild reindeer, and yet another at Gizhiga. Thus . . . Petr Baranov . . . played a significant role in pacifying the native Siberian population, establishing trade, and founding posts which were forerunners of the present-day towns of northeastern Siberia."[70]

Without doubt, the fairs at Ostrovnoe and other places resulted in a sharp increase in the cross–Bering Strait trade because of the availability of highly desired furs in the nearby regions of Alaska. To acquire trade goods the Chukchi had to acquire furs, but Chukotka, as we have seen, is poor in furs. Chukotka's vegetation is mostly arctic and alpine tundra, which does not support many of the furbearers whose pelts were sought at the trade fairs in northeastern Asia; in contrast, the most valuable furs were harvested in the taiga, or boreal forest. A vast area of central Alaska and the Kotzebue Sound drainage is covered by coniferous forests and bogs, which are inhabited by lynx, wolverine, beaver, marten, ermine, otter, mink, and other furbearers.[71]

"Fur animals are not found just anywhere and everywhere," wrote Ray Tremblay, an Alaskan trapper. "A trapper seeking a large catch of marten will trap in hilly country dominated by spruce trees. Here, in the conifer forest, the lemming and the vole, which are the main source of food for marten, make their home, feeding on seeds and grasses. . . . Both the marten trapper and the mink trapper who work the river valleys can expect to take a variety of other furbearers, such as fox, lynx, wolverine, and wolves, as these carnivores roam both hills and valleys in their search for food."[72]

The ethnohistorian Dorothy Jean Ray identified four factors that were central to the expansion of the intercontinental trade: "(1) the cessation of Chukchi-Cossack hostilities . . . which allowed Chukchi traders to serve as middlemen between Russians and Alaskan Eskimos; (2) a sufficient quantity of trade goods, which would not be absorbed by the Russians and Siberians on the long journey across Siberia; (3) a commodity in Alaska that would be of great enough value to the Russians and the Chukchi to make the long and difficult journey from Russia to northeastern Siberia worth the effort; and (4) traders to carry the goods in Alaska. All of these requirements were satisfied with the establishment of a large trading market on the Anyui tributary of the Kolyma River in 1789. Although 800 miles from the strait, it was to have far-reaching effects in Alaska."[73]

In summary, the end of the Chukchi and Koryak Wars and the creation of the trade fairs in northeastern Asia brought about important changes for the native inhabitants on both sides of Bering Strait. The Chukchi expanded their range into depopulated areas in the west and south, and apparently their reindeer husbandry intensified as a result. With the existence of a predictable source of trade goods, some Chukchi began to concentrate primarily on trading, traveling to and from the Ostrovnoe trade fair on trips that took as many as six months of the year. The Alaskan Eskimos also benefited from the newly reliable source of trade goods, and they intensified their efforts to acquire marketable furs, some of which had hitherto been of relatively marginal value to them; hence trapping became far more important for them. The Alaskan native trade fairs also took on a greater importance than previously, when, for the most part, only local products had been exchanged among the various Eskimo nations. As Ernest S. Burch, Jr., has noted, it was ironic that the ferocity of the Chukchi's resistance to the Russians' attacks may have allowed the American Eskimos, who were the Chukchi's historical enemies, to remain free of the burden of yasak imposed by the Russians. And, he wrote, "had it not been for the [existence of Bering Strait], Chukchi reindeer herders, flushed with their victory over the Russians, could easily have expanded eastward into [Alaska]. As it was, they had to expand in the opposite direction."[74]

The intercontinental trade that Eliab Grimes had so astutely analyzed in his letter of September 9, 1819, to Astor's associate John Ebbets was, in fact, a relatively recent phenomenon in the region, a result of the creation of new sources of foreign goods that by then had gone on for only about three decades. Yet in another three decades the structure of the Bering Strait trade would fundamentally change yet again.

4

MARKETING THE FURS

Russian traders in northeastern Asia acquired their furs from several sources: at the Ostrovnoe fair and other native trade fairs, from elsewhere in Siberia, from Russian America, and a few from Canada via London and St. Petersburg. Nevertheless, a substantial amount of furs — fox, beaver, lynx, river otter, marten, and other skins — arrived from the vast forested regions of central Alaska via the native trade at Bering Strait. In fact, the only types of Alaskan furs that did not reach the Asian markets via the Bering Strait trade were sea otters and fur seals: the pelts of these two animals were carried across the North Pacific by ships of the Russian-American Company and its predecessors.

Once the merchants of northeastern Asia had bought the furs, the central task became transporting them to a market and selling them. During the Russian advance across Asia the market for their furs had been Europe, particularly Leipzig, which was a major distribution point for western Europe, but by the time the Russians had expanded into Alaska, the primary market for the Alaskan furs had become China.[1]

THE TREATIES OF NERCHINSK AND KIAKHTA

Unorganized trade between the Russian and Chinese empires had gone on since early in the seventeenth century. When the Russian eastward expansion approached the Amur River, however, the Russians found themselves blocked by Chinese forces, a confrontation which resulted in the Treaty of Nerchinsk in 1689. In that treaty, although the Russians surrendered rights to settlement in the Amur basin, they gained trade concessions allowing them to send fur caravans to Beijing. By providing a point of sale for Russian furs in northeastern Asia, the

Treaty of Nerchinsk thus became one element in the Russian expansion toward Alaska. Basil Dmytryshyn and his associates wrote, "This important first Russo-Chinese treaty was twice amended in the following century . . . but the territorial agreements remained in force until the middle of the nineteenth century, [and] consequently Russia's expansionist energies were redirected toward northeastern Asia, Kamchatka, the North Pacific and eventually the northwest coast of North America."[2]

In their visits to Beijing, the Russian merchants were famous for their bad behavior. According to Governor George Simpson of the Hudson's Bay Company, who visited Irkutsk in 1842, "The Muscovites constantly set so bad an example before the sedate folks of the imperial city in the way of drinking and roistering, that, after exhausting the patience of the celestials during a period of three-and-thirty years, they were entirely deprived of their commercial privileges in 1722. After all intercourse between the two nations had ceased for five years, the Russians, having first made some concessions and apologies, obtained a new treaty . . . , by which, in order to prevent future misunderstanding, the international trade, so far at least as private individuals were concerned, was to be conducted on the international frontier."[3]

Most important, in 1727 a new treaty, the Treaty of Kiakhta, delineated the border between the empires and allowed two forms of trade: caravan trade and frontier trade. The treaty established that no more than two hundred merchants could visit Beijing every three years in a single caravan, and that two frontier posts would be erected at points on the border of the two empires, where the trade between Russian and Chinese merchants could be controlled. For the Alaskan fur trade, however, a more significant event took place in 1728, when the towns of Kiakhta and Mai-mai-ch'eng were built at the principal crossing point on the Mongolian border. More than four thousand miles east of St. Petersburg and more than one thousand north of Beijing, it was "one of the most wretched sites for a town that could be imagined." Even so, in the 1720s for example, 100,000 rubles' worth of furs—primarily sable and red fox pelts, but also ermine, beaver, otter, hare, squirrel, and others—were exported from Kiakhta to China in return for silks and cottons. Tea did not become an important export from China until the end of the eighteenth century.[4]

Although massive smuggling went on, as late as 1762 the trade with China was still officially a Russian government monopoly. "In spite of state limitations and strict prohibitions[,] clandestine private trade on the Russo-Chinese border flourished," and, in fact, the smuggling activities were so great that smuggled furs amounted to 75 percent of the traffic to China. Eventually the Russian government accepted the situation, and in 1762 Empress Catherine II ("Catherine the

Great") permitted the merchants unfettered trade with the Chinese for all furs, including the most valuable ones: sea otters, lynx, squirrels, foxes, and sables. The prices the merchants received in China were about ten times what they bought them for in Siberia, and in some years more than a million skins were traded into China.[5]

China became the main market for Russian furs as a result of Catherine's decision to allow free trade, an act that coincided with the Russian expansion across the Aleutians. The resulting flow of furs to market made the twin border towns of Kiakhta and Mai-mai-ch'eng the center of the Russo-Chinese trade. The fur trade with China made Irkutsk, near Lake Baikal, the storage and staging point for transporting the furs to Kiakhta and also a wealthy city. The merchants of Irkutsk bought furs at market fairs in December and March and then sent them to Kiakhta. By the year 1800, 8,300,000 rubles' worth of goods were exported from Kiakhta. In fact, in the nineteenth century Russian merchants not only sold Alaskan and Siberian furs to China but also imported additional furs from Canada and the Pacific Northwest.[6]

BRINGING THE FURS TO MARKET

Reaching Kiakhta with the furs was very difficult. Once the Russians had abandoned the overland route from Petropavlovsk via Anadyr fort, they carried their Alaskan furs by ship to Okhotsk, where the punishing task began. The furs first were hauled across the height of land into the headwaters of the Lena drainage and on to Yakutsk. There the furs from the Russian-American Company, as well as those from the cross–Bering Strait trade and from elsewhere in eastern Siberia, were sorted.

George Simpson visited Yakutsk in 1842 on his journey around the world. "At one time," he wrote, "Yakutsk engrossed nearly all the fur trade eastward, from the Lena to the farthest bounds of Russian enterprise, thus draining a territory, certainly more extensive, and perhaps not less productive, than all the wilderness of British America." He added, "Nearly all the furs and ivory are sold in the annual fair, which is attended by troops of itinerant dealers from other parts of Siberia and also from Moscow."[7]

At Yakutsk the very best furs were sent on to European Russia. Walrus tusks often went to Turkey and Persia, but some went to China. Even though British and American maritime fur traders were able to undersell the Russian furs via Canton, a huge amount of furs went south from Yakutsk to Irkutsk, where they were stored until they were carried onward to Kiakhta on the Mongolian border.[8]

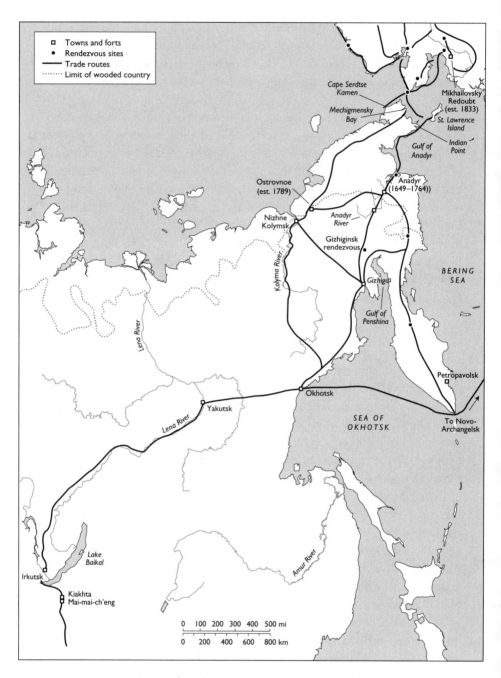

Map 4.1. Selected Asian trade routes and trading sites.

William Coxe, a British clergyman who traveled and studied extensively in European Russia in the latter part of the eighteenth century, and who had unusually free access to manuscripts and journals in St. Petersburg, described the struggle involved in transporting the furs from Okhotsk to Yakutsk, to Irkutsk, and onward to Kiakhta.

> The furs of Kamtchatka and of the Eastern Isles [the Aleutians] are now conveyed from the peninsula by water to Ochotsk; from thence to Yakutsk by land on horse-back, or by rein-deer: the roads are so very bad, lying either through a rugged mountainous country, or through marshy forests, that the journey lasts at least six weeks. Yakutsk is situated upon the Lena, and is the principal town, where the choicest furs are brought in their way to Kiachta, as well as from Kamtchatka as from the northern parts of Siberia, which lie upon the rivers Lena, Yana, and Indigirka. At Yakutsk the goods are embarked upon the Lena, towed up the stream . . . ; from thence they are transported over a short tract of land to the rivulet Buguldeika, down that stream to the lake Baikal, across that lake to the mouth of the Selenga, and up that river to the neighborhood of Kiachta.[9]

The historical geographer James R. Gibson explained the problems of carrying trade goods the other way, from Irkutsk to Russian America. "Provisions were packed in Irkutsk in winter and carted in spring 150 miles . . . to the head of navigation on the upper Lena," he wrote. "The provisions were transferred to flat-bottomed and single decked river vessels propelled by oars and sails. . . . The barge-like river boats left in late spring at high water in strings of two to four vessels, taking from two to six weeks to navigate the 1500 miles downstream [from Irkutsk] to Yakutsk. . . . The number of craft varies, of course, from year to year; in 1830 [one observer] counted 40 riverboats hauling 1800 tons of flour . . . to Yakutsk."

At Yakutsk the cargo was then transferred to horses for the overland slog to Okhotsk. "There the provisions . . . were ferried across the Lena to the rendezvous . . . , where there were several hundred tethering posts and extensive meadows with ample grass for the herds of pack horses and droves of beef cattle. In spring and summer, the animals proceeded to Okhotsk via the Yakutsk-Okhotsk Track. This irregular and indefinite trail . . . stretched 600 to 750 miles in a southeasterly direction. Its route varied in accordance with the vagaries of the weather and the memories of the Yakut guides and lead horses. . . . Convoys consisted of 100 to 150 animals; they were grouped in strings of 10 to 12 horses with one conductor and took from one to two months to make Okhotsk, depending on the condition of the trail. During the first half of the nineteenth century 10,000 to 15,000 pack horses were employed annually on the Yakutsk-Okhotsk Track to convey state and private freight."[10]

George Simpson traveled westbound over the Okhotsk-Yakutsk trail. On his first day out of Okhotsk he met one of the eastbound convoys. "During the afternoon, we met an apparently interminable line of about six hundred horses, carrying goods," he wrote. On the fourth day he added, "We met several herds of cattle and caravans on their way to Okhotsk. The caravans generally march at the rate of four or five miles an hour for twelve hours at a stretch. . . . The animals are taught to travel in single file, a certain number being tied together by a rope from the tail of one to the mouth of another, and so on from front to rear." The following day, after Simpson had crossed the height of land from the Okhotsk Sea drainage into the Lena drainage, he noted, "Our road was absolutely alive with caravans and travellers, all proceeding to Ochotsk with goods, provisions, and cattle; and of flour alone not fewer than five thousand loads had passed us before the close of our fifth day."[11]

Then at Okhotsk the cargo was loaded aboard ships for the passage to Russian America. "At Okhotsk . . . which was reached between mid-June and mid-August, the [provisions] were put aboard company vessels for trans-shipment to New Archangel. . . . Under the Russian-American Company a ship usually left New Archangel in the middle of May and reached Okhotsk in late June or early July, standing there until late August, when the last pack trains and cattle droves arrived from Yakutsk. The furs from Russian America . . . , as well as colonial reports and discharged employees, were unloaded and replaced with supplies, dispatches, and recruits from Russia and Siberia. The ship left Okhotsk in late August or early September and, sailing under favorable northeasterly winds, it usually arrived at New Archangel in October."[12]

KIAKHTA AND MAI-MAI-CH'ENG

Kiakhta was not only a center of export and import but also a customs control point and a significant source of revenue for the Russian government.[13] Kiakhta was a "fortress and a small suburb," wrote William Coxe. "There are three gates at which guards are constantly stationed. . . . The principal public buildings are a wooden church, the governor's house, the custom-house, the magazine for provisions, and the guard-house. It contains also a range of shops and warehouses, barracks for the garrison, and several houses belonging to the crown; the latter are generally inhabited by the principal merchants. . . . The suburb, which is surrounded by a wooden wall . . . contains no more than an hundred and twenty houses very irregularly built."

Though only a few hundred yards from Kiakhta, Mai-mai-ch'eng was a world apart. Coxe continued: "The Chinese town is called by the Chinese and Mongols, Maimatschin, which signifies fortress of commerce. . . . It is situated about an hundred and forty yards South of the fortress of Kiachta, and nearly parallel to it. Midway between this place and the Russian fortress, two posts about ten feet high are planted in order to mark the frontiers of the two empires. . . . Maimatschin has no other fortification than a wooden wall, and a small ditch about three feet broad. . . . The town is of oblong form: its length is about seven hundred yards, and its breadth four hundred. On each of the four sides a large gate faces the principal streets; over each of these gates there is a wooden guard-house for the Chinese garrison, which consists of Mongols in tattered clothes, and armed with clubs. . . . This town contains two hundred houses and about twelve hundred inhabitants."

Mai-mai-ch'eng, Coxe reported, was inhabited only by males. "The merchants of Maimatschin come from the Northern provinces of China, chiefly from Pekin . . . and other principal towns. They are not settled at this place with their wives and families: for it is a remarkable circumstance, that there is not one woman in Maimatschin. This restriction arises from the policy of the Chinese government, which totally prohibits the women from having the slightest intercourse with foreigners. No Chinese merchant engages in the trade in Siberia who has not a partner. These persons mutually relieve each other. One remains for a stated time, usually a year . . . and when his partner arrives with a fresh cargo of Chinese merchandize, he then returns home with the Russian commodities."

Transactions between the Russians and Chinese were conducted according to strict protocols.

> The commerce between the Russians and Chinese is entirely a trade of barter. . . . The Russians are prohibited to export their own coin, nor indeed could the Chinese receive it, even should that prohibition be taken off; for no specie is current among them except bullion. And the Russians find it more advantageous to take merchandize in exchange, than to receive bullion at the Chinese standard. The common method of transacting business is as follows. The Chinese merchant comes first to Kiachta, and examines the merchandize he has occasion for in the warehouse of the Russian trader; he then goes to the house of the latter and adjusts the price over a dish of tea. Both parties next return to the magazine, and the goods in question are then carefully sealed in the presence of the Chinese merchant. When this ceremony is over, they both repair to Maimatschin; the Russian chooses the commodities he wants, not forgetting to guard against fraud by strict inspection. He then takes the precaution to leave behind a person of confidence, who remains in the warehouse until

the Russian goods are delivered, when he returns to Kiachta with the Chinese merchandize.

Coxe also reported that the Chinese demand for furs was so strong that the Russians also imported them from other sources to serve the Chinese market. "The greatest part of [the] furs and skins are brought from Siberia and the New-discovered Islands [Alaska]: this supply however is not alone fully adequate to the demand of the market at Kiachta. Foreign furs are therefore imported to St. Petersburg, and from thence sent to the frontiers. England alone furnishes a large quantity of beaver and other skins, which she procures from Hudson's Bay and Canada."[14] It was therefore at least theoretically possible that skins that had been trapped in northwestern arctic North America might have traveled both east and west around the world to reach Kiakhta.

RUSSIAN AND CHINESE TRADE GOODS

The pelts of sea otters and fur seals were most desired by the Chinese merchants, but they were by no means the only items traded into the vast Chinese market. In the north of China the winters were cold and the supply of heating fuel was limited. Squirrels, ermines, several varieties of foxes, sables, muskrats, beavers, lynx, ferrets, rabbits, tanned hides and leathers, lambskins, and Russian cloth and fabrics constituted about 85 percent of the exports from Russia taken to Kiakhta. Hardware, tin, camels, horses, cattle, and hunting dogs were also part of the Russian exports.

For example, P. A. Tikhmenyov, in his history of the Russian-American Company, listed the furs and other products that were exported from Russian America from 1797 to 1821. Some were sent west, but the majority was sold at Kiakhta. Tikhmenyov's figures probably greatly underreported the actual volume of the trade, and of course, he would not have known the total number of Alaskan furs that crossed Bering Strait to the fairs in northeasternmost Asia. His tally:

Sea otters	72,894
Beavers	34,546
Beaver tails	59,530
River otters	14,969
Black and silver foxes	13,702
Blue foxes	21,890
Red foxes	30,950
Sables	17,298
Wolverines	1,151

Lynx	1,389
Minks	4,802
Blue polar foxes	36,362
White polar foxes	4,234
Wolves	121
Bears	1,602
Sea lions	27
Walrus tusks	58,374 pounds
Whalebone	42,357 pounds.[15]

On the other side of the trade, Chinese camel caravans took fifty or fifty-one days to reach Mai-mai-ch'eng from Beijing. They carried not only cottons and silks in various forms—which were among the most valuable products exported by the Chinese—but also loose-leaf tea and brick tea. Brick tea was inferior to loose-leaf tea, but it had a large market in northeastern Asia. It was made in northern China and Mongolia from tea dust, "stalks, large leaves, and refuse matter generally. This is moistened with sheep's or bullock's blood and pressed into brick-shaped cakes." In this form it resisted deterioration and was easy to transport. It was sold primarily to the "Mongols, Bouriats, Tartars, and the Siberian peasantry." George Simpson encountered brick tea in Okhotsk. "Though coarse, strong, and ill-flavoured, it is consumed in great quantities by the lower orders in Siberia," he wrote, "being made into a thick soup, with the addition of butter and salt."[16]

Tea, cottons, and silks made up 90 percent of the exports in the eighteenth century. Tobacco in ball form ("Chinese tobacco") was also traded into the Russian Empire, as was a wide variety of small manufactured goods, including porcelains, earthenware, enamelware, lacquerware, ivory, copper porringers and ladles, iron ladles, ink, incense, rouge, fans, pipes, pearls, artificial flowers, live monkeys, tiger and panther skins, pepper, anise, preserved and jellied fruits, sugar candy, quinine, rhubarb, musk, and Chinese silver.[17]

In assessing the Kiakhta and Mai-mai-ch'eng trade, William Coxe added: "Russia derives great advantages from the Chinese trade. By this traffic, its natural productions, and particularly its furs and skins, are disposed of in a very profitable manner. Many of these furs, procured from the most easterly parts of Siberia, are of such little value that they would not answer the expense of carriage into Russia; while the richer furs, which are sold to the Chinese at a very high price, would, on account of their dearness, seldom meet with purchasers in the Russian dominions. In exchange for these commodities the Russians receive from China several valuable articles of commerce, which they would otherwise be obliged to buy at a much dearer rate from the European powers, to the great disadvantage of the balance of their trade."[18]

DECLINE OF THE TRADE

In the first quarter of the nineteenth century the volume of furs sold from Kiakhta began to decline, and by 1826 furs comprised a little less than half of the transactions, whereas tea had become the most important Chinese export. Furthermore, by 1860, in the aftermath of the Opium Wars and the consequent exposure of China's weakness, the Russian merchants were allowed to trade in Beijing directly, and Russian ships were allowed to enter Chinese ports, thus reducing the flow of furs at Kiakhta. Even in the 1880s, however, Kiakhta continued to be an important transshipment point between Russia and China, although most of the Alaskan furs were by then marketed in San Francisco.[19]

George Kennan, an American who had traveled in northeastern Asia in the 1860s and several decades later returned to study the Siberian exile system, reported on his visit there.

Kiákhta, which stands on the border-line between Mongolia and Siberia, does not appear at first sight to be anything more than a large, prosperous village. It contains a greater number of comfortable-looking two-story log dwelling houses than are to be found in most East-Siberian villages, and it has two noticeable churches of the Russo-Greek type with white walls and belfries surmounted by colored or gilded domes; but one would never suppose it to be the most important commercial point in Eastern Siberia. Through Kiákhta, nevertheless, pass into or out of Mongolia every year Russian and Chinese products to the value of from twenty to thirty million *rúbles* ($10,000,000 to $15,000,000). Nearly all of the famous "overland" tea consumed in Russia is brought across Mongolia in caravans from northern China, enters the Empire through Kiákhta, and after being carefully repacked and sewn up in raw hides is transported across Siberia a distance of nearly four thousand miles to St. Petersburg, Moscow, or the great annual fair at Nízhni Nóvgorod. Through Kiákhta are also imported into Russia silks, crepes, and other distinctively Chinese products, together with great quantities of compressed, or "brick" tea for the poorer classes of the Russian people and for the Kírghis, Buriáts, and other native tribes. The chief exports to the Chinese Empire are Russian manufactures, medicinal deerhorns, ginseng, furs, and precious metals in the shape of Russian, English, and American coins. Even the silver dollars of the United States find their way into the Flowery kingdom through Siberia. Among the Russian merchants living in Kiákhta are men of great wealth, some of whom

Figure 4.1. Mai-mai-ch'eng street scene (Kennan 1891, 109).

derive their commercial transactions in general, and from the tea trade in particular, incomes varying from $75,000 to $150,000 per annum.

Like William Coxe a century earlier, Kennan was struck by the difference between the two towns. He wrote of Mai-mai-ch'eng:

> You can hardly believe that you have not been suddenly transported on the magical carpet of the "Arabian Nights" over a distance of a thousand miles. The town in which you find yourself is no more like the town that you have just left than a Zuñi pueblo is like a village in New England, and for all that appears to the contrary you might suppose yourself to be separated from the Russian Empire by the width of a whole continent. The narrow, unpaved streets are shut in by gray, one-story houses, whose windowless walls are made of clay mixed with chopped straw, and whose roofs, ornamented with elaborate carving, show a tendency to turn up at the corners; clumsy two-wheel ox-carts, loaded with boxes of tea and guided by swarthy Mongol drivers, have taken the place of Russian horses and *telégas*; Chinese traders in scull-caps, loose flapping gowns, and white-soled shoes appear at the doors of the courtyards instead of the Russian merchants in top-boots, loose waistcoats, and shirts worn outside their trousers whom you have long been accustomed to see; and wild-looking sunburned horsemen in deep orange gowns and dishpan-shaped hats ride in now and then from some remote encampment in the great desert of the Gobi, followed perhaps, by a poor Mongol from the immediate neighborhood, mounted upon a slow-pacing ox. Wherever you go, and in whatever direction you look, China has taken the place of Russia, and the scenes that confront you are full of strange, unfamiliar details.[20]

The Treaty of Kiakhta of 1727 had established Kiakhta and Mai-mai-ch'eng as the primary transfer point for Alaskan and Siberian furs, and the volume of the trade grew as the result of Catherine the Great's liberalization of the regulations on trade with China. These two events were important factors in helping the Russian traders to sell the furs they had bought at the Ostrovnoe trade fair and elsewhere. As William Coxe observed, many of these furs were of insufficient value to justify the expense of transporting them to the markets of Europe. Thus, by providing a market for Alaskan and northeast Asian furs, the transfer point of Kiakhta and Mai-mai-ch'eng indirectly stimulated the Chukchi to become the middlemen in the vigorous intercontinental fur trade that Eliab Grimes discovered in 1819 at Bering Strait.

Part 2

The Russian-British Rivalry
in Northern Alaska

The competition between Russia and Britain for knowledge of the northernmost North Pacific began in 1778, when Captain James Cook's ships sailed into waters where previously the Russians had been the only foreign visitors. The Napoleonic Wars interrupted this contest, but in 1816 it was revived with Otto von Kotzebue's expedition to Bering Strait. For the next four decades agents of both nations pushed north with the goals of promoting the fur trade and thus of gaining dominion over the adjacent lands and waters.

5

THE RUSSIANS MOVE NORTH

The Russian commercial expansion to Alaska began in August 1742, when the survivors of Vitus Bering's *Sviatoy Pyotr* reached Petropavlovsk, Kamchatka, from their winter of starvation on the Commander Islands. They brought the skins of the animals whose meat had sustained them: seals, arctic foxes, and 900 sea otters, for which "the Chinese at the Kiakhta border usually pay a price of 80 to 100 rubles," wrote Gerhard Friedrich Müller. Despite the wretched state in which the men returned, their cargo of furs was a powerful enticement for others to push east across the northern North Pacific, and the following year, 1743, Yemelian Basov left Okhotsk with two survivors of the *Sviatoy Pyotr* to return to the Commander Islands.

Empress Elizabeth (r. 1741–61) had, nevertheless, tired of the expense of Tsar Peter's discovery expeditions and had turned her attention to Europe. The movement east along the Aleutians was consequently left to private entrepreneurs, who were charged a tax of 10 percent on the furs they imported from their hunting expeditions to Alaska. Basov's was the first of many small, privately financed fur hunting and trading expeditions that would head east. These pioneers pushed farther and farther along the arc of the Aleutians, and by 1768 all of the islands, with the exception of the Pribilofs, had been scouted for their potential to yield furs.[1]

By 1797 forty-two companies had made a total of 101 voyages in search of furs. As time wore on, however, and as the catches of foxes and sea otters declined, longer and longer voyages were necessary to produce a paying cargo, which consequently increased their capital requirements. Thus the smaller entrepreneurs gradually gave way to those who were better funded, and by the late 1780s most of the activity was financed by only a handful of merchants who competed fiercely—and sometimes violently—against one another.[2]

Finally the merchant Grigory Shelikhov imposed order on the chaos. Previously the fur hunting expeditions had been organized on a voyage-by-voyage basis, but Shelikov joined with Ivan Golikov to form the first permanent company in the North Pacific fur trade. In 1785 they founded the first Russian settlement in Alaska, on Kodiak Island, a base of operations that allowed them to advance farther eastward. Later other merchants joined them to form the first Russian joint-stock company. In 1792 the partners appointed Aleksandr Andreevich Baranov chief manager of the enterprise. Almost single-handedly, Baranov gained control of the Alaskan fur trade, and although Shelikhov died in 1795, Tsar Paul granted the organization a monopoly over the Kuriles and Aleutians and much other North Pacific territory in 1799. Thus the Russian-American Company was born.[3]

But, most important for Russia and for the Bering Strait region, Tsar "Paul and his advisors," Raymond Fisher wrote, "saw the grant of monopoly not as one conferred on the Shelikhov company to the exclusion of its competitors, but as a consolidation of competitors into one company that could bring order into the Pacific fur trade and resist intrusion into the North Pacific by other maritime powers, especially the British. To this end the new company was given quasi-governmental authority, enabling it to provide an administrative apparatus that had been conspicuously lacking in the half century since the fur rush began."[4]

Although Baranov wanted to investigate the potential of the regions north of the Pacific Rim, during his incumbency as chief manager he was preoccupied with a host of other matters, and by 1818, when he was relieved of his duties, he had made only modest progress northward.[5] At the same time the Russian government had been fully occupied with events in Europe, and it was only with the end of the Napoleonic Wars that the North Pacific again gained its attention.

After Billings's explorations in 1791 (see chapter 3), it was not until 1816 that Europeans returned to the Bering Strait region. That year Otto von Kotzebue led the first foreign expedition to Bering Strait in the nineteenth century. A quasi-governmental endeavor, his voyage was privately financed by Count Nikolai Petrovich Rumiantsev, the chancellor of Russia. Kotzebue was sent in search of a northern water route from Bering Strait to Europe and to carry out geographical and scientific research throughout the Pacific. Commanding the 180-ton brig *Riurik*, he left Kronshtadt, in the Gulf of Finland, in summer 1815 and arrived at Bering Strait a year later. There he discovered Kotzebue Sound and met the well-armed Eskimo fur traders. Kotzebue then visited the Asian coast of Bering Strait before heading south. He returned north in 1817, but during a violent storm on the way to the Aleutians he received a painful injury to his chest. On reaching St. Lawrence Island in July he found pack ice barring his way, and the cold and damp so aggravated his injury that he was forced to abandon his search for a northwest passage and head south to a more favorable climate. The *Riurik* touched at Hawaii, where Kotzebue met American traders and no doubt told them of his discovery of Kotzebue Sound. After stopping at Manila for repairs, the *Riurik* rounded the Cape of Good Hope and returned to Kronshtadt in summer 1818.

Even though he had not found a northwest passage to Europe, Kotzebue felt that the sound he had discovered could serve as a forward base for further exploration. Noting that the British were moving northwest toward Russian America, he wrote: "In my opinion, our government might establish several settlements on the coast of Beering's Straits to the north, like the English Hudson's Bay Company, which extends its trade far to the west of Hudson's Bay. It possesses colonies in the interior of the country, at a very little distance from the newly-discovered sound, and will, without doubt, take advantage of trading there."[6]

Then in 1819—the year after Kotzebue had returned to Russia—Eliab Grimes, aboard the *General San Martín*, scouted the Bering Strait region to evaluate its potential for the fur trade. And the same year, the Imperial Russian Navy dispatched another expedition to follow up on Kotzebue's discoveries, again searching for a northwest passage from Bering Strait to the Atlantic. Two ships, the *Otkrytie*, commanded by Mikhail Nikolaevich Vasiliev, and the *Blagonamerenny*, commanded by Gleb Semyonovich Shishmaryov, reached Bering Strait in 1820. There they met the American trading brig *Pedlar* and the hostile Buckland River Eskimos. The Russian ships left the *Pedlar* in Kotzebue Sound and followed the Alaskan coast northward, discovering Mys Rikord and Mys Golovnin (which the British later named Cape Thompson and Point Hope) as they charted the coast from Cape Krusenstern to beyond Icy Cape. The next summer, 1821, they returned north and surveyed the Alaskan coast from Bristol Bay to Norton Sound. Pack ice prevented one of the ships from passing beyond Icy Cape, but the other charted the north coast of the Chukchi Peninsula from Bering Strait to Cape Serdtse Kamen and fixed the position of St. Matthew Island. After a stop in Petropavlovsk, both ships sailed for Kronshtadt via Cape Horn.

THE VOYAGES OF KHRAMCHENKO AND ETHOLEN

Just as Russia's geopolitical objectives sent Vasiliev's and Shishmaryov's expedition to the Bering Strait region, at the same time the Russian-American Company sent its own expeditions north to scout for fur trading opportunities. With the company's returns declining on the Northwest Coast and in the Aleutians, the lands farther north offered the opportunity to revive the trade, and in 1818

Pyotr Korsakovsky went inland from Bristol Bay, north of the Alaska Peninsula, scouting for new sources of furs. The following year the company established Novo-Aleksandrovsky Redoubt at the mouth of the Nushagak River, while Korsakovsky continued his explorations, reaching as far as the mouth of the Kuskokwim River.[7]

On Count Rumiantsev's urging, in 1821 the company sent two experienced mariners to expand on Korsakovsky's reconnaissance. The company's Main Office in St. Petersburg cautioned, however, that the information from this exploration was to be kept strictly confidential: the directors felt that Kotzebue's narrative had stirred up too much foreign interest in lands and waters the company wished to keep to itself.[8] Vasily Stepanovich Khramchenko, who had sailed aboard the *Riurik* with Kotzebue, commanded the brig *Golovnin*, and Arvid Adolf Etholen, the cutter *Baranov*. They sailed from Novo-Arkhangelsk to Bristol Bay, where Khramchenko parted with Etholen, who would explore the Kuskokwim River. Khramchenko kept on north, to Nunivak Island and then to Norton Sound, where he discovered Golovnin Bay (see rear endpaper map).

Khramchenko's and Etholen's success in 1821 encouraged the company to send another expedition north. On April 23, 1822, Matvei Ivanovich Muravyov, the chief manager of the Russian-American colony, ordered Khramchenko to return to Norton Sound. This time, however, Etholen would sail with him aboard the *Golovnin* to gather intelligence about the region, information which the company could use in expanding its trade northward. Muravyov ordered Khramchenko to survey the southern shore of Norton Sound before heading toward Bering Strait. His principal objective was to establish trade relations with the Eskimos and to acquaint them with the goods that they might expect to receive in trade with the Russians. As a secondary assignment, Khramchenko was to investigate the enduring rumor (which was false) of the existence of a Russian settlement on the "Kheuveren" River on the Seward Peninsula.[9]

The *Golovnin* arrived at Stuart Island, northeast of the Yukon River delta, on July 2, 1822. The Eskimos at first were wary of the Russians but quickly lost their distrust, and later they offered to trade beaver, otter, and caribou skins. Soon thirty-five kayaks surrounded the *Golovnin*. "Their joy was unspeakable," wrote Khramchenko. "One of them delivered a long speech in sing-song, often mentioning our ship . . . others, without leaving their [kayaks], ran their hands over their head, face, and chest then turned their hands palm up and extended them toward us, showing thereby that they were as peaceful as we."[10] Khramchenko also learned about the furs that were carried westward, toward Bering Strait, and he felt that these Eskimos hunted for furs during the winter "but only to have something to trade with the Aziagmiut [Sledge Islanders] for pewter pipes, knives, some tobacco, and glass labrets."[11] The Eskimos' joy may have stemmed from the realization that the presence of a trading vessel might break the monopoly that the Bering Strait natives had hitherto enjoyed as the sole source of foreign goods.

The brig then sailed for the north coast of Norton Sound and three days later was in Golovnin Bay. There Khramchenko found two Eskimos whom he had met the year before: "They recognized me immediately," he wrote, "and approached our brig without apprehension. Once aboard, our guests were very happy to learn that we had brought much tobacco and many pewter pipes; in fact they danced up and down with joy and, going up to every sailor, said 'kuyanna-kuyanna' ['thank you–thank you']." The Golovnin Bay Eskimos probably assumed that they would have better trade opportunities with the Russians than with the traders from Sledge Island.

The next day, while the Russians traded knives, spears, and tobacco for beaver and fox skins, Khramchenko met a remarkable Eskimo named Tungan. Although Tungan showed Khramchenko his furs, he would not trade with the Russians: Tungan must have been a trader himself. What amazed Khramchenko, however, was that Tungan told him he had been far southwest of Bering Strait, to the Gulf of Anadyr, where he had met two Russians, "Vasilev" and "Vorobev." Tungan told Khramchenko that while traveling by kayak from Golovnin Bay toward Cape Prince of Wales, a sudden storm had blown him offshore. He was driven before the wind for three days, until he providentially fetched up on "a long island [St. Lawrence Island] inhabited by poor people who live on whale and walrus meat. They traded the walrus skins in the neighboring land, which was one night's journey from the western end of the island. He called this land Kuslit, and it was there that he had seen the aforementioned Russians a number of times."[12]

Tungan then proved the truth of his story by demonstrating his thorough knowledge of the geography of the Bering Strait region. "Tungan, wishing to comment on the places to which his unexpected journey had taken him, found a smooth spot on the sand and sketched the American coast from where we were to Bering Strait; then he sketched the nearby island. The island closest to Golovnin Bay he called Aziyak [Sledge Island]; the next island farther up the coast he called Ukivok [King Island] and said that it was inhabited. The people live on the steep cliffs and for the most part trade furs with the peoples who live in Kuslit; next he delineated two large islands and to the south of them a tiny islet [the Diomedes and Fairway Rock], giving each of them its own name. Finally, he formed the American coast into a cape opposite those islands."

Tungan continued, describing the overland travel routes on the Seward Penin-

sula between Port Clarence and Golovnin Bay and then speaking about the western shore of the Bering Strait region.

He sketched in the Kavsyak [Kuzitrin] River opposite Ukivok Island, saying
that the inhabitants of that island often visit the river and sometimes, toward
autumn, they travel to Golovnin Bay. He then proceeded to draw the land
where he had spent such a long time, designating it as a long island and saying
that the inhabitants call it Chuakak [St. Lawrence Island]. At the eastern end
of St. Lawrence Island he drew three small islands [the Punuk Islands], saying
that the northern island has a steep mountain and that there is a dwelling at its
foot. Finally he drew Kuslit [the Chukchi Peninsula], saying that he had seen
the Russians Vasilev and Vorobev there, and as proof of this he spoke several
words which he had often heard the Russians say. Tungan said the following:
Papush tabaku [a bundle of tobacco leaves], *trubka tabaku* [a pipe of tobacco],
and *proshka tabaku* [snuff] and, in addition, he pronounced some curse words
used by our common people.

As a conclusion to these tales, I must mention that the storm had carried
Tungan to St. Lawrence Island, which is evident from the sketch and undoubtedly he could have visited the east coast of Asia often and have seen Russians,
for, as he had already stated, the inhabitants of St. Lawrence Island often travel
to the Asian coast to trade walrus skins. Taking everything into consideration, it
may be assumed that Tungan could have gone to the Anadyr River where, one
would think, he saw Vasilev and Vorobev who, according to his stories, traded
with the savage peoples, a trade that may have been conducted by private persons.

Tungan related that last year he had left Kuslit with some Ukivok Islanders
and then had crossed the Kaviyayak [Kuzitrin River] and Kweigat Tuksmuk
rivers and had reached his homeland.[13]

Tungan also was aware of mechanical traps. "Tungan begged me for a trap, explaining that he would show his countrymen how to use it; he had told us earlier
that he had often seen traps at Vasilev and Vorobov's place and that he knew how
to set a trap and what safety measures to take in doing so. When our conversa-
tions had ended, I set out for the brig and asked my new acquaintance to visit me
on the ship the next day. The Americans [Eskimos], including Tungan, arrived at
4:00 AM and I invited Tungan into my cabin and repeated last evening's conversation. He drew on paper all those coasts which he had drawn in the sand, exactly
as he had done before. . . . The [Eskimos] stayed aboard the brig until two o'clock,
after which they set off for different points. When Tungan departed, I presented
him with a silver medal from among those given me for distribution among the
savage peoples."

"The [Eskimos] offered us fully equipped [kayaks] in trade," Khramchenko added, "but not one of the Americans wanted to part with his furs, because we could not give them much tobacco, for which and only which they will trade their fox skins. They are great masters of the art of barter; they drive a very hard bargain, always consult each other and, finally, take great pleasure in thinking they have cheated someone."[14] The Eskimos were probably holding out for a better deal with the Bering Strait traders.

Khramchenko then sailed on toward Bering Strait. On July 11, as the *Golovnin* approached Sledge Island, three umiaqs with ten or twelve persons in each approached from the mainland. They lowered their sails and paddled cautiously toward the *Golovnin*, while at the bow and stern of each they raised red fox skins on poles, indicating that their mission was trade, not warfare. "At first they did not approach our vessel for a long time," wrote Khramchenko, "and standing with the [umiaqs] in one place, they raised their hands. I ordered our sailors to do the same, indicating by this that we, too, have no weapons against them. Finally the [Eskimos] timidly came alongside the brig. . . . In the [umiaqs] they had some silver and red foxes, beavers, land otters, and sables which they bartered to us for large knife-like items of the palma type, Chukchi spears, buttons, and Circassian tobacco."[15] Because these Eskimos were carrying furs, they were probably on their way to meet Chukchi traders at one of the native trade fairs, perhaps the one in Port Clarence or the one on Big Diomede Island.

The next day, July 12, the *Golovnin* reached King Island, where Tungan had reported an active group of traders. Five umiaqs, with ten or eleven persons in each, stood out from the island. Like Billings's reception nearby in 1791, in the lead umiaq the natives hoisted an inflated sealskin float from a pole in the bow, while on the others they hung red foxes from poles in the bow and stern, showing that they wished to engage in trade, not warfare. "They very slowly approached the brig and shouted something to us, always raising their hands," he wrote. "I ordered that a white handkerchief be raised on a pole and ordered the interpreter to call them to him aboard the vessel. It seems that the islanders did not understand our interpreter. They stopped paddling, and by their movements it seems they consulted among themselves. Finally they decided to come alongside the vessel."

Khramchenko continued:

Two men, tall and of stately bearing came aboard. . . . One of them offered me a red fox as a gift. I for my part gave him a gift not so generous, only in order not to lower a value on those goods, because the inhabitants of the north in general are great masters at trade. When first meeting a European, they try first to give them gifts of those furs which they want to barter in order, through that, to find out the value of their furs and then they barter them no more cheaply than that. Soon afterwards a barter was established between us and the number of [umiaqs] increased. When up to 50 male [King Islanders] had gathered, I, fearing a superiority in numbers, forbade some to board the vessel, but ordered them to hold a little away from it. . . .

During the barter the islanders many times went to shore and again returned from it with new goods. They always tried to deceive us and if they succeeded they were extremely happy. . . .

With the setting of the sun we saw a large [umiaq] coming from the island. On its drawing near to the vessel, we saw two men who stood near the middle. One of them loudly uttered *Taroma! Taroma!* To which I responded in the same manner. When the [umiaq] approached the vessel the islanders who were with us immediately gave it room. In the [umiaq] were 11 men. All of them were tall and rather stately. Ground squirrel parkas only to the knees, trousers of seal skin, and [reindeer or caribou skin boots] constituted their clothing.

The senior of them, named Anak, whom I considered the leader, boarded our vessel and, approaching me, then several times together with the word *taroma* touched his forehead to mine. Finally, moistening his hand with saliva, he stroked his and my chest. I imitated him in everything. After so friendly a greeting, I invited Anak to my cabin. Two interpreters of the Chukchi and American languages, two shamans Ikaiuk and Iiaiuk, and his nephew Kuna-ginyn followed him everywhere. This person and all the others lacked those ornaments with which in general the [Eskimos] disfigure themselves, i.e., they had neither designs [tattoos] nor slits [for the insertion of labrets] on the face.

The fact that these men did not wear labrets and were accompanied by translators suggests that they may actually have been visitors: Siberian Eskimo or Chukchi traders.

Then Anak showed Khramchenko—as Tungan had done at Golovnin Bay—his knowledge of the Bering Strait region, describing the location of St. Lawrence Island, although he had not been there. "Through the interpreters we could converse about much with the old man Anak," Khramchenko wrote. "The others sat quietly and listened to us with attention. I here learned from Ankh about one large island about which he related that this island is to the S of the island inhabited by them. Old man Anakh called that island Chuakak [Sivuqaq] and said that he had not been there but only heard about it from Chukchi from Ualak-mut [Uelen people]."[16] He continued:

We would have engaged in conversation with old man Anak still longer if a sailor who had entered the cabin had not interrupted them with unexpected news. This messenger from the watch reported to me that the islanders were stealing. I and my guests went above. The Ukivoktsy [King Islanders] who still remained after bartering were stopped by me. Anak for his part undertook a strict search, but for all his efforts we could not find many things. The islanders, having noted so strict an action, covertly returned the shot they had stolen. Regarding the other things that we could not find, they said that those islanders who took them had already left for shore. In that case I at first thought to detain the old man Anak until the loot was returned, but, having thought it over, I decided to treat the Ukivoktsy as peaceably as possible. Meanwhile, I gathered all the islanders on the vessel and talked about their behavior with us, saying that we will take nothing from them without [paying?]. I calculated exactly what things were given to them for their goods, trying thus to express how shameful it is for them to rob us when we are their friends. Finally I ordered that a falconet be fired, saying to them that, should they not find the stolen things, I will pursue the thief with this weapon. Then, having taken leave of all, we parted. Old man Anak, leaving the brig, assured me that all will be returned tomorrow, saying that the Ukivoktsy live in a single place and consequently it is impossible to keep a secret. He promised without fail to find what had been lost.[17]

Khramchenko's even-handed treatment of the King Islanders' thefts—and Anak's cooperation—was an intelligent response by both men to a provocation. It illustrates the Eskimos' perception of theft and modes of exchange among the Iñupiaq Eskimo nations. As Ernest S. Burch, Jr., has stated, although the Eskimos considered intra-national theft to be unacceptable, inter-national theft was acceptable.[18] Those King Islanders who stole the goods from the Russians had viewed them as foreigners from whom theft was acceptable. This was the worldview that the Buckland River Eskimos displayed to Shishmaryov in Kotzebue Sound in 1820 when they cut buttons from his uniform and later threatened a shore party from the *Blagonamerreny* (see chapter 1).

Khramchenko then moved the brig closer to King Island.

When we approached the settlement of the Ukivoktsy . . . I ordered that a blank charge be fired from the cannon, due to which an extraordinary rumbling resounded along the cliffs. Not much after that we saw two single-hatch [kayaks] which with extraordinary quickness hurried toward the vessel. The islanders shouted something from afar and every minute showed the things which had been stolen from us the day before. One must suppose that they were giving advance notice in order that we receive them in a friendly manner. As soon as these islanders came alongside the vessel, both immediately boarded it and handed me our spyglass and shot which yesterday we could not find. These envoys remained not long at the vessel, and, having bartered a few red foxes, left again for shore. It seems the Ukivoktsy long feared us, because no one of them arrived from shore until they were convinced of our friendliness.

At sunrise we again were surrounded by inhabitants of the barren rocks who bartered to us foxes, lynxes, beavers, land otters, sables [martens], mink parkas, and walrus tusks of various qualities. For everything they accepted from us in payment tobacco, Chukchi spears, long knives, Russian axes, sky blue beads, and lead. . . .

Toward the end the islanders bartered their weapons and [kayaks] to us, for which they accepted various trifles from us. Anak and his nephew visited me three times and always conversed with me for several hours. I asked him how far they go and in what direction they go more, with what people they trade, what exactly they trade and what things they receive. Anak answered all such questions always with pleasure. His knowledge, it seems is rather broad. I say this because he knows very well the position of the shore of Bering Strait.[19]

Then Khramchenko learned of the existence of a firearm among the King Islanders. This was most likely the gun that William J. Pigot, aboard the *Pedlar*, had traded to the chief in 1820 (see chapter 1). "Kunaginyn told me about some gun and asked me for powder, but I did not want to give it to him until he shows it. Later I found out that Kunaginyn is the son of the former leader. The islanders, it seems, listened to him more. Therefore, as a sign of our favor toward the Ukivok people, I gave him a silver medal. He asked me to call him by a Russian name. When I named Kunaginyn Vasily the islanders began to rejoice and every minute pronounced this name."[20]

"I do not have sufficient information about the female sex of Ukivok Island," Khramcheno added. "Though we did see one woman during barter, one cannot draw general conclusions about all of them from this one. . . . Her ears were pierced in one place, in which she had earrings made up of varicolored beads. Her hair was plaited into two braids hanging on either side which were interwoven with beads of sky blue color."

He then described the span of the King Islanders' trade network, which extended beyond the territories of the Iñupiaq Eskimos, crossing well past the linguistic boundary to the Yup'ik Eskimos near the Yukon delta. "The islanders' arms consist in large knives or Chukchi spears which they wear in sheaths purposely sewn to their trousers on the right-hand side. . . . The chief industry of the inhabitants of Ukivok island is based for the most part on barter with the Chukchi, from whom they receive various Siberian articles and Circassian tobacco. In exchange for these things they buy furs from the Americans [Eskimos], for which they go to Stuart Island and from there along the coast to the Gvozdyov [Diomede] Islands. . . . The language of the islanders is entirely one with those Americans who live between Cape Rodney and Kotzebue Sound."[21]

Thus Khramchenko learned that the King Islanders had themselves become middlemen in trade across Bering Strait. The King Islanders brought furs from as far south as the Yukon delta and carried these furs to the Diomede Islands, where they exchanged them with Chukchi traders, who, as we have seen, were themselves middlemen in the trade that originated out of the Ostrovnoe fair and perhaps other fairs in northeastern Asia.

The brig then passed through Bering Strait and turned toward Kotzebue Sound. Near Shishmaref Inlet, on the north coast of the Seward Peninsula, the Russians spotted two umiaqs, with ten persons in each, hurrying toward the *Golovnin*. "They frequently stopped paddling, and shouted something, always raising their hands. One must think that by this they let us know in advance that they were unarmed. I ordered the sailors to do exactly the same. On the [umiaqs] in the bow on poles were raised white rabbits, with which they waved every minute. Before reaching our vessel, the [Eskimos] stopped and, it seems, scrutinized it with extraordinary curiosity. I ordered my interpreter to call them to him on the brig, but these savages still did not trust us. Having consulted among themselves, however, they decided to come alongside."

"These [Eskimos] are all a little taller than average and dressed very poorly. They somewhat understood our interpreter but our conversation still was not great because certain words they did not understand at all."[22] Perhaps these Eskimos were Tapqaġmiut, the nation that inhabited the lands near Shishmaref Inlet. It may have been that the interpreter understood the Yup'ik Eskimo dialects but was unfamiliar with Iñupiaq Eskimo languages.

"The skin of a white rabbit proffered to me as a gift was the beginning of barter. . . . For five foxes, which they long did not show us, we paid one iron kettle; and weapons and various articles they bartered to us for small pieces of hoop iron and other trifles." He continued: "During the barter our sailors joked much and through that furnished us no little amusement because from certain [Eskimos] they bartered nearly all their clothes for a leaf of tobacco. The savages, remaining entirely naked, willingly parted with clothing only in order to have in its place some tobacco, which they extraordinarily love. My intention was to call at Kotzebue Sound, but a wind that soon came up from the SE hindered me in this. Therefore, I decided not to penetrate farther into Bering Strait, but proposed before the onset of the bad fall season to hurry my arrival at the Pribilof Islands because I could assume that I would have to pick up cargo from there and deliver it to the Novo-Arkhangelsk office. And so, coming about, we began to sail toward the SW."[23]

In the same frame of mind as Eliab Grimes had written to John Ebbets in 1819, Khramchenko concluded his report to Muravyov with a summary of his achievements and of the commercial intelligence he had gained: "I may be allowed to say that this year's [1822] expedition was not useless. Besides the important advantage of verifying and correcting all the discoveries and surveys made last year, in 1821, with the visit to Ukivok Island the precise route of the trade of America and Asia in these latitudes is discovered. . . . Repeated dealings with the inhabitants extended knowledge of their customs and way of life. Also received is much information about the shores and even with the interior of the land, and now, with sufficient precision, one can define what one should hope from trading with the inhabitants of these regions."[24]

The voyages of 1821 and 1822 sponsored by the Russian-American Company thus provided a solid basis of commercial knowledge, knowledge that the company would exploit in its move northward and that would prove valuable in the last forty years of the company's existence.

6

The British Response

With the end of the Napoleonic Wars, the British government was as sensitive to Russia's activities in the North Pacific as the Russian government was to Britain's. One result was that Britain's Royal Navy, like the Imperial Russian Navy, devoted a substantial portion of its energies to surveying and exploration, and one objective was the discovery of a northwest passage between the Atlantic and Pacific oceans.[1]

In London, John Barrow, the ambitious and energetic second secretary of the Admiralty, was concerned about the Russians' efforts to find a northwest passage. He wrote in 1817: "The Russians have for some time been strongly impressed with the idea of an open passage round America. . . . It would be somewhat mortifying if a naval power but of yesterday should complete a discovery in the nineteenth century, which was so happily commenced by Englishmen in the sixteenth."[2]

As Trevor Levere wrote, "Encouraged by the Admiralty and the Royal Society, Parliament in 1818 passed an act offering substantial rewards for the discovery of a northwest passage . . . in the twin interests of commerce and science." In 1818 and 1819 Barrow outfitted three expeditions to search for a northwest passage. Although these efforts were not successful, they did at least help to delineate the land masses where a northwest passage might be found, and because of this Barrow worried that Russia might capitalize on the British discoveries—an attitude quite similar to the Russian-American Company's anxiety that foreigners might profit from Kotzebue's explorations.[3]

Within this climate of anxiety Captain John Franklin, who had served with the previous arctic expeditions, in 1823 proposed an expedition that would travel overland in North America, descend the Mackenzie River to the Arctic Ocean, and then travel west to Bering Strait, where it would rendezvous with a naval ship and return to Great Britain. Franklin promoted his expedition by stating that its objectives were for "advancing geographical knowledge and the fur trade, as well as preventing the encroachment of Russia," and his proposition fell on fertile ground at the Admiralty. The outcome was a bold and complicated tripartite expedition for charting and traversing a northwest passage. William Edward Parry would lead two ships into the Arctic west of Greenland; John Franklin would descend the Mackenzie in boats and head west along the continental coast, and both expeditions would rendezvous in Kotzebue Sound with HMS *Blossom* under the command of Frederick William Beechey, who had formerly served under both Parry and Franklin in the Arctic.[4]

As early as 1824, however, the Russians had learned of the plans for the British expedition, and that year Count Nikolai Petrovich Rumiantsev, who had financed Kotzebue's voyage, proposed to the Russian-American Company that they should jointly outfit an expedition, sending Khramchenko to complete the surveys begun by Kotzebue and Vasilev and Shishmaryov. "If Russia should undertake nothing," Rumiantsev wrote to Matvei Ivanovich Muravyov, the chief manager of the Russian-American colony, "and the English should succeed in reaching Bering Strait, then the short distance of these regions from our Asiatic and American possessions will give Europe the right to reproach us for leaving such pursuits, in our own waters and around our shores, to other nations." Unfortunately for the Russians, the expedition—which in any case would have arrived too late to meet Franklin—did not take place because of Rumiantsev's death.[5]

On May 25, 1825, the sloop-of-war *Blossom*, under the command of Frederick William Beechey, sailed for the Pacific Ocean. In addition to carrying out surveys and undertaking a broad program of scientific studies, Beechey was ordered to meet the Franklin and Parry expeditions in Kotzebue Sound. The *Blossom* rounded Cape Horn, visited a number of Pacific islands and reached Petropavlovsk, Kamchatka, late in June 1826. At Petropavlovsk, Beechey learned that Parry had been unable to complete a traverse of a northwest passage and had returned to Britain. The *Blossom* then pushed on to Kotzebue Sound to meet Franklin.[6]

JOHN FRANKLIN'S EXPEDITION

In the meantime, Franklin had gone overland from New York and had wintered at Great Bear Lake in northern Canada. In June 1826, he and his men descended the Mackenzie River in four boats, two of which Franklin sent east along the arctic coast under the command of Dr. John Richardson, while he, leading a party of fifteen in two boats (the *Lion* and *Reliance*), headed west from the Mackenzie delta (see rear endpaper map).

On July 7, at Tent Island in the western corner of the delta, Franklin's party came upon a large encampment of Eskimos, members of the Kuukpaŋmiut nation, one of seven Eskimo nations that formed the Tchiglit ("Mackenzie Eskimos"; today, Inuvialuit), who occupied the arctic coast and nearby lands, from the border with Russian America to Cape Parry in the east. The home territory of the Kuukpaŋmiut was the central Mackenzie delta, and Franklin's encounter with this group resembled the reception that Shishmaryov had received from the Buckland River Eskimos in Kotzebue Sound six years before.[7]

Decent and reliable, but a somewhat colorless and unimaginative man, Franklin was burdened by ponderous prose. His description of his nearly fatal encounter with the Mackenzie Eskimos is important because the narrative is one of the few detailed descriptions of encounters that took place in the early nineteenth century when small parties of Europeans met superior numbers of Eskimos.

The expedition's boats grounded in shallow water about a mile from the Eskimo camp. Immediately the natives launched their boats and paddled toward the explorers. Franklin counted seventy-three kayaks and five umiaqs in the approaching fleet. His Eskimo interpreter Augustus announced to the natives that they would receive presents from the strangers and that if they could find a navigable channel to the ocean, they could expect to develop trade with the foreigners.

But things immediately started to go wrong for Franklin and his men. A crowd of 250 to 300 Eskimos surrounded Franklin's boats clamoring to trade their labrets, bows and arrows, spears, and other things in return for Franklin's trade goods. Then came the flashpoint. One of the boats' oars inadvertently capsized a kayak, and the sailors hauled the shivering Eskimo into the boat, where the Eskimo spotted its trade goods.

> He soon began to ask for everything he saw, and expressed much displeasure on our refusing to comply with his demands; he also, as we afterwards learned, excited the cupidity of others by his account of the inexhaustible riches in the Lion, and several of the other men endeavored to get into both our boats, but we resisted all their attempts. Though we had not hitherto observed any of them stealing, yet they showed so much desire to obtain my flag, that I had it

Figure 6.1. Franklin's party meeting the Mackenzie Eskimos
(Franklin 1828, pl. 7).

furled and put out of sight, as well as everything else that I thought could prove
a temptation to them. They continued, however, to press upon us so closely,
and made so many efforts to get into the boats, that I accepted the offer of
two chiefs, who said that if they were allowed to come in, they would keep the
others out.

For a time they kept their word, and the crews took advantage of the respite
thus afforded, to endeavour to force the boats towards the river into deeper
water. The Reliance floated, but the Lion was immovable, and Lieutenant
Back dropping astern again made his boat fast to the Lion by a rope. At this
time one of the Lion's crew perceived that the man whose kaiyack had been
upset had a pistol under his shirt, and was about to take it from him, but I
ordered him to desist, as I thought it might have been purchased from the Loucheux [Gwich'in]. It had been, in fact, stolen from Lieutenant Back, and the
thief, perceiving our attention directed to it, leaped out of the boat and joined
his countrymen, carrying with him the great coat which Augustus had lent
him.[8]

Like Shishmaryov's party at Kotzebue Sound in 1820, Franklin and his men
had met a vastly superior number of Eskimos who believed that it was acceptable behavior to steal from members of foreign nations; and like the Eskimos
of Kotzebue Sound, when they outnumbered the foreigners, they pressed their

Figure 6.2. Franklin's encounter (Franklin 1828, pl. 8).

Figure 6.3. Franklin's escape (Franklin 1828, pl. 9).

advantage and became hostile and aggressive. Four decades later Father Émile
Petitot reported on a visit to the Mackenzie Eskimos: "By their Spartan code
theft is a form of prowess and is sanctioned."[9]

But the tide continued to ebb, grounding the boats even more firmly. Franklin
described their predicament:

> The water now ebbed so far that it was not knee deep at the boats, and the
> younger men wading in crowds around us, tried to steal everything in their
> reach; slyly, however, and with so much dexterity, as almost to escape detec-
> tion. The moment this disposition was manifested, I directed the crews not to
> suffer anyone to come alongside, and desired Augustus to tell the two chiefs,
> who still remained seated in the Lion, that the noise and confusion occasioned
> by the crowds around the boats greatly impeded our exertions; and that if they
> would go on shore and leave us for the present, we would hereafter return
> from the ship which we expected to meet near this part of the coast, with a
> more abundant supply of the goods. They received this communication with
> much apparent satisfaction, and jumping out of the boats repeated the speech
> aloud to their companions. From the general exclamation of "teyma," which
> followed, and from perceiving many of the elderly men retire a distance, I con-
> ceived that they acquiesced in the propriety of the suggestion, and that they
> were going away, but I was much deceived.

Teyma and *taima* were greetings given to a number of early explorers by Eskimos. Similar to the *taroma* with which Khramchenko was greeted, it presumably
meant that their encounter would be peaceful, but in this case it was a bluff.

Franklin continued: "They only retired to concert a plan of attack, and returned in a short time shouting some words which Augustus could not make out.
We soon, however, discovered their purport, by two of the three chiefs who were
on board the Reliance, jumping out, and, with the others who hurried to their
assistance, dragging her toward the south shore of the river. Lieutenant Back
desired the chief who remained with him to tell them to desist, but he replied by
pointing to the beach, and repeating the word *teyma, teyma* with a good natured
smile. He said, however, something to those who were seated in the [kayaks] that
were alongside, on which they threw their long knives and arrows in the boat,
taking care in so doing, that the handles and feathered ends were turned towards
the crew, as an indication of pacific intentions."[10]

Augustus, who was a Caribou Eskimo from the west coast of Hudson Bay, may
have incorrectly translated Franklin's statement about his promise that a ship that
would come nearby with a large supply of trade goods, or it may have been that
the Eskimos misunderstood his message, thinking instead that Franklin's boats

contained the trade goods that he mentioned. In any case the situation soon turned very dangerous.[11]

"As soon as I perceived the Reliance moving under the efforts of the natives," Franklin went on,

I directed the Lion's crew to endeavour to follow her, but our boat remained fast until the Esquimaux lent their aid and dragged her after the Reliance. Two of the most powerful men, jumping on board at the same time, seized me by the wrists and forced me to sit between them; and as I shook them loose two or three times, a third Esquimaux took his station in front to catch my arm whenever I attempted to lift my gun, or the broad dagger which hung by my side. The whole way to the shore they kept repeating the word "teyma," beating gently on my left breast with their hands, and pressing mine against their breasts.

As we neared the beach, two oomiaks, full of women, arrived, and the "teymas" and vociferation were redoubled. The Reliance was first brought to shore, and the Lion close to her a few seconds afterwards. The three men who held us now leaped ashore, and those who had remained in their [kayaks], taking them out of the water, carried them to a little distance. A numerous party then drawing their knives, and stripping themselves to the waist, ran to the Reliance, and having first hauled her as far up as they could, began a regular pillage, handing the articles to the women, who, ranged in a row behind, quickly conveyed them out of sight.

Lieutenant Back and his crew strenuously, but good-humouredly, resisted the attack, and rescued many things from their grasp, but they were overpowered by numbers, and had even some difficulty in preserving their arms. One fellow had the audacity to snatch Vivier's knife from his breast, and to cut the buttons from his coat, whilst three stout Esquimaux surrounded Lieutenant Back with up-lifted daggers, and were insistent in their demands for whatever attracted their attention, especially for the anchor buttons which he wore on his waistcoat. In this juncture a young chief coming to his aid, drove the assailants away. In their retreat they carried off a writing desk and cloak, which the chief rescued, and then seating himself on Lieutenant Back's knee, he endeavoured to persuade his countrymen to desist by vociferating "teyma teyma," and was indeed very active in saving whatever he could from their depredations.

The Lion had hitherto been beset by smaller numbers, and her crew, by firmly keeping their seats on the cover spread over the cargo, and by beating the natives off with the butt-ends of their muskets, had been able to prevent any article of importance from being carried away. But as soon as I perceived that the work of plunder was going on so actively in the Reliance, I went with Augustus to assist in repressing the tumult; and our bold and active little interpreter rushed among the crowd on shore, and harangued them on their treacherous conduct, until he was actually hoarse.

In a short time, however, I was summoned back by Duncan, who called out to me that the Esquimaux had now commenced in earnest to plunder the Lion, and, on my return, I found the sides of the boat lined with men as thick as they could stand, brandishing their knives in the most furious manner, and attempting to seize every thing that was moveable; whilst another party was ranged outside ready to bear away the stolen goods. The Lion's crew still kept their seats, but as it was impossible for such a small number to keep off such a formidable and determined body, several articles were carried off. Our principal object was to prevent the loss of the arms, oars, or masts, or any thing on which the continuance of the voyage, or our personal safety, depended. Many attempts were made to purloin the box containing the astronomical instruments, and Duncan, after thrice rescuing it from their hands, made it fast to his leg with a cord, determined that they should drag him away also if they took it.

But the Eskimos pressed their advantage, and Franklin's crew only narrowly avoided bloodshed.

In the whole of this unequal contest, the self-possession of our men was not more conspicuous than the coolness with which the Esquimaux received the heavy blows dealt to them with the butts of the muskets. But at length, irritated at being so often foiled in their attempts, several of them jumped on board and forcibly endeavoured to take the daggers and shot-belts that were about the men's persons; and I myself was engaged with three of them who were trying to disarm me. Lieutenant Back perceiving our situation, and fully appreciating my motives in not coming to extremities, had the kindness to send to my assistance the young chief who had protected him, and who, on his arrival, drove my antagonists out of the boat.

Then I saw that my crew were nearly overpowered in the fore part of the boat, and hastening to their aid, I fortunately arrived in time to prevent George Wilson from discharging the contents of his musket into the body of an Esquimaux. He had received a provocation of which I was ignorant until the next day, for the fellow had struck at him with a knife, and cut through his coat and waistcoat; and it was only after the affair was over that I learned that Gustavus Aird, the bowman of the Lion, and three of the Reliance's crew, had also narrowly escaped from being wounded, their clothes being cut by the blows made at them with knives.

No sooner was the bow cleared of some of the marauders than another party commenced their operations at the stern. My gun was now the object of the struggle, which was beginning to assume a more serious complexion, when the whole of the Esquimaux suddenly fled, and hid themselves behind the drift timber and [kayaks] on the beach. It appears that by the exertions of the crew, the Reliance was again afloat, and Lieutenant Back wisely judging that this was the proper moment for more active interference, directed his men to level their muskets, which had produced the sudden panic.

The Lion happily floated soon after, and both were retiring from the beach, when the Esquimaux having recovered from their consternation, put their kai-yacks in the water, and were preparing to follow us; but I desired Augustus to say that I would shoot the first man who came within range of our muskets, which prevented them.[12]

Unlike the Eskimos that Kotzebue met in 1816, this group knew about fire-arms. Later, Franklin learned that the Eskimos had encountered them in the hands of their enemies, the Loucheux (Gwich'in), who lived south of the Mac-kenzie Eskimos.[13]

"It was now about eight o'clock in the evening," Franklin continued, "and we had been engaged in this harassing contest for several hours, yet the only things of importance which they had carried off were the mess canteen and kettles, a tent, a bale containing blankets and shoes, one of the men's bags, and the jib-sails. The other articles they took could well be spared, and they would, in fact, have been distributed amongst them, had they remained quiet. The place to which the boats were dragged is designated as Pillage Point."

Franklin's boats were only able to move about a quarter of a mile before they grounded again. The sailors waded out, seeking deeper water, but found none, so they secured the boats side by side and waited. Augustus then bravely went ashore to address the Eskimo throng.

Shortly after the boats had been secured, seven or eight of the natives walked along the beach, and carrying on a conversation with Augustus, invited him to a conference on shore. I was at first very unwilling to permit him to go, but the brave little fellow entreated so earnestly that I would suffer him to land and reprove the Esquimaux for their conduct, that I at length consented, and the more readily, on seeing that the young chief who had acted in so friendly a manner was amongst the number on the beach. By the time Augustus reached the shore, the number of Esquimaux amounted to forty, and we watched with great anxiety the animated conversation he carried on with them.

On his return he told us that its purport was as follows: — "Your conduct," said he, "has been very bad, and unlike that of all other Esquimaux. Some of you even stole from me, your countryman, but that I do not mind; I only regret that you should have treated in this violent manner the white people who came solely to do you kindness. My tribe were in the same unhappy state in which you now are, before the white people came to Churchill, but at present they are supplied with every thing they need, and you see that I am well clothed; I get all I want, and am very comfortable. You cannot expect, after the transactions of this day, that these people will ever bring goods to your country again, unless you show your contrition by returning the stolen goods. The white people love the Esquimaux, and wish to shew them the same kindness that they bestow upon the Indians; do not deceive yourselves, and suppose that they are afraid of you; I tell you they are not, and that it is entirely owing to their humanity that many of you were not killed to-day; for they have all guns, with which they can destroy you either when near or at a distance. I also have a gun, and can assure you that if a white man had fallen, I would have been the first to have revenged his death."

The veracity of Augustus was beyond all question with us; such a speech delivered in a circle of forty armed men, was a remarkable instance of personal courage. We could perceive, by the shouts of applause with which they filled the pauses in his harangue, that they assented to his arguments, and he told us that they had expressed great sorrow for having given us so much cause of offence, and pleaded, in mitigation of their conduct, that they had never seen white people before, that every thing in our possession was so new to them, and so desirable, that they could not resist the temptation of stealing, and begged him to assure us that they never would do the like again, for they were anxious to be on terms of friendship with us, that they might partake of the benefits with which this tribe derived from their intercourse with white people. I told Augustus to put their sincerity to the test by desiring them to bring back a large kettle and the tent, which they did, together with some shoes, having sent for them to the island whither they had been conveyed.

After this act of restitution, Augustus requested to be permitted to join a dance of which they had invited him, and he was, for upwards of an hour, engaged in dancing and singing with all his might in the midst of a company who were all armed with knives or bows and arrows.[14]

At last the tide began to rise, and the boats floated again. Franklin's party moved on six miles before going ashore. After posting sentries they got their first sleep in twenty-four hours. When the men woke the next morning they began to mend the sails from which the Eskimos had cut the metal fittings, but while this work was underway, Lieutenant George Back spotted another group of Eskimos paddling toward them. Knowing that they would be more vulnerable on shore, the men launched their boats through the surf.

"We had scarcely pulled into deep water," Franklin wrote, "before some of the kaiyacks had arrived within speaking distance, and the man in the headmost one, holding out a kettle, called aloud that he wished to return it, and that the oomiak which was some distance behind, contained the things that had been stolen from us, which they were desirous of restoring, and receiving in return any present that we might be disposed to give."

But Franklin smelled a rat. "I did not deem it prudent, however, for the sake of the few things in their possession which we required, to hazard their whole party collecting around us, and, therefore, desired Augustus to tell them to go back; but they continued to advance until I fired a ball ahead of the leading [kayak], which had the desired effect—the whole party veering round, except four, who followed us a little way, and then went back to join their companions."[15]

Shortly thereafter, and farther along the coast, the explorers met a group of friendly Eskimos, who were probably members of the Kigiqtaġuġmiut nation, whose territory included the lands between the Mackenzie delta and, approximately, the border with Russian America, within which was a prominent settlement on Herschel Island. Augustus told them about the encounter at Tent Island: "Those are bad men," they said, "and never fail either to quarrel with us, or steal from us, when we meet. They come, every spring from the eastern side of the Mackenzie, to fish at the place where you saw them, and return as soon as the ice opens. . . . If you are obliged to return by this way, before the people remove, we, with a reinforcement of young men, will be in the vicinity, and will willingly accompany you to assist in repelling any attack."

A month later Franklin discovered that his suspicions about the Eskimos' motives in offering to return the stolen equipment had been well founded:

We learned that up to the time that the kaiyack was upset, the Esquimaux were actuated by the most friendly feelings towards us, but the fellow whom we had treated so kindly after the accident, discovering what the boats contained, proposed to the younger men to pillage them. This suggestion was buzzed about, and led to the conference which the old men held together when I desired them to go away, in which the robbery was decided upon, and a pretty general wish was expressed that it should be attended with the total massacre of our party.

Providentially a few suggested the impropriety of including Augustus; and for a reason which can scarcely have been imagined. "If we kill him," said they, "no more white people will visit our lands, and we shall lose the opportunity of getting another supply of their valuable goods; but if we spare him, he can be sent back with a story which we shall invent to induce another party of white people to come among us."

This argument prevailed at the time; but after the interviews with Augustus at the dance, they retired to their island, where they were so much inflamed by the sight of the valuable articles which they had obtained, that they all, without exception, regretted that they had allowed us to escape. While in this frame of mind the smoke of our fire being discovered, a consultation was immediately held, and a very artful plan laid for the destruction of the party, including Augustus, whom they conceived to be so firmly attached to us that it was in vain to attempt to win him to their cause. They expected to find us on shore; but to provide against the boats getting away if we should have embarked, they caused some kettles to be fastened conspicuously to the leading kaiyack, in order to induce us to stop. The kaiyacks were then to be placed in such a position as to hamper the boats, and their owners were to keep us in play until the whole party had come up, when the attack was to commence. Through the blessing of Providence, their scheme was frustrated.

THE HERSCHEL ISLAND ESKIMOS

Franklin and his men then pushed on west along the arctic coast into uncharted territory. Near Herschel Island, Franklin began to learn about the native trade of the region: a group of friendly Eskimos told him that they received iron, knives, and beads from two sources, but primarily from Eskimos "who reside a great distance to the westward, and to meet whom they send their young men every spring with furs, seal-skins, and oil, to exchange for those articles, and also from the Indians, who come every year from the interior to trade with them by a river that was directly opposite our encampment; which I have therefore named the Mountain Indian River." The Mountain Indian River is today the Firth River, which enters the Beaufort Sea near the western end of Herschel Island.

Franklin learned that these trade encounters were carried out with considerable mutual suspicion.

These Indians leave their families and canoes at two days' march from the mouth of the river, and the men come alone, bringing no more goods than they intend to barter. . . . They also said that the Esquimaux to the westward, speak a dialect so different from theirs, that at the first opening of the communication, which was so recent as to be within the memory of two of our present companions, that they had great difficulty in understanding them. Several quarrels took place at their first meetings, in consequence of the western party attempting to steal; but latterly there has been a good understanding between

Figure 6.4. Herschel Island Eskimo, 1826.
This Herschel Island man had pierced not
only his cheeks but also his septum. The beads
that were fastened to the labrets were made in
China and had reached him via the cross–Bering
Strait native trade. The beads then changed
hands again at the Sheshalik, the Niġliq,
and the Barter Island rendezvous
(Franklin 1828, detail of pl. 13).

them, and the exchanges have been fairly made. . . . Our visitors did not know
from what people either the Indians or the Esquimaux obtained the goods, but
they supposed from some "Kabloonacht" (white people) who reside far to the
west. As the articles we saw were not of British manufacture, and were unlike
those sold by the Hudson's Bay Company to the Indians, it cannot be doubted
that they are furnished by the Russian Fur Traders, who receive in return for
them all the furs collected on this northern coast. Part of the Russian iron-work
is conveyed to the Esquimaux dwelling on the coast east of the Mackenzie.[16]

Although the North Alaskan Eskimos were almost certainly receiving their
trade goods via the Sheshalik trade fair and then via an inland route, it is possible
that the "Mountain Indians" (Gwich'in) received theirs via different routes: there

were at least fifty overland travel routes in northwestern Alaska. A more compelling possibility is that these goods may have come via Sheshalik—or possibly via the native trade in Norton Sound—and then to the Koyukon who traded them onward to the western Gwich'in groups. These Gwich'in could have traded them to other Gwich'in—Franklin's "Mountain Indians"—who then carried them to the rendezvous with the Eskimos near Herschel Island. It is less likely that these goods entered the native trade network from the Russian-American Company's Novo-Aleksandrovskii Redoubt, which had been established in southwestern Alaska at the mouth of the Nushagak River in 1819.[17]

"The western Esquimaux use tobacco," Franklin wrote, "and some of our visitors had smoked it, but thought the flavour very disagreeable. Until I was aware of their being acquainted with the use of it, I prohibited my men from smoking in their presence, and afterwards from offering their pipes to the Esquimaux at any time." Thus Franklin established the location of the "tobacco frontier," which had been at Bering Strait nearly half a century before, when Captain Cook had touched there. Tobacco's eastward advance was almost certainly the result of the greater amounts entering the native trade network via the trade fairs in Chukotka.

"At the conclusion of this conference our visitors assured us, that having now become acquainted with white people, and being conscious that the trade with them would be beneficial, they would gladly encourage further intercourse, and do all in their power to prevent future visitors from having such a reception as we had on our arrival in these seas."[18]

A few days later Franklin's party crossed the 141st meridian: the boundary that Russia and Great Britain had agreed upon in the treaty of 1825. They were now in Russian America, and soon they met the Eskimo traders who had traveled west from Herschel Island to meet the "western Esquimaux" traders. The Herschel Islanders were then on their way back from the encounter. Franklin learned that the exchange had taken place only a few days before and named his next campsite Barter Island.[19]

FRANKLIN'S RETURN

Hampered by bad weather and heavy ice, Franklin and his crew made slow progress west. After six weeks of travel, on August 16 they were still only halfway to Icy Cape, which marked Captain Cook's farthest advance on the northwest coast of arctic Alaska. Icy Cape was the northernmost point of which Franklin was aware on the northwest coast of Alaska. He sensibly concluded that he had little chance of reaching his rendezvous with Beechey in Kotzebue Sound before the onset of winter. Naming the barrier islands at his westernmost point of advance Return Reef, he headed back toward the Mackenzie River, not knowing, of course, that the *Blossom's* barge was at that time sailing north. On August 23 the *Blossom's* men would discover Point Barrow, about 175 miles from Franklin's westernmost advance. But in view of the reception that the Point Barrow Eskimos gave the *Blossom's* boat party only a few days later, Franklin was probably lucky to have turned back.[20]

By charting the coast and reporting about the natives, Franklin, whose expedition had been sent out as a result of Great Britain's competition with Russia, was also enabling the fur trade to expand northward. And the fur trade, too, carried territorial claims for the host nation. Furthermore, Franklin had learned that the regular trade encounters between the Mackenzie Eskimos and those nations to the west had begun only recently and that the goods that the Eskimos acquired were Russian. He also noticed that tobacco was only just beginning to work its way eastward via the traders.

Although irregular trade exchanges had probably gone on between the North Alaskan Eskimos and the Mackenzie Eskimos before the establishment of the Ostrovnoe trade fair in 1789, after that date substantial amounts of trade goods began to flow east across Bering Strait from Ostrovnoe and other fairs in northeastern Asia, and it is likely that the Barter Island exchange became an annual rendezvous as a result of this.[21]

The Ostrovnoe fair had far-reaching effects. The intercontinental trade across Bering Strait that Kotzebue (1816), Grimes (1819), Pigot (1820), Vasiliev and Shishmaryov (1820), and Khramchenko (1822) witnessed was now drawing furs from as far south as the Yukon delta and beyond, and as far east as the Mackenzie delta. Furs were exchanged in return for iron, knives, and beads; and tobacco was also spreading into arctic America. These commodities moved via existing native trade routes and trade fairs that were becoming increasingly important to the Eskimos. Alaskan furs were flowing to China via Kiakhta, and goods from the Ostrovnoe trade fair, and perhaps other fairs in northeastern Asia, were now being carried more than two thousand miles eastward.

FREDERICK WILLIAM BEECHEY'S EXPEDITION

While the Franklin expedition was underway in 1826, the *Blossom* stopped at Petropavlovsk on her way north, and there Captain Beechey learned that Parry's expedition had returned to Britain. Beechey's principal objective was now to rendezvous with John Franklin's boats. Of course Beechey did not meet Franklin, but the knowledge he gained in surveying the northwestern coast of Alaska yielded a highly accurate chart of the region and produced valuable intelligence for the Admiralty.

THE EXPEDITION IN BERING STRAIT AND NORTHWESTERN ALASKA, 1826

On July 17, 1826, the same day that Franklin was approaching Herschel Island, the *Blossom* reached the southwestern tip of St. Lawrence Island. At once twenty-four men and women in four umiaqs approached the ship and offered to trade nets, walrus ivory, skin shirts, harpoons, bows and arrows, small birds, and skins in return for tobacco. "The first word they uttered was 'tobacco' . . . but they would only take that weed in the leaf," wrote James Wolfe, the Admiralty mate. "The women seemed only to wish for beads, the blue colour being the most prised, yellow they would not have. From their making it a rule to bite them we conceived that they had been duped with compositions of wax."[22]

The *Blossom* pushed on toward the rendezvous with Franklin in Kotzebue Sound. On July 21, at Shishmaref Inlet, on the north coast of the Seward Peninsula, two umiaqs came to the ship. "They willingly sold everything they had," Beechey noted, "except their bows and arrows, which, they implied were required for the chase on shore; but they could not resist 'tawac' (tobacco) and iron knives, and ultimately parted with them."[23]

Beechey was not involved in the fur trade, but he had been ordered to collect ethnographic and natural history specimens throughout the Pacific, and to do so he carried a substantial cargo of trade goods: "50 yards of blue and read broadcloth, iron in the form of hoops and bars, 500 hatchets, nails, saws, 4 cases of beads, jewelry and trinkets of different colours but mainly blue, 500 knives, 100 printed handkerchiefs, 50 kaleidoscopes, 100 bundles of needles, 40 pair of scissors, 80 looking glasses, 36 common shirts, 1,000 fish hooks of different sizes, 10 bundles of vermillion." The *Blossom* carried an ample stock of tobacco.[24]

When the *Blossom* reached Chamisso Island in Kotzebue Sound, the sailors found no trace of Franklin, and the crew began a series of coastal surveys. On July 22, in the northeastern corner of the sound, six or seven umiaqs, with about ten men and women in each, approached the ship. The first boat sold salmon and capelin to the men, but the others offered polar bear, caribou, ermine, white and red fox, muskrat, and bird skins that "were far superior to any before even seen at Kamschatka," in return for blue beads, tobacco, knives, and pewter rings, "but they preferred the beads."[25]

The *Blossom* also carried a small schooner-rigged barge for coastal surveys, and while the ship was in deeper water, the barge's crew carried out inshore reconnaissance and discovered Hotham Inlet. Although the sailors did not know

Figure 6.5. Eskimo traders in Kotzebue Sound. James Wolfe, 1826. The Eskimo
man in the stern of the umiaq (left) is raising his arms to show that he does not have
knives concealed in his sleeves. The man to his left holds up a fox skin, and the man
on the right displays his bow, showing that he does not have an arrow ready on the
bowstring. The Eskimos made these gestures to show the British sailors that they
were not hostile but rather wished to engage in trade (Wolfe MSa).
Beinecke Rare Book and Manuscript Library, Yale University.

it, three rivers—the Noatak, Kobuk, and Selawik—flow into Kotzebue Sound.
These watersheds were the homelands of several Eskimo nations. Much of these
lands was within the tree line and hence supported populations of valuable fur
bearing animals.

On July 30 the barge rejoined the *Blossom* at Chamisso Island and the men
reported that they had met a large number of umiaqs near Hotham Inlet. The
sailors were unaware that the *Blossom* and the barge had been very near Sheshalik
(*Sisualiq*), on the north shore of Kotzebue Sound. The reason that the *Blossom's*
men had met a large number of umiaqs in Hotham Inlet—and had been offered
furs of high quality—was that members of many of the Eskimo nations of northern and western Alaska were converging on Sheshalik for the great annual trade
fair. There, as we have seen in chapter 1, 1,700 or more natives from the nations
of northwestern Alaska as well as some from the Seward Peninsula, King Island,
Norton Sound, and as many as five boats (forty-five to sixty-five persons) from
the Chukchi Peninsula—and occasionally a few Koyukon and Gwich'in—met
annually, in a season of general truce, to dance, feast, and engage in athletic
competitions, among many other activities, but principally to engage in trade.[26]

With the barge in company, on July 30, 1826, the two vessels immediately set
off for a survey of the northwestern coast of Alaska. On August 1, as they rounded
Cape Krusenstern at the northwest corner of Kotzebue Sound, Eskimos in three
umiaqs paddled at least ten miles to reach the ship and trade for beads, knives,

and tobacco. Then the two vessels continued on, stopping at Cape Thompson and Point Hope (which the British believed they had discovered, although Vasiliev's and Shishmaryov's expedition had, in fact, already named them Mys Rikord and Mys Golovnin). At Icy Cape, they bought four hundred pounds of caribou meat for four pounds of tobacco. There Beechey remarked that the Eskimos "expressed no surprise at the appearance either of the ship or of [the barge], and that they were provided both with knives and iron kettles." As we have seen, Russian explorers had been there as recently as 1821, and those "knives and iron kettles" probably entered the native trade network in Chukotka.[27]

On August 15, now beyond Vasiliev's and Shishmaryov's farthest point, three umiaqs came out to the *Blossom* near Point Franklin. The British were startled to find that once again the Eskimos, some of whom readily climbed aboard, "far from being surprised at the sight of a ship, they on the contrary began immediately to make signs for Tobacco and knives, and a traffic was speedily commenced." Word-of-mouth information from members of other Eskimo nations may have given these Eskimos confidence in approaching the expedition, or possibly they may have visited ships at points farther south during their excursions to the trade fair at Sheshalik. It is less likely that there may have been other trading vessels that we know nothing about visiting the coast.[28]

Although the barge had been sailing in company with the *Blossom*, on August 17, Beechey ordered it to head north alone, searching for Franklin's party along the coast. But Franklin, on that same day, was then only at Return Reef. He concluded that he had no hope of reaching the rendezvous at Kotzebue Sound in time to meet Beechey that year and began his return voyage to the Mackenzie River. Once the barge was underway, the *Blossom* headed back to Kotzebue Sound to continue her surveys.

On August 29 in Kotzebue Sound, Beechey met a group of Eskimos at their camp on the Choris Peninsula and gained an insight into how they conducted their bartering, "They commenced a brisk traffic with dried salmon, of which we procured a great quantity," he wrote. "Generally speaking, they were honest in their dealings, leaving their goods with us, when they were in doubt about a bargain, until they had referred it to a second person, or more commonly to some of the old women. If they approved of it, our offer was accepted; if not, they took back the goods. On several occasions, however, they tried to impose upon us with fish-skins, ingeniously put together to represent a whole fish, though entirely deprived of their original contents: but this artifice succeeded only once: the natives, when detected in other attempts, laughed heartily, and treated the affair as a fair practical joke." These Eskimos were no doubt returning from the Sheshalik fair toward their homelands. They soon left the Choris Peninsula, having surreptitiously dug up a cache that Beechey's men had buried for Franklin and taken the iron hoops from a barrel of flour. Ten years earlier Kotzebue had had a similar encounter in Kotzebue Sound. The Eskimos, Kotzebue wrote, "treated us very contemptuously, offering us little rags of rats' and dogs' skins in exchange; but when they observed that we laughed at their goods, they also joined heartily in the laugh, talking much to each other, and at last advised us to put the rags in our noses and ears."[29]

Each national group departed from the Sheshalik fair at a different date. Once they had concluded their business at Sheshalik, they headed for their homelands, allowing themselves sufficient time to arrive before the onset of winter. Beechey's men soon discovered that another traveling group had camped nearby on Chamisso Island. These people, Beechey noted, "differed in several particulars from those [who had camped on the Choris Peninsula]." One of the women had "the septum of the nose pierced, and a large blue bead strung upon a strip of [baleen] passed through the orifice, the bead hanging as low as the opening of the mouth. One of them, on receiving a large stocking needle, thrust it into the orifice, or, as some of the seamen said, 'spritsail-yarded her nose.'"[30]

Yet another group of Eskimos then arrived at the Choris Peninsula. This one was heading toward their home at Cape Prince of Wales. Five families with seven umiaqs set up camp in five tents. When Beechey and his shore party visited their camp, the Eskimos greeted the British warmly, but they would not allow the men to approach their tents; instead, they locked arms with the sailors and led them to higher ground, where they were seated on planks and skins. The Eskimos presented each man with a dried fish and then offered them a bowl containing a mixture of berries, greens, and fat, an Eskimo delicacy that the British declined. The Eskimos prepared for dancing by donning their best clothes (which they were unwilling to sell until the dance was finished) and seated themselves in two concentric circles, the men in the inner circle and the women in the outer circle. "In addition to their usual costume," Captain Beechey observed, "some had a kind of tippet of ermine and sable skins thrown over their shoulders, and others wore a band on their heads, with strips of skin suspended to it at every two inches, to the end of which were attached the nails of seals."

It appears that this group of Eskimo traders approached the *Blossom's* sailors as they would have approached members of a sovereign Eskimo nation at Sheshalik. The Sheshalik fair took place in a time of general truce, when warfare and animosity among Eskimo nations was temporarily suspended in favor of international trade. These Eskimos, most likely members of the Kiŋikmiut nation from Cape Prince of Wales, may have viewed their encounter with the men from the *Blossom* in some way as an extension of the Sheshalik fair, which explains their peaceful behavior, and which stands in contrast to the receptions that other groups of Europeans had often received—and would receive—in the same region. When the dance ended the Eskimos began bartering with the sailors, and Beechey mentioned that the Eskimos were greatly excited by a mirror, which they held before the face of a blind man. The British bought 172 pounds of dried fish for hatchets, knives, and red and blue beads.[31]

Once again the Europeans learned that the Eskimos were skillful traders. Admiralty Mate James Wolfe wrote: "We concluded that they were more in the habit of intercourse with other people than any we had before seen. They understood two or three of the Kamtschadale words and appeared perfectly aware of the value of several articles offered in barter; of which however blue beads were in the highest estimation." During the trading the Eskimos tried to steal things from the British, but when the sailors spotted their pilfering, the particular item was returned with "a hearty laugh." One of them cut a button from the tail of Captain Beechey's coat but returned it when discovered.[32]

The Eskimos also showed that they were well acquainted with the qualities of iron and understood that it varied in hardness. They tested the British knives and hatchets "by hacking at them with their own. If they stood the blow, they were accepted, but if, on the contrary, they were notched, they were refused." Captain Beechey noticed that the women in this group wore broad iron bracelets, which the British had not seen adorning the women of other groups. "By their having four or five of them upon each wrist," Beechey wrote, "it appeared that this metal, so precious with the tribes to the northward, was with them less rare."[33]

Although iron by then had become relatively plentiful to the native nations adjacent to Bering Strait, the Eskimos still particularly wanted adzes, which, to them, were far more useful for woodworking than were axes. "Some small hatchets, which in that shape had been but little prized," James Wolfe observed, "were by the armourer converted into adzes, and for these they would have given anything. They hugged them and showed the greatest eagerness to possess them. This was a great point gained, and as the captain wished to purchase a baydair (Kaiyak or Oomiak) he offered two for a new one. They would readily have consented but signified that they should not have enough left to carry their party."[34]

During a visit to the *Blossom* the Eskimos' leader marveled at the workmanship of the vessel, but Beechey remembered that "he seemed to regret that so much iron had been expended where thongs would have served as well." One day the Eskimos drew a map in the sand for Beechey. It was an accurate delineation of the coast from Cape Krusenstern, on Kotzebue Sound, to Cape Darby, on Norton Sound. The map also showed a feature that the British had not known of, the great embayment of Port Clarence on the southwestern Seward Peninsula.

On September 2 the Eskimo party headed onward, toward their homeland, but on September 3 another umiaq in the long procession of boats returning from Sheshalik reached the ship. And three days later two umiaqs carrying two families arrived under full sail. Through the fog the British at first thought that the boats might be Franklin's party. Each boat was carrying its own equipment, and from their language Beechey thought they might also be from Cape Prince of Wales.[35]

Beechey admired the amount of cargo the umiaqs carried. "From two of these they landed fourteen persons," he noted, "eight tent poles, forty [caribou] skins, two kyacks, many hundredweight of fish, numerous skins of oil, earthen jars for cooking, two living foxes, ten large dogs, bundles of lances, harpoons, bows, and arrows, a quantity of [baleen], skins full of clothing, some immense nets made of hide for taking small whales and porpoises, eight broad planks, masts, sails, paddles, &c., besides [walrus] hides and teeth, and a variety of nameless articles always to be found among the Esquimaux."

This group appeared to be poorer than the previous one heading toward Cape Prince of Wales but nevertheless was well supplied with foreign trade goods. Beechey noted that they made fire not with a traditional bow drill, but with iron and pyrites. The women wore beads hanging from their ears and attached to their clothing, and the sailors were surprised that some of the women had bells sewn under their parkas: "When they moved," Beechey noted, "several bells were set ringing, and on examining their persons, we discovered that they had each three or four of these instruments under their clothes, suspended from their waists, hips, and one even lower down." Later, one of the Eskimos showed Beechey a Russian coin imprinted with the head of Empress Catherine and a halberd head that had been converted into a knife. Beechey concluded that this was "evidence of the communication that must exist between their tribe and those of the Asiatic coasts opposite."[36] Catherine the Great reigned from 1762 to 1796; this coin may have reached the region via Billings's visit to Bering Strait in 1791.

The next day the sailors and Eskimos did some trading, and in return for about one hundred pounds of fish and other things, the Eskimos received necklaces of blue beads, brooches, and cutlery. On shore, the captain's younger brother, Richard Beechey, noted that the Eskimos showed "surprise at my knocking off a small wooden bowl from the top of a post with my gun, particularly when they afterwards found it pierced with shot."[37]

On September 10 the barge rejoined the *Blossom* in Kotzebue Sound. After the barge separated from the *Blossom* at Icy Cape it had followed the coast north, and on August 23 had reached 71°23′ N. The British sailors saw no land to the east, west, or north. They were at the northernmost point of Alaska and nearly the northernmost point of continental North America. The men called it "World's End." Beechey renamed it Point Barrow in honor of the second secretary of the Admiralty. The barge's crew reported that the village there was the largest they had seen in the barge's voyage north from Icy Cape. Two umiaqs came out to the sailors, and their passengers seemed unsure whether they should approach the little schooner. The British gave the Eskimos tobacco and beads and later others visited the barge. The sailors bought some artifacts, but the natives tried to steal from them, and the British broke off contact, concluding that the Eskimos' aggressive behavior made it unsafe for them to go ashore to leave a message for Franklin.[38]

Elson then took the barge a mile northwest of the point for astronomical observations, but on its return to the point about twenty Eskimos armed with bows and arrows and spears confronted the barge. According to William Smyth, the Eskimos thought the British wished to land, and "they made signs for us to remain on board. They appeared quite prepared for hostilities, some of them nearly naked and, preserving a more than ordinary silence, but one spoke at a time, seemingly interrogating us with regard to our intentions. The natives kept walking abreast to us" as the barge worked its way south along shore. After several miles "our friends having tired of the chase stopped and after watching us for some time longer, returned." These Eskimos clearly regarded the British as a hostile force and were prepared to defend themselves.[39]

Twenty miles down the coast at Refuge Inlet things were entirely different for the explorers. After the sailors threw presents ashore and gave leaves of tobacco, the small group of natives received the sailors warmly, and later, when the pack ice closed in around the barge, trapping it near shore, they offered them food. One old man, after receiving beads and tobacco, offered what they "concluded to be a prayer, at the same time blowing with his mouth, as if imploring an east wind and the dispersion of the ice. — In the afternoon the wind had increased to a gale." The Eskimos later helped the men to haul the boat south with a track line.[40]

As soon as the barge returned to the *Blossom* at Chamisso Island Beechey sent it on a short exploratory trip through Eschscholtz Bay to the Buckland River. On the return, seven kayaks confronted the barge near Elephant Point. The Buckland River Eskimos—the same Eskimo nation that Shishmaryov had met in 1820—were "very troublesome, pestering [the British for tobacco and receiving it] in the most ungracious manner, without offering any [thing] in return."

On October 1, 1826, while searching for a channel into Hotham Inlet, Beechey landed at Sheshalik. The Eskimos there were very interested in the sailors' firearms, and to "satisfy one of them," Captain Beechey wrote, "I made him fire off a musket, that was loaded with ball. . . . The explosion and the recoil . . . so alarmed him, that he turned pale, and put away the gun. As soon as his fear subsided he laughed heartily, as did all his party, and went to examine the wood, which was found to be perforated by the ball."[41]

Later, on October 10, the barge's crew came upon three umiaqs carrying thirty or forty of the local Buckland River Eskimos. The Eskimos drew their knives and tried to board the vessel. "In their attempts to steal they were unusually daring: one of them on being forced back immediately drew his knife, accompanied with some threats. Mr. Elson declared that he never would have allowed himself to be treated in such a manner with impunity, had he not recollected the obstacles which might be thrown in the way of Capt. Franklin, should a rumor of hostilities between us and the natives get abroad." It appears that the Buckland River Eskimos were as aggressive as ever in the face of foreigners whom they outnumbered—and their ability to threaten Shishmaryov's party in 1820 may have contributed to this behavior with the British in 1826, with disastrous consequences in 1827, as we shall see.[42]

Later Beechey summarized his understanding of the Alaskan Eskimos' fondness for tobacco. "Smoking is their favorite habit," he wrote, "in which they indulge as long as their tobacco lasts. Parties assemble to enjoy the fumes of this narcotic, and the pipe passes round like the calumet of the Indians, but apparently without the ceremony being binding. Their pipes are short, and the bowls of some contain no more tobacco than can be consumed in a long whiff; indeed the great pleasure of the party often consists in individuals endeavouring to excel each other in exhausting the contents of the bowl at one breath, and many a laugh is indulged at the expense of him who fails, or who, as is very frequently the case, is thrown into a fit of coughing by the smoke getting into his lungs."

Elsewhere he described their pipes.

We witnessed a smoking party in which the women and children partook equally with the men. The pipe used on this occasion was small, and would contain no more tobacco than could be consumed with a whiff. To these instruments were attached a pricker and a strip of dog's skin, from the last of which they tore off a few hairs, and placed them at the bottom of the bowl of the pipe to prevent the tobacco, which was chopped up very fine, being drawn into the mouth with the smoke. The tobacco which they used had pieces of wood cut up fine with it, a custom which is no doubt derived from the Tschutschi, who use the bark of the birch-tree in this manner, and imagine it improves the quality of the herb. The pipe being charged with about a pinch of this material, the senior person present took his whiff and passed the empty pipe to the next, who replenished it and passed it on, each person inflating himself to the fullest extent, and gradually dissipating the fumes through the nostrils. The pungency of the smoke, and the time necessary to hold the breath, occasioned considerable coughing with some of the party, but they nevertheless appeared greatly to enjoy the feast.

Beechey added, "They seldom use tobacco in any other way than this, though some natives whom we saw to the southward of Beering's Strait were not averse to chewing it, and the St. Lawrence islanders indulged in snuff. Their predilection for tobacco is no doubt derived from the Tschutschi, who are so passionately fond of it, that they are said by Captain Cochrane to snuff, chew, and smoke, all at the same time. The practice of adulterating tobacco is common with the Tschutschi, and has, no doubt, passed from them to the Esquimaux, who often adopt it from choice. That which finds its way to this part of America is of a very inferior quality, and often has dried wood chopped up with it."[43]

STRUCTURE OF THE NATIVE TRADE

After his return to England, Beechey compared notes with Franklin and accurately concluded that a reliable trade must have been in operation, transporting goods from Siberia to a point of exchange in northern Alaska, and he predicted, in effect, the existence of the trade fair at Niġliq in the Colville River delta of northern Alaska. "It was remarked that the inhabitants of Point Barrow had copper kettles, and were in several respects better supplied with European articles than the people who resided to the southward," he wrote.

Captain Franklin found among the Esquimaux near the Mackenzie several of these kettles, and other manufactures, which were so unlike those supplied by the North-west Company [which merged with the Hudson's Bay Company in 1821], as to leave no doubt of their being obtained from the westward.
    Connecting these facts with the behaviour of the natives who visited us off Wainwright Inlet, and the information obtained by Augustus [Franklin's interpreter], it is very probable that between the Mackenzie River and Point Barrow there is an agent who receives these articles from the Asiatic coast, and parts with them in exchange for furs. Augustus learned from the Esquimaux that the people from whom these articles were produced resided up a river to the westward of Return Reef. The copper kettles, in all probability come from the Russians. . . . From the cautious manner in which the whole tribe dispose of their furs, reserving the most valuable for larger prices than we felt inclined to give, and sometimes producing only the inferior ones, we were induced to suspect that there are several Esquimaux acting as agents upon the coast properly instructed by their employers in Kamschatka, who, having collected the best

furs from the natives, cross over with them to the Asiatic coast, and return with the necessary articles for the purchase of others.[44]

A digression is necessary to understand the flow of trade goods that Beechey and Franklin had perceived. Depending on the location of their home territories, most of the Eskimo nations of northwestern Alaska were primarily oriented to exploiting the resources of either the sea or the interior; hence their trade was central to acquiring those commodities that were not available in their own homelands. For example, at the Sheshalik rendezvous the visitors from the nations of the interior brought products that the coastal dwellers required: caribou and Dall sheep hides, furs (marmot, ground squirrel, beaver, black and brown bear skins, ermine, fox, hare, lynx, marten, mink, muskrat, river otter, wolf, and wolverine), minerals for tools and weapon points, soapstone lamps and cooking pots, birch bark and other plant products, and ready-made clothing, among many other items. Likewise, the coastal dwellers traded to the inlanders whale and seal oil, sealskin rope, boot soles, sinew, waterproof boots, whale skin and blubber, dried seal meat, walrus ivory, certain varieties of driftwood, and other things as well. The visitors from the Chukchi Peninsula brought not only tobacco, beads, knives, pots, scissors, and needles, but also reindeer skins, which were highly prized for their distinctive color patterns, and wolverine and wolf skins. In return, the Asian traders mostly bartered for furs for the Asian markets but also for dried fish, ready-made clothing, soapstone lamps and pots (some of which the Alaskan Eskimos had acquired from other Eskimo traders farther east and which originated in Canada), and a variety of wooden utensils.[45]

The Sheshalik fair was, however, not the only point of exchange in northern and western Alaska. In the south, a summer rendezvous took place at Pastuliq, near the northernmost branch of the Yukon delta. There traders from the nearby Yup'ik-speaking Eskimo nations met with each other and with traders from Sledge Island, and probably with King Islanders as well. Traders also gathered at a winter fair at Aniliukhtapak, where the Yukon and Kuskokwim rivers most closely converge, and where Yup'ik peoples met the Athapascan-speaking Ingalik. Farther up the Yukon, at Nuklukayet, where the Tanana River enters, Koyukon met Tanana and Gwich'in in the summer. Native groups also met at a large fair in Port Clarence near Bering Strait, where traders from Eskimo nations on the Seward Peninsula and Norton Sound, King Island, and the Diomedes met Asian Eskimos and Chukchi traders. And as we have seen, traders from King Island and Sledge Island also met Chukchi traders on Big Diomede Island in Bering Strait.

In the north, smaller fairs took place. In the summer at Icy Cape traders from

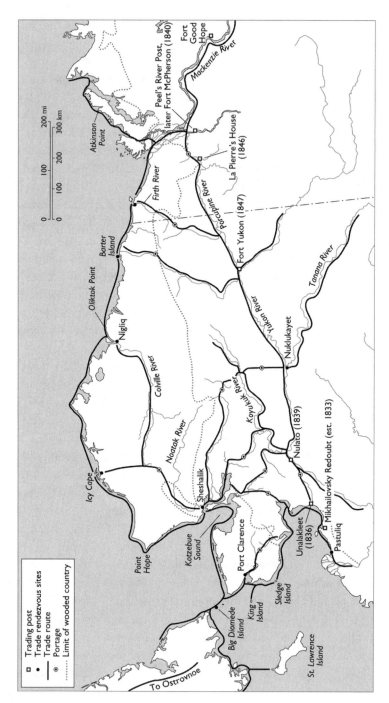

Map 6.1. Selected trade routes and portages in Alaska and adjacent regions.

nearby inland and coastal nations converged briefly, and in the winter, representatives of several interior-dwelling Eskimo nations gathered for similar exchanges near the headwaters of the Noatak and Colville rivers. But the largest fair north of Sheshalik took place near the arctic coast of Alaska at Niġliq in the Colville River delta, where, for the most part, representatives of the Eskimo nations dwelling in the Colville River drainage and adjacent areas met representatives from the lands surrounding Point Barrow. As with the fair at Sheshalik, at Niġliq the coastal-dwelling Eskimos brought maritime products, and the interior dwellers brought inland products. A single trader from the interior, often acting as an agent for others, might bring as many as five hundred to six hundred caribou hides to Niġliq.[46] Some of the traders from the interior might have visited the Sheshalik fair the summer before and, in that case, would have brought tobacco, beads, and metal products to exchange. In 1854 Dr. John Simpson noted that seventy-four persons, with fourteen umaiqs on their sleds, left Point Barrow in early July, bound for Niġliq.

Dr. John Simpson, the surgeon aboard HMS *Plover*, was the first European to understand the structure of the flow of trade goods in the Bering Strait region and northern Alaska.[47] Based on his experiences from 1848 to 1854 with the fleet searching for Sir John Franklin's Northwest Passage expedition, which had vanished in 1845, he wrote:

> At the Colville, the Nu-na-tang'-meun [interior-dwelling Eskimos] offer the goods procured at Se-su'-a-ling [Sheshalik] on Kotzebue Sound from the Asiatics, Kokh-lit' en'-yu-in [Chukotkans], in the previous summer, consisting of iron and copper kettles, women's knives (o-lu'), double-edged knives (pan'-na), tobacco, beads, and tin for making pipes; from their own countrymen on the Ko'-wak [Kobuk] River; stones for making labrets, and whetstones, or those ready made, arrow heads, and plumbago [graphite]. Besides these, are enumerated deer [caribou] and fawn skins, and coats made of them, the skin, teeth, and horns of the [Dall sheep], black fox, marten, and ermine skins, and feathers for arrows and head dresses.
>
> In exchange for these, the Point Barrow people . . . give the goods procured to the eastward the year before, and their own sea produce, namely, whale or seal oil, whalebone [baleen], walrus tusks, stout thong made from walrus hide, seal-skins, &c., and proceed with their new stock to [Barter Island]. Here they offer it to the . . . Western Mackenzie Esquimaux, and receive in return, wolverine, wolf, [Dall sheep], and [beluga whale] skins, thong of deerskin, [soapstone lamps]. . . .
>
> In the course of the winter, occasional trade takes place with the people of

Point Hope, but most of the knives, beads, [soapstone lamps], and wolverine skins, are taken to the Colville the following year, and, in the next after, make their appearance at Kotzebue Sound and on the coast of Asia.[48]

The soapstone lamps probably came from the Copper Eskimos, who quarried the soapstone near Tree River in Coronation Gulf in arctic Canada. Although Alexander Mackenzie reported a soapstone pot in an Eskimo encampment in the Mackenzie River delta in 1789, it is likely that, west of the Mackenzie River, the soapstone trade was carried on vigorously only from about 1800 to 1860. The trade probably began once the regular rendezvous between the Point Barrow Eskimos and the Mackenzie Eskimos began near Barter Island, around the beginning of the nineteenth century. This rendezvous, as we have seen, may well have become more important as a result of the increased flow of trade goods from Chukotka after the Ostrovnoe trade fair was established in 1789. The soapstone trade probably declined when metal pots and pans became readily available in the Western Arctic, although it may have continued in some form until the latter part of the nineteenth century.[49]

And it seems that this greater volume of trade goods may have been important in the increasing social stratification within Eskimo nations in northwestern Alaska in the early and middle nineteenth century. Wealthy individuals are known to have arisen among both the coastal and interior-dwelling nations at this time, indicating a shift "from the accumulation of food resources to trade — in skins, furs, and whale bone (baleen)," writes Ernest S. Burch, Jr. "The wealthy inlanders all seem to have lived near the upper reaches of large rivers, and they all seem to have come from families whose members specialized as traders." The inlanders, located as they were at the headwaters of important watersheds, would have had the advantage in trading both south to Sheshalik and north to Niġliq. George M. Stoney, who carried out explorations in the Kotzebue watershed in 1883 and 1884, described how some inland Eskimos traveled to the Sheshalik trade fair. "When the river breaks traveling begins, some go to the mountains, and others to the coast. Those going to the coast carry their families and all their possessions in large skin-boats (oomiaks) the owner steering and the others paddling enough to keep in the stream while the current takes the boat down. Two or three small families often go in one large boat. They follow a day or so behind the ice, reaching Hotham Inlet before it gets clear. Stops are made on the journey to catch fish for immediate use and for use at the trading station [Sheshalik]. A rich man travels in state; he never takes any other family than his own; he hires paddlers and a steersman; and enjoys all the luxuries he can."[50]

Once the Point Barrow people had finished trading at Niġliq, near the end of July some moved on, to Oliktok Point, east of the Colville delta. There they prepared to travel farther east, to the rendezvous near Barter Island, where, as Franklin had discovered in 1826, they met the westernmost Mackenzie Eskimos, members of the Herschel Island nation. The north coast of Alaska east of the Sagavanirktok River—which enters the Beaufort Sea near Prudhoe Bay—is relatively poor in resources and hence at that date did not support a permanent, year-round population:[51] Gwich'in hunted caribou there in the summer, while at the same time the Point Barrow Eskimos traveled along the coast to reach their trade rendezvous near Barter Island.

The Point Barrow traders usually left their women and children and many of their boats at Oliktok before they headed east. Unlike the Sheshalik and Niġliq fairs, the trade encounter at Barter Island in the early years was, as Franklin reported, overlain by intense mistrust between the visiting parties. "The conduct of the Point Barrow people in their intercourse with those of the Mackenzie . . . seems to be very wary," John Simpson wrote at midcentury, "as if they constantly keep in mind that they were the weaker party, and in the country of strangers. They describe themselves as taking up a position opposite the place of barter on a small island to which they can retreat on any alarm, and cautiously advance from it making signs of friendship."

Simpson was also shown a cuirass of lamellar armor that a Point Barrow Eskimo wore under his parka during the exchange at Barter Island. The owner, "Erk-sin-ra," said that it had come from Asia. It was composed of iron plates "about three inches long and ¾ of an inch broad perforated at the sides & stitched together with leather thongs. The iron plates formed four circles round the body which they fitted closely allowing perfectly free motion. He put it on next to his skin and over it a coat—then said he did not fear the thrust of a Kang-ma-li [Mackenzie Eskimo] knife when thus protected."[52]

Unlike the trading procedure that took place at the other fairs, wherein substantial portions of the goods were exchanged between established trading partners—and only after these exchanges were concluded would open-market trading take place—the Barter Island exchanges were carried out by open-market trading and as soon as the trade was done, the traders immediately retraced their steps. By the mid-nineteenth century, however, things were changing: "They say that great distrust was formerly manifested on both sides by the way in which goods were snatched and concealed when a bargain was made; but in later years more women go, and they have dancing and amusements, though they never remain long enough to sleep there."[53]

A summer trade rendezvous was nevertheless not the only mode of exchange between native groups in northern and western Alaska. Another highly important element in facilitating the flow of trade goods was the Messenger Festival. In a Messenger Festival members of one community invited another, usually in the depth of winter, via messengers, to visit them for a festival of dancing, feasting, entertainment, and trading. The trading usually took place between persons who had an established trading relationship.[54]

Apart from the trade fairs and Messenger Festivals, inter-national trade also took place between established trading partners on their own. Sidney Huntington, a Koyukon, described one of these inter-national trading relationships that went on in the last quarter of the nineteenth century.

Each March Grandfather traveled from the Koyukuk River up the Dakli River into Zane Hills, where he camped on the Dakli side of a low pass. This was as far as it was safe for him to venture. The mountainous land that lay before him, between Eskimo and Athapascan country, was then known as "No Man's Land."

Meanwhile Schilikuk would make his way up the Selawik River on the other side of the pass, his dogsled full of coastal products—sealskins, fawn caribou skins, mukluks (both waterproof and warm winter types), seal oil, salt, and walrus ivory. He would camp on the Selawik side, for he dared go no farther.

My grandfather would walk, alone and unarmed, to the pass, carrying a long pole. If he saw no sign of Schilikuk, he thrust his pole into the deep snow and returned to camp. Every day he snowshoed to the pass to see whether a second pole was planted in the snow beside his—the signal that Schilikuk had arrived and trading could begin.

When there were two poles in the snow, Grandfather took his loaded sled to the pass to meet Schilikuk. Each would lay everything out for the other's inspection. The Eskimo especially wanted fine wolverine furs, prized for use as a face liner in wolf-fur ruffs in the hoods of parkas. . . .

My grandfather was eager to get caribou fawn skins, which are easily made into soft winter undergarments and socks. Also in demand in the Koyukuk valley were seal oil, which is a high-energy food, walrus ivory tusks from which items could be carved, sealskins for winter outer garments, and tough-as-iron ropes made from walrus skin.

Each trader always went through the motions of being offended at the offers of the other. My grandfather, for example, would act insulted at an offer of three caribou fawn skins for one wolverine skin. He would pick out of the Eskimo's pile two or three more fawn skins and add them to the stack, insisting that this particular wolverine skin was worth at least five, maybe six fawn skins. Time wasn't important. They might haggle for days.[55]

Trade goods traveled a vast distance in northeastern Asia and northwestern North America. Hypothetically, the Russian trade goods that the Mackenzie Eskimos bought at Barter Island in 1826 might have been sent from Russia or China in 1823 and reached Yakutsk in 1824. Russian traders would then have carried them down the Kolyma River to Nizhne Kolymsk and onward to the Ostrovnoe fair in the early spring of 1825. From there Chukchi traders would have hauled them across Chukotka by reindeer sled to Cape Dezhnev, where they were traded to other Chukchi, who were probably joined by Asian Eskimos, carrying the goods in their umiaqs across Bering Strait to the Sheshalik fair on Kotzebue Sound in the summer of 1825. Inland-dwelling Eskimos might then have hauled the goods north and perhaps exchanged them at a winter Messenger Festival or in the summer of 1826 at Niġliq in northern Alaska. From Niġliq, Point Barrow Eskimos would have taken them by boat to the rendezvous with the Mackenzie Eskimos at Barter Island. From there the goods might have been traded eastward, to other Mackenzie Eskimos—or to Athapascan traders who would have carried them south, over the mountains. In 1848 Sir John Richardson reported that he saw Eskimos using Russian trade goods as far east as Atkinson Point, east of the Mackenzie delta. Other trade goods were no doubt passed on by the Mackenzie Eskimos to the Copper Eskimos.[56]

And the trade goods that Beechey's men exchanged with the Eskimos near Sheshalik in July 1826 may have been traded onward in any number of directions: over the inland route to Niġliq; up the rivers that drain into Kotzebue Sound; northwest along the coast to Point Hope and beyond; across Bering Strait to Asia; over the inland route from Kotzebue Sound to the Yukon drainage; to the trade fair at Port Clarence for distribution throughout the Seward Peninsula or, even farther, along the shores of Norton Sound via the Sledge Island traders or King Island traders, as far as Pastuliq, near the Yukon delta, and from there into the Yukon drainage to Aniliukhtapak and into the Kuskokwim River drainage or to Nuklukayet and up the Yukon.

Similarly, the westward flow of furs and other products that passed from North America to Asia could have originated as far east as the Mackenzie delta and then changed hands at Barter Island, Niġliq, and Sheshalik. At Sheshalik they would have been carried by Chukchi or Siberian Eskimo traders to the western shore of Bering Strait, where Chukchi traders would have carried them to Ostrovnoe or other fairs in northeastern Asia. Furs from the lower and middle Yukon might have been exchanged at Nuklukayet or another trade rendezvous. They then might have reached the coast of Norton Sound, at Pastuliq or Unalakleet, where they passed into the hands of King Islanders or Sledge Islanders who carried them to Port Clarence or Big Diomede. From there the Chukchi and Siberian Eskimo traders would have carried them across Bering Strait.

Once the furs had been collected at the Ostrovnoe fair, they would have been carried to Nizhne Kolymsk and then to Yakutsk, on the Lena. There they would have been sorted, with some of the best skins going to St. Petersburg and to Leipzig (where they would possibly have been mingled with some skins that had been carried out of Alaska eastbound via the Hudson's Bay Company), but the majority would have gone south to Irkutsk and onward to Kiakhta, Mai-mai-ch'eng, and to Beijing. A skin from the Mackenzie delta might have traveled more than six thousand miles to reach Beijing, and, later, as we shall see in chapter 10, once the Hudson's Bay Company's trade goods reached the arctic coast, the eastern end of the trade network became Great Britain. Thus, barring the distance between St. Petersburg and London, the globe had been girdled by a boreal trade network, a substantial portion of which was in native hands.

THE EXPEDITION IN PORT CLARENCE AND KOTZEBUE SOUND, 1827

When the *Blossom* departed Kotzebue Sound in 1826, Beechey took it to San Francisco, to Honolulu, and to Macau. The following spring the *Blossom* stopped again in Petropavlovsk, Kamchatka, where the crew surveyed and sounded the harbor, work which produced charts that were valuable to the Anglo-French fleet in 1854 and 1855 during their assaults on the town in the Crimean War. On August 2, 1827, the *Blossom* anchored off Cape Rodney on the southwestern Seward Peninsula. There the crew hoisted out the barge. Under Elson's command the barge was to continue its coastal surveys. Beechey wanted to explore the coast between capes Rodney and Prince of Wales and, in particular, to check on the Eskimos' reports that there was a large bay southeast of Bering Strait.

A few days later the barge entered the large body of water that is enclosed by Point Spencer's long sandspit. They were not the first foreigners to appreciate its size and protection. Eliab Grimes had visited it aboard the *General San Martín* eight years before. Beechey would later name it Port Clarence in honor of his godfather, the duke of Clarence, who later became King William IV. On August 5, on the east shore of Port Clarence, the barge came upon two umiaqs carrying twenty men and two women. The British tried to trade with them for a fine otter skin, but "the owner seemed well aware [that it] was valuable," wrote James Wolfe. "Beads he entirely rejected, a hatchet was then offered, which I think would have gained it, had he not unfortunately espied a small sauce pan; afterwards nothing else would please him; but as the useful utensil could not be spared, he went away with his skin." When the barge returned to the *Blossom* at Chamisso Island on August 11, Elson confirmed to Captain Beechey the existence of Port Clarence. He added that one of the natives there had drawn a map of the area that corresponded to the outline drawn at Chamisso the summer before by one of the Eskimos from Cape Prince of Wales.[57]

On August 13 at Chamisso Island two umiaqs containing some of their "old friends" (Buckland River Eskimos) arrived at the ship. One man offered to trade a muskrat skin for Beechey's epaulettes. The sailors recognized that some members of this group had been among the thirty or forty Buckland River Eskimos who had threatened to attack the barge near Elephant Point on October 10, 1826. The next day the natives visited the ship again and one of them drew a knife on Lieutenant George Peard, who wrote that "one or two of them [were] inclined to be troublesome." The Captain, not trusting them, thought this group was "dirty, noisy, and impudent." They left the ship late at night but returned a few hours later and found the sailors washing the decks. "They probably expected that we should be fast asleep," he wrote, "and that they would have an opportunity of appropriating to themselves some of the moveable articles upon deck. There was otherwise no reason for returning so soon; and from what we afterwards saw of these people, there is every reason to believe that was their real motive."[58]

In company with the barge, the *Blossom* left Kotzebue Sound on August 14 for the north, again searching for Franklin's party. When they were south of Icy Cape, Beechey gave Lieutenant Edward Belcher command of the barge and ordered it to continue north. The *Blossom* then headed south to explore Port Clarence. The *Blossom* spent a week surveying and charting Port Clarence, and the men noted that the Eskimos there were well supplied with iron. "Among the inhabitants of the village on the northern shore," Captain Beechey wrote, "there were several girls with massive iron bracelets. One had a curb chain for a necklace, and another a bell suspended in front, in the manner described in the preceding year at Choris Peninsula." Others had brass-inlaid iron-headed spears in the shape of halberds, which the Eskimos must have received from the Chukchi traders. The sailors also found that the Eskimos had a good idea of the relative value of their furs: the price for a silver fox or an otter skin was a hatchet apiece.[59]

One girl had a musket's hammer hanging from her neck "and held it so sacred that she would scarcely submit it to examination, and afterwards carefully concealed it within her dress." It is tempting to speculate that this hammer may have come from the gun that William J. Pigot, aboard the *Pedlar*, had sold to the King Island chief in 1820. King Island is close to Port Clarence, and if the gun's owner had been unable to procure ammunition for the firearm, as is likely, he may have broken it up for the metal. The hammer may have been traded to the Port Clarence Eskimos.

In Grantley Harbor, an inner embayment of Port Clarence, the men learned about the extent of the Eskimos' summer travel. The sailors came upon some Eskimos who were tending their fishing nets and remembered that they had met them at Chamisso Island the summer before. It was also here that they saw another group from Cape Prince of Wales that they had encountered in Kotzebue Sound the same summer.

On September 10 the *Blossom* returned to Chamisso Island, and Beechey learned that the barge had been wrecked in a gale and was a total loss. The barge had returned from Icy Cape, and three days before the *Blossom*'s arrival the crew had been working ashore on the Choris Peninsula, hauling driftwood to build an observatory. Belcher had anchored the barge in shallow water very near shore. Suddenly a strong southwest wind sprang up, sending heavy seas onto the barge. The steep waves soon had the barge pounding on the bottom and swamped it. Belcher, in command, tried to save the crew on board by going out to her with a small boat, but while they were launching, the breakers swiftly destroyed it. Some Eskimos were nearby with an umiaq. They apparently understood the futility of trying to launch a boat against the wind in the gale. Belcher, however, forced them at pistol point to carry the boat to the water. With a crew of Eskimos and sailors he then launched it twice, but the seas drove it ashore. Because of Belcher's lack of foresight three of the crew drowned and the barge was pounded to pieces.[60]

The remains of the barge now littered the shore, and the Eskimos began salvaging the wreckage. Belcher, "an able if disagreeable officer" who was at once "active, intelligent, bombastic, querulous, warlike and forthright," considered this to be an act of vandalism and forced them to return as much of the flotsam as he could. "The natives picked up what things drifted on shore," James Wolfe reported, "particularly pleased with the iron and copper and even went off to get what they could from the wreck. This very natural conduct appears to have excited the displeasure of Lieut. Belcher, and when our cutter [from the *Blossom*] landed he made signal for more assistance & fire arms, he supposing that if one of the natives were seized and taken on board every thing would be returned."[61]

Belcher did, in fact, seize one of the Eskimos—who ironically had been trying to cooperate with him in retrieving some of the wreckage—and forcibly took him aboard the *Blossom* to be held in captivity until the goods were returned. The man's family came out to the *Blossom* in an umiaq, offering to return some of the wreckage and ransom him for furs, but Belcher refused to release him until most of the salvage from the wreckage was turned over to the British.[62]

Some of the *Blossom*'s officers were appalled at Belcher's ham-handed actions. Three days later, on September 13, the British released that Eskimo prisoner and sent him ashore. James Wolfe summarized his thoughts on the incident:

> We found no benefit arising from the method we had pursued. The fact was Lieut. Belcher was a great loser by this unfortunate accident and among other things was a valuable theodolite which he suspected was in the hands of these natives, but I believe it was not the case. Whilst the hostage was detained on board, he was treated with the greatest kindness, and many presents made him, yet he evinced a very natural dislike to his situation, and would frequently burst into tears; probably the idea of captivity was before unknown to him, and the uncertainty of his fate with the absence of his family & friends must have awakened a new train of feelings, powerful enough to unman a mind supported by the aid of religion or philosophy. When he was liberated many contributed to make up a quantity of beads, tobacco &c &c and I confess I was heartily glad to see him free.[63]

Later two umiaqs full of Buckland River Eskimos came alongside the *Blossom*, and Captain Beechey recognized some of the men who had threatened the crew of the barge near Elephant Point on October 10, 1826. They were the same men who had again acted aggressively when aboard the ship on August 14, 1827. The group came aboard, but later, when the sailors ordered the natives to leave the ship, "They took no notice of our signs," George Peard wrote, "but when the Gunner motioned to them with a cutlass, they got ready their bows and shewed they were determined to have their own way. However, on a musket being levelled at them they made off, but held up their weapons in defiance, pointing to shore, and uttering what we constructed from their gestures to be threats and imprecations." The next day on Chamisso Island they threatened both a watering party and a group of five sailors who were digging a grave for one of the drowned sailors.[64]

On September 29, the tensions that had smoldered for a fortnight erupted. A watering party was ashore at Chamisso when the sailors aboard the *Blossom* spotted an umiaq with eight Buckland River Eskimo men and a boy heading toward the island. Worried that the shore party might be in danger, Lieutenant George Peard sent a cutter with an armed crew under Belcher's command to protect the sailors there. Peard ordered Belcher to drive the Eskimos away if they "proved to be any of the same party that had so lately distinguished themselves for daring and insolence." Once the cutter reached the island things seemed to be going well, with the Eskimos offering to trade some furs for tobacco, which none of the sailors had with them at the time. The sailors recognized only one of the Eskimos who earlier had threatened the shore party, but Belcher, spotting an Eskimo carrying away a piece of wreckage holding some nails, ordered him to put it down — although, unknown to Belcher, one of the midshipmen had given it to the native.[65]

The Eskimos then went back to their umiaq, and the sailors pushed it off. But the natives paddled back to shore, to be pushed out again. This was repeated several times, while at the same time the Eskimos, according to Captain Beechey, "were occupied in preparations for hostility, by putting on their eider-duck frocks over their usual dresses, and uncovering their bows and arrows." They then started paddling their umiaq sideways toward shore and Belcher fired a musket ball between the boat and the beach, waving at them to leave. Instead, the Eskimos ran the boat ashore, wrapped other skins around themselves and ran up a steep bank. They fired their arrows at the sailors from more than one hundred yards and wounded one or two of the men.

The sailors returned fire and hit an Eskimo who had inexplicably remained behind to disable the umiaq by cutting a hole in its skin cover. A bullet struck him in the thigh but he managed to limp away to join the others, all of whom retreated into one of the gullies in the hillside, occasionally firing arrows as they went.[66]

James Wolfe, aboard the *Blossom*, described what happened next.

By this time we had a gun ready from the Ship and perceiving the natives crawling over the brow of a cliff fired a shot at them, which tho' it fell short, evidently threw them into the greatest consternation, and they ran to & fro not knowing where to go. When the firing had ceased Mr. Belcher divided his party now of 21 . . . into two intending to proceed to the assistance of the Master & Purser who were on the other side of the island in the direction which some of the natives seem to have taken, when the second Cutter arrived . . . [with] the Captain . . . he took command and ascended the hill, proposing to secure the persons of the natives and take them on board the Ship.

A small party consisting of the Serjeant & four marines was detached along the edge of the Cliff to reconnoitre, while the main body was about 30 yards within them; in this manner they had not advanced more than 20 yards, when a cry was heard, and three of the five marines were seen stretched on the ground, one of them had received an arrow thro' the arm which transfixed it to his side, another in the head and a third a little above the wrist and then; a fourth was also struck on the wrist but owing to his being very thickly clothed just on the spot the arrow scarcely raised the skin.[67]

The natives were lying in a small ravine, concealed by tall grass. They fired on the marines from only five or six yards away. The marines returned fire, "shot away two of their bayonets and were ordered to fall back," George Peard reported. "Mr. Elson hastening to the spot where he observed the firing, and approaching close to the same ravine but on the other side of it saw three fellows adjusting their arrows; he immediately leveled his piece at one of them not more than half a dozen yards off, gave the poor wretch the contents (a ball over a charge of duck shot) and retreated to the rest of the party."[68]

After the gunfire, Beechey ordered his men to lay down their arms. He then walked alone toward the Eskimo positions, making signs of friendship. Meanwhile the Eskimos were busy building a low breastwork of mud and clumps of sod. After an hour an Eskimo elder, covered in mud, came forward and motioned for the British to leave. Beechey then ordered his men to return to the ship. They towed the natives' umiaq with them to keep them isolated on Chamisso Island. "I thought that by detaining them," he wrote, "we should be able to convince them our resentment was unjustifiably provoked, and that when they conducted themselves properly, they should command our friendship."[69]

The following evening the temperature fell to 30°F, and the captain sent the natives' skins and some seal meat to the island. The sailors left these in front of a fire, and they returned to the ship for the night. In the morning they found that the Eskimos had not taken the meat or skins. The Eskimos probably suspected a trap. The sailors then left the umiaq, which they had repaired, and some tobacco and beads to pay for three knives and some bows and arrows that Beechey had confiscated.[70] The next day the British noticed that the umiaq had been moved and was now hidden in some bushes.

On October 5, the last day the *Blossom* was in Kotzebue Sound, George Peard went ashore:

At 5 PM. Mr. Elson, Mr. Collie and myself obtained leave to examine the ravine[,] the scene of action on Chamisso Island. We found that part of it where the marines were wounded, three or four feet deep, and two holes on one side and three on the other dug partly under the bank, free from snow, large enough to hold one or two persons in a sitting posture, and in a single instance communicating with each other under ground.

Here we discovered a poor fellow laying under the snow athwart the ditch most likely in the same position he fell after receiving the fatal wounds, three of which we remarked on his face, as if from buck shot. His quiver full of arrows remained slung at his back and his bow had been placed under his head. My companions recognized him as one of the leaders in the late fray; and no doubt he met his death from Mr. Elson's gun. Several broken arrows were laying about the Spot.[71]

It was the first recorded killing of an Eskimo by a European in northwestern Alaska. Later in the evening the *Blossom* sailed from Kotzebue Sound. No British ships would return to Bering Strait for twenty-one years, and when they did, they were in search of Sir John Franklin's Northwest Passage expedition, which vanished in the Arctic in 1845.

7

MIKHAILOVSKY REDOUBT

FYODOR PETROVICH LITKE'S EXPEDITION

While Beechey was at Bering Strait with the *Blossom*, a Russian naval expedition was also under way to the North Pacific. In August 1826, the *Moller*, commanded by Mikhail Nikolaevich Staniukovich, and the *Seniavin*, commanded by Fyodor Petrovich Litke, a widely experienced arctic navigator, left Kronshtadt for the Pacific Ocean. Among other tasks, the *Moller* was to survey the Aleutians and Alaska Peninsula, while the *Seniavin* was to concentrate on the Bering Sea and eastern coasts of Asia. The government sent this expedition to carry out hydrographic surveys of the coasts of Russian America and northeastern Asia, but just as Franklin's explorations were valuable to the Hudson's Bay Company, Litke's observations, both cartographic and ethnographic, would prove useful to the Russian-American Company in its plans to expand its trading operations toward Bering Strait.

The *Seniavin*, with a cargo for the Russian-American Company, reached Novo-Arkhangelsk in June 1827, but there was no manpower to spare to unload the *Seniavin*, so the *Seniavin*'s crew, in addition to carrying out their own repairs, was forced to move thirty-five tons of goods from the lowest tier in the ship's hold and replace them with rock ballast. After five weeks in Novo-Arkhangelsk, Litke headed west and surveyed the coasts of Unalaska, the Pribilof Islands, and St. Matthew Island before the autumn weather forced him to sail for Petropavlovsk, Kamchatka, where Beechey in HMS *Blossom* had touched only a few months before.

In July 1828, the *Seniavin* reached Bering Strait and put into St. Lawrence Bay to rate the ship's chronometers and carry out repairs. To the Russians' surprise, Chukchi came out to the ship and were extremely friendly—and ready to trade.

Figure 7.1. Chukchi summer camp at St. Lawrence Bay, 1828. When the *Seniavin* visited St. Lawrence Bay in 1828, the expedition's artist recorded a number of details of the natives' lives. Three of the Chukchi wear *kamleikas*, sea mammal intestine rain shirts. Inflated intestines, the raw material for rain shirts, are drying at the base of the tent. The women wear their usual reindeer-skin overalls and are adorned with beads.
Salmon are drying on the ridgepole of the tent and rack, out of reach of the dogs. The man at the right holds a harpoon. An inflated sealskin drag float, which is shown stored on the top of the tent, would have been attached to a harpoon head by a long line for use in capturing whales, walruses, and seals. A gutted seal is on the ground at the right, and intestines are on the ground at the left. Another sealskin is shown in the foreground; it probably contained sea mammal oil. Several foreign trade items are also shown—among them, a bottle, a metal knife, and a metal pot. The Chukchi may have acquired these by trading walrus tusks, which are scattered about in the foreground (Litke 1835, pl. 45).

Five days later the *Seniavin* carried its surveys down the coast to Mechigmen-sky Bay. There a group of St. Lawrence Bay Chukchi joined them again, having traveled overland. Some of the natives wore the silver medals that Shishmaryov had given them when the *Blagonamerenny* visited the Chukchi Peninsula in 1821. Litke continued his survey among the islands on the eastern coast of the Chukchi Peninsula and then proceeded along the shore of the Gulf of Anadyr.

Next he headed to Petropavlovsk and on to Kronshtadt, where he ended the voyage in 1829.

It was clear to Litke that things had changed substantially at Bering Strait in the twelve years since Kotzebue's visit of 1816. It is a measure of how well acquainted the natives had become with the visits of foreign ships that in Holy Cross Bay (Zaliv Kresta) in Anadyr Gulf the Chukchi could not understand why the *Seniavin*'s company was not interested in buying walrus tusks from them. Litke reported that those Chukchi who had interacted with the Russians at the Gizhiga fair and at Ostrovnoe had developed what he called a "russo-tchouktchi" style of dress that incorporated manufactured fabrics. And he noted that whereas Kotzebue had met a few Chukchi at Cape Dezhnev who did not use tobacco, all of the Chukchi he saw were so passionately fond of it that they would prefer a leaf of tobacco in trade to an axe or a metal pot. Each Chukchi, he reported, carried a wooden pipe, inlaid with lead or tin designs, in his or her boot. The Chukchi smoked pulverized tobacco leaves; they filled the inside of the pipe with wood shavings to filter the tobacco oils from the smoke, so that when they had finished puffing their tobacco they could then smoke the oily shavings.[1]

Litke also confirmed the existence of the cross–Bering Strait trade. He found that those "sedentary" Chukchi who lived on the coast closest to Bering Strait were in regular contact with the natives on the American shore. The sedentary Chukchi received their trade goods from the nomadic "reindeer" Chukchi, who spent about half of the year in the lands near the sedentary Chukchi. The sedentary Chukchi, Litke noted, provided the reindeer Chukchi with walrus hides, seal skins, whale and seal oil, and walrus tusks in return for knives and halberds, iron and copper pots, and tobacco.

Litke learned that the commerce of the region involved several trade fairs. The reindeer Chukchi could now visit three trade fairs: one on the Kolyma (Ostrovnoe on the Maly Aniui River), another near Gizhiga, and the third on the Anadyr River. The Ostrovnoe fair was the largest. The poorest of the three was the Gizhiga fair, which took place in February on the open tundra, about 250 miles northeast of Gizhiga. Only two or three merchants went there, accompanied by a few dozen Cossacks, a commissar, and sometimes a cannon for protection from the Chukchi (which was no longer necessary). They left Gizhiga in January, searching for the Chukchi. A few "sedentary" Koyaks also joined them. When the two parties met, they set up their tents and the fair began, lasting a few days. To this fair the Chukchi brought fox and marten skins, walrus tusks, reindeer skins, and live reindeer, which they traded mostly for tobacco but also for iron articles, pots, and cloth, some of which would be traded to the sedentary natives in the eastern Chukchi Peninsula. Litke could not have known it, of course, but he had thus confirmed Eliab Grimes's report of 1819 to John Ebbets that Chukchi, carrying Alaskan furs, were known to visit trade fairs both on the Kolyma watershed and near Gizhiga.

The third fair took place on the Anadyr River about 150 miles from its mouth. Litke reported that this fair was the domain of a "merchant of Kargopol," Pyotr Baranov, the brother of Aleksandr Baranov, the first chief manager of the Russian-American colony. Litke may have gotten some of his facts wrong, but he noted that the Baranov brother hired about twenty hunters, who with their wives and children lived in a settlement protected by several cannons, which had not been fired in living memory. In January and February groups of reindeer Chukchi, Koryak, and Even (Lamut) visited the settlement for a fair that lasted about three weeks. He understood that the Russians traded the usual items for red fox, sea lion, beaver, sable, otter, arctic fox (both blue and white), walrus tusks, and marten and ground squirrel parkas.

Litke also stated that sedentary Chukchi from the coasts of the entire Gulf of Anadyr participated in a fourth rendezvous, at the mouth of the Anadyr River. Fifty Chukchi umiaqs, or more, gathered there in the summer to trade and hunt. Some boats then headed upriver to Baranov's post, bringing walrus tusks to trade for tobacco. Litke learned that on the return downriver, a forty-pound parcel of tobacco "that would not cost more than 50 roubles in Izhiga, [the hunters] paid 20 red fox, 30 pairs of walrus tusks and some arctic fox, a price that, in local terms, was equivalent of at least 500 roubles."

"This is a pretty good trade," Litke added, "even allowing for the cost of overland transport from Izhiga to Anadyr. Moreover, the [Russian] workers themselves trap fox, sable and wolverine in winter and in summer hunt reindeer and catch fish, providing an abundant supply throughout the summer."[2]

ETHOLEN, TEBENKOV, AND WRANGELL

While Litke's expedition was underway from Russia, Matvei Ivanovich Muravyov became the chief manager of the Russian-American colony. Muravyov had only recently arrived in Novo-Arkhangelsk in 1820 when William J. Pigot and the *Pedlar* touched there, just ahead of the orders from St. Petersburg that forbade foreign vessels from trading in the territories and waters that Russia claimed in the North Pacific. As a result of these strictures, during much of Muravyov's incumbency he was forced to concentrate on obtaining supplies to feed the colony, which was often on the "brink of starvation." These efforts and his own declining health prevented him from vigorously expanding the company's operations northward, although he did send out Khramchenko and Etholen in 1821 and 1822 (see chapter 5).[3]

By the time Pyotr Yegorovich Chistiakov replaced Muravyov at the end of 1825, the problem of supplying food to the colony had improved somewhat: the treaties with the United States (1824) and Great Britain (1825) opened the coast again to foreign commerce. In St. Petersburg the Main Office of the Russian-American Company, recognizing that the exports of sea otter skins had declined steeply, recommended that Chistiakov expand the company's activities northward into the interior and to the shores of Norton Sound to find new sources of furs, especially beavers and river otters.[4]

Building on the reconnaissance of 1821 and 1822, Chistiakov sent Etholen on his third northern voyage in 1830. This time Etholen took command of the brig *Chichagov* to survey the perimeter of Norton Sound and to call at Sledge Island and King Island. Etholen was also ordered to "visit the settlements of the Chukchi on the Asiatic coast, attempting everywhere to expand the company's trade relations and to gather data on the most suitable means for bartering furs." He was instructed to impress upon the coastal natives that "henceforth a vessel will come to them for trade every year in order to wean them from taking their furs to the Chukchi."[5]

Etholen departed Novo-Arkhangelsk in June and headed for St. Lawrence Island, but foul weather forced him east, to Golovnin Bay in Norton Sound, and from there he touched at Sledge Island and King Island before crossing back to the Asian coast and entering St. Lawrence Bay. In St. Lawrence Bay dangerous drifting pack ice kept the *Chichagov* constantly on the move for fifteen days; nevertheless the Chukchi from a wide area came to the brig with walrus ivory and furs. Etholen then sailed to St. Lawrence Island, where he identified five native settlements and learned that the natives there mostly hunted walruses, whose tusks were their main commodity in their trade with the Chukchi. From there Etholen moved on to St. Matthew Island and the Pribilofs before returning to Novo-Arkhangelsk.

At Novo-Arkhangelsk Etholen reported to the new chief manager, Baron Ferdinand Petrovich Wrangell. Etholen advised Wrangell that the company should establish a station on Stuart Island, northeast of the Yukon delta, for trade with the natives of Norton Sound and the Yukon River.[6] Wrangell agreed with Etholen. Wrangell, as we have seen in chapter 3, had carried out his own explorations in northeastern Siberia and on the Chukchi Peninsula and understood the realities of life in those regions. Wrangell knew that Alaskan furs and walrus ivory flowed to the Chukchi via two main routes. He understood that once the Chukchi had become traders, their formerly hostile relations with the Alaskan natives had been replaced by "friendly trade," and that the Diomede Islands had become a point of exchange between the Eskimos and the Chukchi. The Chukchi traveled there "by baidar [umiaq] in summer and by dogsled in winter, bringing Russian goods and reindeer skins." They also traveled to St. Lawrence Island, "leaving warm clothing and tobacco in return for large walrus tusks." They also established trade with the King Islanders who received tobacco, beads, and, especially, reindeer clothing for their walrus ivory. Most important, however, Wrangell knew that the Chukchi also had forged close trade relations with the Sledge Islanders.

The following year, 1831, Wrangell sent Lieutenant Mikhail Dmitrievich Tebenkov north in command of the brig *Chichagov* to trade at Golovnin Bay, Stuart Island, Sledge Island, King Island, St. Lawrence Island, and Mechigmensky Bay on the Chukchi Peninsula. Etholen had allowed the natives of Golovnin Bay to buy trade goods on credit, and Tebenkov was ordered to try to acquire beaver and river otter pelts in repayment. If he was successful, he was to offer them twice the amount of tobacco that Etholen had given them—with the goal of receiving payment the following year.

Wrangell offered these generous advances because he wanted to capture the furs that the Chukchi traders were carrying out of Russian America to the Asian fairs. His understanding of the structure of the intercontinental native trade at Bering Strait was that the Sledge Islanders had by that date become the dominant middlemen in the trade between Norton Sound and the rendezvous with the Chukchi on Big Diomede Island. Wrangell stated:

Aziak [Sledge] Island . . . is no greater in circumference than Ukivok [King Island]. . . . The inhabitants call themselves Aziakmiuts. . . . They surpass all their neighbors in trading ability, and were in consequence employed by the Chukchi as agents. The Aziakmiuts met the Chukchi on the island of Imaklit [Big Diomede Island] . . . receiving Russian goods and warm clothing which they were to barter for furs along the American coast.

Every year, during the first few days of July, about 10 [umiaqs] with 100 fully armed men set out to trade along the coast to the south, following the rivers and bartering furs with tribes living there. Finally they reached the mouth of the Pastol [Pastuliq], where the proceeds from the hunt in the interior, particularly from the rivers Kvikpak [Yukon] and Kuskokvim and from the sea coast as far as Nunivok [Island] and the mouth of the Kuskokvim, were assembled. During the course of the year, the Pastolmiuts [Pastulirmiut] (people living on the Pastol) handled all the furs and walrus tusks produced by the tribes and awaited the arrival of the Aziakmiuts, who returned to Imaklit [Big Diomede] as soon as they had loaded their baidars with the goods bartered.

In this way the Chukchi provided the inhabitants of a coastal strip about [1,100 miles] in length with Russian goods, and this takes into account only the coastal fringe. If the Russian-American Company had not erected forts at Nushagak and in the bay of Kenai, there is no doubt that the Russian goods brought by the Chukchi from Kolymsk [the Ostrovnoe trade fair], i.e., cauldrons, knives, tobacco and glass beads, would have reached Kenai after traveling more than [1,900 miles] (the goods are brought across the land of the Chukchi by reindeer and later transported in open boats). Thus far did Chukchi trade influence extend.[7]

Wrangell had a two-part plan for gaining control of the flow of furs that were crossing Bering Strait to Asia: not only would he try to intercept the Asian products that were heading to Alaska by buying them from the Chukchi at Mechigmensky Bay, but also he would try to intercept the Alaskan furs that were heading to Asia. To do the former, Wrangell instructed Tebenkov to try to persuade the Mechigmensky Bay Chukchi that it would be more convenient to trade with the company's ships than to visit the Ostrovnoe trade fair or to go to Anadyr. Wrangell saw his opportunity to do the latter when Tebenkov reported that he had found an anchorage near Stuart Island, about sixty miles from the Yukon delta, and that the natives had asked for a Russian trader to be stationed there. No doubt the natives near Stuart Island recognized the advantages of having access to a source of trade goods other than from the Sledge Islanders. Tebenkov added prophetically that a trading post on Stuart Island should be well manned and fortified because the Sledge Islanders and the Chukchi were likely to take hostile action against any attempt to undercut their positions as middlemen in the intercontinental native trade, as they annually swept up the furs on their way to the rendezvous at Pastuliq, near the Yukon delta.

At first the native trade from the company's ship was substantial and profitable. In 1831, for example, from the Nushagak River north, Tebenkov in the *Chichagov* collected 239½ beavers, 4 river otters, 12 cross foxes, 96 red foxes, 4 blue foxes, 40 white foxes, 11 lynxes, 86 martens, 6,840 pounds of walrus tusks, and 756 pounds of baleen. The value of these commodities at Irkutsk was 31,636 rubles in return for goods valued at 1,016 rubles in colonial prices.[8]

To break into the Chukchi trade at Mechigmensky Bay—and thus to seize the role of middleman in the cross–Bering Strait trade—Wrangell requested the following trade goods: 100 smoking pipes (copper and tin); 200 Russian axes; 700 Yakutsk knives with sheaths; 30 iron ladles; 50 ship carpenter's saws and bow saws; 540 pounds of iron kettles; 200 fire steels; several types of beads, belt buckles, and needles; 50 spears; 100 scissors; 200 thimbles; 300 combs; 300 earrings with large pendant beads; 300 bracelets; and small bells and jingles.[9]

Although Wrangell also wanted to break the trade link between the Sledge Islanders and the Chukchi, he did not have sufficient manpower to set up the post in Norton Sound at once, but he did send Tebenkov north again in the *Chichagov* in 1832 to try to buy furs at Stuart Island and nearby before the Sledge Island traders arrived there. Wrangell also asked for information about the Yukon River peoples. Tebenkov carried out his orders, visiting the same places that he had the previous year, collecting furs and issuing goods on credit. Wrangell furthermore instructed Tebenkov to buy reindeer-skin clothing at Mechimensky Bay for resale to the King Islanders and St. Lawrence Islanders. This was another effort to become the middleman. Wrangell added that the Kolyma merchants "value foxes much more in comparison with other goods, and walrus tusks lower, than accepted in our trade. This circumstance should be turned to our advantage by bartering from the Chukchi primarily walrus tusks (of large and medium size) and reindeer clothing, paying 2 and 2¾ times less than the Kolyma prices, 4 times less than the Kolyma prices for foxes and arctic foxes. . . . In this way the Chukchi, in hope of obtaining good receipts for foxes at Kolyma, will more willingly let us have walrus tusks and reindeer clothing at reduced prices. . . . It is also no advantage for us to attract the Chukchi completely away from Kolyma, where they receive such high payment for foxes of all sorts. We should try to obtain through trade, both on the Asian coast and the American, goods produced locally and not resold goods." Wrangell also sent "a small quantity of rum for regaling the toyons [chiefs] on the Asian coast but added, "do not accustom the [Eskimos] to the use of spirits."[10]

FOUNDING MIKHAILOVSKY REDOUBT

By the end of 1832 Wrangell had received enough supplies and men to set up a post near the Yukon delta, and in 1833 he again sent Tebenkov north, this time in command of the bark *Urup*, carrying precut timbers to build the trading post, not at Stuart Island but nearby. He found a site close to the mainland on the southeastern shore of a small treeless island (see front endpaper map). As soon as the fort was well underway Tebenkov sailed to Golovnin Bay, Sledge Island, King Island, and then crossed to Mechigmensky Bay and St. Lawrence Island. On his return to Norton Sound he found that the construction of Mikhailovsky Redoubt (in honor of Tebenkov's name saint) was going well, and he left seventeen men there under the command of Ivan Kuzmin, with instructions to develop a trade with the natives.

At the end of the summer Kuzmin sent Andrei Glazunov up the coast to investigate a report that the natives near Unalakleet, on the eastern shore of Norton Sound, had plenty of furs to trade. At Unalakleet Glazunov met a group of Koyukon who had portaged over from the Yukon via the Unalakleet River to await the arrival of the Sledge Island traders. Glazunov went back to Mikhailovsky to collect sufficient trade goods, but when he returned to Unalakleet, the Sledge Islanders were already there; protecting their monopoly, they threatened Glazunov and forced him to retreat quickly to save his own life. Later, a group of Sledge Islanders passed Mikhailovsky, heading for the native trade rendezvous at Pastuliq, and rumors were abroad that they, with the aid of local Eskimos, would attack the post. The attack did not take place in 1833, but the Russians had little success that winter in establishing trade relations with the natives.

The next summer, 1834, Wrangell sent two vessels north: the brig *Okhotsk*, commanded by D. F. Chernov, and the schooner *Kvikhpak*, under Aleksandr Filippovich Kashevarov. Because they assumed that the Alaskan natives would begin trading at Mikhailovsky, the brig was to deliver supplies to the redoubt and then sail directly to Mechigmensky Bay without stopping at the usual places on the American side. The *Kvikhpak* was ordered to assist in exploring the area near Mikhailovsky and to hurry south to Pastuliq, near the Yukon delta, before the Sledge Island traders arrived. The *Kvikhpak*'s captain was to scout the area and to find out how many furs the Sledge Islanders collected at Pastiliq, how much they paid for them, and whether it would be practical to set up an outpost there.[11]

The Russians quickly learned the lesson that the natives had taught Eliab Grimes when he tried to break into their trade monopoly at Big Diomede in 1819: the Sledge Islanders strongly opposed any intrusion into the native trade network. Wrangell reported to the Main Office, "The inhabitants of the river *Pastol'* (where furs flow together from the interior and are bought by the Aziiakmiuts [Sledge Islanders] for the Chukchi), being incited by the Aziiakmiuts and not believing assurances of the redoubt commander's friendliness, not only have not brought furs to the redoubt, but have universally announced that they consider the Russians their enemies and will not let the latter [come] to them."

Wrangell added that, in 1833, when Glazunov had taken a longboat to Unalakleet, he had met a group of Sledge Islanders in six umiaqs and had "found himself in obvious danger from the ill intentions of the latter, so that he had to save himself by fleeing into the dark and stormy night." The same Sledge Islanders, probably on their way to Pastuliq, then arrived at Mikhailovsky "and had an argument with our people there, taking the guns from the sentries, but through Kuzmin's resoluteness and caution, the important consequences that could have come from the impudence of these savages were averted."[12]

In winter 1834–35 Kuzmin sent Glazunov overland from Mikhailovsky to the Yukon, to scout for a location to set up a small outpost near the portage where the

Yukon and Kuskokwim rivers most closely converge. Glazunov found that the site of the native trade fair at Anilukhtakpak (near the present village of Holy Cross, Alaska) was a less suitable location than one farther downriver at Ikogmiut (today, Russian Mission). Kuzmin consequently planned to send a man there with trade goods once the summer's supplies had arrived from Novo-Arkhangelsk.

THE SLEDGE ISLANDERS' ATTACK ON MIKHAILOVSKY

The following summer, 1835, the brig *Polifyom* served as the northern supply ship. After departing from Mikhailovsky in July with the fur returns, the brig went to Indian Point, Mechigmensky Bay, and King Island, collecting 4,266 walrus tusks in all. Near the end of July the brig headed to Sledge Island, but the crew found the settlement completely deserted. The entire population was away, presumably on trade.[13]

In 1833 the company's Main Office in St. Petersburg, ignorant of the realities of the Bering Strait trade, had questioned Wrangell about why he felt it necessary to keep so many men to protect Mikhailovsky Redoubt, reasoning that "in their fragile boats and without firearms [the Chukchi and Sledge Islanders] are scarcely in a position to threaten our settlement."[14] Wrangell, displaying the classic exasperation of a veteran field man at the ignorance and naïveté of a distant headquarters staff, was amazed at the stupidity of this question and growled in response:

> *First*, the Chukchi and [Sledge Islanders] in their "fragile boats," which only seat ten men each, go annually, despite the great distance to Pastol' [Pastuliq] and stop in at Stuart [Mikhailovsky] in whole flotillas of ten or more boats to barter furs. *Second*, savages without firearms are not dangerous to a settlement as long as the people are protected inside a fortification with cannons, etc., but in the summer the greater part of the garrison has to be dispersed to lay in a supply of food.
>
> Remember: in the time of many companies [prior to the formation of the Russian-American Company] for the last half century, the Aleuts, not having firearms took whole vessel crews; and Captain Beechey in very recent times experienced the impudence of the North American savages within sight of a man-of-war.[15]

And Wrangell was proved absolutely right. After the *Polifyom* had headed south from Mikhailovsky in August 1835, the strained relations between the Russians and the native traders broke out into open hostility when a group of Sledge Islanders ambushed nine company employees while they were collecting driftwood. The Eskimos killed one Russian and with the exception of one man wounded all the others. Seven years later the explorer Lavrenty Alekseevich Zagoskin recorded the details of the ambush, which he may have heard from Ivan Zvonaryov, the only man who escaped unharmed.[16]

> The [Sledge Islanders], seeing their influence weakened year by year . . . determined to destroy the fort. They arrived . . . in 10 skin boats under the guise of seeking barter, and set up a watch with the help of the natives, whom they intimidated, to discover when the force at the post should be divided to carry out the various tasks. An occasion soon presented itself. Nine of the company men were sent in a longboat to collect wood. They were not expecting to be set upon, but had with them, as prescribed by regulations, their weapons, ball cartridges, and small shot for geese.
>
> On the 10th of August with a contrary wind the boat with the collected floatage was halted in the strait. . . . The [Sledge Islanders] decided to destroy this handful of people first and then to turn their attention to the fort. But Providence had decreed otherwise. When the attack came, one company man was left on the field but seven who were wounded owed their lives to the valiant behavior of . . . Kurepanov. Intelligent, and of great physical strength, he realized in the heat of the fighting that the only salvation lay in dragging the enemy's skin boat into the water. This skin boat was the only one used to deliver the pick of the [Sledge Islanders'] young men while the rest, some two hundred in number, were hiding behind the coastal hills. When the circle of attackers fell back before our guns, Kurepanov cried, "After me, boys, and may God help us!" and alone shoved the skin boat into the water.
>
> The rest followed him closely, and the skin boat was pushed off. The savages shouted when they saw this desperate action, and let fly a cloud of arrows. But it was too late: the defenders heeled the boat over and the walrus hide deflected the bone points. The paddles, which fell out from the inside of the boat, were used to get to a safe distance. Three men soon fainted from loss of blood. They all supposed that the fort had been destroyed, and Kurepanov took it upon himself to reconnoiter its condition; about midnight he arrived at the gates. All possible help was immediately given to the injured, and they all recovered. The fort was saved, and from that time on the [Sledge Islanders] have never dared show their faces on the southern shore of Norton Sound.[17]

THE RUSSIAN RESPONSE TO THE
ATTACK ON MIKHAILOVSKY

Kuzmin's report did not reach Novo-Arkhangelsk until the following spring, 1836. The new chief manager of the colony, Ivan Antonovich Kupreianov, immediately sent Mikhail Tebenkov to investigate the incident and dispatched a second vessel, the *Kvikhpak*, under the command of Aleksandr Kashevarov, to assist him. They were ordered to capture as many Sledge Islanders as possible and to bring them to Novo-Arkhangelsk to deter any future hostile action.

After conducting his inquiries Tebenkov concluded that the Russian party had not kept up their guard while collecting driftwood and was inadequately armed as well. He was unable to find any Sledge Islanders for interrogation but instead took five local natives who had known about the attack but had not participated in it. Unfortunately they reached Novo-Arkhangelsk when smallpox was epidemic there. All contracted the disease, and one died. The survivors were returned to their homeland the following summer.[18]

By summer 1836 the Russians had also set up a small outpost and fishing station on the eastern shore of Norton Sound at Unalakleet, an effort to intercept the furs that reached the coast via the overland native trade route from the Koyukon on the Yukon. In 1837 Andrei Glazunov then traveled up the Unalakleet River and over the portage to the middle Yukon. The next year, 1838, Pyotr Malakhov, with a trade outfit, reached Nulato, near where the Koyukuk River joins the Yukon. He collected 350 beaver pelts from the Koyukon, and because of his success, in 1839 the company built an outpost there. At the Nulato outpost, the Koyukon traders who had bought their furs from natives in the surrounding country received in exchange "red and white beads, shells, pots, copper jugs, and different articles of iron."[19]

Thus, by building Mikhailovsky Redoubt, the Russians not only had begun to intercept one branch of the flow of furs heading west across Bering Strait to the Kolyma but also had used it as a base for reaching farther, to penetrate the fur-rich lands of the lower and middle Yukon. From 1842 to 1860 Mikhailovsky and its outposts exported 43,398½ beaver pelts, 4,954½ river otters, 10,216 red foxes and its color variants, 1,403½ arctic foxes, 183 bears (probably black bears), 1,007 lynx, 8,253 marten, 4,668 muskrat, 330 mink, 53 wolverine skins, 1 wolf skin, 3,315½ pairs of beaver castors, and a little more than 100 pounds of walrus ivory.[20]

8

THE EXPEDITIONS TO POINT BARROW

PETER WARREN DEASE AND THOMAS SIMPSON

In the 1830s, both the Russian-American Company and the Hudson's Bay Company continued to probe northward. As John Franklin had predicted in 1823 in proposing his expedition, the information he acquired in 1826 was indeed useful "for advancing . . . the fur trade," and it sparked the interest of the Hudson's Bay Company in the lower Mackenzie River and adjacent Arctic coast. In 1827, Chief Factor Peter Warren Dease, a veteran northern trader who had assisted Franklin's expedition, was put in charge of Fort Good Hope, the company's northernmost post on the Mackenzie River. One of Dease's duties was to gather intelligence about the lands and peoples to the north. Dease advocated building a trading post northwest of Fort Good Hope, on the Peel River, a tributary of the Mackenzie delta. From the Gwichyaa Gwich'in, the easternmost of the Gwich'in groups, whom the traders called *Loucheux*, or "Squint Eyes," he had learned that

> no other tribe but themselves frequent that Stream, they generally remain to the Westward between it and where the Mountains dip into the Ocean which is their hunting grounds, they tell us that towards the Sources of that River, Beaver is to be found pretty numerous, but the distance great for them to hunt and bring their hunts to this establishment; that was a post established for them they would be able to make better hunts, but at the same time the Whites would require to be strong, as they would be subject to the visits from the Esquimaux who they represent as a very treacherous and hostile People; they come up the river annually in barges as far as [Arctic] Red River to traffic with the Squinteyes, and the last accounts from the latter Tribe, they had every rea-

son, they said, to think the Esquimaux were hostilely inclined towards them—
some shots with arrows were exchanged in the Spring between the two Tribes,
and in the Fall they say two Esquimaux in a Canoe came up to their Camp
apparently as Spies and without going on shore or speaking to them turned
back—this they look upon as a certain mark of hostile intentions.[1]

Soon after he wrote that report, the company stationed Dease upriver at Fort
Simpson, where he and Edward Smith reported on the state of affairs between
the Gwich'in and the Eskimos and about its effect on the company's trade: "The
Esquimaux last Summer treacherously murdered one of the Loucheux Indians,
an insult which the latter will not forgive. Any hostilities between those Tribes
will affect the Trade of [Fort Good Hope] and should the former prove Victors
will endanger the safety of the Establishment, as in the latter case there is no barrier between us and the Esquimaux who are now acquainted with our residence
near their lands." William Barr, the editor of Dease's journal, added, "It would be
another decade before a post (Peel's Post, later, Fort McPherson) was established
on the Peel River, near the head of the Mackenzie Delta right at the southern
margin of Inuit [Eskimo] territory, and for several decades thereafter the post
operated under the constant threat of Inuit aggression."[2]

Despite Dease's and Smith's advice, it was not until 1836 that George Simpson, the Hudson's Bay Company's governor in North America, sent out an expedition. One reason for the company's renewed push northwestward was that the
market for beaver pelts had become very soft, in part because cheaper silk hats
had replaced beaver hats as the headwear of choice in Britain, leaving the company with a vast overstock of beaver, which had to be sold at a loss. "To counter
this serious loss of markets, the HBC began promoting luxury furs—mink, fox,
and especially marten." George Simpson ordered Dease, with Thomas Simpson
as his assistant, to proceed out onto the Arctic coast to complete the exploration
of the unknown region that lay between Franklin's farthest advance at Return
Reef and Elson's probe to Point Barrow during the Beechey expedition. On
June 1, 1837, Dease and Simpson, with eight men in two boats, the *Castor* and
Pollux, left Fort Chipewyan on Lake Athabasca. They descended the waterways
to the Mackenzie River and reached Fort Good Hope (see rear endpaper map).
There the Gwich'in told them that the Eskimos had killed three of their people
and severely wounded another only a month before. Simpson wrote, "They expressed their sorrow at our determination to expose the lives of so small a party
among such a treacherous people as the Esquimaux [and] earnestly cautioned
us to be on our guard in every meeting with these perfidious savages, especially
in the act of *embarking*, the moment they usually select for an attack. [They]

declared that if the latter injured us . . . the whole tribe would combine to exact a terrible vengeance."

But as Simpson added:

It is but justice to the Esquimaux to state, that, from our inquiries, the Loucheux appear to have drawn the above chastisement upon themselves. For several years they had exacted, and received, a gift, as "blood-money," from the former, on account of a Loucheux whom they asserted to have died of his wounds in an old encounter. On this last occasion three of the Loucheux repeated the annual demand, with which the Esquimaux were about to comply, when unfortunately the very man, so long reported dead, made his appearance. On this, the Esquimaux, after reviling the Loucheux for their falsehood and extortion, fell upon them; and, of the four one only escaped, wounded by flying to the woods. The traders have long been at great pains to effect a permanent reconciliation between these hereditary enemies. For this purpose, in 1817, and again in 1819, Mr. Dease gave considerable presents to the Loucheux chief to negotiate a peace, which lasted for several years.[3]

It was, of course, very much in the best interests of the Hudson's Bay Company to end the hostilities between the Eskimos and the Gwich'in so that the natives could bring their furs in peace to the trading post. But the Gwich'in hardly saw it that way because they wanted to preserve their profitable role as middlemen. Shepard Krech III has written: "The Gwich'in, armed with guns, successfully prevented the Inuvialuit [Mackenzie Eskimos] from having direct access to European traders, which heightened the tension among all three ethnic groups."[4]

Farther downriver, on July 7, 1837, Dease and Simpson visited the northernmost of the Loucheux (Gwich'in) encampments, and they noticed that the Gwich'in had what appeared to be Russian knives and buttons, which they had received in trade from the Eskimos "during their intervals of amicable intercourse," evidence that trade alternated with hostilities between the two groups.[5]

On July 9, in the western part of the Mackenzie delta, they met the first Eskimos, who probably assumed that Dease's and Simpson's party were their enemies, the Loucheux: "About 8 AM, on turning a sharp point, we came suddenly upon an Esquimaux oomiak, containing four women and a couple of dogs. The ladies, throwing off their coverings, leaped ashore, and fled through the willows with the utmost precipitation. We did not land, but passed on under full sail."[6]

Two hours later when the explorers went ashore to make breakfast, they were "hailed in a very rough manner" by a naked Eskimo in a kayak who threatened them with a long knife, but after the explorers shouted "teyma," which they believed to be a friendly greeting, he paddled to their camp and put on his clothes. Simpson wrote, "He . . . soon gave us to understand, by words helped out by signs, that he was the chief who interfered to stop the plunder of Sir John Franklin's party by his countrymen at Pillage Point. He likewise told us that it was his wives who, terrified by our sudden appearance, abandoned the oomiak, which was laden with reindeer meat.

"We presented our new friend with an axe, a knife, and several other articles, besides a liberal share of our repast. But not withstanding our generosity, he was immediately detected in the set of concealing, in the breast of his dress, a knife and fork, having previously secreted a tin dish among the willows, where on a search it was discovered. He laughed at all this as a good joke." Dease noted, "It does not appear that he considered the violation of the 8th Command as a very heinous offence."[7]

Later that afternoon the boats reached the Arctic Ocean. Immediately at Tent Island, where Franklin's party had had trouble in 1826, fifteen or twenty kayakers from an Eskimo encampment put off and followed them, moving fast. These were probably members of the Kuukpaŋmiut nation, the group that lived in the central Mackenzie delta. The kayakers came alongside the boats, and the explorers gave each man "a knife, a file, some rings, beads, and awls," Simpson wrote. "They then became importunate to trade for their bows, arrows, darts, lip-ornaments, in fact, everything they had." The Hudson's Bay Company men "had no desire to enter into this kind of traffic." They were, after all, looking for furs, not curios, but Simpson noted that "to quiet them we traded for a few of these articles."[8]

The Eskimos began to pilfer from the boats and tried to convince the explorers to camp with them, but Dease and Simpson, no fools, understood full well the dangers of this and pushed on. "We therefore peremptorily ordered them back, but to no purpose. Two or three guns were shown, which alarmed them a little." The Eskimos still followed, "even after one or two blank shots, till I fired with ball over them; upon which they instantly ducked their heads, veered round, and, after paddling out of reach, halted to hold a consultation,—more canoes now appearing in the distance."[9] The two boats outran the Kuukpaŋmiut kayaks and thus probably avoided an encounter similar to the one that John Franklin's party had had to endure. It was not until they reached Shingle Point that the explorers went ashore to pitch their tents.

On July 11 the men sailed as far as Kay Point, where they found pack ice hard ashore. Making camp once again, they spotted a group of Eskimos who approached them cautiously. These persons were, no doubt, members of the Herschel Island nation, with whom Franklin had enjoyed friendly relations. Dease, recognizing that this group behaved in a far different manner than the one they had just passed, wrote, "Each of them was gratified with a Small present. . . . They did not show the prying disposition that I expected, or attempt to purloin anything True, they were too few to act out with any boldness."[10]

A week later, just west of today's Barter Island, the explorers found a camp of about sixty friendly men, women, and children. These Eskimos must also have been Herschel Island Eskimos on a trading voyage to meet the North Alaskan Eskimos. "They were very keen traders," Dease noted, "always offering the least valuable articles first and holding out to get as much as they can for them." Dease added, "They are apparently on their way to the Westward to meet a party from that Quarter to barter with them."[11]

It is interesting that this group of Eskimos had their families with them, although they must have been very near the place where they annually met the Alaskan Eskimos. The Alaskan traders, who feared the eastern Eskimos, usually left their women and children at Oliktok Point, east of the Colville River delta, when they went to the trading rendezvous with the Mackenzie Eskimos. Ernest S. Burch, Jr., has written that at the Barter Island trade rendezvous, "Fear and distrust were so great [between the groups from the east and from the west] that no one slept during the proceedings. . . . Then, their business concluded, the various parties immediately headed homeward."[12] When Franklin visited Barter Island in 1826, he believed that regular trade encounters between the Alaskan and Mackenzie Eskimos had begun only recently (see chapter 6). Perhaps in the eleven years between Franklin's visit and that of Dease and Simpson the two groups had become more trustful of one another as the volume of their trade grew; hence their interdependence. And this, of course, may have been a result of an increasing volume of trade goods that flowed east from the Ostrovnoe fair and other Asian fairs, and possibly because of an increase in Russian goods moving north from the Russian-American Company's operations.

Dease and Simpson distributed presents to the men ("axes, trenches, knives, files, and fire-steels") and to the women and children ("awls, needles, rings, beads, and scissors") and traded for waterproof boots and for labrets, which contained large blue beads. They noted that the Eskimos had iron kettles, "which they said they procured from the westward for two skins of the wolverine."[13] The beads were probably Chinese and had reached the Herschel Islanders by changing hands at Mai-mai-ch'eng and Kiakhta and at the Ostrovnoe fair. The Chukchi traders carried the beads and other manufactured goods to Sheshalik in Kotzebue Sound, and from there interior-dwelling Eskimos probably carried them over the mountains of the Brooks Range to the trade fair at Niġliq. At Niġliq these goods were exchanged again and taken onward by the Point Barrow Eskimos to Barter Island.

The iron kettles were probably Russian, but they may have reached the Eskimos at Barter Island from another source. In 1826 and 1827, Frederick William Beechey's men mentioned iron kettles once and reported that the Eskimos had copper kettles (which must have come from Ostrovnoe or other Asian fairs), but the iron kettles that Dease and Simpson saw may have been traded by the Russian-American Company at Mikhailovsky or from its ships. The iron kettles then would have reached first the Sheshalik fair and then the Niġliq fair, or, less likely, they may have been carried up the Yukon and reached Herschel Island via the "Mountain Indians" at the Firth River rendezvous.

On July 23 Dease's and Simpson's party arrived at Return Reef, the point where John Franklin had turned back toward the Mackenzie in 1826. They were by then only about 175 miles east of Point Barrow, and from there they pushed on into uncharted territory. Just west of Smith Bay, about 50 miles from Point Barrow, the pack ice was hard against the land. Dease and Simpson reasoned that there was no surety of reaching Point Barrow with the two boats. They decided to split the party, sending Simpson ahead on foot while Dease would remain there, guarding the boats. Simpson and five men started off to the west on August 1, carrying only a few personal possessions, their guns, "a few trinkets," a sextant and artificial horizon, and, most important, a canvas canoe.[14]

Along the way they passed a number of sleds. Simpson correctly assumed that they had been left by Eskimos traveling eastward in the late spring, who would collect the sleds on their return in the autumn. These Eskimos carried their boats on the sleds until they found open water, then proceeded onward by boat toward the trading rendezvous at Niġliq in the Colville River delta.

Two days later, southwest of Tangent Point in Dease Inlet, Simpson and his men came upon a camp of four Eskimo tents. As Simpson recounted:

> We immediately directed our steps toward them, . . . but, on our approach, the women and children threw themselves into their canoes, and pushed off from the shore. I shouted "Kabloonan teyma Inueet," meaning "We are white men, friendly to the Esquimaux"; upon which glad news the whole party hurried ashore, and almost overpowered us with caresses. The men were absent, hunting, with the exception of one infirm individual, who, sitting under a reversed canoe, was tranquilly engaged in weaving a fine whalebone net. Being unable to make his escape with the rest, he was in an agony of fear; and, when I first went up to him, with impotent hand he made a thrust at me with his long

knife. He was, however, soon convinced of our good intentions; and his first request was for tobacco, of which we found men, women, and even children inordinately fond. This taste they have, of course, acquired in their indirect intercourse with the Russians; for the Esquimaux we had last parted with [the Herschel Island Eskimos] were ignorant of the luxury.[15]

If Simpson was correct about the Herschel Island Eskimos not using tobacco, then it seems that the "tobacco frontier" had not advanced significantly eastward during the eleven years between Franklin's exploration and that of Dease and Simpson.

Simpson continued:

I told them that I required one of their oomiaks, or large family canoes, to take us two or three days' journey—or sleeps, as they term it—to the westward; after which we should return. . . . These skin boats float in half a foot of water. No ice was visible from the tents; and, from the trending of the coast, it was more than doubtful that our journey could have been accomplished in any reasonable time on foot. They acceded to my demand, without a scruple. We selected the best of three oomiaks; obtained four of their slender oars with lashings; and arranged our strange vessel so well that the ladies were in raptures, declaring us to be genuine Esquimaux, not poor white men.

Whilst my companions were thus employed, I procured, from the most intelligent of the women, a sketch of the inlet before us, and of the coast to the westward, as far as her knowledge extended. She represented the inlet as very deep; that they make many encampments in travelling round it. . . . She also drew a bay of some size to the westward; and the old man added a long and very narrow projection, covered with tents, which I could not doubt to mean Point Barrow.[16]

Simpson and his men reached the Point Barrow sandspit on August 4: "Seeing the ocean spreading far and wide to the south-west, we unfurled our flag, and with three hearty cheers took possession of our discoveries in his Majesty's name." They had closed the gap between Franklin's and Beechey's discoveries of 1826. Simpson, nevertheless, was fully aware of the hostile reception the men in the *Blossom*'s barge had received at Point Barrow and decided not to go as far as the village on the point itself. Instead, leaving a guard with the umiaq, he turned south and walked to a nearby tent camp near the base of the spit, probably at Piġniq, where the Eskimos gathered to capture eider ducks on the birds' southern migration, taking them on the wing with bolas weighted with walrus teeth. "To prevent surprise we marched along the highest shingle ridge; and, drawing

near the tents, could see the men, armed with bows and arrows, conceal themselves behind the mounds. . . . As soon as we got within hearing, I stepped forward, and called out that our visit was a friendly one; upon which our antagonists
immediately started up, and advanced to meet us with loud acclamations. . . .
The women and children now issued from their tents, and a brisk traffic opened;
but, as I felt anxious about our canoe, I signified my intention of immediately
returning to the landing-place. The whole party accompanied us; their patriarch
headed the grotesque procession, carrying our flag upon a long fish-spear; and
every article we had purchased found a willing bearer."

Simpson went on to explain why he believed his small party had received a
more friendly reception than the men in the *Blossom's* barge: "We had scarcely
established a boundary line on the beach, when the inhabitants of the other village [at the northern tip of the sandspit], who had been watching our motions,
swelled this throng, and welcomed us with an equal show of pleasure. I explained
how we happened to be in possession of a vessel so familiar to them; and I believe that its evident emptiness rendered them much less troublesome than they
would have been had our riches appeared greater.

"All were eager to trade; and we were soon loaded with seal-skin boots, kamleikas, or water-proof shirts, weapons, and gimcracks, some of which had figures
of marine mammals rudely carved in ivory. But what most attracted our curiosity
was an ingenious and novel contrivance for capturing wild fowl. It consists of six
or eight small perforated ivory balls, attached separately to cords of sinew three
feet long; the ends of which being tied together, an expanding or radiating sling
is thus framed, which, dexterously thrown at the birds as they fly past, entangles
and brings them to the ground."

But most of all the Point Barrow Eskimos wanted tobacco.

The grand article in demand here was tobacco, which, as in Dease Inlet, they
call tawāc, or tawācah, a name acquired of course from the Russian traders.
Not content with chewing and smoking it, they swallowed the fumes till they
became sick, and seemed to revel in a momentary intoxication. Beads, rings,
buttons, fire-steels, everything we had, were regarded as inferior to tobacco, a
single inch of which was an acceptable equivalent for the most valuable article
they possessed.

When in the course of this barter some of the younger people became forward and troublesome, the seniors at once restrained them. . . . Meanwhile the
old flag-bearer . . . paraded a roll of raw meat, fashioned like a huge sausage
severing therefrom sundry slices, or rather junks, which he imparted most liberally to everyone who chose to partake of his good cheer. . . . When the means

of buyers and sellers were at length exhausted, some of the women and girls ranged themselves in a circle, to gratify us with an exhibition of their national dances.[17]

"The Esquimaux of Point Barrow have unquestionably an indirect trade with the Russians," Simpson observed, "whom they call 'Noonatagmun.'" The "Noonatagmun" were not Russians but rather members of an Eskimo nation from the lands surrounding the main stream of the Colville River, with whom the Point Barrow Eskimos traded at Niġliq each summer and less regularly via Messenger Festivals in the winter.

Simpson continued, "The old man readily took charge of, and promised to convey, a letter which I addressed to them, or to any other whites on the western coast, containing a brief notice of the success of the expedition; and I made him a small present to confirm his seeming good will."[18]

It is interesting that Simpson's party had enjoyed a relatively amicable visit, during which the elders suppressed the aggressive behavior of the younger men and shared food and offered a women's dance. Perhaps the Point Barrow Eskimos did not view this small group of foreigners—who had traveled via umiaq and without significant property—to be a threat. Similarly, the elders may have behaved in that manner because they saw an advantage in opening direct trade relations with a source of foreign goods. Ernest S. Burch, Jr., believes, however, that "the Barrow people may have been peaceful because there weren't very many of them there. Probably the most dynamic individuals were to the east, trading and hunting caribou."[19]

Simpson and his men left Point Barrow on September 4 and headed back toward their "boat extreme." When they reached Dease Inlet the next day, they found the Eskimos whose umiaq they were using, and Simpson invited them to travel with his party to the place where they had left their boats. Four Eskimos in their kayaks set off with them, but at Tangent Point, where they found another group of Eskimos, the kayakers refused to go farther, and Dease bought the umiaq for an axe. He also gave his remaining stock of tobacco to the former owner.

The explorers got ready to shove off, but nine Eskimos grabbed the umiaq and tried to pull it ashore. They stopped when Simpson pointed his gun at them, "but quick as thought they snatched their bows and quivers, expecting to take us by surprise," Simpson wrote. "When, however, they saw the whole crew ready for the combat, they lowered their tone of defiance." He added, "When the threatened fray was blown over, I explained, as well [as] I could, to the aggressors, that the visit and intentions of the whites were altogether friendly; but we parted in mutual distrust."

A day later, when Simpson and his men reached Dease's camp, Simpson learned that the Eskimos who had tried to drag the umiaq ashore at Tangent Point had been at Dease's camp two days before and had stolen a few silver tea spoons and other things while the men slept. Dease thought that the owners of the umiaq had refused to go farther west because, having learned of the theft of Dease's equipment, they feared they might be punished for it when they reached the boat camp.[20]

Dease noted that the Eskimos who had tussled with the explorers over the umiaq were returning from a trading rendezvous, and were "very fond of Smoking, but seldom inhaling more than six or seven draughts of the Smoak which is retained and all drawn into the lungs, when it produces Coughing and a kind of Sickness which appears to be the Chief Enjoyment and Object with them using it."[21]

The explorers kept on east, and on August 16 were at Shingle Point, near the western edge of the Mackenzie delta. There they came upon several Eskimo families. As before, the Mackenzie Eskimos—probably the Kuukpaŋmiut again—tried to steal from the boats, and Simpson noticed that a frying pan was missing. "Upon my demanding restitution," he wrote, "the offender was pointed out; and I was in the act of going up to him, when he drew his long knife upon me, and at the same moment [one of the men] called out that one of his accomplices was bending his bow to transfix me through the back. I turned round in time to prevent the treacherous design, and, as our people were prepared to support us, the Esquimaux were glad to submit; and an old man produced the bone of contention from under a pile of drift wood."

Simpson then summarized his understanding of the Eskimos' behavior toward small parties of foreigners: "We invariably found the arrogance of the natives to increase in due proportion with their numbers. The moderation and forbearance of the whites are, in their savage minds, ascribed to weakness or pusillanimity; while the fierceness of the Loucheux and Mountain Indians [both Gwich'in] inspires terror. Notwithstanding the deceitful good-humour of the Esquimaux, I have no hesitation in asserting, that, were they in possession of fire-arms, it would require a stronger force than ours to navigate their coasts."[22]

Dease's and Simpson's party reached the Mackenzie on August 17, ascended it, and wintered on Great Bear Lake. The next year they turned east and, carrying out an equally impressive and productive voyage, advanced as far as the Boothia Peninsula, thereby nearly completing the mapping of the northern coast of continental North America.

ALEKSANDR KASHEVAROV

While the Hudson's Bay Company was organizing the Dease and Simpson expedition, the Russian-American Company, unaware of the British project, was developing an expedition of its own with exactly the same goal: closing the gap between Franklin's and Beechey's explorations. In 1824, Count Rumiantsev had proposed sending a joint expedition (with the Russian-American Company) to meet Franklin on the Arctic coast, but this initiative ended with Rumiantsev's death. Some years later, in 1836, when Baron Ferdinand Petrovich Wrangell had completed his tenure as chief manager of the Russian-American colony and returned to St. Petersburg, he promoted the idea to the company's board of directors, calling for an expedition to examine the unknown section of coast between Point Barrow and Return Reef. It is unlikely that the Russian-American Company would have been able to exploit any discoveries so far from its northernmost activities, which at that date were in Norton Sound and on the lower and middle Yukon; rather, the purpose of this expedition was part of the great geopolitical contest for dominion between Russia and Great Britain.

The Russian-American Company assigned Aleksandr Filippovich Kashevarov, an educated Creole whose mother was a Kodiak Eskimo, to lead the effort. The expedition was ingeniously planned, comprising one twelve-oared baidara (a large Aleutian skin-boat) and five three-man baidarkas (three-hatch Aleutian kayaks). To assist Kashevarov, the crew included "an assistant head of the expedition, a medical student, thirteen Russians and Creoles [offspring of Russian fathers and native mothers], one of which might serve as interpreter, and ten Aleuts." The expedition would go north as far as possible aboard one of the company's ships and then proceed, as Count Rumiantsev had proposed in 1824.

In Novo-Arkhangelsk, Ivan Antonovich Kupreianov, the new chief manager of the colony, strongly supported the project. In addition to a first-class outfit of surveying instruments, he supplied warm clothing and specially made wooden and leather containers that would fit in the baidarkas in the event that the larger boat was lost. He assigned the brig *Polifyom* to carry the expedition north.[23]

The *Polifyom* paused at Mikhailovsky to resupply the post and to collect two interpreters for the expedition. The brig then touched at King Island but found that the entire population was away, probably for trade. Beyond Bering Strait near Cape Lisburne pack ice stretched across the horizon, halting the *Polifyom*. On July 5, 1838, the Kashevarov expedition disembarked from the brig and began to work north close inshore (see rear endpaper map).[24] Nearing Icy Cape, the explorers not only found the pack ice blocking their way but also discovered that the lagoon inside the barrier island was so shallow that the baidara could go no farther. Kashevarov sent it south with fifteen men. He ordered the baidara party to wait at one of the southern entrances to the Kasegaluk Lagoon and to build a hut in case the expedition might be forced to spend the winter there. Kashevarov then pushed ahead carrying four weeks' provisions for the fifteen men paddling the five baidarkas.

Not far from Icy Cape they found a large village of Siḷaliñaġmiut Eskimos, the Eskimo nation that lived on the northwestern coast of arctic Alaska. Their encounter was friendly, but the Eskimos warned Kashevarov that the next Eskimo nation up the coast, the Point Barrow Eskimos, which they referred to as the "Kakligmiuts," were "evil." Two days later the expedition came upon another Siḷaliñaġmiut settlement at the end of the lagoon. The Eskimos must have turned out ready for a fight because Kashevarov wrote, "In error, they took us for their enemies the Kakligmiuts, but we placated them by giving each person a leaf of tobacco."[25]

On July 21, at the village of Atanik, near Point Franklin, the Russians had their first encounter with members of the "Kakligmiut" nation. Through his interpreter, Kashevarov learned that these people were acquainted with the coast as far south as Chamisso Island. Kashevarov also heard a garbled report about Dease's and Simpson's expedition of the previous year, although he was, of course, unaware that it had taken place. "We learned that in the past summer people similar to us . . . had arrived at [Point Barrow] from the east. One of the savages immediately showed us a scrap of paper obtained from [an] . . . inhabitant of Point Barrow. This proved to be from our manuscript calendar of 1836 and on it a half diameter of the sun was indicated. This scrap of paper was one of those which the Nusha-gak interpreter, the creole Lukin, had distributed to coastal inhabitants of North America in 1836, to whom he had gone at that time with the sole purpose of expanding the trade of his post on the Kuskokwim River with the natives, wishing by distributing these papers to leave evidence behind him."[26]

Kashevarov's informant must have conflated the arrival of Thomas Simpson at Point Barrow with the arrival of Lukin's paper. The very existence of Lukin's paper near Point Barrow gives a glimpse of how quickly trade goods could move over long distances in the North. Semyon Ivanovich Lukin, a Creole employee of the Russian-American Company, was very active on the Kuskokwim River, but he apparently never traveled north of Mikhailovsky Redoubt. It is possible that Lukin's paper reached the coast of Norton Sound in 1836 and then passed to other hands at the Sheshalik fair that summer or in 1837, from whence it could have reached Point Barrow early in 1838 via either an exchange at a winter Messenger Festival or, possibly, the Niġliq rendezvous.[27]

Rounding Point Barrow on July 23, Kashevarov's men found that most of the inhabitants of the settlement on the point were inland, hunting caribou. The Russians then headed east, along the north coast of Alaska. In Dease Inlet two days later they passed a summer camp of Point Barrow Eskimos. The Eskimos, in three umiaqs, followed the Russians and landed where they had stopped. Kashevarov, like Dease and Simpson the year before, encountered the form of behavior common when a group of Eskimos met a smaller number of foreigners. "They tried to steal our chronometer, thermometer, and expedition log, but we forced them to return the things they had stolen. Following this the savages began to threaten to attack us in large numbers and they tried to talk Utuktak, the [interpreter] who accompanied us, into leaving us, threatening that in a few days, when all the Kakligmiuts were to gather at Point Barrow for the whale hunt . . . we would be taken prisoner; they said that more than 20 [umiaqs] would gather at the point and they all would attack us."[28]

Later, forty Point Barrow men approached the Russian camp. "Each carried a bow in hand and had a quiver full of arrows on his back, in addition to a knife — which the savage is never without and which hangs from his side in a sheath," Kashevarov added.

The savages continued to approach us one by one and the number of natives kept increasing and increasing, and as their numbers increased so did their audacity. As each new savage arrived, they all insistently demanded that we give them tobacco, and although we had already given them tobacco, they let us know that they were dissatisfied or they laughed at their presents. The Chpagmiut, Utuktak, who accompanied us, became convinced, after our negotiations with the Kakligmiuts, that if we tarried here any longer the savages would attack us to steal our things, which they had not seen but imagined to be copious and were tempted by them. We were led to believe or at least strongly suspect that the intentions of the savages were unfriendly or inclined that way, as evidenced not only by their behavior with us, but by the fact that they had not brought their women or children with them. Further, the respected Kakligmiut, Negubanna, who tried more than the others to talk Utuktak into leaving us, repeated that his kinsmen had evil intentions toward us and that they were only waiting until there were enough of them to attack us. At that time [an umiaq] with four men and a woman arrived from the east; they approached our baydarkas without invitation and began examining them boldly.

We could halt the audacity of the savages only with force; our kind treatment of them had not disposed them toward friendship. The position of the expedition had become highly doubtful, the more so because the Aleuts who rowed our baydarkas were convinced that the savages were invincible because of their numbers, their powerful builds, the fact that they were used to danger, and besides they were not tired as were the Aleuts. For these reasons, at 4:30 we set out to the south to change our position. However the savages pursued us in their [umiaqs], and asked us where we were going. In passing the summer camp of the natives, we noticed unusual activity there. New ones were probably arriving (for all those we knew were chasing us); they were taking down their tents rapidly and loading their things post-haste into their [umiaqs]. Several savages ran along shore, carrying [kayaks]. At 5:30, in trying to elude the [umiaqs] that were chasing us, we moved out from shore. . . . At this moment a very thick fog suddenly set in, limiting visibility to less than 150 ft. and we followed our previous course along the coast southward for 2½ miles.[29]

Recognizing that his expedition was in a very dangerous situation, Kashevarov headed back toward Point Barrow. "The large numbers and very unfriendly attitude of the inhabitants put an end to further progress of the expedition; we were forced to return," he wrote. Even so, the explorers had difficulties with high winds and encroaching pack ice as they worked their way south along shore. Near the southern end of Kasegaluk Lagoon the men rejoined the crew of the baidara, who had built a hut on Kashevarov's orders. Kashevarov's expedition then continued south, reaching Chamisso Island in Kotzebue Sound on August 29.

On September 5 the *Polifyom* arrived to carry them back to Novo-Arkhangelsk.[30] While the *Polifyom* was at Chamisso a shore party had a dangerous encounter with the local Eskimos, presumably the Buckland River Kaṇiġmiut, who behaved with their usual aggressiveness. "The bravery of the Creole Klimovskiy saved the lives of the people in the sloop of the Russian-American company's brig 'Polifem' which had been sent for water to the mouth of the river when the brig was in Kotzebue Sound in 1838," wrote L. A. Zagoskin.[31]

Like Franklin and Dease and Simpson, Kashevarov had carried out an important voyage of exploration despite hardships and hostile encounters with the Eskimos, but the Russian-American Company would never capitalize on his discoveries.

9

ZAGOSKIN'S EXPEDITION TO THE YUKON

The smallpox epidemic that struck Novo-Arkhangelsk in 1835 and 1836 reached the lower and middle Yukon while Kashevarov's expedition was under way in 1838. Although the company vaccinated as many natives as possible, the disease spread to the southern and eastern coasts of Norton Sound, killing as much as half the population in some settlements. Four years later only 283 Eskimos remained alive on the coast of Norton Sound. The natives believed that this scourge had arrived via the Russians, and in spring 1839 a group attacked the outpost at Ikogmiut on the lower Yukon, killing the trader and two employees.[1]

ETHOLEN'S INSTRUCTIONS

In this period of instability Arvid Adolf Etholen became chief manager of the colony. Etholen understood the potential of the northern trade: he had surveyed in the northern Bering Sea in the 1820s and realized that it was essential for the company to reorganize its operations to gain control of the fur trade on the Yukon and in Norton Sound. Among other things, he complained to the Main Office in St. Petersburg about the quality of the company's tobacco and trade goods. "Aboard colonial vessels annually sent from Novo-Arkhangelsk to trade with the Chukchi and other savage tribes at Bering Strait it is constantly noted that they pay no attention to and do not care a bit for our Circassian tobacco in comparison with that supplied to them by the merchants on the Kolyma, because in strength, freshness, and overall quality the tobacco sent to the colonies via Okhotsk is much worse than that [from the Kolyma], as are all the iron- and copperware such as knives, kettles, etc. This greatly damages the company's trade with those peoples, who for these reasons primarily keep their best furs and largest walrus tusks to barter for Kolyma goods."[2]

Etholen noted that the fur returns of Mikhailovsky Redoubt had declined since its founding in 1833. Although the smallpox epidemic of 1838–39 almost certainly contributed to the decline, the Sledge Islanders, the King Islanders, and perhaps others as well continued to carry a substantial amount of fur to the Chukchi traders at Big Diomede and to the Port Clarence fair. The Chukchi traders also collected furs at the Sheshalik fair, furs that Etholen wanted to capture for the Russian-American Company. He directed the captain of the company's brig *Promysel* to visit Port Clarence to scout its potential for acquiring furs and to establish friendly relations with the local Eskimos.[3]

Judging from Etholen's correspondence, although the Russians at Mikhailovsky and the native traders had probably confronted one another in some way in summer 1841, he decided that it would be in the company's best interest to offer the native traders small presents and to allow them to travel past Mikhailovsky to the native trade fair at Pastuliq, if they would agree to sell their furs at Mikhailovsky on their return; nevertheless, he ordered that any who refused to cooperate would not be allowed to pass the island in the future. To enforce this plan Etholen suggested sending an armed barge to block the Sledge Island traders on their way to Pastuliq and to warn them that they risked being taken prisoner if they disobeyed the Russians' orders. This confrontation apparently did not take place, although Etholen did repeat these instructions the following year.[4]

Etholen also studied the problem of supplying the company's outposts. First, however, he needed to know much more about the land and about native trade routes. Russian probes out of Michailovsky had thus far been somewhat haphazard. In 1840, however, Lavrenty Alekseevich Zagoskin proposed to Etholen that he should undertake a more systematic investigation of the lower and middle Yukon and of the intercontinental Bering Strait native trade.

Recognizing the potential of the proposal, in 1842 Etholen ordered Zagoskin to go north. Unfortunately, Etholen's orders to Zagoskin were so broad that they were impossible to carry out completely: not only was Zagoskin to inspect Eschscholtz Bay in Kotzebue Sound, where—the Russians correctly suspected—furs were reaching the Chukchi traders overland from the Yukon, but he was also to search the vast area of the Yukon and Kuskokwim rivers to their headwaters to determine the location of the best portages between the two.[5]

ZAGOSKIN'S TRAVELS

Although things started badly for Zagoskin, ultimately he achieved a highly important exploration of a barely known region of Russian America. In May 1842, Zagoskin set out from Novo-Arkhangelsk aboard the company's brig *Okhotsk*.

After stops in the Aleutians and Pribilofs, in late June the *Okhotsk* encountered heavy pack ice seventy miles south of St. Lawrence Island. It was not until June 27 that the brig rounded the western end of the island and headed toward Sledge Island. Again pack ice surrounded the ship, this time accompanied by a herd of bellowing walruses. For nine days the brig sailed back and forth between the Asian and American coasts, reaching Mikhailovsky only on July 10.[6]

At Mikhailovsky Zagoskin had planned to recruit Feofan Utuktak, the interpreter who had been a mainstay of Kashevarov's expedition in 1838, but Utuktak "flatly refused" to join Zagoskin. "He declared that he had formerly been a bachelor," Zagoskin wrote, "but that now he had two beautiful wives, and because of them . . . his wants were fulfilled." To make matters worse, Zagoskin then found that he could not buy enough dogs to pull his sleds for the planned winter expeditions. Meanwhile the *Okhotsk* sailed on a short trading mission to Mechigmensky Bay on the Chukchi Peninsula and to the Diomede Islands. But when the brig returned to Mikhailovsky, Zagoskin was forced to conclude that the summer's heavy ice would almost certainly make the planned voyage to Kotzebue Sound impossible and would interfere with his preparations for the winter journeys. The brig sailed south on August 15.[7]

In December 1842, Zagoskin set out by dogsled up the Yukon to Nulato and continued up the Koyukuk as far as the Kateel River, where he believed he had identified the native overland trade route to Kotzebue Sound (see rear endpaper map). In summer 1843 he worked his way up the Yukon by boat for about one hundred miles and then went downstream to Ikogmiut (today, Russian Mission).[8]

In the meantime, while Zagoskin was at work, Etholen had set his sights farther north, intent on scouting the western end of the Kotzebue-Yukon trade network. In 1843 the *Okhotsk* sailed north again to supply Mikhailovsky. Etholen ordered Captain Netsvetov to head to Kotzebue Sound. "Drop anchor in a safe place, behind the Chamisso Island, as close as possible to the *Choris* Peninsula," he wrote.

> Engage in trade with the natives and with the traders who travel annually from the Gvozdyov [Diomede] Islands from the Kaviak Bay [Port Clarence] and from other localities south of the Bering Strait in order to buy the furs in the entire region, which later reach the Kolyma. These traders always assemble there [Kotzebue Sound] on their return trips from the North. It is very desirable that you should try to attract them to us, but you are not to trust them beyond measure. Captain Beechey had a rather unpleasant business with them and was compelled to use firearms.

You are to try to learn in detail the resources and enterprise of the area, most of all the extent of the rivers and what are the river resources there. Also you are to pay attention to any suitable localities where we could establish a Settlement. For this purpose it is especially necessary to know the following: is there in the vicinity of either standing timber or of driftwood; are the streams rich in fish; or is it possible to obtain sufficient store of caribou meat.

In the last year I ordered Lieutenant Zagoskin to investigate the course of the Buckland River, which the natives call Kanyk. Do question the natives about this river in detail (but you yourself are not to ascend the Buckland River, because of the distances involved which could be much too prolonged absence from your vessel). Information obtained by you, combined with the information which I hope presently to receive from Mr. Zagoskin, should suffice for my future decisions.

I should also like very much to obtain through you this season detailed information about the streams which empty into the bay named by captain Beechey [Hotham Inlet]. According to information formerly obtained by Mr. Kashevarov, and last year by Mr. Zagoskin, one must suppose that these rivers penetrate far into the interior and that three days' travel upstream much timber is found; wherever there is forest along the river banks, there are also beavers, as the natives reason. The natives call the northern of these rivers *Kubok* [Kobuk] and the southern *Chilivyk* [Selawik]. As the mouths of these rivers are not too far from the location where the brig Okhotsk is to stand at anchor, . . . it is desirable that you personally inspect [them]. However . . . only if there is absolute certainty that . . . the vessel will remain safe from any . . . attempts on the part of the Natives.[9]

As ordered, Captain Netsvetov resupplied Mikhailovsky. Continuing onward, he passed through Bering Strait, but at Cape Espenberg on the north coast of the Seward Peninsula pack ice stopped the *Okhotsk*. Kotzebue Sound appeared to be full of ice, so Netsvetov, who had other tasks to complete that summer, headed instead to Mechigmensky Bay on the Chukchi Peninsula. After a short stop there he returned to Mikhailovsky and then went south, arriving back at Novo-Arkhangelsk in late October.[10]

During that winter and the following summer, Zagoskin surveyed parts of the Kuskokwim River, returning in June 1844 to Mikhailovsky, where he boarded the *Okhotsk* and sailed to Novo-Arkhangelsk in September. Although Zagoskin did not reach Kotzebue Sound and was unable to accomplish all of his objectives, he nevertheless had carried out a highly important exploration of a poorly known part of Russian America and collected an impressively large amount of ethnographic, geographic, and biological information for the company.[11]

ZAGOSKIN'S REPORT

On his return Zagoskin wrote a detailed report to Etholen. Among many other observations he confirmed that before the Russians had established Mikhailovsky Redoubt some manufactured goods had reached the natives of that region from a company post on Bristol Bay. He added, however, that they received most of their "metal pots, knives and lances" and tobacco via the trade route that started at the Ostrovnoe fair. From there, the route continued eastward via the Chukchi traders who passed the goods on to the King Islanders and Sledge Islanders and others, who then carried them to the southern shore of Norton Sound. He reported, however, that these traders had ceased traveling to the southern shore of Norton Sound in 1837.[12] This suggests that Wrangell's idea of setting up Michailovsky Redoubt had indeed helped to stem some of the flow of Alaskan furs that were going to the Chukchi traders.

Zagoskin reported that the natives on the southern coast of Norton Sound supplied the peoples on the Yukon with sea mammal skins and oil, skin boats, tobacco, and iron. They received in return beaver, river otter, marten, wolf, wolverine, and fox skins, as well as wooden bowls and other utensils. The natives dwelling on the Yukon above the delta reached the east shore of Norton Sound via the Anvik and Unalakleet rivers, and among other things, they traded for beluga whale oil (which was highly prized because it was tasteless) in seal bladder containers. Depending on the size of the bladder, the price varied from 4 to 15 prime beavers.

He added that an average of 1,000 reindeer or caribou skins reached the area via the Malimiut traders. They, for example, would buy 1 prime black fox for 12 winter skins and 10 unborn fawn skins or a pound of tobacco and an umiaq cover; 22 martens for 11 skins; 1 first-class beaver for 2 skins; 1 wolf or wolverine for 12 to 17 skins; and "for two matched, clear, flawless greenish-blue beads" 3 or 4 skins. "The best parkas," Zagoskin continued, "both in the quality of skins and the beauty of decoration, come from the [Malimiut], who obtain the skins of domesticated deer from the Chukchi, and make them into garments with great taste. A woman wearing Chukchi hand-sewn boots, white pants of domesticated deerskin, a [Malimiut] parka . . . and with spanking-new native-style headdress will please the eye of any European who sees her."[13]

The natives who traded at Mikhailovsky, Zagoskin continued, traded for "tobacco, European iron and copper products, and a small number of manufactured trifles." In return the post received 350 to 500 beaver pelts, 100 otter skins, and about 150 fox skins. He added that this trade was undercut by competition from the Russian-American Company's other outposts on the Yukon.[14] Zagoskin thus echoed Wrangell's plan, adding that it would be highly desirable to intercept more of the furs that the Chukchi traders were still carrying to the Kolyma.

In fact, at that time the amount of furs that the Chukchi traders were selling at Ostrovnoe was indeed substantial: Waldemar Bogoras found a report from 1837 in the Kolyma archives stating that 100 beaver pelts, 395 marten, 30 lynx, "31 marten garments, etc." from Alaska were traded at the fair, as well as approximately "one-half of the 580 red foxes, 80 gray foxes, 13 black foxes, 268 white foxes, 8 blue foxes, and 1,563 walrus-tusks" that were sold that year. "These figures, moreover," Bogoras added, "must be at least doubled to reach the real trade value, because the merchants of Kolyma always greatly underestimate data for official records."[15]

Zagoskin advised that the Russians had to usurp the role of middlemen from the native traders and proposed that this could be done by establishing regular trading relations with the natives. "First, we must without fail buy up every kind of pelt, whether fox, otter, arctic fox, muskrat, rabbit, swan, or whatever. Second, we must try to have on hand [at Mikhailovsky], and especially on the Yukon, all the commodities necessary to the native way of life. These . . . consist of all the local products of the country. By buying from one and selling to the other we must take upon ourselves the role of middleman in the trade between the peoples of the coast and those of the Yukon."[16]

In the aftermath of the smallpox epidemic of 1838–39 which had devastated Eskimo and Koyukon nations near the Yukon, the structure of the native trade in Norton Sound changed significantly: Iñupiat traders ("Malimiut") began moving south, primarily from the Kotzebue Sound area and a few from the Seward Peninsula, into the depopulated lands of the Yup'ik Eskimos on the eastern shore of Norton Sound, becoming middlemen in supplying furs overland to the Sheshalik fair and thus from there to the Chukchi. Consequently it appears that the role of the Sheshalik fair was enhanced, while simultaneously the volume of the exchanges at Big Diomede and Port Clarence was somewhat diminished—as was the role of the Sledge Island and King Island traders—by the arrival of these new traders.

The coastal natives of Norton Sound then traded these goods onward, to the natives living on the Yukon, "always adding one or more leaves of tobacco to each hide of a fur-bearing animal: one doe hide or winter buck hide for 2 prime beaver pelts; two fall skins of young [caribou] for six beaver; one buck or doeskin for a prime [river] otter; one spring buck skin or doeskin, depending on the whiteness of the feet, for 1 or 2 beaver; six winter [caribou] and two fall skins of young [caribou] for a *tulun* (22 pieces) of [marten]; . . . four winter [caribou] skins for one Arctic red fox; 6, 8, or 10 [caribou] skins for a dark brown or black one."[17]

Zagoskin noted that the presence of Russian trading posts had interfered with the Malimiut control of the trade with the Yukon peoples and that they "encourage hostility towards us," but he suggested to Etholen that "if we can satisfy their needs by regularly trading our European products with them, then we can be sure of developing them into trusty helpers for collecting the trade products of the natives living north of Bering Strait."[18]

Zagoskin reported that the Athapascans (Koyukon), who inhabited the middle Yukon east of Norton Sound and whom the Eskimos called "Ulukagmyut," also acted as middlemen in the trade with the Malimiut Eskimos, adding that when the Russians learned of the richness of the fur yields on the middle Yukon and sent Andrei Kondratievich Glazunov from Mikhailovsky to investigate the region's potential, his Koyukon guides had led him over long and difficult trails, concealing the easiest route to Nulato. It was only in 1838 that a young boy inadvertently showed Pyotr Vasilievich Malakhov the best portage to the interior.[19]

Zagoskin advised that until the company could set up a post near Bering Strait or in Kotzebue Sound, "We must remember that every piece of fur that once slips by our northern posts in the interior crosses to the Asiatic shore, and undermines the trade of the Company." The reason for the strength of the cross–Bering Strait trade was, he felt, that the merchants on the Kolyma and Anadyr rivers paid four to six times as much for the furs as the Russians did at Mikhailovsky. He also advocated increasing the activities of the Nulato post for the same reason, acknowledging "how pervasive the influence of the Chukchi is, and how detrimental it is to our budding trade in that area."

Zagoskin went on to state that the company was, in effect, competing against itself by trading large amounts of tobacco at Mechigmensky Bay on the Chukchi Peninsula for walrus ivory and furs at four to six times the price it was paying for the same at Mikhailovsky. "When we visited the natives of the [lower Koyukuk River] we found them in possession of a supply of articles, numerous in comparison to those from Kolyma [Ostrovnoe] that were exports to the colonies and which had reached them through the [Malimiut] of Kotzebue Sound. The tobacco which is so well known in the north under the name of Azyagmyut [Sledge Islanders] tobacco is pure Cherkass tobacco given to the Chukchi from our boats, and prepared by them in some special fashion. We even happened on some shreds of tobacco pouches stamped with R.A.K. (Russian-American Company)."

Zagoskin also explained that Mikhailovsky was itself part of the problem in obtaining furs from the interior: the Russians often kept the best trade goods at Mikhailovsky for trade with the visiting natives and released far too little to supply the interior posts, which were, after all, near where the furs originated. This situation encouraged native middlemen to come to Mikhailovsky, and, Zagoskin continued, if insufficient trade goods were supplied to the outposts, then the flow of furs would be diverted to the Sheshalik fair, where the Chukchi purchased them and ultimately carried them to the Ostrovnoe fair. Zagoskin advocated increasing the pay and provisions of the outpost personnel and sending them out into the surrounding country to trade directly with the trappers and thus to prevent native middlemen from acquiring the furs.[20]

Although in 1839 the company had built a seasonal outpost at Nulato on the middle Yukon, near its confluence with the Koyukuk River, it was not until 1841 that Vasily Maksimovich Deriabin became the first resident manager. When he arrived, Deriabin found that the company's cabin had been burned down. He was unable to learn who had put it to the torch. It is tempting to speculate that the local Koyukon middlemen resented this intrusion into their trade monopoly. Deriabin rebuilt the post, but to make matters worse, for the next four years the manager at Mikhailovsky neglected to send sufficient trade goods to Nulato. It was not until Zagoskin's return to Novo-Arkhangelsk in 1844 that Etholen learned about the situation. Etholen ordered a new manager to make Nulato's supply a priority, particularly so because, when Zagoskin had been there, he had seen a group of Koyukon with a large number of marten, beaver, and wolverine pelts that they had bought on a trading trip upstream on the Yukon.[21]

In 1845 Deriabin returned to Novo-Arkhangelsk to discuss the situation at Nulato with the new chief manager of the colony, Mikhail Dmitrievich Tebenkov. Tebenkov, of course, had himself established Mikhailovsky Redoubt in 1833, and he recognized the importance of the Nulato outpost, both as a key to the middle Yukon and as a way of intercepting the furs that were being carried to Kotzebue Sound. By 1846 the Russian-American Company was able to report to its shareholders that "the chief concern of the colonial authorities is now focused on entirely stopping, to the degree possible, the transfer of American furs to the Chukchi and through them to the Yakutsk merchants."[22]

Deriabin was well supplied when he returned to Nulato in 1846. In the following summers he made several trips upriver—as far as the vast wetland basin called the Yukon Flats—to collect beaver, lynx, marten, mink, muskrat, and river otter pelts from the natives there before the Koyukon middlemen could get hold of them. These trips also helped to diminish the stream of furs that reached the Chukchi traders.

Tebenkov's predecessor, Etholen, had understood the difficulties of setting up a post in Kotzebue Sound and of keeping it reliably supplied by sea. He had only been able to instruct the captain of the annual Mikhailovsky supply ship to try to intercept the Chukchi traders at Bering Strait and to buy their furs. This idea was identical to the advice that Eliab Grimes had given to John Ebbets in his report of 1819. Tebenkov also wrestled with this problem and explored the idea of setting up an outpost on one of the Diomedes to intercept the flow of furs to the Kolyma. Although he felt that the attempts to reach Kotzebue Sound by sea in 1842 and 1843 had been half-hearted, Tebenkov considered the possibility of supplying an outpost in Kotzebue Sound from Nulato. He ordered Deriabin to scout for a possible route overland from there to Kotzebue Sound. Deriabin and a party set out in November 1847, but they must have headed too far to the west: instead of crossing the height of land and finding a river system that drained into Kotzebue Sound, after seventeen days of travel they met a group of Malimiut who were three days' march upriver from Shaktoolik, a settlement on eastern Norton Sound. The Eskimos may have been gathered for a Messenger Festival with a group from the interior. The natives greeted the Russian party cordially, but Deriabin was suspicious about the possibility of being attacked, and he returned to Nulato. The plans to find an overland route to Kotzebue Sound from Nulato apparently ended there.[23]

Had the Russians persisted, the initiative might have been very profitable. If the company had been able to supply sufficient trade goods to the Kotzebue Sound outpost and protect it—it is not at all certain that they would have been able to do this—the Russians might have broken into the native trade network and undersold the price of goods coming from Asia. Furthermore, if they had been able to maintain a well-supplied outpost in Mechigmensky Bay, thus positioned—athwart the main route to Ostrovnoe from Bering Strait—they would probably have ended the cross–Bering Strait native trade by supplying the natives on both shores with the goods they sought.

In 1847 the company continued its efforts to intercept the Chukchi furs by trading on the Asian coast, but a survey of the mouth of the Anadyr River, where it was thought they could trade profitably, turned up nothing. Tebenkov reported to the Main Office, "If there even are foxes, wolves, arctic foxes, and other fur bearers there, we cannot withstand the competition in the price the local traders give the natives at Anadyrsky ostrog, Gizhiga, and Kolyma or Ostrovny." The company, which forbade the sale of alcohol to the northern natives, reported to its shareholders, "Unfortunately, the visit to the Anadyr River in 1847 also convinced one that the development of the company's trade with the Chukchi presents an important obstacle in that the necessary basis of their trade with the Siberian merchants is strong drink, and this item is entirely abolished in the company's dealings with native tribes. This circumstance may for a considerable time postpone the attainment of useful results from trade with the Chukchi."[24] The Russian-American Company's next challenge would come, not from the Chukchi traders in the west but rather from the east, from the Hudson's Bay Company.

10

The British Expansion Northwestward

In the latter eighteenth century the rivalry between the Hudson's Bay Company and its principal competitor, the North West Company, which was based in Montreal, focused on developing new sources of furs. Whereas sables and, later, sea otters had driven the Russian expansion eastward, it was primarily beavers that drew the British traders west. The largest market for beaver skins was not for clothing but rather the hat industry, which used the pelt's underfur in felt making.[1]

Because the Hudson's Bay Company enjoyed a chartered monopoly over the lands within the Hudson Bay drainage, its competitors in Montreal, who at first were mainly French, focused their attention on the St. Lawrence River and Great Lakes drainage. By the 1750s, however, the supply of beavers near the Ottawa River declined, forcing the traders to seek new areas, and in 1778, the same year that Captain James Cook's ships were charting the coasts of Alaska and Bering Strait, Peter Pond crossed the height of land between the Hudson Bay and Mackenzie River drainages at Methye Portage (Portage La Loche) and wintered near Lake Athabasca, a region lying beyond the chartered lands of the Hudson's Bay Company. Pond's historic exploration opened to the Montrealers the fur-rich Athabasca region, which has been called "the Eldorado of the fur trade."[2]

Eleven years later, while Billings's expedition was underway—and the same year that the Ostrovnoe trade fair began—Alexander Mackenzie set off from Fort Chipewyan. He descended the waterways to Great Slave Lake and became the first European to travel down the Mackenzie River. Mackenzie was searching for a waterway to the Pacific Ocean, to link his explorations with Cook's. But on this journey he was severely discouraged: he found that the Mackenzie River flowed not west but northwest, and in mid-July 1789 he reached tidewater at the shore of the Arctic Ocean in the Mackenzie delta. Ten days later, on his return upriver, Mackenzie met a group of Gwich'in and learned that they were "continually at variance" with the Eskimos. The Gwich'in claimed that the Eskimos were "a people who take every advantage of attacking those who are not in a state to defend themselves; and though they had promised friendship, had lately, and in the most treacherous manner, butchered some of their people. . . . They also declared their determination to withdraw all confidence in the future from the Esquimaux, and to collect themselves in a formidable body, that they might be enabled to revenge the death of their friends."

Although Mackenzie misunderstood part of the message, he learned that some trade did in fact go on between the Gwich'in and Eskimos. The Gwich'in had received small amounts of iron from the Eskimos, which, he was told, the Eskimos had acquired eight or ten years before from other Eskimos farther to the west. Thus some form of trade relations must have existed between the Mackenzie Eskimos and those farther to the west prior to the commencement of the regular trade exchanges at Barter Island. The early exchanges may well have been sporadic because of the scarcity of manufactured goods that were available to the Alaskan Eskimos, and of course they may have been broken off because of warfare between the Alaskan and Mackenzie Eskimos.

In any case, those exchanges at Barter Island began — or were revived — near the very end of the eighteenth century or in the first years of the nineteenth century (see chapter 6). This was probably a result of the commencement of the Russian trade fairs in Chukotka and the consequent increase in the availability of foreign manufactured goods in the Bering Strait region. Before that time small amounts of iron may have reached the Mackenzie Eskimos from the Anadyr fort, which had been built in 1649 and was abandoned in 1764.[3]

The North West Company did not attempt to exploit Mackenzie's discoveries until 1799, when traders Duncan Livingston and James Sutherland, along with seven others, including three native guides, reached the lower Mackenzie by canoe. All but one of the party were killed, but there are conflicting accounts of their deaths: it is unclear whether they were killed by Eskimos or by their own guides.

Despite these murders, fur traders continued to descend the Mackenzie, and in 1800 the North West Company built a post on Great Bear Lake. In 1804 it advanced farther, building Fort Good Hope at the mouth of the Hare Indian River. In 1809, another trader went far downriver, to the head of the Mackenzie delta, but there "a numerous party of Eskimaux, occupying both banks of the river, put themselves in such a menacing attitude, that it was deemed prudent to return, without making any attempt either to land or to proceed farther."[4]

By 1815, the North West Company's trade on the Mackenzie was declining, and the company abandoned its posts on the river, temporarily leaving the region without a European presence, "a fact that caused hardship and anger among the Indians." But in 1816 Willard-Ferdinand Wentzel canoed as far as Fort Good Hope with some trade goods. He was greeted "with extravagant demonstrations of joy" and promised to try to have some posts reestablished. The next year another Nor'wester, Charles Grant, went downriver and traded successfully. By 1820, three posts were back in operation on the river, and two more were reopened in 1821, coinciding with a significant event in the history of Canada: the amalgamation of the North West Company and the Hudson's Bay Company.[5]

PEEL'S RIVER POST

It was John Franklin's expedition of 1826 that ultimately led the Hudson's Bay Company to explore farther northwest. On the expedition's return from the Arctic coast, as the boats neared the Mackenzie delta, Augustus, the expedition's Eskimo interpreter, learned from the Herschel Islands Eskimos that they might be ambushed by the "Mountain Indians." Those Eskimos told Augustus that after the expedition had passed Herschel Island bound west, seven Gwich'in men had traveled overland to the mouth of the "Mountain Indian River" (the Firth River), near Herschel Island, to trade. According to Augustus, upon seeing the goods that Franklin had given to the Eskimos, the Gwich'in realized that the presence of foreigners "should ruin their trade with the Esquimaux." They learned that the expedition had not yet returned from the west and heard of the Eskimos' attempt to capture the party near Tent Island. Lacking canoes, they planned to attack Franklin's men when they camped at the mouth of the Mackenzie. The Eskimos, wrote Franklin, "urged us to make all speed, and not to halt in the night, nor to go to sleep; but, if the crew became tired, to put up on an island out of gun-shot of the main shore, because the Gwich'in were armed with guns as well as bows. They instructed Augustus minutely as to the course we were to steer . . . and directed us to keep along the main shore until we should come to a large opening, which was the western outlet of the Mackenzie, and had a deep channel."

The Eskimos may have been trying to keep the explorers' trade to themselves, but whether or not this information was true, Franklin followed the Eskimos' advice and kept to the western shore as he entered the Mackenzie delta. After several days, Franklin realized that he was ascending a tributary, not the main channel of the Mackenzie. He named the tributary Peel River and reported that it appeared to flow from the mountains to the west.[6]

One result of the merger of the Hudson's Bay Company and the North West Company was that the British Parliament granted the new company a trading monopoly over not only the Hudson Bay watershed but also the Mackenzie and Pacific drainages. At the same time George Simpson, then governor of the company's Northern Department, faced the problem of having too many posts whose trading areas overlapped. He closed a number to eliminate competition among them, and he established trading posts in other areas where the furs originated, thus forcing the middlemen to become trappers themselves.[7]

But by 1821 the newly merged company's opportunities for expansion were essentially limited to the farthest northwest and to lands west of the Rocky Mountains. In 1823 the company recognized that Fort Good Hope was too far upriver to allow the Gwich'in ease of access and moved the post farther downstream to the Travaillant (Trading) River, on the border of the Gwich'in and Hare Indian territories. But the lack of local game presented problems when it came to provisioning the post, so in 1827 it was relocated upriver to its old site, which again made it difficult for the Gwich'in to visit. Nevertheless, "when the Hudson's Bay Company expanded along the lower Mackenzie River," wrote Kenneth Coates, "the eastern bands of the [Gwich'in] now found themselves with a consistent supply of European goods and were able to set themselves up in a strong middleman position *vis-á-vis* the western [Gwich'in] and Han Indians. Although the pre-contact institutions remained in existence after the arrival of European traders on the periphery, the actual trading networks proved to be highly variable, with considerable reorientation occurring as native groups moved to exploit new sources of European commodities."[8]

Even so, the company did not begin to look farther north until 1837, when Dease and Simpson were sent to follow up on Franklin's explorations. They returned with the news of the discovery of the Colville River, which seemed to have potential for access to the interior. Two years later John Bell set out from Fort Good Hope to investigate Franklin's report of the Peel River. Bell spent two months on the river and apparently ascended it for at least ninety miles, until it became too shallow and fast for further progress. He then returned downriver and explored a tributary of the Peel, the Rat River (see rear endpaper map). Bell ascended the Rat and met a large group of Gwich'in with whom he traded successfully and who told him about a portage at its headwaters to the lands of the "Tramontane Loucheux" (Gwich'in) and their furs.[9]

The explorer Vilhjalmur Stefansson saw Bell's meeting as a historic moment, for it took place at the height of land between the headwaters of the Rat and Bell rivers, between the Mackenzie and Yukon watersheds: "So there Bell was on the continental divide . . . and camped at a swampy meadow where the waters seep in two directions, one trickle bound for the Yukon and the Pacific, another for the Mackenzie and thus to a navigable water connection southeast to the middle regions of North America."[10]

In June 1839 the council of the Hudson's Bay Company's Northern Department, chaired by George Simpson, resolved to "take the necessary steps to establish in the summer of 1840 a post on Peel's River, under the direction of Mr. Bell, and in 1841 another post on the head waters of Colville River." The Pelly had been explored in 1840 by Robert Campbell. It was later found to be a tributary of the upper Yukon River, but briefly it was thought that the Pelly might in fact be the upper Colville River, the mouth of which Dease and Simpson had located on the Arctic coast in 1837. If so, the thinking went, the Colville had the possibility of allowing access to the interior, not only as a transportation route for the fur trade but also as a navigable route to the Pacific. In spite of this, it was not until 1851 that Robert Campbell descended the Pelly and reached Fort Yukon, conclusively establishing that the Yukon was not the Colville.[11]

Bell, in scouting for a suitable location for a trading post, reported his concerns about the Eskimos. "The Proximity of the barbarous and savage Esquimaux may probably prove vexatious in the beginning as they shall no doubt visit the Establishment some time or other. They generally come up once a year to the mouth of the Peel, and on these excursions they invariably quarrel with their neighbors the Loucheux Indians, who inhabit that part of the country and with whom they are on the worst terms. Since my return off the voyage in August last I have heard that the Esquimaux had cruelly murdered six men of the Loucheux Indians whom they accidentally met with inland on a hunting expedition."[12]

The anthropologist Shepard Krech III has summarized the state of affairs between the Gwich'in and the Mackenzie Eskimos (today, Inuvialuit) in the first half of the nineteenth century. Between 1789 and the last recorded bloodshed (in 1850), the Gwich'in and Eskimos "fought each other in the lower Mackenzie and Peel River drainages at least twelve times. When they did not fight, they traded with each other, occasionally they hunted together for a week or more. In trade the [Gwich'in] were interested in whale bone for their nasal septa ornaments, seal oil, and sealskins. As their trade developed in the first half of the nineteenth century, the [Gwich'in] traded for . . . foxes . . . that the [Eskimos] trapped. The [Eskimos] desired mainly wolverine skins . . . and European trade goods."[13]

Elsewhere Krech has written:

The Inuvialuit tended to be coastal and the Gwich'in to remain inland, but they both exploited the resources of the Mackenzie Delta. Moreover, the Inuvialuit needed flint for projectile and spear points and knives, and several excellent and favoured sources were located well within Gwich'in territory. Gwich'in and Inuvialuit met annually and their meetings were potentially volatile. The Inuvialuit were contemptuous of all their Northern Athapascan neighbors, including the Gwich'in. Hostilities erupted with regularity and people on both sides were killed—on four occasions in the 1820s alone. But the Gwich'in and Inuvialuit also traded and hunted with each other, and the Gwich'in used their geographical location and possession of guns to control the terms of the trade, possibly exacerbating hostilities. . . .

A fundamental difference between Gwich'in and Inuvialuit was that the former possessed guns and the latter did not. Armed, the Gwich'in answered Inuvialuit contempt with firepower and prevented Inuvialuit from having access to HBC posts—first Fort Good Hope, later Peel River Post. Without guns, it is unlikely that they could have maintained their balance of power and their middleman trading position in the face of Inuvialuit assertiveness.[14]

Bell's superior, Chief Factor Murdoch McPherson, cautioned him about trading with the Eskimos at the new fort. "Their visits, it is well known, are not for the purposes of trade and there consequently can be no harm in discouraging them at least till they are found to be more profitable," he wrote. In May 1840, Bell left Fort Good Hope in a party of eighteen. At the mouth of the Peel a group of Gwich'in was waiting for them "with a view of acting as an escort to our party," Bell wrote, "in the event of a collision with the Esquimaux, whose uniform hostility to the whites rendered a meeting with them anything but desirable." Bell gave the Gwich'in presents but declined their offer of escort.[15]

On June 15, about forty miles up the Peel, he reached the site of what would be known first as Peel's River Post and later as Fort McPherson. In December he reported to George Simpson: "I did not see any of the Esquimaux as I anticipated on my passage down the Mackenzie, as none of them came up during the summer. The *Loucheux* Indians who had a severe blow to avenge, paid them a very unwelcome visit soon after the opening of the navigation in the spring; and without shewing them the least mercy massacred a whole camp of them."

Bell added that soon after he reached the site of the post a large party of muskrat hunters visited from "across the Western Mountains." "With them [was] a strange Indian whose lands are still more remote than theirs. He gave me a flattering description of that distant country which he represents to be rich in Beaver. It is now evident that most of the Beaver procured from the Rat Indians [bands of Gwich'in from the upper Porcupine River and Crow Flats] have been, and are still, bartered with that distant nation."

Peel's River Post began well. By August 25, 1840, Bell had sent to Fort Good Hope 590 beavers, 163 martens, 15,000 muskrats, 2 otters, 1 bear skin, 1 lynx, and 70 dressed moose skins. By December 9, he had in store at the post 350 beavers, 360 martens, 6 wolverines, 2 wolves, 2 otters, 1 silver fox, 1 red fox, 1 bear skin, and 300 muskrats.[16]

In the autumn, several small groups of Athapascans visited the post, and Bell reported "an Indian of the Tribe called by the Interpreter 'Les Gens Fou' [*Gens de Fou*, or Han] made his appearance here and gave a very favorable account of the country he inhabits. He appeared to be pleased with the treatment he received and promised faithfully to conduct a party of his relations here on the last Ice." He added that in October a group of the "Rat Loucheux" brought in 220 beaver and 100 muskrats. Bell ended his report with a plea for more trade goods. "I have further to beg you will be as liberal as possible in the supply of guns and large kettles for the trade, there being an extraordinary demand for these articles."[17]

In July 1841, Bell recounted that in the spring "a large party of the Rat Indians from the westward Rocky Mountains" had arrived with a valuable catch of furs, but Bell had "scarsely any thing in Store to pay for their Hunts." Nevertheless, the Gwich'in waited at the post until the "Outfit" arrived from the Mackenzie, and "they were immediately equipped to the full extent of their demands, and . . . they took their departure highly satisfied. Out of the 25 guns that came down this party alone took 20, all paid in fine Beaver." They also bought a large amount of ammunition and beads, but few dry goods.[18]

By December 1841, although Bell's trade was developing well and the number of beaver and marten skins was increasing, he had been unsuccessful in inducing the "strange tribe of Indians lately discovered" to visit the post. He assumed that their trapping lands were so far to the west that it was not practical for them to travel to the post "carrying their furs across a long chain of Mountainous country." He added that "those strangers from the Westward were in the habit of bartering with another nation more remote than themselves; and who apparently received their supplies from the Russian Establishment." Thus Bell was developing an understanding of the flow of furs that were going west. Athapascan middlemen were most likely carrying these furs toward the Bering Strait region, and after passing through other hands, the furs were probably reaching both Mikhailovsky Redoubt and the trade rendezvous at Sheshalik.[19]

In 1842 Bell continued his explorations across the height of land, searching for

Figure 10.1. Fort McPherson (formerly Peel's River Post), 1847. Alexander Hunter
Murray Journal, Beinecke Rare Book and Manuscript Library, Yale University.

the native group from whom he had been receiving beaver skins via middlemen.
This time he crossed the Richardson Mountains via another route. On a difficult
five-day march he descended the Bell River. Nevertheless Bell returned to the
Peel's River Post believing that the overland route was too difficult to be used
for moving supplies in the fur trade. In fact, without knowing it, he had been at
a much easier portage between the Rat and Bell in 1839, a portage that was only
about a thousand feet above sea level, but which would not be used for another
thirty years and would become known as McDougall Pass.[20]

Bell, however, informed his superior that in December 1842 a group of "Musquash Indians" ["Rat Indians"—Gwich'in] had visited the post and traded for
guns and ammunition, paying with beaver and marten skins. The Gwich'in told
Bell that they had met a party of "Mountain Tribe Indians more remote than
themselves." Bell hoped that this group would visit the post at the end of May.[21]

The following summer, 1843, James Pruden and John Lee Lewes also failed to
find a practicable route through the Richardson Mountains because of the "Mis-
conduct of the Indian Guide," who deserted the party. Bell felt that the "Musquash Indians" had no desire to have the Hudson's Bay Company enter their
territory because the company's presence would destroy their role as middlemen
in the trade. "It appears to me a very extraordinary and mysterious proceeding
on the part of the Musquash Indians," he reported to George Simpson, "who
have been repeatedly told of our wish to establish a Post beyond the Mountains,
was principally for their own interest and comfort, that it would be the means
of exempting them in future from carrying their hunts upon their backs across
the Mountains to the Peel River. It seems they are not very desirous that we
should extend our trade beyond its present limits. They are no doubt aware that
an Establishment upon their lands would put a stop to the lucrative trade which
they carry on with the strange tribes inhabiting the Inland country more remote
than their own hunting grounds."[22]

At Peel's River Post, John Bell encountered the same reception that Eliab Grimes had received from the Chukchi middlemen at Big Diomede Island in 1819 and that Andrei Kondratievich Glazunov had met with the Koyukon while searching for portage from the Unalakleet River to the Yukon: the natives were protecting their role as middlemen and, in fact, without knowing it, were resisting George Simpson's initiative to place posts were the furs were located, which would have forced the native middlemen to become trappers themselves. The result, of course, was that as each new post advanced farther into virgin fur territory, one group of natives became fur hunters while other groups, farther away, themselves became the new middlemen.

Shepard Krech III put it this way: "Middlemen positions did alter some Kutchin [Gwich'in] who had participated indirectly in the Fort Good Hope trade [and] now came directly to Peel River Post. Mackenzie Flats, Peel River and Upper Porcupine River Kutchin were the most frequent direct participants. All were also middlemen, and the Upper Porcupine River Kutchin and Crow River Kutchin to their west became known as quite aggressive traders."[23]

No doubt for their own advantage, the Gwich'in lost no time in telling Bell about Russian trading activities farther west, perhaps referring to the Russian-American Company's Nulato outpost.

The Peel and Musquash Indians have often mentioned to me the existence of an Establishment at great distance inland, in the direction, or probably beyond, the Colvile River; and lately discovered by the Strange Tribe with whom my Indians traffic. I have seen a quantity of large Blue, Red and Cut Beads, and long Columbia Shells [dentalium shells], likewise a course Cotton Shirt of divers Colours, and made like our Guernsey Frocks, but of sufficient length to fit a Man of 6 feet.

The Strange Indians are inviting my Musquash Hunters to accompany them to that new Establishment, being nearer to them than the Peel, and where they assured them to get a handful (the Indians expression) of Beads for a MB [Made Beaver] skin. Should this report prove correct, the Musquash Indians may probably be prevailed upon by the importunity of their neighbours, to make that Fort (if any such) their future resort, and thus their valuable hunts be lost to this place.

In yr. last much valued communication, you had the goodness to inform me that the Russians "had pushed their establishment from Norton Sound in the direction of the Colvile River." Might it not be from one of their advanced inland Posts, that the distant Strange Indians received the Beads and other trading articles I have already mentioned[?][24]

FORT YUKON

By the end of 1844 John Bell was ready to make a third attempt to explore west-ward from Peel's River Post. In summer 1845 he took the route he had covered in 1842. This time, however, following Governor George Simpson's advice, he hired guides who were ignorant of the lands to the west; hence "had no self-interest conflicting with the purposes of exploration," wrote the historian Kenneth Coates. He crossed through the Richardson Mountains to the Bell River, where he built canoes, then descended the Bell to what would be called the Porcu-pine River and descended the Porcupine to its confluence with the Yukon. Bell's highly important journey brought the Hudson's Bay Company to within about three hundred miles of the Russian-American Company's explorations on the middle Yukon.[25]

On his journey Bell met only a few Gwich'in because most "were absent on trading excursions to another tribe at some distance down the River." Neverthe-less he learned that the area was rich in fish, game, and furs because he had seen salmon weirs and "several Deposits of valuable Furs hung up in trees along with other property and the vestiges of Moose Deer was seen in every point and Island on which we landed."

"I have made particular enquiries respecting the existence of any trading Establishment in the vicinity of that River," he wrote to George Simpson about his discussions with the natives.

> It is evident from their reply there are no trading posts in any part of the Inland Country, but they admit that white People (Russians, I suppose) have been seen by the natives inhabiting the Banks of the River below them. These whites ascend the lower part of the River on trading excursions among the Inland natives, and are represented to be very liberal in distributing their goods for the Furs which they procure.
>
> The Esquimaux to the westwards likewise ascend the "Youcon" and carry on a trade with the Natives, as well as with the Musquash Indians who come an-nually to our Establishment on the Peel. I have seen a large camp of the latter tribe on the Rat River who had about a doz. of beat iron Kettles of Russian manufacture which they bartered from the Esquimaux. . . .
>
> The Musquash Indians came in a large party to the Ft. this summer with excellent hunts. They have apparently great aversion to the extension of trade to the west side of the Mountains, as such a step would no doubt put a stop to the lucrative trade they carry on with the natives in that quarter.[26]

So Bell confirmed that Russian trade goods were reaching the Yukon via both Athapascans and Eskimos. The natives' manufactured goods no doubt originated from the Russian-American Company; the Eskimos' manufactured goods, however, may have come via the Ostrovnoe, Port Clarence, and Sheshalik fairs. Bell also confirmed that the native middlemen did not welcome the company's intrusion into their monopoly.

Echoing Peter Warren Dease's concerns of twenty years before, Bell worried about the vulnerability of the Peel's River Post to attack from the Eskimos. He was convinced that Eskimo-Gwich'in hostilities were hurting trade. Nevertheless, at the end of 1843 Bell had sent some surprising news to John Lee Lewes. Bell reported that a group of Mackenzie Eskimos wanted to establish trade relations with the post. He learned from one of the Mackenzie River Gwich'in that in September a group of eight Eskimos had traveled from the coast to Arctic Red River and camped with the Gwich'in for a week "apparently on friendly terms, the result of which has been a lasting peace concluded between these hostile tribes. Whether this long wished for reconciliation is feigned or sincere on the part of the Esquimaux, time only can show. They are seemingly very desirous of opening a friendly intercourse with the Whites," Bell wrote. He noted that the Eskimos planned to meet with the Gwich'in the following summer and to visit the post. He added, "I do not apprehend any danger from their presence, especially when they are accompanied by our friendly Indians of McK. River."[27]

Bell's hopes were soon dashed. "During my absence, hostilities broke out between the two rival tribes, the Peel Indians [Gwich'in] and the *Esquimaux* and blood has been shed not withstanding the recent peace concluded between the hostile parties," he continued in his report to Simpson.

This much wished for reconciliation was not of long duration and it is from the Esquimaux's conduct was feigned, and a mere cloak to cover their treachery. Two men, two women and two children of the Peel Indians have been killed and three men of the esquimaux were shot on the spot. This unfortunate affair took place near the mouth of the Peel. The *Huskies* [Eskimos] were the aggressors, having committed this cowardly exploit by a nocturnal surprise. Three of our men coming down from Ft. Good Hope . . . had a narrow escape as those savages were watching for them. . . .

It needs no acute penetration to divine the wicked design of the Esquimaux which was evidently to attack the Establishment; or they would not have massacred Indians with whom they seemed to be in terms of friendship, and who had frequently endeavoured to bring them to the Fort. I am apprehensive of the safety of the Establishment, especially when it is so weakly guarded during the people's absence on the voyage to Fort Simpson with the returns. . . . It would therefore be very desirable that half a dozen Muskets be sent in to Peel's River, not with the intentions of blowing up the Huskies, but with the view of defending our lives and the honble. Company's property, in the event of these savages attacking us.[28]

But in 1846, although the Hudson's Bay Company men had built a halfway house (La Pierre's House) at the headwaters of the Bell River, they were unable to follow up on John Bell's expedition to the Yukon because of a lack of boats. In 1847, however, after Bell had been reassigned to a post farther south, Alexander Hunter Murray was ordered to build a post at the confluence of the Yukon and Porcupine rivers. On April 1, 1847, he wrote to Murdoch McPherson that all the necessary goods had already been stored at La Pierre's House and that the men were cutting timber to build a boat to descend the watershed to the Yukon in the summer.[29]

Murray left Peel's River Post on June 11, 1847, and immediately found that "the labyrinth of swamps and lakes" was flooded. A punishing journey lay ahead: "We waded most of the way knee deep, but often to the middle in sludge and water, the day was clear and warm, and the mosquitos had already begun their ravages, which rendered the commencement of the voyage anything but pleasant." The next day he wrote, "Although stiff in the joints and otherwise fatigued I could sleep little, from my moss bed having sunk into the water, and from a severe attack of heartburn occasioned by eating raw pemmican which generally disagrees with my stomach." Murray found the Bell River in flood and was forced to rope his way across it. He reached La Pierre's House on June 14.[30]

Murray left La Pierre's House on June 18 and descended the Bell and the Porcupine. When he reached the Yukon on June 25, he turned upstream and found a site to build Fort Yukon about three miles above the confluence, which was "a central location to the surrounding tribes of Indians." "No time was lost in commencing with the necessary operations," he wrote to Murdoch McPherson in November, "and the whole of my people have been constantly employed ever since." They had built a dwelling house and storehouse before the onset of winter, and during the winter of 1847–48 he planned to prepare timber for other houses and the stockade's wall.

"News of our arrival soon spread among the Natives, and in a few days therefore we were visited by several large parties," Murray continued, "all of whom, except a few that had seen the Russians, never before met with White people." The presence of a trading post on the Yukon meant that the Upper Porcupine River Gwich'in (the "Rat Indians") lost their position as middlemen between the Hudson's Bay Company and the Gwich'in bands farther west. "The Rat Indians are enraged at our being here," he wrote.[31]

Shepard Krech III put it this way: "The establishment of Fort Yukon led to a

Figure 10.2. Alexander Hunter Murray's expedition crossing the
Bell River, 1847. Alexander Hunter Murray Journal, Beinecke Rare Book
and Manuscript Library, Yale University.

great deal of stress. The Upper Porcupine River [Gwich'in] were upset at the loss
of their middleman position and the evaporation of their lucrative trade; the
Yukon Flats [Gwich'in] immediately capitalized on their newly strategic position. . . . Many of the furs that had flowed into Peel River Post from the west were
now redirected to Fort Yukon." And some Gwich'in began to manipulate the
company's credit system in which goods were advanced to certain Gwich'in to
encourage them to trade at a certain post. In 1848, Krech continued, "an Upper
Porcupine River [Gwich'in] who had traded at Peel River Post since 1840, took
his furs to Fort Yukon where he convinced company traders to accept them. . . .
In another instance, a Crow River [Gwich'in] traded high-value marten at Fort
Yukon and low-value, high transport-cost muskrats at Peel River Post, a situation
that infuriated the Peel River Post clerk."[32]

Alexander Hunter Murray described a visit by Rat Indians to Fort Yukon in
August 1847. "They had a few Martens and Beaver, and a large quantity of rat
skins notwithstanding they all knew that no rats would be traded here; but these
fellows had debts at Peels River which they intended to evade paying and expected to receive payment for all they brought. I did not wish to encourage any
of the Indians to leave Peels River, particularly those that were nearer to it than
this, and refused to trade their Musquash [muskrat]. . . . They were greatly dis-
pleased at this of course, and two of them flung about forty skins (480 rats) into
the fire."[33]

The Gwich'in lost no time in telling the British about the Russians and twisting the information to their own best advantage. "They had a great quantity of beads, kettles, guns, powder, knives and pipes and traded all the furs from the bands, principally for beads and knives, after which they traded dogs, but the Gwich'in were unwilling to part with their dogs, and the Russians rather than go without gave a *gun* for each." It was, as we have seen, against the policy of the Russian-American Company to trade guns to the northern natives.[34]

Although by November 20 Murray had the post well provisioned with game for the winter and had collected prime beaver and marten skins that he valued at £1,403, he had almost exhausted his supply of trade goods and was forced to try to persuade the Gwich'in to hold onto their skins until he received his next outfit in the summer. The problem, he wrote, was that the Gwich'in had "hitherto been in the habit of trading with another band of Indians between [here] and the Coast, who dispose of the Furs to the Russians." He added that he expected two bands, which usually traded with the Russians, to visit his fort, and he asked for tobacco and knives from Peel's River Post. Although the lands nearby were "reported to abound in Beaver and Martens," and although the local Gwich'in appeared willing to hunt for the post's provisions and trap the furbearers, he needed to have an "extensive Outfit" of "Beads, Axes, Blankets, Guns and ammunition and Tobacco, which are greatly in demand here" to pay for the furs and food. Otherwise, he wrote, "it will be impossible to prevent the greater part of the Furs being taken to the Russians."

When the trade outfit reached Murray in January 1848, he was shocked to discover "so limited a supply of articles most needed (beads and guns) being sent; . . . there are only a quarter of a box of beads (16 lbs.). I would have been better satisfied had none at all been sent, as then I could have settled with the Indians alike, without displeasing one more than another. I am now at a loss what to do. There is one man of the upper band [Upper Porcupine River Gwich'in] who has between 90 and 100 skins in martens and beaver which he is keeping *all* for beads on our return. *Two men* would take more that what are sent, and how am I to settle with 300?" He added, "Without *beads* and plenty of them you can do little or no good here."[35]

"Beads are the riches of the Kutchin [Gwich'in]," wrote the explorer-scientist Sir (formerly Dr.) John Richardson, "and also the medium of exchange throughout the country lying between the Mackenzie and the west coast, other articles being valued by the number of strings of beads they can procure." According to Shepard Krech III, "Beads became a general purpose money, especially in fairly ordinary economic transactions. They were used to pay, for example, for furs, moose skins, and other items exchanged from Indians living farther from trading posts, and some bands, like the Yukon Flats Kutchin, were said almost to

Figure 10.3. "Saveeah, chief of the Kootcha-Kootchin," 1847. Alexander Hunter
Murray Journal, Beinecke Rare Book and Manuscript Library, Yale University.

have ceased hunting and to have become even more intense traders than they
had been before." William L. Hardisty, who succeeded Murray at Fort Yukon,
thought that some of the Gwich'in had become "essentially a commercial people,
and live by barter, supplying their wants by exchanging their beads, which form
the circulating medium, for the peltries of neighboring tribes." Thus the cycle
continued: as the posts advanced farther into unexplored territory, one group of
middlemen supplanted another.[36]

Despite his shortage of trade goods, when Murray reached La Pierre's House
in June 1848, he carried with him furs which he valued at £1,557, fifteen shillings,
and three pence, a sum the geographer C. Ian Jackson calculates to have been

worth £121,000 in 2001. Murray advised Murdoch McPherson that he could not bring out more furs because of the lack of trade goods. "Owing to the want of goods it was impossible for me [to] increase that sum, although an immense quantity of furs were already collected by the Natives, the greater part of which, I regret to say, I will not be able to procure, as I find my present Outfit so very limited in the articles most required."[37]

THE TRADE CIRCUIT BETWEEN FORT YUKON AND LONDON

It would be a long time before the furs that Murray collected at Fort Yukon during the winter of 1847–48 reached the market in London. First they had to be packed for the long journey. Before 1865 the Hudson's Bay men packed them in ninety-pound parcels. The skins were carefully arranged in a fur press, which was a lever apparatus that worked like a giant nutcracker. When the parcels were sufficiently compressed they were covered with other skins and heavy burlap to make them water-resistant, tightly sewn together, and then lashed with rope. Each bale was marked with the post of origin.

After 1865 the weight of a bale was reduced to eighty pounds. According to Martin Hunter, who had worked for the company, an eighty-pound bale might contain 40 large beavers and 20 small beavers; 8 large bears and 4 small bears; 500 spring muskrats; 720 large and small fall muskrats; 2 beavers for covers and 60 lynx skins; 2 beavers for covers and 30 otters; 2 beavers for covers and 50 fox skins. "A well-made pack would withstand all the hundreds of handlings in making a journey," wrote Hunter.[38]

If all went well, for example, in spring 1848 the Fort Yukon furs would be carried by boat to La Pierre's House, where they would be cached until winter, when they would be carried by dogsled to Peel's River Post. In summer 1849 the furs would go by boat up the Mackenzie and its tributaries to Fort Chipewyan on Lake Athabasca, then up the Athabasca and Clearwater rivers to the twelve-mile Methye Portage (Portage La Loche) rendezvous. There the "Mackenzie Brigade" would exchange the furs for trade goods that the "Athabasca Brigade" had hauled west from Norway House on Lake Winnipeg.[39] The furs would be stored for the winter at Norway House and in summer 1850 hauled by boat to York Factory, at tidewater on Hudson Bay. At York Factory the furs would be exchanged for inward-bound trade goods from the company's ship that had arrived from Great Britain. The ship would then depart with the furs, arriving in England in late autumn. The furs that reached London would be sold during the winter, with many going to Leipzig, where they might join some Alaskan furs that had been hauled westward across Bering Strait via the native trade network and onward, via Yakutsk and Irkutsk.

The following spring, 1851, trade goods destined for Fort Yukon were sent from England to York Factory on Hudson Bay. There they were hauled by York boats to Norway House and stored for the winter. In 1852 the Athabasca Brigade moved the goods to Methye Portage and swapped them for furs from the Mackenzie Brigade, who carried them downriver to Peel's River Post. In spring 1853 the trade goods would be hauled to La Pierre's House and stored until the men from Fort Yukon arrived there by boat in late June and exchanged their furs for the outfit. If everything went according to plan, the cycle that began in autumn 1847 would be completed in autumn 1853. "It took a minimum of seven, and sometimes eight or nine years for trade goods in London to be replaced by furs from Fort Yukon," writes C. Ian Jackson.[40]

Murray, writing from the end of the Hudson's Bay Company's line at Fort Yukon, reflected on his isolation: "I must say that we passed the summer very comfortably, although in the midst of a heathen land, and so far removed from civilized country. Fort Simpson, for instance, we Youconians consider as a partly *civilized* place, and talk of it as you would of Red river settlement. Rat Portage is to us what Portage la Loche [Methye Portage] is to the [people?] of the McKenzie, and we look upon Peel's River as being near home; but this is now our home, a home in the 'far west' with a vengeance."[41]

THE HUDSON'S BAY COMPANY IN RUSSIAN AMERICA

Murray also passed on a report from the Gwich'in about Russian activities on the Yukon. This information was somewhat confused in the retelling, and although the Gwich'in probably altered it to gain their best advantage in trade with the Hudson's Bay Company, the report probably referred to the Nulato post, near the confluence of the Koyukuk and Yukon rivers, where Vasily Maksimovich Deriabin had become the first resident trader in 1841. "The Russians, who have been in the habit of visiting the Youcon annually for the last four years, arrived last summer [1847] at their usual rendezvous between us and the mouth of the river, and having heard of our being in the Country commenced to build and a party of them passed the winter there. Their prices were immediately lowered and they have been opposing us as much as possible and endeavouring to incite the Indians against us."

Murray may also have heard a garbled report of the Russian use of the overland shortcut from Norton Sound to Nulato via the Unalakleet River. Again the Gwich'in may have altered the information to their advantage. "Several small parties of Indians of the lands between [here] and the S.W. Coast, arrived previous to my departure [for La Pierre's House]. During the winter they had been at one of the Russian Forts and by them I learned that our opponents have discovered a nearer Route to the Youcon, by a river that joins it above where we are established, and that it is their intention to visit us in the Summer. By last account they were making every preparation for the trip, and having their goods etc. brought over a narrow portage to the banks of the river they will descend. My informant knew or said nothing of their intentions towards us but they may easily be supposed, as a large party of 'Hankootchii' [Han] were to accompany them."[42]

The Gwich'in also told Murray that the Russians had ascended the Yukon in 1846 and 1847 to within eight days' travel from Fort Yukon and that they had intended to move farther up the river but were unable to do so. Murray was convinced that the Russians knew of the presence of the Hudson's Bay Company at Fort Yukon, and he asked Murdoch McPherson for instructions on how to deal with them if they reached the fort.[43]

In fact the Russians had indeed been getting closer to Fort Yukon. Ivan Zakharov had made an upriver trading expedition in 1845, and when Vasily Deriabin returned to Nulato in 1846, he carried with him instructions that the chief manager of the Russian-American colony, Mikhail Dmitrievich Tebenkov, had formulated on the basis of Zagoskin's and Deriabin's advice. Because of native reports of fur rich lands at the confluence of the Tanana and Yukon rivers, and farther upriver at "Lake Mintokh" (the Yukon Flats), Tebenkov ordered Deriabin to scout upriver for trading opportunities and to try to intercept furs that were being carried by native middlemen to the trade fair at Kotzebue Sound. Deriabin made several trips upriver between 1846 and 1851, just as the Hudson's Bay Company was beginning its operations at Fort Yukon.[44]

And the Russians had indeed confirmed the British presence on the river. In May 1849 Deriabin had left Nulato on his upstream trading expedition. When he was less than seventy miles from the Yukon Flats he encountered thirty canoes heading downstream. As a greeting, the natives fired a volley from their muskets. Deriabin responded in kind. Because the Russian-American Company prohibited the sale of firearms to the northern natives, it must have come as a shock to Deriabin that the natives had twelve guns among them. Deriabin learned that the natives had bought the guns from white men who had settled upstream on the river. The natives' muskets were of good quality, and they had beads unlike those sold by the Russian-American Company as well as twist tobacco and English knives. As Katherine Arndt has pointed out, "This was the first concrete evidence that . . . rumors [which had reached Mikhailovsky about six white foreigners on the river] had some basis in fact."[45]

But at Fort Yukon Murray had more on his mind than the matter of competition with the Russians: he was well aware that he had built Fort Yukon in Russian America. Murray kept a private journal of his activities in 1847 and 1848, which he sent to Murdoch McPherson. On June 21, 1847, as he descended the Porcu-pine River toward the Yukon, he wrote, "We are now, according to my reckoning, *across the Boundary Line*, and I have been on the look-out as we came along, for a site whereon to build; should it so happen, that we are compelled to re-treat upon our own territory." In the treaty of 1825, Russia and Great Britain had agreed to make the border between their territorial claims in North America at the 141st meridian west of Greenwich (see chapter 1). The treaty stipulated that "no establishment shall be formed by either of the two parties within the limits assigned . . . to the possession of the other; consequently British subjects shall not form any establishment, either upon the coast or upon the border of the conti-nent comprised within the limits of the Russian possessions."[46]

In fact Fort Yukon was four degrees, sixteen minutes (117 statute miles) west of the international border, although Murray calculated it as being even farther west, "six degrees of longitude across the Russian boundary." In describing Fort Yukon's stockade he noted that the walls were made of tree trunks sunk three feet into the ground and standing more than fourteen feet above ground. He added, "When all this is finished, the Russians may advance when they d——d please."[47]

Murray was also worried that he could not match the Russian prices. "We can-not begin to compete with the Russians as to prices, nor can I tell what the result will be after the full force of the opposition will be felt. I should like much to know what are the H.B. Company's intentions respecting this country, whether it will be leased from the Russians . . . or if we are to continue here regardless of them. In the latter case we shall in all likelihood get into some trouble, but if we have goods sufficient for the demands of the Indians, I doubt not but we might fight our way for a few years, unless the Russians build nearer to us than where they are now; as for their coming here in summer, I have great hopes, that the dis-tance and difficulty of navigating the river will be sufficient preventation."[48]

For the same reasons that the Gwich'in were quick to tell Murray about the Russians' activities, it did not take long for them to tell the Russians about the British presence on the river. In summer 1849 some of the natives who had visited Fort Yukon the year before, trying to find the best prices for their furs, had instead descended the river to meet the Russian traders, and after having done so, one of the "Gens de Bute" (Tanana) went upriver to Fort Yukon in August, carrying a letter that Deriabin had paid him to carry to the British traders.[49]

Murray could not read Russian, so he forwarded the letter to John Rae at Fort Simpson and to George Simpson. Neither Rae nor Simpson could read Russian, so the letter was forwarded to London, where it was translated. The translation was sent back over the usual route, a circuit of several years. In fact, however, the "letter" that the Tanana had presented to Murray was probably only the cover sheet of a letter from Vasily Deriabin, the contents of which were lost on its way to Murray:

The Russian-American Company's
baidarshchik [post manager] of Nulato
odinochka [outpost] Vasily Deriabin/ Kvivpak [Yukon] River
1849 June 17th

Deriabin's letter caused neither Murray nor Simpson great anxiety. Murray thought that the fact that a native was paid to carry the letter to Fort Yukon was evidence that the Russians were unable to do so themselves. Simpson decided to hold the course, and John Rae advised Murray to undersell the Russians by offering better prices for the furs.[50]

Murray replied to Deriabin's letter the following summer:

Youcon R. June 9th 1850.

Sir,

I have the honor to inform you that your note sent by an Indian has been received, but if there was anything of importance contained therein, I regret from ignorance of the Russian language and characters that I am unable to reply to you.

In case there be anything of importance to communicate to me, will you have the goodness to write to me in English or French, and I shall endeavour to send you an answer.

Alex. H. Murray[51]

In 1849 Deriabin had sent a report about the rumors of foreigners on the upper river to Novo-Arkhangelsk. From there it was forwarded to St. Petersburg on a circuit as slow as that of their British counterparts. By 1851 the directors in St. Petersburg had concluded that the foreigners on the river were agents of the Hudson's Bay Company. Although the Russian-American Company began again to focus on the upriver trade, especially the Yukon Flats, and intended to determine the location of Fort Yukon, in the 1850s it was hampered by declining revenues, weak chief managers, and the Crimean War. "The net result of the Russian-American Company's difficulties in the 1850s," wrote Katherine Arndt, "was an overall contraction of its activities in Alaska's interior. That its fur returns did not drop as sharply as might be expected must be credited to the activities of various native middlemen. Throughout the decade the company grew much more dependent upon their services to carry its trade to the far reaches of the colonies."

In 1860, however, an energetic new chief manager, Johan Hampus Furuhjelm, reinvigorated the Russian-American Company's activities, and one result of this was the resumption of spring trading expeditions upriver from Nulato. But, most important for Fort Yukon, the manager at Mikhailovsky sent Ivan Semyonovich Lukin, whose mother was probably an Athapascan, to "find the English settlement" on the Kvikhpak River. For a number of years the Russians had been sending trading parties upstream to the native trade rendezvous at Nuklukayet, where the Tanana River enters the Yukon. Lukin pushed on from Nuklukayet with a party of Athapascans and reached Fort Yukon, where, it is said, he pretended to be a defector from the Russian-American Company. "Ivan Lukin's arrival at Fort Yukon in the summer of 1862 . . . did not generate the panic it might have some fifteen years earlier," wrote Katherine Arndt, "for the post was now too well established to be threatened by the presence of a single Russian in a canoe. Indeed the Russian creole, by ancestry more than half native himself, may have blended in so well with the post's other visitors that [the Hudson's Bay Company men] learned of his presence only after the fact."[52]

Lukin returned downstream to Nulato, thereby establishing that the Kvikhpak and the Yukon were the same river, but the Russian-American Company, having for a time suspected that the two rivers were identical, did not broadcast his discovery and, probably because of a shortage of manpower, took no action against the Hudson's Bay Company or Fort Yukon.[53]

In 1864 the Hudson's Bay Company began sending trading parties downriver past Nuklukayet, thus taking over the role of the Fort Yukon Gwich'in, who had formerly acted as middlemen. These journeys, as well as the Russians' annual upriver expeditions, resulted in the entire middle and lower Yukon being covered by foreign traders, although the Hudson's Bay Company's traders enjoyed an advantage by being able to descend the river right after breakup and thus to arrive at the rendezvous several days before the Russians were able to reach it from downriver. At the beginning of the twentieth century, Archdeacon Hudson Stuck paused near Nuklukayet during a trip from his mission at Fort Yukon. He learned that the visits by the Hudson's Bay Company traders were remembered fondly: "Old natives at Tanana still tell with admiration of the bateaux with six pairs of oars which brought them guns and blankets and powder and shot and tea and tobacco, and gave them better terms than the Russians from Nulato gave."[54]

George R. Adams traveled with Russian-American Company personnel on the Yukon from 1865 to 1867 as a member of the Western Union Telegraph Expedition. He described the Russian-British contest for trade on the river. "The Russians on their trading trips only went up and down the river in a barge, with several armed men and a small cannon on the bow, which upon coming to a village or river encampment, they would fire, to make a great noise and properly intimidate the Indians."

> The Russian Company knew that the British Company had no right to be trad-ing at Fort Yukon, and as they expressed it "were stealing the Russian Com-pany's furs," but were helpless in the matter, as there had been no surveys made to prove that the British had invaded the Russian territory, they could not make it an international question and Fort Yukon was too far up the Kvihpak [Yukon] River for the Russians to take a force and drive the "thieves" away.
>
> So the English Company sat back with a "what are you going to do about it?" air and continued the profitable trade. What are particularly vexatious to the Russians was the fact that the upper part of the Kvihpak River was free of ice sooner in the spring than that below, so that the British would come down the river to Nuklukiate [Nuklukayet] and get most of the spring trade in furs there and be away before the Russians could get up the river to that point, a trip that they made at that time every year from Nulato with their "gun barge."[55]

Frederick Whymper visited Nuklukayet with a Russian trading party in 1867. "This place is the furthest point ever reached by the Russian traders, and is about 240 miles above Nulato. Within the last two or three years some of the Hudson Bay Company's men have come down with trading goods to this village. Hither come Indians from all quarters. Co-Yukons, Newicarguts, Tananas, and even the Kotch-á-kutchins from Fort Yukon. On some occasions their gatherings have numbered 600 persons. . . ." "On landing at this village a ceremony had to be gone through, possibly to test whether we had 'strong hearts' or not. The Indians already there, advanced whooping, yelling, and brandishing their guns till they reached us, and discharged them in the air. We, with the Indians just arrived, returned the compliment."[56]

But neither the Hudson's Bay Company nor the Russian-American Company was able to dominate the trade; furthermore, a substantial quantity of furs still reached Kotzebue Sound via native middlemen. For the Hudson's Bay Com-pany, Katherine Arndt has written, "There persisted only a small, nagging worry that the Russians might some day verify that Ft. Yukon was in trespass and de-mand its removal."[57] The Hudson's Bay Company would remain at Fort Yukon until 1869, but in 1849 and 1850, when Deriabin and Murray exchanged their mutually unintelligible letters about their operations on the Yukon, the person-nel of both companies were unaware of the great changes and challenges they would face as the result of the massive invasion by foreign fleets at Bering Strait, an invasion that had begun in 1848 and which would change the Bering Strait fur trade forever.

Part 3

FOREIGN FLEETS REACH BERING STRAIT

At midcentury the pace of change accelerated sharply in the Bering Strait region. Whereas the year 1847 marked the end of occasional visits by foreign vessels, the year 1848 marked the beginning of a sustained foreign presence, a presence that would forever change both the fur trade and the lives of the natives themselves. Two foreign fleets were the agents of this change: the British fleet searching for Sir John Franklin and the whaling and trading fleet, which was primarily American.

The searching fleet operated in the region only from 1848 to 1854, and it was focused solely on finding Sir John Franklin's ships and, later, on finding HMS *Investigator* and HMS *Enterprise*. The careful reports that the British sailors gathered during the Franklin Search in the Western Arctic provide an invaluable glimpse of the state of native life as it existed on the threshold of the massive invasion by the commercial fleets. Whereas the presence of the searching fleet among the natives was for the most part benign, the whaling and trading fleet was aggressively intrusive and caused wrenching change.

11

THE SEARCH FOR SIR JOHN FRANKLIN

In 1845, with high hopes of capitalizing on more than three centuries of British efforts to discover a northwest passage, the Royal Navy sent Sir John Franklin, in command of two sturdy and well-outfitted ships, to complete the search. The expedition sailed into Baffin Bay and vanished forever, but because Franklin's provisions were ample for three years—and could be stretched to four—there was little concern for the expedition's safety until two years had passed without word from him. In 1847, with anxiety growing, the Lords Commissioners of the Admiralty made plans to send searching expeditions to meet Franklin the following summer. They were nevertheless forced to confront the fact that Franklin's orders had been drafted so loosely that it was impossible to know where he had gone. Depending on how successful Franklin had been, his ships might be anywhere in the vast area between Baffin Bay and Bering Strait.

SPRING 1848 THROUGH SPRING 1849

To cover all possibilities, the Admiralty sent out three expeditions in spring 1848. One expedition followed Franklin's presumed route via Baffin Bay. Another, led by Sir John Richardson and assisted by Dr. John Rae of the Hudson's Bay Company, was to concentrate on the central area by descending the Mackenzie River and following the coast east as far as the Coppermine River. A third expedition was to enter the Arctic via Bering Strait.[1]

The Admiralty assigned two ships to the Bering Strait search. One, HMS *Herald*, under the command of Captain Henry Kellett, was at that time charting the west coast of Central America. Additionally, in January 1848, the Admiralty sent out from England HMS *Plover* under Commander Thomas E. L. Moore to assist the *Herald*. Laden with supplies, the *Plover* was to winter at Bering Strait as a depot ship for Franklin.

The Lords Commissioners ordered the *Plover* to meet the *Herald* at Panama in spring 1848 and then to sail in company to Petropavlovsk, Kamchatka, where the ships were to take aboard interpreters for their northern cruise. It was planned that the ships should reach Bering Strait at the beginning of July 1848, after which four boats would proceed north along the Alaskan coast in search of a good winter harbor for the *Plover*. The *Herald* would then transfer additional supplies to the *Plover* before heading south for the winter. The Lords Commissioners sent Lieutenant W. J. S. Pullen to join the *Plover* at Panama. Pullen was to lead a boat expedition, searching for Franklin along the north coast as far as the Mackenzie River. These western expeditions were thus intended to cover the entire continental coast of North America from Bering Strait to the Coppermine River in summer 1848.

The *Plover*'s orders were changed at once, probably in recognition of the fact that only one ship would be needed to collect intelligence and interpreters at Petropavlovsk, while the other's time could be more profitably spent at Bering Strait. The *Herald* alone would visit Petropavlovsk while the *Plover* would go directly to Bering Strait from Panama.

From the start things went badly for the western search. Captain Kellett believed that there were insufficient fresh provisions available at Panama for both ships, and by the end of March 1848, time was getting short for the expedition to reach Bering Strait during the brief season of open water. Recognizing this, the commander-in-chief of the Royal Navy's Pacific Station in Valparaiso, Chile, sent a steamer to Panama to tow the *Herald* west, out of the calms of the Gulf of Panama, to allow it to sail to Hawaii for provisions. There the *Herald* would await the *Plover* before starting north. Although the *Plover* was already at sea, it was thought that it would touch at one of the ports on the west coast of South America and receive the new orders. This change of plans meant that Lieutenant Pullen arrived in Panama only to learn that the *Plover* would not touch there. In fact, as we shall see, Pullen would not reach Bering Strait until 1849. But the *Plover* herself was forcing a change in the already much-changed plans. Although it proved to be sea-kindly, the *Plover* was slow, even when driven by a press of sail in gale-force winds. By May, when it should have been near Hawaii, it had just reached the Falkland Islands.[2]

Contrary to Kellett's assumptions, however, the *Herald* had indeed secured sufficient provisions in Panama, so he headed directly to Kamchatka, sending another ship to Hawaii to await the *Plover*. But the *Plover* was moving so slowly that it did not reach Lima's seaport until July, and by then the *Herald* was six thousand miles ahead of it. The *Herald*, also a slow sailer, reached Petropavlovsk at the beginning of August, a month after her planned arrival at Bering Strait. Kellett waited there for a week, hoping that the *Plover* might catch up to him, but he knew that the autumn weather in Bering Strait is brutal and if he was to do any searching for Franklin that summer, he had to push on at once.[3]

At the beginning of September the *Herald* arrived at Mikhailovsky Redoubt in Norton Sound to recruit an interpreter. Kellett hired Pavel Akliaiuk (Oglayuk), a Creole from Kodiak Island who had spent some time at Fort Ross, the Russian-American Company's post in Bodega Bay, California. Although Pavel spoke no English and the British spoke no Russian, they could communicate somewhat in Spanish. The British soon gave him a nickname: "Bosky," apparently because of his fondness for alcoholic refreshment.[4]

On September 14, the *Herald* reached Chamisso Island in Kotzebue Sound. The men climbed to the top of the island and found monument posts carved with records of Kotzebue's discovery of the sound in 1816 and of subsequent visits by the *Otkrytie*, *Blagonamerenny*, and *Blossom*—but there was no record of Franklin.[5]

Mid-September is late in the arctic autumn. Most of the Eskimos who had camped at Chamisso on their return from the Sheshalik trade rendezvous had already returned to their winter quarters. The sailors found only four natives, and they were too frightened to be of much use as informants. One of them, however, told Bosky a tantalizing story, which no doubt was somewhat mangled in the multistep translation from Iñupiaq Eskimo to Koniag Eskimo, to Russian, to Spanish, to English. "Our Russian interpreter was here informed by an old man, that he had heard from a person who had just arrived from the head of the Buckland river, that he had seen a party of men dressed like sailors, with an officer, having a gold band on his cap and brass buttons. They had come from a main body who were further inland, and had brought up all the venison; they could not speak, nor make themselves understood to any of the natives; the spot where they are is ten days' journey from this overland, but a boat could reach it in a very short time."[6]

This may have been a report of Zagoskin's explorations up the Koyukuk River from Nulato in winter 1842–43. More likely, it referred to Alexander Hunter Murray's expedition to establish Fort Yukon in 1847. In any case, it was, according to Berthold Seemann, a naturalist aboard the *Herald*, "a piece of information which opened a field for various but fruitless endeavours."[7]

The *Herald*'s men quickly scouted Eschscholtz Bay to check on the rumor, but the weather turned so cold that Kellett feared that they might be frozen in. The *Herald* weighed anchor on September 29. Heavy weather prevented it from stopping at Mikhailovsky, so Kellett headed to Petropavlovsk, where Bosky was put ashore and paid off at the rate of one dollar per day for his summer's service, plus some winter clothes from the *Herald*'s stores. It would be a year before Bosky returned to Mikhailovsky. The *Herald* headed for Central America to resume her surveying duties.[8]

In the meantime, no one knew where the *Plover* was. The *Plover* had, in fact, left Hawaii on August 25, and Commander Moore headed toward Bering Strait by the safest but longest route, sailing west of the Aleutians, thus adding a thousand miles to the voyage. The *Plover* reached St. Lawrence Island in mid-October and found it covered with snow. Everyone aboard knew that winter would not be long in coming. Moore pressed on, but he was working under a severe handicap: he had not received the charts of the Bering Strait region that the Admiralty had sent out to him. Moving cautiously and sounding frequently, he closed with the south coast of the Chukchi Peninsula and began searching for a sheltered winter anchorage.

Commander Moore was a lucky man. Almost at once the men spotted a cleft in the high hills ahead. Moore sent two boats to scout it. They reported a deep bay with a safe inner anchorage behind a low sandspit. A few days later the water began to freeze. With a local Chukchi leader acting as the pilot Moore moved the *Plover* into the bay and to an inner embayment. The large outer bay—which would become generally known as "Plover Bay"—he named Providence Bay, an inner bay, Plover Bay, and the anchorage behind the sandspit, Emma Harbour. Emma Harbour was protected from moving ice and had fresh water. Nearby was a Chukchi settlement, and reindeer were grazing on the surrounding hills. Moore reasoned that he would be able to barter for fresh meat during the winter and thus combat the onset of scurvy.[9]

The British got along well with the local Chukchi. Throughout the winter they visited the ship almost daily, often bringing reindeer meat. The Chukchi no doubt welcomed this new source of trade goods. Commander Moore, in fact, not only kept a Chukchi woman in his cabin during the winter but also traded a musket to the chief for twelve reindeer. Other than meat, the sailors traded for "sable" (probably Alaskan marten), fox, and other skins, paying mostly with saws, knives, needles, beads, and tobacco. The *Plover* also carried a supply of alcohol, which the natives called *tanuk*. It was said that the name originated with Commander Moore, who when he was on the trail would occasionally stop for a drink of rum, saying to his guide, "Come, Joe, let's take our tonic."[10]

Moore sent out traveling parties in search of the missing Franklin expedition and, whenever natives visited the ship, the sailors quizzed them for information about any foreigners that might be in the country. On one trip to Cape Chaplin

(Mys Chaplina, or "Indian Point" to the whalers and traders) the men heard a report that four ships had been seen in the area, all of them headed south. Two had three masts; the others had two. The sightings of the three-masted vessels were probably the *Herald* and the American whaling bark *Superior*. In summer 1848, the *Superior* cruised for whales in Bering Strait (see chapter 12). Unless an unknown vessel was in Bering Strait in 1848, the report of two-masted ships was probably multiple sightings of the Russian-American Company's brig *Veliky Kniaz Konstantin* (*Grand Duke Constantine*). The brig had resupplied Mikhailovsky Redoubt and then visited St. Lawrence Island, Mechigmensky Bay, and King Island.[11]

William Hulme Hooper, the *Plover*'s mate, led a search party to Cape Dezhnev to check on the report of a ship near there. On his way to St. Lawrence Bay, Hooper came upon a Russian cross that had been erected in 1821 to mark the grave of one of the crew of Shishmaryov's *Blagonamerreny*. Nearby Hooper stayed with a Chukchi headman, Ahmoleen, a whaling captain and trader who had visited the Ostrovnoe fair many times. "He possessed much . . . property, of immense value . . . obtained by barter at the annual fair. Wealthy was he too in reindeer and other Tuski goods."[12]

Hooper described what he had learned about the Ostrovnoe fair. "The journey to Kolyma occupies, we were told, a period of six months; that to the other place they visit, conjectured to be the Fort on the Anadyr, takes four. . . . Ahmoleen . . . described, and even named, two or three of the Russian traders. . . . The journeys to Kolyma are undertaken with reindeer and large covered sledges; furs and ivory are taken to be exchanged for tobacco in the leaf, of a very inferior nature; common rough beads, generally of a dull opaque blue; knives; printed cottons, of which loose flowing dresses are made to go over the fur clothes . . . probably also a little sugar, and I rather think very small quantities of spirits, as . . . ayak-memil (fire water) was by no means unknown to them and eagerly sought for. To obtain it no sacrifice was considered too great."[13]

Ahmoleen also drew a map of the Bering Strait region for Hooper. It appears that Ahmoleen had visited St. Lawrence Island, Port Clarence, and the Sheshalik trade fair as well. He also showed Hooper his lamellar armor cuirass. The cuirass "consisted of back and breast plates of walrus-hide, at least a quarter of an inch thick, and in some places double. . . . Upon these were flattened flat and thin iron plates overlapping each other." It was, "as Ahmoleen explained, too heavy to be worn in combats where activity was required. Hence his desire for one of lighter make. He seemed in some way to have heard of chain mail, as he described it by locking his crooked fingers into one another."[14]

Hooper also learned of a reported shipwreck on the Alaskan shore, stating that

Ahmoleen's Map of Bering Strait

Ahmoleen's map was reproduced in William Hooper's book with north at the bottom of the page. It is shown here with north at the top of the page. On the Asian side, among other features are Plover Bay, St. Lawrence Island, St. Lawrence Bay, and Cape Dezhnev. The two Diomede Islands and Fairway Rock are shown in their correct spatial orientations in the middle of Bering Strait. It appears that Ahmoleen had traveled on the American side of Bering Strait from Kotzebue Sound to Port Clarence (and into the Imuruk Basin as far as the village of Kauwerak—Qaviaraq—on the Kuzitrin River) and King Island. Most interesting, if the traced line on his map is correct, it appears that he may have sailed between Port Clarence, Plover Bay, and St. Lawrence Island.

the natives of that coast had "obtained knives, pots, and guns from the wreck. These news were said to have come from Po-orten [a village at Cape Dezhnev], whither they were brought from E-mah-leen [Big Diomede Island] . . . about eight months since." Later, near Cape Dezhnev, Hooper was told that "only fragments of a hull and stern frame had been thrown up, from which, in place of pots or knives, only nails had been drawn." Hooper tried to hire guides to take him to the wreck, but no one would agree to go because the natives were feuding with their neighbors and were of a "fierce intractable disposition." This may have been a fabrication; nevertheless, apart from an unknown vessel having been wrecked on the Alaskan shore or a ship having lost its boat near Bering Strait before 1849, this report may refer to the loss of the *Blossom*'s barge at Chamisso Island in 1827.[15]

SUMMER 1849 THROUGH SPRING 1850

Despite the efforts of the *Herald*'s and *Plover*'s crews, by spring 1849 the sum of their hard work had revealed only that Franklin's men were not near Kotzebue Sound, nor were they on the Chukchi Peninsula. On June 13, 1849, the *Plover* was again afloat in relatively clear water, although floating ice in the bay prevented it from going to sea. Almost at once the natives reported that they had

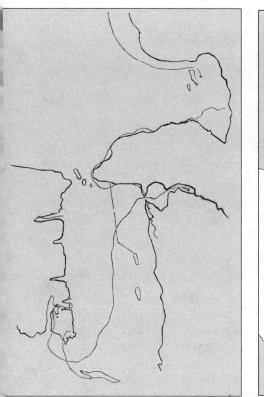
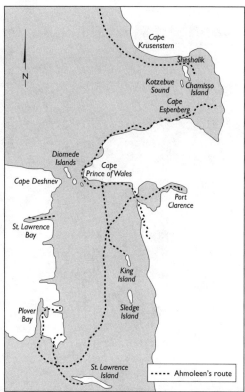

Map 11.1. (left) Ahmoleen's map of Bering Strait, 1848–49
(W. H. Hooper 1853, 162–63).
Map 11.2. (right) Geographical key to Ahmoleen's map.

sighted two ships nearby. Moore sent Henry Martin, the second master of the *Plover*, to investigate. A few days later Martin boarded the American whaleship *Tiger* of Stonington, Connecticut, and the British sailors learned that they would have plenty of company in the Arctic. Reports of the *Superior*'s whaling success in 1848 drew fifty whaleships to Bering Strait in 1849 (see chapter 12).[16]

The *Plover* finally reached the designated rendezvous at Chamisso Island on July 13, 1849, a year and a half after its departure from Britain. Moore climbed to the top of the island, found the posts with the names of the ships that had been there before, and thus learned that the *Herald* had been in Kotzebue Sound in 1848. But the *Plover* was still out of touch with the rest of the world, and, more important, during the winter of 1848–49 the Lords Commissioners of the Admiralty had not heard from any of the search expeditions. No better off than they

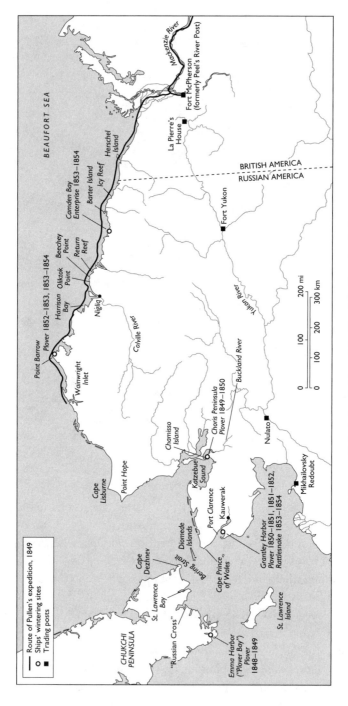

Map 11.3. Selected activities of the Franklin Search, 1848–54.

had been in 1848, they were forced to plan for any number of contingencies as the navigation season of 1849 approached.[17]

The Lords Commissioners ordered Captain Henry Kellett, who was again surveying with the *Herald* at Panama, to return north with a year's provisions for the *Plover*. Kellett was instructed to stop at Honolulu and Petropavlovsk—in case the *Plover* had wintered at either place—and then to head to Kotzebue Sound. If he should meet the *Plover*, he was to help it establish itself in a suitable wintering site and then depart for Honolulu, to be ready to return to Bering Strait in 1850.

Cholera was epidemic in Central America, and few supplies were available when Kellett received his orders, so the *Herald* went to Honolulu, which by then had become the major port of resupply for the Pacific whaling fleet. There he took aboard not only fresh provisions but also Lieutenant William J. S. Pullen, who, as we have seen, had missed his connection with the *Plover* the year before. The *Herald* reached Petropavlovsk on June 23. The *Plover*, of course, was not there, but Kellett did hear a rumor that it had wintered somewhere to the north. To the sailors' amazement, however, amid several American whaleships in the harbor was a British yacht, the schooner *Nancy Dawson* of the Royal Thames Yacht Club. The owner, Robert Shedden, had brought her north from Hong Kong on his own initiative to help in the search for Franklin. The two vessels left the harbor together. The *Herald* arrived at Chamisso Island on July 14, and the crew immediately began transferring supplies to the *Plover*. A few men were exchanged as well, and principal among them was Lieutenant Pullen, who was joining his ship fourteen months after he had left Britain.[18]

Several days later the *Herald* and *Plover* stood out of Kotzebue Sound in company and almost at once met the *Nancy Dawson*. By July 19 the three ships were off Point Hope with bowhead whales spouting all around and American whaleships in sight. While their boats scouted close inshore, the ships worked their way north through shoals of birds, seals, and whales, amid the "continual bellowing" of vast herds of walruses. Eskimos frequently boarded the ships, and Kellett reported that they came alongside "fearlessly, and disposed of every article they had, the women selling their fur dresses, even to the second pair of breeches, for tobacco and beads."

The ships reached Wainwright Inlet on July 25. By then Franklin's expedition had been out of touch for four years. It was assumed that Franklin's men were at the end of their supplies and possibly were somewhere between Wainwright Inlet and the Mackenzie River. Kellett, however, judged that it would be too dangerous for his deep-draft squadron to proceed farther up this coast, where no ships had ever been. He knew from the reports of Beechey, Franklin, and Dease and Simpson that the water was very shoal near shore as far as the Mackenzie. Kellett ordered Pullen to depart for the Mackenzie. While the ships waited off Wainwright Inlet, the men loaded four boats. The largest was the *Owen*, the *Herald's* pinnace, a thirty-foot decked schooner. The *Plover's* half-decked yawl-rigged pinnace was also to go, as were two partially covered twenty-seven-foot whaleboats. Pullen's small squadron was outfitted with seventy days' provisions for the twenty-five crew and carried extra rations for Franklin's men.

Pullen was ordered to sail as far as the head of the Mackenzie delta and then to return to the *Plover* at once. This was clearly impossible: he would have had to cover more than a thousand miles in the short arctic summer. His orders did state, however, that if he should find himself unable to return, he was to ascend the Mackenzie to a trading post from which he could send messages to the Admiralty.

By July 29 Pullen's boats were within ten miles of Point Barrow, but there the pack ice blocked them. The men secured the boats to a large grounded piece of ice and found, to their surprise and comfort, that the *Nancy Dawson* had arrived to wait with them. It of course was not under Kellett's command, and the schooner probably drew far less water than Kellett's ships. "Pullen went on board that vessel," reported Dr. John Rae, who spent the following winter with Pullen. "During his absence Hooper and nearly all the men scattered themselves among the Esquimaux women on the floes, when an opportune rupture of the ice took place, and caused a number of very ludicrous exposés."[19]

The boats worked their way to Point Barrow on August 1 but were again stopped by pack ice, which was hard on the land. Pullen used the time to go ashore and trade with the natives, buying a walrus-skin umiaq to carry some of the supplies. It cost him "a large butcher's knife, a looking-glass, and a quantity of tobacco and beads." After several hours the ice began to lift; just as they were getting underway, the *Nancy Dawson* came into sight once again. Unsure whether the Eskimos were hostile, Shedden was doing his best to keep an eye on the boat expedition. The *Nancy Dawson* then rounded the point and became the first ship to enter the Beaufort Sea. There Shedden was forced to turn back. Despite his noble endeavor, the *Nancy Dawson's* crew was near mutiny from fear of the Arctic.[20]

Pullen pushed on and was at Cape Simpson two days later, but the two larger boats were a handicap in the shallow water near the coast. He ordered both the *Owen* and the *Plover's* pinnace to return to the ships and continued east with thirteen men in the two whaleboats. The umiaq, heavily laden with provisions, was under tow. As they crossed Harrison Bay, off the Colville River delta a gale nearly swamped Pullen's overloaded squadron. Flying spray soaked the men to the skin, and they stopped to dry out on the east side of the bay. Not far from there, at Oliktok Point, they came upon a camp of about one hundred Eskimos with thirteen tents. These people were Point Barrow Eskimos. They had completed their annual trade with the inland Eskimos at Niġliq in the Colville delta and were preparing to travel farther east, to meet the Mackenzie Eskimos at Barter Island.

At Oliktok Pullen's men buried a cache of provisions for Franklin. Pullen wrote: "We met here a great many natives, all friendly and glad to see us, to whom I made presents, and made our cache without their observing it; the direction post we could not hide, but set it very deep into the soil. On shoving off we missed our shovel, and one of the men observed a native bury something in the sand and stand on it; I walked up to him, fully expecting it was the missing article, and on trying to find out what it was he resisted. When Mr. Hooper pushed his hand completely through the sand, got hold of the shovel, and hauled it from under him." Hooper added, "We could not spare the implement, so dislodged the thief from his position over it, and recovered the article; but our friend was not satisfied with his deprivation, and seized the prow of the boat to prevent our departure, while his companions seemed much inclined to make a rush upon us . . . a couple of guns were levelled at the man in an instant, and their aspect quickly changed his views; he let go of the boat and retreated hastily. We hoisted sail and ran along shore, until a mark was observed, which we landed to examine, and while so engaged, were visited by an oomiak, containing twenty-four men, and only one woman. As they came from [Oliktok] we distrusted their honesty, and a line was therefore drawn in the sand between the parties, as a Rubicon to each."

Underway again, the sailors spotted an umiaq full of natives following them. They put ashore on one of the barrier islands. The natives also landed and seemed "quite friendly." To the sailors' surprise, the group's headman—who the British would later know as O-mi-ga-loon—had a musket and wanted ammunition. "I gave them a few beads and small pieces of tobacco, but one of them[,] apparently a chief was very desirous of getting [gun] powder. He had a musket of English manufacture, Barnet[t] the name on it, also a powder horn with about a quarter pound of powder in it, but no shot."[21]

This must have been the first firearm among the Point Barrow people, and O-mi-ga-loon was not yet well acquainted with its operation. "He had a long gun, of English manufacture," Hooper recalled. "The name on the lock was Barnet: it was very shaky; but notwithstanding, evidently highly prized. . . . He was permitted to fire one of the fowling-pieces, for we wanted to see how far his knowledge of the use of firearms extended; and his proceeding caused much amusement: he kneeled down in the sand, shut his eyes, and compressed his lips firmly; and after a slight pause, during which he was doubtless resolving upon the performance of the great achievement, pulled the trigger, and received a smart tap, having held the gun loosely from the shoulder. Mightily was he relieved when the exploit was concluded, and, with his companions, breathed freely once more; for they, like him, had been in all-engrossing suspense until the deed was done."[22]

Because the British thought no firearms had reached the region, they were very concerned about O-mi-ga-loon's gun. The Barnett firm sold trade guns to the Hudson's Bay Company from 1821 onward, and some of these guns were sold at Peel's River Post and Fort Yukon. It is worth noting that in 1850—the summer following Pullen's encounter at Oliktok—Captain Robert M'Clure of HMS *Investigator* also met O-mi-ga-loon, armed with his gun, near there. M'Clure noted that the mark on the gun's lock was "Barnett 1840." In view of the fact that when O-mi-ga-loon met Pullen's party in 1849, he was not yet well acquainted with firearms and that he was on his way to the trade rendezvous at Barter Island, it is likely that he had acquired the gun only the year before, 1848, at the Barter Island rendezvous and may not have been able to buy much powder then. Because of the time required for the gun to reach the lower Mackenzie from England and then to reach O-mi-ga-loon, the gun could not have been sold to a Gwich'in at Peel's River Post earlier than 1844. It is less likely that the gun was traded from Fort Yukon, which was established in 1847.[23]

Where O-mi-ga-loon acquired the gun is important: he almost certainly would not have traveled father west than the trade rendezvous at Barter Island. It is likely that he was able to buy the gun because relations between the Gwich'in and the Mackenzie Eskimos had begun to improve; in fact, in 1849 the Gwich'in and Eskimos traded peacefully at the mouth of the Peel River. O-mi-ga-loon's possession of a gun thus suggests either that the Gwich'in traders had by then begun visiting Barter Island instead of—or in addition to—the rendezvous that Franklin had reported at the mouth of the Firth River, near Herschel Island, or that the Mackenzie Eskimos had carried the gun to Barter Island after an exchange with the Gwich'in, hence their relations with the Mackenzie Eskimos must have gotten better.[24]

Pullen's boats shoved off again, passing several Eskimo camps as they moved on to the east, but when they reached Beechey Point, which Franklin had named in 1826, a rising sea and a strong northeast wind forced them to go ashore. At 3 AM August 12 the natives approached again, Pullen wrote,

> walking along shore from their camp about two miles off, having certainly watched us all the time. They now mustered in large numbers; there could not have been less than eighty, among whom I recognized our friend [from Olik-

tok] who tried to steal our shovel, and the chief [O-mi-ga-loon] with the musket carried by his wife, and several other women present beside. I felt no apprehension, but at the same time had all ready to embark at a moment's notice, drawing a line for their boundary, and saw them all seated on their proper side, when the man with the musket crossed over and made many demands for powder, which I would not give him, and motioned him off; when on seeing me resolute in refusing, he gave the gun to his wife, walked a short distance to their camp, and returned almost immediately with his bow and arrows, the whole of the men doing the same.

Pullen realized that it would be best to put some distance between his expedition and O-mi-ga-loon's group.

I gave the word to get into the boats, but to do it leisurely, and show them we are ready: Mr. Hooper, two marines, and self, kept a sharp look out with musket in hand, when I ordered [one whaleboat and the umiaq] to shove off and get into deep water. In the meantime the chief tried hard to get on the bank and to windward of us, but I would not allow him, when the remainder of us made a move to the [other whaleboat], they made a rush for the bank, and I expect hoped to catch us at disadvantage, but we were all in the boat, Mr. Hooper and I with our double barrels at the present, while the men were shoving off, and pulling out to the [first whaleboat]. One fellow had an arrow on the string, and the bow at full stretch, when, fortunately, I covered him, and he dropped down under the bank immediately. We lost our anchors, otherwise everything was all right.[25]

But a strong easterly wind forced Pullen to drop back west, to Return Reef. The Eskimos followed, keeping to windward. The sailors went ashore, built a low breastwork from driftwood, and posted sentries. The Eskimos landed about five hundred yards away and built their own breastwork. They "did not dare to advance in the face of the fire-arms," Hooper remembered. "They made treacherous signals of amity, and erected a skin frock on a pole, an invitation to barter and fraternise, but we were not so easily deluded. By and by two natives ventured to approach, making all sorts of friendly gestures, but timid enough under the mask; for when about two hundred yards distant, they were sent to the rightabout in an instant by Sullock, the sentinel-marine, who charged them with fixed bayonet, and they scampered back in haste to their defenses and companions." The next morning the British slipped away in a fog and kept on to the east, but when they landed to build a fire and dry out, two large umiaqs, with forty armed men, followed them and fired a few arrows. Pullen and Hooper returned fire, and the Eskimos dropped to the ground. With a following breeze the boats put off and continued east.[26]

The size of the Eskimo groups that Pullen and his men encountered between Oliktok and Return Reef suggests that the importance of the trade rendezvous at Barter Island had grown in the years since Dease's and Simpson's visit of 1837. The growth in the size of the rendezvous probably was a result of the increased amount of trade goods that were reaching the coast. Initially they came from Asia, later from the Russian-American Company, and more recently, from the Hudson's Bay Company. At Icy Reef, east of Barter Island, for example, the British met a group who must have been Mackenzie Eskimos. Hooper thought they looked unlike Point Barrow Eskimos. "One of them had a broad and short double-edged knife, on which the names 'I. and H. Sorby' were imprinted: this must have been obtained by barter from the Indians, as it was of the kind called dagues, supplied by the Hudson's Bay Company to those people."[27]

In the exchange of local resources between the Point Barrow Eskimos and the Mackenzie Eskimos, both groups were primarily coastal dwellers with rich marine resources of their own. Unlike the inland-coastal trade, wherein local products that were scarce to the other group were exchanged, in the exchanges between the Point Barrow and Mackenzie peoples the opportunity to acquire manufactured goods was far more likely to have been the reason.

On August 21 Pullen's boats reached Herschel Island and on September 5 they arrived at Fort McPherson, which had formerly been called Peel's River Post. Pullen and his men had thus carried out an important open boat voyage, but they had learned only that there were no signs of Franklin on the coast west of the Mackenzie River.[28]

In the meantime the *Herald, Plover, Nancy Dawson,* and the boats that Pullen had sent back from Point Barrow had all reached Chamisso Island. Both Commander Moore and Captain Kellett made boat excursions up the Buckland River and enjoyed excellent relations with the Eskimos there. They, of course, knew about the hostilities that had taken place between the Buckland River Eskimos and the crew of the *Blossom* in 1827 and were puzzled by the fact that these natives were so friendly. Captain Kellett believed that the change in the natives' attitude was because of the presence of Bosky, the interpreter, who had been taken back aboard the *Herald* after his winter at Petropavlovsk. Kellett thought that Bosky had told the Buckland River Eskimos that the British had come in peace. It is equally likely that the lure of trade goods and the presence of three ships at Chamisso Island—as well as a large number of well-armed men—kept the Eskimos quiet.

By September 26 carpenters from both the *Herald* and *Plover* had finished building a supply house on shore and had completed the initial winter preparations for the *Plover*. The *Plover* would winter on the east side of the Choris Peninsula, near Chamisso Island. The *Herald* then departed for the south.

All winter Commander Moore sent out parties to search for news of Franklin. Lieutenant Bedford Pim undertook one of the most interesting journeys. In November 1849, Moore heard a vague rumor about two ships being east of Point Barrow—most likely a report about Pullen's expedition. Pim volunteered to go overland to Mikhailovsky Redoubt to learn whether any such news had filtered down the river to the Russian-American Company's traders. With Bosky interpreting, he set out in March 1850 and reached Mikhailovsky twenty-six days later. There he learned that "some white men were living on the banks of a river called by the Indians 'Ekko' [Yukon] and that the Russian trade had already suffered on that account." Pim at first assumed that the report referred to Hudson's Bay Company personnel who were searching for Franklin but later changed his mind. "Subsequent information induced me to alter this opinion. First, they were badly supplied with provisions, and had bartered their percussion guns in order to obtain food; as the company only exchange flint guns, of which they have plenty in store. . . . Secondly, the spot where they were supposed to be, I am led to believe, is two or three hundred miles within the Russian boundary-line, and moreover up a river, —a most improbable place for any Englishman to penetrate in search of gain. Lately the party was said to consist of two officers and ten men, evidently the crews of two small boats, the departure of whom from the Mackenzie River I had reason to believe impossible." This was, of course, a reasonably accurate account of Alexander Hunter Murray and his men having established Fort Yukon in 1847.[29]

Meanwhile, in winter 1849–50 in Britain nothing whatever was known of Franklin's whereabouts. Sir John Richardson and Dr. John Rae had surveyed the continental coast from the Mackenzie delta to the Coppermine River and found no signs of the expedition; nor had the searches in the Eastern Arctic. Franklin had been provisioned for three years; he had by then been gone four and a half. Completely baffled, the Lords Commissioners of the Admiralty ordered two ships, the *Enterprise* and *Investigator*, which had recently returned from the Eastern Arctic, to return north, this time via Bering Strait. Captain Richard Collinson would lead the expedition and be in command of the *Enterprise;* Captain Robert M'Clure would command the *Investigator*. Five other expeditions would enter the Eastern Arctic via Baffin Bay. The *Plover*, no longer in the van, would become a depot ship in support of the searching expeditions.[30]

SUMMER 1850 THROUGH SPRING 1851

The *Herald* returned to Chamisso Island on July 15, 1850, and the crew immediately began transferring supplies to the *Plover*. Moore reported to Kellett about the rumors of white men in the Alaskan interior. Kellett thought they might refer to Pullen's group and ordered Moore to take the *Plover* north along the coast to investigate.

The *Plover* reached Icy Cape on July 23. Moore immediately set off with thirteen men, including an interpreter, in two boats, hoping to run up to Point Barrow in a lead of open water between the pack ice and the shore. He arrived at Wainwright Inlet the same evening and found a group of Eskimos camped in twenty-one tents. The natives surrounded the sailors and "became very troublesome, thieving all they could." Having learned nothing about Franklin, he pushed on, with the natives following along the shore.

Four days later Moore reached Point Barrow and estimated that there were more than three hundred Eskimos there. "One native gave information that a number of people like ourselves had arrived at a river called Coo-pack, at what time I could not ascertain; that they had bartered their muskets for food, were now dead, and had been buried by the natives there; also that . . . the ship or boat was washed away." This most likely was a garbled report of the skirmish between the Point Barrow Eskimos and Pullen's expedition near Beechey Point in 1849. Commander Moore discounted the rumor; nevertheless he offered the highest price possible — a musket and tobacco — to be led to the spot, but no one took him up on his offer.[31]

Meanwhile M'Clure in the *Investigator* had made a fast passage from Hawaii to Bering Strait — only twenty-six days — by heading directly through the Aleutian chain rather than skirting their western end (as the *Enterprise* was then doing), thus saving a thousand miles. When the *Herald* met the *Investigator* north of Bering Strait, Kellett suggested that M'Clure should wait for Collinson, who was M'Clure's commanding officer, but M'Clure pressed on into the Beaufort Sea regardless. He is believed to have been intent on capturing a reward for the first traverse of a northwest passage.

Later, off Cape Lisburne, Moore consulted with Kellett, then took the *Plover* to Port Clarence to winter in Grantley Harbor. After waiting in vain for the *Enterprise*, Kellett took the *Herald* to Mikhailovsky to check on the rumors that Bedford Pim had reported during the winter. To Kellett's disappointment, he found that Pim's informants had been transferred to Novo-Arkhangelsk. But it seemed to Kellett that the Russian-American Company's post at Nulato would be an ex-

Figure 11.1. Mikhailovsky Redoubt, 1850–51. Edward Adams wintered at Mikhailovsky during the search for Sir John Franklin's expedition. Scott Polar Research Institute, University of Cambridge, image 83/11/54.

cellent place to obtain information firsthand about the white men who had been reported in the interior.[32]

Kellett then returned to Port Clarence to check on the *Plover's* preparations for the winter and was surprised to find the *Enterprise* there. He had assumed that it had passed the *Herald* unseen and gone into the Beaufort Sea, but Collinson had arrived so late in the season that he was unwilling to pass Point Barrow. The *Herald* then departed for Great Britain, and Collinson, heading south for the winter, touched at Mikhailovsky to put ashore a search party. Lieutenant John J. Barnard, Assistant Surgeon Edward Adams, and Thomas Cousins, a sailor who had been a member of Sir John Richardson's searching party in 1848, were to spend the winter and try to get to Nulato to check on the rumors that Pim had reported. Edward Adams was not only a talented artist and diarist; he proved to have a keen ethnographer's eye as well. In his detailed journal he noted, among many other details, that Eskimos from Kotzebue Sound and Buckland River occasionally traveled to Mikhailovsky during the winter, bringing beaver and otter skins to trade.[33]

At Port Clarence the *Plover's* men settled in for their third northern winter. Apart from an outbreak of scurvy, the winter passed without significant problems, thanks in part to the good relations that the sailors enjoyed with the local Eskimos, who refused to believe that the *Plover* was not there for trade. The natives kept the sailors well supplied with food, selling them "six thousand pounds of caribou, several thousand ptarmigan, and fish, hares, and berries."[34]

One surprising event of the winter was the arrival of a party of Chukotkan natives who had crossed Bering Strait. This traverse demanded great skill and endurance: It was an extremely dangerous journey of more than fifty miles across moving pack ice. "During the month of April we were visited by several natives from the Asiatic shore," wrote Gunner's Mate John Matthews. "They wanted rum in exchange for their articles, but Captain Moore would not allow anyone to give it them on any account." In assessing the natives' motivation for undertaking such a hazardous trip Matthews added, "I believe since that the Americans have found these seas to abound in whale, they have been in the habit of trading with them for liquor and I think it, morally speaking, to be very wrong so to do."[35]

In February Moore sent a party to Mikhailovsky to check on Lieutenant Barnard's group. It was not until April 2, 1851, that he received word, and it was deeply shocking. At first the winter had gone fairly well for the three. Bosky, formerly the expedition's interpreter, was living there and helped the sailors to question the natives who visited the post. Initially the British heard only repetitions of the rumor that white men had been murdered on the north coast of Alaska, but on December 23, 1850, the baidarshchik Vasily Maksimovich Deriabin, the factor in charge of the Russian-American Company's outpost at Nulato, arrived at St. Michael and confirmed the stories of white men to the east of Nulato, but he believed—correctly, as it turned out—that the men were traders, not Franklin's men.

In the summer of 1849, Deriabin had gone on a trading expedition upriver from Nulato. There he met Koyukon who were well supplied with trade goods. Edward Adams wrote to Collinson that they had "muskets, powder and shot, English knives, beads, tobacco, and a few preserved meat tins. On being questioned, they stated that they received them from a party of five white men who had been living for two years upon their river. Upon hearing this Maxemoff [Deriabin] gave them a letter to take to the Englishmen from whom they received the goods. . . . All the goods appear to correspond with those used by the Hudson's Bay Company for bartering, except the preserved meat tins, which I have since found came from the 'Plover' through the Buckland River natives. Maxemoff purchased one of the muskets, which corresponds exactly with the Hudson's Bay ones." In reporting about the meat tins that the Buckland River

Eskimos had carried away from the *Plover* in Eschscholtz Bay in 1849–50 Adams also confirmed the existence of the overland trade route between the Eskimos of Kotzebue Sound and the Koyukon of the middle Yukon. This of course was the trade route that Zagoskin sought to find in 1842 and the one that Tebenkov ordered Deriabin to search for in autumn 1847.[36]

Lieutenant Barnard planned to investigate the report about foreigners on the Yukon. Leaving Adams and the sailor at Mikhailovsky to interrogate any natives who might visit, he hired Bosky to accompany him as interpreter. Barnard, Deriabin, and Bosky set off at the end of December, and Adams had no word from Barnard until February 24, 1851, when a native appeared at the post with an alarming letter.

> Dear Adams
>
> I am dreadfully wounded in the abdomen, my entrails are hanging out. I do not suppose I shall live long enough to see you. The Cu-ú-chuk Indians made the attack whilst we were in our beds. Boskey is badly wounded, and Darabin dead.
>
> I think my wound would have been trifling had I medical advice. I am in great pain; nearly all of the natives in the village are murdered. Set out for this in all haste.
>
> John Barnard

When Adams reached Nulato he pieced the story together. Barnard had arrived there on January 16, 1851, and stayed in the trading post, where he learned that a few days before, on January 10, "a Russian accompanied by a native servant, was sent to the Koukok [Koyukuk] River to trade for skins, and to bring back the chief of the village, with whom Mr. Barnard and Maxemoff [Deriabin] wished to have some conversation," wrote Edward Adams. "Mr. Barnard expressed a great wish to accompany these men, but was dissuaded from doing so by his interpreter [Bosky], who, mistrusting the Koyukon, refused. On February 15 at about five o'clock in the morning Deriabin happened to go outside his log cabin and found about eighty armed Koyukon there. They grabbed him and stabbed him with a knife, but he broke free and staggered mortally wounded into his room in time for his native wife to bar the door. The Indians then burst into Barnard's room."[37]

Adams continued,

> It appears that Mr. Barnard was awoke by the noise of their approach, and asked what it was? Pavil [Bosky] answered, "The Indians are come; take your gun and shoot them." Both barrels of his gun had been left loaded with small shot; these were fired; but from the direction of the shot-marks on the wall, I

Figure 11.2. Nulato, 1851. Edward Adams led the search party to Nulato, where Lieutenant Barnard and Vasily Deriabin had been murdered by Koyukon. Scott Polar Research Institute, University of Cambridge, image 83/11/20.

think they must have gone off whilst he was struggling with the Indians. He then appears to have struck with the butt until the stock broke, and he fell dreadfully wounded.

Before Pavil had time to get out of bed, an attempt was made to stab him; but the knife, badly aimed in the dark, passed between his arm and side. Being without a gun or other weapon, he warded off the spears with a blanket, and took five of them away, with one of which he wounded some of the Indians, and ultimately cleared the room, although badly wounded with three arrows which were sticking in his body.

The Indians then left the house, and congregated on the bank of the river, planting their shields in a row so as to form a wall, as if intending to attack the other building. At the time of the arrival of the Indians, a woman was in the cooking house, boiling her kettle; she saw them, but dared not to go out until they were in Maxemoff's house, when she ran to the barracks, and alarmed the men, who were all asleep. By this time the Indians had collected outside, and one of the men fired from a window and killed one of them, when the rest immediately snatched up their shields, and made off for the woods.

They then went down to the village, and finding the unsuspecting inhabitants asleep succeeded in murdering all but four; one man, who made his escape, and three women, whom they took away as captives. They killed men, women, and children, fifty-three in number; and after eating part of one of the men, set fire to the houses, and took their departure, carrying one man, who had been wounded by Pavil, on a sledge. The Indian who was killed they left behind; he was pitched down upon the river, and afterwards eaten by the dogs.

The man who escaped from the village says, that they threatened to return to Darabin with more men, burn the houses, kill all the inhabitants, and then proceed to Michaelowski on the same errand. They also said they had killed the two men who were sent to their village.

One of the Indians had remained in Maxemoff's house after the others had left. A woman saw him lying on the floor covered with his shield, and called one of the Russians, who fired a pistol at him at the distance of a yard, but he was shaking so much from fright that he missed his aim, and the man jumped up and made his escape. . . .

Mr. Barnard lived till the morning of the following day, but was too severely wounded to be able to write any account of the affair. . . .

I buried Mr. Barnard on the 16th March, in the burial ground at Darabin, some of the Russians, at my request, firing a volley over his grave, at the head of which I placed a board, inscribed with his name, the cause of his death, etc.[38]

Adams was at a loss to explain why the Koyukon had attacked Nulato. In all, the Koyukon killed fifty-six persons in the village, more than fifty of whom were Koyukon. In light of recent research it appears that Barnard may have stumbled into an intra-Koyukon feud which was "only one of a continual series of raids between the Koyukuk and Lower Yukon division [groups]," wrote the ethnohistorian Annette McFadyen-Clark. This incident may have arisen because the Koyukuk group was angry that its trade monopoly was threatened by the Lower Yukon people, who were cooperating with the Russians.

Adams left Nulato on March 18, carrying Bosky, whose wounds had healed sufficiently to allow him to ride on the sled. Ten days later they reached Mikhailovsky, but Bosky's health began to deteriorate and on April 20, 1851, Bosky (Pavel Akliaiuk) died there.[39]

During the same winter, 1850–51, the Lords Commissioners of the Admiralty were increasingly frustrated as they planned the future of the search. By then Franklin's expedition had been gone for more than six years. The Lords Commissioners ordered Collinson to take the *Enterprise* into the Arctic, searching for the *Investigator*, so that the two ships could explore west of the Arctic islands. The *Plover* was to remain north as a depot ship for the other two. The *Daedalus* would resupply the *Plover*, and if the *Plover* was found to have been wrecked, the *Daedalus* would replace her as a depot ship.

SUMMER 1851 THROUGH SPRING 1852

Pack ice stopped the *Enterprise*, in company with more than one hundred whaling vessels, in June in the Gulf of Anadyr. Several Chukchi umiaqs came out to the ship, offering to trade furs and walrus tusks for alcohol and tobacco. "When one of them was given about one-eighth of a pint of rum, he swilled it several times around his mouth, then squirted it into his neighbour's mouth, who then passed it on to the next in line, including women, so that they could all get at least a taste."[40]

The ship reached Port Clarence on July 3, 1851. The next day the *Enterprise* and the *Plover* were joined there by three whaleships: the *Lagoda* of New Bedford, Massachusetts, the *Nancy* of Havre, France, and the *Sheffield* of Sag Harbor, New York. The latter was under the command of Captain Thomas Roys, who had discovered the Bering Strait whaling grounds only three years earlier. Because of Roys's success in 1848, he was now accompanied by nearly two hundred whaleships. He and several other whaling captains had offered to search for Franklin along the margin of the pack ice in the Arctic Ocean. These ships were joined in Port Clarence by several trading vessels: the schooner *Eliza* (Captain John Archer) of Hobart, Tasmania; the schooner *The Lady Franklin*; the *Rêna* (Captain John Simpson), a *lorcha* from Hong Kong; and the *Juno*, a German brigantine out of Honolulu. These small ships, and probably others as well, had come north not only to trade for furs and ivory but also to sell fresh provisions among the whaling fleet.[41]

Aboard the *Plover* in summer 1851, Commander Moore reported that the presence of the large foreign fleet had created problems both for the natives and for the British sailors. The natives at Grantley Harbor were "constantly drunk," he said, adding that the great increase in trade goods from the foreign ships had inflated prices: whereas the *Plover*'s men had bought five reindeer from a native at Plover Bay in winter 1848–49, by summer 1851 the same man had acquired a whole case of tobacco from one of the whaleships and would not trade any meat to the British. "I am sorry to inform their Lordships," Moore continued, "that the whalers have been the means of doing the natives (along the coast on both sides of the straits) a vast deal of injury, by the introduction of a vast quantity of spirits which they have supplied them, and the extravagant manner in which they have given them tobacco that I feel certain the supplies of venison, etc., which I have hitherto been able to procure for the crew will be most materially curtailed, besides which, we shall have to travel considerably further for what little we may procure."[42]

The Russian-American Company's bark *Kniaz Menshikov* (*Prince Menshikov*) was also in Port Clarence that summer. It had been sent north with three tasks: to scout the bay for setting up an outpost; to report on the whaling fleet's activities; and to learn whether the ships were trading with the natives. It must have greatly concerned the Russian-American Company that so large a foreign presence was suddenly in waters where the company's ships had been virtually alone only four years before. It was the company's policy not to trade firearms or alcohol to the northern natives, but these new arrivals were under no such constraints.[43]

The *Enterprise* sailed from Port Clarence on July 10, 1851, but at Point Barrow the ship was beset between pack ice and grounded floes on shore. A number of Eskimos, both men and women, walked over the shore-fast ice to the ship. "Upon being refused admittance," wrote one of the officers, "they revenged themselves by exposing their persons and performing ludicrous and indecent gestures." He concluded that "the morals of these people have not improved by intercourse with the Whalers." The *Enterprise* soon rounded Point Barrow, entered the Beaufort Sea, and disappeared into the Arctic for three years.[44]

The *Plover* made a quick trip to Mikhailovsky to collect dispatches, and when the ship returned to Port Clarence, HMS *Daedalus* was at anchor. The crews transferred supplies while the ships' carpenters caulked the *Plover*'s hull. Because the entire crew of the *Plover* had been aboard since she had sailed from Great Britain in 1848, and some of them had served even longer, having started out aboard the *Herald* in 1845, twenty-seven new men transferred to the *Plover*. The *Daedalus* then left the *Plover* in Port Clarence for its fourth northern winter.[45]

The winter passed uneventfully for the crew of the *Plover*. On January 9, 1852, the men were once again surprised by visiting Asian natives who had endured the dangerous fifty-five-mile winter crossing of Bering Strait. John Matthews recorded the encounter. "Five natives arrived from the coast of Asia. Each man had his own five dogs and it is astonishing to see them sitting in the small sledges and coming along like so many ponies, guided only by the whip." Although there is no report of the purpose of their visit, the men had probably crossed to Alaska seeking alcohol, as some had done the previous winter.

One of the local headmen, Kimouky, sold the ship quantities of caribou meat, and Captain Moore even lent him a musket and ammunition to help him hunt. As spring approached, the sailors also paid with tobacco for "large quantities of

seals . . . captured by the Esquimaux." Because of the quality of their fresh provisions the *Plover's* men avoided scurvy, but they learned nothing of Franklin's
whereabouts.[46]

SUMMER 1852 THROUGH SPRING 1853

In Great Britain, the year 1852 brought only gloom. Franklin had been missing for nearly seven years and there remained little hope for his survival. The
Plover had become the fall-back supply ship for the *Enterprise* and *Investigator*,
whose whereabouts also were unknown. The *Amphitrite* sailed north to resupply
the *Plover*. Aboard the *Amphitrite* was Commander Rochfort Maguire. Maguire
would replace Commander Moore, who had by then spent four northern winters
aboard the *Plover*. Maguire was directed to put the *Plover* into winter quarters at
Point Barrow. His orders stated that if Maguire should hear no word from the
Enterprise or *Investigator* in the winter of 1852–53, he was to remain north for
another winter as well.[47]

The *Amphitrite* reached Port Clarence on June 30, 1852. There the crew found
the 135-ton schooner *Koh-i-noor* (Captain George Levine) from Hong Kong,
buying furs and walrus ivory, and also the Russian-American Company's brig
Okhotsk, which had resupplied Mikhailovsky and was now on a northern trading
voyage.

The *Amphitrite's* surgeon examined the *Plover's* crew. Those who were judged
unfit for further service and those who did not wish to spend another northern
winter were exchanged for volunteers. One notable return to the *Plover* was
the surgeon Dr. John Simpson. He had been aboard the *Plover* for its first three
northern winters (at Plover Bay, Kotzebue Sound, and Port Clarence) but had
left for Great Britain in 1850 aboard the *Herald*. His fluency in Iñupiaqtun —
and his basic understanding of the state of relations among the native nations of
the Bering Strait region and northwestern Alaska — allowed the sailors to gain an
understanding of the Eskimos that other expeditions had lacked.[48]

The *Plover's* crew cached provisions at Grantley Harbor and left for the north.
At Point Barrow they settled into an unpleasant winter. Scurvy broke out, and the
Eskimos were aggressive and overbearing, frequently stealing from the ship. "We
are obliged to keep sentries under arms to prevent [the Eskimos] from cutting the
lead from our scupper holes or, in fact, any loose thing lying around the ship in
the shape of iron or copper," wrote John Matthews. "They will, if possible, take
the lead they use to make the pipes, copper for their women, who have copper
ear-rings and rings around their wrist. I have seen some with eight or ten round
each wrist."[49]

The sailors made a few exploratory trips but turned up nothing about Franklin. The only intelligence they gathered was from an Eskimo who arrived from the east, carrying a letter from M'Clure, who had given it to him nearly three years earlier on one of the barrier islands east of Oliktok, when the *Investigator* was on its way into the eastern Beaufort Sea. The letter carrier was probably a member of one of the interior-dwelling Eskimo nations who was visiting his trading partner at Point Barrow.[50]

Almost as soon as the *Plover* had reached the winter anchorage, Maguire learned the distressing news that one of the Eskimos had a gun. As we have seen, it was O-mi-ga-loon who owned the gun. "This I considered the worst piece of information amongst many unpleasant circumstances," he wrote. "As the Chief [O-mi-ga-loon] expressed a wish to see me, I went up, and found a large, power-ful, old man, with a very bad expression of countenance. He had a Hudson's bay Musket, with the name of Barnett on the lock, it was a good deal worn, but fit for service. He had a powder horn slung over his right shoulder, and hanging hunter fashion under his left arm, he had neither ball or shot, for which he was very anx-ious, and would not part with any thing except for Ammunition."[51]

O-mi-ga-loon, "the principal man at Point Barrow," was probably the first to own a gun there. He had threatened Pullen's boat expedition near Oliktok in 1849 and had met a party from the *Investigator* near there in 1850. The British thought that O-mi-ga-loon had bought his gun from Athapascans, but by 1854 three Point Barrow men bought Hudson's Bay guns from the Mackenzie Eski-mos at Barter Island. The Mackenzie Eskimos almost certainly acquired these guns via Gwich'in middlemen.[52]

As we have seen, the natives used fifty or more overland travel routes in north-western Alaska. Because of Dr. John Simpson's fluency in Iñupiaqtun, Maguire was able to learn about the routes that trade goods followed to reach Point Bar-row. Maguire noted, for example, that all the Eskimos had knives with the same maker's mark on the blade (a Maltese cross over the letter "I"), which he assumed were of Russian origin. (It is more likely that these knives were made by the firm of John Wilson in Sheffield, England.) "They told us they got them from the Ko-Yu-Kuk Indians. . . . Upon enquiring if these people had guns, we were told they had, the old chief [O-mi-ga-loon] informing us that he purchased his from them. We endeavoured to find if the Esquimaux here knew anything of the Russian post in the country—or where the people they bartered with to the East[war]d got their supplies. The only answer we could get was they got them a long way off. And that the Ko-Yu-Kuks had not much gun powder." It is more likely that O-mi-ga-loon bought his gun from Gwich'in traders, not the Koyukons.[53]

During that winter a Point Hope Eskimo traveled to Point Barrow to visit his trading partner. When the Eskimo, Sam-ma-ru-ma, visited the ship, Dr. Simpson asked him about trade with "the Asiatics." He replied that "he gave the Martin (Sable), Fox, Wolverine, Wolf, and other Skins and sometimes whale oil and fish for Kettles, tobacco, beads and Knives. . . . He said that he had only one . . . bartering friend at this place [Point Barrow], and that he brought three kettles to barter getting . . . wolverine skins in return." Thus Simpson learned that in addition to receiving Russian goods from Sheshalik, via the trade fair at Niġliq, the Point Barrow Eskimos also received them via a coastal route in the winter through established trading partnerships and that the Point Barrow people then carried some of these goods to Barter Island, to trade with the Mackenzie Eskimos. Dr. Simpson found that the Mackenzie Eskimos traded "wolverine, wolf, martin and a variety of deer skins together with knives of English manufacture which they procure from the Indians . . . for which they receive copper kettles, beads[,] tobacco and large knives which come from the Asiatic coast, and walrus tusks."[54]

At the beginning of July 1853, a large number of Eskimos headed east, past the *Plover*, toward the Niġliq rendezvous. Their umiaqs were hauled on sleds pulled by women and dogs, while the men dragged "five or six small (truck) sledges [that] carried their barter which appeared to be seal and Whale blubber." Maguire estimated that from July 4 to July 7, 150 persons, with twenty-seven to thirty umiaqs, passed the *Plover*. The winter population of the village at Point Barrow was approximately three hundred persons.

"It appears," he added, "to be a tour of pleasure as far as the Colville River [Niġliq], where they meet their friendly Nuna-tagmutes who they seem very fond of and speak in raptures of the dancing and eating they enjoy togeather from thence a select party extend themselves to barter Island, leaving much of their lumber and perhaps smaller children until their return, the women go on until a day's journey or so, of meeting the Eastern people, when the men advance and conclude their business as expeditiously as possible."[55]

Despite Simpson's statement that the Point Barrow traders concluded their business quickly at Barter Island and promptly returned west, it is clear from the map in his report that some Point Barrow people had by then traveled farther east on the coast, past the site of the trade rendezvous. This rendezvous took place not at today's Barter Island but a few miles west of there, on a low sand island, which is today Arey Island. In a map showing the natives' place names on the north coast of Alaska, Simpson added an annotation: "Siko Island, farthest visited by Pt. Barrow natives." *Siko* or *Siku* (ice) denotes the barrier island that Franklin named Icy Reef, in reference to the "semi-permanent ice, *aufeis*, that is found on the delta of the Kongakut River," about fifty miles east of the site of the Barter Island trade rendezvous. The fact that some Point Barrow people had traveled this far, in an area they had in the past considered to be hostile territory, suggests, once again, that the lure of trade was breaking down what had formerly been deeply mistrustful relations between native groups.[56]

SUMMER 1853 THROUGH SPRING 1854

The *Plover* broke out of Elson Lagoon at Point Barrow on August 9, 1853. The next day it met the *Amphitrite* south of Icy Cape, and the two headed to Port Clarence for the usual surveys, caulking, and transfers of men and supplies. On August 22, HMS *Rattlesnake* appeared. Under the command of Commander Henry Trollope, who had been Maguire's shipmate aboard the *Herald*, the *Rattlesnake* was sent north to serve as a depot ship for the winter at Port Clarence. The Russian-American Company's bark *Kadiak* also arrived to collect driftwood for the company's post on the Pribilof Islands. The company had instructed her captain, V. G. Pavlov, to scout the Buckland River area for the possibility of establishing an outpost, but this part of the voyage apparently did not take place.[57]

The Hong Kong schooner *Koh-i-noor* also returned to Port Clarence. One of the men aboard the *Amphitrite* described the scene: "On the spit that separates Grantley Harbour from Port Clarence was a quite populous village, the various tribes generally congregating here about June, for the purpose of barter, the upper water tribes bringing down reindeer skins, and furs of all kinds to exchange for walrus hides, seal skins and. . . . Tobacco was in great demand, TAWAC was loudly demanded on all sides, it formed in fact the great circulating medium."[58]

The *Plover* was ordered to return to Point Barrow as an advance support ship for the crews of the *Enterprise* and *Investigator*, while the *Rattlesnake* was to serve as a fall-back depot for the crews of all three ships in case the *Plover* might be lost. At Grantley Harbor, Trollope was directed to build a house large enough to hold seventy men. Thus, by 1853, the Admiralty had abandoned the search for Franklin, and British naval activities near Bering Strait had become a watch for the *Enterprise*, now gone two years, and the *Investigator*, now gone three.[59]

NORTHERN ALASKA, 1853–1854

The crew warped the *Plover* into her anchorage in Elson Lagoon at Point Barrow for the second time, and the ship began its sixth northern winter. Fortunately, the relations between the sailors and the Eskimos had by then improved, and there was much visiting between the groups—thanks in part to Dr. John Simpson's presence and Commander Rochfort Maguire's firm but gentle leadership. As I have noted previously, the British also found that three more guns (making

Figure 11.3. Interior of an Eskimo house at Point Barrow, 1852–54. Dr. John Simpson,
the *Plover*'s surgeon, made this sketch. On the wall the man's musket holds pride
of place. John Simpson Papers, Perkins Rare Book, Manuscript, and
Special Collections Library, Duke University.

a total of four, including O-mi-ga-loon's gun) had by then reached the Point Barrow Eskimos.[60]

One of the guns, belonging to Maguire's friend Erk-sin-ra, was in poor condition: "several threads of the screws [in the lock] being worn, and bound round
with fibres of deer sinews to make them hold." Dr. Simpson told Erk-sin-ra that
"the Indians Knew all about it, and Knew his ignorance of such matters. . . . Erk-
sin-ra answered that when he bought one again he would be wise and take off the
lock previously." A native trader had sold a worn-out gun to Erk-sin-ra.[61]

When the ice was thick enough for travel in autumn 1853, Maguire set out
east with a sledge party in search of the *Enterprise* and *Investigator* but learned
nothing new. The winter proceeded without serious incident, and he went east
again in April. This time, however, Maguire turned back near the Colville River
delta when he met a party of armed Gwich'in who began following his sled with,
he thought, every intention of killing the sailors. "Our unexpected return," he

wrote, "was in consequence of having met a party of four Ko-yu-Kuk Indians, or rather they followed our track from (I suppose) the neighbourhood of the Colville. And they were armed with a musket each, and had no apparent object in their journey to [Oliktok Point] where they overtook us, I was rather puzzled as to my future proceedings as I intended to have continued my journey for two days longer—but having only a rifle and a double barraled gun with Ammunition only for a chance supply of game. I thought it proper under the circumstances to return to the ship. . . . From all our knowledge of them they are not considered over scrupuluous." After Maguire returned to the *Plover*, he learned from the Eskimos that these "It-Kal-ge" [Indians] were considered to be friendly and that they would have been greeted warmly in the village.[62]

Maguire incorrectly assumed that these natives were Koyukon, members of the nation that had carried out the Nulato massacre, but it is likely that they were not Koyukon but were Gwich'in—and if Maguire had kept on for another week, he would have found the *Enterprise* in Camden Bay.[63]

Collinson and his crew had spent two winters in harbors on the coast of Victoria Island, one of them in Cambridge Bay, not far, as it turned out, from where Franklin's ships were abandoned. But on the way back toward Point Barrow in 1853 the *Enterprise* was caught by the ice and forced to winter in Camden Bay, Alaska, only 250 miles east of Point Barrow. In early July 1854, Collinson got word of the *Plover* when a party of Mackenzie Eskimos visited the *Enterprise*. Three were carrying Hudson's Bay Company muskets and powder horns. "On the evening of the 1st of July a large party of the natives were seen coming towards the ship from the eastward. . . . In a short time a printed paper dated H.M.S. Plover, July 4th, 1853, Point Barrow, was produced. . . . I therefore determined to open communication with Captain Maguire as soon as the ice would admit a boat to proceed to the westward. Our new visitors, forty-one in number in two *oomiaks*, soon made themselves quite at home . . . showing a strong disposition to appropriate every article. They brought a good many fox and brown bear skins, but neither venison nor fish; these, however, they promised to return with, and produced three muskets, one of which had a date, 1850, on the lock." The Eskimos must have acquired the gun very recently. The fact that Mackenzie Eskimos were carrying papers that had been printed aboard the *Plover* at Point Barrow in July 1853 suggests that these Eskimos had probably received them from Point Barrow Eskimos at the Barter Island trade rendezvous the previous summer or perhaps from Gwich'in traders.[64]

On July 20, 1854, just as the *Enterprise* was breaking out of her winter quarters, the Eskimos returned accompanied by a group of Gwich'in. Collinson wrote:

We soon found out that they had several strangers with them, the chief of whom produced a paper, on which was written:—

> The printed slips of paper delivered by the officers of H.M.S. *Plover* on the 25th of April, 1854, to the Rat Indians, were received 27th of June, 1854, at the H.B. Company's establishment, Fort Youcon. . . . The Rat Indians are in the habit of making periodical trading excursions to the Esquimaux along the sea-coast. They are a harmless, inoffensive set of Indians, ever ready and willing to render every assistance they can to whites.
>   Wm. Lucas Hardisty
>   Clerk in Charge

Collinson continued, "These people were entirely different-featured from the Esquimaux, and were clad in blankets, and wore as necklaces and ornaments through the septum of the nose dentalium." One of Collinson's men added other details about the Gwich'in. "There were 2 females with them and nearly all had their faces painted in red streaks, besides a great profusion of Beads round their necks and wrists. . . . They had ten muskets with them and we gave them some powder and shot."[65]

Thus the group of "Rat Indians" (Gwich'in) that Maguire had met near the Colville delta had carried his message to Fort Yukon, and they, or others, had returned to the Arctic coast and joined with a group of Mackenzie Eskimos who were on their way to a trading rendezvous with the Point Barrow Eskimos. The fact that the Gwich'in were now traveling in company with the Eskimos reveals that the formerly hostile relations had improved considerably. Although until the mid-nineteenth century Eskimo-Gwich'in relations had whipsawed between trade and warfare, in 1847 the Upper Porcupine River Gwich'in told the Hudson's Bay Company men that they wanted to have trade goods advanced to them so that they could trade with the Eskimos. The following year the Mackenzie Flats Gwich'in traded peacefully with the Eskimos at the mouth of the Peel River. The reasons for this change in attitude were that muskrats had become an important trade item for the Gwich'in and epidemic diseases had drastically reduced the natives' numbers. Firearms were now reaching the Eskimos regularly from the Hudson's Bay Company through Gwich'in middlemen, first from Fort McPherson (formerly Peel's River Post) and later from Fort Yukon. From the perspective of the Gwich'in as middlemen in the trade with the Eskimos, Shepard Krech III has written: "By 1850, guns were in strong demand throughout the [Gwich'in] area. Those who did not carry these costly items (at 20 Made Beaver [the Hudson's Bay Company's unit of value], the most expensive item in the Hudson's Bay

Company inventory) traded nonetheless for powder and ball which they would exchange in turn with gun carriers."[66]

> The Gwich'in put great stock in their middleman position. They maintained it until mid-century . . . but not after mid-century. By then many had died from disease and the demographic balance of power had shifted. Those who survived valued peace and direct access to muskrats, whose optimum habitat was the upper Mackenzie Delta, a dangerous no-man's land separating Gwich'in and Inuvialuit [Mackenzie Eskimos], more highly than feuding and middleman profits. HBC [Hudson's Bay Company] traders also changed their attitude toward the Inuvialuit. Formerly suspicious and antagonistic toward them, they groomed Gwich'in interpreters to translate and open trade and became bold enough themselves to overcome their traditional attitude.[67]

The growing volume of trade goods that was now entering the region from several sources—from the Mackenzie River, from the trade rendezvous at Sheshalik, and from foreign ships—must have been a significant factor in the warming of relations between the groups. And the fact that the group of Gwich'in traders that visited Collinson aboard the *Enterprise* was already *west* of Barter Island (as was the group that Maguire had met), where the exchange between the Point Barrow Eskimos and the Mackenzie Eskimos had formerly taken place, suggests that the party was on its way to rendezvous with them farther west, possibly at Collinson Point or beyond, perhaps at Oliktok, near the Colville delta.

As Rochfort Maguire noted on July 1, 1854, the Point Barrow people had now begun to anticipate a source of guns from the Mackenzie Eskimos. Although they received first-class caribou skins from the Eskimos from the interior of Alaska, he wrote, "from the Eastern people they exchange Kettles, and now that they are so well supplied with tobacco by us, it may be bartered also for Kap-wick [wolverine] skins, sable [marten] skins, muskets, and beads [etc]."[68]

Near Return Reef on July 27, 1854, while the *Enterprise* was making slow progress toward Point Barrow, a group of forty Point Barrow Eskimos—men, women, and children in several kayaks and umiaqs—arrived from the west carrying papers, printed aboard the *Plover* as recently as July 1 and 2. The papers stated that the *Plover* had been ordered south. It is worthy of note that a large number of Point Barrow Eskimos were by that date proceeding east of Oliktok with their families, presumably toward the trade rendezvous with the Mackenzie Eskimos, whereas previously the women and children usually would have stayed at Oliktok or a little farther east while the men proceeded. This confirms that the former tensions between the two groups had relaxed considerably.[69]

PORT CLARENCE, 1853–1854

At Port Clarence during the winter of 1853–54 things were relatively uneventful, although the Eskimos refused to believe that the *Rattlesnake* was not there for trade. Captain Trollope sent traveling parties out from the ship all over the western Seward Peninsula but, of course, learned nothing about Franklin. Unknown to the sailors, in January 1854 the Admiralty had published a notice stating that if by the end of March no word had been received that Franklin's men were alive, their names would be removed from the navy's roster and their heirs would receive their back pay. By then, apart from Franklin's ships, only the *Enterprise* remained to be accounted for. The *Plover* and *Rattlesnake* were ordered to remain in the North for another winter. If no word had been received from the *Enterprise* by the end of winter 1854–55, both the *Plover* and the *Rattlesnake* were to head south, for no supply ship would be sent north in 1855. Thus the Admiralty was preparing to abandon hope of Collinson, as it had of Franklin.[70]

On June 25, 1854, HMS *Trincomalee* arrived from Honolulu with orders and supplies. Most important, it brought news of the *Investigator*, which had spent two winters frozen in on the north coast of Banks Island. The crew was on the verge of starvation when they were discovered by a patrol led by Lieutenant Bedford Pim. Pim, who had wintered aboard the *Plover* in Kotzebue Sound in 1849–50, was then serving aboard HMS *Resolute*, which was wintering in the Eastern Arctic. M'Clure and his men abandoned the *Investigator* and walked to the *Resolute* and HMS *Intrepid* in spring 1853, but these ships were also beset by ice during the summer and forced to winter again. They were abandoned in spring 1854, and their crews, along with the *Investigator*'s men, walked to the depot ship *North Star*, which was wintering at Beechey Island under the command of W. J. S. Pullen. The men returned to Britain aboard the *North Star*, and the *Investigator*'s crew thus became the first Europeans to traverse a northwest passage.[71]

SUMMER 1854

At the beginning of July umiaqs began arriving at Grantley Harbor in Port Clarence for the annual trade rendezvous. "About 12 [umiaqs] came in today from Cape Price of Wales, the Asiatic side, and King's Island," noted Philip Sharpe, aboard the *Rattlesnake*, "so that the troublesome time is about to commence; already there are 20 or 30 huts [tents] on the spit end." Later the little 93-ton trading schooner *Pfeil* (Captain Corsen) of Bremen arrived from Honolulu, as did the schooner *Koh-i-noor* from Hong Kong. The *Pfeil* had been trading at St. Lawrence Island, Cape Rodney, and Mys Chaplina (Indian Point) for "skins, whalebone, and tusks." "She had collected 4000 lbs. of tusks, 3000 lbs. of whale-bone, and 200 or 300 skins—marten, sable, and others."[72]

For the British ships the usual transfers of supplies went on, and the *Plover* re-turned to Point Barrow on August 28 to resume the vigil for the third winter there. But to the surprise of all, Eskimos boarded the ship with news that the *Enter-prise* had reached Point Barrow. In fact, unknown to either, the ships' paths had crossed a few days before. The southbound *Enterprise* was becalmed in Bering Strait on its way to Port Clarence when a fleet of forty-two umiaqs passed the ship on their way to, presumably, the Sheshalik rendezvous. They offered to trade furs and walrus tusks but would accept only rum and brandy in payment.[73]

At Point Barrow five whaleships—the first whaleships to reach there—were cruising nearby, and they confirmed the report to the *Plover*'s men. The *Plover* headed back south, and near Point Hope the *Enterprise* itself hove into sight. The two ships headed to Port Clarence, where Maguire transferred fresh stores to the *Enterprise*. The *Enterprise*'s gunroom steward, Richard Shingleton, was shocked at the change that had come over the Eskimo traders in the three years since the *Enterprise* had last been at Port Clarence. He noted that liquor was the item most sought by the natives, and next in demand was firearms; furthermore the price of trade goods had increased steeply. In describing the purchase of caribou legs he wrote, "weighing about 30 lbs. each which 3 years previous when we were down here I could have purchased for a string of Beads or a knife or a few Buttons each, but today I was forced to give them a 2 lb. Cannister of fine [gun] powder for each one I purchased which was 3. The meat certainly was cheap and most excellent but before they would have been content with a few trinkets of little or no value."[74]

The British ships then left for the south, ending the western search for Sir John Franklin. The *Plover* sailed to San Francisco, where it was found unfit for further service and was sold at auction to a ship breaker. The *Plover*'s crew moved aboard the Russian-American Company's bark *Sitkha*, which had been captured in an Anglo-French assault on Petropavlovsk during the Crimean War. Shortly before the *Plover*'s men left San Francisco for England they read in an American news-paper that near King William Island, more than one thousand miles east of Point Barrow, Dr. John Rae had found the remains of some of Franklin's men.[75]

12

TRADING ACTIVITIES FROM 1848 TO THE SALE OF RUSSIAN AMERICA

Almost twenty-nine years to the day after two hundred Chukotkans confronted Eliab Grimes and the crew of the *General San Martín* in Bering Strait, Captain Thomas Roys and the crew of the whaling bark *Superior* found themselves in a similar predicament. On July 23, 1848, when the *Superior* lay becalmed near Big Diomede Island, forty natives in seven umiaqs headed toward the small whaleship. The approaching flotilla made Roys very uneasy because for all he knew they might be hostile—and the *Superior* had no firearms except "one Blunt and Sims revolver that would not go unless you threw it."[1]

But much had changed at Bering Strait in the three decades since Grimes's voyage, and unlike the encounter with the *General San Martín* in 1819—when the Eskimos and Chukchi saw the presence of a foreign ship as a threat to their trade monopoly—by 1848 the natives had been in fairly regular contact with the Russian-American Company's ships and no doubt viewed the *Superior*'s visit as a welcome opportunity to acquire trade goods. But no one—foreigner or native— could have foreseen that the year 1848 marked the end of the natives' relative isolation and that within a year Bering Strait would be overrun by foreign fleets and awash in foreign products.

THE FIRST DECADE

Like Eliab Grimes in 1819, Roys had arrived at Bering Strait on a commercial reconnaissance. In Petropavlovsk seven years before, a Russian naval officer had told him about the large numbers of whales in Bering Strait, and sensing an opportunity, Roys bought copies of Litke's surveys of the area. Later, in Hawaii, Roys met with John Meek, who was then Honolulu's harbormaster and who had been the captain of the *Pedlar* during the cruise to Bering Strait in 1820. Meek no doubt confirmed the Russian's report, leading Roys to consult Frederick William Beechey's narrative of the voyage of HMS *Blossom*. Roys concluded that the whales reported in Bering Strait were the same species as the "Greenland whales" that Europeans had been capturing in the northern North Atlantic for three centuries.[2]

The *Superior* sailed north alone and had phenomenal success at Bering Strait. Roys quickly captured eleven whales and filled the ship's hold with 1,600 barrels of oil. The news of his discovery was soon published in the *Friend*, a Honolulu missionary newspaper. By early 1849 many marine journals picked up the story, and Roys's success set off a flurry of excitement among the world's whalemen, whose catches had been declining elsewhere.

In 1849 fifty whaleships went north to good success. The fleet increased each year until 1852, when 224 ships—from most of the whaling ports of the United States, as well as a few ships from Australia, Germany, Hawaii, and France—cruised there. In fact, throughout the sixty-five year history of the Bering Strait fishery, whaleships would make more than 2,700 cruises to the arctic whaling grounds.[3]

When the whaling fleet reached the Chukchi Peninsula in 1849 the whalemen thought it odd that the natives showed little surprise at the presence of the ships. Near Plover Bay, Mary Brewster, the wife of the captain of the ship *Tiger* of Stonington, Connecticut, witnessed one of the first encounters. She was falling asleep at 11 PM on June 25, 1849, when she was jolted awake by one of the officers shouting, "The bloody Indians are coming."

> We did not feel much pleased as we preferred to form our first opinion by day. . . . I asked my husband what he should do. Said he should not allow them to come on board till he could see something of them—a few spades was got down—four old muskets was loaded neither of them though would go off—or not more than one—They came alongside and when motioned to leave and go back they went—and we went to bed.
>
> This morning several canoes came off and the first one which came said good morning with the word *English*. We said America. They wanted towack [tobacco] and not instantly taking their meaning a slight tap on their face with one of their number speaking more plain tobak, the tobacco was got and liberally distributed to them and the great joy exhibited by them shewed they were well acquainted with the weed.
>
> They had their women with them, and were dressed alike in trowzers made of seal skin and a skin garment similar to a shirt. I was quite pleased with their appearances, and we all concluded they were harmless. . . .

Towards 6 we saw a small schooner coming, much to our surprise, concluded it must be a Russian trader, proved to be a barge from ship Plover which had anchored and wintered in a bay 30 miles from us by sea and about 5 by land. The indians had travelled across and told them a ship was on the coast and as they were expecting their consort to bring supplies they thought it must be her. Judge of their surprise when they found an American whaler to the north of them bound into the Arctic and they certainly were amazed when they saw me.[4]

The next day eleven umiaqs towed the *Tiger* to anchor in Plover Bay. Two days later the natives came aboard.

A very pleasant day, plenty of native company. We have had callers from the whole coast I believe, a chief by the name Notochen with his wife and child, then another chief who is the greatest man of the nation I expect. We are caressed, touched noses together, and as near as we can understand they are to be our friends. They were well dressed in seal skin trousers and a coat made from deer skin made loose and belted round them. The women dressed the same save their hair is long and braided. Two of the women were very pretty. Their skin which had not been exposed was as white as mine, black eyes and red cheeks. . . .

Their chief food is seals' flesh—walrus and blubber with fish. The blubber is cut up in slits and I could not help laughing to see a child about 6 months old in the bottom of one of their canoes lying on his back with a strip of blubber as much as it could hold in both hands sucking it and apparently very happy—

They stopped nearly all day. We gave them bread, combs, needles, thread, and knives and at 4 they left all pleased with their visit.[5]

By then the natives of the Chukchi Peninsula had become reasonably comfortable with the presence of foreign vessels. In fact, on August 2, 1849, when the whaleship *Richmond* of Cold Spring Harbor, New York, went aground twelve miles south of St. Lawrence Bay, the natives helped the whalemen in their unsuccessful attempt to refloat her and then cared for them for four days until they were rescued. And in 1852, when the *Citizen* of New Bedford was lost on the north coast of the Chukchi Peninsula in a terrible autumn gale, the natives housed, fed, and clothed the crew for the entire winter. But even in 1849 Mary Brewster foresaw problems. Near Cape Dezhnev on August 3 she wrote: "Several of the natives came on board. . . . Their demand is usually for rum but as we have no liquor they have to get it somewhere else—I think if the whaling continues good here they will not be the happy people they are now. They will naturally learn many ways which will not be for their good. Liquor will only cause them to quarrel. It is a great pity that they should ever get accustomed to the use of it and I wish we had more temperance ships and more temperate commanders so that the influence could be better."[6]

The whalemen are often accused of having introduced alcohol into the Bering Strait region, but the natives of Chukotka were already well acquainted with it by the time the first whaleships arrived. Mary Brewster's remarks indicate that the natives had a taste for rum. In fact, alcohol had been reaching Bering Strait from the Kolyma region for a number of years. Alcohol was distilled in Kamchatka in the eighteenth century, and the Chukchi were aware of it by the beginning of the nineteenth century. In 1816 Kotzebue noted that the natives of Cape Dezhnev liked brandy.[7]

Nevertheless, alcohol was still relatively scarce at the Ostrovnoe fair in the 1830s, even though the explorer Ivan Kobelev was allowed to sell some spirits there. "The price of the liquor was a marten-skin for a glassful," wrote the ethnographer Waldemar Bogoras. "Because of this traffic, he [Kobelev] was greatly loved by all the people. At the same time, however . . . Nishne-Kolymsk had a regular saloon, where even fruit brandy . . . was sold. In 1842 . . . the saloon . . . sold thirty barrels of undiluted alcohol, and in 1847 even fifty barrels. In 1864 the price of alcohol at the [Ostrovnoe] fair was two beaver-skins for one bottle. From that time on, the imports of alcohol into the Kolyma country increased quite regularly until they reached three hundred barrels yearly." In fact, by 1847 the chief manager of the Russian-American Company reported to the Main Office in St. Petersburg that the company's "trade with the Chukchi presents an important obstacle in that the necessary basis of their trade with the Siberian merchants is strong drink."[8]

During the winter of 1848–49 the crew of the *Plover* also traded alcohol to the natives who visited the ship in Plover Bay. "Moore says nothing [in his official report] of their selling spirits to the natives," wrote the explorer Dr. John Rae, "and cheating them as much or more than the most rascally fur trader ever heard of. The plan was this, the trader pro. tem. gradually diluted the spirits very much, but this the poor Tchukchi had no means of finding out until the seamen (who were probably parties interested) put them 'up to' a plan of discovering the imposition by holding a little of the liquid to a light, if it took fire all was right, if not the 'brown skin' went back to have his 'drap o' drink' strengthened. But the acute trader was still too knowing for the native, as on future occasions he reduced the strength of the grog as before or rather more, and then poured carefully on the top a little strong rum or alcohol, which being of less specific gravity remained on the surface."[9]

Just as the frontier for the tobacco market had steadily proceeded eastward in the Bering Strait region, the natives' desire for alcohol moved in the same direction. The geographer Don C. Foote believed that before 1848 the "alcohol frontier" was at Cape Dezhnev, but four years later, it was in northwestern Alaska. Apart from the cruises of the *General San Martín*, the *Pedlar*, and the Russian-American Company's ships, it is unlikely that other trading vessels visited the Bering Strait region prior to 1849.[10]

What drew the traders there in 1849 was Thomas Roys's report. In his widely disseminated article in the *Friend*, Roys had mentioned that the Asiatic natives were "well supplied with valuable furs that could easily be purchased." This lured some vessels to Bering Strait in 1849 to trade—not only with the natives but also with the whaling fleet and the ships participating in the Franklin Search. These traders would have carried the usual Pacific Ocean inventory of fresh produce, manufactured goods, tobacco, and rum, and by summer 1851 several trading vessels—from Australia, Hong Kong, and Hawaii—were operating at Bering Strait, among them, the *Koh-i-noor* of Hong Kong, trading for "walrus teeth and furs, with plenty of rum on board."[11]

During the first decade of the Bering Strait whale fishery the encounters between whalemen and natives mostly took place on the Chukchi Peninsula, at the Diomede Islands, at Cape Prince of Wales, and to a lesser extent at Port Clarence. The whalemen, many of whom did not care to trade, often freely gave the natives needles, pins, iron, and other small manufactured goods. The natives, however, were accustomed to strict reciprocity in trade encounters. This behavior was at first puzzling to them; later they grew to consider it their right to receive gifts when they visited a ship, and if they did not receive such things, they asked for them. Thus grew the foreigners' perception that most of the natives of the Bering Strait region were bothersome beggars.[12]

"The non-native generosity of giving without expected return was entirely foreign to an Eskimo whose activities were based on a complicated system of reciprocal relationships," wrote the ethnohistorian Dorothy Jean Ray. "In the native trading operations there were well-established procedures, routines, and units of exchange through trading partnerships, formalized ceremonial exchanges such as the messenger feast and feasts of the dead . . . but when the white man came in person with unfamiliar objects as well as large quantities of familiar and much-desired items like knives and tobacco, the exchange became skewed."[13]

Apart from the trading vessels, in the early years of the bowhead fishery a few whaleships did trade in rum, but most ships did not carry much alcohol other than the captain's and officers' private stocks, and some vessels were strictly "temperance" ships, carrying none at all. Those who traded with the natives at that time usually purchased furs, walrus tusks, clothing and boots, whalebone, and fish and game. The natives often asked for payment in rum, tobacco, and knives. But as early as 1852 it seemed to many whalemen that the natives mainly wanted rum.[14]

In fact, when the whaleship *Citizen* of New Bedford was wrecked on the north coast of the Chukchi Peninsula, and the crew was forced to spend winter 1851–52 with the natives, Lewis Holmes described the Chukchi drinking habits:

> At the time of our visiting the wreck with the natives, they were very inquisitive to know whether we had any thing to drink which would make them dance and sing, and such like. From their gestures, words, and actions, we knew they meant *rum*. In addition to our previous knowledge of their habits in this particular, our further acquaintance with them, for half a year or more, confirmed us in the opinion that they loved ardent spirits, and whenever and wherever they could get it they would drink to excess.
>
> We found there were no half-hearted, occasional, genteel drinkers. They had no idea of making a quantity of spirits continue its enlivening and kicking effects through several days and weeks; but they wanted, and they would have, if furnished with the means, one grand "burst up," one tremendous "spree," and that would end it for the present, until the next supply could be obtained. They went on the principle that many others tolerate, "they could not have too much of a good thing."
>
> Some spirits had been brought to the settlement, obtained probably by way of traffic from other tribes in the interior. . . . When the "fire water" arrived at the settlement, it happened to be in the night time. . . . By morning, many of the natives who had drunk to excess were laid away as those who belong to the class of quiet ones; but others were noisy, confident, and brave—full of their gabble—rich—possessing the whole creation, and a little more. . . .
>
> Again the natives would display, in the most boisterous manner, their skill in harpooning or lancing the whale, or walrus, and thus brandish their weapons with uplifted arms, as if they were about to strike their prey. One of this class was so stimulated with alcoholic strength and courage, that suiting his action to the word or impulse, he threw his spear with all his might into the broadside of one of the huts, and it passed within a short distance of the captain's head.

"In the month of May [1852]," Holmes continued, "Captain Norton took a short cruise into the interior, about one hundred miles, with the head man and several others, accompanied by their dog teams. The settlement he visited was called *Souchou*. The principal food among the natives there was deer [reindeer] meat; in return the natives bring to the coast deer meat, tobacco, spirits, etc."[15]

And rum was the cause of the first recorded clash between whalemen and natives in the Bering Strait region. On July 10, 1851, the whaleship *Armata* of New London, Connecticut, was running with all sails set along the edge of the ice on the east coast of the Chukchi Peninsula near Arakamchechen Island. At about 10 AM it struck hard on a reef. The crew could not free it, and the ship began to go to pieces. Several whaleships soon gathered round her. On the thirteenth, while the crew of an Australian whaleship, the *Emu*, was salvaging the gear and cargo, a large group of natives boarded the *Armata*, and in the confusion immediately made for the captain's supply of rum. The natives may have been drunk on arrival, because the *Koh-i-noor* had recently sold them "plenty of rum." In any case they were soon visibly drunk and began plundering the wreck.

The *Emu*'s captain had probably bought part, or all, of the *Armata*'s oil, baleen, and equipment via the standard practice of a hastily convened auction among nearby whaling captains; hence he had purchased the salvage rights. The natives, of course, would not have known of these protocols and probably viewed the wreck as fair game. The fight broke out when one of the *Emu*'s crew tried to prevent a native from carrying off a piece of equipment, and struck him. The native then stabbed the sailor with his knife, mortally wounding the man. Chaos ensued: the whalemen fought with harpoons, lances, hatchets and cutting spades, and when it was over, a number of natives and one sailor lay dead. "Rum was the cause of the trouble," wrote Asa Tobey.[16]

Although the story quickly spread throughout the fleet, and the sailors were on their guard for trouble, the profits were so alluring that traders and some whalemen continued to sell alcohol to the natives. In 1853 one of the crew of HMS *Amphitrite* reported: "While in Port Clarence a whaler arrived the captain of which told me that a few days previously he had landed at a village on the Asiatic shore and was horrified at discovering the whole village in confusion and the unfortunate villagers reeling about in various stages of intoxication, men and women all were drunk, even little children were reeling and rioting in a most disgraceful state. . . . Men were lying about as insensate as logs."[17]

In the years following the *Armata* incident there were many reports of natives of the Chukchi Peninsula coming aboard whaleships "drunk" and "saucy." For example, the captain of the whaleship *Julian* of New Bedford wrote in 1859:

> Come near having some trouble with [the natives] while my boats were off [replenishing the ship's water casks], after a couple of chiefs went on board the Good Return and Capt. Fish gave them some rum and they got a little tight and wanted more rum and [he] wouldn't give them anymore, and they come on board of my ship and wanted rum. I saw they were half drunk and told them

no and made motions that they were drunk. They said no and coaxed a long time but no use, I wouldn't let them have any and they told me if I didn't let them have some rum, they would go on shore and cut my raft rope and destroy my [water] casks. I went down below and loaded my revolver and went on deck and told them to go and cut it if they wanted to and showed them my revolver. I heard no more about rum or raft ropes after that day. If they had done it I should have shot everyone that had a hand in it.[18]

The whaling fleet largely deserted the Bering Strait region from 1854 through 1857 because of declining catches in those waters and the report of abundant bowheads in the Sea of Okhotsk. While there had been 168 whaling cruises to the Bering Strait region in 1853, in 1854 there were 45; in 1855 there were 7; in 1856, 9; and in 1857, 12. It was not until 1858 that the Okhotsk fishery declined, and with few other productive whaling grounds in the Pacific, the fleet returned to Bering Strait.[19]

Of course during the whaling fleet's absence the natives did not lose their taste for alcohol: when USS *Vincennes* carried out surveys there in 1855, the natives they met on the Chukchi Peninsula requested rum. And while the whaling fleet was concentrating its efforts in the Sea of Okhotsk, the bulk of the maritime trade in Bering Strait was carried out by perhaps a dozen brigs and schooners from Hawaii, Hong Kong, and other ports. Unfortunately there is little information on the extent of their activities. In 1854 the little German-owned schooner *Pfeil* of Honolulu brought home 4,000 pounds of walrus tusks, 3,000 pounds of whalebone, and "200 or 300 skins—marten, sable, and others."[20]

THE SECOND DECADE

When the whaling fleet returned to Bering Strait in the late 1850s the nature of the whalemen's trade had changed. The price of whalebone (baleen) had doubled—due in part to its use in Victorian fashion for corset stays and skirt hoops, among other things—and many captains found that trading for it made sense. The whalemen and traders experimented with several new strategies to take advantage of this new opportunity.

WHALER-TRADERS

Several of the vessels in the Hawaiian whaling fleet were traders as much as whalers. In 1858, for example, the brig *Agate* of Honolulu returned with 22,000 pounds of ivory and 1,200 skins. One whaleman discovered that he could "buy a hundred dollars' worth of bone [whalebone] or fur for a gallon of rum which cost

Siberian Eskimo Pictograph of the Bering Strait Region, 1860s

This important document (fig. 12.1), drawn on sealskin, records both the geographical knowledge and the events in the life of a Siberian Eskimo who probably lived on the coast of the Chukchi Peninsula in the settlement of Uŋaziq on Cape Chaplin (Mys Chaplina—"Indian Point" to the whalers and traders). Judging from the information on the sealskin, the person who drew it was probably a wealthy hunter who was not only a whaling captain but also a trader who had traveled throughout the Bering Strait region and dealt with foreigners in several locales. Among much other information, the pictograph contains scenes of hunting for bowhead whales, gray whales, beluga whales, walruses, seals, reindeer and caribou, and bears.

Most important, the drawing depicts events that probably took place in the 1860s, and it delineates landforms on both sides of Bering Strait (fig. 12.2). On the Asian coast the shore is traced from west of Plover Bay in the Gulf of Anadyr to Cape Dezhnev at Bering Strait. On the American coast, the shoreline runs from approximately Cape Krusenstern in the Chukchi Sea to Point Spencer in the Bering Sea. Native traders on both sides of Bering Strait would have been acquainted with these coasts.

More specifically, the large lobe on the left side of the sealskin (here shown at 9 o'clock) represents the artist's home village at Indian Point (Cape Chaplin), the Siberian Eskimo settlement of Uŋaziq, with its several rows of dwellings and a row of storage racks closer to shore. To the left of the settlement is the Cape Chaplin lagoon, Lake Naivan, and to the left of the lagoon are high hills and hunters. Below the lobe of Cape Chaplin is Tkachen Bay ("Marcus Bay" of the whalers and traders), and near Tkachen Bay umaiq crews are shown hunting gray whales (*Eschrichtius robustus*).

Below this bay (at approximately 7 o'clock) is Zaliv Providenia ("Plover Bay" of the whalemen). A hook-shaped sandspit represents the site of the Eskimo settlement of Yryrak (V. V. Bychkov et al. 2002, 133). Nearby, a three-masted ship, which is almost certainly a whaling vessel, is at an-

continued

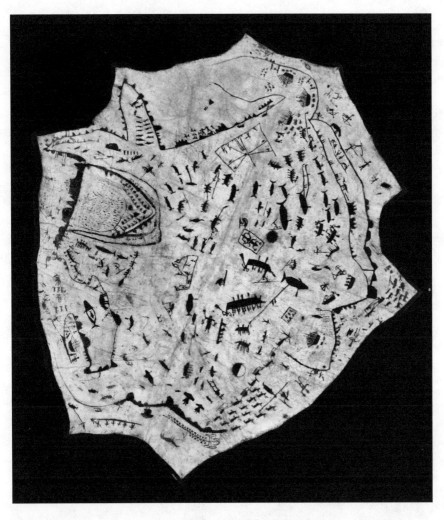

Figure 12.1. Siberian Eskimo pictograph of the Bering Strait region, 1860s. Pitt Rivers Museum, University of Oxford, 1966.19.1.

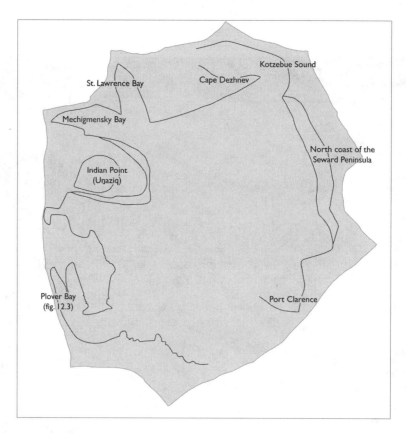

Figure 12.2. Geographical key to Eskimo pictograph.

Figure 12.3. Detail of Eskimo pictograph: trade with foreigners in Plover Bay. Pitt
Rivers Museum, University of Oxford, 1966.19.1.

chor behind another sandspit representing Emma Harbor (fig. 12.3). The ship's anchor line extends to the shore, a precaution often taken when wintering in a location where the harbor ice might shift. Two dog teams pulling sleds approach the vessel, indicating that it is a winter scene and thus that the ship is probably in winter quarters there. On the shore, two figures—one of which is not wearing native clothing—are apparently engaged in trade. Native artists always carefully depicted a ship's rig: three-masted ships are known to have wintered alone in Plover Bay only in 1861–62 and 1862–63 (Bockstoce and Batchelder 1978b, 83).

Curving to the right of "Plover Bay" the coastline is shown as high hills, which probably represent the steep southern coast of the Chukchi Peninsula that extends west as far as Cape Yakun (which is shown as very bold, at about 6 o'clock).

To the right of the bold coastline (from about 4 o'clock to 5:30), a person is leading a train of five reindeer hauling sledges, on one of which another person is riding. This scene depicts a group of traders heading toward a trade fair. Near the reindeer train is a reindeer herd. Near the herd a man is shown harpooning a seal at its breathing hole in the winter ice. To the left of these are three figures wearing Chukotkan armor, suggesting the memory of a hostile encounter. It is interesting that St. Lawrence Island is apparently not shown. Perhaps the person who drew the map did not consider its trade to be of importance.

Directly above the lobe of Cape Chaplin (at 9 o'clock) two embayments appear. The lower one, which extends farther to the left, conflates Seniavin Strait (Proliv Seniavina), Arakamchechen Island, and Mechigmensky Bay. The other embayment (at approximately 10 o'clock) is St. Lawrence Bay, with its bold shoreline and the settlement of Nunyagmo (Nuniamo) at its northeastern corner. From there, the relatively straight line is probably the coast from St. Lawrence Bay to Cape Dezhnev. Three settlements are shown on the shore. At the top of the sealskin the shoreline then curves back (at approximately 12 o'clock) and there are five habitations shown on shore. This most likely is the Chukchi village of Uelen, which lies on a sandspit just west of Cape Dezhnev. This shoreline then ends.

continued

Another shoreline starts directly above the first. It represents the American coast from approximately Cape Krusenstern (at 1 o'clock) in the north to Port Clarence and Point Spencer (at approximately 4 o'clock) in the south. Three two-masted vessels—which are probably trading brigs or schooners—are shown (toward 1 o'clock), each with a number of umiaqs nearby. This scene probably represents trading activities in Kotzebue Sound. On shore two pairs of figures are engaged in trade. Trading vessels began visiting the Sheshalik trade fair in Kotzebue Sound in the 1850s.

A small hook in the American shoreline appears on the right of two of the trading vessels (at approximately 1 o'clock). This no doubt represents Cape Espenberg, which lies at the northeastern corner of the Seward Peninsula. Traders from Chukotka would have passed Cape Espenberg when visiting the trade fair at Sheshalik. At that point on the pictograph the shoreline divides into two roughly parallel lines (running from 1 o'clock to 3 o'clock), one of which depicts the long chain of barrier islands that enclose lagoons on the north coast of the Seward Peninsula; the other is the shoreline inland of the lagoons. Several settlements are on the barrier island shore. At the western end of the inner line is the short chain of mountains that ends at Cape Prince of Wales.

Near the inner line (from 1 to 2 o'clock) are three groups of human figures. One group, to the right of the line, is hunting a wounded animal with bow and arrow and spear. To the left of the line a second group is engaged in wrestling, dancing, and perhaps rope pulling, suggesting the festivities that often accompanied trading encounters between native groups. To the right of the line a third group apparently engages in warfare or some hostile activity: three men armed with spears and bow and arrow surround a fourth who is armed with a spear. Ernest S. Burch, Jr. (2005, 141, 259–73), has identified seven sites where armed conflicts took place in Alaska between Chukotkans and Seward Peninsula Eskimos. He states that warfare between native groups in the Bering Strait region had ceased by the 1860s or 1870s and speculates that when the region suddenly became well supplied with manufactured goods, the natives concluded that the advantages from trade outweighed any pos-

continued

sible gains from inter-national warfare (234). Waldemar Bogoras also found that trade was responsible for the decline in warfare in Chukotka at about the same time (1904–9, 44, 49–50, 53–54).

The headland of Cape Prince of Wales is on the right (at approximately 3 o'clock). The shoreline continues from there with the cliffs of the York Mountains. Then (at about 4 o'clock) a large embayment is enclosed by a sandspit. The sandspit is likely Point Spencer and the bay is Port Clarence. On shore are habitations, and in the shallow water near shore is perhaps a net for capturing beluga whales (*Delphinapterus leucas*).

In the bay is a two-masted ship with several umiaqs nearby. Two larger umiaqs are approaching from the vicinity of Cape Prince of Wales. One of these umiaqs has a mast up, indicating that it is probably on a long-range traveling expedition. These two umiaqs may represent traders arriving from the Asian side of Bering Strait. On the inland side of the shoreline are two figures in foreign dress, one of which is apparently wearing a broad-brimmed European-type hat. In the 1850s and 1860s Port Clarence was visited by whalers and traders, Russian-American Company supply vessels, and the Royal Navy's fleet searching for Sir John Franklin.

For an earlier analysis of this document see Walter J. Hoffman's description (1897).

40 cents at home." Their dual purpose made sense: if one of those whaler-traders took a whale or two, then the oil and whalebone covered the costs of the voyage and the results of the trading were pure profit. Rum was essential for this trade. A whaleman remarked in 1852 at Cape Dezhnev: "One canoe of Indians came along side to trade. They had skins, walrus tusks etc, etc. but want nothing but rum, once in a while some tobacco but will take nothing else if they can get rum and you can get anything they have got for a drink of rum. Two good drinks will get them drunk and then they are happy." Six years later, at St. Lawrence Island, a whaleman aboard the *South America* found that "the bone from a bowhead was packed alongside of the [chief's] hut which he would not trade, unless he could obtain rum." Near Plover Bay in 1858 another wrote, "Towards evening, a canoe

load came down from the upper bay where the head chief 'Pelekante' lives. They were, most of them, intoxicated and we came very near having serious trouble with them."[21]

In 1858 the bark *Harmony* of Honolulu cruised in the Bering Strait region, and its trading master, B. F. Denham, recorded a glimpse of operations at the beginning of the second decade of the fleets' presence at Bering Strait. At Plover Bay he wrote, "[We] had probably over an hundred natives on the deck. A few brought trade with them but the majority seemed to have come from curiosity and to get what they could by begging and stealing. They are certainly the most unblushing 'out and out' thieves I ever saw. They will pat you on the shoulder with one hand in token of friendship, and with the other relieve your pocket of anything you may have been unguarded enough to leave in it. Nor are they at all backward about asking for what they want. All day I have been pestered for tobacco, beads, knives etc. by rascals that had nothing to trade for. I think if they had the ship and cargo they would be unsatisfied."[22]

The *Harmony* traded at the west end of St. Lawrence Island and along the coast of the Chukchi Peninsula to Arakamchechen Island, where, Denham noted, "A person unacquainted with these people can have no idea of the shrewdness and caution with which they make their bargains. A large stock of patience and good nature is required in order to get along smoothly in trading with them. They invariably at first . . . double the price they expect to get. Our trade thus far has been profitable, but we could make much better bargains if the [brig] 'Oahu' was not so near us. Competition is said to be the life of business, but the rule does not apply to this latitude for here we find it a great hindrance." When the bark passed Mechigmensky Bay, Denham wrote, "Capt. Waterman thinks [this] is a good place for whaling and trading. Water is shoal. Natives live mostly about the mouth of the Bay." At Cape Dezhnev Denham reported, "Our friend 'Tinunte' came off to see us. He reported his coadjutors 'Namedeman' and 'Zonea,' as being ashore drunk on some liquor they recently obtained from some vessel."

The *Harmony* then arrived in Port Clarence and was joined by another Hawaiian whaleship, the German-owned brig *Wailua*. There they learned that they were not the first visitors that summer. "Several canoes and kayaks have been off from shore this afternoon, but the natives seem to have but little trade to dispose of. It is quite likely that some vessel has been here before either the *Wailua* or ourselves, and obtained about everything they had." Two days later the *Harmony* anchored off Cape Prince of Wales. "While at anchor this morning two canoes came alongside. They were some of those we traded with at Port Clarence and were bound to the Diomedes and East Cape [Cape Dezhnev] though they live on Kings Island. They had a few furs but I was unable to buy them as I had no percussion guns and they would take nothing else." There Denham learned that there was an active cross–Bering Strait native trade and that by 1858 the desire for percussion firearms had already replaced the demand for the less effective flintlock muskets.

"The people on the American side seem to be more warlike than their Asiatic brethren," Denham continued. "Guns, powder, shot, and bullets are about the only articles of trade they care for, but whether they use them for fighting or for hunting I had no means of ascertaining. From the little I saw I should not think they were very fierce or treacherous, although they have a pretty hard name among the traders. I had no trouble in dealing with them and as regards begging they bear no comparison to the natives on the other side."[23]

WINTERING VOYAGES

After its return to Bering Strait in the late 1850s, the whaling and trading fleet also experimented with wintering voyages. The heavy weather and increasing cold at the end of the whaling season usually forced the ships to depart Bering Strait in October. But the whalemen knew that they were missing an opportunity to catch whales in the late autumn. The natives had told them that from late October to early December the bowheads, migrating south, were found on the coast of the Chukchi Peninsula, and in the spring they returned north on the same route. Consequently, the idea of wintering a ship on the coast of the Chukchi Peninsula appeared to offer the advantage of hunting whales in the spring and fall and trading for furs during the winter. So, in September 1859, the New Bedford whaleship *Cleone* and the brig *Wailua* of Honolulu entered Plover Bay to begin the first planned commercial wintering voyages in the Bering Strait region.[24]

The whalemen were woefully ill prepared. Lacking the experience and resources of the Royal Navy, the crews of the *Cleone* and *Wailua* suffered appalling hardships. In mid-October the whalemen saw a number of bowheads, but young ice prevented the *Cleone*'s crew from capturing more than two; the *Wailua* took none. One of the *Wailua*'s boat crews was blown away in a late autumn gale, and when a search party found the boat, only three men were alive.

During the winter at Plover Bay the temperature fell to −29°F. Ice formed everywhere inside the hull, even with four stoves burning constantly in the ship. Scurvy broke out and progressively weakened many of the men on both ships. To make matters worse, they ran out of firewood and had to burn their spare spars, but the last straw was when the whales finally began passing north in April 1860.

The weakened men found that the open water was so far from the ships that they lacked the strength to haul their boats to the ice edge. The *Wailua* lost fifteen men to scurvy, and the *Cleone*, two. The death toll would have been higher were it not for the help of the natives. The arrival of several whaleships in mid-June probably saved the rest: the whaleships sent medicine and fresh vegetables across two miles of solid ice to the wintering ships. The crews began cutting a channel to the open water in early July; even so, they did not get out until July 14, and by then most of the whales had already passed them. Together, the two ships took only 200 barrels of oil, and some of that they were forced to trade to the natives for food.[25]

By early 1861, however, Captain Benjamin H. Sisson of the New Bedford bark *Coral* was ready to try again in Plover Bay, but he was far better prepared and his strategy was different. Upon reaching the bay in the autumn he sent his summer's catch to Hawaii aboard another ship: if the *Coral* were to be lost during the winter, at least something would be saved from the voyage. Most important, Sisson carried a full supply of trade goods, which allowed him to buy not only food and fuel from the natives but also whalebone. By the end of the winter he had traded for 9,500 pounds of whalebone, mostly in return for rum and tobacco. The men saw plenty of whales in the autumn, but there is no report of their having taken any. It didn't matter—the *Coral*'s "trade bone" amounted to the yield of four or five whales. The crew enjoyed good health all winter, and the bark broke out of Plover Bay at the end of June.[26]

In 1862 the bark *Zoe* of Honolulu—under the command of Captain John Simmons, who had commanded the *Cleone* on the wintering of 1859–60—went into winter quarters in Plover Bay, while at the same time the *Kohola* of Honolulu settled in at St. Lawrence Bay. To keep their food requirements as small as possible both ships sent most of their Hawaiian deckhands and a few others south to Honolulu aboard the trading brig *Victoria*.

Although the *Zoe* returned to Honolulu in 1863 with 350 barrels of whale oil, 6,000 pounds of baleen, and "good Arctic trade," the winter went badly for the crew of the *Kohola* at St. Lawrence Bay. A tragic misunderstanding with the natives about the accidental drowning of a native leader resulted in Captain Brummerhoff's murder.[27]

Barney Cogan, the *Kohola*'s first mate, reported the events.

Soon after we anchored the sailors went ashore, stole some whisky from one of the native huts, got drunk, and came aboard resolved to take the ship. We put them in irons and under guard. The native of whom they stole the liquor came aboard afterward and remained two or three days. Meanwhile a strong gale sprang up. Some of the sailors told him they had seen the wind carry off his hut and destroy everything. This set the fellow crazy. He insisted upon going ashore. We knew it would be impossible to land him, and tried in vain to dissuade him.

While we were at dinner one day, he jumped overboard and started to swim ashore. I threw a line to him, but he brushed it away and started off. He had almost reached shore, when he encountered young ice, lost his strength and was drowned, his body never being seen again.

After the gale subsided, his father and two brothers came aboard inquiring for him. We told them the truth, but the sailors, who sought revenge on the captain, told them that the captain had stabbed him and thrown the body overboard. They ignored our story and believed theirs. The [natives] then told the captain they would kill him if he came ashore. On account of this affair, cheating in trade, giving poor rum mixed with pepper, etc. a strong hatred naturally sprang up among all the natives against him, and they refused to come aboard and trade.

While I was on one of my expeditions, the captain traded for six deer. The natives took their trade—a keg of rum—in advance, and went ashore to get the deer, which were inland. I returned at this juncture, and the captain asked me to go and get the deer; but when I found what trade he had given them, I suggested that we wait until the liquor and its effects had disappeared. He then said he would go himself, and, in spite of warnings from the rest of us and the friendly natives, he started off.

We followed him with the glass and soon saw there was trouble. We could see the team returning in great haste and a crowd following. Afterward we learned that the friends of the man that had been drowned and a few other natives, incensed at the captain's treatment of them, had followed his team and sought revenge. The captain fired at them with his revolver, then threw it away and fled toward the ship, but soon was overtaken, pierced by an arrow, and then stabbed to death. I endeavored to recover the body, but could not find a trace of it, the natives saying that it had been given to the dogs; but I recovered his clothing.[28]

Barney Cogan also reported that the three murderers, "Ranau, Rakou, and Wapus, blood relations of the drowned man," had "struck down their huts" and left the area immediately. "The [natives] then assured us that now all was settled according to their custom of man for man, and that they would not molest any one of us, which promise they faithfully kept. The chief sent us also the deer the captain had bought, and we received considerable trade from them afterwards." The *Kohola* returned to Honolulu with 600 barrels of whale oil and 10,000 pounds of whalebone. Eight Hawaiian sailors died of scurvy and other diseases during the winter. In the early 1870s merchants sent a few more small vessels on wintering voyages to the region, but the experiment apparently ended there.[29]

TRADING ON THE ALASKAN SHORE

During the late 1850s and throughout the decade of the 1860s, the market for whalebone remained fairly strong, and, along with furs and ivory, it became an important source of profits to the captains and officers of the whaling vessels, who sometimes traded on their own accounts. In general they had previously avoided trading on the "East Shore" because they believed that the Eskimos there were aggressive and treacherous. By then the traders had identified Kotzebue Sound (hence the Sheshalik trade rendezvous) as a lucrative site, and some trade must have gone on there because in autumn 1853, when HMS *Plover* was wintering at Point Barrow, her captain, Rochfort Maguire, learned that those Point Barrow traders who had visited the rendezvous at Niġliq in the Colville River delta had been introduced to "wine" and sulfur matches, probably via native traders who had visited the Sheshalik fair the summer before.[30]

In 1858 B. F. Denham, the trading master of the whaleship *Harmony*, wrote: "Memorandum. Kotzebue Sound. Capt. Waterman says the shores of this sound are thickly inhabited. That is[,] he has heard so, but never was there himself. The natives are more fierce than on the Asiatic Side. Capt. Corsen of the [brig] 'Victoria' [of Honolulu] told him he would go there (last season) if he could depend upon his crew, but as they were mostly Kanakas [Hawaiians] he did not like to trust them—Thinks it is a first rate place for trading."[31] The *Harmony*'s crew of thirty-six included twenty-five Hawaiians. Among the whaling and trading fleets Hawaiian sailors had a reputation for passivity and lack of initiative.

Port Clarence was another productive trading site. Although the *Harmony* did not enter Kotzebue Sound, she did visit Port Clarence, where Denham noted, "At this place the Victoria got a large quantity of walrus ivory." In the summer of 1859 at least six whaleships visited Port Clarence to trade for furs and ivory in return for "guns, rum, powder, knives," as one trader put it.

It was not until the 1860s that the whalemen began deliberately to expand their trading activities north of Bering Strait along the Alaskan shore, and in part this took place because they were finding bowheads there. They learned, however, that from Point Hope northward the quality of the trade was generally low: probably the Eskimos were doing most of their trading at the Sheshalik fair in Kotzebue Sound. When the *George and Susan* touched at Icy Cape in 1859—one of the first whaleships to attempt to trade there—the men found that "the inhabitants had no furs and but little of anything except canoes and dogs."[32]

By the mid-1860s whaleships and whaler-traders began to push deep into the Chukchi Sea, regularly cruising not only along the Alaskan coast as far as Point Barrow but also along the northwest coast of the Chukchi Peninsula. For example, in June 1866 Captain Eduard Dallman aboard the German-owned Hawaiian brig *W. C. Talbot* cruised in the Bering Strait region, particularly St. Lawrence Island and Norton Sound, where he visited Mikhailovsky Redoubt. Then from July to September he crisscrossed the Chukchi Sea, cruising along the Chukchi Peninsula before heading north with the retreating pack ice. On that voyage he became the first European to see Wrangel Island, coasting on its southeastern corner before heading east along the ice margin as far as Point Franklin in Alaska, and then visiting Kotzebue Sound in September.[33]

The whalers and traders were also aware that on the Alaskan coast north of Bering Strait some groups could be very dangerous. In 1859, aboard the whaleship *Julian*, Samuel P. Winegar wrote: "Most of [the natives near Bering Strait] are friendly and hospitable. Farther north, off Point Barrow and Icy Cape they are very treacherous. [You] have to be on your guard." But the Point Hope Eskimos were considered to be especially aggressive. On July 16, 1868, for example, the whaleship *Cornelius Howland* of New Bedford, Massachusetts, touched at Point Hope and had a difficult encounter: "The natives come on board of us, and they was very noisy. They had some few walrus tusks and a good lot of whalebone and some skins for trade," wrote Captain B. F. Hohman. "There is a great many people on this point. The natives filled our deck full, so there was danger of taking our ship, and they was very saucy and they stole several things, breaking open carpenter's chest and stole 2 saws, a square, and stole all they could get hold of. At 2 PM. the natives was so saucy and was taking everything they could lay their hands on and was in a fair way to take the ship. We called all hands on deck and drove the natives forward and hauled out the big gun and pointed it at them. They hallowed and went over the sides fast. There was over a hundred natives on board and plenty more on the beach coming off."[34]

The Point Hope Eskimos, according the whaler John W. Kelly, "have often attacked parties of whalemen who have been on shore after casks of water or driftwood for fuel." "Four instances are mentioned: once when the natives were driven off with clubs; another time when they surrounded a boat's crew, pricked the men's throats with knives, stole their tobacco, and cut buttons from their clothes; again, when they pursued the departing boats, caught hold of their painters, and tried to pull the boats ashore, which was frustrated by cutting the painter. Upon the last occasion, when they attacked a boat in force, the officer in charge stood them off with a whaleman's cutting spade, inflicting many wounds, but it is not known whether any were killed."[35]

The lure of trade, nevertheless, seems eventually to have overcome some of the Point Hopers' aggressiveness. Captain E. F. Nye wrote to the *New Bedford Standard* in 1879 that Captain Barney Cogan thought that the Eskimos there were "getting quite civilized; a few years ago they were quite wild and very rude and had to be watched, now they behave very well indeed; they know how to trade and know the value of whalebone and skins."[36]

OTHER SOURCES OF MANUFACTURED GOODS

At the same time a modest amount of non-Russian goods was also reaching the Bering Strait region from other sources. From 1865 to 1867 the Western Union Telegraph Expedition attempted to link Europe to America via a telegraph line that was planned to run through northeastern Siberia, across Bering Strait, and across Alaska. The project was abandoned when the Atlantic Cable was successful. In the Bering Strait region the expedition maintained camps at Plover Bay, Port Clarence, and Mikhailovsky. The men bought meat and fish from the natives, and when they shut down operations, they abandoned the wire, insulators, poles, and a variety of manufactured goods. Among other things, the Eskimos made bracelets from the wire.[37]

Shipwrecks also contributed some foreign goods to the natives. From 1849 to 1867 approximately twenty-five vessels were lost in the northern Bering Sea and Chukchi Sea. Furthermore the Confederate States cruiser CSS *Shenandoah* burned twenty whaleships and caused the loss of another in 1865. The natives on both sides of Bering Strait collected flotsam from these wrecks.[38]

DECLINE OF WARFARE

At about this time firearms and metal traps also began to reach the coastal Eskimos north of Bering Strait. Although the Russian-American Company did not trade firearms to the northern natives, by the 1850s, as we have seen, guns had reached Point Barrow via the Mackenzie River, and John Murdoch, who lived there from 1881 to 1883, noted a few Russian muskets as well. Dr. John Driggs, who arrived at Point Hope as its first missionary in 1890, believed that the Point Hope Eskimos acquired firearms about 1860. By the 1870s metal traps were also in use throughout the region.[39]

One result of these new trading opportunities with the ships on the northwest coast of Alaska was an increase in the east-west flow of trade between the North Alaskan Eskimos and the Mackenzie Eskimos. The increased availability of trade goods on the Alaskan shores of the Chukchi Sea was felt as far away as Fort McPherson, the Hudson's Bay Company's post on the Peel River. William L. Hardisty reported that the fur returns there from the Eskimos were less than he had expected for 1869 because they were saving their furs to trade at the rendezvous at Barter Island. "Unfortunately," Hardisty wrote, the Mackenzie Eskimos "opened up a trade with the Americans thro' the medium of other parties of Esquimaux living on the coast west of the Mackenzie," and in 1865 the Roman Catholic (Oblate) missionary Émile Petitot noticed that one Mackenzie delta Eskimo had a knife that came from an American whaleship that probably had traded it in northwestern Alaska. Five years later, the Anglican missionary William C. Bompas, describing trade in the Mackenzie delta, wrote, "American vessels already trade with the western Esquimaux. In fact I see here tobacco, knives, beads, and kettles obtained from the Americans which the Esquimaux have traded along the coast from the more western natives. Two men of this band [Mackenzie delta Eskimos] have started along the coast to the west this present winter with a parcel of furs intending to return next winter bringing supplies from the same source." Charles Brower, a whaleman at Point Barrow, reported that in the 1880s native traders regularly traveled between the Mackenzie delta and Point Barrow.[40]

A result of this influx of foreign goods and the increasing foreign trade was that warfare between national groups was in decline by the 1860s and ceased entirely in the 1870s. Edward William Nelson, who was stationed at St. Michael from 1877 to 1881, noticed the change.

> In ancient times, . . . intertribal communication along the coast was irregular and uncertain, owing to the hostile attitude of the people toward one another. Now the old barriers have been broken down, and active barter between the different communities has become a marked feature of their life. This is particularly the case among the people living between the Kuskokwim and Kotzebue sound. The numerous fur trading stations which have been established among them, and the visits of trading vessels and whaling ships to the coast of Bering strait, have served to quicken and encourage among them the spirit of trade. In summer the people of Bering strait make visits to the head of Kotzebue sound and to the mouth of the Yukon, carrying the skins of tame reindeer purchased from the people of the Asiatic coast, for which they receive in barter skins of various fur-bearing animals that are used in turn for trading with vessels in Bering strait or with their Asiatic neighbors.[41]

Ernest S. Burch, Jr., speculates that the increased volume of foreign trade was an important factor in this change. He writes:

> It seems to me, . . . that the Iñupiaq obsession with trade, which they considered so important that they could meet peacefully with inveterate enemies at least once a year at trade fairs, is one part of the answer. The other part is the

Figure 12.4. Mackenzie Eskimo leader, Noulloumallok-Innonarana, ca. 1865
(Petitot 1887, 78–79).

vastly increased opportunity for commerce opened up around the mid-century by the sudden proximity of Westerners with goods to trade. Western goods acquired previously via the Chukchi had to come a vast distance overland. They were probably so expensive that it was not worth sacrificing other important activities to acquire the means, that is, the furs, to buy them. However, goods brought by ship to Mikhailovskii Redoubt (Saint Michael) and Bering Strait . . . must have been cheap by comparison. From then on, substantial benefits could be achieved through the international trade in furs. Warfare was an obvious impediment to this trade and, after a few unsuccessful confrontations between groups trying to control it, simply was not worth pursuing anymore.[42]

The last recorded bloodshed between Mackenzie Eskimos and Gwich'in occurred in 1856, and by 1868 the flow of goods and people along the north Alaskan coast and throughout northwestern Alaska had increased to such a degree that at Fort McPherson Father Petitot noted that Eskimos from the Colville River were visiting the fort in company with Mackenzie Eskimos, and he reported that among the visitors was a mixed-race Eskimo with red hair, freckles, and a full beard, who, Petitot assumed, was of Russian parentage from somewhere near Mikhailovsky Redoubt. On the Chukchi Peninsula the ethnographer Waldemar Bogoras wrote: "'These are peaceful times,' said one of the wandering Chukchee traders to me at Indian Point. 'Wars have ceased, everybody thinks only of gain, and all tribes and nations intermingle.'"[43]

THE RUSSIAN RESPONSE

The Russian-American Company understandably viewed the activities of the whalers and traders with great concern, but at the same time it was distracted by a host of other problems. Unfortunately for the company, the decade of the 1850s was a time of difficulties, especially for its northern operations. After the Koyukon attack on Nulato in 1851, although relations with the natives improved somewhat, the company suspended its upriver trading trips, and the manager at Mikhailovsky failed to resume the trade. In summer 1854 the company made its last attempt at intercepting the flow of furs at Kotzebue Sound. After resupplying Mikhailovsky and taking aboard eighty-two bales of beaver pelts, eleven sacks of fox, and four boxes of beaver castors, in addition to the returns from Kolmakov Redoubt (twenty-four bales of beaver, four casks of fox, and one box of beaver castors), the bark *Kadiak* sailed to Kotzebue Sound. It anchored near Chamisso Island and disembarked a small expedition of eleven persons (including an interpreter, one Tlingit, and four Aleuts) in a whaleboat and two baidarkas. The exploratory party went to scout the Buckland River for a site to establish a redoubt or an outpost. The party returned only two days later, and the company made no further effort to operate in Kotzebue Sound.

The Crimean War further complicated the company's operations. Even though the Russian-American Company and the Hudson's Bay Company had entered into a private treaty of neutrality, an Anglo-French expeditionary force assaulted Petropavlovsk in 1854 and again in 1855. The Russian defenders drove off the allied force in the attack of 1854, but the British captured the company's new bark *Sitkha* and returned her to England under the command of Rochfort Maguire. In 1855 the Russian-American Company did not send its own ship to resupply its northern posts because of fear that it might be captured as a war prize; instead the company chartered the American bark *Cyane* of San Francisco to do the work.

"While the colonies escaped serious privation during the war years," the ethno-historian Katherine Arndt has written, "the restrictions on shipping decidedly crimped [Chief Manager] Voevodskii's plans for strengthening the company's competitive position in the north. Not only did the Main Office [in St. Petersburg] fail to ship the goods he had specially ordered from Siberia, but Circassian tobacco, an item vital to the northern trade and available only from Russia, was in critically short supply. Uncertain as to when more might be available, Voevodskii reserved the last of the preferred tobacco for barter on the Alaskan mainland; for all other purposes, post managers would have to issue the Virginian variety, locally considered to be inferior. Other staples of the northern trade were more readily available in [Novo-Arkhangelsk] but, for lack of space aboard the single vessel sent to supply all the western districts, could not be shipped to Mikhailovskii in their usual quantity in 1855. . . .

"Also curtailed were any projects which would require an increase in personnel for their implementation," Arndt continued. "With the colonies already chronically short of qualified personnel, and no new company employees being sent from Russia, Voevodskii could only advise his post managers to make do with the men they had. At the same time, he cancelled all plans to establish a new post on Kotzebue Sound . . . a post at that location would be difficult to provision even in the best of times. Now, however, he simply could not spare enough men to ensure the safety of such a post in the likely event of an attack by jealous local native competitors."[44]

In 1856 Voevodsky, who did not know whether the Crimean War had ended, hence was proceeding with caution, wrote about the plan to establish an outpost in Kotzebue Sound: "The main obstacles . . . are the inconvenient location and difficult provisioning, and also the fact that this [outpost] must compete in respect to trade with the savages living in the neighborhood who [act as middle-men] with distant savages and then transfer the bartered furs to the Chukchi with profit for themselves and, although it is not yet known for certain, judging from the stories of the savages themselves and the firearms and other things they have, they even conduct trade with foreigners. Therefore in settlement there, especially at first, a rather significant garrison will be required, and, as the Main Office will please see from my dispatch of the same date . . . our means in workers will be in-sufficient even for undertakings already begun." Had the company been able to maintain a post near the Buckland River, it might not only have cut deeply into the native trade into the interior of Alaska but also into the trade at the Sheshalik rendezvous and across Bering Strait.[45]

CAPTAIN VERMAN'S REPORT

In the midst of this period of difficulties for the company and swift change in the Bering Strait region, Captain Fyodor Karlovich Verman, an officer in the Russian-American Company's fleet, reported on the inroads that the whaling and trading fleets were making on the company's effort to secure the cross–Bering Strait trade: "One must attribute the lack of development of our trade [at Bering Strait] to the following reasons: (1) the way of life of the local inhabitants, fixed by climatic and local circumstances; (2) their trade relations with the Chukchi; and (3) the impossibility of the Company supplying them with what they need. Recently, especially since the end of the [18]40s, the following circumstances have been added: (1) the natives' dealings with foreign whaling vessels and (2) the furnishing of our natives with firearms and supplies by those vessels and by our English neighbors. . . .

"In former times," Verman continued, "when all the furs of the American coast that had been [carried across Bering Strait and] bartered by the seden-tary Chukchi, passed from them through the hands of the nomadic or reindeer Chukchi into the hands of the Siberian merchants [at the Ostrovnoe fair on the Maly Aniui River], the Chukchi brought our natives certain Russian goods and Circassian tobacco, but since the times when these furs have for the most part been yielded by them to foreign vessels, very few of those goods appear among them, and in their place firearms and their appurtenances are bought. Following that, of the items the natives need, they take from the Company only tobacco, iron kettles, knives, axes, fire steels, plain sewing needles and faceted needles for sewing baidarkas and waterproof clothing, and some other items classed as luxu-ries."

Echoing Tebenkov's and Wrangell's advice of decades before, Verman felt that it was essential that the company should supply the Alaskan natives with the

Chukchi products they desired, thus interrupting the native trade across Bering Strait. He advocated setting up a station on the Chukchi Peninsula in Mechigmensky Bay to buy reindeer and whale products from the natives. "It is necessary to have a vessel which, though small, is sufficiently supplied with all trade goods and which from early spring until fall would visit King Island, the Diomedes, Port Clarence and Kotzebue Sound, and then during the summer the Company could purchase both furs and Chukchi products." This was, of course, exactly what the trading fleet from Hawaii and San Francisco was already doing.

Recognizing that the foreign vessels were also trading firearms, Verman urged the company to change its policy against selling guns to the northern natives.

> The sale of firearms and their appurtenances would advance our trade most of all, since this item is especially loved by the natives, and supplying it would be very profitable for the Company because all the guns seen by me on our mainland and on the Asian coast are of poor quality and low price: they are for the most part American in the manner of soldiers' guns and cheap English guns of the carbine type but without rifling. Also encountered are double-barreled guns and pistols, but all of not very good workmanship.
>
> According to the Malegmiut, from foreign vessels they receive a rifle or a fowling piece in exchange for a silver fox. They themselves barter these guns to other savages for 18 to 20 beaver skins. For a box of 100 cartridges or for a 1-funt [approximately one pound] tin of powder or for 40 bullets they take a good otter or a good cross fox or three or even four beaver skins. From these prices it is seen that such trade has a good profit. Our neighbors the English, not restraining themselves in type of trade, as is demonstrated by the appearance of firearms from the upper reaches of the Kvikhpak [Yukon] River, enjoy these profits.

Verman added that the Russian-American Company was not alone in suffering from the intrusion of the whalers and traders: their influence reached as far west as the Kolyma River.

> If the interference of foreign vessels in our trade is felt in this manner, then the trade of the Siberian merchants with the Chukchi is suffering still more from it, and in time all the harmful effects of these dealings will prove still more apparent on the inhabitants of the American coast, and especially of the Asian coast, themselves, who are being accustomed to strong drink, which constitutes their main trade good. On the American coast the foreign vessels visit for a short time primarily Kav'iaiak Bay [Port Clarence], Cape Nykhta [Cape Prince of Wales], and Kotzebue Sound, sometimes Golovnin Bay, and now and then appear at the shores of Nukivok [Nunivak] Island. On this island there are good

foxes and near its shores there are walrus. Such visits to our shores are early in the spring, immediately after the ice breaks up, and after that they set sail for the Arctic Ocean, where they stop in Kotzebue Sound.

The Asian coast is visited by them, and especially by whalers, much more often, since whales primarily hold to this coast, which is richer in good bays and harbors, and besides they are completely sure that here no one will bother them. These shores are much better known to them than to us because they visit them annually and winter in St. Lawrence Bay and in one large bay in the Gulf of Anadyr. . . . This bay is called Port Providence ["Plover Bay"].

Verman gained much of his knowledge of the Bering Strait trade from Captain Heinrich Hackfeld. Hackfeld, a native of Bremen, was one of several German merchants who operated out of Hawaii in the nineteenth century. Hackfeld settled in Honolulu in 1849 and soon founded H. Hackfeld and Company, a general trading company that, among other activities—which included whaling and trading in the North—served as the agent for the Russian-American Company. Verman understood that the whalers were heavily involved in trading with the natives of the Bering Strait region and that much of the traffic came via the Hawaiian Islands. He wrote: "Every whaling vessel engages in trade, too, when the opportunity arises, and other vessels, equipped strictly for trade, also engage in whaling to the degree possible. These vessels are primarily outfitted from San Francisco and Honolulu (Sandwich Islands). During my sojourn in this latter place in 1861, eight different vessels from that port were engaged in trade in the Bering Sea and Arctic Ocean according to information I received from our Company's agent Mr. Hackfeld and others. The extent of this trade can be determined by the following indications. In 1860 the schooner *Sea Witch* exported from our North 9,000 dollars' worth of furs which were acquired by Mr. Hackfeld wholesale."

But Hackfeld was not the only merchant with his eyes on Bering Strait, and Verman learned that the competition was working in the natives' favor by raising the price of furs.

Subsequently I chanced to become acquainted there with a certain skipper [Corsen], who was captain aboard the first vessel outfitted for trade by the house of Hofschleger, in 1849, and he told me that the vessel was bought for 3,000 dollars and equipped with goods worth 2,000 dollars. The first experiment proved successful and from that time on he engaged in this trade aboard Hofschleger's vessels on a nearly annual basis. After all expenses, he managed to accumulate capital of 12,000 dollars for himself in the course of eight years. Despite the fact that furs in the North, according to him have so risen in price that now for a gun costing 6 Hamburg thallers only 20 sables are received, whereas before it was 80 to 120 sables, he set out with me to Bremen with the intention of building a small screw vessel and continuing to engage in this trade independently. The trade is more profitable for those who manage to be among the first at the savages' gathering places after the ice opens, which one can do most easily in a screw vessel.

Forecasting by almost two decades the call for government patrols in the Bering Strait region, Verman advocated sending a naval cruiser for the "protection of our coasts and islands." "If cruisers will make these vessels leave our shores and if we ourselves will supply the natives with firearms, then one may hope that our trade will noticeably strengthen."

Verman also understood that the threat to the Russian-American Company's trade did not end with the foreign fleets; it included the Hudson's Bay Company: "Besides, since the removal of foreign vessels from our shores will not stop the delivery of firearms to the natives from the English possessions, we should ourselves supply them with this weapon in order to prevent the transfer of our furs into the hands of the English."[46]

THE TWILIGHT OF RUSSIAN AMERICA

Despite Captain Verman's sound advice, the future of Russian America was uncertain. As early as 1850 a number of the tsar's advisors had questioned whether Russian America could "survive sustained Yankee curiosity," wrote Howard I. Kushner. And in 1853, N. N. Muravyov-Amursky, the governor general of Eastern Siberia, recognizing the vigor of the American expansion across the continent, wrote to the tsar, "The North American States inevitably will spread over all North America, and *we cannot avoid the expectation that sooner or later we must cede our North American possessions to them.*"[47]

Later, after the Opium War with Great Britain (1839–42) had exposed China's weakness, Russia turned her attention to the fertile lands of the Amur drainage. Then, as John J. Stephan has noted, the Crimean War "taught Russia the supreme importance of possessing the Amur basin both for communications to Kamchatka and for its strategic value in the defense of Eastern Siberia." As we have seen in chapter 4, Russia had ceded these lands to China in the Treaty of Nerchinsk in 1689 but recovered them in 1860 with the Treaty of Beijing. The Treaty of Beijing also allowed Russian merchants to trade directly in Beijing, thus bypassing Kiakhta and Mai-mai-ch'eng and the arduous overland supply route from Okhotsk. Because "its maritime province [now] stretched to the borders of Korea and the Sea of Japan," wrote Ronald J. Jensen, "Russia needed no other colony on the Pacific."[48]

But the Crimean War had also revealed the vulnerability of Russia's American colony. In 1857 Grand Duke Constantine, Tsar Alexander II's brother, advised him that it would be best to sell the colony to the United States before the Americans seized it themselves. Recognizing that the company's twenty-year charter would expire on January 1, 1862, the government undertook a comprehensive analysis of the condition of Russian America and of the Russian-American Company. Accordingly, the grand duke arranged for Pavel Nikolaevich Golovin to conduct an independent review of the state of the colony and its value to the Crown. In Russian America the company's senior staffers—who strongly supported the continuing existence of the colony—were aware of the grand duke's antipathy toward the company and regarded Golovin merely as a spy, who "made mischief in diverse ways."[49]

In any case, on his return to Russia in October 1861 Golovin submitted his assessment of the state of affairs in Russian America. Among other things, Golovin noted that although the company's fur returns were declining overall, the northern trade was worse. For example, from 1842 to 1848 the company's annual trading voyages to Bering Strait—which took place after the ship had resupplied Mikhailovsky—had collected a modest total of 45 beaver pelts, 3 river otters, 187 red foxes and their color variants, 1,167 arctic foxes, 27 martens or sables, and more than 35,000 pounds of walrus ivory. But worse, the competition from the foreign whalers and traders had been so intense that from 1849 to 1860 the company's ships had collected *in total* only 3 beaver pelts, 40 red foxes and its color variants, 16 arctic foxes, and a small amount of walrus ivory. "The Company has tried to promote some sort of trade with the Chukchi and the [Diomede, King, and Sledge] islanders, but like the others they demand vodka, firearms and gunpowder."

Because of the activities of the foreign trading fleet, Golovin wrote, "even the Lower Kolyma merchants cannot trade profitably with the Chukchi, so they sell them Russian goods and vodka just as they did formerly, and they also buy foreign goods from them." Thus the foreign fleet's trading activities were reversing the traditional direction of the flow of trade goods in Chukotka, changing it from west-to-east to east-to-west.

Confirming Verman's assessment, Golovin reported that American and Hawaiian trading vessels—among them he identified the *Kohola, Nero, Victoria,* and *Zoe*—"trade in the north mainly with such items as rum, low-grade cognac, tobacco, gunpowder and firearms," in exchange for furs, whalebone, and walrus ivory. Most importantly, he added, "Any time American newspapers mention

Figure 12.5. Mikhailovsky Redoubt, ca. 1867 (Dall 1870, 11).

whalers they state that such and such a ship, engaged in whaling in the north, had an unsatisfactory catch but nevertheless found business *very good.*" Golovin noted that some of these foreign vessels had also engaged in poaching fur seals in the Pribilof and Aleutian islands.

Like Verman, Golovin advocated sending naval vessels to patrol those waters, adding, "It would seem useful to completely revoke from the charter the prohibition against the Company selling alcoholic beverages, weapons and gunpowder to the natives. . . . The harm has already been done. All the savages have firearms, carbines, pistols, revolvers, powder, shot and vodka. There is no possibility of completely halting this illicit trade. Cruisers will be able to prevent its growth and protect the inhabitants from the lawlessness of foreigners, but the contraband trade will continue to some degree in spite of this." Golovin's assessment of the state of affairs in Russian America no doubt found sympathetic ears in St. Petersburg. When the company's charter expired in 1862 it was "extended only provisionally" by the Crown, which was increasingly unenthusiastic about the cost of maintaining the colony.[50]

The explorer-scientist William Healey Dall, like Golovin, was an independent witness to the Russian-American Company's operations. A participant in the Western Union Telegraph Expedition, Dall described Mikhailovsky Redoubt in 1866, giving a glimpse of a company post during the last years of Russian America.

The fort is composed of log buildings with plank roofs, placed in the form of a square, and with the intervals filled by a palisade about ten feet high, sur-mounted by a *chevaux-de-frise* of pointed stakes. This is also continued round the eaves of the buildings. There are two outlying bastions, pierced for cannon and musketry, and containing a number of pieces of artillery of very small cali-ber and mostly very old-fashioned and rusty, except two fine brass howitzers of more modern manufacture. The principal buildings are the commander's house, consisting of two private rooms, an armory and a counting-room, or *contórum*, a couple of buildings used as storehouses, a bath house, and separate houses for the married and unmarried workmen. There is a flag-staff leaning apologetically as if consciously out of place, and a gallery for the watchman, who is on duty day and night, with relicfs, and who tolls a bell on the hour stroke to notify the inmates that he is not asleep. One of the bastions is without cannon, and is used as a guard-house for refractory subjects.

Outside of the stockade are several other buildings, a small storehouse used for furs, a large shed where boats are drawn up in winter, a blacksmith's shop, and a church. The latter is octagonal in shape, with a small dome, surmounted by a cross, and a beam bearing a bell at the side of a small porch which covers the doorway. Other small buildings are scattered about; a sun-dial is to be found not far from the church, and a noticeable feature in the fall is the stacks of bleached driftwood, which, from a distance, look not unlike tents or bas-tions.[51]

Nor was Dall impressed by the quality of the company's personnel at Mikhai-lovsky.

The inmates of the fort—with the exception of Sérgei Stepánoff Rúsanoff, an old soldier, who commands not only this, but all the trading posts in the Dis-trict of St. Michael, under the title of Uprovalísha—may be divided into three classes: convicts, creoles, and natives.

The workmen of the Russian American Company were, almost without ex-ception, convicts, mostly from Siberia. . . . They were men convicted of such crimes as theft, incorrigible drunkenness, burglary, and even manslaughter. These men, after a continued residence in the country, naturally took to them-selves wives, after the fashion of the country, since Russian subjects in the Com-pany's employ were prohibited from legal marriage with native women. . . .

There are a few Yakúts in the service of the Company, and these, with some native workmen, who are generally of the tribe which inhabits the immediate vicinity of the post, compose the garrison.

The regular workman gets about fifty pounds of flour, a pound of tea, and three pounds of sugar a month; his pay is about twenty cents a day. Some of the older men get thirty cents and a corresponding addition to the ration of flour. They work with little energy and spirit as a general thing, but can accomplish a great deal if roused by necessity. Small offenses are punished by confinement in the guard-house, or *boofka*, and greater ones by a thrashing administered by the commander in person; those who commit considerable crimes are forced to run the gauntlet, receive one or two hundred blows with a stick, or in extreme cases are sent for trial to Sitka, or, in case of murder, to St. Petersburg.

Frederick Whymper, Dall's associate, had a similar view on the quality of the company's personnel. "They were not a satisfactory body of men," he wrote. "The inhabitants of the fort—all servants of the company—were a very mixed crowd, including pure Russians and Finlanders, Yakutz, from Eastern Siberia, Aleuts, from the islands, and creoles from all parts. . . . In fact, it is said that some of them had been criminals, who had been convicted in St. Petersburgh, and offered the alternative of going to prison, or in the service of the Russian American Company! We found them—as did Zagoskin many years before—much given to laziness and drunkenness. Fortunately, their opportunity for the latter was limited, usually, to one bout per annum, on the arrival of the Russian Ship from Sitka [Novo-Arkhangelsk] with their supplies; whilst the 'Provalishik,' Mr. Stephanoff, the commander of the fort, who had charge of the whole district, stood no nonsense with them. . . . His arguments were of a forcible character: I believe the knout formed no part of his establishment, but he used his fists with great effect!"[52]

Dall also assessed the regional manager, Stepánoff. "The present Uprovalísha, Stepánoff, has been in office about four years. He is a middle-aged man of great energy and iron will, with the Russian fondness for strong liquor and with ungovernable passions in certain directions. He has a soldier's contempt for making money by small ways, a certain code of honor of his own, is generous in his own way, and seldom does a mean thing when he is sober, but nevertheless is a good deal of a brute. He will gamble and drink in the most democratic way with his workmen, and bears no malice for a black eye when received in a drunken brawl; but woe to the unfortunate who infringes discipline while he is sober, for he shall certainly receive his reward; and Stepánoff often says of his men, when speaking to an American, 'You can expect nothing good of this rabble: they left Russia because they were not wanted there.'"

Dall also evaluated Stepánoff's subordinates: "The commanders, or *bidárshiks*, of the smaller posts in the District of St. Michael are appointed by Stepánoff, who has absolute authority over them, and does not fail to let them understand it, making them row his boat, when the annual supply-ship is in port. . . . But

Stepánoff trembles before the captain of the ship or an old officer of the Company, much in the same way that his workmen cringe before him. This sort of subservancy, the fruit of a despotic government, is characteristic of the lower classes of Russians; and to such an extent is it ingrained in their characters that it seems impossible for them to comprehend any motives of honor or truthfulness as being superior to self-interest."[53]

Dall went on to explain his understanding of how trade was conducted at Mikhailovsky.

The prices paid by the Russian American Company for furs in the District of St. Michael were substantially as follows. The trade was carried on by barter entirely. To the original cost of the goods in Hamburg or St. Petersburg, from forty-two to seventy-five percent was added for expenses. A marten was worth one paper ruble, or twenty cents. A mink was valued at ten cents; foxes, from thirty cents to five dollars; stone-foxes [arctic foxes], ten cents; lynx, at sixty cents; beaver at forty cents; the castoreum, at five cents a pair; otter, from forty to eighty cents; black bear, at sixty cents; and muskrats or walrus-tusks at one cent each.

But in many respects the natives did not receive even the whole value of this insignificant tariff. The goods were delivered at their appraised value to the bidárshik of a trading post. All expenses of winter journeys, of native servants in the fort, and, in fact, everything except the cost of constructing the buildings and the wages of the Russian workmen, must come out of the trading goods. Hence, while the Company's price of a pound of Circassian tobacco was thirty cents, and the bidárshik was expected to balance his account with the Uprovalísha of his district by returning, say, three mink for the tobacco; yet the native received nothing like a pound for three mink skins. The tobacco comes done up in small bundles called *papóoshki*. There may be from two to six small of these in a pound; yet for each one, large or small, the native must give a marten skin or two mink skins. Again, the Company's price for lead was twenty cents a pound. Their bullets were about thirty-six to the pound. Yet the native only received ten balls for his marten, or five for a mink skin.

Like Captain Verman, it was no surprise to Dall that the competition from the whalers and traders and from the Hudson's Bay Company was cutting deeply into the Russian-American Company's fur returns.

In the season of 1867–68, there were collected in the District of St. Michael, by Stepánoff, sixteen thousand martens. . . . During the same time, not less than fourteen thousand found their way to the traders at Kotzebue Sound and Grantley Harbor [Port Clarence], and ten thousand to Fort Yukon. This makes a total of forty thousand, which may be averaged to be worth at least two dollars and a half each. In their purchase, not over twenty thousand dollars were expended, in every way. The profits of such a business are evident.

Since 1850, traders from the Sandwich Islands, have visited Kotzebue Sound and Grantley Harbor every spring. These traders are usually small vessels, brigs or schooners. They load at Honolulu with ammunition, double-barrelled Belgian fowling pieces, hardware, and rum or alcohol. They follow up the melting ice, and usually reach Bering Strait in the latter part of June. Their tariff of prices amounts to about fifty cents apiece for marten, in goods. They are usually provided with whaling implements, and manned by Kanakas [Hawaiians]. A single whale will pay the expenses of the voyage, and leave the profits of the trade clear. The large quantities of liquor which are obtained in this manner by the natives have a very demoralizing effect.[54]

Dall's associate, Frederick Whymper, noted that the whalers who visited Port Clarence paid much higher prices for the furs than did the Russian-American Company—the whalers were acquiring furs, via native middlemen, from "high up the Yukon"—and that Chukchi reindeer skins were found there as well, having been traded in the opposite direction.[55]

The American Civil War (1861–65) delayed discussions about the sale of Russian America, but by 1866 the Russian-American Company was in steep decline: the value of its shares stood at only 15 percent of their value a decade earlier, and the company, facing bankruptcy and with debts amounting to more than one million rubles, sought relief from the Crown. Appraising the situation, the minister of finance, Mikhail Reutern, concluded: "After seventy years of existence the company has not achieved either any Russification of the [native] male population or any lasting entrenchment of the Russian element. . . . The company does not even bring material benefits to its shareholders."[56]

Tsar Alexander and his senior advisors, worried about the potential for clashes with the large American whaling and trading fleet and about the expense of maintaining control of the northeasternmost waters of the Pacific, agreed to pursue the sale "not because of the impact of the proceeds on Russia's depleted finances or of the straightened circumstances of the Russian-American Company but primarily because of a desire to strengthen relations with the burgeoning United States and the conviction that Russia's Pacific future lay not on the eastern but on the western side of the ocean in the contiguous territory of the more promising Amur valley."[57]

The 126 years of Russian America were drawing to a close as the tsar's government confronted the decision to sell the colony, a decision that would elementally alter both Russia and the United States. Howard I. Kushner put it this way: "The Russian government concluded that the retention of Russian-America was an overextension of the Russian empire and that the colony's value was not sufficient when measured against the cost of defending it against continued American encroachments."[58]

Shortly after the sale of Russian America, Thomas W. Knox, an American journalist traveling in eastern Siberia, thought the sale made sense and was in Russia's best interest: "The sale of his American property was an excellent transaction on the part of the Emperor. The country brought no revenue worth the name, and it threatened to be an expensive ornament in coming years. It required a sea voyage to reach it, and was upon a continent which Russia does not aspire to control. It had no strategic importance in Muscovite policy, and was better out of the empire than in it."[59]

13

Chaos and Transformation in the Latter Third of the Nineteenth Century

THE ALASKA PURCHASE

News of the sale of Russian America reached Prince Dmitry Petrovich Maksutov, the chief manager of the colony, in Novo-Arkhangelsk in late spring 1867. Maksutov learned that on March 30 in Washington, DC, representatives of Russia and the United States had signed a treaty stipulating that Russia would sell its American colony to the United States for $7,200,000. Russia ratified the treaty on May 14, the United States two weeks later. "News of the sale took [Maksutov] by surprise," wrote Molly Lee. "When the word reached him . . . Maksutov found himself in the unenviable position of not only breaking the news to Alaskans but also overseeing the transfer itself." His orders were to conclude the company's business and to wait for the delegates of the United States and Russia to arrive for the formal transfer of the colony.[1]

On October 18, USS *Ossipee* arrived at Novo-Arkhangelsk with commissioners from both nations aboard. The transfer took place the same day: Russian America became the Territory of Alaska; Novo-Arkhangelsk became Sitka; and General Jefferson Columbus Davis of the United States Army became the commander of the Department of Alaska. But although the United States had purchased the land and the government property from the Crown, the Russian-American Company's assets—which included warehouses; trading posts; ships; trade goods; furs, including 80,000 fur seal skins; and 30,000 gallons of liquor— were to be sold on behalf of the shareholders. "The hastily-written treaty was vague, however, regarding the distinction between government and private property, a fact which was to lead to misunderstanding later," wrote the historian Richard Pierce. "Thrust into a new and unwelcome role," Prince Maksutov remained in Alaska for a year while he liquidated the company's assets. Rumors about the possible sale of Russian America had been circulating since the mid-1850s, and a number of entrepreneurs arrived in Sitka scrambling for bargains. For $350,000 Hutchinson, Kohl and Company of San Francisco acquired the Russian-American Company's physical assets and goodwill. After merging with several competitors, Hutchinson, Kohl became the Alaska Commercial Company and was "in an economic sense the successor of the Russian-American Company."[2]

CHANGES ON THE YUKON

The new owners moved quickly to occupy the Russian-American Company posts, and in summer 1868, accompanied by Prince Maksutov aboard the steam bark *Alexander* (formerly the *Imperator Aleksandr II*), they landed George R. Adams at St. Michael (formerly Mikhailovsky Redoubt). "Adams was impressed with the possibilities of trade in land furs . . . and engaged a number of creoles to hunt furs on a year's contract."[3]

But although the Alaska Commercial Company had secured the assets of the Russian-American Company, it was impossible to claim its monopoly: a rush of independent traders soon moved upriver to set up their own operations. In 1868, with remarkable foresight, Frederick Whymper, who had recently traveled from Norton Sound to Fort Yukon, viewed it this way: "Free traders, doubtless now the country is open to them, will play great havoc. Soon the record too of the interior, as of the coast trade already, will be—to use the words of a well-known traveller—'White men, whiskey, guns, powder and ball, small-pox, debauchery, extermination.'"[4]

A group of American traders spent winter 1867–68 at the site of the summer trade fair at Nuklukayet, near where the Tanana River enters the Yukon. In the spring, when the Hudson's Bay Company's traders arrived from Fort Yukon to meet the natives, the Americans warned them that they were trespassing on American soil. American traders also quickly moved upriver to Fort Yukon and protested the company's presence there too.[5]

In contrast to the scruffy appearance of some of the Russian-American Company's posts, in the last years of the Hudson's Bay Company's occupation of Fort Yukon, several visitors remarked on its tidy orderliness. William Healey Dall wrote:

> The present buildings consist of a large house, containing six rooms, for the commander; a block of three houses, of one room each, for the workmen; a

Figure 13.1. Fort Yukon, 1867. By 1867 three of the stockade's walls
had been removed (Whymper 1868, 219).

large storehouse; a kitchen; and four block-houses, or bastions pierced for musketry, at the corners of the proposed stockade. Outside of the fort is a small
house of two rooms, belonging to Antoine Houle the interpreter.

All the houses were strongly built, roofed with sheets of spruce bark pinned
and fastened down by long poles. The sides were plastered with a white mortar
made from shell-marl, obtainable in the vicinity. Most of the windows were of
parchment, but those of the commander's house were of glass. The latter was
provided with good plank floors, and the doors and sashes were painted red
with ochre. The yard was free from dirt, and the houses, with their white walls
and red trimmings, made a very favorable comparison with any of those in the
Russian posts.[6]

Frederick Whymper added, "After our experience with the rather dirty Russian
forts, [it] was quite a relief to find newly plastered walls, glazed windows, capital
floors, open fire-places, and a general appearance of cleanliness." "The fur room
of the fort was a sight not to be witnessed every day," he continued, "thousands
of marten skins hanging from the beams, and huge piles of common furs lying
round. They also get a very respectable number of silver-grey and black foxes."[7]

Nevertheless, it was not until July 31, 1869, that Captain Charles W. Raymond
of the United States Army, aboard Parrott and Company's little river steamer, the
fifty-foot sternwheeler *Yukon*, traveled upriver more than 1,200 miles from St.

Figure 13.2. Sternwheel steamboat *Yukon*, 1883. For many years the Alaska Commercial Company's *Yukon* was the only powered vessel on the Yukon River (Schwatka 1900, 314).

Michael to determine Fort Yukon's geographical position. The *Yukon* had been carried to St. Michael aboard the company's ship *Commodore* and had set off from that settlement on July 4.[8] "At Fort Yukon, notwithstanding the somewhat unpleasant character of our errand," Raymond wrote, "we were cordially welcomed by Mr. John Wilson, the agent of the Hudson Bay Company."[9]

Raymond reported on the trade goods at the fort.

At Fort Youkon . . . there has been established a regular scale of prices, the beaver skin being the standard. Thus the price of a gun is eighteen skins. If marten skins are offered, they are taken at the rate of two to a skin, and inferior skins are received in the same way, according to their value.

The following list shows the kind of goods at Fort Youkon during the last season: guns, double and single barrel, London made; pocket knives, one and two blades; pants, ordinary and fine; white flannel shirts, red flannel shirts, calico shirts, yacht shirts, heavy cloth, blue striped drugget, white striped drugget, shawls, large and small; cotton drill; bullets, twenty-eight to the pound; shot, No. 4; butcher knives; tin pans, various sizes; tin cups, metal buttons, pearl buttons, linen thread, skeins; linen thread, spools; silk handkerchiefs, cotton handkerchiefs, silver rings, capotes, (overcoats,) neckhandkerchiefs, (black)

Paris neckties, English belts, Canadian belts, powder, ribbon (wide), ribbon (narrow).

Raymond added that the Hudson's Bay Company imported 1,200 pounds of gunpowder annually to Fort Yukon and that the quality of the English firearms was far superior to the Russian guns.

Most important, however, after taking sun sights to establish his longitude, Raymond handed the following letter to John Wilson:

> Fort Youkon, Alaska Territory, August 9, 1869
>
> Sir: It having been ascertained that Fort Youkon is within the territory of the United States, it becomes my duty, under the instructions of the Treasury Department of the United States, to inform you that it is unlawful for you to trade with Indians within this territory, and that all such trading will subject you to the penalties of the laws of the United States against smuggling. Such trade must, therefore, immediately cease.
>
> It is my duty to inform you that, under the treaty for the transfer of this country by Russia to the United States, the buildings heretofore occupied by your company have become the property of this government.
>
> I must also call your attention to the fact that our laws prescribe that no foreigner shall enter or remain in the Indian country of the United States without a passport from the War department or an authorized officer, under penalty of one thousand dollars. You will, therefore, see the necessity of removing your company's employés beyond our boundary at as early a time as convenient.
>
> I am, sir, very respectfully, your most obedient servant,
>
> CHAS. W. RAYMOND
>
> Inspector of Customs United States Treasury Department.[10]

He then raised the Stars and Stripes on the fort's flagpole.

Raymond had the law on his side. A congressional act of 1834, which was later deemed to include Alaska, provided that "no person shall trade with any of the Indians (in the Indian country) without a license . . . ; that no license to trade with the Indians shall be granted to any persons except citizens of the United States; that a foreigner going into the Indian country without a passport from the War Department . . . shall be liable to a fine of $1,000; finally that [a government representative] shall have the authority to remove from the Indian country all persons found therein contrary to law."[11]

Lewis B. Parrott of San Francisco—the nephew of the owner of Parrott and Company, which would soon merge with Hutchinson, Kohl and Company to form the Alaska Commercial Company—had arrived at Fort Yukon with Raymond.[12] "Under [Parrott's] watchful eye . . . the Company's servants ceased all trading."[13] Ferdinand Westdahl and Moise Mercier took charge of the post for Parrott.[14]

The Hudson's Bay Company had ordered that Fort Yukon was to be put to the torch to prevent the Americans from using the post, but those orders did not reach the fort until after the Americans had taken possession of it, and because the season was so far advanced, the Hudson's Bay Company men were forced to remain there for winter 1869–70. They were prohibited from trading with the natives, who in turn refused to trade with the Americans. The Gwich'in professed that they would remain loyal to the Hudson's Bay Company.[15]

In the following summer, the Hudson's Bay Company's men left Fort Yukon and moved seventy miles up the Porcupine River, to the foot of the Upper Ramparts, and built Rampart House near Howling Dog Rock, a site the men thought to be well east of the border.[16] The company then decided to relocate their trading activities to La Pierre's House, but in 1872 it relocated the Rampart House post farther upstream. "The manoeuvre served two purposes—offering Yukon Indians an opportunity to continue trade with the H.B.C. and keeping the American traders in the Yukon River basin out of the lucrative trade of the Mackenzie River district."[17]

Nevertheless, "the Americans proved to be intense competitors," wrote Kenneth Coates and William Morrison, "sending native assistants to establish temporary trading posts across the river from Rampart House, escalating prices, and offering generous gifts to Indians who agreed to trade at their stations. . . . In 1866, Fort Youcan had attracted over £6,000 worth of furs, fully one-third of the returns for the entire Mackenzie River district. By the 1880s, Rampart House was bringing in between £425 and £900, representing a scant 2 to 4 per cent of the Mackenzie River take."[18]

In 1887, on the hunch that the post might still be in Alaska, the company burned its buildings to deny them to others and moved again upstream, to a site opposite the mouth of the Salmon Trout River, which seemed to be far enough east. In 1889, however, J. Henry Turner of the U.S. Coast and Geodetic Survey reached there on his expedition to determine the location of the international boundary and found that the post was still within Alaska, so Rampart House was moved yet again to a position "only a few yards east of the Meridian."[19] "The firm resorted [then] . . . to a more passive role," wrote Kenneth Coates, "content to hold on to the limited trade garnered at Rampart House . . . to prevent American encroachment on the lucrative Mackenzie River trade."[20] In 1893 the company abandoned both Rampart House and La Pierre's House.[21]

The Yukon itself quickly became the major transportation route for interior Alaska, and St. Michael, the nearest deep-water port, sixty miles from the Yukon delta, became the trans-shipment point between ocean and river vessels. For a decade the little sternwheeler *Yukon* was the only powered vessel on the river. She often wintered at Fort Yukon and made one round-trip per year, towing barges of furs and people to St. Michael and returning upriver with supplies and trade goods. "Company agent Leroy McQuesten sometimes acted as captain as well as fireman, engineer, mechanic and pilot and was the only white man aboard. He related, 'It is a wonder to me that we didn't blow her up or sink her as I didn't know anything about steamboating.'"[22]

At the same time, San Francisco became the primary market for Alaskan furs, many of which were ultimately sold in London and elsewhere in Europe.[23] One result was a great increase in the amount of trade goods available to the native inhabitants of the region. By 1881, for example, there were eight one-man trading posts on the Yukon between the delta and the international boundary: "Adapting a method long used with considerable success by the Hudson's Bay Company, some Americans hired native 'trippers' to travel to distant tribes and solicit trade."[24]

By then St. Michael was the central point of distribution for the region. Steel traps were now in demand. "In 1870 trade goods worth $16,050 were sent to the Alaska Commercial Company post at St. Michael," wrote Dorothy Jean Ray, "and the Eskimos had one of the largest choices of goods so far: petticoats, hoop skirts, cloth, buttons, beads, American leaf tobacco, flour, seeds, harmonicas, and hardware." The Alaska Commercial Company, like the Russian-American Company before it, did not trade in alcohol. In 1870 the company bought its on-site competition, the firm of Taylor and Bendel.

Two years later François X. Mercier—who had built a trading post at Nuklukayet in 1868—became manager of the Yukon District for the Alaska Commercial Company (ACC). From his headquarters at St. Michael he directed the company's operations, setting up posts and organizing regular transportation throughout the entire Yukon drainage as far as Fort Reliance, the company's post that had been established in 1874 in Canadian territory, 1,600 miles upriver from St. Michael. In 1877 Mercier joined the Western Fur and Trading Company, which the ACC bought in 1882 for $175,000, regaining near monopoly control of the river. "From then until 1892, when a new company, the North American Transportation and Trading Company [NAT&TC], was organized, Saint Michael and the Alaska Commercial Company were almost synonymous." The NAT&TC had lower prices but, unlike the ACC, did not offer credit, costing it a considerable volume of trade.[25]

The summer rendezvous with the ships at St. Michael was as lively as any fur trade congregation, complete with members of many nations showing off their best regalia and their wealth. Athapascans from the river visited St. Michael not only with their furs but also to trade wooden tubs and dishes for seal oil and other coastal products, and umiaqs arrived from Cape Prince of Wales, King Island, and Sledge Island—carrying the occasional Chukchi visitor who would have traveled nearly 500 miles to reach St. Michael—to trade Siberian reindeer skins for furs, which they in turn traded to the whaleships and trading vessels or to the Chukotkans.

Edward William Nelson, who was stationed at St. Michael with the U.S. Army's Signal Corps from 1877 to 1881, noted that beaver and river otter skins were most highly prized by the Chukotkans, who would pay two reindeer skins for one of either. "In the month of August, 1879, we were visited at St. Michael by an umiak from Cape Prince of Wales, and another from King Island. In July 1881, a number of umiaks arrived from the former place. These all brought deerskins [reindeer skins] and tanned hides of seal and walrus for trade. The umiaks in full sail, crowded with fur-clad people, dogs, and their various possessions, made a very picturesque sight. Among the men were some Chukchi from the northern coast of Siberia." It is a measure of how quickly things were changing that in the following summer the ethnographer Johan Adrian Jacobsen noted that when a large skin boat arrived from King Island, those Eskimos would now accept cash for the ethnographic objects he sought; whereas in the interior he still needed to carry trade goods for his purchases.[26]

Nelson described the scene when the ships anchored in the roadstead at St. Michael and the steamer arrived from 1,200 miles upriver, towing a string of boats: "The traders select their stock of goods at Saint Michaels each spring after the arrival of the annual supply vessel, and having loaded them into barges the latter are towed to their respective stations by a small steamer. The year is then passed in trading with the natives, and the succeeding spring they return to Saint Michaels with their boats laden with furs. As each trader brings a crew of natives from his station, all dressed in holiday finery, and the coast traders bring in their Eskimo employés, Saint Michaels becomes the center of an extremely picturesque and animated gathering for a few weeks during the last of June and the first of July."[27]

The naturalist John Muir visited St. Michael in June 1881.

On the nineteenth instant the steamer belonging to the Western Fur and Trading Company arrived from a station fifteen hundred miles up the river, towing three large boats laden with Indians and traders, together with the last year's collection of furs. After they had begun to set up their tents and unload the furs, we went over to the storerooms of the Company to look at the busy throng.

Figure 13.3. Fort Yukon Gwich'in man at
St. Michael, ca. 1880. Edward William
Nelson photographed a Gwich'in man who
had descended the Yukon River 1,200 miles
to trade at the St. Michael fur rendezvous.
He proudly displays his gun and his finest
clothing. National Anthropological Archives,
Smithsonian Institution, Suitland, MD,
image 01431100.

They formed a strange, wild picture on the rocky beach; the squaws pitching
the tents and cutting armfuls of dry grass to lay on the ground as a lining for fur
carpets; the children with wild, staring eyes gazing at us, or, heedless of all the
stir, playing with the dogs; groups of dandy warriors, arrayed in all the colors
of the rainbow, grim, and cruel, and coldly dignified; and a busy train coming
between the warehouse and the boats, storing the big bundles of shaggy bear-
skins, black and brown, marten, mink, fox, beaver, otter, lynx, moose, wolf, and
wolverine, many of them with claws spread and hair on end, as if still fighting
for life. They were wildly suggestive of the far wilderness whence they came—
its mountains and valleys, its broad grassy plains and far-reaching rivers, its forests and its bogs.

The Indians seemed to me the wildest animals of all. The traders were not at
all wild, save in dress, but rather gentle and subdued in manners and aspect,

Figure 13.4. Eskimo traders at St. Michael, ca. 1880. Edward William Nelson captured this image of a family of Eskimo traders on a winter visit to St. Michael. National Anthropological Archives, Smithsonian Institution, Suitland, MD, image 01426300.

like half-paid village ministers. They held us in a long interesting conversation, and gave us many valuable facts concerning the heart of the Yukon country. Some Indians on the beach were basking in the yellow, mellow sun. Herring and salmon were hanging upon frames or lying on the rocks—a lazy abundance of food that discouraged thought of the future.[28]

Edward William Nelson described a typical summertime trading exchange at St. Michael:

The natives brought their dried fish, seal oil, etc. to trade in the morning. It was amusing to watch them barter for the goods they desired. One man would come in with some dried fish and throwing it on the floor would stand unconcernedly as though he had no interest in the proceedings until the trader would ask . . . then he would name the articles he wished. The trader would then show how much he would give . . . but instead of accepting, these natives from the north almost invariably refused at first and haggled for a larger price and in some instances took their things away. Perhaps after an hour or so the same man would come in with something else he wished to trade and so they continued making an exceedingly long-winded affair out of every bargain. After a large amount of talk a water parkie [waterproof parka] was secured for me at about a cost of 50¢.[29]

In the second half of the nineteenth century the post managers often staked native traders with goods to buy furs in the field, and they themselves traveled throughout the country during the winter. They collected those furs—as well as local commodities that other natives would require—and thus captured some of the coastal-inland exchanges that the traditional native traders had performed. One result of this practice was that the use of dogs for pulling sleds spread from the Eskimos to the Athapascans of the interior. Johan Adrian Jacobsen noted that in winter 1882–83 every trader on the Yukon had six to ten dog teams and sleds for these trips. On the lower Yukon, he wrote, "The sleds are loaded with white and colored cotton goods, powder, lead, percussion caps, tobacco, matches, knives and beads." The field trips out of St. Michael ranged from Sledge Island and Kotzebue Sound in the north to Nunivak Island in the south, as well as the lower and middle Yukon, and the Yukon-Kuskokwim delta.[30]

And in 1879 the Alaska Commercial Company established an outpost station at the head of Norton Bay, at the mouth of the Koyuk River, to intercept the furs the natives were carrying south from the Noatak, Kobuk, and Selawik watersheds and to serve as a staging point from which trading expeditions went to the Kotzebue drainage.[31] One native trader, a company agent, traveled from there to the Noatak River and sent back a pictographic report to the Koyuk Station. "The trader is a Mahlemut from here [Koyuk] called *A hal ak* and speaks some English," reported Edward William Nelson. "He sent a piece of paper back giving an account of his expenses and what he had bought thus far. He had drawn upon the paper a dog and about it were rough outlines of the articles he had given in payment for dog feed and surrounded it all by a line. In another place were drawn different kinds of skins with the prices paid drawn underneath and in another place was a map of his route with the villages marked down and the directions northeast and southwest he had copied from a compass laying it down on the map to make a very good sketch of his trip so far."[32]

Sometimes the bartering was extremely tiresome for the resident trader. At Koyuk Station, Edward William Nelson continued: "Last evening we had an example of native trading, the chief from Kotzebue Sound who has been here a long time with a lot of deerskins (Chukchees) and some fancy deerskin boots and other similar articles. He demanded an enormous price for everything and as Tommy has sent the old fellow's son on a trading trip he felt compelled to buy some of the articles, but in selling some half dozen things the old rascal haggled, talked and fussed, now wanting one article and now another and we did not get rid of him until 3 AM. We hurried to bed and had barely extinguished the light when back he came saying he did not want part of the stuff but wished something else. He was told to wait until morning when he again made himself a nuisance for about 2 hours in simply exchanging goods."[33]

The post traders also offered goods on credit, an arrangement that in the 1870s and 1880s the natives scrupulously honored. "In this, however, they were very honest, paying all debts contracted in this manner," wrote Edward William Nelson. "During my residence at St. Michael [1877–81] I saw men trusted for goods who came from distant villages and were scarcely known by sight to the traders. This would often happen when the man lived in a village 100 or 200 miles away. On one occasion an Eskimo came to St. Michael in midwinter from near Kotzebue sound, bringing a mink skin to settle a debt which he had contracted with the trader the previous year. If this man had desired to do so, he need not have come and the trader would have had no means of obtaining his pay. This was one of many such cases that came to my notice"[34]

Despite this convenient arrangement, the whaling fleet undercut the trade. The whalemen did not calculate the cost of transportation in the prices of their trade goods: they were, after all, on a whaling voyage. On the other hand, the trade goods at St. Michael obviously had to be priced to include the cost of transportation; consequently it was sometimes difficult for the St. Michael traders to strike a bargain with natives visiting from the north. "A great many whalers . . . pay almost anything they charge for their goods and thus give them an exaggerated idea of their value," wrote Edward William Nelson in 1877.

And the volume of the foreign fleets' trade at Bering Strait in the 1870s was such that the St. Michael traders did not venture farther west than Sledge Island for their own safety. Beyond Sledge Island the natives were known to buy large amounts of alcohol from the whaling and trading fleets and were considered to be very dangerous. In 1880, at Sledge Island, Edward William Nelson reported about the natives who lived closer to Bering Strait: "The natives along this part of the coast are great rascals and reckless regarding the lives of others. In [the settlement's ceremonial house] we saw four or five livid scars from ugly knife wounds upon the chiefs here and several others were marked the same way. At this place, however, the natives are comparatively inoffensive, but those from King Island are hard cases, and upon the Diomedes and at Cape Prince of Wales they are still worse. This is, to a great extent, a result of the large amount of whiskey they obtain from the whalers and other vessels trading there." "The Malemut at the head of Kotzebue Sound are another vigorous, overbearing tribe," Nelson added. "They buy whiskey from the trading vessels and have drunken orgies, during which several persons are usually hurt or killed. In 1879 a fatal quarrel of this kind took place on Kotzebue sound; the people said it was the fault of the Americans for selling them whiskey, and the relatives of the dead men threatened to kill with impunity the first white man they could in order to have blood revenge."[35]

For trips west of Sledge Island in the 1880s, for example, the Alaska Commercial Company employed a tough Sledge Islander named Saxo, who had re-

**Purchase and Sale Agreement for a Frame House at
Cape Prince of Wales, ca. 1890**

In the early 1890s Harrison R. Thornton and his wife served as missionaries at Cape Prince of Wales. Among his papers is a drawing made by
Kukitak, evidently a wealthy Eskimo trader, who agreed to purchase
a frame house, with two stoves, for 1 cross fox skin, 3 caribou parkas,
2 muskrat parkas, 5 brown bear skins, 1 polar bear skin, 5 pairs of caribou
pants, 5 pairs of waterproof skin boots, 10 medium walrus tusks, 10 large
walrus tusks, 20 mink skins, 20 caribou fawn skins, 20 red fox skins, 20
white fox skins, 10 lynx, 5 beavers, and 5 other foxes. Thornton estimated
the total value of these items to be $321.50.

located to Unalakleet in the early 1870s. Saxo made annual trading expeditions
as far as the eastern tip of the Chukchi Peninsula. "He is friendly to the whites
and is known for his courtesy and helpfulness," wrote Johan Adrian Jacobsen.
"He has this respect in spite of the fact that he has committed a number of murders."[36]

INTRUSIONS AND CATASTROPHES

As we have seen, after the arrival of the foreign fleets in 1849, the natives of the
Bering Strait region were forced to cope with events beyond their control. After
the Alaska Purchase, these intrusions and calamities grew in strength and inten-
sity. They included not only the availability of alcohol in quantity and the reduction of the bowhead whale and walrus populations but also the introduction of
foreign diseases, which coincided with the collapse of the caribou and reindeer
populations. It was a time of intense stress and wrenching change for the native
societies throughout the greater Bering Strait region.

THE MARITIME ALCOHOL TRADE

By the mid-1860s alcohol had become so readily available that the natives of
the Bering Strait region could obtain it from a number of sources. Normally the
alcohol that was traded from ships was consumed quickly and the natives' desire

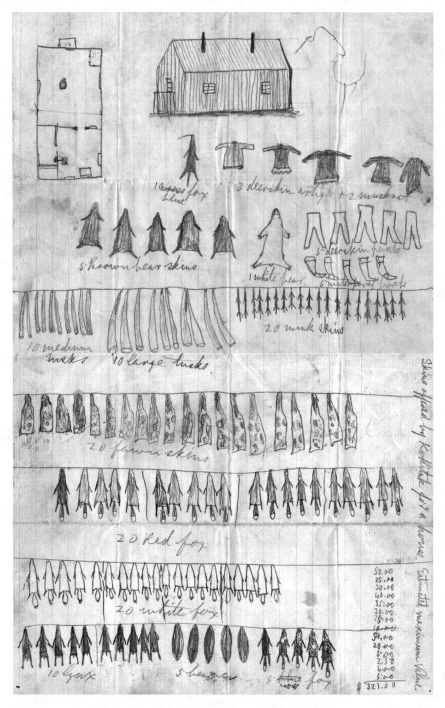

Figure 13.5. Purchase and sale agreement for a frame house at
Cape Prince of Wales, ca. 1890. Peary-MacMillan Arctic Museum,
Bowdoin College, Brunswick, ME (1986.1.21, 22).

for more was met only by the usual wintertime trickle from the Kolyma, but eventually a few natives became wealthy enough through trade to be able to buy sufficient quantities of rum to allow them to keep stocks on hand throughout the entire winter. At the same time some merchants of San Francisco and Honolulu sent a few small trading vessels to overwinter on the coast or simply sent parties of men north to winter on shore with a stock of trade goods. For example, at the end of his Bering Strait trading voyage in 1878, Captain Frederick A. Barker of the schooner *Leo* of San Francisco supplied one group of shore-based traders in Plover Bay with some of the stock he had not sold: 13 barrels of rum, as well as "9 cases all mixed and 35 boxes of tobacco." The rest of his unsold stock—24 casks of rum equaling 1,247 gallons, and 168 boxes of tobacco equaling 3,528 pounds—he had already shipped south aboard the *Syren*, which was bound for Honolulu and therefore outside U.S. Customs control.

Of course the native traders did not welcome this foreign intrusion into the wintertime trade monopoly that they had formerly enjoyed. Gideon Bartlett wrote, "Another schooner [the *Leo*] . . . left three men from San Francisco that Jensen sent up to trade this winter. They built them a nice house about forty feet long and mostly a store house. The natives don't like this much and have threatened to kill them before spring."[37]

The ready availability of alcohol at Bering Strait in the 1860s and 1870s was felt throughout much of northern Alaska and Chukotka. George R. Adams, a member of the Western Union Telegraph Expedition (1865–67), wrote: "I discovered when in the Koyukon country that the Hudson Bay Company was not the only one carrying on illegitimate trade in Russian America. The Koyukon chief showed me two unopened bottles of whiskey, a small bore double barrel shotgun, powder shot and caps which had been traded for with whaling vessels, that carried liquor and goods to trade with the Eskimo of Behring Straits and the Arctic Coast of Russian America, and these had traded them to the Indian tribes next inland and so had passed from tribe to tribe for five hundred miles and brought a high price in furs by the time they reached the Koyukon Country."[38]

And during the winter of 1878–79, when the Swedish exploration ship *Vega* wintered on the north coast of the Chukchi Peninsula en route to the first traverse of the Northeast Passage, her commander, A. E. Nordenskiöld, remembered: "During a visit . . . made in the autumn of 1878 to the reindeer-Chukches in the interior of the country, much diluted American gin was . . . presented, and the tent owner showed his guests a tin drinking-cup with the inscription 'Capt. Ravens, Brig Timandra, 1878.' Some of the natives stated distinctly that they could purchase brandy at Behring's Straits all year round." In fact, unlike the situation in the 1850s, when Asian natives had crossed Bering Strait to Port

Clarence hoping to obtain alcohol from the British ships searching for Franklin, by the 1870s there were reports of the direction of travel having reversed, with American Eskimos crossing Bering Strait in midwinter, bringing furs to Cape Dezhnev to trade for alcohol.[39]

The ethnographer Johan Adrian Jacobsen learned that at St. Michael in the 1870s "an Eskimo named Arnakpeik was a smuggler of Siberian whiskey and was known to have killed Eskimo and Indians after he had gotten them drunk," he wrote.

> To be more invincible he gathered around himself a bodyguard of young people who followed his orders. To prove his absolute invulnerability he acquired an iron cuirass from a whale hunter. He boasted about it and ordered his bodyguard to shoot him. When this happened Arnapeik was not injured. He became so bold that he decided to become the most important power in Alaska.
>
> One day he became very angry at the Alaska Commercial Company and let it be known that the next time he came to Fort Saint Michael he would burn down their trading establishment. Mr. Rudolph Neumann . . . was the agent, and he set a day and night watch on the buildings. One day a small flotilla appeared with Arnakpeik and his fellow murderers. When they were still a musket shot away Mr. Neumann sent a messenger saying that if he did not leave at once he would turn the large cannon on them. Arnakpeik assured him that he had come only to trade, but did turn away.
>
> Since he did not feel powerful enough to defeat the Alaska Commercial Company, he decided to terrorize the Eskimo in the neighborhood and tried to force them to become partners with him. One day when he was drunk with his Siberian whiskey, a few [Koyukon] came to Unalakleet on their way home on the overland trail. In order to gain possession of the goods the [Koyukon] had obtained in trade and distribute it among his retainers, Arnakpeik decided to kill them.

In fact, Saxo, an Eskimo agent of the Alaska Commercial Company, split Arnakpeik's head open with an axe, Jacobsen reported.[40]

In view of alcohol's well-known potential to cause problems, it is not surprising that trouble broke out. Throughout the 1860s and 1870s, ships' logbooks and journals contain reports of drunken and aggressive natives boarding the ships, but by most accounts the Eskimos from Cape Prince of Wales were an exceptionally aggressive group. John W. Kelly, a shore whaler of wide experience in northern Alaska, described them as "a band of hypocrites and shylocks, possessing a large share of brazen effrontery." Captain Calvin Leighton Hooper of the U.S. Revenue Marine considered them to be the "worst on the coast," "great bullies" who traveled "in large numbers compelling smaller bands to trade with them at their own terms." They were, according to George Bailey of the same service, "a bad set, fond of rum." The ethnographer Edward William Nelson reported that on "several occasions the villagers of Cape Prince of Wales fairly took possession of vessels with small crews, and carried off whatever they wished."[41]

In 1873 Frederick S. Hall was appointed as an Indian agent to suppress the whiskey trade, and he set up his headquarters at St. Michael. "Hall's sole duty was to ferret out liquor and to apprehend the culprits who sold it to the natives." Although he left St. Michael the next year, he learned that there was an active whiskey trade from the ships at Cape Prince of Wales, and he foresaw a tragedy, predicting that if trouble were to break out between whites and Eskimos, the trade at Cape Prince of Wales would be its cause.[42]

The Cape Prince of Wales Eskimos doubtless knew of the rough treatment that the Buckland River Eskimos had given to Shishmaryov and his men in 1820 and to the crew of the *Polifyom* in 1838. "They have a traditional story of having driven the Russians out of Kotzebue Sound," wrote John W. Kelly. Their success at bullying foreigners, both native and white, was well known and, aided by alcohol, probably contributed to the tragedy that befell the Cape Prince of Wales Eskimos in 1877. In any case, on July 5, 1877, they met their match in the crew of the trading brig *William H. Allen* of Honolulu. The brig was becalmed in Bering Strait between the Diomedes and Cape Prince of Wales, and Captain George Gilley ordered the anchor down to avoid being carried onto Prince of Wales shoal. There were twenty-four men aboard the ship, most of them Hawaiians. Gilley told Charles Brower about it in 1886.

> In the evening a party of Eskimo came aboard trading and they had a lot of fox skins which they traded for whiskey. . . . Going ashore all the natives at once got drunk and raised cain all night. In the morning all their booze was gone, but not their desire for more. Early in the day a crowd came off for more liquor, but with nothing to trade for it. When Gilley refused them, they got ugly, shoving the crew around, thinking that they were in their power. Gilley had a crew of Kanakas [Hawaiians], who are a peaceable lot to get along with, unless something turns up to make them mad.
>
> The crew stood the shoving around for a long time, all the time trying to get their anchor and get away from the drunken Eskimo. Things went from bad to worse, the Eskimo getting worse all the time. At last the mate struck one of them[.] Another at once drew his knife stabbing the mate, killing instantly.
>
> The crew went crazy, with axes, spades, or anything they could lay their

hands on. They started for the drunken natives, driving those still uninjured and the wounded ones forward under the forecastle head[.] From there they pulled them out with boathooks[,] knocked them over the head with anything they could get their hands on, throwing the bodies into the boat along side, then turned the boat adrift.[43]

John W. Kelly, a whaler and prospector and an astute observer of the state of affairs in the region, also reported about the incident. Kelly traveled widely throughout the Bering Strait region in the 1880s; he spoke Iñupiaqtun and had an Eskimo wife. He wrote:

Beginning about the year 1860, vessels have been fitted out at Honolulu and San Francisco for the purpose of trading in Arctic waters. These are careful not to be surprised or captured by the natives of Cape Prince of Wales.

Soon after the acquisition of Alaska by the United States (1867) these people captured and plundered a San Francisco trading vessel. Encouraged by their success, and having as their leader [a shaman], whom the natives considered invulnerable, they seized and boarded a Hawaiian brig, commanded by George Gilly [Gilley], a Bouin [Bonin] Islander. The natives drove the crew below, killing one man. The chief caught Gilly by the throat and began pressing him back, when Gilly drew a revolver, but was only jeered at by the chief; striking the chief over the head with it and loosening his hold he shot him dead. In the meantime the mate had come on deck with a rifle, but was seized by the second chief, and in the struggle for the gun both fell on the deck. Watching his opportunity the helmsman brained the native with a spare tiller. Gilly and the mate then took up positions at the ports in the forward part of the poop and opened fire on the natives, who swarmed on deck. Becoming panic-stricken, they fled into the rigging, and many sprang over the sides of the vessel, capsizing their canoes, and were drowned. Those that were left sought refuge under the top-gallant forecastle. When drawn out of their hiding places with long boat-hooks, they ran with drawn knives upon the crew and fought until knocked dead with capstan bars. Fifteen natives lay dead on deck. The number drowned is not known.[44]

When the fight was over the crew threw the dead Eskimos into an umiaq, where one woman lay concealed under a tarpaulin. They cast off the umiaq, which drifted ashore. In 1887 Gilley reported, "Afterward I learned that these same men had looted Captain Jacobsen's schooner a week before, and tried to take Captain Raven's brig. . . . No attempt to take a vessel has been made since."

Captain Calvin Leighton Hooper of the Revenue Cutter Service thought that

Figure 13.6. Captain George Gilley. The journalist Herbert Aldrich photographed Captain George Gilley in 1887. Ten years earlier he had been the captain of the trading vessel *William H. Allen* when the fight broke out with the Cape Prince of Wales Eskimos. New Bedford Whaling Museum, New Bedford, MA.

"the lesson taught them at that time seems to have had a beneficial effect." In 1881 the ethnographer Edward William Nelson wrote that the Eskimos "were rewarded with a well-merited punishment. . . . Since then though having frequent rows etc. enough to keep up their reputation as the most villainous lot of natives along the American coast—they have behaved themselves tolerably well to vessels." For many years trading vessels gave Cape Prince of Wales a wide berth, and if they stopped there at all, they did not anchor and, instead, merely backed their sails while they allowed only a few Eskimos aboard at a time.[45]

Nor did the Eskimos forget. In 1888, Charles Brower narrowly escaped being murdered in retribution. "The Gilley Affair" may have been a factor in the 1893 murder of Harrison R. Thornton, a missionary at Cape Prince of Wales. And in 1897, Frank Boyd, a prospector working out of Point Hope, was killed by an Eskimo whose father had died aboard the *William H. Allen*.[46]

REDUCTION OF THE BOWHEAD WHALE POPULATION

While the trade in alcohol ran unchecked, the whaling fleet was facing substantial challenges of its own: challenges that it brought upon itself and which required major tactical changes, changes that brought the fleet in closer contact with the northern natives. After twenty years of intense hunting pressure the whaling fleet had by then reduced the bowhead whale population of the Bering, Chukchi, and Beaufort seas to about one-third of its size twenty years before. The bowheads had become increasingly difficult to find during the summer, and the catches took place mostly in the spring and autumn. To capture whales in these two seasons the ships had to arrive in the North earlier in the spring and stay later in the autumn, and the fleet had to expand its range into dangerous areas at dangerous times of the year.

The result was that sixty-seven ships were lost between 1866 and 1879. These wrecks mostly occurred in the Chukchi Sea, where they provided the natives with considerable salvage material, but at a cost. In 1871, for example, thirty-two ships were abandoned on the northwest coast of arctic Alaska near Point Belcher. The local Eskimos rummaged through many of the ships, searching for stores of alcohol, most of which the whalemen had destroyed before leaving. The natives, however, broke into the ships' medicine chests, and assuming that any liquid in a bottle was alcohol, they drank the contents. Charles Brower, who visited the scene thirteen years later, wrote: "In ransacking the wrecked ships the Eskimos came across the medicine chest and . . . they imagined that anything in a bottle was whiskey. They drank everything that was liquid. Many of them died in their houses." He added that so many died in the village of "Nu-na-reah" that it was abandoned and never inhabited again.[47]

REDUCTION OF THE WALRUS POPULATION

Although the whaling fleet had severely reduced the bowhead whale population by the late 1860s, its hunting activities became far more destructive to the natives' lives when it turned to walrus hunting. In the 1860s a relatively steady market price for animal oils and the greater difficulty of catching bowheads led the whalemen to begin an intensive walrus harvest. The costs of a whaling voyage were fixed, whether or not the crew was whaling; hence, other than engaging in trade with the natives, it was logical to harvest walruses for their oil and ivory to acquire some revenue during an otherwise unproductive time. Whereas the pack ice protected the bowheads from the ships in the "middle season" between spring and fall, the walrus population moved north at the edge of the retreating ice, where it was within reach of the whalemen.

The whalemen quickly reduced the walrus population. From 1866 to 1879 they captured at least 132,000 walruses. But the death toll was far greater because of mortally wounded animals that escaped. It is likely that the whalemen retrieved only 60 to 70 percent of the animals they wounded; hence the total deaths of walruses in those years would have been, perhaps, 190,000 to 220,000 animals. The trading fleet also hunted walruses, but left very few records, so the death toll was even higher. Almost the entire harvest took place in the Bering Strait region and Chukchi Sea.[48]

Of course it was the natives who suffered most from this appalling slaughter. Many of the coastal-dwelling native groups of the Bering Strait region depended on walruses, more than upon the whales, as a highly reliable source of food and raw materials. This was particularly true for the island dwellers on both sides of Bering Strait: they, unlike their mainland neighbors, had no other major resources to fall back on, and during the 1860s and 1870s they watched as the whalemen drove the walrus and whale populations toward extinction.

Not all whalemen were insensitive to this problem. In fact, it was forcefully driven home to Captain Frederick A. Barker after his whaleship, the *Japan* of Melbourne, Australia, was wrecked near Cape Dezhnev in a punishing gale in late autumn 1870. The natives of Uelen and Naukan and other villages took him and the rest of the survivors into their huts and cared for them as best they could.

Barker, an intelligent man and sensitive observer of the natives' lifeways, who paradoxically also became a major supplier of alcohol to the natives, was dependent on their largess all winter, and he saw firsthand how narrow the margin of their existence was and how dependent they were upon the walrus herds. He wrote to New Bedford's *Republican Standard*: "Should I ever come to the Arctic Ocean to cruise again, I will never catch another walrus, for these poor people along the coast have nothing else to live upon. . . . I felt like a guilty culprit while eating their food with them, that I have been taking bread out of their mouths, yet although they knew that the whaleships are doing this, they still were ready to share all they had with us."

Barker's letter was reprinted in New Bedford's *Whalemen's Shipping List and Merchants' Transcript*, and many whalemen agreed with him. No doubt they realized that they too could be shipwrecked in the North and be forced to rely on the kindness of the same people to whom their hunting was causing such hardship. One captain who replied to Barker wrote in New Bedford's *Republican Standard*: "The worst feature of the business is that the natives of the entire Arctic shores . . . are now almost entirely dependent on the walrus for their food, clothing, boats, and dwellings. Twenty years ago whales were plenty and easily

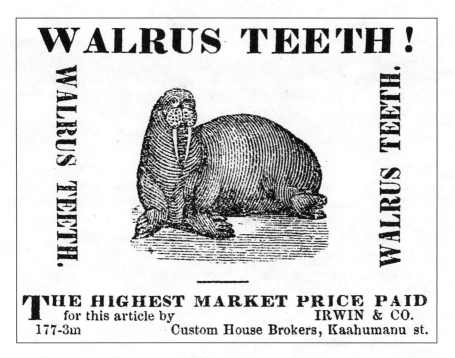

Figure 13.7. Advertisement in a Honolulu newspaper, ca. 1870. From about 1868 to 1880 whaling and trading vessels hunted walruses in the Bering Strait region, severely reducing the population and causing great hardship and famine for the coastal natives. New Bedford Whaling Museum, New Bedford, MA.

caught, but the whales have been destroyed and driven north, so that now the natives seldom get a whale. . . . Several captains lately arrived home have told me that they saw the natives thirty or forty miles from land, on the ice, trying to catch a walrus to eat, and were living on the carcasses of those the whalemen had killed." These concerns were strongly echoed in Honolulu's newspapers as well, but to little effect, and the fleet continued its destruction of the walrus population.[49]

A disaster was inevitable. Although the Bering Strait natives had taken only a few whales and walruses in winter 1877–78 and were described as "very poor," the catastrophe occurred the following winter. The first news reached the outside world when the trading schooner *General Harney* arrived at Honolulu with the report that many natives in the Arctic had died the previous winter as the "result of killing off the walrus by whalers." Soon thereafter another trading vessel, the schooner *Pauline Collins*, touched at Unalaska, and Captain J. J. Nye told the officers of the U.S. revenue cutter *Richard Rush* that he had found all the natives dead at three villages on St. Lawrence Island. "From information he received at another settlement, he learned that they had all died from starvation during the winter and early spring on account of their inability to get seal, walrus, and whale-meat, the ice having broken up early, and a continuance of southerly winds having kept it packed in such quantities against the island, that they were unable to get any food."

The details of the tragedy emerged slowly the following summer. The revenue cutter *Thomas Corwin* visited the island only briefly in 1880, but the Eskimos reported that the weather had been "cold and stormy for a long time, with great quantities of ice and snow, so that they could not hunt walrus and seal," and that they had scraped their way through the winter by eating their dogs and walrus hide coverings on their boats and houses. It was not until 1881, when the *Corwin* returned to St. Lawrence Island, that the full extent of the disaster became apparent: the *Corwin*'s men learned of the deaths of possibly 1,000 persons out of a population of about 1,500 and the extinction or abandonment of six villages. Edward William Nelson, who was traveling aboard the *Corwin* that summer, described the scene at one village on St. Lawrence Island:

> I landed at a place on the northern shore where two houses were standing, in which, wrapped in their fur blankets on the sleeping platforms lay about 25 dead bodies of adults, and upon the ground and outside were a few others. Some miles to the eastward, along the coast, was another village, where there were 200 dead people. In a large house were found about 15 bodies placed one upon another like cordwood at one end of the room, while as many others lay dead in their blankets on the platform.
>
> In the houses all the wooden and clay food vessels were found turned upward and put away in one corner—mute evidences of the famine. Scattered about the houses on the outside were various tools and implements, clay pots, wooden dishes, trays, guns, knives, axes ammunition and empty bottles; among the articles were skulls of walrus and of many dogs. The bodies of the people were found everywhere in the village as well as scattered along in a line toward the graveyard for half a mile inland.[50]

Other native groups also suffered severe hardship at about the same time because of the destruction of the great walrus herds. In 1880 most of the inhabitants of Sianliq, the westernmost Eskimo village on the Chukchi Peninsula, died of starvation. In the same year, William Healey Dall reported that groups of natives from Cape Dezhnev had moved to Archangel Gabriel Bay, north of Cape Navarin, and to Cape Olyutorski because of the "growing scarcity of seal and walrus."

At the same time, natives starved in Plover Bay, and the lack of walruses apparently drove a number of King Island Eskimos to Sledge Island. By then walruses had become extremely scarce throughout the Bering and Chukchi seas. These are the tragedies that were reported; undoubtedly there were more.[51]

INTRODUCTION OF FOREIGN DISEASES

The introduction of exotic diseases to the Bering Strait region was also extremely disruptive for the Eskimos, Athapascans, and Chukchi. The natives had little or no immunity to such foreign diseases as measles, influenza, gonorrhea, syphilis, and scarlet fever, and in Alaska the trade fairs and Messenger Festivals also contributed to their spread.[52] In Chukotka, too, an epidemic of smallpox struck the natives in 1884, and one observer who traveled there in 1891 estimated that about 1,000 Chukchi had died. Ernest S. Burch, Jr., estimates that the Eskimo population of northwestern Alaska fell from more than 5,000 persons in 1860 to about 1,000 in 1890, with a steep decline occurring in the 1880s.[53]

COLLAPSE OF THE CARIBOU AND REINDEER POPULATIONS

To make matters worse for the natives, in northwestern Alaska in the 1870s and 1880s the caribou herds, their most important inland resource, became extremely scarce. In response, Eskimos living in the Brooks Range of northern Alaska increased their reliance on Dall sheep. In the 1880s large numbers of sheep hides were traded at the Sheshalik trade fair.[54]

Although some blamed the traders for selling repeating rifles to the natives who, they claimed, destroyed the caribou through wasteful hunting, it is more likely that the crash of the Western Arctic caribou herd, the Seward Peninsula herd, and the Nulato Hills herd was a natural cyclical decline. One result of this was the Great Famine of 1881 to 1883 in northwestern Alaska, which, as Ernest S. Burch, Jr., has shown, eliminated several Eskimo nations outright.[55]

Another result of the caribou decline was that the "Malimiut"—who had migrated from the Kotzebue drainage to the shores of Norton Sound into lands depopulated by the smallpox epidemic of 1838–39—again moved farther south and "extended their range to Nunevak Island and even to Nushagak and up the Kuskokwim River," as Edward William Nelson wrote from his station at St. Michael in 1880. Nelson added, "They are an energetic people extremely fond of trading and it is also among them that so many murders are yearly committed in this part of Alaska." At about the same time on the Chukchi Peninsula the reindeer and moose populations, as well as other game species, also crashed.[56]

THE SHESHALIK TRADE RENDEZVOUS

Oddly enough, one manifestation of the scarcity of caribou was an increase in interregional trade. This came about not only because the trading fleet was providing substantial amounts of manufactured goods to the natives, particularly to those visiting the Sheshalik rendezvous and the Port Clarence rendezvous, but also because of what Ernest S. Burch, Jr., has called a "clothing crisis in Northwest Alaska." The lack of Alaskan caribou skins available for clothing meant that Siberian reindeer skins, which had hitherto been sought for their exotic color pattern, were in great demand, as were those few skins which were still being taken in the headwaters of the Kotzebue Sound watershed. The cross–Bering Strait trade from Chukotka to Alaska—which might have been expected to have declined in the face of a steady inflow of manufactured products from the whaling and trading vessels—actually remained strong for a while.

Aboard the *Corwin* at Cape Prince of Wales in July 1881, E. W. Nelson saw seven or eight umiaqs approaching from the Diomedes: "I now learned that these boats were the annual trading boats from [Cape Dezhnev] on their way to this place and even across Kotzebue Sound . . . with tame reindeer skins to trade for furs with the American natives," he wrote. "Some of the men in these boats are from Cape Jakan on the north coast of Siberia and they started in early May with dogsleds. . . . The return occupies them till early winter, and then comes a winter visit to the trading fair at Ghighiga [Gizhiga] near the Anadyr Rivere to trade the furs he gets in Alaska for Russian goods." Natives from King Island also participated in the cross–Bering Strait trade, traveling as far as Indian Point on the southeast corner of the Chukchi Peninsula and beyond Cape Serdtse Kamen on the north coast.[57]

The coastal Eskimos paid for the Siberian skins with furs and for the Alaskan skins with marine products. By that time beaver pelts had become some of the most desired furs for the Chukotkans. Less valuable skins were sold in lots sufficient to make a parka: 4 caribou, 40 ground squirrels, or 40 muskrats. George Stoney witnessed the trade rendezvous in the mid-1880s. "The Siberian natives send over for certain skins," he wrote, "especially otter and beaver, in exchange for the tame reindeer, Russian tobacco, whiskey, and firearms. . . . During one of my visits I saw a good many drunken natives. When under the influence of liquor they sometimes kill each other."[58]

In 1880 it was estimated that more than 1,200 persons were at the Sheshalik trade rendezvous. Edward William Nelson described the fair at Sheshalik in 1881. "In July, 1881, we found at Hotham Inlet a row of over 150 conical lodges set up for over a mile along the beach, which were occupied by Malemut from Selawik lake and natives from Kowak and Noatak rivers. . . . When we arrived there we saw a small trading schooner lying off the village, surrounded by umiaks three or four deep and the deck crowded by a dense mass of the Eskimo. Tobacco, drilling, knives, ammunition, and other small articles were used to buy from them the skins of reindeer, wolves, black bear, arctic hare, red, white, and cross foxes etc."[59]

That same year the captain of the *Corwin*, Calvin Leighton Hooper, also described the great Sheshalik trade fair. "These natives, who are from all parts of the coast, visit this place annually for the purpose of meeting the traders and exchanging with each other, and also for the purpose of indulging in a dance and athletic sports. They come from the southward, Cape Prince of Wales, the Diomedes, and King's Island, and from the Siberian shore as far as Cape Yachan [Yakan], from the Alaska coast to the northward as far as Point Hope, and from the rivers emptying into the head of Kotzebue Sound and Hotham Inlet."[60]

Four years later, in 1885, Lieutenant George Stoney of the U.S. Navy was in Kotzebue Sound aboard the *Corwin*. Stoney recorded the trade goods that were most sought. Alcohol, repeating rifles, and fixed ammunition would not, of course, have been sold in the presence of a revenue cutter. The natives were, however, allowed to purchase percussion firearms and ammunition. "The articles most in demand are here given in the order of their importance," Stoney wrote.

Tobacco, the strongest and darkest Kentucky leaf—dark leaf Russian tobacco is still more valuable; [gun]powder in one-half pound cans; lead in one-sixth pound bars; shot, Nos. I. II. BB in six-and-one-quarter and twelve-and-one-half pound bags; double barreled and single barrel shot guns of good material, with small bores, to shoot ball and shot; [percussion] caps, waterproof, one hundred in a box; drilling, the best quality; camp kettles of wrought iron, one to five gallons capacity; sheath knives, blades thick, six to ten inches long and of good metal—as they are good judges; flour twenty-five-pound bags, cheapest quality; pipes, cheap fancy ones; traps, all kinds and sizes; molasses and sugar, the commonest kind; saws, axes, boy's axes; files of all kinds; gimlets; needles, (Glover) Nos. I and II; sulpher matches, in blocks; fancy calico shirts; brown duck overalls; fine and coarse combs; playing cards; beads, blue and black; tin cups; pans; looking glasses; spy glasses; chopping knives and dog chains.[61]

Like the Hudson's Bay Company's custom of using the "Made Beaver" as the basic unit of value, at the Kotzebue rendezvous the standard unit of value became the red fox skin. A red fox skin's value stood slightly below the middle of the scale. In descending order, the most valuable skin was the silver fox, followed by cross fox, river otter, beaver, black bear, wolf, wolverine, brown bear, lynx, marten, red fox, arctic fox, caribou, mink, hare, and squirrel (marmot and ground squirrel). All who were involved in this trade, both native and foreign traders, used this scale of value. In the native inland-coastal product exchanges, for example, a sealskin full of seal oil was sold to the interior dwellers for the equivalent of two to four red fox skins, and an umiaq might be sold for as many as twenty-five to thirty skins.[62]

The value of labor was also established on the same scale: Stoney hired Eskimo helpers for a half-skin per day, and he paid them using the following table of equivalencies, which was the normal value of trade goods in Kotzebue Sound in the mid-1880s.

1 lb [pound] gun powder	1 skin
1 lb lead	¼ "
1 box [percussion] caps	¼ "
1 fathom [six feet] drilling	½ "
25 lb bag of flour	2 "
1 lb sugar	¼ "
1 large axe	3 "
1 boy's axe	2 "
1 gallon molasses	1½ "
1 pound tobacco (6 hands)	1 "
1 pound shot	¼ "
1 large file	1 "
2 small files	1 "
1 camp kettle	4 to 2 "
12 blocks matches	1 "
1 large trap	3 "
1 small trap	2 "
1 knife	1 "
1 tin pan	½ "
1 saw	2 "
1 chopping knife	1 "
1 gimlet	¼ "
1 dog chain	1 "
1 shirt	1½ "
1 suit overalls	5 "
1 looking glass	¼ "
1 fine comb	½ "
1 coarse comb	½ "

1 camp kettle (1 gallon)	1 ″
1 pipe	1 ″
1 pack cards	1 ″
1 paper needles	¼ ″
6 thimbles	¼ ″

Alcohol, repeating rifles, and cartridges—which were contraband—were, of course, highly desired. At that time many of the natives were still using muzzle-loaders. "Breech loading rifles and cartridges are the most valued of all articles and bring extreme prices," Stoney observed. "Whiskey is also in great demand and commands high prices—both of the above are sometimes obtained from the smugglers on the coast."[63]

By the mid-1880s the native societies of the greater Bering Strait region had been assaulted by influences beyond their control: alcohol, the reduction of the whale and walrus populations, the collapse of the caribou and reindeer herds, and the introduction of foreign diseases. In summarizing the situation at Point Hope, Ernest S. Burch, Jr., could well have been describing all of the native nations of the region. "By the late 1870s the fabric of Point Hope life was crumbling," he wrote. "The human population had been drastically reduced. The resource base had been devastated, and a number of new and thoroughly disruptive forces were at work among the people."[64]

14

THE LAST DECADES OF THE
NINETEENTH CENTURY

THE BEGINNING OF GOVERNMENT PATROLS

With such a sorry state of affairs it is not surprising that concerned persons spoke out, calling for governmental control in the North. In the 1870s newspapers on both the East and West Coasts of the United States carried letters and articles about the destructive influence of the foreign fleets upon the natives in Chukotka and Alaska. In 1878, for example, the following report appeared in San Francisco's *Weekly Bulletin:* "The whaling vessels which are now dropping in to this port from the Arctic Seas are officered by very intelligent men, who have some clear perceptions of right and wrong. . . . The masters of these whaling vessels have made from time to time some observations touching an illicit traffic on the coast about Behring Straits, which ought to receive the attention of the Federal Government, as well as that of the Russian authorities. It is well known that no liquor is allowed in Alaska within the jurisdiction of the [Alaska Commercial Company]. This regulation grows out of business considerations. . . . There is also a standing order that no liquor is to be admitted to any port of Alaska."

It was widely believed that the trade in alcohol had increased in the 1870s.

During the last five years there has been a very large increase of the liquor traffic, both upon the American and Russian sides of Behring Straits. A part of this liquor is supplied by Honolulu houses, and a part is sent up [to] Plover Bay . . . Indian Point, St. Lawrence Island, St. Lawrence Bay, Cape East [Cape Dezhnev], and settlements further north. On the American side are Point Hope, Point Belcher, Point Franklin, . . . and Point Barrow. These are all within the Territory of Alaska, and all are within the limits where the liquor traffic is prohibited by the Federal Government. The Russian Government absolutely forbids the landing of liquor in the settlements on the Siberian side. About three years ago the [brig] *Timandra*, owned at this port, was overhauled by a Russian war vessel when about to land liquors at the Russian settlements. Her liquors were taken out and destroyed and the vessel was ordered off. There is no cutter or other American armed vessel which goes into these high latitudes. An occasional Russian armed vessel sails along the Siberian coast looking in upon the various settlements; but this supervision is not close enough to keep down the unlawful traffic in liquors. The Russian Consul at this port refuses to sign manifests where liquor forms any part of the cargo which is to be transported to the Russian settlements.

Nor was it surprising that the alcohol trade was extremely profitable, the article continued:

These half breeds and Indians are rapidly destroyed by indulgence in the cheap and wretched liquor which is taken to them in this clandestine way. There is an immense profit in the business. The liquors are usually exchanged for whale-bone, walrus ivory and fur. The trade is wholly in the form of barter. A thirty dollar rifle is frequently exchanged for whalebone worth from eight hundred to a thousand dollars. A barrel of cheap rum, according to this standard of valuation, would go in a great way in this business of exchange. The liquor taken up from this port is mainly sent by one firm, and is a cheap kind of Central American rum. It is brought to this city [San Francisco] and stored in bond without paying duties, and is sent on its way to impoverish and kill the natives on either coast. As it is nominally taken into a foreign country, the duty is in this way avoided. Honolulu also supplies more or less of this cheap stuff. At Plover Bay a fellow by the name of [Goharren] generally acts as consignee of liquor, and as he can neither read nor write, he is no doubt a very convenient sort of person to see that papers are properly signed, and everything is regular, snug and right. . . .

Now, as this traffic is illegal and utterly destructive to the natives in that region, it ought to be prohibited in some effective way. An armed cutter stationed in that vicinity for six months of each year, would make the business too precarious for that class of traders who have no conscientious scruples about trade where large profits are the result.[1]

In fact on July 27, 1868, the Fortieth Congress had created a customs district for Alaska, extending the laws of the United States for navigation and commerce to the new territory. Among other things, the act prohibited the importation of liquor. In 1873 the act was amended, specifically forbidding the sale of alcohol and breech-loading firearms to Indians. "These two acts," wrote Governor Ernest Gruening, "comprised the only legislation [for the territory] that was to be enacted by the Congress for seventeen years."[2]

Although Alaska was initially under the control of the army, Congress did not organize a civil government for the territory. "Observers referred to Alaska as being under 'military rule,' but the rule was *de facto* and never *de jure*." Smuggling went on unchecked, and there was no force in place to control it, although, echoing Captain Verman's advice to the Russian-American Company, there were many requests for a steamer to do just that. Soon after the Alaska Purchase, George Davidson, who compiled the first coast pilot (sailing directions) for Alaska, wrote prophetically: "In a few years the whole fur trade will degenerate into an illicit traffic with whiskey smugglers, unless the most rigid and inflexible means are employed to regulate it." But apart from one northern cruise in 1870, only in 1879 did revenue cutters begin their regular annual patrols of the Bering and Chukchi seas.[3]

The army ruled Alaska until 1877, when its small force was withdrawn to assist against the Nez Percé uprising in Idaho and "even their shadowy authority and potency ceased to exist," wrote Ernest Gruening. To fill the gap the Treasury Department was given responsibility for the territory. The navy was in control from 1879 until 1884, when the Forty-eighth Congress finally passed the Organic Act, providing for civil control of Alaska and, among other things, prohibiting "the introduction, manufacture, and sale of intoxicating liquor except for medicinal, mechanical, or scientific purposes." The prohibition would not be repealed until 1899, when the act was amended.[4]

By law, any vessel clearing from an American port for Alaska, or transiting its waters with alcohol, firearms, or ammunition aboard, was required to post a bond amounting to twice the value of the products, refundable upon presenting proof of their proper disposal. To avoid problems with the law, some captains either submitted a false cargo manifest or claimed that any alcohol and firearms were for trade on the Siberian shore. "The 'Siberian trade' pretext is a blind," wrote Special Agent Harrison G. Otis. "The contraband goods are notoriously destined in nearly every case for traffic on both the Siberian and American shores." In July 1870, for example, the revenue cutter *Reliance* seized the schooner *Louisa C. Simpson* at Chamisso Island in Kotzebue Sound. The schooner was carrying contraband but had cleared for Plover Bay on the Chukchi Peninsula.[5]

Other vessels cleared San Francisco "purporting to be engaged in fishing and trading" but departed without any whaling or fishing gear. A number of traders simply called at Hawaii, then a sovereign nation, and took on supplies of contraband there. One year the schooner *Loleta* took aboard 1,247 gallons of rum. In

1879 it was carrying 1,600 gallons of rum when a federal agent confiscated it in the Pribilof Islands.[6]

In Hawaii, Frank T. White, aboard the San Francisco whaleship *Jeanette*, wrote: "We take our stores consisting of 50 bbls. of Alcohol, which we afterwards dilute to make 100, and 9000 lbs. of Tabacco, 70 bbls. of water, a tierce of Whiskey, 10,000 cigars, etc. It is taken at Honolulu, . . . so it comes much cheaper than in the U.S. Most of the liquor and tobacco is sent consigned to someone, shipped from the U.S. in bonds, and at Honolulu turned over to the master of the ship."

Some traders sailed directly from Honolulu under Hawaiian registry. In the 1870s the Hawaiian northern whaling and trading fleet annually fluctuated between as few as two and as many as ten vessels. In 1878, for example, the little 86-ton Hawaiian schooner *Giovanni Apiani* traded in the North for 750 pounds of whalebone, 220 pounds of ivory, and "393 packages trade." The traders' profits were assured because they could buy rum in Hawaii at 75 cents per gallon, dilute it by half with water, and trade it for a pound of whalebone, which in 1877 was worth $2.50. Over 11,000 gallons of liquor were shipped north out of Honolulu in 1879.[7]

At last, in 1879 the annual revenue cutter patrols to Bering Strait began with the cruise of the *Richard Rush*, and the cutter's men learned that eleven trading vessels visited Kotzebue Sound and "sold large quantities of liquor, breech-loading arms and ammunition" and that thirty barrels of alcohol had been landed at Cape Rodney on the southwest coast of the Seward Peninsula. When the *Rush* visited the wreck of the trading brig *Timandra* on Nunivak Island, among her cargo the crew seized 56 Winchester rifles, 86,150 Winchester cartridges, 18 sets of reloading tools, and 10,000 primers. J. C. Merrill and Company of San Francisco owned the *Timandra*. "This same vessel, with others fitted out by the same firm," wrote G. W. Bailey to the secretary of the treasury, "has traded in these waters for several years, and invariably traded liquors, breech-loading arms, and ammunition, contrary to and in violation of law, but could not be caught in the act."[8]

In 1880, Captain Calvin Leighton Hooper of the U.S. Revenue Marine seized the schooners *Leo* and *Loleta* for selling alcohol and breech-loading firearms to the natives. In the *Leo*'s hold they discovered 26 cases of alcohol, most of which were labeled "Bay-rum," "Jamaica ginger," "Pain-killer," and "Florida water." The schooner *Loleta*, seized at the end of her cruise, still had 29 Winchester rifles and 24,000 rounds of ammunition aboard. In 1878 the *Loleta* had returned to Hawaii with 290 barrels of oil, 4,719 pounds of whalebone, 4,000 pounds of ivory, and "60 skins etc."[9]

In the first years of the revenue cutter patrols, the officers and others were struck by the strength and pervasiveness of the maritime trade. At St. Lawrence Island the natives seemed "perfect slaves to rum [who would] barter anything they possess[ed] to procure it and remain drunk until it was gone." William Healey Dall visited Plover Bay aboard a U.S. Coast Survey schooner in 1881: "Two canoes . . . came out to meet us, it being the practice to give everybody a drink on their arrival 'to facilitate trade.' They asked for 'lum' (rum) and were informed we had none. 'No got lum! American schooner no got lum! (with rising indignation), Lie! Lum got!' was the exclamation. . . . However, much to their disgust, they were finally convinced we were not traders, and departed, leaving us in peace." In Kotzebue Sound in 1881 the *Flying Mist* was reported to have been selling whiskey by the drink for one fox skin apiece.[10]

But the presence of the revenue cutters did have some effect on the unbridled trade: by the end of the *Corwin's* northern cruise in 1884, Captain Michael A. Healy reported that "the whiskey traffic in northern Alaska has almost entirely ceased." This was certainly an exaggeration; still, the revenue cutters had succeeded at least in suppressing the most flagrant whiskey trading on the American shore. Although the revenue cutters usually arrived in July, by which time much of the trading had concluded, Healy noted that the "masters of the vessels boarded made no secret of having brought large quantities of liquor into the Arctic for trading purposes, but had thrown it overboard before reaching the United States boundary line on learning that a revenue-cutter was in these waters."[11]

Oddly enough, the contraband laws had an unusual side effect on the resident traders at St. Michael. There, in 1881 William Gilder, a journalist with the *New York Herald*, reported: "The neighboring tribes are mild and peaceful . . . unless under the influence of liquor, which they still procure at exorbitant prices from whaling vessels and traders in violation of existing laws, which are so strict that the agents of the American trading companies cannot even bring any kinds of liquors, wines or beer here for their own use. Mr. Lorenz [the Alaska Commercial Company's resident agent] says that, while he cannot land beer here for his table or cartridges for breech-loading guns for his own use, he can buy liquor or cartridges from the natives at any time."[12]

By then, as Lorenz mentioned, repeating firearms had also entered the region in quantity. "At many places from Point Hope to Point Barrow we were offered whalebone, ivory, the skins of reindeer, mountain sheep, Parry's marmot, whistlers [ground squirrels], and many white and red fox skins," wrote E. W. Nelson in 1881. "Whisky and cartridges seemed to be about the only articles desired by these people in exchange." In 1883 John Murdoch reported that at Point Barrow the Eskimos preferred a Winchester fifteen-shot rifle, which the "whalers and traders purchase cheaply at wholesale." "The whalers are also in the habit of buying up all sorts of cheap or second-hand guns for the Arctic trade," he added, and the Eskimos "naturally are most desirous to procure cartridges for the rim-fire Winchester guns, as these are not intended to be used more than once." In fact the Eskimos did devise methods to reload rim-fire cartridges, which were manufactured to be fired once and then discarded.[13]

At Point Barrow by the early 1880s the bow and arrow was used only by hunters who were "too poor to obtain guns." Referring to the coastal natives of northwestern Alaska in the late 1880s, John W. Kelly wrote, "There is scarcely a male Eskimo over twelve years of age who does not own one or more repeating-rifles. . . . As there is much rivalry between different traders, the natives receive full valuation for their products." Kelly estimated that whalers and traders annually sold $30,000 worth of "arms, ammunition, muslin, flour, at San Francisco prices, in exchange for their furs and whalebones."[14]

The high prices that George Stoney reported for repeating rifles and alcohol at the Sheshalik fair in 1885 reflected the success that the revenue cutters were having in suppressing some of the trade in contraband. But although Captain Healy was required to uphold the law, he and many others nevertheless felt that the ban on breech-loading repeating firearms (a result of the Indian uprisings of the 1860s and 1870s in the American West) was a great hardship on the northern natives.[15]

Unsurprisingly, the trade in breech-loading firearms continued, and by 1890, in the village at Cape Prince of Wales, the missionary Harrison R. Thornton reported that among the settlement's 135 males there were 67 breech-loading rifles, 5 breech-loading shotguns, and 27 revolvers. By 1901 on the Chukchi Peninsula, among a population of 440 at Indian Point there were more than 400 modern firearms.[16]

As might be expected, the Alaskan Eskimos did not welcome the revenue cutters' interference with their source of alcohol and firearms, an interference that also impeded them in their role as middlemen to more distant Alaskan customers. In 1881 Captain Calvin Leighton Hooper reported on the second cruise of the revenue cutter *Corwin:* "In the vicinity of Kotzebue Sound they were very bitter against us, and, I am informed, openly boasted . . . that they would capture the vessel and kill all hands if she came again to prevent their getting whiskey. . . . They did not, however, attempt to carry out their dire threats into execution. On the contrary they *appeared* quite friendly." And at Point Barrow in 1882 Patrick Henry Ray, a member of the U.S. Army Signal Service, reported to his superior that although at least three whaleships traded alcohol and other commodities, these visits were not sufficient for the natives to acquire their "usual supply" of "whiskey, arms, and ammunition" and mistakenly assumed that Ray was the

cause of it. Hooper's successor, Captain Michael A. Healy, wrote that the Eskimos learned that the cutter had come north to stamp out the whiskey trade and
that "no liquor can be got on board the Corwin, even if they beg for it on their
knees, as they have frequently done." "The natives cannot understand why the
Corwin interferes with trade in repeating rifles and whiskey," the naturalist John
Muir observed. "They consider it all a matter of rivalry and superior strength."[17]

The revenue cutters of course had no authority to act on the Russian side of
Bering Strait, and this gave the natives of Cape Dezhnev, the Diomedes, King
Island, and Cape Prince of Wales the advantage of acting once again as middlemen: They frequently carried alcohol across Bering Strait and traded it at Kotzebue Sound or Port Clarence. In 1881 Captain Calvin Leighton Hooper visited
a village on Big Diomede Island, in Russian territory: "In many of the houses
we saw piles of whalebone and fine furs of marten, fox, and beaver, which we
learned were intended for the East Cape [Cape Dezhnev] trade to purchase
rifles, cartridges and whiskey," he wrote. "I tried to buy some marten, but could
not induce the natives to part with them, although offered nearly as much as
they would cost in San Francisco." In fact, in the early 1890s natives from Cape
Prince of Wales and King Island made annual summer trading voyages as far as
Indian Point at the southeastern corner of the Chukchi Peninsula to buy whiskey
and reindeer skins, which they then sold to Alaskan natives.[18]

At about the same time the Russian government also became alarmed about
the situation on the Siberian coast. Although the traders were being brought
under a degree of control in Alaska, they continued selling their products on the
coast of the Chukchi Peninsula. This traffic was also in violation of Russian laws.
"St. Petersburg tried to curtail the American presence in 1877 by prohibiting
natives from bartering furs for food, only to relent within a year as famine gripped
Chukotka," wrote the historian John J. Stephan. "By 1879 the prominent jurist
Konstantin Pobedonostev was warning the future Tsar Alexander III that unless
warships were dispatched to the Northeast, local natives 'will altogether forget
that they belong to Russia.'"[19]

In 1881 the Russian government sent a naval vessel, the *Strelok*, to patrol the
Asian coast of Bering Strait. Her crew distributed leaflets, printed in English,
among the coastal natives to give to the foreign ships, informing them that they
were prohibited from coming within three miles of shore; nor were they allowed
to trade guns, ammunition, or alcohol. The following year, 1882, the gunboat
Kreiser went north. But the trading vessels did not fear the Russians: the traders
usually arrived in the Bering Strait region well before the Russian patrols.[20]

For example, in 1881 at St. Lawrence Bay on the Chukchi Peninsula, John
Muir wrote: "Nearly all the natives we have thus far met admitted very readily that

whiskey was not good for them. But Jaroochah was not to be so easily silenced, for he at once began an anti-temperance argument in saloon-and-moderate-drinker style, explaining with vehement gestures that some whiskey was good, some bad; that he sometimes drank five cupfuls of the good article in quick succession, the effect of which was greatly to augment his happiness, while out of a small bottle of the bad one, a small glass made him sick. And as for whiskey or rum causing people to die, he knew, he said, that that was a lie, for he had drunk much himself, and he had a brother who had enjoyed a great deal of whiskey on board of whalers for many years, and that though now a gray old man he was still alive and happy."

"This speech," Muir added, "was warmly applauded by his listening companions, indicating a public opinion that offers but little hope of success for the efforts of temperance societies among the Chukchi."[21]

To control the "foreign interlopers" the governor-general of the region, Baron Korf, created the Anadyr District in 1889. "The first governor succumbed to depression, but his young and energetic successor, Nikolai Gondatti, relished the assignment, studying the Chukchi language, surveying Chukotka, encouraging Russian enterprise, and stocking provisions in government warehouses that natives could buy at subsidized prices," wrote John J. Stephan. But "the fruits of Gondatti's exertions did not long survive his departure in 1897," just as the gold rush swept over the region.[22]

TRADE IN THE 1880s AND 1890s

Whether or not a particular ship made a practice of trading alcohol, by the 1880s the natives on both shores of Bering Strait relied on the whaleships and trading vessels to provide them with the manufactured goods upon which they now depended. One native of Indian Point, recognizing that the survival of the coastal Siberian Eskimos (called *Masinkers* by the whalemen) now depended upon this foreign source of goods, told the journalist Herbert Aldrich, "I b'lieve no whale-ship, Masinker man all die."[23]

Firearms, ammunition, woodworking tools, needles, clothes, knives, and a hundred other things were by that date essential to their lives. In 1887 at Plover Bay, for example, the whaleship *Francis Palmer* did the following trade: sold were 5 boxes of tobacco from Honolulu, 2 packages of leaf tobacco, 1 Winchester rifle, 3 boxes of reloading tools, 2 dozen knives, 700 WCF [Winchester Center Fire] rifle cartridges, 300 fifty-grain loaded cartridges, 2 pieces of white drilling, 27 bags of flour, 300 pounds of bread, 12 packages of matches, 4 hatchets, 2 axes, 1 saw, 1 mechanical toy, 1 whaling bomb lance, 1 dozen thimbles, 1 dozen spools of thread, 1 dozen papers of needles, and 5 pounds of beads. In return the natives paid the trader 237 arctic fox skins, 10 red fox, 1 polar bear skin, 1 brown bear skin, 92 pounds of ivory, 100 pounds of whalebone, 10 pairs of native boots, and 2 fur parkas. This is the report of only one ship at one settlement, amid a fleet of forty whaleships and perhaps a half a dozen traders that were working in the North that year.[24]

In fact, in 1895 Governor Nikolai Gondatti, who was conducting a census of the coastal dwellers on the Chukchi Peninsula, listed the following trade goods that the inhabitants of Avan, a small settlement near the mouth of Plover Bay, had acquired from American ships that year: "4.5 tons of flour, 880 kilograms of biscuits, 800 kilograms of sugar, and other goods, in exchange for one-third of the baleen of a bowhead whale, 43 pairs of walrus tusks (approximately half their estimated annual walrus catch), 5 polar bear skins, 22 fox skins, 36 seal skins, and 140 reindeer skins, in addition to 14 sets of men's fur clothing." Although there are no comprehensive records surviving about the amount of trade goods that were imported to the Bering Strait region, considering the size of the trade at Avan, which was a minor settlement, the total inflow of goods to the region must have been substantial.[25]

TRADE PROCEDURES AND PRACTICES

By then a routine had developed in the trade procedure. Whaling and trading vessels annually passed northward along both coasts, beginning at Cape Olyutorskii on the Asian coast or Nunivak Island on the Alaskan side. When the natives spotted a vessel, if they wished to trade, they set a flag, waved a shirt, or paddled toward the ship with a pelt hoisted on a pole. The ship then hove to by backing one of its sails, or made fast to the ice edge. Only rarely would it anchor. It was customary for the captain to provide each boatload of natives with a bucket of bread and some jam or molasses. The procedure went this way: the natives brought out their furs, whalebone, ivory, skin clothing, boots, and mittens and usually showed their inferior items first so that a price would be established before they presented their prime pieces. But to encourage the natives to engage seriously in the trade, if a square-rigged ship was hove to, she "lay with the topsail to the mast, ready to fill away at any time," wrote Captain Hooper, "and when the trade gets dull, the master orders 'brace forward,' and the natives understanding that to mean the vessel is about to leave, trade becomes more active for a while; and when it slacks the same thing is repeated."[26]

In an extension of the trading partnerships that existed between members of different native nations, each wealthy native usually had a favorite captain with whom he preferred to deal, saving the best pieces for him and getting better

Figure 14.1. Trading schooner *San Jose* icebound, 1886. New Bedford
Whaling Museum, New Bedford, MA.

prices in return, and some captains also basically "staked" natives who, in effect, became their agents ashore. In this meeting of cultures a trade jargon grew up, allowing the traders and natives to communicate via an amalgam of words derived from English, Hawaiian, Chinese, Spanish, Danish, and other languages. Some examples, drawn at random:

mikaninni—small or child
kow-kow—food
mukki—dead or broken
pau—not or none
hana-hana—work
puni-puni—sexual intercourse
wahini—woman
kuni—wife
myr-can—American
mi savi—I know
mi no savi—I don't know
spose—if
ketchem—catch them, get, take
mek-fast—make fast, fasten, tie, hitch up[27]

Figure 14.2. Captain Barney Cogan and friend aboard ship at Indian Point, 1887.
New Bedford Whaling Museum, New Bedford, MA.

Sexual favors were also a profitable trade item, and one of the easiest ways for natives to obtain alcohol. With the exception of the Diomede Islanders, who apparently forbade their women from having sexual intercourse with foreigners, native men on both sides of Bering Strait encouraged the practice to the extent that a few observers reported that some native men had become merely pimps for their wives and daughters. Not surprisingly, sexually transmitted diseases became widespread throughout the region, and by 1890, for example, Henry D. Woolfe estimated that half the population of Point Barrow was "tainted" by secondary or tertiary syphilis.[28]

Chicanery was also part of trading in Bering Strait. Some captains made a practice of carefully pouring alcohol into containers that were partly full of water so that the alcohol floated on the surface; others added pepper to low-strength liquor or gave out samples of full-strength whiskey and sold a heavily diluted mixture. "In order to make it strong enough for the savage palate," wrote William H. Gilder, "after it had been watered sufficiently to gratify the cupidity of the poachers, it is doctored with cayenne pepper, tobacco juice, and other powerful ingredients, until the wonder is that those who drink it are not killed at once."

In return it was not uncommon for the traders to encounter, among other deceptions, fox tails sewn on rabbit skins, or damaged fox skins cleverly patched with rabbit fur, or broken walrus tusks riveted together with lead and the joints concealed by smeared reindeer fat, or stones set in the roots of walrus tusks to increase their weight. At Point Hope, Charles Brower was warned by his friends, the shore whalers Jim Allen and Tom George, who themselves were not innocent of such practices. They told Brower:

> I had to be careful in buying [whalebone] from the Eskimo[s] there. They were a bad lot, and if I did buy any bone to look it over before paying for it. . . . They had a custom of soaking their bone overnight, then covering it with four dry slabs before bringing it off [to the ship] to trade. This of course increased the weight at least 15%, so anyone that bought it from them was buying water and paying bone prices for it. When I asked [Allen and George] if they had ever done a thing like that they swore that no one but an Eskimo would try to beat a friend that way.
>
> Next time they came [aboard] they brought several bundles of bone with them. As I had been in the game longer than they, I thought it just as well to see how far they would go. Long bone only brought top price; small [bone,] according to its length. While I took them in the cabin to give each a drink I had the mate take the lashings off the bone and sort it as it ought to [have been]. On opening their bone, it was just as they told me the native bone would be. While they were having a second drink I [went up] on deck and overhauled the bone. Coming back, I told them what I had done, and if we traded I would take off their weight 20% for water and only pay for long bone what I had agreed. They told me all their bone was first class, [although] only a small amount was long. Every bundle had been filled with calf bone and covered with a few long ones.
>
> They were inclined to be indignant at my not trusting them, but it finally wound up in a laugh, they saying that they hoped to put one over on me, as I was the oldest trader along the line.

Another ploy to add weight to a batch of baleen was to include flat iron bars amid the bundles of whalebone sold to the ships. On arrival in San Francisco a captain might discover that his "trade bone" also contained iron barrel hoops. In 1894 at Indian Point, Frank Russell reported, "The chief will no longer buy a demijohn of alcohol without testing it from the bottom. He remembers the time when he drank the first draft from the vessel and became very 'molly kelly'—

drunk, while his followers quenched their own overpowering thirst with the water on which a pint of alcohol had been carefully poured. Captain Murray told me that he had once purchased two bundles of whalebone, of a native of that coast, in which two heavy iron bars were concealed. When the trick was discovered, the thrifty Eskimo laughed and said, 'alle same white man!'"[29]

TRADING SITES

The regular arrival of the whaleships at prominent places in the Bering Strait region also strengthened the importance of a few native trading congregations at the expense of others. On the Chukchi Peninsula these trading sites were principally Indian Point and Cape Dezhnev. And the trade was so substantial that by the early 1880s at Indian Point it was reported that almost everyone could speak some English. According to Waldemar Bogoras, "The whalers seldom skirt the Arctic coast westward from [Uelen, near Cape Dezhnev] and even then almost never go beyond [Kolyuchin] Bay. All the Maritime people who wish to take part in this trading [travel to the sites where they can meet the ships], those from the Arctic villages, to [Cape Dezhnev]; those from the Pacific villages, to Indian Point. No positive times are set for these gatherings; but, beginning with the middle of March, the dog-teams and reindeer-caravans begin to appear one after another. They keep coming long after the appearance of the first whaling-ships, because the snow melts away only in the late spring. Travelling with skin boats begins at the end of May, and from July on wholly replaces journeying with sledges."[30]

The Alaskan natives also adjusted their routine to acquire trade goods where they were most abundant. In 1881, for example, the revenue cutter *Corwin* met one hundred Point Hope Eskimos in nine umiaks, heading, not south to Sheshalik, but rather north to Point Barrow to trade, and about the year 1885 the natives moved the site of their trade rendezvous in Kotzebue Sound from Sheshalik to Qikiqtaġruk, the location of the present town of Kotzebue, most probably because the trading vessels could approach closer to shore there.[31]

And just as the sites at Cape Dezhnev and Indian Point became predominant in the trade on the Asian side of Bering Strait, Port Clarence on the Alaskan side also took on added importance. At the end of June, when the whales had passed north through Bering Strait but pack ice still blocked the ships' progress, the fleet paused to refit and resupply before resuming its northern cruise, and Port Clarence's large, well-enclosed bay offered good protection. In the first decades of the whale fishery the whaleships did not visit Port Clarence regularly, even though it was the best harbor in the region. At first they used Plover Bay and St. Lawrence Bay on the Chukchi Peninsula to ride out gales, carry out repairs, and to fill their water casks. By the mid-1860s, however, they began to visit Port Clarence more frequently.

By the late 1870s the ships' owners recognized that to secure profitable catches from the declining bowhead population, their ships had to be put at considerable risk; hence the owners began to send tenders north to meet their ships. Tenders not only resupplied the ships in midsummer but also took their cargoes south, thus preventing the loss of the "spring catch," should the ships be lost later in the season. For example, in the 1880s the owners maintained a coal supply at Port Clarence for the steam auxiliary whaleships.[32]

And for the natives, Port Clarence's trade fair allowed access to the congregation of whaleships. In fact, by 1879 the rendezvous had become such an important source of foreign trade goods for the natives that when the Swedish exploration ship *Vega* reached Port Clarence, Lieutenant Pallander wrote, "The whole harbor of Port Clarence was swarming with natives." He noted that the Eskimos had ample supplies of steel axes and knives, as well as American handguns and rifles. Pallander talked with two Eskimo men who spoke English: one had been taken aboard a whaleship to San Francisco; the other, to Honolulu. He noted that they had coconut shells and mats of plaited fronds in their tents. To his amazement, one of the Eskimos presented the captain with a letter. "Upon opening it, the captain found inside the business card of a San Francisco firm, offering their outstanding selection of hunting gear to 'sportsmen in Arctic waters.'" "Only an American firm would spread such advertising among the Bering Strait Eskimo" was Pallander's comment.[33]

In 1887 the journalist Herbert Aldrich witnessed the Port Clarence rendezvous. "Nearly every canoe that came along-side had either fish or furs to trade, those from the vicinity having the former, and those from Cape Prince of Wales, King's Island, Norton Sound, and other distant places, the furs. It is understood at all these places that the ships are at Port Clarence about the first of July, so hither the natives come to trade. In some of the nearer settlements all household goods are packed up, and the whole family moves here to be near the fishing grounds."[34]

Once the whaleships had completed their work at Port Clarence, they headed north, and while searching for bowheads, continued trading on the Alaskan coast. "Point Hope is the first place upon the Alaskan Arctic shores that the whalemen touch after recruiting at Port Clarence," wrote Henry D. Woolfe about the whalers' activities in the latter 1880s.

There the natives having whalebone, walrus ivory, or any products trade with the whalemen. . . . The arrival of the fleet is anxiously looked for, and it is a sea-

Figure 14.3. An Eskimo girl in her finest
parka, aboard ship at Port Clarence, 1887
(detail). A bundle of fox skins, perhaps her
father's, is in the foreground. New Bedford
Whaling Museum, New Bedford, MA.

son when the utmost disregard of all decency prevails. . . . Similar conditions
prevail all along the coast as far as Point Barrow. . . . Off Point Lay, at Icy cape,
Wainwright inlet, and Point Belcher are the points of rendezvous for both the
natives and ships. Quite a motley gathering of clans can be found at these encampments; entire families can be seen living in tents of various sizes, while
in the center of the temporary village is a large structure of deerskin supported
by driftwood that serves as a dancing and general lounging tent. Everything
in their possession, from large bundles of whalebone to the smallest ivory or
bone carving, is brought for trade by these people, and the goods received in
exchange are either carried off to a safe locality or packed in their canoes for
transport home.[35]

The strength of the maritime trade was such that by the early 1880s at Point
Barrow tobacco had become so readily available that the Eskimos had become

very particular about what they bought. "They use all kinds of tobacco," wrote John Murdoch, who was stationed there with the U.S. Signal Service, "but readily distinguish and desire the sorts considered better by the whites. For instance, they were eager to get the excellent quality of 'Navy' tobacco . . . while one of our party who had a large quantity of exceedingly bad fine-cut tobacco could hardly give it away. A little of the strong yellow 'Circassian' tobacco used by the Russians for trading is occasionally brought up from the southwest, and perhaps by the Nunatañmiun, and is very highly prized, probably because it was in this form that they first saw tobacco." He added that in addition to pipes (*pai'pa*), they also smoked cigars (*pai'pa-sigya*) and cigarettes (*mûkpara-pai'pa:* "paper pipe").[36]

CHUKCHI TRADERS

The increased volume of foreign goods available to the natives in the Bering Strait region also helped to create a merchant class of Chukchi who became full-time traders in their own right. A. E. Nordenskiöld, who wintered aboard the *Vega* on the north coast of the Chukchi Peninsula in 1878–79, saw a number of the native traders who traveled from Bering Strait to the Ostrovnoe fair. "Many spend their whole lives in commercial journeys," he wrote. And on the north coast of the Chukchi Peninsula in summer 1881 William H. Gilder reported: "At [Cape Dezhnev] are certain articles which they can procure by trading, and at Nishne Kolymsk are others, so that they go from one end of the line to the other, a distance of about 1,500 miles, as they are compelled to follow the coast in all its tortuous windings. At [Cape Dezhnev] they can get Henry rifles and cartridges, as well as American knives, tobacco and calico; while at Nishne Kolymsk they get Circassian tobacco, a cheap but very strong article, brass smoking pipes, bear spears, and such articles."[37]

Waldemar Bogoras described how the Chukchi organized their trading journeys in the latter part of the nineteenth century:

In the reindeer branch of the Chukchi, a man more active than the others, though oftentimes not over-attentive to his herd of reindeer, of which he has but comparatively few, will want to go to the seashore for barter. . . . He will begin collecting fawn-skins for trading, and pack-sledge reindeer for the journey, his relatives and neighbors loaning him some of the latter. He will go partly as their agent, and will carry skins to sell for them on commission. . . . He will start with a traveling-camp in February or March, and will proceed very slowly, being careful not to over-fatigue his reindeer . . . thence he will advance from one small watershed to another, following the general direction of the seacoast, but all the time keeping a considerable distance from it. With the advance of the season, he will proceed eastward as far as possible, and turn to the shore only when traveling with reindeer becomes impossible. Sometimes he will reach [Cape Dezhnev]; more often he will stop in some other village.

The trader would spend the summer near Bering Strait before starting back in the autumn.

> He will spend the whole summer on the seashore; he will take part in the seal-hunting, so as to have a share in the spoils without paying for it; and he will journey by boat to [Cape Dezhnev]. In exchange for his skins, he will try chiefly to get ground-seal [bearded seal] hides and all kinds of thongs, and American products,—alcohol, Winchester rifles, and cartridges. In the middle fall he will start on his return journey as slowly as before, and will finally go back to his own country in the spring. He will return the borrowed reindeer, for the most part without any particular pay, and will distribute some of the wares he has bought among those whose agent he has been, retaining a considerable share of the profit for himself out of every transaction of this kind. Such a journey will last a whole year, and perhaps even longer; so that a caravan leaving two months before fair-time at Anui [Ostrovnoe] will be back just in time for the next fair. Travelling between Indian Point and the Anadyr is much shorter, and is usually accomplished in one winter, so that a caravan starting in the fall will come back about the middle of the next spring.[38]

According to Bogoras, who carried out his field research in Chukotka in the late 1890s and the first years of the twentieth century, "when a man finds zest and profit in [trade] journeys, he makes them his vocation, and becomes a Kavra´lit."

> The greater part of the Kavra´lit are maritime people who first turned to reindeer-breeding and then to trade, and thus are experienced in both pursuits and in the customs of both parts of the tribe. The Kavra´lit are continually *en route*. In former years they were anxious to visit the Russian fairs. They went down to the seashore to meet the boats coming from the Diomede Islands and America, and often associated with them and made a trip across the sea to secure an additional supply of valuable peltries. Sometimes the father of a family would start westward with a reindeer-caravan. Meanwhile one of his sons would wait till summer and cross Bering Strait in his boat. The next spring father and son would meet, and arrange for the distribution of their wares for new journeys. Even now a few Kavra´lit traders have not restricted the range of their travels, and continue to visit both the Anui fair and the Diomede Islands. Others, however, trade chiefly in fawn-skins, and do not go as far as the Ostrov-noye market-place or the Kolyma settlements. . . .

In former times there were richer men among the Kavra´lit than there are at present. About forty years ago [ca. 1850–60] one of them bought horses and made summer trips between Reindeer camps, carrying his wares on horseback. Another one, at his own request, was sent to Yakutsk by the officials of the Kolyma district. He visited the Russian governor at Yakutsk, and received through him a gold medal and a parade coat adorned with silver lace.[39]

But in fact, during the last decades of the nineteenth century the volume of trade from the ships was so great that fewer and fewer natives chose to attend the trade fair at Ostrovnoe on the Maly Aniui River. In response, the Russian government offered inducements to encourage the natives to visit the fair. The natives, however, quickly began to manipulate the system for their own benefit. Bogoras continued: "At the present time about six or seven hundred people gather together for the Anui fair. One-fourth of these are Russians, Russianized natives, and Yakut, from settlements on the Anadyr, Kolyma, Alaseya, and Indighirka; one-fourth are Kolyma Lamut; and the rest, Reindeer Chukchee and [native traders]. Commerce has fallen off greatly, because American peltries have nearly ceased to come, and part of the peltries from the Asiatic shore are bought by the whalers."[40]

He added: "The number of Maritime Chukchee who attended the Anui fair, which in former times usually amounted to a couple of scores, fell to ten and even less. Then the authorities thought to attract them again by restoring the tribute-presents. . . . Everyone who should bring a companion with him would be entitled to special recompense. . . . In the year 1889 twelve Maritime Chukchee paid tribute at the fair and received for one red fox, for instance, one large kettle, one knife, one spear-head, several pounds of tobacco, beads, candy, and hard-tack. The value of the presents was much higher than that of the tribute. . . . The tributaries would come to the Anui fair without a large amount of peltries for trade, only with their tribute and a few skins for buying liquor; and the whole transaction degenerated into a complete sham."[41]

"TRADING CHIEFS"

At the same time, because of the general population decline throughout the region and the volume of foreign trade goods entering it, it became possible for one man to dominate a village. Previously, at the main settlements—which had larger populations—several persons would have been in competition with one another, thus preventing the supremacy of only one. In the 1860s, 1870s, and 1880s, however, "strong men" consolidated power and wealth in a number of native groups—four are known to have done so in northwestern Alaska—and at some coastal settlements men who might be called "trading chiefs" became the principal middlemen for the villagers' trade with the ships.[42]

The most successful of these trading chiefs was Goharren, an exceptionally entrepreneurial Eskimo of Indian Point on the Chukchi Peninsula. At first he may have been staked by a whaler or trader, but he soon became a trader in his own right. Goharren amassed a fortune in trade goods. At his zenith he owned three wooden store houses that were full of whiskey, firearms, ammunition, and a wide variety of manufactured goods, as well as whalebone, furs, and ivory. With these large stocks of foreign goods he was able to trade throughout the winter, obtaining products at favorable prices. Goharren also offered credit to the natives; consequently many Indian Point natives were in his debt more or less permanently. And during the winter, natives on the Chukchi Peninsula frequently made long trips to trade with him, particularly for alcohol.

In 1891, for example, Goharren is reported to have had in his warehouses 200 sacks of flour, 80 boxes of tobacco, and ivory and whalebone worth between $5,000 and $8,000. He also sold secondhand whaleboats, which he bought from the whaleships on their return south. He outfitted four whaling crews and owned 100 reindeer. At one time he had as much as $75,000 worth of whalebone stored away. By the turn of the century Goharren owned a gramophone.[43]

Goharren, however, suffered a severe but temporary setback in an impressive attempt to outfit a vessel for whaling and trading on his own. In 1886 Captain Benjamin Dexter reached Indian Point in his sixty-foot schooner *Henrietta*. At the time Goharren had two "heads"—about 4,000 pounds—of whalebone in his storehouses. The baleen was worth almost $11,000 and Goharren offered to buy the schooner from Dexter for the whalebone, plus 800 to 1,000 pounds of ivory, 500 fox skins, and 3 polar bear skins. Dexter accepted the offer, but soon a Russian gunboat, the *Kreiser*, appeared on its usual northern patrol. A party boarded the *Henrietta* and found that it was a foreign vessel and that Goharren had not obtained permission from the governor in Vladivostok to be operating in those waters. The Russians seized the *Henrietta* and took it to the Sea of Okhotsk, where she was used as a patrol vessel.[44]

Goharren was not the only native trader on the Chukchi Peninsula. In 1881 the ethnographers Arthur and Aurel Krause reported that two storehouses in the settlement of Uelen, near Cape Dezhnev, were full of guns, axes, saws, powder, and lead. By the last years of the nineteenth century, fourteen Siberian Eskimo traders are reported to have owned storehouses.[45]

At Point Hope, Alaska, another powerful trading chief arose at about the same time as Goharren. Ataŋauraq was a man of exceptional intelligence, strength, aggressiveness, and gall. Like Goharren, Ataŋauraq became the middleman for

Figure 14.4. Goharren and son, Indian Point, 1887. Goharren was a wealthy Siberian Eskimo trader at Indian Point. Here he poses with his son, who wears high-button shoes and a suit of clothes that must have originated in San Francisco. New Bedford Whaling Museum, New Bedford, MA.

most of the trade that went on with the ships, but, unlike Goharren, he achieved his supremacy through fear.

Charles Brower, a pioneering shore whaler, remembered visiting Ataŋauraq ("Attungowrah") with John W. Kelly at Point Hope in 1888:

> Kelley and I went to the village, the chief and all his harem turned out to greet us, making me very welcome, same as they had always done, feasting us with the best there was in the place. I carried a message to Attungowrah from the head man at Point Barrow village, Ounalena. Ounalena wanted Attungowrah to meet him at Icy Cape the coming summer and they would have a wrastleing match. Ounalena had heard he was a very Strong man. He thought he was just as strong and maybe the better wrestler.

Figure 14.5. Ataŋauraq, Point Hope, 1887.
Ataŋauraq was a much-feared "trading
chief" at Point Hope, Alaska. Here he wears
a hybrid costume, with a button-front parka
and mattress ticking trousers. He also wears a
very large and expensive labret in his cheek.
He was murdered in 1889. New Bedford
Whaling Museum, New Bedford, MA.

I sure started something. Attungowrah just got up and declared himself, saying there was no one on the whole coast that could throw him, nor anyone that
could kick as high with both feet. Immediately he started to show his ability as
a kicker. Standing in the center of his igloo, he kicked the window frame in the
top of his house with both feet at once. This was something I had never seen
before, and I believed him. But when he asked me to carry a large rock all the
way to [Point Barrow], just to show Ounalena what he could lift with one hand,
it was too much. I had to decline. . . .

This was the last I saw of Attungowrah. Two years after he was killed in a feud
that lasted the best part of two years, during which time thirteen people were
killed, he being the last to go.[46]

By the early 1880s Ataŋauraq had forged ties with some of the captains of the whaling fleet and with Captain Healy of the Revenue Cutter Service. He is remembered as both a generous man and a tyrant who consolidated power and then was corrupted by it. "It was not uncommon among the Eskimo, particularly about the shores of Bering Strait and northward, for some man of great courage and superior ability to gather around him a certain following and then rule the people through fear," wrote the ethnographer Edward William Nelson, who visited Point Hope in 1881. "Such men usually confirmed their power by killing any one who opposed them."

> In order to keep their followers in a friendly mood, they made particular effort to supply them with an abundance of food in times of scarcity, or to give them presents of clothing at festivals; they also try to secure the good will of white men whenever they think it is to their interest to do so.
>
> At Point Hope we saw such a chief, who had killed four men and had the entire village terrorized. The people were overawed by his courage and cunning, and hated him so much that a number of them went quietly to the *Corwin* and begged [Captain Calvin Leighton Hooper] to carry the man away.
>
> During our stay at Point Hope this fellow was never seen without a rifle in his hand, and the people said he always carried it. During the trading on the *Corwin*, whenever one of the villagers was offered a fair price for one of his articles and began to haggle for a greater one, this man would quietly take the goods offered and give them to the other, who would then accept them without another word.[47]

Captain Hooper also wrote about Ataŋauraq. "He does not hold the position of chief as an hereditary right or by influence of wealth, but by sheer force of arms. He is never without his Sharps rifle, and with it he overcomes all opposition. . . . He is a good shot, and quick to act. It is said that he has killed several of the tribe and has the rest thoroughly cowed."[48]

More than one observer thought that sooner or later someone would murder Ataŋauraq. "He passed from tyranny to assassination," wrote John W. Kelly. On February 14, 1889, he was "shot dead by two brothers whom he had exiled, and who had returned for the purpose of killing him. He inspired such terror that every year people left for distant hunting-grounds, till it seemed that a few more years of his reign would have seen [Point Hope] depopulated." The anthropologist Froelich Rainey, who lived at Point Hope in 1940, saw it this way: "He became a spokesman for the Eskimo in their dealing with white men; his consequent wealth enhanced his self esteem and he assumed dictatorial powers in the village. His eventual loss of prestige was undoubtedly owing to the fact that he began taking other men's wives by force. Finally, exceeding the patience of the men in the village he was shot to death as he lay sleeping among his five wives."[49]

SHORE WHALING STATIONS

During the mid-1880s another major foreign intrusion took place on the coast of northwestern Alaska via the establishment of shore whaling stations at Point Barrow, Point Hope, and a few other places. In the 1880s the whaling fleet had expanded to all of the navigable waters of the Bering and Chukchi seas in their search for the dwindling numbers of bowheads, and one of the few innovations remaining was to establish shore stations on the Alaska coast to try to capture those bowheads that migrated ahead of the ships through the leads in the pack ice in the early spring.

With the price of whalebone high and rising, in 1884 the Pacific Steam Whaling Company of San Francisco set up a shore station at Point Barrow, and in 1887 entrepreneurs built one near Point Hope. Both enterprises had shaky starts, especially at Point Hope, where Ataŋauraq resented the competition and forced the whalemen to set up their station six miles east of the village of Point Hope. "In 1890 whaling took a boom," wrote Jack Hadley, a veteran shore whaler. "Trading stations were established and their proprietors made from 500 to 1,000 per cent profit."[50]

To the natives' advantage, however, these shore stations also served as trading posts, offering the Eskimos a year-round opportunity to sell their furs and baleen, whereas previously the trade fairs, Messenger Festivals, and ships' visits had been their only markets. At Point Barrow in 1886 the presence of the shore station—and its market for furs—brought about a change in the Eskimos' trading journeys, allowing them to dispose of their pelts there, rather than at one of the native trade fairs. Charles Brower, who was a member of the crew of the first shore whaling station, recalled the year 1886, when the Point Barrow natives returned from the trade fair at Niġliq in the Colville River delta. The Eskimos "brought back lots of fur, mostly fox skins, although they had others as well, beaver, marten, mink, black bear, and lynx. . . . [The station] bought all the fur that they had, everyone was satisfied, the Eskimo thankful that they had a place where they could dispose of their furs without having to keep them a year."

In fact a number of the interior-dwelling Eskimos soon began traveling to Point Barrow in the summer, to Piġniq, a site a few miles south of the point, "to trade their furs for oil and ammunition, tents and all the other truck they need, many of the people coming from the Kobuk River. At this time there was no . . .

store nearer than St. Michaels," wrote Brower. In 1887 eighteen umiaqs from the interior, with at least six persons in each, arrived at Piġniq to trade.[51]

By that time the market value of whalebone had risen so much that it brought about a change in the native sharing practices in their whale hunt. Four decades earlier, when whalebone had been of little commercial value, it was usually shared relatively equally among the hunters who had participated in capturing the whale. But in the last quarter of the nineteenth century baleen's value rose sharply, and on the Chukchi Peninsula Waldemar Bogoras, from his perspective at the end of the century, described the change in the sharing procedure: "I was told that in former times, as many as fifty years ago, after each successful catch [of a bowhead whale], a large part of the best whalebone was distributed among all the inhabitants of the village. . . . At present good whalebone is too valuable and rare to be thus distributed. . . . In most cases, however, the whale is killed, not by a single boat, but by two, three, or several boats. One of the boats that has acted foremost, is considered as the 'principal boat,' the others are only 'assistant boats.' Then the whalebone is divided along the middle line into two equal parts. . . . The principal boat takes one half. The other half is divided among the assistant boats; and each boat distributes its portion among the crew. When a whale has drifted ashore, the meat and blubber are carved and taken by all present; but the whalebone belongs, as a rule, to the one who first noticed the whale." The stations also proved to have a positive aspect by providing extra whale meat and products to the local natives at a time when the walrus and caribou resources were scarce.[52]

The increased amount of trade goods also helped to reduce the tensions and distrust that had existed among nations in northern Alaska (see chapter 13). In fact, sometime before 1889 an Eskimo group had made a pioneering trip of more than 700 miles by umiaq from Point Barrow into Canada, as far as Cape Bathurst, east of the Mackenzie delta. One of the Point Barrow men took a wife at Cape Bathurst and returned with her to Barrow. "After this Point Barrow people frequently came as far as Baillie [Cape Bathurst]," Vilhjalmur Stefansson learned, "bringing tobacco and labrets which they exchanged for copper and [soapstone] for [lamps]." The round-trip from Point Barrow to the Mackenzie required two or three years to complete, and some Mackenzie Eskimos also visited Point Barrow. Stefansson added that at about this time traders carried Siberian reindeer skins as far east as Cape Bathurst, where "they were considered much more 'stylish' than caribou because of their rarity and cost."[53]

Henry D. Woolfe, the enumerator for the seventh district of Alaska in the Eleventh U.S. Census (1890), described the state of trade relations. "It is a general rule that but few females [have accompanied] the trading parties to any point

Figure 14.6. John W. Kelly with a visiting Gwich'in trader at Point Barrow, Alaska.
John W. Kelly (right), a veteran shore whaler, was photographed at Point Barrow with
two visiting Gwich'in (center), ca. 1886. These Gwich'in were probably on a trading
expedition, far from their usual hunting and trapping territories. They stand out
from the Eskimos surrounding them by their long hair, lack of labrets, and
the decorated jacket on the taller Gwich'in. Sheldon Jackson Collection,
Presbyterian Historical Society, Philadelphia.

where meetings with the Itchali or Upper Yukon and Porcupine river Indians take place. Within the past few years the custom has been relaxed, and in 1890 4 families left Point Barrow to reside at Herschel island and several women accompanied the trading parties to Barter island." In fact, to judge from a photograph—probably taken in 1886—in Woolfe's report, a Gwich'in had traveled as far west as Point Barrow, most likely to visit his Eskimo trading partner (fig. 14.6).[54]

The trading rendezvous at Barter Island also lost its importance as the flow of persons back and forth along the north coast of Alaska increased. About 1890 "the old trading residence of Barter Island was given up and Collinson Point took its place," wrote Vilhjalmur Stefansson. There Point Barrow Eskimos met Gwich'in and Mackenzie Eskimos at this new rendezvous, which was somewhat farther west than Barter Island. Among other things they traded ammunition and sought wolverine skins. By then, however, trade—both from the whaling fleet which had recently expanded its cruises into the eastern Beaufort Sea, and from the Hudson's Bay Company, which was trying to recapture some of the trade it had lost to the fleet—reduced the importance of that rendezvous. The summer of 1901 was the last in which Gwich'in from Rampart House are reported to have visited Collinson Point.[55]

LOCAL DISTILLERIES

Sadly, another result of the presence of the shore whaling stations was that the Eskimos learned how to make their own alcohol out of a mash of molasses and flour. Charles Brower wrote that in 1888 Peter Bayne, a corrupt shore whaler at Point Hope, taught Ataŋauraq how to make hooch. Ataŋauraq then taught his allies, and they passed along this knowledge until there was "not a single village on the coast from Point Barrow south that did not have one or more distilling apparatus going whenever the natives could procure the necessary flour and molasses," wrote Lieutenant E. P. Bertholf of the U.S. Revenue Marine. During the winter of 1897–98 Bertholf destroyed twenty stills at Point Hope alone but believed there were many more that he did not discover. Stills reached St. Lawrence Island in 1896, when a Point Hope woman landed there from a whale-ship.[56]

Henry D. Woolfe wrote about stills at Point Barrow in 1890: "Within the past 2 years Kotzebue sound and Point Hope natives have instructed the Point Barrow natives how to distill alcohol from molasses, sugar, and flour. A mixture of these articles with water is boiled in an old coal oil or any other available can, into which is inserted an old gun barrel, fitted with dough or clay to render the joint air-tight. The barrel passes through a block of ice, and as the mixture boils the vapor condenses as it leaves the tube into a crude spirit, and is caught in a receptacle. The utmost care is taken to avoid losing a drop of this precious mixture. Attempts to check the making of this vile mixture prove abortive, as the law does not prohibit the sale of sugar, molasses, or flour to these natives."[57]

At Cape Prince of Wales, Thomas Lopp reported in his newspaper, the *Eskimo Bulletin*, that during the winter of 1896–97 four hundred gallons of molasses were made into rum and that "a bottle full of 'moonshine,' 'Aurora Borealis,' or 'Midnight-sun' brand, can be readily exchanged for a red fox skin." In fact, locally distilled alcohol undercut the cross–Bering Strait trade in foreign liquors, a trade in which the Chukotkan natives had become the middlemen because of the U.S. revenue cutters' suppression of the trade on the Alaskan coast. In 1898 the *Eskimo Bulletin* reported, "Some East Cape [Cape Dezhnev] natives took a quantity of liquor to Kotzebue Sound to trade at the summer rendezvous; but finding it unprofitable to compete with the crude alcohol which was being distilled there from molasses, sugar and flour, they carried their liquor back to Siberia."[58]

Not only did the whalers buy whalebone, furs, and ivory from the natives, but also they paid for large numbers of boots and fur clothing to equip their crews for the arctic cruise. The trade for boots, mittens, and parkas provided the natives of the Chukchi Peninsula, St. Lawrence Island, and the Diomede Islands with a substantial source of income at a time when other marketable commodities were declining.[59]

The whalemen also signed on natives at St. Lawrence Island and the Chukchi Peninsula, as well as at Point Hope and Point Barrow, to work as ordinary seamen on the northern cruise. If the ships were embarked on wintering voyages to the eastern Beaufort Sea, entire families were often signed aboard for two years or more, the men serving as ordinary seamen, hunters, and dog drivers, and the women as seamstresses. If a native man signed aboard for a single summer's cruise without taking his family along, the captain usually sent food ashore to his wife to tide the family over for the summer. This advance would be deducted from the native's pay at the end of the summer. On the ship's return south the natives were paid off with trade goods, whaling gear, and used whaleboats, which were highly prized. Some also traded directly for whaleboats. In 1886 the price was 230 pounds of whalebone, more than $600.

When a whaleship landed its native crew at its village in the autumn, the captain also gave them for food the flukes (the tail) of the last whale the ship had caught. But in the heavy weather and growing ice of October, for safety's sake it was sometimes impossible to land the natives. To avoid being caught on a lee shore in a dangerous season, the captain occasionally had no choice but to keep on. In such cases the natives had to go to San Francisco with the ship. They would be on their own in San Francisco, usually taking wage employment, and would be returned to their homes six months later, on the ship's next northern cruise. Some chose to go south in any event. One native had spent two years as a dishwasher in San Francisco. Another "sturdy young fellow from the [Chukchi Peninsula] had gone to San Francisco with a vessel and remained all winter," wrote Edward William Nelson. "He liked the country there, he said; but, as he expressed it, 'Merican too damn much work.'"[60]

In the 1890s whaling vessels made more than seventy winterings on the coast of the Beaufort Sea, the majority of them at Herschel Island. The whalemen not only sent out their own hunters to take caribou but also bought meat from other natives. The whalemen considered the most effective hunters to be the "Nuna-

tarmiuts," those inland Eskimos whose original homelands had been in the central Brooks Range of Alaska but who had moved east, nearer Herschel, because
of the decline in the Alaskan caribou herds in the 1880s. It is likely that they
reached the Arctic coast near the international boundary only a few years before
the whaleships began to overwinter. A number of Gwich'in also hauled meat
to Herschel Island from their homelands near Rampart House and La Pierre's
House, posts that the Hudson's Bay Company abandoned in 1893. One of the
hunters in each Gwich'in band was appointed to be a "trading chief" for the
group in negotiations with the whaling captains.[61]

Natives were drawn to Herschel because of the ready access to manufactured goods: gunpowder, primers, lead, rifles, fixed ammunition, flour, sugar,
tea, calico, tobacco, soap, knives, combs, files, whaleboats, small stoves, clothing, and many other items, including alcohol. The whalemen bought meat from
the natives for about six or seven cents a pound, paying in trade goods that they
priced at San Francisco wholesale cost. Because the whalers did not add the cost
of transportation to these goods, the prices they asked were only 20 or 30 percent
of those charged at Fort McPherson, the Hudson's Bay Company's post on the
Peel River, a fact which the Gwich'in immediately noted.

This point was dramatically made to John Firth, the clerk in charge at Fort
McPherson, in summer 1892 when a party of Eskimos arrived in a whaleboat
loaded with trade goods. They bartered with the locals and headed back to Herschel with the furs. The fur returns from Fort McPherson had declined significantly since 1890, when the whaling fleet began wintering at Herschel. In response Firth sent word to the whalers that unless they abandoned trading for furs,
the company would no longer forward mail to the fleet. Most of the whalemen
ceased trading for fur at Herschel; they valued receiving news from home more
than profits from the fur trade.[62]

At the time the whaleships were overwintering at Herschel Island and other
places on the coast of the Beaufort Sea, the shore whaling stations also needed
large numbers of whalemen to man their whaling crews. This labor shortage
brought about a shift in the native population: in the 1890s, after the whaling
fleet had recruited a large number of Point Barrow natives to serve on wintering
voyages in the eastern Beaufort Sea, a number of Point Hope Eskimos moved
to Point Barrow to hunt for the Pacific Steam Whaling Company, and Eskimos
from the Seward Peninsula and the rivers that drain into Kotzebue Sound moved
to the Point Hope area to fill the void at the shore stations there.

At Point Hope the stations were mostly clustered about six miles east of the
native village, and that settlement comprised so many persons of different native
groups and foreign nationalities that the polyglot community became known as

"Jabbertown." By winter 1897–98 there were thirteen small stations in operation within fifty miles of Point Hope.[63]

The price of baleen was very high in the last years of the nineteenth century and the first years of the twentieth. At first the Eskimos worked for very little pay, receiving such things as tobacco, lead, flour, matches, rifles, and ammunition, and the stations were very profitable, but as more stations were set up and as competition increased among them, so did the natives' pay, and the cost of running a station rose as high as $20,000 per year. The shore stations, as well as a number of entrepreneurial Eskimo whaling captains, outfitted several whaling crews. Consequently the wages rose for the native whalemen, who were, in effect, paid a full year's supplies to reserve their labor for the spring whaling season. By 1890 several wealthy Eskimos at Point Barrow had wooden houses "of a civilized type" with iron cooking stoves.[64]

This in turn stimulated and skewed the trade with the natives of the interior. The market for whalebone collapsed in 1908, but the news had not yet reached the North. That year Vilhjalmur Stefansson described the peculiar development in native-to-native trade, when he encountered a group of native traders who were returning to Point Barrow from their summer rendezvous at Niġliq in the Colville River delta.

> This camp turned out to be returned traders who had been to the Colville and even to Flaxman Island to exchange ammunition, flour, tea, cloth, and other commodities—which they get cheaply at Point Barrow—for skins of caribou, mountain sheep and foxes. At Point Barrow these men work for the Cape Smythe Whaling & Trading Company, and for other white and Eskimo whalers. Some of the Eskimo at Point Barrow now carry on whaling on a large scale, maintaining as many as five or six boat crews. Irrespective of whether their employers are white or Eskimo, these men get each year as wages about two hundred dollars' worth of supplies. . . . The whaling season in the spring is six weeks. . . . For all the rest of the year the men have nothing to do . . . and can go wherever they like, while their employers must not only pay them a years' wage for six weeks work, but also furnish them houses to live in, usually, and rations for the entire year.

Stefansson continued with an analysis of the strange price structure at Point Barrow, where the whaling stations virtually gave firearms and food to the Eskimos in return for their participation in the station's spring whale hunt.

> Of course the men are expected to get their own fresh meat, which they do by seal and walrus hunting, and by cutting in the whales,—only the bone (balleen)

[*sic*] of which goes to their employers. The employer supplies them with cloth for garments, and such suitable provisions as flour, tea, beans, rice, and even condensed milk, canned meats and fruits. Each man each year gets, among other things, a new rifle with loading tools and ammunition. The result is that firearms are probably nowhere in the world cheaper than they are at Point Barrow . . . [where] you could buy a new Winchester rifle of any type, with loading tools, five hundred rounds or so of smokeless powder ammunition, and a considerable quantity of powder, lead, and primers for five dollars in money; had you bought the same articles wholesale at the factory in New Haven, the price would have been in the neighborhood of twenty dollars. . . . The reason for all this is that whaling was . . . so fabulously profitable an industry that the whaling companies cared scarcely at all what they paid for the services as long as they got the whales.

And the odd environment at Point Barrow in turn had odd effects at the native trade rendezvous at Niġliq in the Colville River delta.

The pay-day of the Point Barrow Eskimo comes in the spring, and their employer hands them out rifles, ammunition, cloth, provisions, and various things which the people scarcely know what to do with. So they load them into their skin boats and take them east along the coast to sell them at any point in the Colville or at Flaxman Island. To give some idea of the scale of prices it is worth while to say that one of the men whom we met returned with ten deerskins, which was all he had received in the Colville River for a boat-load of supplies consisting of two new rifles, two cases of smokeless powder ammunition for these, twenty-five pounds of powder and a corresponding supply of lead and shot, three bolts of cloth, a case of carpenter tools, some camp gear, three hundred pounds of flour, sixty pounds of good tea, two boxes of tobacco, and various other articles too numerous to mention. The ten caribou skins were of varying quality. The best of them were worth that year about five dollars apiece, and the total value of the ten skins could not have been more than thirty dollars. In other words, had this same Eskimo stayed at Point Barrow during the summer and been able to board a whaling ship with thirty dollars in his pocket, he could have bought ten deerskins of a corresponding quality, had they been carried by the ship, although of course the ships carry only fairly good skins, averaging much better than the ten which he had secured in the Colville.[65]

Earlier Stefansson wrote, "Even after spending a whole summer on the trading journey and paying such prices as this for skins, the Barrow traders seemed pretty well pleased if they could only hear of some rival who had got fewer skins for his boatload than they had."[66]

Stefansson also reported about the Eskimos' perception of their responsibilities as wage laborers for the whaling stations.

> The wage idea such as they have is quite different from ours. Indeed, this might be considered as our idea misunderstood. . . . A concrete instance I know of illustrates a variant of this idea. The man Kuala was hired on these terms: he was furnished fifteen (or twenty) sacks of flour, besides rice, beans, tea, coal oil, etc., a new rifle, and a thousand cartridges, tent material, etc., and promised certain things at the end of the year, if he should do as follows: trap energetically with (fifteen) traps furnished for the purpose, and deliver all fox skins, half his deerskins, and the saddles of all deer and sheep killed, to his employer.
>
> *Unalike* [an Eskimo] trapped six foxes and sold the skins, ate the saddles of all deer killed, and used all deer and sheepskins, in fact, willfully and openly broke every item in his agreement. Now he expects to receive, and his neighbors expect he will receive, the things promised to him at the end of the year.
>
> These views of wages and bargains have been fostered, perhaps engendered by whalers and with other white men who have been so dependent on the service of Eskimo that they have put up with anything. A man who tried to do differently would become known as a "bad man" and the object of an informal boycott.[67]

With such an abundance of foreign trade goods flooding the Bering Strait region, a similar development took place in Chukotka. "At the mouth of the Anadyr," Waldemar Bogoras wrote, "American wares are bartered away by the Chukchee for commodities that, according to our scale of prices, are worth less than what is paid to the whalers for them. One rifle is sold for from 20 to 30 pieces of brick-tea, i.e., 8 to 12 rubles; one whale-boat, for 70 pieces of brick tea, 30 pounds of sugar, 20 pounds of tobacco, — in all, about 50 rubles. Smaller articles, such as powder, percussion-caps, cotton goods, are bought by the Cossacks at still cheaper rates. The reason is that in former times the Russians did not accept whalebone, and set on their wares high prices in peltries; so that the Maritime natives who barter at present for American wares with whalebone are accustomed to regard them as of lesser value in comparison with Russian wares."[68]

15

End of the Century

THE GOLD RUSHES

In the very last years of the nineteenth century the structure of the trade at Bering Strait changed yet again, a result of the massive invasion of foreigners seeking gold. During the 1870s a trickle of prospectors and traders had entered the Yukon, men who occasionally worked for—or in competition with—the Alaska Commercial Company. In the 1880s and early 1890s, miners made a series of small strikes near the Alaska-Canada boundary—at the same time that the Alaska Commercial Company and its competitors introduced several larger stern wheelers to supply their posts on the river.[1]

But the year 1896 marked the end of the region's relative isolation—and by then there may have been as many as 1,000 miners working on the river—when miners found pay dirt on Bonanza Creek in the Klondike, near the Alaska-Canada boundary. That winter, word of their success spread throughout the local area, which was soon completely staked with mining claims that yielded big returns. It was said that the average yield per claim in 1897 was $600,000.

After the Yukon broke up in spring 1897, many of the miners headed downriver to St. Michael to take passage south. In 1897 the riverboats of the Alaska Commercial Company and the North American Transportation and Trading Company are reported to have descended the river carrying a ton and a half of gold. The news broke to the outside world when the ACC's steamer *Excelsior* reached San Francisco on July 14 with more than $500,000 of gold aboard. Three days later the NAT&TC's *Portland* was off Seattle with $964,000, and the rush was on. That summer twenty steamers left West Coast ports for Alaska and the Yukon, and 10,000 persons are reported to have left Seattle alone. The stampeders reached the Klondike by several routes. Many boomers marched over the mountains from the Pacific via Chilcoot Pass; others went down the Mac-kenzie via the "all Canadian route" and over the mountains to the upper Yukon; some descended the Mackenzie and ascended the Rat River via the old fur trade route; and large numbers took passage to St. Michael and went up the Yukon in boats.[2]

The Klondike gold rush was at its peak in 1898. That year 20,000 "98ers" passed through St. Michael, and prospectors roamed widely throughout the en-tire region. Several observers agreed that "speculators and transportation com-panies had conspired to broadcast to the world an endless bonanza in the Klon-dike. Thus lured, the unwary and inexperienced came in droves to buy worthless claims."

These frantic searches led to a spurious gold rush in the Kotzebue drainage in 1898, when 800 miners wintered on the Kobuk River. By spring 1899 it was clear to the prospectors in the Kotzebue area that there was little or no gold to be found there, but this realization coincided with a report that three men had staked claims on Anvil Creek, thirteen miles west of Cape Nome on the south coast of the Seward Peninsula. Many of the Kotzebue prospectors headed to Nome, as did 8,000 from the Klondike. The lucky ones found gold by washing it from the beach sands there, taking out $2 million that year alone. It was said that digging gold from Nome's beaches was easier than stealing it. That winter Nome had a population of 5,000, including twenty drinking establishments. Shortly thereafter gold was discovered in the Tanana River drainage, leading to the founding of the town of Fairbanks, and miners made another strike on the Yukon near Ruby in 1907.

In the last decade of the nineteenth century the population of Alaska was esti-mated to have doubled, reaching more than 60,000. By then the development of a large non-native population that had taken up residence in the region led to the establishment of a number of general merchandise stores in settlements at coastal points from St. Michael to Kotzebue, at several places in the Yukon and Kobuk watersheds, and throughout the Seward Peninsula.[3]

The impact of the gold rushes was felt even in Chukotka. Waldemar Bogoras noted that it was forcing another change in the natives' trade on the Chukchi Peninsula by creating a market for the natives' crafts.

At the present time the chief source of income of the natives are [reindeer] fawn skins, which are much needed by the American [gold rush] miners for making garments; also skins of full-grown reindeer for sleeping bags, ready-made garments even of poor quality, and, most of all, various kinds of seal-skin boots, which are used both by the whaling-crews and by the miners. Asiatic and American natives sell these boots by the thousand every summer; but the demand keeps increasing, and in 1901 the price at Indian Point was a sack of flour per pair.

The chief places for trade continue to be [Cape Dezhnev], and especially Indian Point. . . . Two or three native traders in both places have acquired year by year a larger amount of native products, until finally they are able to obtain by exchange each summer a sufficient amount of European wares to last for the trade of the whole year. They have even bought wooden storehouses brought on purpose from San Francisco. At the present time the whole number of such storehouses on the Pacific shore is fourteen.[4]

DECLINE OF THE CROSS–BERING STRAIT NATIVE TRADE

In this time of swift change, the volume of the cross–Bering Strait native trade declined steeply because the whalers and traders had by then largely usurped the role of middlemen: by working on both coasts they achieved what Wrangell, Tebenkov, and Zagoskin had advocated for the Russian-American Company decades before. In fact, a few American traders had begun carrying beaver pelts from San Francisco to trade with the Chukchi. "At the present time," wrote Waldemar Bogoras, "the American Eskimo have not enough peltries and sealskins to trade with the Asiatic natives, because all such things go to the local white traders."[5]

The American trade even undercut the Russian merchants, Bogoras wrote:

American wares [on the Chukchi Peninsula] are generally twice as cheap as those brought from the interior of Siberia. Even those brought from Vladivostok by sea cannot compete with them, because most of them are of American origin, and have come by a more circuitous route. American granulated sugar forms an exception. It is inferior to the well-refined, hard lump sugar of the Russians. American cutlery is not always so well adapted to the uses of the natives as are the rough strong knives made for this purpose in Yakutsk, Sredne-Kolymsk, Markova, etc. Moreover whalers do not trade in brick-tea, because they do not visit any Chinese or southern Siberian ports. . . .

After the native stock of whalebone became exhausted, the whalers began to accept instead walrus ivory and the skins of white foxes and of black and polar bears. Other Asiatic peltries, such as those of red and cross foxes and of wolves, also skins from America, like the beaver and marten, are taken to the Russian fairs because they fetch a much higher price in Asia than would be paid by the whalers.

But the Americans' trade was still very profitable. Bogoras listed the prices that trade goods were fetching on the coast of the Chukchi Peninsula at the end of the nineteenth century. "In trading with the whalers, a storehouse that is worth $100 in San Francisco, is sold for 100 slabs of whalebone (about 400 pounds), worth from $2.50 to $3.50 per pound; i.e., for $1000-$1400. A second-hand whaleboat, with equipment, is sold for 20–30 slabs of whalebone, or from $200 to $420; a shotgun or a Winchester rifle with reloading tools, for 4–6 slabs; a small box of chewing-tobacco (6 ¼ pounds), for 2 pairs of boots; a keg of black molasses, for 1–2 pairs of boots; an embroidered garment, to a slab of whalebone; etc."[6]

Shortly after the turn of the century, merchants in Nome began to outfit small schooners, sending them throughout the region, from Nunivak Island to Point Barrow and beyond, as well as to the Chukchi Peninsula, trading the usual commodities in return for furs, ivory, whalebone, and native clothing. Although a few Asian Eskimos continued to cross Bering Strait in their umiaqs, it was now to visit the new town of Nome with its huge supply of trade goods, rather than the trade fairs in Kotzebue Sound or Port Clarence. These native traders themselves sold furs, clothing, boots, walrus ivory, and curios to the large community of foreigners in Nome.

THE BEGINNING OF STABILITY

As the twentieth century drew near, the chaos and disruption that had beset the region began to abate. The American and Russian patrols in the area did in fact force a decline in alcohol trade in the last decades of the century, making it more difficult for traders to sell alcohol with impunity. At the same time many of the whalemen concluded that it was simply not in their best interest to trade alcohol to the natives. By 1901 only two whaleships regularly traded alcohol out of the ten that visited Indian Point. This came about because of a sincere spirit of temperance on the part of a number of captains and hard-and-fast rules against the trade by some companies, particularly the Pacific Steam Whaling Company and the Alaska Commercial Company. But by then, of course, the natives knew how to distill their own alcohol.

In the last years of the nineteenth century a number of the shore whaling stations went out of business because of the scarcity of whales, and most of the rest closed after the market for whalebone collapsed. But those shore whalers who remained—at Point Hope, Point Barrow, and one or two other places—actually became forces for stability. These persons, plus the presence of schoolteachers and missionaries who arrived in the 1890s at Point Barrow, Point Hope, Kotzebue, Cape Prince of Wales, Port Clarence, St. Lawrence Island, St. Michael,

Figure 15.1. Cape Dezhnev traders visiting Nome, ca. 1903. In 1899, when the town of Nome was established on the south coast of Alaska's Seward Peninsula, natives from throughout the region began to visit it, rather than native trade rendezvous sites, to acquire manufactured goods. Here natives from Cape Dezhnev, having crossed Bering Strait in their umiaq, are in Nome's Snake River, probably embarking on their return journey. Beverly Dobbs Collection, Special Collections, UW26276, University of Washington Libraries, Seattle.

Tanana, Fort Yukon, and other settlements, exerted a positive influence as the century drew to a close.[7]

CONCLUSION

The vigorous intercontinental fur trade that Eliab Grimes and the crew of the *General San Martín* encountered at Bering Strait in 1819 had existed for only thirty years and was itself an outgrowth of the Russian expansion into northeast-ernmost Asia. Thirty years after Grimes's visit, foreign fleets reached the region, and the trade among natives grew because of the increased availability of manu-factured goods—but at a severe cost. The latter half of the nineteenth century was highly stressful and destructive for the native societies of the region: the ready availability of alcohol, the introduction of foreign diseases, and the suppression of the whale and walrus populations, with the collapse of the caribou and reindeer populations, together forced the native populations into steep decline and resulted in the outright elimination of several Eskimo nations, while those that remained scrambled to adapt to situations they had never before encountered.

As the second half of the nineteenth century wore on, a vast amount of foreign trade goods became available to the inhabitants of the region, and to seize these new trading opportunities, the natives changed their trade routes and the locations of their trade fairs. The Sheshalik rendezvous was moved to a place in Kotzebue Sound for easier contact with the ships, and Port Clarence, Indian Point, Cape Dezhnev, Point Hope, Icy Cape, Wainwright Inlet, and Point Barrow took on new importance as sites that offered access to ships and hence to manufactured goods. Wage employment became available both aboard the whaleships and at shore whaling stations.

These changes were felt far beyond the Bering Strait region. At the Ostrovnoe fair on the Maly Aniui River in Chukotka the supply of American furs declined drastically, and in western arctic Canada, Fort McPherson, the Hudson's Bay Company's post on the Peel River, lost furs to the changing trade patterns on the north coast of Alaska, where many more furs were now going to the stations and to the ships at Point Barrow.

Although the whaling industry collapsed in the early years of the twentieth century, as World War I approached, prices for furs were rising, causing the natives to return to a closer involvement with the fur trade as their primary source of income. This in turn led to a dispersal of the population from the main settlements and helped to create a number of small independent trading posts throughout the region. These factors, along with the rise of Nome and Kotzebue as population centers and trans-shipment points, once again changed the nature of the arctic fur trade.

Appendix: The Introduction of Firearms to the Eskimos of the Bering Strait Region

There is disagreement about when the Eskimos of Bering Strait first obtained firearms. In 1820 Midshipman Karl Karlovich Gillesem (Hillsen) reported that the Buckland River Eskimos (Kaŋiġmiut) used firearms in their encounter with Shishmaryov and the party from the *Blagonamerenny* at Elephant Point. Gillesem stated that a few of the Eskimos possessed muskets and that they wished to trade for gunpowder and lead. He also described an incident wherein Lazarev's pistol was accidentally discharged into an Eskimo's face. Furthermore, Gillesem recounted that as the Russians rowed toward their ship in their longboat, the Eskimos fired their guns at them and the Russians returned the fire with their falconet. Neither Aleksei Lazarev nor Nikolai Shishmaryov mentioned these details.[1]

Regarding the possibility that the Buckland River Eskimos already possessed firearms in 1820, Ernest S. Burch, Jr., has pointed out that the Eskimos of the same region were ignorant of firearms four years earlier (1816) when Kotzebue visited the area. Kotzebue described a tense encounter with the Eskimos at Shishmaref Inlet in 1816: "I myself threatened them with my gun, pointing it sometimes at one, and sometimes at another; but this had no effect on them; they laughed heartily, and only waited for more troops to attempt a serious attack upon us. As our firearms, with which they were wholly unacquainted gave us superiority, and protected us from every danger, we patiently bore all their provocations." Later, near the mouth of the Nugnugaluktuk River in Goodhope Bay, he wrote, "I observed a snipe, and wishing to know if my companions [the Eskimos] were acquainted with fire-arms . . . I was induced to shoot it. The sound occasioned the greatest fright, they looked at each other, not knowing whether to stay or fly. . . . The dead snipe . . . inspired . . . the greatest respect for the [gun], and they could not get over their astonishment." As we have seen from Eliab Grimes's report to John Ebbets about the 1819 cruise, the only firearms that were reported to have been traded from the *General San Martín* were a pair of old pistols, somewhere in the North Pacific.[2]

Gillesem's account of his voyage in the Pacific seems to be reliable in many other details—and in some cases can be verified by the other reports—but his mention of the Eskimos possessing firearms in Kotzebue Sound cannot be confirmed. Gillesem's narrative was published twenty-seven years after the event, and he may have written his account some years after the voyage took place. In the passage of time, it seems probable that Gillesem confused some of the details of the encounter with the Buckland River Eskimos because in his description of events in 1820 he mentions meeting American trading brigs three times (in Kotzebue Sound, in Novo-Arkhangelsk, and in Hawaii) and apparently recalled having met two separate vessels. In fact, all three encounters were with the *Pedlar* (which he does not identify by name). In the Kotzebue Sound and Hawaiian encounters he identifies the brig's captain as Pigot (who was actually the *Pedlar*'s supercargo), but in the Novo-Arkhangelsk encounter the brig's captain is correctly identified as Meek. My earlier references to Eskimos possessing firearms in the incident in 1820 were based on Gillesem's account.[3]

In 1826 and 1827, when the Beechey expedition was in the Bering Strait region, no Eskimos were reported to have possessed firearms. Nevertheless, firearms had undoubtedly been working their way toward the Bering Strait region. Kotzebue noted that a native near Cape Dezhnev had a musket, and at St. Lawrence Bay he met a Chukchi from Mechigmensky Bay with a musket in "miserable condition." He assumed that the natives had acquired firearms from Russian traders—presumably via one of the trading centers in northeastern Asia. At that date there must have been very few firearms on the Chukchi Peninsula because Fedor Petrovich Litke, who surveyed its eastern shore in 1828, stated that the Chukchi did not have firearms and pointed out that it was forbidden to sell these weapons to them at the trade fairs.[4]

It is doubtful that firearms had reached Bering Strait from the east. In 1820 the British trading posts in the Mackenzie watershed were located too far away to have been the source of the guns. On the assumption that it is unlikely that any trading vessels had preceded Kotzebue's ship to Bering Strait, the only probable source for the muskets would have been via native trade, north from the Okhotsk Sea region. The first recorded sale of a musket to an Eskimo in the Bering Strait region was in 1820 at King Island. Because the Russian-American Company did not sell firearms or ammunition to the northern natives, the next firearms probably reached the natives of Bering Strait after 1848, when the British fleet searching for Sir John Franklin was operating in the region and the whaling and trading fleets began annual cruises to Bering Strait.[5]

CHRONOLOGY

1632	Yakutsk is founded on the Lena River.
1639	Udsk is founded on the coast of the Sea of Okhotsk.
1644	Nizhne Kolymsk is founded on the lower Kolyma River.
1648	Semyon Dezhnev and associates, on a voyage from the Kolyma River to the Anadyr River, are the first foreigners to reach Cape Dezhnev, the easternmost point of Asia.
	Okhotsk is founded.
1649–1764	Anadyr fort is in operation.
1670	The Hudson's Bay Company receives its charter.
1689	The first Treaty of Nerchinsk establishes trade relations between Russia and China on the Mongolian-Siberian border.
1727	The Treaty of Kiakhta delineates the border between the Russian and Chinese empires and establishes both a caravan trade and a frontier trade.
1728	Vitus Bering and crew pass through Bering Strait on a voyage from Kamchatka.
	The trading centers Kiakhta and Mai-Mai-Ch'eng are built on the Russian-Chinese border.
1731	Dmitry Pavlutsky carries out his first campaign against the Chukchi.
1732	Mikhail Gvozdyov and Ivan Fyodorov explore the Bering Strait region and reach King Island.
1741	Bering and Chirikov reach the Alaskan mainland.
1743–99	Expeditions from Kamchatka and Okhotsk hunt for furs in the Commander and Aleutian islands and mainland Alaska.
1763–65	Nikolai Daurkin explores the Chukchi Peninsula and visits Big Diomede Island.
1764	The end of armed hostilities between the Russians and Chukchi.
	Anadyr fort is abandoned.
1778	Peter Pond crosses the height of land at Methye Portage into the Mackenzie watershed.

1778–79	Captain James Cook's expedition charts the shores of northwestern North America, the Bering Strait region, and northwestern Alaska.
1779	Captain James Cook's men discover that the sea otter pelts they acquired for trifles on the Northwest Coast fetch phenomenal sums in Canton, China. Ivan Kobelev explores the Chukchi Peninsula and visits the Diomede Islands.
1783	John Ledyard's unauthorized account of Cook's voyage to the Northwest Coast helps to bring American merchants into the trans-Pacific fur trade.
1789	Alexander Mackenzie descends the Mackenzie River to the Arctic Ocean. The Ostrovnoe trade fair is established on the Maly Aniui River, 800 miles west of Bering Strait.
1791–93	Joseph Billings's expedition explores Chukotka and Bering Strait.
1795–1810	Regular trade exchanges between the Point Barrow and Mackenzie Eskimos begin at Barter Island.
1799	The Russian-American Company is granted a twenty-year charter by the tsar.
1804	Fort Good Hope is established on the Mackenzie River.
1810	The supply of sea otter pelts is declining on the Northwest Coast of North America.
1812	War of 1812 results in a British blockade of American ports and capture of American merchantmen.
1815	Americans return to the trans-Pacific trade.
1816–17	Otto von Kotzebue explores the Bering Strait region and charts Kotzebue Sound.
1817	José de San Martín crosses the Andes and defeats a Spanish army, leading to Chile's independence.
1818	An American merchant fleet reaches Coquimbo, Chile. John Ebbets purchases the brig *General San Martín*. Eliab Grimes takes command and sails to Petropavlovsk, Kamchatka.
1819	Pyotr Rikord is appointed commandant of Kamchatka. William J. Pigot, William Heath Davis, John Ebbets, and Thomas Meek conclude a contract with Rikord and Dobell, acting for the Russian government, for exclusive rights to conduct a whale fishery on the coast of Siberia for ten years, commencing in 1821. Eliab Grimes returns to Petropavlovsk with the *General San Martín*. He carries out a commercial reconnaissance of the Bering Strait region.
1820	William J. Pigot aboard the brig *Pedlar* visits Bering Strait to confirm the results of the *General San Martín*'s cruise of 1819. The tsar orders eastern Siberia closed to foreigners and nullifies the whaling contract with Pigot, Davis, Ebbets, and Meek.
1820–21	Vasiliev and Shishmaryov carry out explorations in the Bering Strait region.
1821	The tsar issues an *ukaz* closing the shores of the northern North Pacific to foreign vessels. This is followed by separate *ukaz*, granting the Russian-American Company another twenty-year charter.

The Hudson's Bay Company and the North West Company merge.

1821–22 Etholen and Khramchenko explore the Bering Strait region for the Russian-American Company.

1822 The *Apollon* reaches Russian America, carrying the orders that close Russian America and northeastern Asia to foreign trade.

1824–25 The Russian government concludes conventions with the United States and Great Britain, confirming the eastern boundary of Russian America at the 141st meridian west of Greenwich and granting rights of commerce to American and British vessels for ten years.

1826 Captain John Franklin and crew descend the Mackenzie River and proceed west, along the Arctic coast, as far as Return Reef.

1826–27 Frederick William Beechey is sent (but fails) to rendezvous with John Franklin in Kotzebue Sound and carries out explorations in the Bering Strait region and northwestern Alaska.

1828 Fyodor Petrovich Litke charts the shores of the Chukchi Peninsula.

1830 A. K. Etholen surveys Bering Strait and Norton Sound for fur trade potential.

1831–32 M. D. Tebenkov surveys the Bering Strait region.

1832 Kolmakovsky Redoubt is founded on Kuskokwim River.

1833 M. D. Tebenkov in the bark *Urup* founds Mikhailovsky Redoubt near the Yukon delta and trades in the Bering Strait region.

1834 Aleksandr Kashevarov in the schooner *Kvikhpak* delivers supplies to Mikhailovsky and trades in the Bering Strait region.
The brig *Okhotsk* delivers supplies to Mikhailovsky.
Sledge Island Eskimos attack Mikhailovsky.

1835 The brig *Polifyom* resupplies Mikhailovsky and trades in Bering Strait region.

1836 D. F. Chernov and M. D. Tebenkov in the brig *Polifyom* resupply Mikhailovsky and trade in Bering Strait region.
By this date the Unalakleet outpost is in operation.
Aleksandr Kashevarov in the schooner *Kvikhpak* visits Mikhailovsky.

1837 Peter Warren Dease and Thomas Simpson chart the north coast of Alaska between Franklin's and Beechey's farthest advances.
The brig *Polifyom* resupplies Mikhailovsky and trades in the Bering Strait region.

1838 The *Polifyom* resupplies Mikhailovsky and takes the Kashevarov expedition to Cape Lisburne.
Aleksandr Kashevarov's expedition rounds Point Barrow.
The *Polifyom* collects the Kashevarov expedition at Chamisso Island.

1838–39 Smallpox is epidemic in the lower and middle Yukon and Kuskokwim drainages, killing as much as half of the native population.

1839 The *Polifyom* resupplies Mikhailovsky and trades in Bering Strait region.
The Nulato outpost is established and later burned.

1840	The Hudson's Bay Company establishes Peel's River Post (later called Fort McPherson) near the Mackenzie delta.
	The *Polifyom* resupplies Mikhailovsky and trades in Bering Strait region.
1841	The brig *Promysl* resupplies Mikhailovsky and trades in Bering Strait region.
	The Nulato outpost is permanently manned.
1842	The brig *Okhotsk* resupplies Mikhailovsky, trades in Bering Strait region, and attempts to survey Kotzebue Sound.
1843	The brig *Okhotsk* resupplies Mikhailovsky, trades in Bering Strait region, and attempts to survey Kotzebue Sound.
	L. A. Zagoskin ascends Yukon from Nulato.
1844	The brig *Okhotsk* resupplies Mikhailovsky, trades in Bering Strait region, and attempts to survey the mouth of the Anadyr River.
	Ivan Zakharov ascends Yukon from Nulato.
1845	Sir John Franklin's expedition departs from England in search of a northwest passage.
	John Bell of the Hudson's Bay Company crosses the height of land between the Mackenzie and Yukon drainages and descends the Porcupine River.
	The brig *Okhotsk* resupplies Mikhailovsky and trades in the Bering Strait region.
	Ivan Zakharov ascends the Yukon from Nulato.
1846	The *Okhotsk* resupplies Mikhailovsky, trades in Bering Strait region, and surveys Big Diomede for an outpost site.
	The Hudson's Bay Company establishes La Pierre's House, at the headwaters of the Bell River, to serve as a halfway house when Fort Yukon is built.
1846–50	Vasily Maksimovich Deriabin makes several trading expeditions upriver from Nulato.
1847	The brig *Okhotsk* resupplies Mikhailovsky and surveys the mouth of the Anadyr River for its trade potential.
	The Hudson's Bay Company's post, Fort Yukon, is founded by Alexander Hunter Murray more than one hundred miles inside Russian America.
1848	HMS *Herald* reaches Kotzebue Sound and returns south, having failed to meet HMS *Plover*.
	Thomas Roys in the bark *Superior* discovers the Bering Strait whaling grounds.
	The brig *Veliky Kniaz Konstantin* resupplies Mikhailovsky and trades in the Bering Strait region.
1848–49	HMS *Plover* winters in Plover Bay on the Chukchi Peninsula.
1849	The *Herald*, with supplies, meets the *Plover* at Chamisso Island in Kotzebue Sound. The yacht *Nancy Dawson* joins them in northwestern Alaska.
	Pullen's boat expedition travels from Wainwright Inlet to the Mackenzie River.
	The brig *Promysl* resupplies Mikhailovsky.
	Approximately fifty whaleships cruise in Bering Strait region.

1849–50	HMS *Plover* winters near Chamisso Island.
1850	The *Herald* resupplies *Plover* in Kotzebue Sound.
	HMS *Investigator* rounds Point Barrow and enters the Beaufort Sea.
	HMS *Enterprise* reaches Point Barrow and returns south.
	The brig *Okhotsk* resupplies Mikhailovsky.
1850–51	The *Plover* winters in Port Clarence.
1851	Vasily Deriabin and Lieutenant Barnard are murdered by Koyukon at Nulato.
	HMS *Daedalus* resupplies the *Plover* at Port Clarence.
	The *Enterprise* rounds Point Barrow and enters the Beaufort Sea.
	The bark *Kniaz Menshikov* resupplies Mikhailovsky, trades in the Bering Strait region, and visits Port Clarence.
1851–52	The *Plover* winters in Port Clarence.
1852	HMS *Amphitrite* resupplies *Plover* at Port Clarence.
	The brig *Okhotsk* resupplies Mikhailovsky and trades in the Bering Strait region.
	More than 200 whaleships cruise in Bering Strait region.
1852–53	The *Plover* winters at Point Barrow.
1853	The *Amphitrite* resupplies the *Plover* at Port Clarence.
	The bark *Kadiak* resupplies Mikhailovsky and visits Port Clarence.
1853–54	The *Plover* winters at Point Barrow
	The *Enterprise* winters in Camden Bay.
	HMS *Rattlesnake* winters at Port Clarence.
1854	HMS *Trincomalee* resupplies the *Plover* at Port Clarence.
	The *Enterprise* reaches Port Clarence.
	All British ships leave the Western Arctic, concluding the Franklin Search in the west.
	The bark *Kadiak* resupplies Mikhailovsky and scouts Kotzebue Sound for an outpost site.
1854–55	During the Crimean War an Anglo-French force assaults Petropavlovsk, Kamchatka.
1855	The American bark *Cyane* resupplies Mikhailovsky.
	USS *Vincennes* carries out surveys on the coast of the Chukchi Peninsula and in the Chukchi Sea.
1855–57	Very few whaleships cruise in the Bering Strait region. The focus of whaling activity is in the Okhotsk Sea.
1856	The American steam-auxiliary bark *Astoria* resupplies Mikhailovsky.
1857	F. K. Verman in the bark *Kniaz Menshikov* resupplies Mikhailovsky.
1858	The steam-auxiliary bark *Imperator Aleksandr II* (ex. *Astoria*) resupplies Mikhailovsky.
	The whaling fleet returns to the Bering Strait region.
1859	The bark *Kniaz Menshikov* resupplies Mikhailovsky.
1859–60	The whaleships *Wailua* and *Cleone* winter in Plover Bay on the Chukchi Peninsula.

1860	The *Imperator Aleksandr II* resupplies Mikhailovsky.
1861	The *Imperator Aleksandr II* resupplies Mikhailovsky.
1861–62	The American whaleship *Coral* winters in Plover Bay.
1862	The bark *Nakhimov* (ex. *Cyane*) resupplies Mikhailovsky.
	The Russian-American Company resumes upriver trading expeditions from Nulato. Ivan Lukin reaches Fort Yukon.
1862–63	The Hawaiian whaling brig *Kohola* winters in St. Lawrence Bay, on the Chukchi Peninsula. The *Zoe* winters in Plover Bay.
1863	The bark *Kniaz Menshikov* resupplies Mikhailovsky.
	A Russian trading expedition goes upriver from Nulato.
1864	J. Hanson in brig *Shelikhov* resupplies Mikhailovsky.
	A Russian trading expedition goes upriver from Nulato.
	The Hudson's Bay Company begins sending trading parties downriver from Fort Yukon as far as Nuklukayet.
1865	The bark *Nakhimov* resupplies Mikhailovsky.
	CSS *Shenandoah* burns 20 whaleships in the Bering Strait region.
1865–67	The Western Union Telegraph Expedition operates in the Bering Strait region.
1866	The steam-auxiliary brig *Veliky Kniaz Konstantin* resupplies Mikhailovsky.
1867	The bark *Kniaz Menshikov* resupplies Mikhailovsky.
	Russia sells Russian America to the United States. Hutchinson, Kohl and Company of San Francisco buys the assets of the Russian-American Company.
1867–77	The period of army rule in Alaska.
1868	Congress creates a customs district for Alaska.
	The Alaska Commercial Company is founded, amalgamating Hutchinson, Kohl and Company and several other groups.
	The Alaska Commercial Company's steam bark *Alexander* (ex. *Imperator Aleksandr II*) visits St. Michael.
1869	The Hudson's Bay Company is forced to cease trading at Fort Yukon.
1869–70	The trading schooner *Hallie Jackson* of San Francisco winters in Plover Bay.
1870	The first cruise of a U.S. revenue cutter to Bering Strait.
1870s–80s	Caribou become extremely scarce in northern and western Alaska.
1870–71	The trading schooner *Hannah B. Bourne* winters in Plover Bay. It is abandoned in the spring.
1871	Thirty-two whaleships are abandoned between Icy Cape and Point Franklin, Alaska. One is successfully salvaged in 1872.
1871–72	Eskimos plunder the whaling wrecks, and many die from drinking the medicine found aboard.
1877–79	The period of Treasury Department rule in Alaska.
1879	The beginning of regular annual patrols to Bering Strait by U.S. revenue cutters.
1879–84	The period of navy rule in Alaska.

1884	Alaska's first Organic Act is passed, establishing civil rule for the Territory of Alaska.
	The first commercial shore whaling station is built at Point Barrow, Alaska.
1887	A commercial shore whaling station is established at Point Hope, Alaska.
1890–91	The beginning of whaleships' wintering voyages at Herschel Island. Winterings by whaleships continue for two decades.
1893	The Hudson's Bay Company abandons La Pierre's House and Rampart House.
1894–95	Fourteen whaleships winter at Herschel Island.
1896	Gold is discovered near the Alaska-Canada boundary on the Yukon River.
1898	The Yukon gold rush brings a massive influx of foreigners and shipping to the Bering Strait region.
1898–99	A spurious gold rush brings 800 miners to overwinter on the Kobuk River.
1899	The founding of Nome, Alaska. A resident fleet of small schooners soon begins to trade throughout the Bering Strait region.

GLOSSARY

arshin   A Russian linear measure equal to 28 inches (approximately 71 cm).

Athapascan   A member of the native North American groups that speak
              Athapascan, including, but not limited to, the Gwich'in, Han, Tanana,
              Koyukon, and Ingalik peoples.

baidar   An open-framed Aleutian boat, the hull of which is made of sea
              mammal hides, often sea lion (*Eumetopius jubatus*) skins.

baidarka   A small Aleutian decked boat, similar to a kayak, with openings for one
              to three paddlers, the hull of which is covered with sea mammal skins.

baidarshchik A boat captain or, in the Russian-American Company, the head of a
              small trading post.

baleen   Also called "whalebone," "bone," or "whale fins." The keratinous plates
              that grow from the upper jaw of baleen whales, with which they filter
              plankton from the water.

bark   A three-masted vessel, square-rigged on the fore and main masts and
              fore-and-aft rigged on the mizzenmast.

barkentine   A three-masted vessel, square-rigged on the foremast and fore-and-aft
              rigged on the main and mizzen masts.

brig   A two-masted vessel square-rigged on both masts; also often used to
              refer to a brigantine, which has a square-rigged foremast and fore-and-
              aft sails on the mainmast.

brigantine   A two-masted vessel square-rigged on the foremast and fore-and-aft
              rigged on the mainmast.

Chukchi   A native group of northeasternmost Asia, which comprised both
              "sedentary" coastal dwellers and nomadic reindeer herders.

Chuvan   A native group of northeastern Asia, descendants of Yukagir and
              Russian parentage.

Cossack   A Siberian military frontiersman in the tsar's service.

Creole   A person of mixed Russian and native parentage.

espontoon	A halberd, a pointed blade with transverse stops at the base, mounted on a pole.
Even	A nomadic people of northeastern Asia, formerly referred to as *Lamut*, who hunted and practiced reindeer husbandry.
Evenk	A widespread native group of northeastern Asia, formerly referred to as *Tungus*.
funt	One-fortieth of a *pud*.
Gwich'in	An Athapascan-speaking people inhabiting the Porcupine River and adjacent regions of the Yukon and Mackenzie drainages.
halberd	A weapon mounted on a pole, the blade of which contains transverse stops at its base.
Han	An Athapascan-speaking people living along the Yukon River near the Alaska-Canada boundary.
hundredweight	A hundredweight (cwt.) was equal to 112 pounds (50.8 kg).
Ingalik	An Athapascan-speaking people living in the lowlands of the upper Kuskokwim River drainage and the Anvik and Innoko rivers, which are tributaries of the lower Yukon River.
Iñupiat	A group of Eskimo nations inhabiting the Seward Peninsula and northern Alaska.
Italian mile	A nautical mile (one degree of latitude) or 1.15 statute miles (approximately 1.85 km).
Julian calendar	In the nineteenth century the Julian ("old style") calendar, in use in Russia, was twelve days behind the Gregorian ("new style") calendar, in use in Europe. Thus, for example, July 10, 1820, in the Julian calendar was July 22 in the Gregorian calendar.
kamleika	A term, perhaps originating in Kamchatka, often used by the Russians to denote rainwear made from sea mammal intestines.
Koryak	A native group of northeastern Asia. Some Koryak were reindeer herders; others were sedentary coastal dwellers who fished and hunted marine mammals.
Koyukon	An Athapascan-speaking people inhabiting the Koyukuk River drainage.
labret	An item of personal adornment, piercing the lower lip, often worn by Iñupiaq males.
Lamut	See Even.
Made Beaver	Or MB. A unit of measurement used by the Hudson's Bay Company to equate the value of furs and trade goods in relation to the value of a prime beaver pelt.
musketoon	A short, large-bore musket.
new style	A date listed according to the Gregorian calendar.
odinochka	A small outpost manned by one trader.
old style	See Julian calendar.
Ostrovnoe	The trade fair established in 1789 on the Maly Aniui River, a tributary of the Kolyma River.

ostrog	A Russian fortified outpost or stronghold.
palma	A single-edged knife used alone or mounted on a shaft. It was made by native blacksmiths and traded throughout northeastern Asia and into Alaska.
picul	A Chinese measure of mass equal to 133 ⅓ pounds.
pinnace	A ship's tender, a small craft.
prikashchik	In the Russia-American Company, a clerk in charge of a trading district. Also a supercargo.
promyshlenniki	Frontiersmen, hunters, and entrepreneurs in the Russian conquest and occupation of Siberia.
pud or pood	A Russian measure of mass equal to 36.11 pounds (approximately 16.38 kg). A *pud* comprised forty *funts*.
Sakha	See Yakut.
sazhen	A Russian unit of linear measure equaling 7 feet (approximately 2.134 m).
schooner	A sailing vessel rigged with fore-and-aft sails on all of its two or more masts.
ship	Used to designate any large water-borne vessel or, in referring to the rig of whaleships, to a three-masted vessel, square-rigged on all three masts.
Slavey	An Athapascan-speaking people living in the boreal forest of northwestern Canada near the confluence of the Liard and Mackenzie rivers and western Great Slave Lake.
sotnik	A commander of a *sotnia*, 100 men.
supercargo	A clerk in charge of cargo aboard a merchant vessel.
Tanana	An Athapascan-speaking people inhabiting the watershed of the Tanana River.
Tungus	See Evenk.
verst	A Russian unit of linear measure equaling .66 statute miles (1.07 km).
ukaz	A decree issued by the tsar.
whalebone	See baleen.
Yakut	One of the largest nonindigenous peoples of Siberia, a Turkic people from Central Asia inhabiting the Sakha Republic and adjacent regions. The Yakut raised horses and cattle and in the north part of their range practiced reindeer husbandry. They also were hunters and fishermen.
yasak	Tribute to the tsar, customarily paid in fur, by the native peoples of Siberia and the Urals.
Yukagir	A native group of hunters and fishermen in northeastern Asia.
Yupik	Eskimos of St. Lawrence Island and a few settlements on the coast of the Chukchi Peninsula.
Yup'ik	Eskimos of southwestern Alaska.
zimove	A small winter hut.

NOTES

1. Eliab Grimes to John Ebbets, September 21, 1819. Eliab Grimes Business Letter Book, State Archives of Hawai'i, Honolulu. An earlier version of this chapter appeared in the American Philosophical Society's monograph series in 2005 and is used with its permission.

2. Gibson 1976, 3–5; 1992, 22–23; Malloy 1998, 24–25; Ledyard 1783, 70. These were Spanish dollars, and Ledyard may have overstated the actual price by as much as two-fold. Lower 1978, 34–35; D. A. Wilson 2004. See also E. G. Gray 2007, 104–14.

3. Paul Johnson 1997, 256; Phillips 1961, 290.

4. Gibson 1992, 252.

5. Howay 1973, 105.

6. Collier and Sater 1996, 37.

7. Vagin 1872, 73; Pierce 1990a, 399–400; Howay 1973, 150. I am very grateful to Dr. Katherine Arndt for translations of many of the Russian passages quoted herein.

8. Porter 1932, 280; Pierce 1986, 232–33.

9. Porter 1931, 654; Vagin 1872, 73–75; Howay 1973, 96; Pigot to John Jacob Astor, January 7, 1816, and October 26, 1818, John Jacob Astor Collection, Baker Library, Harvard Business School, Allston, MA. William J. Pigot was probably related to John Ebbets by marriage (Porter 1932, 261, 274).

10. Grimes 1920; MS; Pierce 1990a, 132, 399–400; Malloy 1998, 83, 97, 100–101; Howay 1973, 119–21, 150; Porter 1931, 676, 680; Kotzebue 1821b, 2:195, 198, 203.

11. Cochrane 1824, 1:426; Dobell 1830, 1:314–16, 2:121; H. B. Morse 1926, 3:8, 137, 145; Pierce 1990a, 271–73; Wenger 1984, 26–27; Tikhmenev 1978, 87, 125–28; Stephan 1994, 38.

12. Gibson 1969, 211–12; F. W. Beechey 1831, 238–39, 524–29; Vagin 1872, 39.

13. Pierce 1990a, 400; Vagin 1872, 61–62. Rikord had served under Kruzenshtern and may have met Dobell in 1805 (Dmytryshyn et al. 1989, 67).

14. Vagin 1872, 75. Gregorian calendar date. The Julian calendar date, used in Russia, was June 4.
15. Vagin 1872, 425–27, 441–43; Golder 1917, 111. See also Golder 1917, 16, 113, 140.
16. Vagin 1872, 79.
17. Dmytryshyn et al. 1989, 329–30.
18. Dmytryshyn et al. 1989, xxxiv, li; Vagin 1872, 64–68, 75–84, 86; Tikhmenev 1978, 126–28, 463–65n19; Golder 1917, 16, 17, 39, 105, 107, 111, 113.
     "Under ideal conditions, with the transport available at the time, a trip from St. Petersburg to New Arkhangel [Russian America] could not be completed in under seven months" (Dmytryshyn et al. 1989, liii). After the completion of the transcontinental railroad in the United States in 1869 "the quickest way to get from [St.] Petersburg to Kamchatka was by taking a ship across the Atlantic to New York, a train across America and a second ship across the Pacific" (Reid 2002, 43–44).
19. Efimov 1964, maps 182, 184, 185; Kotzebue 1821b, 1:209–11, 228–29; VanStone 1960, 148.
20. Chamisso 1986, xvii–xviii; Pierce 1965; 1990, 445–46; Daws 1968, 51–52; Kotzebue 1821a, 2:116; 1821b, 2:195, 198, 203; Chamisso 1874, 206–7; 1986, 191–92; Barratt 1988, 155–56n2. Grimes to John Ebbetts, September 21, 1819, Eliab Grimes Business Letter Book. I am grateful to Dr. Ernest S. Burch, Jr., for bringing this document to my attention. A *picul* was a Chinese measure of mass equal to 133 ⅓ pounds.
21. Barratt 1988, 19–25; Pierce 1990a, 435–36; Kotzebue 1821a, 2:148; 1821b, 2:287; Grimes to Rikord, December 15, 1819, Eliab Grimes Business Letter Book; Kotzebue 1821b, 8–9.
22. Based on other analyses of Russian accounts, in earlier publications (Bockstoce 1977a, 6–7; 1988, 2) I incorrectly identified Grimes as "Gray."
23. Eliab Grimes, journal, *General San Martín*, June 29 and 30, 1819, in Eliab Grimes Business Letter Book (hereafter Grimes journal). I have inserted paragraph indentations and some punctuation throughout the letter. Novo-Arkhangelsk is today Sitka, Alaska.
24. Grimes journal, July 4 and 5, 1819.
25. Grimes journal, July 7, 1819; Kotzebue 1821b, 1:195–96; Grimes to John Ebbets, September 21, 1819, Eliab Grimes Business Letter Book. I have added punctuation and capitalizations to the quotations from Grimes's letter to Ebbets here and in subsequent quotations.
     This was the settlement of *Sivuqaq;* today Gambell, Alaska. An umiaq is a large, open-framed Eskimo boat, the hull of which is formed by a covering of hides. The St. Lawrence Island Eskimos covered their boats with walrus hides. See Braund 1988.
     "Sea horse" teeth are walrus tusks. Grimes bought more than 3,300 pounds of walrus ivory. A hundredweight (cwt.) is equal to 112 avoirdupois pounds, or approximately 50.8 kg.
26. Grimes's "Chesmurofs straits" is Shishmaref Inlet, the embayment on the north coast of the Seward Peninsula (66°15′ N, 166°05′ W) about halfway between Bering Strait and Kotzebue Sound. Otto von Kotzebue thought it might have potential as a water-

way to the interior and named it after his lieutenant, Gleb Semyonovich Shishmaryov (Kotzebue 1821b, 199–203; Orth 1967, 867).

27. *Imaqłiq* is Ostrov Ratmanova, Russia, often called "Big Diomede Island." Today the International Date Line runs between Big Diomede and Little Diomede, Alaska, which are about two miles apart.

28. Tebenkov MS.

29. Kotzebue 1821b, 1:204. Grimes's determination of the latitude was accurate within two nautical miles. Cape Krusenstern is officially placed at 68°08′ N (Orth 1967, 546).

30. Eliab Grimes to John Ebbets, September 21, 1819, Eliab Grimes Business Letter Book. Mr. "Dyrkee" (Durkee) was probably the mate of the *General San Martín*. Mr. Durkee was, perhaps, Thomas Durkee, a merchant mariner who operated out of Hawaii at that time (see, for instance, William J. Pigot and John Meek, contract with George Tamoree, June 23, 1820, State Archives of Hawai'i, Honolulu). See also Barman and Watson 2006, 304 (Kaumuali'i, George, Prince).

    At that time the North Magnetic Pole was located in the vicinity of the Boothia Peninsula in arctic Canada. Because of the considerable magnetic variation from true north, in Kotzebue Sound Grimes's "northern shore" was probably the coast of today's Baldwin Peninsula.

31. Burch 1998a, 203, 259–78. Under the term "northwestern Alaska" I include the lands lying west of a line from Norton Bay, on the Bering Sea, to the Colville River delta, on the Beaufort Sea. This area includes the Seward Peninsula and about half of northern Alaska, which roughly coincided with the territories of the Iñupiaqtun-speaking Eskimo nations.

32. The knives were probably *palmas* (see glossary), perhaps made by Evenk (Tungus) blacksmiths.

33. This is the entrance to Kotzebue Sound. Grimes is probably referring to Cape Espenberg.

34. Burch 1998b, 151–62.

35. Grimes had sailed along the face of the York Mountains.

36. The *General San Martín* probably lay off the beach that encloses Brevig Lagoon.

37. Burch 1998b, 162–63; D. J. Ray 1964, 75. In 1827 Captain Frederick William Beechey, aboard HMS *Blossom*, would rediscover this bay and name it in honor of the Duke of Clarence, later King William IV. See chapter 6.

38. Unlike western Alaska, the Chukchi Peninsula, lacking much forested land, yields comparatively few furs (Schweitzer and Golovko 1995, 19–22; CAVM Team 2003).

39. Kotzebue 1821b, 1:262.

40. Grimes first visited the settlement of *Sivuqaq*, today Gambell, Alaska. Cape Anadyr does not appear on modern maps, although on some Russian maps of the eighteenth century it was identified as the southeastern promontory of the Chukchi Peninsula (Efimov 1964, 55, 74). I believe that Grimes is referring to Cape Chukotsky. Lying near the southeast point of the Chukchi Peninsula, it is the nearest continental land to St. Lawrence Island.

    The *General San Martín* may have then visited the settlement of *Qiighwaaq*

(Kivak) near Cape Chukotsky (Krupnik 1993, 30). Grimes was referring to the annual Russian trade fairs that were held at several sites in northeastern Asia, as we shall see in chapter 3.

Whalebone is baleen, the keratinous plates that grow from the upper jaw of baleen whales and with which they filter plankton from the water. Because of its flexibility and durability baleen was highly sought for manufacture into corset stays, among many other uses (Bockstoce 1986, 208, 220, 353). This baleen was probably from a bowhead whale (*Balaena mysticetus*).

41. Grimes to Ebbets, September 21, 1819, Eliab Grimes Business Letter Book.

St. Lawrence Island was named by Vitus Bering, who visited it on St. Lawrence Day, August 10, 1728. In addition to a copy of Kotzebue's map, Grimes also carried a chart of the Bering Strait region that was based on Captain Cook's surveys. On Cook's chart of Bering Strait (Cook and King 1784, vol. 2, between 466 and 467) there are four islands: "Saint Lawrence Island," is in fact only the northwestern tip of St. Lawrence Island. Two others, the "Clerke's Islands" are also part of St. Lawrence Island. Grimes found that the fourth island, "Anderson's Island," does not exist.

Aaron Arrowsmith published a nine-sheet atlas of charts of the Pacific Ocean in 1798, with corrections in 1810 and 1814. The charts were widely used by mariners in the early nineteenth century. The version that Grimes was using indicated an island, "Preobragenia [Transfiguration] of the Russians Charts," a substantial island lying southwest of Saint Matthew Island. The information about this island probably originated from the charts that resulted from Ivan Syndt's voyage of 1764 (Black 2004, 80; Hayes 2001, 80, map 115), one of which was published in London in 1780 (Coxe 1780, between 300 and 301). I am grateful to Andrew David and Susan Danforth for their assistance and information regarding Arrowsmith's charts.

42. Howay 1973, 114; Malloy 1998, 100–101; Ogden 1941, 79; Porter 1931, 1163–64.

43. Kotzebue 1821b, 1:209–11, 228–29.

44. Coxe 1780.

45. Zimmerman 1994.

46. Red, silver, black, and cross foxes are color phases of the red fox (*Vulpes vulpes*), which live in most parts of Alaska. White and blue foxes are color phases of the arctic fox (*Alopex lagopus*). Arctic foxes are found throughout most of the Bering Sea's and Arctic Ocean's coasts and far out on sea ice as well. For a description of these and other marketable furs see chapter 2.

47. Grimes to Ebbets, September 21, 1819, Eliab Grimes Business Letter Book.

The *Sultan* was owned by Boardman and Pope of Boston. A pood, or pud, was a Russian measure of mass equal to 36.11 pounds avoirdupois (approximately 16.38 kg). Grimes acquired the tobacco in Petropavlovsk.

48. Grimes to Ebbets, September 21, 1819, Eliab Grimes Business Letter Book.

Grimes, writing from Petropavlovsk, Kamchatka, refers to a voyage to the Northwest Coast of North America. The net profits from the voyage would have been much less.

49. See chapter 4.

50. Grimes (from Canton) to Dobell (Manila), March 11, 1820, Grimes to Joseph H.

Gardner (Okhotsk), September 21, 1819, Grimes to Meyer and Bruxner (St. Petersburg), September 21, 1819, and Grimes to Ebbets, September 21, 1819, Eliab Grimes Business Letter Book; Lazarev 1950, 214–15; Porter 1932, 281; Pierce 1990a, 399–400; Daws 1968, 55.

51. Grimes to Rikord, December 15, 1819, Eliab Grimes Business Letter Book.

52. Grimes to Pigot, March 10, 1820, and Grimes to Dobell, March 11, 1820, Eliab Grimes Business Letter Book; Howay 1973, 120–21; Malloy 1998, 97.

Grimes reached Boston and sailed again for the Pacific in command of the brig *Inore*, which reached Hawaii in May 1821, having been damaged by a storm. After repairs it was sold to the king of Hawaii. Grimes then took command of the *Eagle* and departed for the coast of California on a smuggling cruise (Howay 1973, 147–48).

53. Porter 1931, 607; Grimes to Pigot, March 10, 1820, Eliab Grimes Business Letter Book. In autumn 1820 Ebbets sailed from New York aboard the *William and John*, reaching Honolulu with a full cargo in April 1821 (Porter 1931, 655). Among other reasons, Astor traveled to Europe for his own health and to seek psychiatric treatment for his eldest son, John Jacob Astor, Jr.

54. Porter 1930, 224–25; 1931, 653; 1932, 282; John Walters MS, 5–7.

The *Pedlar* is listed as the *Pedler* in some sources. The boatswain, or bosun, was a ship's officer, or warrant officer, in charge of sails, rigging, anchors, cables, and all work on deck. A supercargo was a superintendent of a merchant ship's cargo and essentially chartered the vessel that carried it. The supercargo was responsible for all commercial business during a voyage. The ship's captain was responsible for operating the vessel according to the supercargo's directives. I have added punctuation and capitalizations to Walters's manuscript. I am grateful to Dr. Mary Malloy for bringing this manuscript to my attention.

55. Porter 1931, 654; William J. Pigot and John Meek, contract with George Tamore, June 23, 1820, State Archives of Hawai'i, Honolulu; John Walters MS, 9–10.

"The straits" was a term loosely and variously used by nineteenth-century American mariners to include the waters lying between the approximate latitudes of St. Lawrence Island (63° N) and Bering Strait (66° N) (Bockstoce and Batchelder 1978a, 260).

56. Grewingk 2003, 213; Lazarev 1950, 383–84. Vasiliev records the date as July 13, which I have converted to the "new style" (Gregorian) calendar. I am grateful to Ethan Pollock for the translation of *Blagonamerenny*.

57. John Walters MS, 10.

58. Khramchenko MS, 93; Black 2004, 260.

59. John Walters MS, 12.

60. Nikolai Shishmaryov listed his dates per the Julian (old style) calendar, which in the nineteenth century was twelve days behind the Gregorian (new style) calendar. I have added twelve days to Shishmaryov's dates to convert them to the Gregorian date; thus Shishmaryov's July 10 is given here as July 22. Shishmarev MS, microfilm reel 15, item 101, Shur Collection, Alaska and Polar Regions Department, University of Alaska, Fairbanks. The original is in the Russian State Naval Archive (RGAVMF), fond 203, op. 1, d. 730[b].

61. The captain of the *Blagonamerenny* had been there before. Captain-Lieutenant Gleb Semyonovich Shishmaryov had served as senior officer under Otto von Kotzebue aboard the *Riurik* on the voyage of 1815 to 1818. I assume that he was a relative of Nikolai Shishmaryov. Shishmarev MS, fond 203, op. 1, d. 730[b], fos. 54v–55v.

    Axes were not part of the traditional Eskimo tool kit. It is probable that the Eskimos wanted the axe heads to haft them horizontally—not vertically, as the blade of an axe would be fastened to its handle—thus creating adzes. See, e.g., Bockstoce 1977a, 72.

62. Lazarev 1950, 199–200. Lazarev gives the date as July 21 (new style). Labrets, piercing the lower lips, were often worn by Iñupiaq males. Large blue beads, which were probably made in China (P. G. Miller 1994, 18–24; Francis 1994, 288–89), were particularly valued and, cut in half, were fixed to the labrets (Bockstoce 1977a, 87–90).

63. A *baidarka* is similar in construction to a kayak; a *baidara* is similar to an umiaq. Falconets were light cannons, usually mounted on swivels.

64. In 1826, referring to the frozen remains of mammoths that were eroding from its bluff, Frederick William Beechey named it Elephant Point (F. W. Beechey 1831, 232).

65. Lazarev 1950, 201–2.

66. Kotzebue 1821b, 218–22. For details of the Kaŋigmiut beluga hunt, see, e.g., Burch 1998a, 273–77.

67. Lazarev 1950, 202–4. I have added punctuation. Lazarev uses the term "Americans." To avoid confusion I have inserted "Eskimos" throughout. In 1826 Frederick William Beechey was the first person to positively identify the natives of northwestern Alaska as Eskimos (Bockstoce 1977a, 16).

68. Musketoon: a short, large-bore musket. An arshin is equal to 28 inches (approximately 71 cm). Lazarev 1950, 206. See the appendix for a discussion of the possibility of the Buckland River Eskimos possessing firearms.

69. Fienup-Riordan 1994, 321; Burch 1975, 59; Burch 1998b, 476–47, 49.

70. Lazarev 1950, 206–7.

71. "Agalakhmut": Lazarev is probably referring to the Aglurmiut, an Eskimo society that inhabited the northeastern part of the Alaska Peninsula (VanStone 1984, 225, 241).

72. Lazarev 1950, 207–9. I have added paragraph indentations.

73. It is unlikely that the Hudson's Bay Company was the source of these weapons. At that date the nearest British trading post was at Fort Good Hope on the Mackenzie River (Usher 1971, 73), but the closest abundant source of metals, *with a well established trade network*, would have been the Russian trading centers in northeastern Asia. See chapter 3.

74. Lazarev 1950, 210–11.

    Lazarev identifies it as *bagulnik*, which is *Ledum* (s.), a small circumpolar shrub which is occasionally used as a substitute for tea and is variously called "Hudson Bay tea" or "Labrador tea." *Ledum palustre*, which is abundant in the Kotzebue Sound region, contains ledol, "a poisonous substance causing cramps and paralysis" (Hultén 1968, 717).

75. Lazarev 1950, 213; John Walters MS, 13.

    Walters's journal and the Russian reports of the meeting of the three ships in Kotzebue Sound in 1820 do not agree precisely as to the date, when adjusted for the Julian-Gregorian difference of twelve days. These discrepancies, I assume, arose from the fact that Walters's account was apparently written later, from notes, and the Russian accounts were kept in both nautical time (wherein the new day was reckoned to start at noon) and civil time (wherein the new day began at midnight). Furthermore, the Russians had sailed to Bering Strait eastward, via the Cape of Good Hope, whereas the *Pedlar* had sailed from New York westward, via Cape Horn, thus adding the uncertainly of the calculation of the date change near what was later to become the International Date Line.

76. Lazarev was recording his journal in nautical time. The second hour is between 1 and 2 PM. The ships were rated as sloops.

77. Lazarev 1950, 214. He is referring to Peter Dobell. As we have seen, Dobell was not, in fact, the Russian consul in Manila because his credentials had been rejected by the Spanish government. Clark had been his agent in Petropavlovsk while Dobell was in St. Petersburg (Porter 1932, 272).

78. Lazarev identifies the man's name as "Gray." He is referring to Eliab Grimes. The vessel was the *General San Martín*. In fact, her nominal owners were William Heath Davis and Thomas Meek. Eliab Grimes was both her captain and supercargo. Pigot bought the vessel after her return to Hawaii. As noted earlier, it seems clear that Rumiantsev had, in fact, encouraged a subsequent reconnaissance. A *sazhen* is a Russian linear measure equaling seven feet (approximately 2.134 m).

79. Lazarev 1950, 214–15.

80. Lazarev 1950, 215–16. Approximately 132 statute miles. A *verst* is a Russian unit of linear measurement equal to .66 statute miles (1.07 km).

81. Gillesem 1849, vol. 55, no. 10; D. J. Ray 1983, 38.

82. John Walters MS, 13–14. Pinnace: a ship's small craft, or tender.

83. Ernest S. Burch, Jr., personal communication, received April 15, 2004.

84. John Walters MS, 14–15. Liudmila Ivanova Rikorda was admired and respected by all who knew her.

85. Lazarev 1950, 389–90; Rikord to Naval Ministry, November 10, 1820, fond 166, d. 660, ch. 2, ll. 269–70, Rossiiskii Gosudarstvennyi Arkhiv Voenno-Morskogo Flota (RGAVMF) [Russian State Naval Archive]. Muravyov to Main Office, no. 8, January 18, 1821, Records of the Russian-American Company, Correspondence of the Governors General, Communications Sent, vol. 2 [fos. 130–133v], in Fur Seal Arbitration 1895, 8:388.

86. Muravyov to Main Office; John Walters MS, 15; Pierce 1990a, 368–71; Khlebnikov 1976, 58.

87. T. Armstrong 1994, 133; Doyle 1990; Raeff 1956, 43.

88. Kushner 1975, 31; Okun 1979, 75, 78; Vagin 1872, 80–87.

89. Old style (Julian calendar) date.

90. The ships were the *Otkrytie* and *Blagonamerenny*. As we have seen, Pigot had sold a gun to a native at King Island. Muravyov to Board of Management, January 21, 1821, in Fur Seal Arbitration 1895, 8:388. Muravyov was justifiably suspicious about the

Pedlar: in 1815, at Novo-Arkhangelsk, the Russians had seized her briefly for trading gunpowder to the Indians (Pierce 1986, 235, 241; Porter 1930, 229; Malloy 1998, 149).

91. An *ukaz* was a decree from the tsar. This is the old style (Julian calendar) date. For a discussion regarding Bering Strait as the northern limit of Russia's claims, see Foote (1965, 32–33). An Italian mile was equal to a nautical mile (one degree of latitude), or 1.15 statute miles. Dmytryshyn et al. 1989, 339–52.

92. Dmytryshyn et al. 1989, 339–69; Gibson 1991, 107.

93. Galbraith 1977, 19–20; Wenger 1984, 35–36; Barratt 1983, 5–6. See also chapters 4 and 12.

94. Barratt 1990, 149.

95. This was the sloop-of-war *Apollon.* Fur Seal Arbitration 1895, 8:388. Katherine L. Arndt explains the slow pace of communications thusly: "A letter from the Main Office [in St. Petersburg] dated, say, March of 1831, was received by the colonial Chief Manager [in Novo-Arkhangelsk] in the autumn of that year, the Chief Manager sent his response in May of 1832, and the Main Office likely received the response in the autumn of 1832, but could not respond in turn until March of 1833" (Katherine L. Arndt, personal communication, February 17, 1997).

96. Schabelski 1826; Farris 1993, 47; Khlebnikov 1976, 59; Pierce 1986, 7–8; Barratt 1981, 223.

97. Tompkins 1989, 63; Walker 1999, 81; Bancroft 1886, 536–45; International Boundary Commission [1918], 202–11; Hine and Faragher 2007, 72.

98. Porter 1931, 672, 669–70.

99. D. J. Ray 1983, 2.

100. Tikhmenev 1978, 178; Kusov 1993.

2. TRAPPING AND HUNTING FOR MARKETABLE FURS

1. Belden 1917, 250; Sale 2006, 385; Hudson's Bay Company 1967, 11; Burt and Grossenheider 1976, 75; Fox 1983, 155; Pamperin et al. 2006; Pielou 1994, 273–74; Harding 1942, 162.

2. Sale 2006, 387; Harding 1942, 36, 45–46; Slim Semmler, personal communication, Inuvik, N.W.T., July 1990.

3. E. P. Bailey 1992; Burt and Grossenheider 1976, 72–73; Hawbacker 1944, 43–44; Pielou 1994, 274–75.

4. Tetso 1970, 34, 36.

5. Burt and Grossenheider 1976, 70; Pielou 1994, 275–76; Stephenson and Boertje 1994; Golovin 1979, 194.

6. Burch 2005, 213; Hash 1987; John C. George, personal communication, October 30, 2006; E. W. Nelson 1887, 249; Pielou 1994, 278–79.

7. MacFarlane 1906, 707; Mair and MacFarlane 1908, 203.

8. R. M. Anderson 1928, 524–25; Stefansson 1914a, 217.

9. Kennicott 1869, 186, 189. The emphasis is Kennicott's.

10. E. W. Nelson 1887, 249; Golovin 1979, 194.

11. Petersen 1914, 175; C. M. Beaver 1955, 131.
12. Burt and Grossenheider 1976, 54; Shepherd and Melchior 1994.
13. Burt and Grossenheider 1976, 60–63; R. K. Nelson 1983, 146–48; Petersen 1914, 196–98; Solf and Golden 1994.
14. Burt and Grossenheider 1976, 55–58; Pielou 1994, 277–78; David Gray 2005.
15. E. W. Nelson 1887, 245.
16. McCowan 1926, 148; R. K. Nelson 1983, 143–44; Anderson et al. 1977, 379–80; Burns 1994; Hawbacker 1944, 59; Eagle and Whitman 1987; Petersen 1914, 181; Golovin 1979, 194.
17. Tollemache 1912, 163; Berrie, Ernest, and Stephenson 1994; Burt and Grossenheider 1976, 80–81; R. K. Nelson 1983, 153–56; Petersen 1914, 139–40; Harding 1942, 306–7.
18. Burt and Grossenheider 1976, 151–53; Novak 1987; Pielou 1994, 283–84.
19. E. W. Nelson 1887, 280; Sale 2006, 349.
20. Boutin and Birkenholz 1987; Burt and Grossenheider 1976, 193–94; Earnest 1994a; Golovin 1979, 194.
21. Burt and Grossenheider 1976, 91, 94, 100–101; Curby 1994; Pielou 1994, 281–83; Sale 2006, 352–53.
22. Burch 2006, 174; Earnest 1994b; Pielou 1994, 279–81.
23. Burch 2005, 213; Stefansson 1914a, 218; E. W. Nelson 1887, 280; Pielou 1994, 266–71; Valkenburg 1999.
24. Sale 2006, 375.
25. J. A. Allen 1912; Pielou 1994, 262–64.
26. R. M. Anderson 1928, 508–10; C. L. Hooper 1884, 40; E. W. Nelson 1887, 284; 1899, 119; Pielou 1994, 264–66; Sale 2006, 376–80.
27. Kolenosky 1987; Lentfer and Lowry 1994; E. W. Nelson 1887, 254; Pielou 1994, 257–60.
28. Eide, Miller, and Reynolds 2003; Jonkel 1987; Pielou 1994, 260–62.
29. Petersen 1914, 119; Dall 1870, 498; Loyal Johnson 1994; Kolenosky and Strathearn 1987, 442–54; Golovin 1979, 194.
30. The soapstone lamps came from the Coronation Gulf region of arctic Canada. Tebenkov MS; Arsenev 1927; Burch 2006, 165–67; Burns 2005; Phebus 1972, 27–33; Golovin 1979, 194.
31. Pfizenmayer 1939, 184–85; Camman 1954, 21; Digby 1926, passim; Jochelson 1926, 432; Laufer 1913, 335, 345; Simmonds 1877, 344–46.
32. Phebus 1972, 19–26.
33. See, e.g., E. Adams 1850–51; Anderson et al. 1977, 373, 378; Bane 1982, 61, 77; Bogoras 1904–9, 138–42; Campbell 1998, pl. 46; Cooper 1938; Giddings 1961, 132; Harding 1935; McKennan 1965, 34; Murdoch 1892, 260; Paneak 2004, 26; Tollemache 1912.
34. Tetso 1970, 53–54.
35. Camsell 1954, 39.
36. Gubser 1965, 95–96.
37. Maguire 1988, 1:108.

38. Bogoras 1904–9, 140–41; Burch 2006, 137; John C. George, personal communication, October 30, 2006; Matthews MS, April 1853; Murdoch 1892, 268; R. K. Nelson 1969, 172; Paneak 2004, 27.
39. Murdoch 1892, 268.
40. Ostermann and Holtved 1952, 113.
41. Sonnenfeld 1957, 167–68. See also Van Valin 1941, 105–6.
42. Pfizenmayer 1939, 186–87.
43. R. K. Nelson 1969, 173; Frank 1995, 316.
44. R. K. Nelson 1973, 116–17; McKennan 1965, 33–34.
45. Rausch 1951, 170. See also McFadyen-Clark 1974, 162–63.
46. E. W. Nelson 1899, 119.
47. E. Adams 1850–51.
48. Gubser 1965, 93–94.
49. Bane 1982, 76; Burch 2006, passim; Campbell 1998, pls. 34, 44–45; Murdoch 1892, 268; Tollemache 1912, 223–24. See also McFadyen-Clark 1974, 63.
50. E. W. Nelson 1899, 121–22. See also Wells and Kelly 1890, 25; Van Valin 1941, 107–8.
51. Preble 1908, 209–10.
52. Phebus 1972, 48–49.
53. Burch 2006, 172–74; Campbell 1998, pls. 47–50; Sonnenfeld 1957, 169n.
54. Bogoras 1904–9, 132–34; Burch 2006, 134–36; Campbell 1998, pls. 35–36; Phebus 1972, 19.
55. Stoney 1900, 93–94. See also Burch 1998a, 41–43.
56. Stoney 1900, 94.
57. Ingstad 1954, 60–63; Wells and Kelly 1890, 25.
58. E. Adams 1850–51.
59. Pfizenmayer 1939, 189–91.
60. Bogoras 1904–9, 141–43; Jochelson 1975, 557; Pfizenmayer 1939, 191–92.
61. Pfizenmayer 1939, 192–93.
62. Gubser 1965, 96.
63. Rausch 1951, 171–72; Doty 1900, 206; Zagoskin 1967, 220.
64. Guillemard 1889, 88; Paneak 2004, 27; E. W. Nelson 1899, 123; Zagoskin 1967, 221.
65. Gerstell 1985, 22–23; Bogoras 1904–9, 138–39; E. W. Nelson 1899, 122–23; Zagoskin 1967, 220. See also E. W. Nelson MS, December 7, 1877.
66. Murdoch 1892, 259–60. See also Bogoras 1904–9, 14; E. W. Nelson 1899, 121, 242; and Zagoskin 1967, 112.
67. Phebus 1972, 38–42.
68. Burch 2006, 169–71; Krasheninnikov 1972, 123; Murdoch 1892, 263.
69. Rausch 1951, 169–70.
70. Jochelson 1926, 381; 1975, 554; E. W. Nelson 1887, 256; R. K. Nelson 1973, 121.
71. Mair and Macfarlane 1908, 179.
72. Phebus 1972, 43–45, 54–55.
73. Zagoskin 1967, 221; Anderson et al. 1977, 375–77; Bogoras 1904–9, 137; Burch 2006, 174–75; Jochelson 1975, 555; E. W. Nelson 1887, 279–80.
74. E. W. Nelson 1887, 280.

75. R. K. Nelson 1973, 267; Bane 1982, 65.

76. E. W. Nelson 1887, 248.

77. Gubser 1965, 289.

78. Stefansson 1914a, 389; Bogoras 1904–9, 138; Murdoch 1892, 263.

79. Belden 1917, 227, 352–53.

80. Ruttle 1968, 18–22; Harding 1942, 48, 96, 146.

81. Tremblay 1983, 121–23; Harding 1942, 142; Epler 2008, 14.

82. Ruttle 1968, 86; Tremblay 1983, 127.

83. Ruttle 1968, 29; Harding 1942, 21.

84. Hall and Obbard 1987; Obbard 1987; Stains 1979; Tremblay 1983, 53; Harding 1942, 172.

3. THE RUSSIAN EXPANSION TOWARD ALASKA

1. Warnes 1999, 8–11; Lantzeff and Pierce 1973, 72.

2. Kerner 1946, 35.

3. Crownhart-Vaughan 1972, v; Fisher 1943, 1; Kerner 1946, 85–86.

4. T. Armstrong 1965, 14–19; 1975; 1994, 120–21; Crownhart-Vaughan 1972, x–xi; Lantzeff and Pierce 1973, 93–128; Kerner 1946, 66–75; Bychkov 1994.

5. Gibson 1968–69, 204.

6. Krasheninnikov 2004; Kerner 1946, 84; T. Armstrong 1994, 122.

7. Belov 2000, 26–27; Fedorova 1973, 41; Müller 1986, 55.

8. Kamchatka, however, was not annexed until 1697, when Vladimir Atlasov sent a force there from Anadyr and founded the first permanent foreign settlement (T. Armstrong 1994, 124). Dmytryshyn 1991, 24; Fisher 1990, 27; Weiss 2006, 145.

9. Efimov 1964, no. 55; Fisher 1977; Jefferys 1761, xxiv–xxv; D. J. Ray 1975, 14–15.

10. Golder 1922–25, 1:10–11.

11. Müller 1986, 71; Golder 1922–25, 1:18–19; Du Halde 1735, 4:457–58.

12. Fisher 1977; Golder 1922–25, 1:18–19.

13. Belov 2000, 41; Black 2004, 26, Golder 1922–25, 1:22–23.

14. Black 2004, 23–26; Divin 1997; Golder 1922–25, 1:24; Holland 1994, 98.

15. Black 2004, 20–22; Fisher 1981; Frost 2003, 29–64; Holland 1994, 93–94; Kushnarev 1990; Pierce 1990a, 53–55.

16. Black 2004, 40; Gough 2007, 93.

17. Black 2004, 29–56; Frost 2003; Golder 1922–25, vol. 2; Holland 1994, 99–101.

18. Medushevskaya 1975, 81–85; Masterson and Brower 1948, 64–67; Pierce 1990a, 110–11; D. J. Ray 1983, 68–69; 1992, 28–31.

19. See, e.g., Williams 2002, 287–334; Ellis 1782, 1:329–31.

20. Beaglehole 1967, 1:411–12, 431, 438–40.

21. Hanson 1980; Jochelson 1933, 168; 1975, 613–22, 677; Konstantinov 1971, 121–24; Levin and Potapov 1964, 251, 257, 635; Zagoskin 1967, 148, 161, 247, 331; Zykov 1989, 73.

22. Chernenko 2000, 107; Masterson and Brower 1948, 95.

23. Masterson and Brower 1948, 95; D. J. Ray 1971, 1–8; 1992, 45.

24. Quoted in Belov 2000, 49.
25. I have converted the date to the Gregorian calendar from the Julian.
26. It is more likely that these people were Iñupiaq Eskimos who understood the language of the Chukchi. Many natives of the Bering Strait region were bilingual or multilingual. As we have seen, Gvozdyov, Daurkin, and Kobelev were able to communicate with the Iñupiaq speakers on the Diomede Islands in Chukchi (Burch 2005, 151–52). That they were local Eskimos, not traveling Chukchi, is confirmed by the fact that Billings was able to purchase their umiaq: had they been travelers from afar, it is unlikely that they would have parted with it (Sarychev 1806–7, 2:45).
27. Sauer 1802, 244–45. I have inserted paragraph indentations in this quotation.
28. Merck 1980, 189, 191–92, 209. See chapter 2.
29. Emphasis added.
30. Sarychev 1806–7, 2:45; Bockstoce 1977a, 87–90.
31. I am grateful to Ernest S. Burch, Jr., for this transliteration. D. J. Ray 1976, 146–53.
32. D. J. Ray 1983, 72; Hough 1895; VanStone 1983.
33. Burch 2005, 131–32. See also Gurvich 1994.
34. Quoted in Chernenko 2000, 117–18.
35. Count Rumiantsev was chancellor of Russia and Otto von Kotzebue's patron. Alekseev 1990, 85; Dee Longenbaugh, personal communication, May 15, 2002.
36. Sauer 1802, 250.
37. Black 2004, 94; Holland 1994, 152–53; Pierce 1990a, 57–59; Sauer 1802; Sarychev 1806–7, 2:51.
38. Sarychev 1806–7, 2:47–48; Sauer 1802, 250–52. "Whales' fins" was a common term for whalebone (baleen) in the early eighteenth century (Barr 1994).
39. It is probable that the "reindeer's entrails" were actually sea mammal intestines. Sarychev 1806–7, 2:49.
40. Kotzebue 1821b, 1:209; VanStone 1960, 148.
41. Corti 1996; Price 1961, 19; D. J. Ray 1992, 101–2; Fortuine 1996, 4; Goodman 1993, 51–52; Laufer 1924, 16–18; Sayce 1933, 205–6.
42. I thank Igor Krupnik for calling my attention to the different spellings of Siberian Yupik and Alaskan Yup'ik.
43. Jochelson 1975, 783–88.
44. Belov 2000, 39.
45. Golder 1914, 156–57.
46. Jochelson 1975, 788–89.
47. Müller 1986, 78.
48. Golder 1914, 164.
49. Jochelson 1975, 784; Lantzeff and Pierce 1973, 218; Nordenskiöld 1881, 2:77, quoting Georgi 1777, 2:350.
50. Jochelson 1975, 794.
51. Bogoras 1904–9, 697.
52. Bogoras 1904–9, 693–701; Forsyth 1992, 145–51; Lantzeff and Pierce 1973, 218–19; Znamenski 1999, 26.
53. Chernenko 2000, 121.

54. Hickey 1979; Larsen and Rainey 1948, 83, 254; Okladnikov 1964, 92; McCartney 1988; Rudenko 1961; Arutiunov and Sergeev 2007, 192, 203.

55. Bogoras 1904–9, 54, 162–68; Jochelson 1933, 168; 1975, 582; Brisee 1987, 4; Hanson 1980; Konstantinov 1971, 121–24; Levin and Potapov 1964, 251; Zykov 1989, 73.

56. Bogoras 1904–9, 53; Kennan 1870, 286–87.

57. Kotzebue 1821b, 1:228.

58. Golder 1922–25, 2:98–99.

59. Bogoras 1904–9, 56; Chernenko 2000, 114, 128n18.

60. Bogoras 1904–9, 703; Slezkine 1994, 17; Buxton 1903, 110; CAVM Team 2003.

61. Sarychev 1806–7, 2:50.

62. Wrangell 1840, 89–90.

63. Ibid., 114–18.

64. Cochrane 1824, 1:315–16.

65. Ibid., 322–23.

66. Tebenkov MS.

67. Jochelson 1975, 802–3n1.

68. Bogoras 1904–9, 703.

69. Ibid., 704.

70. Pierce 1990a, 25.

71. Hoffecker and Elias 2007, 23–44.

72. Tremblay 1983, 22.

73. D. J. Ray 1992, 98.

74. Znamenski 1999; Burch 2005, 227.

4. MARKETING THE FURS

1. Allen 1903, 103; Fitzhugh and Crowell 1988, 236–37.

2. Dmytryshyn et al. 1985, 497n.

3. George Simpson 1847, 2:371.

4. Crownhart-Vaughan 1972, xix; Dmytryshyn et al. 1985, 497–501; Makarova 1975, 112; Mancall 1971, 249–54; Sladkovsky 1974, 99–103; Lincoln 1994, 144.

5. Makarova 1975, 112; Lincoln 1994, 146. Not until the mid-nineteenth century did China allow Russian ships to enter her ports; hence Russian exports had to be sent overland.

6. Lincoln 1994, 147–48; Makarova 1975, 111–14; Sladkovsky 1974, 146, 170–71.

7. George Simpson 1847, 2:301–2, 304.

8. Fisher 1943, 172–73, 222–29; Gibson 1968–69; 1976, 36; 1990; 1991.

9. Coxe 1780, 247.

10. Gibson 1976, 57–59.

11. George Simpson 1847, 2:260, 268, 270.

12. Gibson 1976, 57–59.

13. Gibson 1976, 37.

14. Coxe 1780, 212–19, 230–35.

15. Tikhmenev 1978, 153.

16. Knox 2007, 318; George Simpson 1847, 2:256.
17. Coxe 1780, 234–40; Foust 1969, 346–59; Gibson 1990, 42; Moxham 2004, 57–58.
18. Coxe 1780, 240.
19. Pierce 1990b, 76–77; Knox 2007, 317.
20. Kennan 1891, 103–4, 107–9.

5. THE RUSSIANS MOVE NORTH

1. Black 2004, 61ff.; Müller 1986, 120.
2. Gibson 1976, 3; Fedorova 1973, 104–10; Fisher 1990, 30–34; Postnikov 1995, 11.
3. Fisher 1990, 32–34; Pierce 1990a, 172–73, 454–59.
4. Fisher 1990, 33.
5. VanStone 1967, 4–6; 1988, 7.
6. Kotzebue 1821b, 1:238–39.
7. Khramchenko MS, 117–21; D. J. Ray 1964; Tikhmenev 1978, 158–59, 467; VanStone 1967, 5–6.
8. Foote 1965, 60.
9. VanStone 1973, 7, 10–13; D. J. Ray 1983, 67–78.
10. July 2 is the old style (Julian) calendar date; it was July 14 in the Gregorian calendar. These Eskimos were Tačirmiut, the Yup'ik nation inhabiting the southeastern corner of Norton Sound (Burch 2005, 38–39). VanStone 1973, 69.
11. These Eskimos were Ayaqsaaġiaaġmiut, the Iñupiaq Eskimo nation inhabiting the southwestern corner of the Seward Peninsula, including Sledge Island (Burch 2005, 38–39). VanStone 1973, 72.
12. "Kuslit" is *Qutlich Nuna*, the Iñupiaq Eskimo toponym for Chukotka (Bockstoce 1988, 1:122; Burch 2005, 40; Murdoch 1892, 44). Tungan, if he was a native of Golovnin Bay, was probably a Yup'ik Eskimo.
13. Tungan probably reached his homeland in Golovnin Bay via Port Clarence, the Tuksuk Channel, the Kuzitrin River, and the Niukluk River (Orth 1971, 557, 691–92).
14. VanStone 1973, 77–85.
15. July 11 is the old style (Julian) calendar date; it is July 23 in the Gregorian calendar. Khramchenko MS, 86–87.
16. "Sivuqaq" appears to have been used in reference both to St. Lawrence Island and to the settlement on the island that is today Gambell, Alaska. "Ualak-mut" refers to persons living in the settlement of Uellyt (Uelen), on the north coast of the Chukchi Peninsula, close to Cape Dezhnev (Burch 2005, 38–39). Khramchenko MS, 90–91.
17. Khramchenko MS, 91.
18. Burch 2005, 20, 38–39.
19. Khramchenko MS, 92–93.
20. Ibid., 93.
21. Ibid., 93–94.
22. Ibid., 100.
23. Ibid., 100–102.
24. Ibid., 115.

6. THE BRITISH RESPONSE

1. See, e.g., C. Ian Jackson 2007.
2. Kirwan 1959, 77.
3. Levere 1993, 44.
4. Gough 1971, 31–32; 1973, 11; VanStone 1977, 7. See also Levere 1993, 111.
5. Kusov 1993; D. J. Ray, personal communication, n.d.; Tikhmenev 1978, 178.
6. Bockstoce 1977a, 9–14.
7. Petitot 1876, xii–xxiv; 1999; Smith 1984, 357; Alunik et al. 2003, 14–15; Morrison 1991a, 85. Betts 2005.
8. Franklin 1828, 99–102.
9. Petitot 1999, 105.
10. Franklin 1828, 102–3; Edna MacLean, personal communication. March 10, 2009.
11. I am indebted to Ernest S. Burch, Jr., for this information about Augustus (personal communication, February 21, 2008).
12. Franklin 1828, 103–7.
13. These natives were the easternmost Gwich'in (see front endpaper map). The Gwich'in for the most part lived in the Subarctic, within the boreal forests in northeastern interior Alaska and northwesternmost Canada, between the middle Yukon and Anderson rivers. They lived in nine or ten regional bands that spoke related dialects. They hunted caribou, moose, and beaver and fished for salmon, trout, and whitefish in rivers and lakes. Their trading and hunting activities occasionally took them north, out on the tundra, as far as the shore of the Beaufort Sea. (Krech 1996, 188–89; Slobodin 1981).
14. Franklin 1828, 107–10.
15. Ibid., 111.
16. Smith 1984, 348–49; Franklin 1828, 111–12, 118, 120, 174.

    When Franklin met Dr. John Richardson again in autumn 1826, he learned that on the same day that Franklin's encounter took place, Richardson's party had had a tense meeting with an aggressive group of Eskimos on the east side of the Mackenzie delta. As with Franklin's party, things quieted down when Richardson's men aimed their muskets at the Eskimos: "Happily there was no occasion to fire at all," Richardson wrote. "The contest of the Esquimaux with the Indians had taught them to dread fire-arms, and on the sudden sight of every man armed with a musket, they fled to the shore" (Richardson 1828, 201).

    When John Richardson encountered a group of Eskimos on the east side of the Mackenzie delta in July 1826, he noted that they were ignorant of tobacco and were amazed when Ooligbuck, Richardson's Eskimo assistant, lighted his pipe and exhaled smoke from his mouth (Richardson 1828, 195).

    I have added paragraph indentations in quoting Franklin.
17. Burch 1976; Arndt 1996, 79; Black 2004, 194. I am grateful to Ernest S. Burch, Jr. (personal communication, April 17, 1997) and to Craig Mishler (personal communication, December 19, 2006) for their help with Gwich'in synonymy.
18. Franklin 1828, 129–31. I have added paragraph indentations.

19. Franklin thought that the feature that is today named Barter Island was, in fact, part of the mainland and named it "Point Manning." Franklin's "Barter Island," which is a low sand island a few miles west of today's Barter Island, was renamed Arey Island by Ernest de Koven Leffingwell (Leffingwell 1919, 93; Orth 1967, 108).

20. Bockstoce 1977a, 113–14; Franklin 1828, 142–47, 160–65. Today Return Reef is the Return Islands, a thirteen-mile chain of barrier islands lying northwest of Prudhoe Bay (Orth 1967, 802).

21. See chapter 10.

22. Wolfe MSa, 110–11.

23. F. W. Beechey 1831, 1:247–48.

24. Gough 1973, 22.

25. Wolfe MSa, 113–14; Belcher MS, 29.

26. Belcher MS, 30; Burch 2005, 180–87.

27. F. W. Beechey 1831, 1:262, 272; Wolfe MSa, 117.

28. Belcher MS, 40; Bockstoce 1977a, 108.

29. F. W. Beechey 1831, 1:285; Kotzebue 1821b, 1:222.

30. Burch 1998a, passim; 2005, 180–92; F. W. Beechey 1831, 1:286–87.

31. F. W. Beechey 1831, 1:286–89; Wolfe MSb, 83, 131–32. These bracelets were, perhaps, the product of Koryak blacksmiths (Jochelson 1975, 624).

32. Wolfe MSb, 75–76.

33. F. W. Beechey 1831, 1:289, 293.

34. Wolfe MSb, 82.

35. F. W. Beechey 1831, 1:292, 294; Richard Beechey MS, 92.

36. F. W. Beechey 1831, 1:295, 297–98; Richard Beechey MS, 92; Wolfe MSb, 136. In 1821 Etholen and Khramchenko bought a copper bell on the shore of Norton Sound (Muravev to Main Office, January 17, 1822, Correspondence of the Governors General, Communications Sent, vol. 2 [reel 27], no. 42, fos. 313–14, Records of the Russian-American Company, National Archives, Washington, DC).

37. F. W. Beechey 1831, 1:297; Richard Beechey MS, 92. For a discussion on the introduction of firearms to the Eskimos of the Bering Strait region see the appendix.

38. Elson 1973, 161–62; Smyth 1831, 1:308. This took place a week after Franklin had started back toward the Mackenzie from Return Reef, about 175 miles east of Point Barrow. The northernmost point of the North American continent is only a few miles closer to the North Pole than Point Barrow. Zenith Point, at Bellot Strait, lies at the tip of the Boothia Peninsula in eastern arctic Canada.

39. Smyth MSa, 118.

40. Smyth 1831, 1:314, 316.

41. F. W. Beechey 1831, 1:322–23, 333.

42. Richard Beechey MS, 101.

43. F. W. Beechey 1831, 1:300, 2:571. Beechey refers to John Dundas Cochrane, who visited the fair at Ostrovnoe on the Maly Aniui in 1821 (Cochrane 1824). See chapter 3.

44. F. W. Beechey 1831, 2:572–73. I have added a paragraph indentation.

45. Burch 2005, 208–14; McFadyen-Clark 1974, 219–30.

46. Spencer 1959, 203.
47. Ernest S. Burch, Jr., personal communication, n.d.
48. John Simpson 1988, 539–40. I have added paragraph indentations.
49. Lamb 1970, 199; Jenness 1922, 44; 1946, 55–64; E. W. Nelson 1899, 63; Stefansson 2001, 117. David Morrison (1991b, 239–46) believes that the trade for soapstone pots and lamps may have begun as late as 1840. Beechey nevertheless bought a small soapstone lamp, which may have been a girl's toy made from a fragment of a broken pot, at Kotzebue Sound in 1826 or 1827 (Bockstoce 1977a, 91).
50. Burch 1975, 220, 222; Stoney 1900, 92.
51. Paneak 2004, 26.
52. Maguire 1988, 1:295; John Simpson MS, October 16, 1853.
53. Burch 2005, 180–202; John Simpson 1988, 537–39; Spencer 1959, 198, 204–5, 208.
54. Burch 2005, 172–180; Spencer 1959, 210–28.
55. Huntington 1993, 16.
56. Richardson 1851, 257, 354. For an early discussion of trade routes see John Simpson (1988, 539–40) and Stefansson (1914b).
57. Wolfe MSa, 195; F. W. Beechey 1831, 2:534.
58. F. W. Beechey 1831, 2:535–36, 555–59; Peard 1973, 228; Wolfe MSa, 196.
59. F. W. Beechey 1831, 2:541–42; Peard 1973, 231.
60. Belcher MS, 211, Wolfe MSa, 200–201.
61. Gough 1973, 24; Ritchie 1967, 258–59; Wolfe MSa, 200–201.
62. Belcher MS, 229–32.
63. Wolfe MSa, 200–201.
64. F. W. Beechey 1831, 2:555; Peard 1973, 235.
65. Peard 1973, 239; Wolfe MSa, 203. In 1850 Dr. John Simpson confirmed that this group of Eskimos was from the Buckland River (Kaŋiġmiut) nation (Burch 2005, 302n40; John Simpson 1850).
66. F. W. Beechey 1831, 2:556–57; Peard 1973, 239; Wolfe MSa, 203.
67. Wolfe MSa, 203. I have added a paragraph indentation.
68. Peard 1973, 239–40.
69. F. W. Beechey 1831, 2:557.
70. Peard 1973, 240; Wolfe MSa, 204.
71. Peard 1973, 241.

7. MIKHAILOVSKY REDOUBT

1. Alekseev 1996; Erman 1843, 464; Litke 1835, 2:265, 277–78. See also Litke 1987.
2. Litke 1835, 2:277–84. I am grateful to William Barr for this translation.
3. Pierce 1990a, 90, 369.
4. Arndt 1996, 27.
5. Tikhmenev 1978, 182; Chistiakov to Main Office, May 26, 1830, Correspondence of the Governors General, Communications Sent, vol. 7 (reel 32), no. 142, fos. 175–177v, Records of the Russian-American Company, National Archives, Washington, DC.
6. Tikhmenev 1978, 181–83.

7. Wrangell 1980, 31–32.
8. Wrangell to Main Office, May 6, 1832, Correspondence of the Governors General, Communications Sent, vol. 9 (reel 34), no. 125, fos. 97–98, Records of the Russian-America Company, National Archives, Washington, DC.
9. Wrangell to Yakutsk Commissary, May 4, 1832, Correspondence of the Governors General, Communications Sent, vol. 9 (reel 34), no. 94, fos. 65v–66, Records of the Russian-American Company, National Archives, Washington, DC.
10. Arndt 1996, 26–33; Wrangell to Tebenkov, June 4, 1832, Correspondence of the Governors General, Communications Sent, vol. 9 (reel 34), no. 293, fos. 242–247v, Records of the Russian-American Company, National Archives, Washington, DC.
11. Arndt 1996, 35–38; Wrangell to commander of the schooner *Kvikhpak* . . . , May 8, 1834, Correspondence of the Governors General, Communications Sent, vol. 11 (reel 36), no. 262, fos. 238–244v, Records of the Russian-American Company, National Archives, Washington, DC.
12. Wrangell to Main Office, April 30, 1835, Correspondence of the Governors General, Communications Sent, vol. 12 (reel 37), no. 153, fos. 147–149, Records of the Russian-American Company, National Archives, Washington, DC.
13. This date is converted to the new style (Gregorian calendar). Wrangell to Main Office, October 5, 1835, Correspondence of the Governors General, Communications Sent, vol. 12 (reel 37), no. 328, fos. 311v–315, Records of the Russian-American Company, National Archives, Washington, DC. During the latter nineteenth century Mys Chaplina was usually called "Indian Point" by whalemen and traders (Bockstoce and Batchelder 1978a).
14. Main Office to Chief Manager Wrangell, March 31, 1833, Correspondence of the Governors General, Communications Received, vol. 8 (reel 8), no. 260, fos. 312–314, Records of the Russian-American Company, National Archives, Washington, DC.
15. Wrangell to Main Office, April 10, 1834, Correspondence of the Governors General, Communications Sent, vol. 11 (reel 36), no. 58, fos. 35–43, Records of the Russian-American Company, National Archives, Washington, DC. I have added a paragraph indentation.
16. Arndt 1996, 38–39.
17. Zagoskin 1967, 97.
18. Arndt 1996, 30–41; Fortuine 1989, 230–238; Kupreianov to Tebenkov, May 14, 1836, vol. 13 (reel 38), no. 297, fos. 188–193; Kupreianov to Chernov, May 14, 1836, no. 298, fos. 193–196v; Kupreianov to Main Office, August 13, 1836, no. 400, fos. 279v–287; Kupreianov to Main Office, June 14, 1837, no. 320, fos. 363v–370v, Correspondence of the Governors General, Communications Sent, Records of the Russian-American Company, National Archives, Washington, DC.
19. Arndt 1996, 42–45, 47n24; Zagoskin 1967, 146–47, 183–84.
20. Golovin 1979, 176–77. Castors are scent glands located near the beaver's anus. They were believed to have medicinal properties and were also used in the manufacture of perfume.

8. THE EXPEDITIONS TO POINT BARROW

1. Barr 2002, 7–11; Ernest S. Burch, Jr., personal communication, April 17, 1997; Ives Goddard, personal communication, October 7, 1997; Slobodin 1981, 530–31.

   The location of Fort Good Hope changed several times. First it was sixty miles north of the Great Bear River, but in 1811 it was moved downstream to the mouth of the Hare Indian River. From 1823 to 1827 it was farther downstream still, near the mouth of the Travaillant River, but from 1827 on it was again located at the mouth of the Hare Indian River (Krech 1996, 190–91).

2. Barr 2002, 11.

3. Coates 1993, 23; Thomas Simpson 1843, 9–102.

4. Krech 1996, 213.

5. Thomas Simpson 1843, 103.

6. Ibid., 105. Dease mentions that a man was also in the umiaq (Barr 2002, 74–75).

7. Thomas Simpson 1843, 106–7. I have inserted a paragraph indentation. Barr 2002, 75.

8. Thomas Simpson 1843, 109; Barr 2002, 76.

9. Thomas Simpson 1843, 110–11.

10. Barr 2002, 76–77; Thomas Simpson 1843, 112–14.

11. Barr 2002, 79.

12. Jenness 1991, 9; Burch 2005, 200.

13. Thomas Simpson 1843, 119, 171.

14. Barr 2002, 84; Ruggles 1991, pl. 34; Thomas Simpson 1843, 141–45.

15. Thomas Simpson 1843, 146–47. I have added paragraph indentations.

16. Ibid., 148–49. I have added a paragraph indentation. Sixteen years later the woman was identified by Rochfort Maguire as the wife of O-mi-ga-loon, from Point Barrow (Maguire 1988, 1:314–15).

17. Thomas Simpson 1843, 153–58. I have added paragraph indentations.

18. Burch 1998b, 9; 2005, 37; Thomas Simpson 1843, 161.

19. Ernest S. Burch, Jr., personal communication, February 21, 2008.

20. Thomas Simpson 1843, 162–67; Barr 2002, 86. Dease's and Simpson's narratives disagree by one day as to the date.

21. Barr 2002, 85.

22. Thomas Simpson 1843, 182–83.

23. VanStone 1977, 8–9; Tikhmenev 1978, 178–79.

24. This date is in the old style (Julian calendar). Kupreianov to Main Office, November 4, 1838, Correspondence of the Governors General, Communications Sent, vol. 16 (reel 41), no. 499, fos. 227v–231v, Records of the Russian-American Company, National Archives, Washington, DC.

25. Kashevarov 1977, 18–27.

26. Ibid., 33.

27. Burch 2005, 170–212; Pierce 1990a, 320–21; VanStone 1977, 72–73n46.

28. Kashevarov 1977, 42.

29. Ibid., 42–43. Feofan Utuktak was an Eskimo from southwest Alaska near the Yukon

delta. Not uncommonly, he was bilingual in both Yup'ik and Iñupiaq Eskimo languages (Pierce 1990a, 514–15; VanStone 1977, 66n5).

30. Kashevarov 1977, 43–65.
31. Zagoskin 1967, 126.

9. ZAGOSKIN'S EXPEDITION TO THE YUKON

1. Fortuine 1989, 230–38; Zagoskin 1967, 100. Ikogmiut is today the village of Russian Mission, Alaska.
2. Etholen to Main Office, May 13, 1841, Correspondence of the Governors General, Communications Received, vol. 13 (reel 13), no. 254, fos. 268v–270, Records of the Russian-American Company, National Archives, Washington, DC.
   Etholen later concluded that the tobacco probably spoiled on the road to Okhotsk. (Etholen to Main Office, May 10, 1843, Correspondence of the Governors General, Communications Sent, vol. 22 [reel 47], no. 314, fos. 302v–304, Records of the Russian-American Company, National Archives, Washington, DC.)
3. Etholen to Netsvetov, May 12, 1841, Correspondence of the Governors General, Communications Received, vol. 13 [reel 13], no. 282, fos. 295–300, Records of the Russian-American Company, National Archives, Washington, DC.
4. Arndt 1996, 41–50; Etholen to Donskoi, May 12, 1841, Correspondence of the Governors General, Correspondence Received, vol. 13 (reel 13), no. 304, fos. 313–316; Etholen to Donskoi, May 1, 1842, Communications Sent, vol. 21 (reel 46), no. 177, fos. 124v–126v, Records of the Russian-American Company, National Archives, Washington, DC.
5. Chernenko et al. 1967, 15; Zagoskin 1967, 82; Etholen to Zagoskin, May 1, 1842, Correspondence of the Governors General, Communications Sent, vol. 21 (reel 46), no. 169, fos. 109–115v, Records of the Russian-American Company, National Archives, Washington, DC.
6. This is the old style (Julian) calendar date. Zagoskin 1967, 83–89.
7. Zagoskin 1967, 89; Arndt 1996, 52–59; Etholen to Main Office, May 10, 1843, Correspondence of the Governors General, Communications Sent, vol. 21 (reel 46), no. 289, fos. 265v–269, Records of the Russian-American Company, National Archives, Washington, DC.
8. Zagoskin 1847–48, end map; McFadyen-Clark 1981, 586.
9. Etholen to Netsvetov, April 27, 1843, Correspondence of the Governors General, Communications Sent, vol. 22, no. 164, fos. 110v–118v, Records of the Russian-American Company, National Archives, Washington, DC. I am grateful to the late Lydia Black for bringing this letter to my attention (Lydia Black, personal communication, June 11, 1982). I have added paragraph indentations.
10. Alekseev 1987, 37–46.
11. Arndt 1996, 52–59; Pierce 1990a, 549–50; Tikhmenev 1978, 348–51; Zagoskin 1967.
12. Zagoskin 1967, 100.
13. Zagoskin 1967, 101, 112.
14. This problem was by no means unique to the Russian-American Company. In 1821,

after the Hudson's Bay Company merged with the North West Company, it was found that the company was trading against itself in areas where posts' territories overlapped. See chapter 10.

15. Bogoras 1904–9, 56–57.
16. Zagoskin 1967, 102.
17. Burch 1998a, 8–10; Zagoskin 1967, 101.
18. Zagoskin 1967, 125.
19. Ibid., 136–37.
20. Ibid., 183–84.
21. Arndt 1996, 57, 66–67.
22. Russian-American Company 1847, 44. See chapter 7.
23. Tebenkov to Main Office, May 14, 1849, Correspondence of the Governors General, Communications Sent, vol. 30 (reel 55), no. 273, fos. 181v–182v, Records of the Russian-American Company, National Archives, Washington, DC.
24. Arndt 1996, 67–70; Tebenkov to Main Office, May 12, 1847, Correspondence of Governors General, Communications Sent, vol. 27 (reel 52), no. 335, fos. 499–501v, Records of the Russian-American Company, National Archives, Washington, DC; Russian-American Company 1848, 42.

10. THE BRITISH EXPANSION NORTHWESTWARD

1. Anonymous 2004.
2. Jackson 2005; Phillips 1961, 328; Rich 1967, 155.
3. Lamb 1970, 192, 199–201, 207–9; Mackenzie 1801, 74–75. See also Honigmann 1970, 21–22. See chapter 3.
4. Wentzel 1823, 78–80; Yerbury 1977, 189–90.
5. Holland 1994, 178–90; Karamanski 1983, 19.
6. Franklin 1828, 177–83. Franklin saw trade goods that the Herschel Island Eskimos had obtained from the Mountain Indians, which were unlike the Hudson's Bay Company's trade goods and which he assumed had originated from the Russians. The Eskimos told Franklin's interpreter that these Indians had guns, which may not have been true. Knowing that the Russian-American Company had a policy against trading firearms to the northern natives, he was at a loss to explain how the Indians had obtained their guns (Franklin 1828, 180–81).
7. Ruggles 1991, 77; Yerbury 1986, 94–99.
8. Arthur Ray 1988, 344–45; Coates 1982, 55–56.
9. Wright 1976, 45; B.200/b/11–12, Hudson's Bay Company Archives, Provincial Archives of Manitoba, Winnipeg, Manitoba (hereafter HBCA).
10. Stefansson 1958, 175.
11. Minutes of a council held at Red River Settlement, Northern Department of Rupert's Land, June 6– 12, 1839. B.239/k/2, fo. 176, HBCA; Stefansson 1958, 174; John Lee Lewes to John Bell, October 7, 1840, B.200/b/13, fo. 18, HBCA; Ruggles 1991, 78–79.
12. Bell, quoted in Stefansson 1958, 172–73.
13. Krech 1984b, 56.

14. Krech 1996, 199. I have added a paragraph indentation.
15. Murdoch McPherson to John Bell, June 2, 1840. B.200/b/12, fo. 9d, HBCA; Bell, quoted in Wright 1976, 46.
16. Bell to George Simpson from Peel's River, December 10, 1840, Peel's River Correspondence, D.5/5, fos. 396–97, HBCA. See also B.200/b/12, B.80/a/17, HBCA.
17. Ives Goddard, personal communication. Craig Mishler, personal communication. See also Crow and Obley 1981, 511–12. The Han inhabited lands on the upper Yukon River which today include the towns of Eagle, Alaska, and Dawson, Yukon Territory; Bell to John Lee Lewes, December 8, 1840, B.200/b/13, fo. 51a, HBCA.
18. Bell to John Lee Lewes, from Peel's River, July 14, 1841, B.200/b/14, HBCA.
19. Bell to George Simpson from Peel's River, December 20, 1841, Peel's River Correspondence, D.5/6, fos. 341–42, HBCA.
20. Bell to John Lee Lewes, from Peel's River, August 23, 1842, B.200/b/15, fo. 26, HBCA. Holland 1994, 219; Jackson 2005, 8; Stefansson 1958, 178–80; Wright 1976, 48–49.
21. Bell to John Lee Lewes, from Peel's River, December 31, 1842, B.200/b/15, fo. 44 Ad, HBCA.
22. Bell to George Simpson from Peel's River, August 11, 1843, Peel's River Correspondence, D.5/8, fos. 421–24, HBCA.
23. Krech 1979, 107–8.
24. Bell to George Simpson from Peel's River, August 11, 1843, Peel's River Correspondence, D.5/8. fos. 421–24, HBCA. I have added paragraph indentations.

    Narrow, tube-like dentalium shells were a valuable trade item that reached the Gwich'in from the Tlingit and Tsimshian tribes on the Northwest Coast of North America, "steadily increasing in value as they diffused eastward through the Cordillera." They "may reasonably be regarded as the aboriginal equivalent of European beads" (Krech 1987, 261). They were important and valuable items of personal adornment (Karklins 1992, 145–52; Mackie 1997, 284–85; Osgood 1936, 47–48). The Russian-American Company also dealt in them.

    "Made Beaver" or "MB" was a unit of measurement used by the Hudson's Bay Company to equate the value of beaver skins, trade goods, and other pelts. The MB was originally a prime beaver pelt that had been worn for a season, hence had lost its guard hairs. The underfur could then be easily removed from the skin and used in felt making.

25. Bell to Murdoch McPherson, December 31, 1844, B.200/b/20, fo. 24, HBCA; Coates 1982, 58.
26. Bell to George Simpson from Peel's River Post, August 1, 1845, Peel's River Correspondence, D.5/14, fos. 212–15, HBCA. I have added paragraph indentations.
27. Bell to John Lee Lewes from Peel's River, December 31, 1843, B.200/b/19, fo. 54, HBCA.
28. Bell to George Simpson from Peel's River Post, August 1, 1845, Peel's River Correspondence, D.5/14, fos. 212–15, HBCA. I have added paragraph indentations.
29. Murdoch McPherson to George Simpson and others from Portage La Loche, July 30, 1846, B.200/b/21. fo. 2d, HBCA; Alexander Hunter Murray to Murdoch McPherson from Peel's River, April 1, 1847, B.200/b/21, fo. 15d, HBCA; Murray MS.

30. Murray 1910, 21–25.

31. Ibid., 55; Murray MS.

32. Krech 1976, 220.

33. Murray 1910, 58.

34. Ibid., 45.

35. Ibid., 93–94; Murray MS.

36. Richardson 1851, 1:391; Krech 1987, 256–57; Hardisty 1872, 311; Krech 1979, 107–8.

37. Jackson 2005, 15. Jackson made this calculation based on "the British House of Commons Research paper 03/82: 'Inflation: The Value of the Pound 1750–2002,'" available online at www.parliament.uk/parliamentary_publications_and_archives/research _papers.cfm. (Jackson 2005, 23–24, n36).

38. Martin Hunter 1907, 77, 78, 81.

39. E. W. Morse 1969.

40. Jackson 2005, 14–15; Dennis Johnson 2006, 71–84; E. W. Morse 1969, 97–102; Murray to Murdoch McPherson, from La Pierre's House, June 24, 1848, B.200/b/23, fo. 9, HBCA; Murray MS.

41. Murray 1910, 53; Murray MS.

42. Arndt 1990b, 181; Murray to Murdoch McPherson from La Pierre's House, June 24, 1848, B.200/b/23, fo. 9, HBCA; Murray MS.

43. Murray to Murdoch McPherson, from Fort Yukon, November 20, 1847, B.200/b/22, fo. 15, HBCA; Murray MS.

44. Arndt 1990b, 182–83; 1996, 67–70. See chapter 9.

45. Arndt 1996, 94–95.

46. Murray 1910, 35; Murray MS; United States Senate 1869, 3. Murray's emphasis.

47. Orth 1967, 348; Murray 1910, 54, 67; Murray MS.

48. Murray 1910, 95; Murray MS.

49. Murray to John Rae, from Fort Yukon, November 16, 1849, B.200/b/24, fo. 43, HBCA; Murray MS; Rae 1953, 329.

50. Arndt 1996, 90–92; John Rae to Murray from Fort Simpson, February 23, 1850, B.200/ b/24, fo. 39, HBCA.

51. E. Adams 1850–51, 58–59. I am grateful to William Barr for bringing this passage to my attention. U.K. House of Commons 1852a, 74.

52. Arndt 1990a, 106; 1990b, 185; 1996, 123–39, 155.

53. Arndt 1996, 151–55; Pierce 1990a, 318–19.

54. Coates 1982, 67–68; Stuck 1917, 136–37.

55. G. R. Adams 1982, 68, 73; Lindsay 1993.

56. Whymper 1868b, 210–11; Lindsay 1993.

57. Arndt 1990b, 185.

11. THE SEARCH FOR SIR JOHN FRANKLIN

1. Both Franklin and Richardson had been knighted in recognition of their arctic explorations.

2. Bockstoce 1985; Pullen 1979, 27–30.

3. Seemann 1853, 2:5–9.

4. U.K. House of Commons 1849a, 16; Seemann 1853, 2:8.

5. D. J. Ray 1983, 95–102.

6. [Chimmo] 1860, 228–29.

7. Seemann 1853, 2:70.

8. *Herald* logbook; Seemann 1853, 2:70.

9. U.K. House of Commons 1850, 35; W. H. Hooper 1853, 12; HMS *Plover* logbooks.

10. Rae 1953, 174–75; W. H. Hooper 1853, 95, 149; Rosse 1884, 186.

11. Bockstoce and Batchelder 1978a; W. H. Hooper 1853, 108–9.

12. W. H. Hooper 1853, 148–52. See chapter 1. The cross was still standing but was very weather-beaten in winter 1870–71 when Frederick A. Barker, a shipwrecked whaling captain, passed through Mechigmensky Bay (Barker n.d.; Wilkinson n.d., 260 and pl. 14).

13. W. H. Hooper 1853, 185–86.

14. W. H. Hooper 1853, 160–62. Body armor was worn in the Bering Strait region until the 1870s. The ethnographer Johan Adrian Jacobsen learned of its use by an Eskimo at St. Michael, Alaska (Jacobsen 1977, 120).

15. W. H. Hooper 1853, 164–67. See chapter 6.

16. Bockstoce 1986, 93–99; U.K. House of Commons 1850, 35–37; HMS *Plover* logbooks; *Tiger* MS.

17. The Chamisso Island visitors' posts are now in the collections of the Burke Museum at the University of Washington, Seattle.

18. U.K. House of Commons 1849a.

19. Rae 1953, 175.

20. U.K. House of Commons 1850, 13; 1852a, 23–33; W. H. Hooper 1853, 226; A. G. E. Jones 1958. Although Shedden died at Mazatlán on the way back to Britain, the *Nancy Dawson* became the first yacht to circumnavigate the world.

21. The British called Oliktok "Point Berens" (Orth 1967, 722). Maguire 1988, 1:82, 2:252n1; U.K. House of Commons 1852a, 23–33; W. H. Hooper 1853, 238.

22. W. H. Hooper 1853, 239–40.

23. Gooding 2003, 20; Hanson 1992, 17–18, pl. 3B, no. 1; Alexander Armstrong 1857, 109; M'Clure 1853, 6.

24. See, e.g., Krech 1979, 109.

25. Franklin 1828, 166; U.K. House of Commons 1852a, 24–30. I have added a paragraph indentation to the parliamentary report.

26. W. H. Hooper 1853, 245–46. Today Return Reef is the Return Islands, a thirteen-mile chain of barrier islands northwest of Prudhoe Bay (Orth 1967, 802).

27. Burch 2005, 213; W. H. Hooper 1853, 255–58. The firm of I and H Sorby were cutlery manufacturers in Sheffield, England. It is also possible that this knife reached the Eskimos via Richardson's and Rae's expedition the year before (Richardson 1851, 1:237).

28. U.K. House of Commons 1852a, 23–30.

29. U.K. House of Commons 1850, 29ff.; Pim 1853, 143–44. See chapter 10.

30. U.K. House of Commons 1850, 74–79.

31. U.K. House of Commons 1851, 36–40.

32. Bockstoce 1985; U.K. House of Commons 1851, 22.

33. Bockstoce 1985; Barr 2007, 50–51; Collinson 1889, 80–81; U.K. House of Commons 1852a, 12–13, 66, 68–69.

34. Seemann 1853, 183; Bockstoce 1985; U.K. House of Commons 1852a, 84, 201–3; Matthews MS; D. J. Ray 1975, 145.

35. Matthews MS.

36. U.K. House of Commons 1852a, 74. See chapters 9 and 10.

37. U.K. House of Commons 1852a, 73–78; E. Adams 1850–51.

38. E. Adams 1850–51; U.K. House of Commons 1852a, 75–77. I have added paragraph indentations.

39. U.K. House of Commons 1852c, 168.

40. Barr 2007, 81, 83.

41. A lorcha was a sailing vessel with a Chinese junk rig and a European-shaped hull.

42. Quoted in Foote 1965, 184.

43. U.K. House of Commons 1852a, 82–83, 88; Matthews MS; Correspondence of the Governors General, Communications Sent, vol. 32 (reel 57), no. 543, June 7, 1851, fos. 400–405, Records of the Russian-American Company, National Archives, Washington, DC.

44. Barr 2007, 88–89; Bockstoce 1985; Collinson 1889, 132–40; U.K. House of Commons 1852a, 79–80.

45. U.K. House of Commons 1852b, 48–59.

46. Matthews MS; D. J. Ray 1975, 147.

47. U.K. House of Commons 1852a, 147, 187.

48. I am grateful to Ernest S. Burch, Jr., for this observation.

49. Matthews MS, September 1852.

50. The letter was given to Attua on August 11, 1850. Attua was apparently a member of the Kuukpigmiut nation, which lived on the lands surrounding the Colville River drainage (Alexander Armstrong 1857, 109; Burch 2005, 37; Miertsching 1967, 45).

51. Maguire 1988, 1:82. See also Miertsching 1967, 46.

52. Maguire 1988, 1:82n2, 213, 215n1.

53. Burch 1976; Maguire 1988, 1:156. Maguire wrote that the maker's mark was the letter "I" over a Maltese cross. (For examples of John Wilson's maker's marks, see Anonymous 2008.) Dr. John Simpson recorded it as the letter "L" (Simpson Papers, Special Collections, William R. Perkins Library, Duke University, Durham, NC).

54. Maguire 1988, 1:171; John Simpson MS, May 25, 1853. Evidence for this trade has also been established by the presence among the Mackenzie Eskimos of a copper medal that an Inuvialuit had converted into a pipe bowl. The Hudson's Bay Company trader Roderick MacFarlane collected the pipe at the company's Anderson River post, east of the Mackenzie River, in 1866. The medal—which lists the *Investigator*'s and *Enterprise*'s movements and the location of food caches (Daitch 2007, 26–27)—was almost certainly given to the Point Barrow Eskimos by the *Plover*'s men sometime between 1852 and 1854.

55. Maguire 1988, 1:237–41, 241n4; U.K. House of Commons 1854a, 182.

56. Maguire 1988, 2:500–501; U.K. House of Commons 1855, 917–42; Orth 1967, 442,

874. Franklin thought that the feature that is today named Barter Island was, in fact, part of the mainland, and he named it "Point Manning." Franklin's "Barter Island," which is a low sand island a few miles west of today's Barter Island, was renamed Arey Island by Ernest de Koven Leffingwell (Leffingwell 1919, 93; Orth 1967, 108).

57. Correspondence of the Governors General, Communications Sent, vol. 34 (reel 59), no. 490, June 20, 1853, fos. 169v–171, and vol. 35 (reel 60), no 68, May 1, 1854, fos. 20–24, Records of the Russian-American Company, National Archives, Washington, DC.

58. Sharpe MS, September 10, 1853; *Friend* (Honolulu), November 16, 1853.

59. Bockstoce 1985; U.K. House of Commons 1854a, 147–48, 156–58, 160–85; U.K. House of Commons 1853, 1.

60. Maguire 1988, 1:275; Petitot 1887, 197.

61. Maguire 1988, 2:392.

62. Ibid., 2:367–69. I have added punctuation.

63. Matthews MS, May 1854; Murdoch 1892, 50–51.

64. Barr 2007, 208; Collinson 1889, 313.

65. Collinson 1889, 320; Barr 2007, 214.

66. Krech 1978; 1983; 1984b, 58–59; 1979, 107–9.

67. Krech 1996, 200.

68. Maguire 1988, 2:408.

69. Barr 2007, 217.

70. D. J. Ray 1975, 151; Foote 1965, 192–93; Sharpe MS, June 28, 1854.

71. U.K. House of Commons 1855, 905–13; 1854b, 2; Markham 1875, 42–43.

72. Sharpe MS, July 3, 1854, August 24, 1854; U.K. House of Commons 1855, 861, 868.

73. Barr 2007, 219.

74. Bockstoce 1985; U.K. House of Commons 1855, 859–60, 900–901; Barr 2007, 222.

75. Matthews MS, November 1854; Grainger 2008, 47, 80.

12. TRADING ACTIVITIES FROM 1848 TO THE SALE OF RUSSIAN AMERICA

1. Roys MS; *Friend* (Honolulu), November 1, 1848.

2. *Nautical Magazine and Naval Chronicle* (London) 23(10) (1854):545; *Pacific Commercial Advertiser* (Honolulu), December 15, 1866; Charles M. Scammon Papers, PK 206, vol. 1, p. 70, Bancroft Library, University of California–Berkeley; David A. Henderson Papers, New Bedford Whaling Museum, New Bedford, MA.

3. *Friend*, November 1, 1848; Bockstoce 1986, 21–26; Bockstoce and Botkin 1983.

4. Brewster 1992, 379–80; *Tiger* MS. I have added punctuation and paragraph indentations.

5. Brewster 1992, 382; *Tiger* MS. I have added punctuation and capitalization. Notochen was from Cape Chaplin ("Indian Point").

6. Lund 2001, 640; *Friend*, October 1, 1849; *Whalemen's Shipping List and Merchants' Transcript* (New Bedford, MA), January 1, January 22, 1850; Holmes 1857, passim; Brewster 1992, 391–92; *Tiger* MS. I have added punctuation and capitalization.

7. Foote 1965, 185.
8. Bogoras 1904–9, 711; Russian-American Company 1848, 42. As we have seen in chapter 3, Kobelev had explored the Bering Strait region in 1779 and again in 1791. He is reported to have lived for more than a century (Boyakova 2005, 1102–3).
9. Rae 1953, 175.
10. Foote 1965, 185–86. See chapter 1.
11. *Whalemen's Shipping List and Merchants' Transcript*, February 6, 1849, December 9, 1851, July 4, 1853; *Cossack* MS, August 1, 1851; *Phillipe de la Noye* MS, July 23, 1851; Collinson 1889, 132; *Mount Vernon* MS, May 31, 1851; John Matthews MS.
12. Lawrence 1966, 106.
13. D. J. Ray 1975, 180.
14. *South Boston* MS, July 29, 1852; Munger 1852, 31; *Samuel Robertson* MS, July 25, 1851; *Constitution* MS, July 16, 1851; *Whalemen's Shipping List and Merchants' Transcript*, July 4, 1853; *Friend*, December 6, 1853.
15. Holmes 1857, 182–86.
16. *Tamerlane* MS, July 14, 1851; *Wolga* MS, July 25, 1851; *Emu* MS, July 10, 1851; *Montreal* MS, August 4, 1851; *Cossack* MS, July 21, 1851; Asa Tobey, *Whalemen's Shipping List and Merchants' Transcript*, July 4, 1853.
17. *Friend*, December 6, 1853.
18. *Julian* MS, July 31, 1859.
19. Bockstoce and Botkin 1983, 115; Bockstoce et al. 2007.
20. USS *Vincennes* MS, August 1855; Nourse 1884, 120; U.K. House of Commons 1855, 868.
21. *Friend*, November 8, 1858; Dall 1870, 502–3; unidentified newspaper clipping, Scrapbook T-1, New Bedford Whaling Museum, New Bedford, MA; *South America* MS, July 1, 1858; Hegarty 1959, 48–50; *Friend*, November 8, 1858; *Antilla* MS, June 5, 1858; Rosse 1884, 186; *Harmony* MS, June 23, 1858.
22. *Harmony* MS, June 23, 1858.
23. Ibid., June 29, July 26, July 28, 1858. Percussion guns were firearms that, like flintlock muskets, were loaded from the muzzle by first pouring a charge of gunpowder down the barrel and then ramming a bullet and/or a load of shot down after it. Flintlock muskets were fired when the gun's hammer (which held a piece of flint) struck a steel plate, thus producing a spark that ignited the charge of gunpowder. Percussion guns were ignited when the gun's hammer struck a percussion cap—a small copper cup containing fulminate of mercury—which produced a spark that ignited the powder charge. Percussion guns were more reliable than flintlocks, being less prone to misfire (Gregg 2000, 126).
24. *Tamerlane* MS, June 3, 1851; Osbon 1902, 366. The first commercial vessel that is reported to have wintered in the Bering Strait region was the trading brig *Swallow* of Hong Kong, which went north "to buy furs and walrus ivory" and was caught by the ice and frozen in at St. Lawrence Bay for the winter of 1850–51. The *Swallow's* wintering was accidental.
25. *Cleone* MS, 1859–60; *Nimrod* MS, June 23 and 27, 1860; *Jireh Swift* MS, June 19, 1860; *John Howland* MS, June 19–June 23, 1860.

26. *John Howland* MS, June 23, 1862; *Thomas Dickason* MS, September 22, 1861; *Pacific Commercial Advertiser*, September 25 and October 9, 1862; *Ocean* MS, June 22, 1862; *Friend*, November 2, 1863.

27. Thrum 1912, 65.

28. Aldrich 1889, 229–34; *Friend*, November 2, 1863.

29. *Pacific Commercial Advertiser*, September 17, 1863; Thrum 1912, 65; Bockstoce and Batchelder 1978b.

30. Maguire 1988, 1:275.

31. *Harmony* MS, memorandum. William B. Waterman was master of the bark *J. D. Thompson* of New Bedford (Lund 2001, 340).

32. *George and Susan* MS, August 4, 1859; *John Howland* MS, September 20, 1859; *Julian* MS, August 23, 1859; *Sharon* MS, July 19, 1859; Whymper 1869, 169.

33. Pawlik 1996, 32–38; unidentified newspaper clippings, March 31, 1881, and passim, William H. Dall Papers, box 44, record unit 7073, Smithsonian Institution Archives, Washington, DC. Dallmann also claimed to have landed on Wrangel Island. The next year, 1867, Captain Thomas Long in the New London whaling bark *Nile* cruised as far west as Chaun Bay (Chaunskaya Guba) on the north coast of Asia before turning north and sailing along the south coast of Wrangel Island. Unaware of Dallman's precedence, he believed he had discovered the island.

34. *Julian* MS, July 31, 1859; *Cornelius Howland* MS, July 16, 1868. I have added punctuation.

35. Kelly 1890b, 10.

36. E. F. Nye to *New Bedford Standard* from Cape Lisburne, August 2, 1879.

37. Dwyer 2001.

38. Bockstoce 1986, 103–28; Bockstoce 2006.

39. E. W. Nelson 1899, 125; Murdoch 1892, 193, 260; Driggs 1905, 95; Thornton 1931, 139.

40. W. L. Hardisty to The Governor etc., p. 101, Fort Simpson Correspondence Inward, 1869–72, B.200/b/38, Hudson's Bay Company Archives, Provincial Archives of Manitoba, Winnipeg, Manitoba (hereafter HBCA); Petitot 1876, 15; Brower MS, 328–29; Bompas MS, 20. See also Bompas (from La Pierre's House) to Church Missionary Society, December 6, 1872, file C.C.1./o., 11–12, Church Missionary Society Archives, University of Birmingham Library, Birmingham, U.K.

41. E. W. Nelson 1899, 229.

42. Burch 2005, 234.

43. Krech 1979, 110; Petitot 1887, 138–39; Bogoras 1904–9, 44–45.

44. Arndt 1996, 109–12, 115–16. Maguire took command of the *Sitkha* after HMS *Plover* was sold to a shipbreaker in San Francisco in October 1854 (Bockstoce 1988, 47).

45. Logs of Company Ships, 1850–1867, reel 75; Log of bark *Kadiak*, 1854–59; and Communications Sent, vol. 35 (reel 60), nos. 232–33, June 17, 1854, and June 21, 1854, fos. 100–3, and Voevodsky to Main Office, May 3, 1856, vol. 37 (reel 37), no. 236, fo. 97, Correspondence of the Governors General, Records of the Russian-American Company, National Archives, Washington, DC. See also Grainger 2008, passim.

46. Verman 1863, 593–600. Hackfeld and Co. still exists and after several transformations

is today Liberty House retail stores (Prusser 1966; Weiner 1982, 16–17). There is no record of Captain Corsen having returned to Bering Strait with an auxiliary-powered vessel.

47. Kushner 1975, 92; Bolkhovitinov 1996, 84–85.
48. Stephan 1969, 274; Bolkhovitinov 2003, 254; Jensen 1975, 23, 51; Norlander 1994, 21–22; Jensen 1975, 51. Emphasis in the original.
49. Farrar 1966, 13; Furuhjelm 2005, 178, 219, 254.
50. Golovin 1979, 93–94, 180–81; Pierce 1986, 46; 1990a, 328–29. Emphasis original.
51. Dall 1870, 10–11. I have altered the punctuation.
52. Whymper 1868b, 128–29.
53. Dall 1870, 11–13.
54. Ibid., 500–501, 502. The company must have relaxed its prohibition on trading ammunition to the natives.
55. Whymper 1868b, 137–38.
56. Bolkhovitinov 1996, 193; Farrar 1966, 14; quoted in Bolkhovitinov 2003, 256.
57. Bolkhovitinov 1996, 187–88; 2003, 254, 257; Grinev 2004. See also Christensen and Møller 2005, 20–21, and O'Grady-Raeder 1994, 334.
58. Kushner 1975, 157.
59. Knox 2007, 55. See also Stephan 1994, 54; Grainger 2008, passim.

13. CHAOS AND TRANSFORMATION IN THE LATTER
    THIRD OF THE NINETEENTH CENTURY

1. Lee 1996, 21.
2. Kushner 1975, 34; Pierce 1990a, 330–32; 1986, 47; Wright 1976, 119.
3. Bockstoce 1977b, 90; Kitchener 1954, 85.
4. Whymper 1868a, 227.
5. Emanuel 2002, 43.
6. Dall 1870, 103.
7. Whymper 1868b, 221, 225.
8. Antonson and DeArmond 2002, 28–29; Sherwood 1965, 91; U.S. Senate 1869; Wilson 1969, 48; Barry Anderson 1983, 37; Lain 1977, 14.
9. Raymond 1900, 23.
10. Raymond 1870.
11. U.S. Senate 1869, 4.
12. Mercier 1986, 71; Lee 1998, 61; Wilson 1969, 50.
13. Lain 1974, 39.
14. Mercier 1986, xiii; Lain 1977, 15.
15. Coates and Morrison 1988, 38; B.240/a-z, Hudson's Bay Company Archives, Provincial Archives of Manitoba, Winnipeg, Manitoba (hereafter HBCA).
16. Governor McTavish to W. L. Hardisty, November 1869, p. 9, James McDougall to W. L. Hardisty, January 3, 1870, p. 16, Fort Simpson Correspondence Inward, 1869–72, B.200/b/38, HBCA.
17. Coates and Morrison 1988, 41–42.

18. Ibid., 43–44; B.200/b/37 and 38, B.200/b/43, HBCA.

19. International Boundary Commission [1918], 227; Wright 1976, 119.

20. Coates 1982, 72.

21. Coates and Morrison 1988, 45. B.200/b/43, fos. 597–598, D.13/15, fo. 234, D.25/17, fo. 320, D.25/9, fo. 97, B.220/e/24, fos. 2–3, D.21/4, fo. 254, HBCA.

22. B. Anderson 1983, 37.

23. Jacobsen 1977, 87.

24. Coates 1982, 73.

25. Mercier 1986; Sherwood 1965, 45; Clark 1996; Jacobsen 1977, 99; D. J. Ray 1975, 195–96.

26. E. W. Nelson 1899, 229–32; Jacobsen 1977:88.

27. E. W. Nelson 1887, 13.

28. Muir 1917, 90–91.

29. E. W. Nelson MS, August 20, 1877.

30. Hosley 1981, 549; Jacobsen 1977, 93–94, 120, 153–60; E. W. Nelson MS, December 7, 1879, and passim; E. W. Nelson 1887, 240.

31. E. W. Nelson MS, November 18, 1879, February 16 and 18, 1880; Jacobsen 1977, 153–66.

32. E. W. Nelson MS, February 18, 1880.

33. Ibid., February 25, 1880.

34. E. W. Nelson 1899, 294.

35. E. W. Nelson MS, March 19, 1880; E. W. Nelson 1899, 301.

36. Jacobsen 1977, 120.

37. Bartlett MS, October 2, 1878. See, e.g., Krause and Krause 1882, 130; Bockstoce and Batchelder 1977b.

38. G. R. Adams 1982, 73.

39. Nordenskiöld 1882, 484–85.

40. Jacobsen 1977, 120–21.

41. E. W. Nelson MS, August 26, 1877, and August 29, 1877; Jacobsen 1884, 268; J. W. Kelly 1890a, 11; Elliott 1886, 431; C. L. Hooper 1881, 20; G. W. Bailey 1880, 15; E. W. Nelson 1899, 299; Aldrich 1889, 30; *Whalemen's Shipping List and Merchants' Transcript*, September 25, 1877.

42. McCoy 1956; D. J. Ray 1975, 189–90.

43. See chapters 1 and 8. J. W. Kelly 1890b, 11; Brower MS, 225–26. I have altered Brower's punctuation.

44. J. W. Kelly 1890b, 12–13.

45. A number of accounts of this incident have been published and many contain half-truths and errors. In general, those that were written farther in time from the event contain the most hyperbole. It is regrettable that no contemporary account by an Eskimo has survived. George Gilley gave his own account of the incident to Charles Brower in 1886 and to Herbert Aldrich in 1887. Aldrich was a journalist and may have colored Gilley's account, which itself would, no doubt, have been self-serving. Charles Brower's report of Gilley's account is probably more accurate, and it agrees in most

details with John W. Kelly's account, with Thomas Lopp's account, with the Revenue Cutter Service report, and with Edward William Nelson's account.

E. W. Nelson MS, August 26, 1877, August 29, 1877, July 12, 1881; J. W. Kelly 1890b, 12–13; Lopp MS. "Gilley Affair"; unidentified newspaper clipping, Atlantic Mutual Insurance Company Collection, the Atlantic Companies, New York, NY, September 20, 1877; *Chronicle* (San Francisco), November 6, 1877; Brower MS, 226;.; J. W. Kelly 1890a, 12–13; Thornton 1931, 38; Aldrich 1889, 30, 142–46; C. L. Hooper 1881, 20; *Whalemen's Shipping List and Merchants' Transcript*, September 25, 1877; *Pacific Commercial Advertiser*, October 27, 1877.

46. Montgomery 1963; D. J. Ray 1975, 215; G. W. Bailey 1880, 15; *Chronicle*, April 13, 1898; Brower MS, 315; *Eskimo Bulletin* (Cape Prince of Wales), May 1892; *American Missionary*, October 1891, 360.

47. Bockstoce and Botkin 1983, 136; Bockstoce and Burns 1993; Bockstoce 2006; 2007; 1986, 151–66; Brower MS, 142, 230. I am grateful to Dr. Ernest S. Burch, Jr., for his help with this information.

48. Bockstoce and Botkin 1982.

49. F. A. Barker n.d.; *Whalemen's Shipping List and Merchants' Transcript*, April 8, 1872; "Shipmaster" *Republican Standard* (New Bedford), reprinted in *Friend*, March 1, 1872, November 1, 1871; *Hawaiian Gazette* (Honolulu), November 1, 1871; Wilkinson, n.d., passim.

50. *Pacific Commercial Advertiser*, September 6, 1879; G. W. Bailey 1880, 19; C. L. Hooper 1881; 1884, 8–9; Muir 1917, 117–23; Wardman 1884, 147–51; unidentified newspaper clipping, Bartlett scrapbook, 12, New Bedford Whaling Museum; E. W. Nelson 1899, 269.

51. V. V. Bychkov et al. 2002, 132; W. H. Dall, Hydrographic Notes, William Healey Dall Papers, Smithsonian Institution Archives, Washington, DC; E. W. Nelson 1899, 296; Krause and Krause 1881, 263–64; 1882, 130–35; Aldrich 1889, 54; *North Star* MS, May 27, 1882; DeWindt 1899, 191; M. A. Healy to Secretary of the Treasury (Report of USRC *Bear*, 1891), M. A. Healy Papers, Sheldon Jackson College, Sitka, AK; P. H. Ray 1885, 46; Woolfe 1893, 146.

52. Burch 1998a, 148–49; Fortuine 1989, 211–12, 250; Jacobsen 1884, 303; J. W. Kelly 1890b, 21; Krupnik 1990; Woolfe 1893, 143.

53. Bogoras 1904–9, 40; Shklovsky 1916, 6; Burch 1998a, 325.

54. C. L. Hooper 1884, 40; E. W. Nelson 1887, 284; 1899, 119.

55. Burch 1998a, 47, 77, 133, 166, 187, 303, 373; E. S. Burch, Jr., personal communication, n.d. See also Skoog 1968, 329–32; Amsden 1979, 402; E. W. Nelson 1887, 237–38; Muir 1917, 27.

56. E. W. Nelson MS, March 8, 1880. See also Fortuine 1989, 230–39; Krupnik 1993, 153.

57. E. W. Nelson MS, July 12, 1881; J. W. Kelly 1898, 82; Rosse 1883, 185; J. T. White MS, September 2, 1894. See also Bogoras 1904–9, 53; Muir 1917, 133.

58. Burch 1998a, 148; E. W. Nelson 1899, 232; Stoney MS, 160.

59. E. W. Nelson 1899, 231.

60. C. L. Hooper 1884, 39.
61. Stoney MS, 157–58.
62. Ibid., 158–59; VanStone 1962, 126–28.
63. E. W. Nelson 1899, 163–64; Cruikshank 1986, 6–7; Stoney MS, 159.
64. Burch 1981, 16.

14. THE LAST DECADES OF THE NINETEENTH CENTURY

1. *Weekly Bulletin* (San Francisco), December 12, 1878, William Healey Dall Papers, box 44, record unit 7073, Smithsonian Institution Archives, Washington, DC.
2. Gruening 1954, 35.
3. Lain 1974, 45, 51, 202; Davidson 1869, 40.
4. Gruening 1954, 36, 50; McCoy 1956, 364; Lain 1974, 343; Antonson and DeArmond 2002, 34; Wright 1976, 120.
5. King 1996, 28; USRC *Reliance* MS, July 18, 1870, Revenue Cutter Service Collection, record group 26, National Archives, Washington, DC.
6. G. W. Bailey 1880, 17–20; Honolulu Harbormaster, Register of Entries and Clearances, vol. 3, State Archives of Hawai'i, see, e.g., *General Harney*, *Timandra*, and *Loleta*.
7. Thrum 1912, 68; Otis 1880, 43–44; F. T. White MS, April 4, 1994.
8. George Williams to T. B. Sherman, October 24, 1879, Alaska File, U.S. Revenue Cutter Service, record group 26, National Archives, Washington, DC; G. W. Bailey 1880, 12–13.
9. King 1996, 47; Thrum 1912, 68; *Loleta* MS, 1878, Honolulu Consular Records, record group 84, National Archives, Washington, DC.
10. C. L. Hooper 1881, 38.
11. Healy 1889, 11, 17; Thrum 1912, 68.
12. Gilder 1883, 50.
13. E. W. Nelson 1899, 231; Gregg 2000, 165; Woolfe 1893, 146.
14. Murdoch 1892, 193–94; Wells and Kelly 1890, 26.
15. King 1996, 41. See also Prucha 1995, 437–61.
16. Thornton 1931, 139; Bogoras 1904–9, 62.
17. C. L. Hooper 1884, 23 (the emphasis is Hooper's); P. H. Ray to Chief Signal Officer, Washington, July 23, 1882, August 13, 1882, August 23, 1882, September 22, 1882, record group 111, National Archives, Washington, DC; Healy 1889, 17–18.
18. Otis 1880, 43–44; Wardman 1884, 148–50; G. W. Bailey 1880; Dall 1881, 104; Healy 1887, 15; C. L. Hooper 1884, 32–33, 76; 1881, 11–12, 21; E. W. Nelson 1899, 231; Woolfe 1893, 145–46; *Eskimo Bulletin*, 1892, 1897; J. W. Kelly 1898, 82; Harrison R. Thornton to M. A. Healy, June 3 and July 21, 1893, Harrison R. Thornton Collection, Peary-MacMillan Arctic Museum, Bowdoin College, Brunswick, ME.
19. Stephan 1994, 88.
20. Bogoras 1904–9, 62–63; Krause and Krause 1881, 277; 1882, 31.
21. Muir 1917, 133.

22. Stephan 1994, 88.

23. Aldrich 1889, 134.

24. *Francis Palmer* (whaleship) MS, 1878; Woolfe 1893, 137; *Montreal* (whaleship) MS, September 15, 1852; *Henry Taber* (whaleship) MS, July 7, 1869; E. W. Nelson 1899, 263; Brower MS, 212; Rosse 1884, 186–88; Aldrich 1889, 49–50; J. A. Cook 1926, 229.

25. Krupnik 1993, 57.

26. C. L. Hooper 1884, 33.

27. Gilder 1883, 159; Reuse 1994, 319–29; Rosse 1884, 186–88; Murdoch 1892, 55; Wells and Kelly 1890; Hammerich 1958, 636; S. Jackson 1902, 89; Drechsel and Makaukāne 1982; Stefansson 1909a; Schumacher 1978; Krause and Krause 1993, 45, 69.

28. Wells and Kelly 1890, 19, 21; James T. White MS, July 16, 1894; *Governor Troup* MS, June 20, 1864; Murdoch 1892, 54; Borden MS, 18–19; Edson MSS. Edson to Langford July 3, 1895, Episcopal Church Historical Society, Austin, TX.

29. Brower MS, 612; Gilder 1883, 50–51; Russell 1898, 155.

30. Krause and Krause 1882, 137; Bogoras 1904–9, 63–64.

31. E. W. Nelson 1899, 231; Burch 1998a, 215; Stoney MS, 159.

32. Bockstoce 1986, 222–23.

33. Kish 1973, 189–90.

34. Aldrich 1889, 74–75.

35. Woolfe 1893, 137.

36. Murdoch 1892, 66, 70.

37. Nordenskiöld 1881, 2:14; Gilder 1883, 159.

38. Bogoras 1904–9, 65–66.

39. Ibid., 66–67.

40. Ibid., 57–58.

41. Ibid., 708–9.

42. Arthur James Allen 1978, 158; Burch 1975, 222.

43. W. B. Jones 1927, 119.

44. Krause and Krause 1882, 140; Bogoras 1904–9, 62–64; unidentified newspaper clipping, M. A. Healy Collection, Huntington Library, San Marino, CA; *Weekly Bulletin*, October 13, 1886; Aldrich 1889, 50–51; J. T. White MS, August 18, 1886; Herbert Apposingok, Gambell, AK, personal communication, August 1969; Kelly 1890b, 9; Muir 1917, 31; Serghei Aroutiounov, personal communication, March 1976; *Chronicle*, October 16, 1890; U.S. Commission of Education 1894, 950; S. Jackson 1896; Sheldon Jackson diary, Presbyterian Historical Society, Philadelphia, PA, p. 70; DeWindt 1899, 197–98, 204–5, 233; "Seizure of the Henrietta," unidentified news-paper clipping, William Healey Dall Papers, box 46, record unit 7073, Smithsonian Institution Archives, Washington, DC.

45. Krause and Krause 1882, 28–29; Hughes 1964, 9.

46. Brower MS, vol. 2, pt. 2:109 (310). I have altered Brower's punctuation.

47. Laurie Uyuġaluq Kingik, personal communication, May 1979, Point Hope, Alaska; E. W. Nelson 1899, 303.

48. E. W. Nelson 1899, 303; C. L. Hooper 1884, 41.
49. J. W. Kelly 1890b, 11; Rainey 1947, 243.
50. Hadley 1915, 917.
51. Brower MS, 241, 283, 287. I have altered Brower's spelling and punctuation. See also Stoney MS, 59; Burch 2005, 196; Jarvis 1899, 99.
52. Bogoras 1904–9, 632.
53. Stoney 1900, 76; Brower MS, 328; Stefansson 1914a, 172–73, 356; E. P. Herrendeen to W. H. Dall, May 18, 1887, William Healey Dall Papers, box 11, folder 34, Smithsonian Institution Archives, Washington, DC.
54. Woolfe 1893, 138; photograph of Gwich'in visitors in Woolfe 1893, opposite p. 145, third figure from right.
55. Stefansson 1914a, 186–87.
56. Bertholf 1899, 20–21; Bockstoce 1986, 20; Fortuine 1989, 296; Mitchell 2003, 154–55.
57. Woolfe 1893, 145.
58. Lopp 2001, 146; *Eskimo Bulletin* (Cape Prince of Wales), July 1898.
59. See, e.g., *John Wells* MS, June 30, 1870, *Mary and Helen* MS, May 25, 1880.
60. Bockstoce 1986, 201; E. W. Nelson 1887, 293.
61. Bockstoce and Batchelder 1978b; B.200/e/24, fos. 2–3; D.25/9, fo. 97; D.13/15, fo. 234; D.25/17, fo. 320, Hudson's Bay Company Archives, Provincial Archives of Manitoba, Winnipeg, Manitoba (hereafter HBCA). I am indebted to Adeline Peter Raboff for this information.
62. Bockstoce 1986, 272–76; Stewart 1955, 262; Russell MS, July 13, 1894; B.157/e/1, fos. 11–12, 13, 14, A.12/FT 202/1, fos. 1–6, HBCA.
63. Bertholf 1899, 25.
64. Bockstoce 1986, 231–54; Burch 1981, 16–19; Hadley 1915; VanStone 1958; Woolfe 1893, 145.
65. Stefansson 1924, 60–62.
66. Stefansson 1909b, 609.
67. Stefansson 1914a, 219.
68. Bogoras 1904–9, 68.

15. END OF THE CENTURY

1. B. Anderson 1983; Emmanuel 1997, 43–47; Wright 1976, 13–133, 138–39, 161; Rennick 2002, 32–47.
2. B. Anderson 1983, 43–44; Sherwood 1965, 147; Marks 1994, 49; Rennick 2002, 32; Emmanuel 1997, 18, 49.
3. Brown 2007, 65; Marks 1994, 50; B. Anderson 1983, 49; Emmanuel 1997, 11, 33; Cole 1984, 38; Rennick 2002, 35; Burch 1998a, 149.
4. Stephan 1994, 88; Bogoras 1904–9, 63–64.
5. Krause and Krause 1881, 278; Bogoras 1904–9, 64.
6. Bogoras 1904–9, 68.
7. F. T. White MS, May 21, 1894; E. P. Beaver 1988, 442–43.

APPENDIX

1. Gillesem 1849, 1971; D. J. Ray 1992, 68–69; Lazarev 1950; Sishmarev MS.
2. Burch 2003, 412–13; Kotzebue 1821b, 1:205, 229. See chapter 1.
3. D. J. Ray 1975; 1983, 63, Bockstoce 1977a, 6–7; 1986, 180; 1988, 2; Ray and Josephson 1971.
4. Bockstoce 1977a, 104–32; Kotzebue 1821a, 1:156; 1821b, 1:245, 259; Gregg 2000, 116; Litke 1835, 2:266–67.
5. See also Gregg 2000.

Bibliography

Adams, Edward. 1850–51. *Journal Kept Ashore in and near St. Michael's Alaska, 12 October 1850–3 July 1851, During Collinson's Franklin Search Expedition, 1850–1855.* Scott Polar Research Institute, University of Cambridge, Cambridge, UK. Archives MS 1115.

Adams, George R. 1982. *Life on the Yukon, 1865–1867.* Kingston, ON: Limestone. Alaska History 22.

Aldrich, Herbert L. 1889. *Arctic Alaska and Siberia, or Eight Months with the Arctic Whalemen.* Chicago: Rand McNally.

Alekseev, A. I. 1987. *The Odyssey of a Russian Scientist: I. G. Voznesenskii in Alaska, California and Siberia.* Ed. Richard A. Pierce. Trans. Wilma C. Follette. Kingston, ON: Limestone.

———. 1990. *The Destiny of Russian America, 1741–1867.* Kingston, ON: Limestone.

———. 1996. *Fedor Petrovich Litke.* Ed. Katherine L. Arndt. Trans. Serge LeComte. Fairbanks: University of Alaska Press.

Allen, Arthur James. 1978. *A Whaler and Trader in the Arctic.* Anchorage: Alaska Northwest.

Allen, J. A. 1903. "Report on the Mammals Collected in Northeastern Siberia by the Jessup North Pacific Expedition, with Itinerary and Field Notes, by N. G. Buxton." *Bulletin of the American Museum of Natural History* 19:101–84.

———. 1912. "The Probable Recent Extinction of the Musk-ox in Alaska." *Science* 36 (934): 720–22.

Alunik, Ishmael, Eddie D. Kolausok, and David Morrison. 2003. *Across Time and Tundra: The Inuvialuit of the Western Arctic.* Vancouver: Raincoast.

Amsden, Charles W. 1979. "Hard Times: A Case Study from Northern Alaska and Implications for Arctic Prehistory." In *Thule Eskimo Culture: An Anthropological Retrospective.* Ed. Allen P. McCartney. Ottawa: National Museum of Man. Mercury Series, Archaeological Survey of Canada, Paper 88, pp. 395–410.

Anderson, Barry C. 1983. *Lifeline to the Yukon: A History of Yukon River Navigation.* Seattle: Superior.

Anderson, Douglas D., Ray Bane, Richard K. Nelson, Wanni W. Anderson, and Nita Sheldon. 1977. *Kuuvaŋmiit Subsistence: Traditional Eskimo Life in the Latter Twentieth Century.* Washington, DC: U.S. Department of the Interior, National Park Service.

Anderson, Rudolph Martin. 1928. "Report on the Natural History Collections of the Expedition." In Vilhjalmur Stefansson, *My Life with the Eskimo.* New York: Macmillan, pp. 436–527.

Anonymous. 2004. "A Day at a Hat-Factory." *Museum of the Fur Trade Quarterly* 40 (1): 2–16. Reprint from *Penny Magazine* 10:567 (1841): 41–48.

———. 2008. "I. Wilson Knife Markings in 1831." *Museum of the Fur Trade Quarterly* 44 (1): 10–11.

Antilla (whaleship). MS. Journal of Charles Quinn, March 13, 1858–November 1, 1858. Providence Public Library, Providence, RI.

Antonson, Joan, and Robert DeArmond. 2002. "Chronology from Purchase to Statehood." *Alaska Geographic* 29 (3): 28–39.

Arctic Bibliography. 1959. Ed. Marie Tremaine. Washington, DC: U.S. Department of Defense. Vol. 8 (contains Parliamentary reports on the Search for Sir John Franklin).

Armstrong, Alexander. 1857. *A Personal Narrative of the Discovery of the North-West Passage. . . .* London: Hurst and Blackett.

Armstrong, Terence. 1965. *Russian Settlement in the North.* Cambridge: Cambridge University Press.

———. 1975. *Yermak's Campaign in Siberia.* London: Hakluyt Society.

———. 1994. "Russian Penetration into Siberia up to 1800." In *The European Outthrust and Encounter. The First Phase c. 1440–c. 1700: Essays in Tribute to David Beers Quinn on His 85th Birthday.* Ed. Cecil H. Clough and P. E. H. Hair. Liverpool: Liverpool University Press. Liverpool Historical Studies 12:118–39.

Arndt, Katherine Louise. 1990a. "Russian Exploration and Trade in Alaska's Interior." In *Russian America: The Forgotten Frontier.* Ed. Barbara Sweetland Smith and Redmond J. Barnett. Tacoma: Washington State Historical Society, pp. 95–107.

———. 1990b. "Russian-American Company Trade on the Middle Yukon River, 1839–1867." In *Russia in North America: Proceedings of the 2nd International Conference on Russian America . . . 1987.* Ed. Richard A. Pierce. Kingston, ON: Limestone.

———. 1996. "Dynamics of the Fur Trade on the Middle Yukon River, Alaska, 1839 to 1868." PhD diss., University of Alaska–Fairbanks.

Arsenev, V. K. 1927. *Tikhookeanskii Morzh* [The Pacific Walrus]. Khabarovsk-Vladivostok: Knizhnoe Delo.

Arutiunov, Sergei, and Dorian A. Sergeev. 2007. *Problems of Ethnic History in the Bering Sea: The Ekven Eemetery.* Trans. Richard L. Bland. Anchorage: U.S. Department of the Interior, National Park Service.

Bailey, Edgar P. 1992. "Red foxes, *Vulpes vulpes,* as Biological Control Agents for Introduced Arctic Foxes, *Alopex lagopus,* on Alaskan Islands." *Canadian Field-Naturalist* 106 (2): 200–205.

Bailey, George W. 1880. Letter to the Hon. John Sherman, Secretary of the Treasury, in letter from the Secretary of the Treasury, U.S. Senate, 46th Cong., 2nd sess., Executive Document 132.

Bancroft, Hubert Howe. 1886. *History of Alaska, 1730–1885*, New York: Bancroft.

Bane, G. Ray. 1982. "The Nature of Subsistence Activities." In *Tracks in the Wildland: A Portrayal of Koyukon and Nunamiut Subsistence*. Ed. Richard K. Nelson, Kathleen H. Mauner, and G. Ray Bane. Fairbanks: University of Alaska. Anthropology and Historic Preservation, Cooperative Park Studies Unit.

Barker, Frederick A. MSa. Journal, 1870–71. Turnbull Library, Aukland, New Zealand.

———. MSb. Journal, schooner *Leo*, March 2, 1878–September 12, 1878, New Bedford Whaling Museum, New Bedford, MA. Old Dartmouth Historical Society Collection, no. 936.

———. n.d. *20 Months in Siberia, Behrings Straits and Alaska by a Shipwrecked Whaling Master*. Typescript. New Bedford Whaling Museum, New Bedford, MA. Kendall Collection, no. 866 A-D.

Barman, Jean, and Bruce McIntyre Watson. 2006. *Leaving Paradise: Indigenous Hawaiians in the Pacific Northwest, 1817–1898*. Honolulu: University of Hawai'i Press.

Barr, William. 1994. "The Eighteenth Century Trade between the Ships of the Hudson's Bay Company and the Hudson Strait Inuit." *Arctic* 47 (3): 236–46.

———, ed. 2002. *From Barrow to Boothia: The Arctic Journal of Chief Factor Peter Warren Dease, 1836–1839*. Montreal: McGill–Queen's University Press.

———. 2007. *Arctic Hell Ship: The Voyage of HMS Enterprise, 1850–1855*. Edmonton: University of Alberta Press.

Barratt, Glynn. 1981. *Russia in Pacific Waters, 1715–1825*. Vancouver: University of British Columbia Press.

———. 1983. *Russian Shadows on the British Northwest Coast of North America, 1810–1890*. Vancouver: University of British Columbia Press.

———. 1988. *The Russian View of Honolulu, 1809–26*. Ottawa: Carleton University Press.

———. 1990. "A Note on Trade between Oahu and the Russian Northwest Coast, 1806–1826." In *Russia in North America: Proceedings of the 2nd International Conference on Russian America*. Ed. Richard A. Pierce. Kingston, ON: Limestone, pp. 144–56.

Bartlett, Gideon. MS. Journal, September 21, 1878–October 21, 1878. New Bedford Whaling Museum, New Bedford, MA. Old Dartmouth Historical Society Collection, no. 524.

Bates, Lindon, Jr. 1910. *The Russian Road to China*. Boston: Houghton Mifflin.

Beaglehole, J. C., ed. 1967. *The Journals of Captain James Cook on His Voyages of Discovery. The Voyage of the* Resolution *and* Discovery, *1776–1780*. 2 vols. Cambridge, UK: Hakluyt Society.

Beaver, C. Masten. 1955. *Fort Yukon Trader: Three Years in an Alaskan Wilderness*. New York: Exposition.

Beaver, E. Pierce. 1988. "Protestant Churches and the Indians." In *Handbook of North American Indians*, vol. 4, *History of Indian-White Relations*. Ed. Wilcomb E. Washburn. Washington, DC: Smithsonian Institution, pp. 430–58.

Beechey, Frederick William. 1831. *Narrative of a Voyage to the Pacific and Beering's Strait, to Co-operate with the Polar Expeditions; Performed in His Majesty's Ship Blossom . . . in the years 1825, 26, 27, 28*. 2 vols. London: Henry Colburn and Richard Bentley.

Beechey, Richard. MS. "Remarks on a Voyage of Discovery to the Pacific and Bherings's

Straits on Board H.M.S. Blossom by Rich. Beechey Midn., Aged 15." Belfast: Public Record Office of Northern Ireland.

Belcher, Edward. MS. "Private Journal, Remarks, etc. HM Ship Blossom on Discovery during the Years 1825, 6, 7 . . . and Continuation of Private journal. . . ." Typescript copy. University of British Columbia Library, Vancouver.

Belden, A. L. 1917. *The Fur Trade of America and Some of the Men Who Made and Maintain It. . . .* New York: Peltries.

Belov, M. I. 2000. *Russians in the Bering Strait, 1648–1791.* Ed. J. L. Smith. Trans. Katerina Solovjova. Anchorage: White Stone.

Berrie, Peter, Jeannette Ernest, and Bob Stephenson. 1994. "Lynx." Wildlife Notebook Series. Juneau: Alaska Department of Fish and Game.

Bertholf, E. P. 1899. Report of Second Lieut. E. P. Bertholf, R.C.S. In [Francis Tuttle]. *Report of the Cruise of the U.S. Revenue Cutter* Bear *and the Overland Expedition for the Relief of the Whalers in the Arctic Ocean from November 27, 1879 to September 13, 1898.* Washington, DC: Government Printing Office, pp. 18–27, 103–14.

Betts, Matthew W. 2005. "Seven Focal Economies for Six Focal Places: The Development of Economic Diversity in the Western Canadian Arctic." *Arctic Anthropology* 42 (1): 47–87.

Black, Lydia T. 2004. *Russians in Alaska, 1732–1867.* Fairbanks: University of Alaska Press.

Blomkvist, E. E. 1972. "A Russian Scientific Expedition to California and Alaska, 1839–1849: The Drawings of I. G. Voznesenskii." Trans. Basil Dmytryshyn and E. A. P. Crownhart-Vaughan. *Oregon Historical Quarterly* 73 (2): 101–70.

Bockstoce, John R. 1977a. *Eskimos of Northwest Alaska in the Early Nineteenth Century.* Oxford: Pitt Rivers Museum, University of Oxford. Monograph Series 1.

———. 1977b. *Steam Whaling in the Western Arctic.* New Bedford, MA: Old Dartmouth Historical Society.

———. 1985. "The Search for Sir John Franklin in Alaska." In *The Franklin Era in Canadian Arctic History, 1845–1859.* Ed. Patricia D. Sutherland. Ottawa: National Museum of Man. Mercury Series, Archaeological Survey of Canada Paper 131:93–113.

———. 1986. *Whales, Ice and Men: The History of Whaling in the Western Arctic.* Seattle: University of Washington Press.

———, ed. 1988. *The Journal of Rochfort Maguire, 1852–1854: Two Years at Point Barrow, Alaska, Aboard HMS* Plover *in the Search for Sir John Franklin.* 2 vols. London: Hakluyt Society.

———. 1991. *Arctic Passages: A Unique Small-Boat Journey through the Great Northern Waterway.* New York: William Morrow.

———. 2003. *High Latitude, North Atlantic: 30,000 Miles through Cold Seas and History.* Mystic, CT: Mystic Seaport Museum.

———. 2005. "The Opening of the Maritime Fur Trade at Bering Strait." *Transactions of the American Philosophical Society* 95(1).

———. 2006. "Nineteenth Century Commercial Shipping Losses in the Northern Bering Sea, Chukchi Sea, and Beaufort Sea." *Northern Mariner/Le Marin du Nord* 16 (2): 55–68.

Bockstoce, John R., and Charles F. Batchelder. 1978a. "A Gazetteer of Whalers' Place-

Names for the Bering Strait Region and the Western Arctic." *Names: Journal of the American Name Society* 26 (3): 258–70.

———. 1978b. "A Chronological List of Commercial Wintering Voyages to the Bering Strait Region and Western Arctic of North America, 1850–1910." *American Neptune* 38 (2): 81–91.

Bockstoce, John R., and Daniel B. Botkin. 1982. "The Harvest of Pacific Walruses by the Pelagic Whaling Industry, 1848–1914." *Arctic and Alpine Research* 14 (3): 183–88.

———. 1983. "The Historical Status and Reduction of the Western Arctic Bowhead Whale (*Balaena mysticetus*) Population by the Pelagic Whaling Industry, 1848–1914." *Report of the International Whaling Commission, Special Issue* 5 (SC/32/PS16): 107–41.

Bockstoce, John R., Daniel B. Botkin, Alex Philp, Brian W. Collins, and John C. George. 2007. "The Geographic Distribution of Bowhead Whales, *Balaena mysticetus*, in the Bering, Chukchi, and Beaufort Seas: Evidence from Whaleship Records, 1849–1914." *Marine Fisheries Review* 67 (3): 1–43.

Bockstoce, John R., and John J. Burns. 1993. "Commercial Whaling in the North Pacific Sector." In *The Bowhead Whale*. Ed. John J. Burns, J. Jerome Montague, and Cleveland J. Cowles. Lawrence, KS: Society for Marine Mammology. Special Publication 2:563–77.

Bogoras, Waldemar. 1904–9. *The Chukchee*. Jessup North Pacific Expedition, Memoirs of the American Museum of Natural History, vol. 11.

Bolkhovitinov, Nikolai N. 1996. *Russian-American Relations and the Sale of Alaska, 1834–1867*. Trans. and ed. Richard A. Pierce. Kingston, ON: Limestone. Alaska History 45.

———. 2003. "The Sale of Alaska: A Russian Perspective." *Polar Geography* 27 (3): 254–57.

Bompas, William C. MS. "The Esquimaux of the Mackenzie River." Church Missionary Society Collection, C.C.1./o., University of Birmingham Library, Birmingham, UK.

Borden, Gilbert B. MS. Journal, August 15, 1889–August 23, 1891. Beinecke Rare Book and Manuscript Library, MS S-265, Yale University, New Haven.

Boutin, Stan, and Dale E. Birkenholz. 1987. "Muskrat and Round-Tailed Muskrat." In *Wild Furbearer Management and Conservation in North America*. Ed. Milan Novak et al. Toronto: Ontario Ministry of Natural Resources, pp. 314–25.

Boyakova, Sardana. 2005. "Ivan Kobelev." In *Encyclopedia of the Arctic*. Ed. Mark Nuttall. New York: Routledge.

Braund, Stephen R. 1988. *The Skin Boats of St. Lawrence Island, Alaska*. Seattle: University of Washington Press.

Brewster, Mary. 1992. *"She was a sister sailor": The Whaling Journals of Mary Brewster, 1845–1851*. Ed. Joan Druett. Mystic, CT: Mystic Seaport Museum.

Brisee, Paula. 1987. "Museum Exhibit Crossroads of Continents: Bering Strait Trade Networks." Typescript. Washington, DC: Smithsonian Institution, Department of Anthropology.

Brooks, Alfred Hulse. 1953. *Blazing Alaska's Trails*. College, AK: University of Alaska and Arctic Institute of North America.

Brower, Charles D. MS. "The Northernmost American. An Autobiography." Rauner Special Collections Library, Dartmouth College Library, Hanover, NH.

Brown, William E. 2007. *History of the Central Brooks Range*. Fairbanks: University of Alaska Press.

Burch, Ernest S., Jr. 1975. *Eskimo Kinsmen: Changing Family Relationships in Northwest Alaska*. St. Paul, MN: West.

———. 1976. "Overland Trade Routes in Northwest Alaska." *Anthropological Papers of the University of Alaska* 18 (1): 1–10.

———. 1979. "Indians and Eskimos in North Alaska, 1816–1977: A Study in Changing Ethnic Relations." *Arctic Anthropology* 16 (2): 123–51.

———. 1981. *The Traditional Eskimo Hunters of Point Hope, Alaska: 1800–1875*. Barrow, AK: North Slope Borough.

———. 1983. *Peoples of the Arctic* (map). Washington, DC: National Geographic Society.

———. 1998a. *The Iñupiaq Eskimo Nations of Northwest Alaska*. Fairbanks: University of Alaska Press.

———. 1998b. *International Affairs: The Cultural and Natural Heritage of Northwest Alaska*, vol. 7. Prepared for NANA Museum of the Arctic, Kotzebue, and U.S. National Park Service, Anchorage.

———. 2003. *The Organization of National Life: The Cultural and Natural Heritage of Northwest Alaska*, vol. 6. Prepared for NANA Museum of the Arctic, Kotzebue, and U.S. National Park Service, Anchorage.

———. 2005. *Alliance and Conflict: The World System of the Iñupiaq Eskimos*. Lincoln: University of Nebraska Press.

———. 2006. *Social Life in Northwest Alaska: The Structure of Iñupiaq Eskimo Nations*. Fairbanks: University of Alaska Press.

———. 2007. "Traditional Native Warfare in Western Alaska." In *North American Indigenous Warfare and Ritual Violence*. Ed. Richard J. Chacon and Rubén G. Mendoza. Tucson: University of Arizona Press, pp. 11–29.

Burns, John J. 1994. "Mink." Wildlife Notebook Series. Juneau: Alaska Department of Fish and Game.

———. 2005. "Walrus." Wildlife Notebook Series. Juneau: Alaska Department of Fish and Game.

Burt, William H., and Richard P. Grossenheider. 1976. *A Field Guide to the Mammals of America North of Mexico*. 3d ed. Peterson Field Guide Series. Boston: Houghton Mifflin.

Buxton, N. G. 1903. "Itinerary and General Description of the Country." In J. A. Allen. "Report on the Mammals Collected in Northeastern Siberia by the Jessup North Pacific Expedition, with Itinerary and Field Notes, by N. G. Buxton." *Bulletin of the American Museum of Natural History* 21:104–19.

Bychkov, Oleg V. 1994. "Russian Hunters in Eastern Siberia in the Seventeenth Century: Lifestyle and Economy." *Arctic Anthropology* 31 (1): 72–85.

Bychkov, V. V., et al. 2002. *Catalog of Objects of Material and Spiritual Culture of the Chukchi and Eskimos of the Chukchi Peninsula in the Provideniya Museum Collections*. Trans. Richard L. Bland. Barrow: North Slope Borough and U.S. National Park Service.

Cammann, Schuyler. 1954. "Carvings in Walrus Ivory." *University Museum Bulletin* 18 (3): 3–31. Philadelphia: University of Pennsylvania, University Museum.

Campbell, John Martin. 1998. *North Alaska Chronicle: Notes from the End of Time: The Simon Paneak Drawings.* Santa Fe: Museum of New Mexico.

Camsell, Charles. 1954. *Son of the North.* Toronto: Ryerson.

Camsell, Charles, and Wyatt Malcolm. 1919. *The Mackenzie River Basin.* Canada Department of Mines, Geological Survey, Memoir 108. Ottawa: King's Printer.

Cantwell, J. C. 1902. *Report of the Operations of the U.S. Revenue Steamer* Nunivak *on the Yukon River Station, Alaska, 1899–1901.* Washington, DC: Government Printing Office.

Carpenter, Edmund. 1997. "Arctic Witnesses." In *Fifty Years of Arctic Research: Anthropological Studies from Greenland to Siberia.* Ed. R. Gilberg and H. C. Gulløv. Copenhagen: National Museum of Denmark. Ethnographical Series 18:303–10.

CAVM Team. 2003. *Circumpolar Arctic Vegetation Map.* Conservation of Arctic Flora and Fauna, Map 1. Anchorage: U.S. Fish and Wildlife Service.

Chamisso, Adelbert von. 1874. *Chamissos Werke.* 2 vols. Ed. Heinrich Kurz. Leipzig: Bibliographischen Instituts.

———. 1986. *A Voyage around the World with the Romanzov Exploring Expedition in the Years 1815–1818 in the Brig Rurik, Captain Otto von Kotzebue.* Trans. and ed. Henry Kratz. Honolulu: University of Hawaii Press.

Chernenko, M. B. 2000. "Travels to the Land of the Chukchi and Voyages to Alaska by the Cossack Sotnik (Leader of a Hundred Men) Ivan Kobelev in 1779 and 1789–91." In *Russians in Bering Strait, 1648–1791.* Russian ed. M. I. Belov. Trans. Katerina Solovjova. Ed. J. L. Smith. Anchorage: White Stone, pp. 107–32.

Chernenko, M. B., G. A. Agranat, and Y. E. Blomkvist, eds. 1967. Introduction to the Russian edition (1956) of *The Travels and Explorations of Lieutenant Lavrentiy Zagoskin in Russian America, 1842–1844.* In Lavrentii Alekseevich Zagoskin. *Lieutenant Zagoskin's Travels in Russian America, 1842–1844.* Ed. Henry N. Michael. Trans. Penelope Rainey. Toronto: Arctic Institute of North America, 1967. Anthropology of the North: Translations from Russian Sources 7.

[Chimmo, William]. 1860. *Euryalus: Tales of the Sea, a Few Leaves from the Diary of a Midshipman.* London: J. D. Potter.

Choris, Louis. 1822. *Voyage Pittoresque autour du Monde, avec des Portraits de Sauvages d'Amérique, d'Asie, d'Afrique, et des Isles du Grand Océan; des Paysages, des Vues é Maritimes, et Plusieurs Objets d'Histoire Naturelle. . . .* Paris: Firmin Didot.

Christensen, Annie Constance, and Peter Ulf Møller. 2005. Introduction. In Anna von Shoultz Furuhjelm. *Letters from the Governor's Wife: A View of Russian Alaska, 1859–1862.* Århus, Den.: Århus University Press.

Clark, Donald W. 1996. "Archaeological Examination of Fort Reliance, Yukon." *Historical Archaeology* 30(2): 93–100.

Cleone (whaleship). MS. Logbook, October 4, 1858–August 4, 1862. New Bedford Whaling Museum, New Bedford, MA. Old Dartmouth Historical Society Collection, no. 413.

Coates, Kenneth S. 1982. "Furs along the Yukon: Hudson's Bay Company—Native Trade in the Yukon River Basin, 1830–1893." *BC Studies* 55 (Autumn): 50–78.

———. 1993. *Best Left as Indians.* Montreal: McGill–Queen's University Press.

Coates, Kenneth S., and William R. Morrison. 1988. *Land of the Midnight Sun: A History of the Yukon.* Edmonton: Hurtig.

Cochrane, John Dundas. 1824. *Narrative of a Pedestrian Journey through Russia and Siberian Tartary, from the Frontiers of China to the Frozen Sea and Kamchatka.* 2 vols. London: Charles Knight.

Cole, Terrence. 1984. "Nome, 'City of the Golden Beaches.'" *Alaska Geographic* 11:1.

Collier, Simon, and William F. Sater. 1996. *A History of Chile, 1808–1994.* Cambridge: Cambridge University Press.

Collinson, Richard. 1889. *Journal of H.M.S. Enterprise on the Expedition in Search of Sir John Franklin's Ships by Behring Strait, 1850–1855.* Ed. T. B. Collinson. London: Sampson, Low, Marston, Searle and Rivington.

Constitution (whaleship). MS. Journal of Obed R. Bunker, September 5, 1847–April 22, 1852. Nantucket Historical Association, Nantucket, MA.

Cook, James 1967. *The Journals of Captain James Cook on His Voyages of Discovery: The Voyage of the* Resolution *and* Discovery, *1776–1780.* 2 vols. Ed. J. C. Beaglehole. Cambridge, UK: Hakluyt Society.

Cook, James, and James King. 1784. *A Voyage to the Pacific Ocean . . . 1776, 1777, 1778, 1779, and 1780.* 3 vols. and atlas. London: G. Nicol and T. Cadell.

Cook, John A. 1926. *Pursuing the Whale.* Boston: Houghton Mifflin.

Cooper, John M. 1938. *Snares, Deadfalls, and Other Traps of the Northern Algonquians and Northern Athapascans.* Washington, DC: Catholic University of America. Anthropological series 3.

Corti, Egon Caesar, Count. 1996. *A History of Smoking.* Trans. Paul England. London: Bracken.

Cornelius Howland (whaleship). MS. Journal of Captain B. F. Hohman, November 12, 1867–November 20, 1870. Providence Public Library, no. 204, Providence, RI,

Cossack (whaleship). MS. Logbook, October 9, 1850–May 10, 1853. New Bedford Whaling Museum, New Bedford, MA. Old Dartmouth Historical Society Collection, no. 92.

Coxe, William. 1780. *Account of the Russian Discoveries between Asia and America. To which are Added, the Conquest of Siberia, and the History of the Transactions and Commerce between Russia and China. . . .* London: T. Cadell.

Crow, John R., and Philip R. Obley. 1981. "Han." In *Handbook of North American Indians,* vol. 6, *Subarctic.* Ed. June Helm. Washington, DC: Smithsonian Institution, pp. 506–13.

Crownhart-Vaughan, E. A. P. 1972. Introduction. In Stepan Petrovich Krasheninnikov. *Explorations of Kamchatka.* Trans. and ed. E. A. P. Crownhart-Vaughan. Portland: Oregon Historical Society.

Cruikshank, Moses. 1986. *The Life I've Been Living.* Comp. William Schneider. Fairbanks: University of Alaska Press, Alaska and Polar Regions Department, Elmer E. Rasmuson Library.

Curby, Catherine. 1994. "Marmot." Wildlife Notebook Series. Juneau: Alaska Department of Fish and Game.

Curtin, Philip D. 1984. *Cross-Cultural Trade in World History.* Cambridge: Cambridge University Press.

Daitch, Clare-Estelle. 2007. "Studying the MacFarlane Inuvialiut Collection." *Arctic*

Studies Center Newsletter 14:26–27. Washington, DC: National Museum of Natural History, Smithsonian Institution.

Dall, William Healey. 1870. *Alaska and Its Resources*. Boston: Lee and Shepard.

———. 1881. "Notes on Alaska and the Vicinity of Bering Strait." *American Journal of Science*, 3d ser., 21 (122).

Davidson, George. 1869. *Coast Pilot of Alaska (first part) from Southern Boundary to Cook's Inlet*. Washington, DC: U.S. Coast Survey, Government Printing Office.

Daws, Gavan. 1968. *Shoal of Time: A History of the Hawaiian Islands*. Honolulu: University of Hawaii Press.

DeWindt, Harry. 1899. *Through the Gold Fields of Alaska to Bering Strait*. London: Chatto and Windus.

Digby, Bassett. 1926. *The Mammoth and Mammoth-Hunting in North-East Siberia*. New York: D. Appleton.

Divin, V. A. 1997. *To the American Coast: The Voyages and Explorations of M. S. Gvozdev: The Discoverer of Northwestern America*. Anchorage: White Stone.

Dmytryshyn, Basil. 1991. "The Administrative Apparatus of the Russian Colony in Siberia and Northern Asia, 1581–1700." In *The History of Siberia from Russian Conquest to Revolution*. Ed. Alan Wood. London: Routledge, pp. 19–36.

Dmytryshyn, Basil, E. A. P. Crownhart-Vaughan, and Thomas Vaughan. 1985. *Russia's Conquest of Siberia, 1558–1700*. Vol. 1 of *To Siberia and Russian America: Three Centuries of Russian Eastward Expansion*. Portland: Oregon Historical Society.

———. 1989. *The Russian American Colonies, 1798–1867*. Vol. 3 of *To Siberia and Russian America: Three Centuries of Russian Eastward Expansion*. Portland: Oregon Historical Society.

Dobell, Peter. 1830. *Travels in Kamtchatka and Siberia; With a Narrative of a Residence in China*. 2 vols. London: Henry Colburn and Richard Bentley.

Dolitsky, Alexander B., ed. 2002. *Ancient Tales of Kamchatka*. Trans. Henry N. Michael. Juneau: Alaska-Siberia Research Center.

Doty, William Furman. 1900. "The Eskimo on St. Lawrence Island, Alaska." In *Ninth Annual Report on Introduction of Domestic Reindeer into Alaska . . . 1899*. Ed. Sheldon Jackson. Washington, DC: Government Printing Office, pp. 186–223.

Doyle, John F. 1990. "Twelve Thousand Miles of Misplaced Motivations: Commercial Management of the Russian-American Company in Alaska and Siberia." Bachelor of Arts thesis, Reed College, Portland, OR.

Drechsel, Emanuel J., and T. Haunani Makuakāne. 1982. "Hawaiian Loanwords in Two Native American Pidgins." *International Journal of American Linguistics* 48(4): 460–67.

Driggs, John B. 1905. *Short Sketches from Oldest America*. Philadelphia: George W. Jacobs.

Du Halde, Jean Baptiste. 1735. *Description Géographique, Historique, Chronologique, Politique, et Physique de l'Empire de la Chine et de la Tartarie Chinoise. . . .* 4 vols. Paris: P. G. Le Mercier.

Dwyer, John B. 2001. *To Wire the World: Perry M. Collins and the North Pacific Telegraph Expedition*. Westport, CT: Praeger.

Eagle, Thomas C., and Jackson S. Whitman. 1987. "Mink." In *Wild Furbearer Management and Conservation in North America*. Ed. Milan Novak et al. Toronto: Ontario Ministry of Natural Resources, pp. 456–73.

Earnest, Jeannett R. 1994a. "Muskrat." Wildlife Notebook Series. Juneau: Alaska Department of Fish and Game.

———. 1994b. "Hares." Wildlife Notebook Series. Juneau: Alaska Department of Fish and Game.

Edson, E. H. MSS. E. H. Edson Collection, Episcopal Church Historical Society, Austin, TX.

Efimov, A. V. 1964. *Atlas Geograficheskikh Otkrytii v Sibiri i Severo-Zapadnoi Amerike, XVII–XVIII vv* [Atlas of Geographic Discoveries in Siberia and Northwest America in the Seventeenth and Eighteenth Centuries]. Moscow: Nauka.

Eide, Sterling, Sterling Miller, and Harry Reynolds. 2003. "Brown Bear." Wildlife Notebook Series. Juneau: Alaska Department of Fish and Game.

Elliott, Henry W. 1886. *Our Arctic Province: Alaska and the Sea Islands*. New York: Charles Scribner's Sons.

Ellis, William. 1782. *An Authentic Narrative of a Voyage Performed by Captain Cook and Captain Clerke . . . between the Continents of Asia and America. . . .* 2 vols. London: G. Robinson, J. Sewell, and J. Debrett.

Elson, Thomas. 1973. *Log of the Voyage of the Barge of H.M.S. Blossom, 1826*. In George Peard. *To the Pacific and Arctic with Beechey: The Journal of Lieutenant George Peard of H.M.S. Blossom, 1825–1828*. Ed. Barry Gough. Cambridge, UK: Hakluyt Society.

Emanuel, Richard P. 1997. "The Golden Gamble." *Alaska Geographic* 24 (2).

———. 2002. "Economic Development of Alaska Territory." *Alaska Geographic* 29 (3): 40–65.

Emu (whaleship). MS. Logbook, January 15, 1851–December 29, 1851. ML A 437, Mitchell Library, Sydney, NSW, Australia.

Epler, John W., Jr. 2008. "The Good, the Bad and the Ugly: How to Handle Raccoon Hides." *Fur-Fish-Game* 105 (8): 14–17.

Erman, A. 1843. *Archiv für Wissenschaftliche Kunde von Russland*. 2 vols. Berlin: G. Reimer.

Euryalus. See Chimmo.

Farrar, Victor J. 1966. *The Annexation of Russian America to the United States*. New York: Russell and Russell.

Farris, Glenn. 1993. "The Russian Sloop Apollo in the North Pacific in 1822." *Sibirica* 1 (1): 47–70.

Fedorova, Svetlana G. 1973. *The Russian Population in Alaska and California: Late Eighteenth Century–1867*. Trans. Richard S. Pierce and Alton Donnelly. Kingston, ON: Limestone. Materials for the Study of Alaska History 4.

Fienup-Riordan, Ann. 1994. "Eskimo War and Peace." In *Anthropology of the North Pacific Rim*. Ed. William W. Fitzhugh and Valérie Chaussonet. Washington, DC: Smithsonian Institution Press.

Finnerty, Edward W. 1976. *Trappers, Traps, and Trapping*. South Brunswick, NJ: A. S. Barnes.

Fisher, Raymond H. 1943. *The Russian Fur Trade, 1550–1700.* Berkeley: University of California Press.

———. 1977. *Bering's Voyages: Whither and Why.* London: C. Hurst.

———. 1981. *The Voyage of Semen Dezhnev in 1648: Bering's Precursor.* London: Hakluyt Society.

———. 1990. "Russia's Two Eastern Frontiers: Siberia and Russian America." *Pacifica* 2 (2): 24–34.

Fitzhugh, William W., and Aron Crowell, eds. 1988. *Crossroads of Continents: Cultures of Siberia and Alaska.* Washington, DC: Smithsonian Institution Press.

Foote, Don Charles. 1965. "Exploration and Resource Utilization in Northwestern Arctic Alaska before 1855." PhD diss., Department of Geography, McGill University, Montreal.

Forsyth, James. 1992. *A History of the Peoples of Siberia: Russia's North Asian Colony, 1581–1990.* Cambridge: Cambridge University Press.

Fortuine, Robert. 1989. *Chills and Fever: Health and Disease in the Early History of Alaska.* Fairbanks: University of Alaska Press.

———. 1996. "Historical Notes on the Introduction of Tobacco into Alaska." *Alaska Medicine* 38 (1): 4–7.

Foust, Clifford M. 1969. *Muscovite and Mandarin: Russia's Trade with China and Its Setting, 1727–1805.* Chapel Hill: University of North Carolina Press.

Fox, M. W. 1983. *The Wild Canids: Their Systematics, Behavioral Ecology, and Evolution.* New York: Van Nostrand Reinhold.

Francis Palmer (whaleship). MS. Journal of Frederick A. Barker, January 11, 1887–November 12, 1887. New Bedford Whaling Museum, New Bedford, MA. Kendall Institute Collection, no. 462.

Francis, Peter, Jr. 1994. "Beads at the Crossroads of Continents." In *Anthropology of the North Pacific Rim.* Ed. William W. Fitzhugh and Valérie Chaussonet. Washington, DC: Smithsonian Institution Press.

Frank, Johnny and Sarah. 1995. *Neerihiinjik: We Traveled from Place to Place.* Ed. Craig Mishler. Fairbanks: Alaska Native Language Center.

Franklin, John. 1828. *Narrative of a Second Expedition to the Shores of the Polar Sea, in the Years 1825, 1826, 1827.* . . . London: John Murray.

Frost, Orcutt W. 2003. *Bering: The Russian Discovery of America.* New Haven: Yale University Press.

Furuhjelm, Anna von Shoultz. 2005. *Letters from the Governor's Wife: A View of Russian Alaska, 1859–1862.* Ed. Annie Constance Christensen. Århus, Den.: Århus University Press.

Fur Seal Arbitration. 1895. *Proceedings of the Tribunal of Arbitration . . . under the Treaty between the United States of America and Great Britain . . . Concerning the Jurisdictional Rights of the United States in the Waters of the Bering Sea,* vol. 8. Washington, DC: Government Printing Office.

Galbraith, John S. 1977. *The Hudson's Bay Company as an Imperial Factor, 1821–1869.* New York: Octagon.

George and Susan (whaleship). MS. Logbook, September 7, 1857–March 1, 1861. New Bedford Free Public Library, New Bedford, MA.

Georgi, Johann Gottlieb. 1777. *Beschreibung aller Nationen des Russischen Reichs*, vol. 2. St. Petersburg: Bey.

Gerstell, Richard. 1985. *The Steel Trap in North America*. Harrisburg, PA: Stackpole.

Gibson, James R. 1968–69. "Sables to Sea Otters: Russia Enters the Pacific." *Alaska Review* 3 (2): 203–17.

———. 1969. *Feeding the Russian Fur Trade: Provisionment of the Okhotsk Seaboard and the Kamchatka Peninsula, 1639–1856*. Madison: University of Wisconsin Press.

———. 1976. *Imperial Russia in Frontier America: The Changing Geography of Supply of Russian America, 1784–1867*. New York: Oxford University Press.

———. 1990. "Sitka-Kyakhta versus Sitka-Canton: Russian America and the China Market." *Pacifica* 2 (2): 35–79.

———. 1991. "Tsarist Russia in Colonial America: Critical Constraints." In *The History of Siberia from Russian Conquest to Revolution*. Ed. Alan Wood. London: Routledge, pp. 92–106.

———. 1992. *Otter Skins, Boston Ships, and China Goods: The Maritime Fur Trade of the Northwest Coast, 1785–1841*. Montreal: McGill-Queen's University Press.

Giddings, J. L. 1961. *Kobuk River People*. College, AK: University of Alaska, Studies in Northern Peoples 1.

Gilder, William H. 1883. *Ice-Pack and Tundra: An Account of the Search for the Jeannette and a Sledge Journey through Siberia*. New York: Charles Scribner's Sons.

Gillesem, Karl Karlovich [Hillsen, Karl K.]. 1849. *Puteshestvie na shliuppe "Blagonamerennyi" dlia Issledovaniia Beregov Azii i Ameriki za Beringovym Prolivom s 1819 po 1822 God* [The Voyage of the Sloop "Good Intent"' to Investigate the Shores of Asia and America beyond Bering Strait, from 1819 to 1822]. *Otechestvennye Zapiski* 55 (10), 67 (11), 67 (12). St. Petersburg.

———. 1971. "[Karl K.] Hillsen's Journal, 'Journey of the Sloop "Good Intent" to Explore the Asiatic and American Shores of Bering Strait, 1819 to 1822.'" Ed. Dorothy Jean Ray. Trans. Rhea Josephson. Typescript. Rauner Special Collections Library, Dartmouth College Library, Hanover, NH.

Goddard, Ives. 1984. "Synonymy." In *Handbook of North American Indians*, vol. 5, Arctic. Ed. David Damas. Washington, DC: Smithsonian Institution, pp. 5–7.

———. 1999. *Native Languages and Language Families of North America* (map). Revised and enlarged, with additions and corrections. Lincoln: University of Nebraska Press.

Golder, F. A. 1914. *Russian Expansion on the Pacific, 1641–1850: An Account of the Earliest and Later Expeditions Made by the Russians along the Pacific Coast of Asia and North America*. Cleveland: Arthur H. Clark.

———. 1917. *Guide to Materials for American History in Russian Archives*. Washington, DC: Carnegie Institution of Washington.

———. 1922–25. *Bering's Voyages: An Account of the Efforts of the Russians to Determine the Relation of Asia and America*. 2 vols. New York: American Geographical Society. Research Series 1.

Golovin, P. N. 1979. *The End of Russian America: Captain P. N. Golovin's Last Report,*

1862. Ed. Basil Dmytryshyn and E. A. P. Crownhart-Vaughan. Portland: Oregon Historical Society.

Gooding, S. James. 2003. *Trade Guns of the Hudson's Bay Company, 1670–1970*. Alexan-
dria Bay, NY: Museum Restoration Service.

Goodman, Jordan. 1993. *Tobacco in History: The Cultures of Dependence*. London: Routledge.

Gough, Barry M. 1971. *The Royal Navy and the Northwest Coast of North America, 1810–
1914: A Study of British Maritime Ascendancy*. Vancouver: University of British Columbia Press.

———, ed. 1973. *To the Pacific and Arctic with Beechey: The Journal of Lieutentant George
Peard of HMS Blossom, 1825–1828*. Cambridge, UK: Hakluyt Society.

———. 1986. "British-Russian Rivalry and the Search for the Northwest Passage in the
Early Nineteenth Century." *Polar Record* 23 (144): 301–17.

———. 2007. *Fortune's a River: The Collision of Empires in Northwest America*. Madeira
Park, BC: Harbour.

Governor Troup (whaleship). MS. Logbook, December 2, 1862–January 3, 1867. MS 339,
Providence Public Library, Providence, RI.

Graburn, Nelson H. H., Molly Lee, and Jean-Loup Rousselot. 1996. *Catalogue Raisonné of
the Alaska Commercial Company Collection, Phoebe Apperson Hearst Museum of Anthropology*. Berkeley: University of California Press, University of California Publications
in Anthropology 21.

Grainger, John. 2008. *The First Pacific War: Britain and Russia, 1854–56*. Woodridge, Suffolk, UK: Boydell.

Gray, David. 2005. "Weasel." In *Encyclopedia of the Arctic*. Ed. Mark Nuttal. New York:
Routledge, pp. 2160–61.

Gray, Edward G. 2007. *The Making of John Ledyard: Empire and Ambition in the Life of an
Early American Traveler*. New Haven: Yale University Press.

Greenfield, William C. 1893. "The Sixth District." In *Report on Population and Resources
of Alaska at the Eleventh Census: 1890*. U.S. House of Representatives, 52nd Cong., 1st
sess., Resources Document 340, pt. 7. Washington, DC: Government Printing Office.

Gregg, David W. 2000. "Technology, Culture Change, and the Introduction of Firearms
to Northwest Alaska, 1791–1930." PhD diss., Department of Anthropology, Brown University.

Grewingk, Constantine. 2003. *Grewingk's Geology of Alaska and the Northwest Coast of
America*. Trans. Fritz Jaensch. Fairbanks: University of Alaska Press.

Grimes, Eliab. MS. Business Letter Book, 1815–25. M-459, Hawai'i State Archives. Honolulu.

———. 1920. "Letters on the Northwest Fur Trade." *Washington Historical Quarterly* 11
(3): 174–77.

Grinev, Andrei V. 2004. "Why Russia Sold Alaska: The View from Russia." *Alaska History*
19 (1, 2): 1–22.

Grinnell, Joseph. 1901. *Gold Hunting in Alaska*. Elgin, IL: David C. Cook.

Gruening, Ernest. 1954. *The State of Alaska*. New York: Random House.

Gubser, Nicholas J. 1965. *The Nunamiut Eskimos: Hunters of Caribou.* New Haven: Yale University Press.

Guillemard, F. H. H. 1889. *The Cruise of the Marchesa to Kamschatka and New Guinea with Notices of Formosa, Liu-Kiu, and Various Islands of the Malay Archipelago.* London: John Murray.

Gurvich, I. S. 1994. "Interethnic Ties in Far Northeastern Siberia." In *Anthropology of the North Pacific Rim.* Ed. William W. Fitzhugh and Valérie Chaussonet. Washington, DC: Smithsonian Institution Press.

Hadley, Jack. 1915. "Whaling off the Alaskan Coast." *Bulletin of the American Geographical Society* 47 (12): 905–20.

Hall, G. Edward, and Martyn E. Obbard. 1987. "Pelt Preparation." In *Wild Furbearer Management and Conservation in North America.* Ed. Milan Novak et al. Toronto: Ontario Ministry of Natural Resources, pp. 842–61.

Hammerich, L. L. 1958. "The Western Eskimo Dialects." *Proceedings of the Thirty-second International Congress of Americanists, Copenhagen 1956.* Copenhagen: Munksgaard, pp. 632–39.

Hanson, Charles E., Jr. 1980. "The Russian Palma." *Museum of the Fur Trade Quarterly* 16 (4): 1–3.

———. 1992. *The Northwest Gun.* Chadron, NB: Museum of the Fur Trade.

Harding, A. R. 1935. *Deadfalls and Snares.* Columbus, OH: A. R. Harding.

———. 1942. *Fur Buyer's Guide.* Columbus, OH: A. R. Harding.

Hardisty, William L. 1872. "The Loucheux Indians: Notes on the Tinneh or Chepewyan Indians of British and Russian America." *Annual Report of the Smithsonian Institution for the Year 1866.* Washington, DC, pp. 311–20.

Harmony (whaleship). MS. Journal of B. F. Denham, March 8, 1858–October 30, 1858. Private collection.

Hash, Howard S. 1987. "Wolverine." In *Wild Furbearer Management and Conservation in North America.* Ed. Milan Novak, James A. Baker, Martyn E. Obbard, and Bruce Malloch. Toronto: Ontario Ministry of Natural Resources, pp. 574–85.

Hauser-Schäublin, Birgitta, and Gundolf Krüger. 2007. *Siberia and Russian America: Culture and Art from the 1700s: The Asch Collection, Göttingen.* Munich: Prestel.

Hawbacker, S. Stanley. 1944. *Trapping North American Furbearers.* 4th ed. N.p.: S. Stanley Hawbacker.

Hayes, Derek. 2001. *Historical Atlas of the North Pacific Ocean: Maps of Discovery and Scientific Exploration, 1500–2000.* Seattle: Sasquatch.

Healy, Michael A. 1887. *Report of the Cruise of the Revenue Marine Steamer* Corwin *in the Arctic Ocean in the Year 1885.* Washington, DC: Government Printing Office.

———. 1889. *Report of the Cruise of the Revenue Marine Steamer* Corwin *in the Arctic Ocean in the Year 1884.* Washington, DC: Government Printing Office.

Hegarty, Reginald. 1959. *Returns of Whaling Vessels Sailing from American Ports, a Continuation of Alexander Starbuck's "History of the American Whale Fishery," 1976–1928.* New Bedford, MA, Old Dartmouth Historical Society.

Helm, June, ed. 1981. *Handbook of North American Indians,* vol. 6, *Subarctic.* Washington, DC: Smithsonian Institution.

Henry Taber (whaleship). MS. Journal of Timothy C. Packard, October 23, 1868–June 29, 1870. MS 371, Providence Public Library, Providence, RI.

Herald, HMS. Logbooks, 1848–50. Royal Geographical Society, London.

Hickey, Clifford G. 1979. "The Historic Beringian Trade Network: Its Nature and Origins." In *Thule Eskimo Culture: An Anthropological Retrospective.* Ed. Allen P. McCartney. Ottawa: National Museum of Man, Mercury Series, Archaeological Survey of Canada, paper 88, pp. 411–34.

Hillsen. See Gillesem.

Hine, Robert V., and John Mack Faragher. 2007. *Frontiers: A Short History of the American West.* New Haven: Yale University Press.

Hoffecker, John F., and Scott A. Elias. 2007. *Human Ecology of Beringia.* New York: Columbia University Press.

Hoffman, Walter James. 1897. "The Graphic Art of the Eskimos: Based upon Collections in the National Museum." *Annual Report of the Board of Regents of the Smithsonian Institution . . . for the Year Ending June 30, 1895, Report of the National Museum, 1895.* Washington, DC: Smithsonian Institution, Government Printing Office.

Holland, Clive. 1994. *Arctic Exploration and Development, c. 500 BC to 1915.* New York: Garland.

Holmes, Lewis. 1857. *The Arctic Whaleman; or, Winter in the Arctic Ocean. . . .* Boston: Wentworth.

Honigmann, John J., and Irma Honigmann. 1970. *Arctic Townsmen: Ethnic Backgrounds and Modernization.* Ottawa: Canadian Research Centre for Anthropology, Saint Paul University.

Hooper, Calvin Leighton. 1881. *Report of the Cruise of the U.S. Revenue Steamer* Corwin *in the Arctic Ocean, 1880.* Washington, DC: Government Printing Office.

———. 1884. *Report of the Cruise of the U.S. Revenue Steamer* Thomas Corwin *in the Arctic Ocean, 1881.* Washington, DC: Government Printing Office.

———. 1885. *Report of the Cruise of the U.S. Revenue Steamer* Thomas Corwin *in the Arctic Ocean in 1881.* Washington, DC: James Anglim.

Hooper, William H. 1853. *Ten Months among the Tents of the Tuski, with Incidents of an Arctic Boat Expedition in Search of Sir John Franklin, as far as the Mackenzie River and Cape Bathurst.* London: John Murray.

Hosley, Edward H. 1981. "Intercultural Relations and Cultural Change in the Alaska Plateau." In *Handbook of North American Indians,* vol. 6, *Subarctic.* Ed. June Helm. Washington, DC: Smithsonian Institution, pp. 546–55.

Hough, Walter. 1895. "Primitive American Armor." *Annual Report of the Board of Regents of the Smithsonian Institution . . . 1893. Report of the U.S. National Museum.* Washington, DC: Government Printing Office, pp. 625–51.

Howard, W. L. MS. "Expedition to Point Barrow under Ensign W. L. Howard." In George Stoney MS. "Report of the 'Northern Alaska Exploring Expedition' Apl. 13, 1884–Nov. 9, 1886." Typescript. MS 2925, National Anthropological Archives, Smithsonian Institution, Suitland, MD, pp. 35–105.

Howay, F. W. 1973. *A List of Trading Vessels in the Maritime Fur Trade, 1785–1825.* Kingston, ON: Limestone. Materials for the Study of Alaskan History 2.

Hudson's Bay Company. 1967. *The Bay Book of Furs*. London: Hudson's Bay Company.

Hughes, Charles C. 1964. "'The Eskimos' from the *Peoples of Siberia*." *Anthropological Papers of the University of Alaska* 12 (1): 1–13.

———. 1984. "Siberian Eskimo." In *Handbook of North American Indians*, vol. 5, *Arctic*. Ed. David Damas. Washington, DC: Smithsonian Institution, pp. 247–61.

Hultén, Eric. 1968. *Flora of Alaska and Neighboring Territories: A Manual of the Vascular Plants*. Stanford: Stanford University Press.

Hunter, Martin. 1907. *Canadian Wilds*. Columbus, OH: A.R. Harding.

Huntington, Sidney. 1993. *Shadows on the Koyukuk: An Alaskan Native's Life along the River*. Comp. Jim Rearden. Anchorage: Alaska Northwest.

Ingstad, Helge. 1954. *Nunamiut: Among Alaska's Inland Eskimos*. New York: W. W. Norton.

———. 1992. *The Land of Feast and Famine*. Montreal: McGill–Queen's University Press.

Innis, Harold A. 1927. *The Fur-Trade of Canada*. Toronto: University of Toronto Library.

———. 1962. *The Fur Trade in Canada: An Introduction to Canadian Economic History*. Toronto: University of Toronto Press.

International Boundary Commission. [1918.] *Joint Report upon the Survey and Demarcation of the International Boundary between the United States and Canada along the 141st Meridian. . . .* Washington, DC: Government Printing Office.

Jackson, C. Ian. 2005. "Fort Yukon: The Hudson's Bay Company in Russian America." London: Hakluyt Society, annual lecture, June 29, 2005.

———. 2007. "Three Puzzles from Early Nineteenth Century Arctic Exploration." *The Northern Mariner/Le Marin du Nord* 17 (3): 1–17.

Jackson, Sheldon. 1896. "The Arctic Cruise of the U.S. Revenue Cutter Bear." *National Geographic Magazine* 7:1 (January).

———. 1898. *Report on the Introduction of Domestic Reindeer into Alaska*. 55th Cong., 2nd sess., Document 30. Washington, DC: Government Printing Office.

———. 1902. *Eleventh Annual Report on Introduction of Domestic Reindeer into Alaska . . . 1901*. U.S. Senate, 57th Cong., 1st sess., Document 98. Washington, DC: Government Printing Office.

Jacobsen, Johan Adrian. 1884. *Reise an der nordwestküste Amerikas, 1881–1883 . . . von Adrian Woldt*. Leipzig: Max Spohr.

———. 1887. *Kaptein Jacobsens reiser til Nordamerikas Nordvestkyst, 1881–1883*. Trans. A. Woldt. Kristiania: Alb. Cammermeyer.

———. 1977. *Alaskan Voyage, 1881–1883: An Expedition to the Northwest Coast of America*. Trans. Erna Gunther. Chicago: University of Chicago Press.

James, James Alton. 1942. *The First Scientific Exploration of Russian America and the Purchase of Alaska*. Evanston: Northwestern University Press. Northwestern University Studies in the Social Sciences 4.

Jarvis, D. H. 1899. Report of First Lieut. D. H. Jarvis. In [Francis Tuttle]. *Report of the Cruise of the U.S. Revenue Cutter Bear and the Overland Expedition for the Relief of the Whalers in the Arctic Ocean from November 27, 1879 to September 13, 1898*. Washington, DC: Government Printing Office, pp. 28–103.

Jefferys, Thomas, ed. 1761. *Voyages from Asia to America . . . Translated from the High Dutch of S. Muller. . . .* London: T. Jefferys.

Jenness, Diamond. 1922. "The Life of the Copper Eskimos." *Report of the Canadian Arctic Expedition, 1913–1918*, no. 12(A). Ottawa: King's Printer.

———. 1946. "Material Culture of the Copper Eskimos." *Report of the Canadian Arctic Expedition, 1913–1918*, no. 16. Ottawa: King's Printer.

———. 1991. *Arctic Odyssey: The Diary of Diamond Jenness, Ethnologist with the Canadian Arctic Expedition in Northern Alaska and Canada, 1913–1916*. Ed. Stuart Jenness. Ottawa: Canadian Museum of Civilization.

Jensen, Ronald J. 1975. *The Alaska Purchase and Russian-American Relations*. Seattle: University of Washington Press.

Jireh Swift (whaleship). MS. Logbook, June 15, 1857–August 20, 1861. New Bedford Free Public Library, New Bedford, MA.

Jochelson, Waldemar. 1926. *The Yukaghir and the Yukaghirized Tungus*. Jessup North Pacific Expedition. Memoir of the American Museum of Natural History, 9.

———. 1933. "The Yakut." *Anthropological Papers of the American Museum of Natural History* 33 (2).

———. 1975. *The Koryak*. Jessup North Pacific Expedition. Memoir of the American Museum of Natural History, 6. New York: AMS Press (reprint).

John Howland (whaleship). MS. Journal of Benjamin Franklin Pierce, October 12, 1858–September 10, 1860. New Bedford Whaling Museum, New Bedford, MA. Old Dartmouth Historical Society Collection, no. 969c.

John Wells (whaleship). MS. Journal of Nathaniel B. Ransom, November 9, 1869–November 14, 1871. New Bedford Whaling Museum, New Bedford, MA. Old Dartmouth Historical Society Collection, no. 769.

Johnson, Dennis F. 2006. *York Boats of the Hudson's Bay Company: Canada's Inland Armada*. Calgary: Fifth House.

Johnson, Loyal. 1994. "Black Bear." Wildlife Notebook Series. Juneau: Alaska Department of Fish and Game.

Johnson, Paul. 1997. *A History of the American People*. New York: HarperCollins.

Joint Federal-State Land Use Planning Commission for Alaska. 1973. *Major Ecosystems of Alaska* (map). Fairbanks: U.S. Geological Survey.

Jones, A. G. E. 1958. "Robert Shedden and the Nancy Dawson." *Mariner's Mirror* 44 (2): 137–39.

Jones, William Benjamin. 1927. *The Argonauts of Siberia*. Philadelphia: Dorrance.

Jonkel, Charles J. 1987. "Brown Bear." In *Wild Furbearer Management and Conservation in North America*. Ed. Milan Novak et al. Toronto: Ontario Ministry of Natural Resources, pp. 456–73.

Julian (whaleship). MS. Journal of Samuel P. Winegar, April 9, 1859–January 1, 1860. Beinecke Rare Book and Manuscript Library, Yale University, New Haven.

Kaplan, Lawrence. 1999. *Inuit or Eskimo: Which Names to Use?* Fairbanks: Alaska Native Language Center (www.uaf.edu/anlc/inuitoreskimo.html).

Karamanski, Theodore J. 1983. *Fur Trade and Exploration: Opening the Far Northwest, 1821–1852*. Norman: University of Oklahoma Press.

Karklins, Karlis. 1992. *Trade Ornament Usage among the Native Peoples of Canada*. Ottawa: Canadian Parks Service. Studies in Archaeology, Architecture, and History.

Kashevarov, A. F. 1977. *A. F. Kashevarov's Coastal Explorations in Northwest Alaska, 1838*. Ed. James VanStone. Chicago: Field Museum of Natural History. Fieldiana Anthropology 69.

Kelly, John W. 1890a. "Ethnographical Memoranda Concerning the Eskimos of Arctic Alaska and Siberia." In *Eskimo-English and English-Eskimo Vocabularies*. Comp. Roger Wells and John W. Kelly. Sitka: Society of Alaskan Natural History and Ethnology 3.

———. 1890b. *Ethnographical Memoranda Concerning the Eskimos of Arctic Alaska and Siberia*. In Eskimo-English and English-Eskimo Vocabularies. Comp. Roger Wells and John W. Kelly. Washington, DC: Government Printing Office. Bureau of Education, Circular of Information 2.

———. 1898. Report of John W. Kelly, Purchasing Agent. In *Report on the Introduction of Domestic Reindeer into Alaska*. Ed. Sheldon Jackson. 55th Cong., 2nd sess., Document 30, pp. 78–87.

Kemp, H. S. M. 1957. *Northern Trader*. London: Jarrolds.

Kennan, George. 1870. *Tent Life in Siberia and Adventures among the Koraks and Other Tribes in Kamchatka and Northern Asia*. New York: G. P. Putnam's Sons.

———. 1891. *Siberia and the Exile System*. New York: Century.

Kennicott, Robert. 1869. "Biography of Robert Kennicott." *Transactions of the Chicago Academy of Sciences* 1 (2): 133–226.

Kerner, Robert J. 1946. *The Urge to the Sea: The Course of Russian History*. Berkeley: University of California Press.

Khlebnikov, Kyrill T. 1976. *Colonial Russian America: Kyrill T. Khlebnikov's Reports, 1817–1832*. Trans. and ed. Basil Dmytryshyn and E. A. P. Crownhart-Vaughan. Portland: Oregon Historical Society.

Khramchenko [Khromchenko], V. S. MS. *Zhurnal vedenyi na brige* Golovnine *v 1822m godu flota michmanom Khramchenko* [Journal Kept on the Brig *Golovnin* in 1822 by Naval Midshipman Khramchenko], microfilm reel 2, item 12, Shur Collection, Alaska and Polar Regions Collections, Rasmuson Library, University of Alaska, Fairbanks. Original in State Archives of Perm Oblast', Russia, fond 445, op. 1 ed. Khr. 74.

Khromchenko, V. S. See Khramchenko.

King, Irving H. 1996. *The Coast Guard Expands, 1865–1915: New Roles, New Frontiers*. Annapolis: U.S. Naval Institute.

Kirwan, L. P. 1959. *The White Road: A Survey of Polar Exploration*. London: Hollis and Carter.

Kish, George. 1973. *North-East Passage: Adolf Erik Nordenskiöld, His Life and Times*. Amsterdam: Nico Israel.

Kishigami, Nobuhiro. 2007. "Indigenous Trade and Social Change of the Siberian Yupik Eskimos in the Bering Strait Region during the Eighteenth to Twentieth Centuries." *Jinbunronkyu (Journal of Liberal Arts)* 76:39–57.

Kitchener, L. D. 1954. *Flag Over the North*. Seattle: Superior.

Knox, Thomas W. 2007. *Overland through Asia: Pictures of Siberian, Chinese, and Tartar Life*. n.p.: Dodo Press.

Kolenosky, George B. 1987. "Polar Bear." In *Wild Furbearer Management and Conservation in North America*. Ed. Milan Novak et al. Toronto: Ontario Ministry of Natural Resources, pp. 474–85.

Kolenosky, George B., and Stewart M. Strathearn. 1987. "Black Bear." In *Wild Furbearer Management and Conservation in North America*. Ed. Milan Novak et al. Toronto: Ontario Ministry of Natural Resources, pp. 442–54.

Konstantinov, I. V. 1971. *Material'naia kul'tura iakutov XVIII veka (po materialam pogrebenii)* [Material Culture of the Yakuts of the Eighteenth Century (from Grave Goods)]. Yakutsk: Iakutskoe Knizhnoe Izdatel'stvo.

Kotzebue, Otto von. 1821a. *Entdeckungs-Reise in die Sud-See und nach der Berings-Strasse zur Erforschung einer nordöstlichen Durchfahrt. Unternommen in den Jahren 1815, 1816, 1817, und 1818 . . . Grafen Rumanzoff auf dem Schiffe Rurick. . . .* Weimar: Gebrüdern Hoffman.

———. 1821b. *A Voyage of Discovery, into the South Sea and Beering's Straits, for the purpose of Exploring a North-East Passage, undertaken in the years 1815–1818 . . . Count Romanzoff, in the ship Rurick. . . .* 3 vols. London: Longman, Hurst, Rees, Orme and Brown.

Krasheninnikov, Stepan Petrovich. 1764. *The History of Kamtschatka, and the Kurilski Islands, with the Countries Adjacent. . . .* Trans. James Grieve. London: T. Jefferys.

———. 1972. *Explorations of Kamchatka.* Trans. and ed. E. A. P. Crownhart-Vaughan. Portalnd: Oregon Historical Society.

———. 2004. "Sable Hunting in Eastern Siberia in the Early Eighteenth Century." *Polar Geography* 28 (2): 147–61.

Krause, Aurel, and Arthur Krause. 1881. "Die wissenschaftliche Expedition der Bremer geographischen Gessellschaft nach den Küstengebieten an der Beringstrasse." *Deutsche Geographische Blätter* 4, Bremen, pp. 245–81.

———. 1882. "Die Expedition der Bremer geographischen Gesellschaft nach der Tschuktschen-Halbinsel." *Deutsche Geographische Blätter* 5, Bremen, pp. 1–35, 111–33.

———. 1883. "Die Bevölkerungsverhältnisse der Tschuktschen-Halbinsel." *Deutsche Geographische Blätter* 6, Bremen, pp. 248–78.

———. 1993. *To the Chukchi Peninsula and to the Tlingit Indians 1881/1882: Journals and Letters by Aurel and Arthur Krause.* Trans. Margot Krause McCaffrey. Fairbanks: University of Alaska Press. Rasmuson Library Historical Translation Series 8.

Krech, Shepard, III. 1976. "The Eastern Kutchin and the Fur Trade, 1800–1860." *Ethnohistory* 23 (3): 213–35.

———. 1978. "Disease, Starvation, and Northern Athapascan Social Organization." *American Ethnologist* 5 (4): 710–32.

———. 1979. "Interethnic Relations in the Lower Mackenzie River Region." *Arctic Anthropology* 16 (2): 102–22.

———. 1983. "The Influence of Disease and the Fur Trade on Arctic Drainage Lowlands Dene, 1800–1850." *Journal of Anthropological Research* 39 (2): 123–46.

———, ed. 1984a. *The Subarctic Fur Trade: Native Social and Economic Adaptations.* Vancouver: University of British Columbia Press.

———. 1984b. "'Massacre' of the Inuit." *The Beaver* (2): 52–59.

———. 1987. "The Early Fur Trade in the Northwestern Subarctic: The Kutchin and the Trade in Beads." In *Le Castor Fait Tout: Selected Papers of the Fifth North American Fur Trade Conference, 1985*. Ed. Bruce G. Trigger, Toby Morantz, and Louise Dechêne. Montreal: Lake St. Louis Historical Society, pp. 236–77.

———. 1996. "Retelling the Death of Barbue, a Gwich'in Leader." In *Reading Beyond Words: Contexts for Native History*. Ed. Jennifer S. H. Brown and Elizabeth Vibert. Peterborough, ON: Broadview, pp. 182–215.

Krupnik, Igor. 1990. "Cultures in Contact: The Population Nadir in Siberia and North America." *European Review of Native American Studies* 4 (1): 11–18.

———. 1993. *Arctic Adaptations. Native Whalers and Reindeer Herders in Northern Eurasia*. Hanover, NH: Dartmouth College, University Press of New England.

Kushnarev, Evgenii G. 1990. *Bering's Search for the Strait*. Trans. and ed. E. A. P. Crownhart-Vaughan. Portland: Oregon Historical Society.

Kushner, Howard I. 1975. *Conflict on the Northwest Coast: American-Russian Rivalry in the Pacific Northwest, 1790–1867*. Westport, CT: Greenwood.

Kusov, Vladimir Svyatoslavovich. 1993. "Count Nikolai Rumiantsev and Russian Exploration of Alaska and North America." *WAML Information Bulletin* 25 (1): 11–22.

Lain, Bobby Dave. 1974. "North of Fifty-Three: Army, Treasury Department, and Navy Administration of Alaska, 1867–1884." PhD diss., University of Texas–Austin.

———. 1977. "The Fort Yukon Affair, 1869." *Alaska Journal* 7 (1): 12–17.

Lamb, W. Kaye, ed. 1970. *The Journals and Letters of Sir Alexander Mackenzie*. Cambridge, UK: Hakluyt Society. Extra Series 41.

Lantzeff, George V., and Richard A. Pierce. 1973. *Eastward to Empire. Exploration and Conquest on the Russian Open Frontier, to 1750*. Montreal: McGill–Queen's University Press.

Larsen, Helge E., and Froelich Rainey. 1948. "Ipiutak and the Arctic Whale Hunting Culture." *Anthropological Papers of the American Museum of Natural History*, 42.

Laufer, Berthold. 1913. "Arabic and Chinese Trade in Walrus and Narwhal Ivory." *T'oung Pao*, 2nd ser., 14:315–64.

———. 1924. *Tobacco and Its Use in Asia*. Chicago: Field Museum of Natural History. Anthropology leaflet 18.

Lawrence, Mary Chipman. 1966. *The Captain's Best Mate: The Journal of Mary Chipman Lawrence on the Whaler Addison, 1856–1860*. Providence, RI: Brown University Press.

Lazarev, Aleksei Petrovich. 1950. *Zapiski o plavanii voennogo shliupa* Blagonamerennogo *v Beringov proliv i vokrug sveta dlia otkrytii v 1819, 1820, 1821 i 1822 godakh* [Notes on the Voyage of the Naval Sloop *Blagonamerenny* in Bering Strait and Round the World for Discoveries in 1819, 1820, 1821 and 1822]. Ed. A. I. Solov'ev. Moscow: Gosudarstvennoe Izdatel'stvo Geografischeskoi Literatury.

Ledyard, John. 1783. *A Journal of Captain Cook's Last Voyage to the Pacific Ocean, and in Quest of a Northwest Passage, Performed in the Years 1776–79*. Hartford: Nathaniel Patten.

Lee, Molly. 1996. "Context and Contact: The History and Activities of the Alaska Commercial Company, 1867–1900." In *Catalogue Raisonné of the Alaska Commercial Company Collection, Phoebe Apperson Hearst Museum of Anthropology*. Ed. Nelson H. H.

Graburn, Molly Lee, and Jean-Loup Rousselot, Berkeley: University of California Press. University of California Publications in Anthropology 21.

———. 1998. "Alaska Commercial Company: The Formative Years." *Pacific Northwest Quarterly* 89 (2): 59–64.

Leffingwell, Ernest de Koven. 1919. *The Canning River Region, Northern Alaska.* Washington, DC: U.S. Geological Survey. Professional Paper 109.

Lentfer, Jack, and Lloyd Lowry. 1994. "Polar Bear." Wildlife Notebook Series. Juneau: Alaska Department of Fish and Game.

Leo (schooner). MS. Journal of Frederick A. Barker, schooner *Leo,* March 2, 1878–September 12, 1878, New Bedford Whaling Museum, New Bedford, MA. Old Dartmouth Historical Society Collection, no. 936.

Levere, Trevor H. 1993. *Science and the Canadian Arctic: A Century of Exploration, 1818–1918.* Cambridge: Cambridge University Press.

Levin, M. G., and L. P. Potapov. 1964. *The Peoples of Siberia.* Chicago: University of Chicago Press.

Lindsay, Debra. 1993. *Science in the Subarctic: Trappers, Traders and the Smithsonian Institution.* Washington, DC: Smithsonian Institution Press.

Litke, Fyodor Petrovich [Lütké, Fedor Petrovich]. 1835. *Voyage autour du monde, executé par ordre de Sa Majesté L'empereur Nicolas Ier, sur la corvette le Seniavine, dans les années 1826, 1827, 1828 et 1829, par Frédéric Lütké. . . .* 3 vols. and atlas. Paris: Firmin Didot Frères.

———. 1987. *A Voyage around the World, 1826–1829.* Ed. Richard A. Pierce. Kingston, ON: Limestone. Alaska History 29.

Lincoln, W. Bruce. 1994. *The Conquest of a Continent: Siberia and the Russians.* New York: Random House.

Loleta (schooner). MS. Logbook, March 17, 1878–July 7, 1879. Honolulu Consular Records (Record Group 84), National Archives, Washington, DC.

Lopp, Ellen Louise Kittredge. MS. Kathleen Lopp, Smith Family Papers, Alaska and Polar Regions Collections, Rasmuson Library, University of Alaska, Fairbanks.

———. 2001. *Ice Window: Letters from a Bering Strait Village, 1892–1902.* Fairbanks: University of Alaska Press.

Lower, J. Arthur. 1978. *Ocean of Destiny: A Concise History of the North Pacific, 1500–1978.* Vancouver: University of British Columbia Press.

Lund, Judith Navas. 2001. *Whaling Masters and Whaling Voyages Sailing from American Ports: A Compilation of Sources.* New Bedford, MA: New Bedford Whaling Museum, Kendall Whaling Museum, and Ten Pound Island Book Company.

Lütké, Fedor Petrovich. See Litke.

MacFarlane, Roderick. 1906. "Notes on Mammals Collected and Observed in the Northern Mackenzie River District, Northwest Territories of Canada, with Remarks on Explorers and Explorations of the Far North." *Proceedings of the U.S. National Museum* 28 (1405): 673–764.

Mackenzie, Alexander. 1801. *Voyages from Montreal, on the River St. Laurence, Through the Continent of North America, to the Frozen and Pacific oceans; in the years 1789 and 1793. . . .* London: T. Cadell, Jun., W. Davies et al.

Mackie, Richard Somerset. 1997. *Trading Beyond the Mountains: The British Fur Trade on the Pacific, 1793–1843*. Vancouver: UBC Press.

Maguire, Rochfort. 1988. *The Journal of Rochfort Maguire, 1852–1854: Two Years at Point Barrow Alaska, Aboard HMS* Plover *in the Search for Sir John Franklin*. 2 vols. Ed. John R. Bockstoce. London: Hakluyt Society.

Mair, Charles, and Roderick MacFarlane. 1908. *Through the Mackenzie Basin: A Narrative of the Athabasca and Peace River Treaty Expedition of 1899*. Toronto: William Briggs.

Makarova, R. V. 1975. *Russians on the Pacific, 1743–1799*. Kingston, ON: Limestone. Materials for the Study of Alaska History 6.

Malloy, Mary. 1998. *"Boston Men" on the Northwest Coast: The American Maritime Fur Trade, 1788–1844*. Fairbanks: Limestone. Alaska History 47.

Mancall, Mark. 1971. *Russia and China: Their Diplomatic Relations to 1728*. Cambridge: Harvard University Press.

Markham, Clements Robert. 1875. *The Arctic Navy List; or, a Century of Arctic and Antarctic Officers, 1773–1873. Together with a List of Officers of the 1875 Expedition, and Their Services*. London: Griffin and Co.

Marks, Paula Mitchell. 1994. *Precious Dust: The American Gold Rush Era, 1848–1900*. New York: William Morrow.

Mary and Helen (whaleship). MS. Journal of Leander Owen, March 27, 1880–October 11, 1880. Rauner Special Collections Library, Dartmouth College Library, Hanover, NH.

Mason, Michael H. 1934. *The Arctic Forests*. London: Hodder and Stoughton.

Masterson, James R., and Helen Brower. 1948. *Bering's Successors, 1745–1780: Contributions of Peter Simon Pallas to the History of Russian Exploration toward Alaska*. Seattle: University of Washington Press.

Matthews, John. MS. Journal of gunner's mate Matthews on board H.M.S. *Plover* 13 Sept. 1850–April 1855, chiefly off northern Alaska coast, in support of Franklin Search expedition. Royal Geographical Society, London.

McCartney, Allen P. 1988. "Late Prehistoric Metal Use in the New World Arctic." In *The Late Prehistoric Development of Alaska's Native People*. Ed. Robert D. Shaw, Roger K. Harritt and Don E. Dumond. Anchorage: Alaska Anthropological Association. Monograph Series 4, pp. 57–79.

McCowan, Dan. 1926. "The Mink." *The Beaver* (September): 148–49.

McCoy, Donald R. 1956. "The Special Indian Agency in Alaska, 1873–1874: Its Origins and Operation." *Pacific Historical Review* 25 (4): 355–67.

McFadyen-Clark, Annette. 1974. *Koyukuk River Culture*. Ottawa: National Museum of Man, Mercury Series, Canadian Ethnology Service 18.

———. 1981. "Koyukon." In *Handbook of North American Indians*, vol. 6, *Subarctic* Ed. June Helm. Washington, DC: Smithsonian Institution, pp. 582–601.

McKennan, Robert A. 1965. *The Chandalar Kutchin*. Montreal: Arctic Institute of North America. Technical Paper 17.

M'Clure, Robert. 1853. *Capt. M'Clure's Dispatches from Her Majesty's Discovery Ship "Investigator."* London: John Betts.

———. 1856. *The Discovery of the North-West Passage*. Ed. Sherard Osborn. London: Longman, Brown et al.

Medushevskaya, O. M. 1975. "Cartographic Sources for the History of Russian Geographical Discoveries in the Pacific Ocean in the Second Half of the Eighteenth Century." In Essays on the History of Russian Cartography Sixteenth to Nineteenth Centuries. *Cartographica*, Monograph 13, supplement 1 to *Canadian Cartographer*, 12:67–90.

Mercier, François Xavier. 1986. *Recollections of the Youcon: Memories from the Years 1868–1885*. Anchorage: Alaska Historical Society.

Merck, Carl Heinrich. 1980. *Siberia and Northwestern America, 1788–1792. The Journal of Carl Heinrich Merck, Naturalist with the Russian Scientific Expedition Led by Captains Joseph Billings and Gavriil Sarychev*. Ed. Richard A. Pierce. Kingston, ON: Limestone.

Miertsching, Johann. 1967. *Frozen Ships: The Arctic Diary of Johann Miertsching, 1850–1854*. Trans. Leslie Neatby. Toronto: Macmillan.

Miller, Gerrit S., Jr. 1916. "Work by Copley Amory, Jr., in Eastern Siberia." Smithsonian Miscellaneous Collections 66 (3): 46–51. *Explorations and Field-Work of the Smithsonian Institution in 1915*. Washington, DC.

Miller, Polly G. 1994. *Early Contact Glass Trade Beads in Alaska*. Altamonte Springs, FL: Bead Society of Central Florida.

Milne, Jack. 1975. *Trading for Milady's Furs*. Saskatoon: Western Producer Prairie.

Mitchell, Donald Craig. 2003. *Sold American: The Story of Alaska Natives and Their Land, 1867–1959: The Army to Statehood*. Fairbanks: University of Alaska Press.

Montgomery, Maurice R., Jr. 1963. *An Arctic Murder: A Cultural History of the Congregational Mission at Cape Prince of Wales, Alaska, 1890–1893*. Master's thesis, University of Oregon–Eugene.

Montreal (whaleship). MS. Journal of Washington Fosdick. 1850–1853, New Bedford Whaling Museum, New Bedford, MA, Old Dartmouth Historical Society Collection, nos. 144–47.

Morrison, David A. 1991a. "The Later Prehistory of Amundsen Gulf." *NOGAP Archaeology Project: An Integrated Archaeological Research and Management Approach*. Ed. Jacques Cinq-Mars and Jean-Luc Pilon. Canadian Archaeological Association, Occasional Paper 1, pp. 77–87.

———. 1991b. "The Copper Inuit Soapstone Trade." *Arctic* 44 (3): 239–46.

———. 2006. "Painted Wooden Plaques from the MacFarlane Collection: The Earliest Inuvialuit Graphic Art." *Arctic* 59 (4): 351–60.

Morse, Eric W. 1969. *Fur Trade Canoe Routes of Canada/Then and Now*. Ottawa: Queen's Printer.

Morse, Hosea Ballou. 1926. *The Chronicles of the East India Company Trading to China, 1635–1834*. 3 vols. Oxford: Oxford University Press.

Mount Vernon (whaleship). MS. Logbook, September 5, 1849–May 18, 1852. New Bedford Whaling Museum, New Bedford, MA. Kendall Institute Collection, no. 149.

Moxham, Roy. 2004. *Tea: Addiction, Exploitation and Empire*. London: Robinson.

Muir, John. 1917. *The Cruise of the Corwin*. Ed. William Frederic Badé. Boston: Houghton Mifflin.

Müller, Gerhard Friedrich. 1986. *Bering's Voyages: The Reports from Russia*. Ed. Carol Urness. Fairbanks: University of Alaska Press. Rasmuson Library Historical Translation Series, 3.

Munger, James F. 1852. *Two Years in the Pacific and Arctic Oceans and China.* Vernon, NY: J. R. Howlett.

Murdoch, John. 1892. "Ethnological Results of the Point Barrow Expedition." *Ninth Annual Report of the Bureau of Ethnology to the Secretary of the Smithsonian Institution 1887–88.* Washington, DC: Government Printing Office.

Murray, Alexander Hunter. MS. Journal of an Expedition to Build a Hudson's Bay Company Post on the Yukon. WA MSS 356, Beinecke Rare Book and Manuscript Library, Yale University, New Haven.

———. 1910. *Journal of the Yukon, 1847–48.* Ed. L. J. Burpee. Ottawa: Government Printing Bureau. Publications of the Canadian Archives 4.

Nassau (whaleship). MS. Logbook, August 7, 1850–May 22, 1853, New Bedford Whaling Museum, New Bedford, MA. Kendall Institute Collection, no. 216.

Nelson, Edward William. MS. Journals, 1877–81. Manuscript Collection, no. 7364, Collection Division 2, box 12, Smithsonian Institution Archives, Washington, DC.

———. 1887. *Report upon Natural History Collections Made in Alaska between the Years 1877 and 1881 by Edward W. Nelson: Arctic Series of Publications Issued in Connection with the Signal Service, U.S. Army.* Ed. Henry W. Kenshaw. Washington, DC: Government Printing Office.

———. 1899. "The Eskimo about Bering Strait." *Eighteenth Annual Report of the Bureau of American Ethnology to the Secretary of the Smithsonian Institution, 1896–97.* Washington, DC: Government Printing Office.

Nelson, Richard K. 1969. *Hunters of the Northern Ice.* Chicago: University of Chicago Press.

———. 1973. *Hunters of the Northern Forest: Designs for Survival among the Alaska Kutchin.* Chicago: University of Chicago Press.

———. 1983. *Make Prayers to the Raven: A Koyukon View of the Northern Forest.* Chicago: University of Chicago Press.

Nimrod (whaleship). MS. Logbook, March 28, 1858–July 11, 1861. New Bedford Whaling Museum, New Bedford, MA. Old Dartmouth Historical Society Collection, no. 946.

Nordenskiöld, A. E. 1881. *The Voyage of the* Vega *round Asia and Europe.* 2 vols. Trans. Alexander Leslie. London: Macmillan.

———. 1882. *The Voyage of the Vega round Asia and Europe.* Trans. Alexander Leslie. New York: Macmillan.

Norlander, David J. 1994. *For God and Tsar: A Brief History of Russian America, 1741–1867.* Anchorage: Alaska Natural History Association.

North Star (whaleship). MS. Journal of Leander Owen, March 3, 1882–July 9, 1882. Rauner Special Collections Library, Dartmouth College Library, Hanover, NH.

Nourse, J. E. 1884. *American Explorations in the Ice Zones.* Boston: D. Lothrop.

Novak, Milan. 1987. "Beaver." In *Wild Furbearer Management and Conservation in North America.* Ed. Milan Novak et al. Toronto: Ontario Ministry of Natural Resources, pp. 282–313.

Novak, Milan, James A. Baker, Martyn E. Obbard, and Bruce Malloch, eds. 1987. *Wild Furbearer Management and Conservation in North America.* Toronto: Ontario Ministry of Natural Resources.

Obbard, Martyn E. 1987. "Fur Grading and Pelt Identification." In *Wild Furbearer Management and Conservation in North America*. Ed. Milan Novak et al. Toronto: Ontario Ministry of Natural Resources, pp. 718–825.

Ocean (whaleship). MS. Logbook, August 7, 1858–November 12, 1863. New Haven Colony Historical Society, New Haven, CT.

Ogden, Adele. 1941. *The California Sea Otter Trade, 1784–1848*. Berkeley: University of California Press. University of California Publications in History 26.

O'Grady-Raeder, Alix. 1994. "The Baltic Connection in Russian America." *Jahrbücher für Geschichte Osteuropas* 42 (3): 321–39.

Okladnikov, A. P. 1964. "Ancient Population of Siberia and Its Culture." In *The Peoples of Siberia*. Ed. M. G. Levin and L. P. Potapov. Chicago: University of Chicago Press, pp. 13–98.

Okun, S. B. 1979. *The Russian-American Company*. Trans. Carl Ginsburg. New York: Octagon.

Orth, Donald J. 1967. *Dictionary of Alaska Place Names*, Washington, DC: Government Printing Office. U.S. Geological Survey, Professional Paper 567.

Osbon, Bradley S. 1902. "Perils of Polar Whaling." In *The White World: Life and Adventures within the Arctic Circle Portrayed by Famous Living Explorers*. New York: Lewis, Scribner. Issued under the auspices of the Arctic Club.

Osgood, Cornelius. 1936. *Contributions to the Ethnography of the Kutchin*. New Haven: Yale University Press. Yale University Publications in Anthropology 14.

Ostermann, H., and E. Holtved. 1952. "The Alaskan Eskimos as Described in the Posthumous Notes of Dr. Knud Rasmussen." *Report of the Fifth Thule Expedition, 1921–24* 10 (3). Copenhagen: Gylendalske Boghandel, Nordisk Forlag.

Otis, Harrison G. 1880. Report of Special Agent H. G. Otis upon Illicit Traffic in Rum and Fire-arms in Alaska. In Letter from the Secretary of the Treasury, March 30, 1880. U.S. Senate. 46th Cong., 2nd sess. Executive Document 132.

Pallas, Peter Simon. 1783. *Neue nordische Beyträge zur physikalischen und geographischen Erd-und Völkerbeschreibung, Naturgeschichte und Oekonomie*, vol. 4. St. Petersburg: Johann Zacharias Logan.

Pamperin, Nathan J., Erich H. Follman, and Bill Petersen. 2006. "Interspecific Killing of an Arctic Fox by a Red Fox at Prudhoe Bay, Alaska." *Arctic* 59 (4): 361–64.

Paneak, Simon. 2004. *In a Hungry Country: Essays by Simon Paneak*. Ed. John Martin Campbell. Fairbanks: University of Alaska Press.

Parry, William E. 1824. *Journal of a Second Voyage for the Discovery of a Northwest Passage*. . . . London: John Murray.

Pawlik, Peter-Michael. 1996. *Von Sibirien nach Neu Guinea. Kapitän Dallman, seine Schiffe und Reisen 1830–1896*. Bremerhaven: Deutsches Schiffahrtsmuseum, Verlag H. M. Hauschild.

Peard, George. 1973. *To the Pacific and Arctic with Beechey: The Journal of Lieutenant George Peard of H.M.S. "Blossom," 1825–1828*. Ed. Barry M. Gough. Cambridge, UK: Hakluyt Society.

Petersen, Marcus. 1914. *The Fur Traders and Fur Bearing Animals*. Buffalo: Hammond.

Petitot, R. P. E. 1876. *Vocabulaire Français-Esquimau dialecte des Tchiglit des bouches de*

Mackenzie et de l'Anderson précédé d'une monographie de cette tribu et de notes grammaticales. Paris: Ernest Leroux.

———. 1887. *Les Grands Esquimaux.* Paris: E. Plon, Nourrit.

———. 1999. *Among the Chiglit Eskimos.* Trans. E. Otto Höhn. Edmonton: Canadian Circumpolar Institute, University of Alberta. Occasional publication 10.

Pfizenmayer, E. W. 1939. *Siberian Man and Mammoth.* Trans. Muriel D. Simpson. London: Blackie and Son.

Phebus, George, Jr. 1972. *Alaskan Eskimo Life in the 1890s as Sketched by Native Artists.* Washington, DC: Smithsonian Institution Press.

Phillipe de la Noye (whaleship). MS. Logbook, June 28, 1848–May 25, 1852. General Services Administration, National Archives and Record Service, Franklin Delano Roosevelt Library, Hyde Park, NY.

Phillips, Paul Chrisler. 1961. *The Fur Trade.* 2 vols. Norman: University of Oklahoma Press.

Pielou, E. C. 1994. *A Naturalist's Guide to the Arctic.* Chicago: University of Chicago Press.

Pierce, Richard A. 1965. *Russia's Hawaiian Adventure, 1815–1817.* Berkeley: University of California Press.

———. 1986. *Builders of Alaska: The Russian Governors, 1818–1867.* Kingston, ON: Limestone. Alaska History 28.

———. 1990a. *Russian America: A Biographical Dictionary.* Kingston, ON: Limestone.

———. 1990b. "Russian America and China." In *Russian America: The Forgotten Frontier.* Ed. Barbara Sweetland Smith and Redmond J. Barnett. Tacoma: Washington State Historical Society, pp. 73–80.

Pim, Bedford. 1853. "The Plover's wintering in Kotzebue Sound—Mr. Pim's journey to Michaelowski." In Berthold Seemann. *Narrative of the voyage of H.M.S. Herald during the years 1845–51, under the command of Captain Henry Kellett . . . being a circumnavigation of the globe, and three cruises to the Arctic regions in search of Sir John Franklin.* London: Reeve, pp. 130–58.

Plover, HMS. Logbooks, 1848–1854. Admiralty Papers 4650–4653, PRO ADM 55/93. National Archives, Kew, UK.

Porter, Kenneth Wiggins. 1930. "Cruise of Astor's Brig Pedler, 1813–1816." *Oregon Historical Quarterly* 31 (3): 223–30.

———. 1931. *John Jacob Astor: Business Man.* 2 vols. Cambridge: Harvard University Press.

———. 1932. "The Cruise of the *Forester.*" *Washington Historical Quarterly* 23:261–85.

Postnikov, Alexei V. 1995. *The Mapping of Russian America: A History of Russian-American Contacts in Cartography.* Milwaukee: University of Wisconsin. American Geographical Society Collection, special publication 4.

Preble, Edward A. 1908. *A Biological Investigation of the Athabasca-Mackenzie Region.* Washington, DC: Government Printing Office. U.S. Department of Agriculture, North American Fauna 27.

Price, Jacob M. 1961. "The Tobacco Adventure in Russia." *Transactions of the American Philosophical Society,* n.s., 51 (1).

Prucha, Francis Paul. 1995. *The Great Father: The United States Government and American Indians*. Lincoln: University of Nebraska Press.

Prusser, Friedrich. 1966. "Heinrich Hackfeld." *Neue deutsche Biographie*, vol. 7. Berlin: Duncker und Humblot.

Pullen, H. F., ed. 1979. *The Pullen Expedition in Search of Sir John Franklin: The Original Diaries, Log, and Letters of Commander W. J. S. Pullen*. Toronto: Arctic History Press.

Rae, John. 1953. *John Rae's Correspondence with the Hudson's Bay Company on Arctic Exploration, 1844–1855*. London: Hudson's Bay Record Society 16.

Raeff, Marc. 1956. *Siberia and the Reforms of 1822*. Seattle: University of Washington Press.

Rainey, Froelich G. 1947. "The Whale Hunters of Tigara." *Anthropological Papers of the American Museum of Natural History* 41 (2): 231–83.

Rausch, Robert. 1951. "Notes on the Nunamiut Eskimo and Mammals of the Anaktuvuk Pass Region, Brooks Range, Alaska." *Arctic* 4 (3): 147–95.

Ray, Arthur J. 1988. "The Hudson's Bay Company and Native People." In *Handbook of North American Indians*, vol. 4, *History of Indian-White Relations*. Ed. Wilcomb E. Washburn. Washington, DC: Smithsonian Institution, pp. 335–50.

Ray, Arthur J., and Donald B. Freeman. 1978. *"Give Us Good Measure": An Economic Analysis of Relations between the Indians and the Hudson's Bay Company*. Toronto: University of Toronto Press.

Ray, Dorothy Jean. 1964. "Kauwerak: Lost Village of Alaska." *The Beaver* (Autumn): 4–13.

———. 1967. "Land Tenure and Polity of the Bering Strait Eskimos." *Journal of the West* 6 (3): 371–94.

———. 1971. "Eskimo Place-Names in Bering Strait and Vicinity." *Names: Journal of the American Name Society* 19 (1): 1–33.

———. 1975. "Early Maritime Trade with the Eskimo of Bering Strait and the Introduction of Firearms." *Arctic Anthropology* 12 (1): 1–9.

———. 1976. "The Kheuveren Legend." *Alaska Journal* 6 (3): 146–53.

———. 1983. *Ethnohistory in the Arctic: The Bering Strait Eskimo*. Kingston, ON: Limestone.

———. 1992. *The Eskimos of Bering Strait, 1650–1898*. Seattle: University of Washington Press.

Ray, Dorothy Jean, ed., and Rhea Josephson, trans. 1971. "[Karl K.] Hillsen's Journal, 'Journey of the sloop "Good Intent" to explore the Asiatic and American shores of Bering Strait, 1819 to 1822.'" Typescript. Rauner Special Collections Library, Dartmouth College Library, Hanover, NH.

Ray, Patrick Henry. 1885. *Report of the International Polar Expedition to Point Barrow, Alaska*. Washington, DC: Government Printing Office.

Raymond, Charles W. 1870. Yukon River and Island of St. Paul. U.S. House of Representatives, 41st Cong., 2nd sess., Executive Document 112. Washington, DC.

———. 1900. "Reconnaissance of the Yukon River 1869." In *Compilation of Explorations in Alaska*. Washington, DC: U.S. War Department, Government Printing Office, pp. 19–44.

Reid, Anna. 2002. *The Shaman's Coat: A Native History of Siberia*. London: Weidenfeld and Nicholson.

Reliance, USRC. MS. Logbook, January 1, 1870–December 31, 1870, U.S. Revenue Cutter Service Collection, record group 26, National Archives, Washington, DC.

Rennick, Penny, ed. 2002. "Territory of Alaska." *Alaska Geographic* 29 (3).

Reuse, Willem Joseph de. 1994. *Siberian Yupik Eskimo: The Language and Its Contacts with Chukchi*. Salt Lake City: University of Utah Press.

Rich, E. E. 1967. *The Fur Trade and the Northwest to 1857*. Toronto: McClelland and Stewart.

Richardson, John. 1828. "Dr. Richardson's Narrative of the Proceedings of the Eastern Detachment of the Expedition." In John Franklin. *Narrative of a Second Expedition to the Shores of the Polar Sea, in the Years 1825, 1826, 1827. . . .* London: John Murray, pp. 187–283.

———. 1851. *Arctic Searching Expedition: A Journal of a Boat-Voyage through Rupert's Land and the Arctic Sea, in Search of the Discovery Ships under Command of Sir John Franklin*. 2 vols. London: Longman, Brown, Green, and Longmans.

Ritchie, G. S. 1967. *The Admiralty Chart: British Naval Hydrography in the Nineteenth Century*. London: Hollis and Carter.

Rosse, Irving C. 1883. "The First Landing on Wrangel Island." *Bulletin of the American Geographical Society* 15:163–214.

———. 1884. "Medical and Anthropological Notes on Alaska." In *Cruise of the Revenue–Steamer Corwin in Alaska and the Northwest Arctic Ocean in 1881: Notes and Memoranda. . . .* Washington, DC: Government Printing Office.

Rousselot, Jean-Loup, and Veronika Grahammer. 2004. *Beyond Bering: The Russian Colonies in the North Pacific, 1741–1867*. Lugano: Galleria Gottardo and Staatliches Museum für Völkerkunde.

Roys, Thomas Welcome. MS. *The Voyages of Thomas Welcome Roys*. Suffolk County Whaling Museum, Sag Harbor, NY.

Rudenko, S. I. 1961. *The Ancient Culture of the Bering Sea and the Eskimo Problem*. Toronto: University of Toronto Press, Arctic Institute of North America.

Ruggles, Richard I. 1991. *A Country So Interesting: The Hudson's Bay Company and Two Centuries of Mapping, 1670–1870*. Montreal: McGill–Queen's University Press.

Russell, Frank. MS. *Journal of Frank Russell, April 26, 1893–August 19, 1894*. National Anthropological Archives, Smithsonian Institution, Suitland, MD.

———. 1898. *Explorations in the Far North: Being the Report of an Expedition under the Auspices of the University of Iowa during the Years 1892, '93 and '94*. Iowa City: University of Iowa.

Russian-American Company. 1847. *Otchet Rossiisko-Amerikanskoi Kompanii Glavnago Pravleniia za odin god, po 1 ianvaria 1847 g* [Annual Report of the Russian-American Company's Board of Directors for One Year, to January 1, 1847]. Trans. Katherine Arndt. St. Petersburg: Russian-American Company.

———. 1848. *Otchet Rossiisko-Amerikanskoi Kompanii Glavnago Pravleniia za odin god, po 1 ianvaria1848 g* [Annual Report of the Russian-American Company's Board of Directors for One Year, to January 1, 1848]. Trans. Katherine Arndt. St. Petersburg: Russian-American Company.

Ruttle, Terence. 1968. *How to Grade Furs*. Ottawa: Queen's Printer. Canada Department of Agriculture Publication 1362.

Sale, Richard. 2006. *A Complete Guide to Arctic Wildlife*. Richmond Hill, ON: Firefly.

Samuel Robertson (whaleship). MS. Journal of George Coggeshall, August 25, 1849–April 22, 1854. New Bedford Whaling Museum, New Bedford, MA. Kendall Institute Collection, no. 330.

Sarychev, Gavriil Andreevich. 1802. *Puteshestvie Flota Kapitana Sarycheva*. . . . 2 vols. St. Petersburg: Schnor's Press.

———— [Sarytschew, Gawrila]. 1806–7. *Account of a Voyage of Discovery to the North-East of Siberia, the Frozen Ocean, and the North-East Sea*. 2 vols. London: Richard Phillips.

Sauer, Martin. 1802. *An Account of a Geographical and Astronomical Expedition to the Northern Parts of Russia . . . by Commodore Joseph Billings*. . . . London: T. Cadell and W. Davies.

Sayce, R. U. 1933. *Primitive Arts and Crafts: An Introduction to the Study of Material Culture*. Cambridge: Cambridge University Press.

Schabelski, Achille. 1826. *Voyage aux Colonies Russes de l'Amerique, fait à bord du sloop de guerre, l'Apollon, pendant les années 1821, 1822, et 1823*. St. Petersburg: N. Gretsch.

Schorger, A. W. 1949. "A Brief History of the Steel Trap and Its Use in North America." *Transactions of the Wisconsin Academy of Sciences, Arts, and Letters* (39): 172–99.

Schumacher, Wilfried W. 1978. "An Eskimo Reflex of South Sea Whaling." *Inter-Nord* 15:233–35.

Schwatka, Frederick. 1900. "Military Reconnoissance [*sic*] in Alaska." In United States, War Department. *Compilation of Narratives and Explorations in Alaska*. Washington, DC: Government Printing Office, pp. 285–364.

Schweitzer, Peter P., and Evgeniy Golovko. 1995. *Contacts across Bering Strait, 1898–1948*. Anchorage: U.S. National Park Service, Alaska Regional Office.

Seemann, Berthold. 1853. *Narrative of the Voyage of H.M.S. Herald during the Years 1845–51, under the Command of Captain Henry Kellett . . . Being a Circumnavigation of the Globe, and Three Cruises to the Arctic Regions in Search of Sir John Franklin*. London: Reeve.

Sharon (whaleship). MS. Logbook, November 25, 1856–November 25, 1859. Providence Public Library, Providence, RI.

Sharpe, Philip. MS. Journal of H.M.S. *Rattlesnake*, 1853–1854. National Maritime Museum, Greenwich, UK.

Shepherd, Peter, and Herb Melchior. 1994. "Marten." Wildlife Notebook Series. Juneau: Alaska Department of Fish and Game.

Sherwood, Morgan B. 1965. *Exploration of Alaska, 1865–1900*. New Haven: Yale University Press.

Shishmarev, Nikolai Dmitrievich [Shishmaryov, Nikolai Dmitrievich]. MS. *Iz zapisok o krugosvetnom plavanii na shliupe* Blagonamerennoi *v 1819–22 godakh* [From Notes on a Round-the-World Voyage Aboard the Sloop *Balgonamerenny* in the Years 1819–22]. Trans. Katherine Arndt. Russian State Naval Archive [RGAVMF]. Fond 203, op. 1,

d. 730[b]. Microfilm copy in Shur Collection, Alaska and Polar Regions Collections, Rasmuson Library, University of Alaska, Fairbanks.

Shklovsky, I. W. 1916. *In Far North-East Siberia.* London: Macmillan.

Simeone, William E. 1995. *Rifles, Blankets, and Beads: Identity, History, and the Northern Athapaskan Potlatch.* Norman: University of Oklahoma Press.

Simmonds, P. L. 1877. *Animal Products: Their Preparation, Commercial Uses, and Value.* London: Chapman and Hall, for the Committee of Council on Education.

Simpson, George. 1847. *Narrative of a Journey Round the World during the Years 1841 and 1842.* 2 vols. London: Henry Colburn.

Simpson, John. 1850. Journal of a Journey from Chamisso Island to Spafarief Bay, January 9 to 12. Box 3, John Simpson Collection, Rare Book, Manuscript, and Special Collections Division, William R. Perkins Library, Duke University, Durham, NC.

———. 1988. "Dr. John Simpson's Essay on the Eskimos of Northwestern Alaska." In *The Journal of Rochfort Maguire, 1852–1854: Two Years at Point Barrow, Alaska, Aboard H.M.S.* Plover *in the Search for Sir John Franklin.* Ed. John R. Bockstoce. London: Hakluyt Society, 2:501–50.

———. MS. John Simpson's Point Barrow Journal. Box 5 (Accounts of Voyages . . . 1851–54), John Simpson Collection, Rare Book, Manuscript, and Special Collections Division, William R. Perkins Library, Duke University, Durham, NC.

Simpson, Thomas. 1843. *Narrative of the Discoveries on the North Coast of America Effected by the Officers of the Hudson's Bay Company during the Years 1836–39.* London: Richard Bentley.

Skoog, Ronald O. 1968. "Ecology of the Caribou (*Rangifer tarandus granti*) in Alaska." PhD diss.,University of California–Berkeley.

Sladkovsky, M. I. 1974. *The Long Road: Sino-Russian Economic Contacts from Ancient Times to 1917.* Moscow: Progress.

Slezkine, Yuri. 1994. *Arctic Mirrors: Russia and the Small Peoples of the North.* Ithaca: Cornell University Press.

Slobodin, Richard. 1981. "Kutchin." In *Handbook of North American Indians,* vol. 6, *Subarctic.* Ed. June Helm. Washington, DC: Smithsonian Institution, pp. 514–32.

Smith, Derek G. 1984. "Mackenzie Delta Eskimo." In *Handbook of North American Indians,* vol. 5, *Arctic.* Ed. David Damas. Washington, DC: Smithsonian Institution, pp. 347–58.

Smyth, William. 1831. "Narrative of the proceedings of the barge of H.M.S. Blossom in Quest of Captain Franklin, and to Explore the Coast N.E. of Icy Cape." In Frederick William Beechey. *Narrative of a Voyage to the Pacific and Beering's Strait.* . . . London: Colburn and Bentley, pp. 307–21.

———. MSa. Journal of the voyage of H.M.S. Blossom, 1826. In Richard Beechey MS. "Remarks on a Voyage of Discovery to the Pacific and Bhering's Straits. . . ." Public Record Office of Northern Ireland, Belfast.

———. MSb. Journal of a Voyage in H.M.S. Blossom. In James Wolfe MS. "Journal of a Voyage on Discovery in the Pacific and Beering's Straits on board H.M.S. *Blossom* Capt. F. W. Beechey." Beinecke Rare Book and Manuscript Library, Yale University, New Haven.

Solf, J. D., and Howard Golden. 1994. "River Otter." Wildlife Notebook Series. Juneau: Alaska Department of Fish and Game.

Sonnenfeld, Joseph. 1957. "Changes in Subsistence among the Barrow Eskimo." PhD diss., Johns Hopkins University, Baltimore, MD.

South America (whaleship). MS. November 2, 1857–May 4, 1859. New Bedford Whaling Museum, New Bedford, MA, Kendall Institute Collection.

South Boston (whaleship). MS. Journal of Samuel Broadbent, July 16, 1851–April 2, 1854. Wethersfield Historical Society, Wethersfield, CT.

Spencer, Robert F. 1959. *The North Alaskan Eskimo: A Study in Ecology and Society.* Washington, DC: Government Printing Office. Smithsonian Institution, Bureau of American Ethnology Bulletin 171.

Stains, Howard J. 1979. "Primeness in North American Furbearers." *Wildlife Society Bulletin* 7 (2): 120–24.

Stefansson, Vilhjalmur. 1909a. "The Eskimo Trade Jargon of Herschel Island." *American Anthropologist* 11:217–32.

———. 1909b. "Northern Alaska in Winter." *Bulletin of the American Geographical Society* 41 (10): 601–10.

———. 1914a. "The Stefánsson-Anderson Arctic Expedition of the American Museum: Preliminary Ethnological Report." *Anthropological Papers of the American Museum of Natural History* 14 (1).

———. 1914b. *Prehistoric and Present Commerce among the Arctic Coast Eskimo.* Canada Department of Mines, Geological Survey, Museum Bulletin no. 6, Anthropological series, no. 3, December 30, 1914. Ottawa: Government Printing Office.

———. 1921. *My Life with the Eskimo.* New York: Macmillan.

———. 1924. *My Life with the Eskimo.* New York: Macmillan.

———. 1958. *Northwest to Fortune: The Search of Western Man for a Commercially Practical Route to the Far East.* New York: Duell, Sloan and Pearce.

———. 2001. *Writing on Ice: The Ethnographic Notebooks of Vilhjalmur Stefansson.* Ed. Gísli Pálsson. Hanover, NH: Dartmouth College, University Press of New England.

Stephan, John J. 1969. "The Crimean War in the Far East." *Modern Asian Studies* 3 (3): 257–77.

———. 1994. *The Russian Far East: A History.* Stanford: Stanford University Press.

Stephenson, Bob, and Rodney Boertje. 1994. "Wolf." Wildlife Notebook Series. Juneau: Alaska Department of Fish and Game.

Stewart, Ethel G. 1955. "Fort McPherson and the Peel River." Master's thesis, Queen's University, Kingston, ON.

Stoney, George M. MS. "Report of the 'Northern Alaska Exploring Expedition' Apl. 13, 1884–Nov. 9, 1886." Typescript. MS 2925, National Anthropological Archives, Smithsonian Institution, Suitland, MD.

———. 1900. *Naval Explorations in Alaska.* Annapolis: U.S. Naval Institute.

Strobridge, Truman R., and Dennis L. Noble. 1999. *Alaska and the U.S. Revenue Cutter Service, 1867–1915.* Annapolis: U.S. Naval Institute.

Stuck, Hudson. 1917. *Voyages on the Yukon and Its Tributaries.* New York: Charles Scribner's Sons.

Sverdrup, Harald U. 1978. *Among the Tundra People.* Trans. Molly Sverdrup. La Jolla, CA: Scripps Institute of Oceanography.

Tamerlane (whaleship). MS. Journal of William Shockley, October 24, 1850–January 12, 1852. Microfilm copy. International Marine Archives, New Bedford Whaling Museum, New Bedford, MA.

Tebenkov, Mikhail D. MS. *Zapiski G. Teben'kova o plavanii k Unalashke i severnym predelam kolonii.* [Mr. Teben'kov's notes on navigation to Unalaska and the northern limits of the colonies]. Trans. Katherine Arndt. Microfilm reel 7, item 55, Shur Collection, Alaska and Polar Regions Department, Rasmuson Library, University of Alaska, Fairbanks. Original in Archives of the Geographical Society of Russia, St. Petersburg, razriad 99, op. 55.

Tetso, John. 1970. *Trapping Is My Life.* Toronto: Peter Martin Associates.

Thomas Dickason (whaleship). MS. Logbook, October 16, 1860–July 12, 1865. Providence Public Library, Providence, RI.

Thornton, Harrison R. MSS. Harrison R. Thornton Collection. Peary-MacMillan Arctic Museum, Bowdoin College, Brunswick, ME.

———. 1931. *Among the Eskimos of Wales, Alaska.* Baltimore: Johns Hopkins University Press.

Thrum, Thomas G. 1912. "Honolulu's Share in the Whaling Industry of By-Gone Days." *Hawaiian Almanac and Annual for 1913* (39): 47–68.

Tiger (whaleship). MS. Journal of Mary Brewster, November 4, 1845–December 19, 1849. MS 716, Mystic Seaport Museum, Mystic, CT.

Tikhmenev, P. A. 1978. *A History of the Russian-American Company.* Trans. and ed. Richard A. Pierce and Alton S. Donnelly. Seattle: University of Washington Press.

Tobuk, Frank. 1980. *Frank Tobuk, Evansville.* Ed. Curt Madison and Yvonne Yarber. North Vancouver, BC: Hancock House.

Tompkins, Stuart R. 1989. "Alaska's Boundaries." In *Interpreting Alaska's History: An Anthology.* Ed. Mary Childers Manguso and Stephen W. Haycox. Seattle: University of Washington Press, pp. 58–84.

Tollemache, Stratford. 1912. *Reminiscences of the Yukon.* Toronto: William Briggs.

Tremblay, Ray. 1983. *Trails of an Alaskan Trapper.* Anchorage: Alaska Northwest.

[Tuttle, Francis]. 1899. *Report of the Cruise of the U.S. Revenue Cutter Bear and the Overland Expedition for the Relief of the Whalers in the Arctic Ocean from November 27, 1879 to September 13, 1898.* Washington, DC: Government Printing Office.

U.K. House of Commons. 1848. Sessional Papers. Accounts and Papers, 1847–48, 41(264) (*Arctic Bibliography,* no. 45216).

———. 1849a. Sessional Papers. Accounts and Papers, 1849, 32(188) (*Arctic Bibliography,* no. 45219).

———. 1849b. Sessional Papers. Accounts and Papers, 1849, 32(497) (*Arctic Bibliography,* no. 45222).

———. 1850. Sessional Papers. Accounts and Papers, 1850, 35(107) (*Arctic Bibliography,* no. 45223).

———. 1851. Sessional Papers. Accounts and Papers, 1851, 33(97) (*Arctic Bibliography,* no. 45226).

————. 1852a. Sessional Papers. Accounts and Papers, 1852, 50(1449) (*Arctic Bibliography*, no. 45229).

————. 1852b. Sessional Papers. Accounts and Papers, 1852–53, 60(82) (*Arctic Bibliography*, no. 45238).

————. 1852c. Sessional Papers. Accounts and Papers, 1852, 50(1435) (*Arctic Bibliography*, no. 45227).

————. 1853. Sessional Papers. Accounts and Papers, 1853, 60(444) (*Arctic Bibliography*, no. 45239).

————. 1854a. Sessional Papers. Accounts and Papers, 1854, 42(1725) (*Arctic Bibliography*, no. 45241).

————. 1854b. Sessional Papers. Accounts and Papers, 1854, 42(171) (*Arctic Bibliography*, no. 45243).

————. 1855. Sessional Papers. Accounts and Papers, 1854–55, 35(1898) (*Arctic Bibliography*, no. 45245).

U.S. Commission of Education. 1894. Report of the Commissioner of Education for the Year 1890–91. Washington, DC: Government Printing Office.

U.S. House of Representatives. 1885. *Report of the International Polar Expedition to Point Barrow, Alaska, in Response to the Resolution of the House of Representatives of December 11, 1884*. Washington, DC: Government Printing Office.

U.S. Senate. 1869. *Message of the President of the United States in Relation to the Encroachments of the Agents of the Hudson's Bay Company upon the Trade and Territory of Alaska.* 40th Cong., 3rd Sess., Executive Document 42, February 3, 1869. Washington, DC.

U.S. Treasury Department, Division of Revenue Cutter Service. 1899. *Report of the Cruise of the U.S. Revenue Cutter Bear and the Overland Expedition for the Relief of the Whalers in the Arctic Ocean from November 27, 1897 to September 13, 1898*. Washington, DC: Government Printing Office.

Usher, Peter J. 1971. *Fur Trade Posts of the Northwest Territories, 1870–1970*. Ottawa: Department of Indian Affairs and Northern Development, Northern Science Research Group, 71–4.

Vagin, V., comp. 1872. *Istoricheskiia svedeniia o deiatel'nosti grafa M. M. Speranskago v Sibiri s 1819 po 1822 god* [Historical Information on the Activities of Count M. M. Speranskii in Siberia from 1819 to 1822]. 2 vols. Trans. Katherine Arndt. St. Petersburg.

Valkenburg, Patrick. 1999. "Caribou." Wildlife Notebook Series. Juneau: Alaska Department of Fish and Game.

VanStone, James W. 1958. "Commercial Whaling in the Arctic Ocean." *Pacific Northwest Quarterly* 49 (1): 1–10.

————. 1960. "An Early Nineteenth Century Artist in Alaska: Louis Choris and the First Kotzebue Expedition." *Pacific Northwest Quarterly* 51 (4): 145–58.

————. 1962. "Notes on the Nineteenth Century Trade in the Kotzebue Sound Area, Alaska." *Arctic Anthropology* 1 (1): 126–28.

————. 1967. *Eskimos of the Nushagak River*. Seattle: University of Washington Press.

————, ed. 1973. "V.S. Khromchenko's Coastal Explorations in Southwestern Alaska, 1822." Trans. David H. Krauss. *Fieldiana Anthropology* 64. Chicago: Field Museum of Natural History.

————, ed. 1977. "A. F. Kashevarov's Coastal Explorations in Northwest Alaska, 1838." Trans. David H. Krauss. *Fieldiana Anthropology* 69. Chicago: Field Museum of Natural History.

————. 1983. "Protective Hide Body Armor of the Historic Chukchi and Siberian Eskimos." *Études/Inuit/Studies* 7 (2): 3–24.

————. 1984. "Mainland Southwest Alaska Eskimo." In *Handbook of North American Indians*, vol. 5, *Arctic*. Ed. David Damas. Washington, DC: Smithsonian Institution, pp. 224–42.

————, ed. 1988. *Russian Exploration in Southwest Alaska: The Travel Journals of Petr Korsakovskiy (1818) and Ivan Ya. Vasilev (1829).* Fairbanks: University of Alaska Press. Rasmuson Library Historical Translation Series 4.

VanStone, James W., and Ives Goddard. 1981. "Territorial Groups of West-Central Alaska before 1898." In *Handbook of North American Indians*, vol. 6, *Subarctic*. Ed. June Helm. Washington, DC: Smithsonian Institution, pp. 556–61.

Van Valin, William B. 1941. *Eskimoland Speaks.* Caldwell, ID: Caxton.

Varjola, Pirjo. 1990. *The Etholén Collection: The Ethnographic Alaskan Collection of Adolf Etholén and His Contemporaries in the National Museum of Finland.* Helsinki: National Board of Antiquities of Finland.

Verman, Fedor Karlovich. 1863. "Zapiska kapitan-leitenanta Vermana o polozhenii Rossiisko-Amerikanskoi Kompanii i torgovle eia na severe kolonial'nykh vladenii" [Memorandum of Captain-Lieutenant Verman on the Position of the Russian-American Company and Its Trade in the North of the Colonial Possessions]. Trans. Katherine Arndt. In *Doklad komiteta ob ustroistve Russkikh Amerikanskikh kolonii* [Report of the Committee on the Organization of the Russian-American Colonies], pt. 2, pp. 586–601. St. Petersburg: Departament vneshnei torgovli.

Vincennes, USS. MS. Logbook, March 21, 1853–July 17, 1856. Records of the Bureau of Naval Personnel, record group 24, microfilm publication 88, roll 10, National Archives, Washington, DC.

Walker, James V. 1999. "Mapping of the Northwest Boundary of the United States, 1800–1846: An Historical Context." *Terrae Incognitae* 31:70–90.

Walters, John. MS. Diary of John Walters. Archival Manuscript Group no. 425, Historical Society of Dauphin County, Harrisburg, PA.

Wardman, George. 1884. *A Trip to Alaska.* San Francisco: S. Carson.

Warnes, David. 1999. *Chronicle of the Russian Tsars.* London: Thames and Hudson.

Webb, Melody. 1985. *The Last Frontier: A History of the Yukon Basin of Canada and Alaska.* Albuquerque: University of New Mexico Press.

Weiner, Frederick Bernays. 1982. "German Sugar's Sticky Fingers." *Hawaiian Journal of History* 16:15–47.

Weiss, Claudia. 2006. "*Nash*: Appropriating Siberia for the Russian Empire." *Sibirica* 5 (1): 141–55.

Wells, Roger, Jr., and John W. Kelly. 1890. *English-Eskimo and Eskimo-English Vocabularies. Preceded by Ethnographical Memoranda Concerning the Arctic Eskimos in Alaska and Siberia by John W. Kelly.* Washington, DC: Government Printing Office, Bureau of Education Circular of Information 2.

Wenger, Donald B. 1984. "Russian-American Relations in Northeast Asia during the Nineteenth Century." PhD diss., Department of History, College of William and Mary.

Wentzel, Willard-Ferdinand. 1823. "Notice of the Attempts to Reach the Sea by Mackenzie's River, Since the Expedition of Sir Alexander Mackenzie." *Edinburgh Philosophical Journal* (8): 77–81.

White, Frank T. MS. "Journal of the Steam Brig Jeanette, E. W. Newth, Master, on a Whaling Voyage to the Arctic and McKenzie River 1893 and 1894." Typescript. New Bedford Whaling Museum, New Bedford, MA, no. LB87-10.3.

White, James Taylor. MS. Diaries, 1889, 1894. Special Collections, Suzallo Library, University of Washington, Seattle.

Whymper, Frederick. 1868a. "A Journey from Norton Sound, Bering Sea, to Fort Youkon (Junction of the Porcupine and Youkon Rivers)." *Journal of the Royal Geographical Society* 38:219–37.

———. 1868b. *Travel and Adventure in the Territory of Alaska. . . .* London: John Murray.

———. 1869. "Russian America or 'Alaska': The Natives of the Youcon River and Adjacent Country." *Transactions of the Ethnological Society of London*, n.s., 7.

Wilkinson, David. n.d. [1906]. *Whaling in Many Seas and Cast Adrift in Siberia.* London: Henry J. Drane.

William H. Meyers (schooner). Journal of Gideon Bartlett, September 27, 1878–October 21, 1878. New Bedford Whaling Museum, New Bedford, MA. Old Dartmouth Historical Society Collection, no. 524b.

Williams, Glyn. 2002. *Voyages of Delusion: The Northwest Passage in the Age of Reason.* London: HarperCollins.

Wilson, Clifford. 1969. "The Surrender of Fort Yukon." *The Beaver* (Autumn): 47–51.

Wilson, Dick A. 2004. "King George's Men: British Ships and Sailors in the Pacific Northwest–China Trade, 1785–1821." PhD diss., University of Idaho–Moscow.

Wolfe, James. MSa. "Journal of a voyage on Discovery in the Pacific and Beering's Straits on board H.M.S. *Blossom* Capt. F. W. Beechey." Beinecke Rare Book and Manuscript Library, Yale University, New Haven.

———. MSb. "Journal kept on board H.M.S. *Blossom;* quoted in Richard Beechey, Remarks on a voyage of discovery to the Pacific and Bhering's Straits on board H.M.S. *Blossom* by Rich. Beechey Midn., aged 15." Public Record Office of Northern Ireland, Belfast.

Wolga (whaleship). MS. Journal of Grafton Luce, January 8, 1851–May 14, 1852, Providence Public Library, Providence, RI.

Woolfe, Henry D. 1893. The Seventh District. In *Report on Population and Resources of Alaska at the Eleventh Census: 1890.* U.S. House of Representatives. 52nd Cong., 1st Sess., Resources Document 340, pt. 7. Washington, DC: Government Printing Office.

Worman, Charles G. 2007. *Firearms in American History: A Guide for Writers, Curators, and General Readers.* Yardley, PA: Westholme.

Wrangell, Ferdinand Petrovich. 1840. *Narrative of an Expedition to the Polar Sea, in the Years 1820, 1821, 1822, and 1823.* Ed. Edward Sabine. London: James Madden.

———. 1980. *Russian America: Statistical and Ethnographic Information with Additional*

Material by Karl-Ernst Baer. Kingston, ON: Limestone. Materials for the Study of Alaska History 15.

Wright, Allen A. 1976. *Prelude to Bonanza: The Discovery and Exploration of the Yukon*. Sidney, BC: Gray's.

Yerbury, J. Colin. 1977. "Duncan Livingston of the North West Company." *Arctic* 30 (3): 189–90.

———. 1986. *The Subarctic Indians and the Fur Trade, 1680–1860*. Vancouver: University of British Columbia Press.

Young, Stephen B. 1989. *To the Arctic: An Introduction to the Far Northern World*. New York: John Wiley and Sons.

Zagoskin, Lavrentii Alekseevich. 1847–48. *Peshekhodnaia opis' chasti russkikh vladienii v Amerikie. Proizvedennaia Leitenantom L. Zagoskinym v 1842, 1843 i 1844 godakh* [Explorations on Foot of Part of the Russian Possessions in America Undertaken by Lieutenant L. Zagoskin in the Years 1842, 1843, and 1844]. St. Petersburg.

———. 1967. *Lieutenant Zagoskin's Travels in Russian America, 1842–1844*. Ed. Henry N. Michael. Trans. Penelope Rainey. Toronto: Arctic Institute of North America. Anthropology of the North: Translations from Russian Sources 7.

Zimmerman, Steven T. 1994. "Northern Fur Seal." Wildlife Notebook Series. Juneau: Alaska Department of Fish and Game.

Znamenski, Andrei A. 1999. "'Vague Sense of Belonging to the Russian Empire': The Reindeer Chukchi's Status in Nineteenth Century Northeastern Siberia." *Arctic Anthropology* 36 (1–2): 19–36.

Zykov, F. M. 1989. *Traditsionnye orudiia truda iakutov (XIX-nachalo XX veka)* [Traditional Implements of Yakut Workmanship (19th–Beginning of 20th Century)]. Novosibirsk: "Nauka" (Sibirskoe Otdelenie).

INDEX

Page numbers in *italics* indicate illustrations.

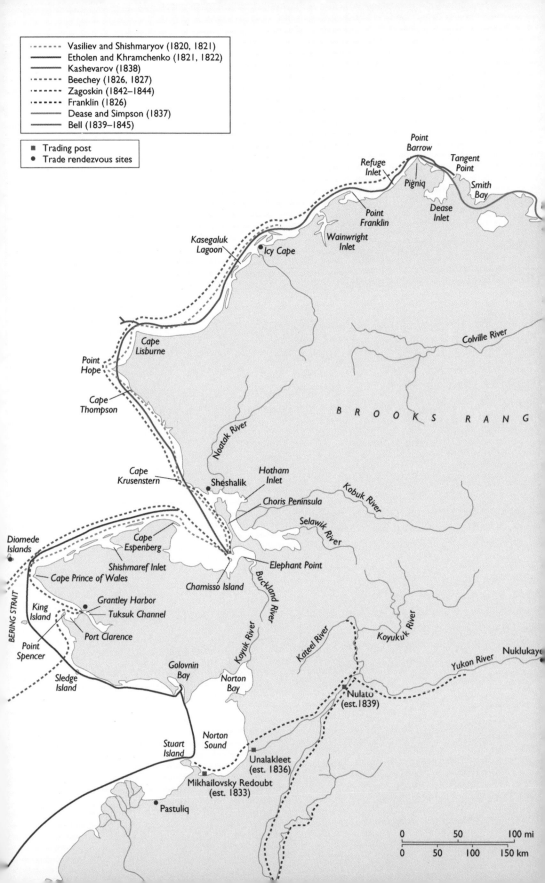

Legend:

- Vasiliev and Shishmaryov (1820, 1821)
- Etholen and Khramchenko (1821, 1822)
- Kashevarov (1838)
- Beechey (1826, 1827)
- Zagoskin (1842–1844)
- Franklin (1826)
- Dease and Simpson (1837)
- Bell (1839–1845)

■ Trading post
● Trade rendezvous sites

Point Barrow
Tangent Point
Refuge Inlet
Pigniq
Smith Bay
Point Franklin
Dease Inlet
Wainwright Inlet
Colville River
Kasegaluk Lagoon
Icy Cape
Cape Lisburne
Point Hope
Cape Thompson
B R O O K S   R A N G
Noatak River
Cape Krusenstern
Hotham Inlet
Sheshalik
Kobuk River
Choris Peninsula
Selawik River
Diomede Islands
Cape Espenberg
Elephant Point
Shishmaref Inlet
Buckland River
Cape Prince of Wales
Chamisso Island
King Island
Grantley Harbor
Tuksuk Channel
Port Clarence
Koyuk River
Kateel River
Koyukuk River
BERING STRAIT
Point Spencer
Sledge Island
Golovnin Bay
Norton Bay
Yukon River
Nuklukaye
Nulato (est. 1839)
Stuart Island
Norton Sound
Unalakleet (est. 1836)
Mikhailovsky Redoubt (est. 1833)
Pastuliq

0   50   100 mi
0   50   100   150 km